DAUGHTERS
OF
THE
CHURCH

DAUGHTERS
OF
THE
CHURCH

WOMEN AND MINISTRY FROM NEW TESTAMENT TIMES TO THE PRESENT

RUTH A. TUCKER
AND
WALTER L. LIEFELD

Academie
Books Grand Rapids, Michigan
Zondervan Publishing House

DAUGHTERS OF THE CHURCH
Copyright © 1987 by Ruth A. Tucker and Walter L. Liefeld

ACADEMIE BOOKS
is an imprint of
Zondervan Publishing House
1415 Lake Drive S.E.
Grand Rapids, Michigan 49506

Library of Congress Cataloging in Publication Data

Tucker, Ruth, 1945–
    Daughters of the church.

    Bibliography: p.
    Includes index.
    1. Women in Christianity—History.   2. Women in
church work—History.   3. Women clergy—History.
I. Liefeld, Walter L.   II. Title.
BV639.W7T83   1987   270'.088042   87-6090

ISBN 0-310-45741-6

Unless otherwise indicated, quotations of Scripture are from the
Holy Bible: New International Version (North American Edition)
copyright © 1973, 1978, 1984 by the International Bible Society,
Used by permission of Zondervan Bible Publishers

Edited by Gerard Terpstra
Designed by Stanley N. Gundry

Printed in the United States of America

87 88 89 90 91 92 93 94 95 96 / AF / 10 9 8 7 6 5 4 3 2 1

In memory of

Kimberly Sue Van Dyke
October 17, 1971–June 21, 1983

A true daughter of the church

whose brief life
had already begun to radiate
the beauty of Christian womanhood

CONTENTS

ILLUSTRATIONS

PREFACE

Why a history of women in the church? Why not a history of *men* in the church? The vast majority of published church histories are histories of men. This was very apparent to us as we perused history books in our research. We considered ourselves fortunate when the index contained the subject "women." How absurd it would have been, however, if the same index had listed the subject "men," which in most cases would have included virtually the entire subject matter of the book.

In many instances the role of women in the church has not been as noteworthy as that of men. After all, it is mainly men who have preached, led church councils, and written theology. But frequently women have been overlooked even when they made outstanding contributions. "As so frequently happens in the writing of history," writes Patricia Hill, "the women have simply disappeared."[1] Their role in religion down through the ages has been flagrantly neglected. And it continues to be neglected, despite longstanding appeals to historians to do otherwise. Indeed, in 1922 Arthur Schlesinger, Sr., called on historians to discard their blatant sexism and take the role of women seriously—an appeal that has yet to be heeded by the vast majority of historians. Perhaps the consciousness-raising that has occurred in recent years will change that, and a book such as this will become obsolete. But until that happens, separate volumes on women in the church are the only means of telling their story.

This is not a feminist history of women—nor is it a "traditionalist" interpretation. Any history suffers when it develops out of a personal philosophy, be it feminist, Marxist, or liberationist. We have tenaciously striven to present an objective account, not only in our effort to represent the truth as accurately as possible but also in our effort to avoid the tendency to magnify our subject. This tendency is particularly acute when a subject has previously been denied a fair coverage.

Because of the varied interpretations of the biblical position of women in ministry—particularly as found in the statements of the apostle Paul—the evaluation of the role of women in ministry has varied considerably. One example is that of Catherine Booth, who was a cofounder of the Salvation Army. She wrote in her book *Female Ministry: Or, Woman's Right to Preach the Gospel:*

> Judging from the blessed results which have almost invariably followed the ministrations of women in the cause of Christ, we fear it will be found, in the great day of account, that a mistaken and unjustifiable application of the passage, "Let your women keep silence in the Churches," has resulted in more loss to the Church, evil to the world, and dishonour to God, than any of the errors we have already referred to.[2]

On the opposite extreme was the evaluation of John R. Rice, fundamentalist radio preacher and evangelist, as he expressed it in his book *Bobbed Hair, Bossy Wives, and Women Preachers:* "Feminism in the churches is a blight that has grieved God and made ineffectual His power and it has disillusioned the people and lost their confidence. I have no doubt that millions will go to Hell because of the unscriptural practice of women preachers."[3]

Another reason for studying the subject of women in the church is to discern the differences between men and women—particularly in their response to spiritual values. Although this volume does not approach the subject from a sociological or psychological perspective, it does seek to shed light on such issues. The question of whether or not women are more inclined to be emotional than men will be touched on, as will the fact that women constitute a higher percentage of church members than do men. Sociologist Peter Berger has attempted to explain this by suggesting that "the impact of secularization has tended to be stronger on men than on women."[4] Because men have traditionally been more involved in the workplace and the public arena than women have, they have been more quickly exposed to new ideas—especially secular thought. Women, on the other hand, who have traditionally been the "keepers of the home," have had fewer challenges to their religious values and have had a greater concern to maintain the religious traditions that uphold domestic stability.

Certain questions repeatedly present themselves to anyone who surveys this history. What cultural factors influenced the role of women? How has biblical exegesis influenced that role? What restrictions and opposition did women face? How did women balance their dual responsibilities for ministry and family or how did they deal with singleness? Are there any discernible trends such as increasing restrictions, increasing opportunities, or growing acceptance followed by reaction?

Such questions reveal that our task is not only to inquire about the actual life and ministry of women in the church but also to observe how they were perceived by men throughout the course of church history. As such, this study is not only a history of women in the church, but also a history of changing perspectives about women.

Before definitive conclusions can be drawn regarding women in church history, much more study needs to be done, but even at this point there are many patterns and trends that have emerged. One obvious generalization that can be made is that women were very prominent in church history. The history of religion is probably the only field of history where women have had such an influential role — even though they were systematically denied positions of authority.

Another pattern indicated by our research suggests that women often had significant leadership positions during the initial pioneering and developmental stages of a movement, only to be replaced by men as the movement became more "respectable." Although this trend has been particularly characteristic of the twentieth century, it was identified a century ago by Frances Willard. In her book *Woman in the Pulpit*, published in 1888, she said essentially the same thing: "In the proportion that any church approaches the dimensions of a hierarchy, the admission of women to the priestly class becomes difficult."[5]

Still another discernible pattern is that throughout the history of the church different views on women have coexisted within the same culture or religion. It is incorrect to assume that leaders or representatives of a particular movement (e.g., the ancient Jewish rabbis) had a monolithic understanding of women. Likewise, we have found that women have been very active in a wide variety of ministries within the institutionalized church despite pronouncements and official decrees to the contrary.

There are many other generalizations that can be made about women in ministry. For example, a personal religious "call" (sometimes accompanied by visions or trances) has been an important factor in justifying ministry for women historically, as it has been for justifying the ministry of lay men who sought preaching roles in the church. It is also true that women appear to have been far more concerned with social needs and the unity of the believers than with doctrinal issues—particularly the "nonessentials" of the Christian creed. As such, we have found that they were often more eager to seek unity across denominational lines. Indeed, women have had a significant influence on ecumenical activities in the church.

We have challenged a number of popularly held assumptions regarding women in the church. The so-called liberal churches, for example, have not always been more open to the ministry of women, nor have the so-called conservative churches been consistently more closed to it.

Another myth that needs to be dispelled is that women are more easily deceived than men and are thus more often the founders of cults and authors of heresies. This view is not supported by historical fact. On the contrary, it appears that women have traditionally been slower than men to adopt unorthodox theology and to accept the kind of biblical criticism that undermines the faith.

Nor is the charge substantiated that it is because women are more emotionally inclined that they turn to sectarian ecstatic religion in larger numbers than men. Many of the leading charismatic "visionaries" throughout history have been men, and the evidence does not appear to indicate that all charismatic religious movements have had a larger percentage of women than noncharismatic mainline churches have had.

One of the most widely held views on women in the church—and particularly on those in leadership positions—is that they have manifested a feminist impulse. Both feminists and traditionalists have lent their support to this view. To the contrary, however, we have found that most women seemed very hesitant to challenge the "rightful" leadership of men. Rarely did they manifest purely feminist qualities; rather, they were cautious about seeking a place of prominence in the church. When they did strive for positions in ministry, their motivation appeared to be to serve more effectively.

The fact that this book has been coauthored by a man and a woman is, we believe, an asset. Approaching the subject from similar backgrounds but "opposite" perspectives has given us a fuller understanding of the role and ministry of women throughout church history. Our religious heritage has been largely in churches where women have not been allowed leadership positions. One of us grew up in Baptist churches with all-male leadership and has since ministered for some thirty years among the Plymouth Brethren, a group whose worship services are often distinguished by their veiled and silent women. The other's early experience was in a male-dominated Christian and Missionary Alliance Church (founded by two women) and her later experience was as a pastor's wife in two independent Fundamentalist Bible churches where women's preaching was anathema.

The vast subject encompassing women in the history of Christianity would be impossible to cover fully in a single volume. The scope of the subject is virtually limitless, considering that it covers two millenniums, has a world-wide geographical breadth, is denominationally pluralistic, and has an endless cast of characters. In numbers, women have dominated the church, and the source material relating to their ministry and status is simply overwhelming. Therefore, any effort to summarize the story must be an exercise in careful selectivity.

Some women or events that have been been previously lost in obscurity will be featured, while others that have achieved a prominent place in the annals of history may appear to be short-changed. Countless others will not find a place at all in this volume; some of them may have made lasting contributions to the church, but, as is the case with many outstanding Christian men, they are not recognized or even mentioned in the annals of history.

What relevence does a history of women in the church have for the church of the late twentieth century? Above all else, it places the current trends of the church in historical perspective. This is crucial for a proper understanding of the church today. Recently a colleague of ours commented that the efforts women are making to enter the pastorate and obtain positions of church leadership are a direct result of the modern feminist movement and that such efforts are thus "of the world, not of God." This is a widely held position in Evangelical churches today. While the feminist movement has had a significant impact on the more liberal churches that have in recent decades granted full equality to women in ministry, it has not necessarily been the motivating force behind the Evangelical women who have sought ordination and leadership positions. Women in Evangelical churches have a long heritage of seeking (and sometimes obtaining) meaningful positions in the church for the purpose of serving God more effectively.

Chapter 1

The Gospel and the World of Jesus: Wives and Mothers

Two contrasting figures appear at the opening of the Christian era: an old man and a young girl.[1] In separate narratives, Luke's literary artistry draws attention first to one and then to the other.

He is Zechariah, resident of Jerusalem, the centuries-old religious center of Judaism. A priest whose knowledge of divine things has been seasoned with the years, Zechariah is astounded by an angel's proclamation that he and Elizabeth would give birth to a son.

She is Mary, resident of Nazareth, a small village removed both in distance and in spirit from Jerusalem. A young teenager whose knowledge of God has been fostered by deep insight into the Scriptures, Mary is astounded by the angel's greeting. Yet she listens intently to his annunciation that she, a virgin, would bear God's Son.

Zechariah doubted,[2] but Mary believed.[3] Perhaps the symbolism is unintentional on Luke's part, but it is there nevertheless: the old era, long past with the close of the Old Testament, receives its final reprise with the incredulity of a man. The new era, about to be proclaimed in the gospel of Jesus Christ, begins with the faith of a woman.

Mary, the Mother of Jesus*

It would be too much to say that ancient Near-Eastern patriarchalism, which embraced even the people of God, ended with Zechariah, or that Mary symbolized the new woman in ministry.[4] The Old Testament did contain positive teachings and examples regarding women, and Mary and other women of her times would therefore have had outstanding models of faithful women of God.

*In order to maintain the flow of historical narration, significant issues concerning the interpretation of the biblical texts will, for the most part, be reserved for appendix B.

Mary and Her Mother. Detail from *The Virgin Mother and Child with St. Anne and John the Baptist* by Leonardo Da Vinci (1452–1519).   National Gallery, London.

Perhaps Mary's poetic nature responded to the invitation of Miriam, Moses' sister, to the Hebrew women to "sing to the Lord" in celebration of the Exodus from Egypt (Exod. 15:20–21). Miriam, described in that passage as a prophetess, appears in what seems to be a leadership role in Micah 6:4, where God says, "I sent Moses to lead you, also Aaron and Miriam."

Deborah was likewise called a prophetess. Even before she led the Israelite troops to a significant victory and before Barak refused to assume leadership, Deborah "was leading Israel" (Judg. 4:4).

Another prophetess, Huldah, was chosen above her contemporaries Jeremiah and Zephaniah to declare God's will for the people when the law was rediscovered in the temple (2 Kings 22:8–20; 2 Chron. 34:14–28).

Mary's biblical models probably also included Esther, who risked her life for her people at a time when God seemed to be silent (the name of God does not even appear in the Book of Esther). King Xerxes' favorite, Vashti, had been discharged because she would not let him use her by having her display her beauty in public. The king also decreed that all women in his realm should respect their husbands. He then found Esther, and she became Vashti's successor. The narrative goes on to trace the various ways in which Esther skillfully used her official and personal relationships with the king to bring good both to her cousin and guardian, Mordecai, and to her people Israel.

Surely, as Mary listened to readings from Genesis, she reflected on the figure of Sarah, that good woman who was a victim of ancient Near Eastern customs, and on Ruth, celebrated for her devotion and faithfulness. There were dark figures of women in the Old Testatament as well. Their stories need not be recounted here, but even in the lives of some of them Mary could find encouraging evidence of the grace of God. One need think only of the prostitute Rahab, who chose to facilitate the invasion of Joshua and his forces against her own pagan city (Josh. 2:1–21; 6:22–25).

The noble wife of Proverbs 31 certainly was an exemplary figure for Mary. In addition to running the household and caring for her family, as one might have expected from a woman of her generation, she involved herself in various profitable commercial ventures. She had "strength and dignity," spoke with wisdom, and gave "faithful instruction" (Prov. 31:25–26).

If there is any doubt about Mary's acquaintance with the Old Testament, that should be dispelled by a study of her song, the Magnificat. It catches not only the spirit but also the vocabulary of Hannah's prayer at the dedication of Samuel. The parallels are obvious as each of these women, though in very different circumstances, celebrated God's gift of a son.

The intertestamental period must have had its heroes for Mary also— women as well as men. The towering figures of this era, especially the Maccabeans, who revolted against foreign pagan oppression, have become more honored with the passing of the years. But certainly in Mary's time there were many traditions— some were factual, some legendary— about the brave people who resisted violence and moral evil. It would be surprising if Mary had not known of these. The story about the outstanding woman of the times, Judith, is an example. It features Judith as a beautiful and devout widow. When her city was under attack, she won her way into enemy headquarters and next to Holofernes, the leader. She killed him and brought his head back to her people. Would Mary not have learned stories like this—even those that were pious legends? Judith seems to be an expression of ideals drawn, at least in part, from the outstanding Old Testament women mentioned above, with additional dashes of heroics that remind us of such characters as the redoubtable Jael and the woman who dropped a millstone on the head of Abimelech in the rowdy days of the judges (Judg. 4:21; 9:52–53).

While the book of Judith specifically intends to show how God worked through weak vessels, nevertheless, Judith is portrayed as a woman of great strength. This applies also to her faith. She sought to live in accordance with laws of ritual purity, and she was faithful in prayer. She is also a model of wisdom. In spite of her questionable use of her beauty and deceitful shrewdness,[5] her story obviously commended itself to the writer's contemporaries and their descendants. As a result, the figure of Judith stands as a model that was greatly admired. She is

Judith With the Head of Holofernes. One of the celebrated women of Jewish tradition. Matteo di Giovanni (c. 1430–1495). Photograph by Michael Cavanagh. Indiana University, Kress Study Collection.

consistently depicted as superior to the men with whom she is associated. . . . The author may be saying that God's power is operative through the weakest of human agents. Nonetheless, Judith is no weakling. Her courage, her trust in God, and her wisdom—all lacking in her male counterparts—save the day for Israel.[6]

Another woman celebrated in the apocryphal writings and perhaps known to Mary was Susanna. The story of her faithful obedience to God is preserved in one of the additons to the Book of Daniel. In yet another apocryphal work, named after the pious Jewish figure Tobit, Mary would have found a rather different citation of a model. In one of Tobit's frequent expressions of praise to God, he lauds God's gift of Eve to Adam as his helper and support.[7] He apparently attributed to Eve a certain amount of moral strength that Adam needed.

Mary would therefore have had several models of faithful women both in Scripture and in the intertestamental stories. The Magnificat shows that as a young woman she had a firm grasp on the nature of God and his work in history and in her own life.[8] Mary speaks there of God's greatness, holiness, mercy, deeds in history, and faithfulness to his covenant. Her reference to the needed reversal of the fate of rich and poor shows her sense of social justice. Mary has been the object of both excessive adulation and unnecessary belittling. But the portrait in Luke's birth narratives and the further unfolding of her experiences in the Gospels reveal a woman who both loved God and needed to grow in faith.[9]

Mary's Growth as a Woman of God

Mary's growth was of a most unusual nature: she had to come to terms with the unique nature of her Son. She had to recognize that his apparent brusqueness (e.g., "Didn't you know . . ." [Luke 2:49] and the address "Woman, . . ." [John 2:4 and 19:26 KJV]) communicated, not disrespect or insubordination in his relationship to her, but rather the difference in their ultimate relationship. In that respect they were not so much mother and son, but woman and divine Savior.

Mary's faith could have been severely shaken if Joseph had taken the customary action when she told him she was pregnant. Jewish custom provided for a legal betrothal as a halfway step between what we now call engagement and the consummation of marriage. The law also mandated divorce as the only way to sever this relationship. Joseph's choice was not whether to divorce Mary or not, but how to do it. He decided on a quiet divorce to avoid bringing Mary into public disgrace. Thus, even though the New Testament opens with a pending divorce (a remarkable fact in itself), the woman is treated with tender consideration. Joseph thought that what seemed to be right must be done—but with the least harm to the woman. While Joseph could be faulted for thinking as a man and apparently assuming Mary's guilt, there was no other alternative at hand. A virginal conception could hardly have come to mind as an option.

Matthew does not say whether Joseph communicated his doubts to Mary, but if he did, it must have been unspeakably difficult for her. But even after that difficulty was resolved by Joseph's complete acceptance of her pregnancy, she was to experience further tensions. When Jesus stayed behind in the Jerusalem temple at the age of twelve, Mary's frustration erupted in the words "Son, why have you treated us like this? Your father and I have been anxiously searching for you" (Luke 2:48). Her question betrays both a mother's natural anxiety and a lack of understanding. Jesus' reply in the following verse— "Didn't you know I had to be in my Father's house?" (or, "about my Father's business?")—implies that she should have gained a sense of his special filial relationship to God the Father. This is the first clue we have that, in spite of the remarkable insights she showed in the *Magnificat*, Mary needed time to absorb the implications of her Son's person and mission.

At the wedding in Cana, Mary was apparently trying to "mother" Jesus, giving rather direct hints that he should do something about the need for more wine (John 2:3). His response has been the subject of much discussion.[10] The question "What have I to do with you?" (v. 4) seems to us like a distancing of himself from his mother. But it is important to realize that in the idiom of the time it could mean "some refusal of an inopportune involvement, and a divergence between the views of the two persons concerned."[11] That is to say, Mary needed to learn that Jesus was on a unique and lonely mission. It was a mission he alone understood. Mary was to learn more about it as time went on.

But we must still face the term "woman." Why both here and at the cross (John 19:26) did Jesus use a term of address that elsewhere he used only in speaking with the semi-foreign Samaritan woman (4:21) and the formerly demon-possessed Mary Magdalene (20:13)? Probably the character of these women in the Gospel of John has nothing to do with it. The fact is that no other woman appears in conversation with Jesus in John's Gospel. Therefore, the simple term "woman" is really the only address we find on the lips of Jesus. It does not seem to carry any negative overtones, as it would today.

Mary as a Disciple

Mary had to learn to follow him as a *disciple*, rather than possessing and directing him as his *mother*. But this spiritual relationship did not obliterate her need of a human relationship. At the cross she was committed to

Jesus and Mary Studying the Torah. From Wallace, "The Boyhood of Christ," *Harpers Magazine*, 74:439 (December 1886), 11.

John's care, as a member of the new spiritual family.

> She must enter the family of faith in full recognition of who she is as a sexual being. She will not lose that sexuality for some spirituality in the community of belief. Rather, she will assume her old role of motherhood and her new role as witness, prophetess and proclaimer of God's word in relationship to believers.[12]

This view of Mary as a disciple in progress fits in with the picture we have of Jesus' family in the Synoptic Gospels. His brothers did not believe in him before the Resurrection. In fact, they attempted to take control of him at one point, saying "He is out of his mind."[13] The fact that this occurs in Mark immediately before the charge that he was in collusion with Satan communicates the idea that *no* one understood him. Although Mary is not mentioned in this passage, there is no indication that she countered the opinion of her other sons. The positive element in this otherwise dismal picture is the statement of Jesus that his true relatives were those who did God's will (or, according to Luke, who heard and did the Word of God).[14] Jesus' seemingly curt response to an unnamed woman in a crowd should be seen in the same way. She had called out, "Blessed is the mother who gave you birth and nursed you," and he replied, "Blessed rather are those who hear the word of God and obey it."[15] This is a not a put-down of either the woman or of his mother. Jesus is simply affirming the tremendously important truth that human relationships are not as important as spiritual responsiveness. There is no reason to think that Jesus would have responded any differently to a man. In fact, he responded in a similar way to the man who wanted him to arbitrate in a matter of inheritance.[16]

In summary, Mary appears in the Gospels as a woman who is highly esteemed, acts like a normal mother, is spiritually more responsive than others but needs to grow as a woman of faith. She is neither exalted above normal womanhood nor looked down on as though her lapses in spiritual understanding had some connection with her being a woman.

Other Women Who Were Associated With Jesus

There are over forty references (not counting repetition in the parallel passages) to women in the Gospels, either in narratives or in the teachings of Jesus. These include allusions to Old Testament events or metaphors (such as Rachel's weeping and the appellation "Daughter of Zion"), parables (the wise and foolish virgins, the woman who used leaven), women as a class (mothers, victims of lust and divorce), or strong characters in the narrative (Jesus' mother, Mary and Martha). The following selections illustrate these.

Elizabeth and Anna

The next two women in the narrative of Luke are the aged Elizabeth and the venerable Anna.[17] Luke accords respect to both. His description of Elizabeth parallels his description of her husband, Zechariah.[18] It does not seem to have been necessary for Luke to include all he said about Elizabeth, since the narrative proceeds to focus on Zechariah. Nevertheless, when he mentions that Zechariah descended from the priestly line, he immediately says, "His wife Elizabeth was also a descendant of Aaron" (1:5). It could be said that the reason for mentioning this is to show that John the Baptist was in the priestly order on both lines. However, Luke goes on to say that *both* of them were "upright in the sight of God, observing all the Lord's commandments and regulations blamelessly" (1:6). He did not need to use the word *both*, but its occurrence emphasizes the fact of Elizabeth's spiritual character. It is hard to think of a higher commendation of spiritual excellence than the one Luke used here to describe Elizabeth. He added that she had not been able to have children, a deficiency that was, of course, in Jewish society a matter of deep regret and embarrassment. The narrative goes on to show how God responded to the devout life of Elizabeth and her husband by giving them a son who would be the forerunner of the Lord Jesus Christ.

Anna seems to have functioned in two roles. One is related to Luke's concern to root Christianity in Judaism. This concern regarding Jewish roots is seen in many ways. The opening scene of Luke's Gospel is set in the Jerusalem temple. There is a reference to Jesus' circumcision and then to the Jewish rites of purification for Mary, Jesus' visit to Jerusalem at the age of twelve, and his custom of attending the synagogue; all these show fidelity to Judaism. Luke also emphasizes Jesus' deliberate progression toward Jerusalem.

Anna's other role may relate to the fact that Jewish law required two witnesses to validate a claim. Given Luke's concern to validate Christianity as the legitimate heir of Judaism, and with his care to provide certainty regarding the facts of Jesus' life (Luke 1:4), the prophet Simeon and Anna seem to have fulfilled this requirement as they testified to Jesus' messiahship.[19] But, if this is the case, there is something remarkable here. One of the witnesses is a woman even though the testimony of women was not acceptable in that society. There is something else striking about the mention of Anna. Luke tends to introduce women and men in pairs in his narrative. Therefore, whether or not this reference to two witnesses is a means of validating Jesus' messiahship on the basis of Jewish custom, it certainly is an example of a pairing of male and female. Luke makes no attempt to lift her out of the customary family role of women, since he identifies her in relationship to her deceased husband. But we should not overlook the fact that he introduces her at the beginning of the passage in terms of her own ministry as a prophetess: "There was also a prophetess, Anna."[20] The Old Testament referred to only three women as prophetesses. But here at the point of transition from the old age to the new age, a woman stands out as a devout servant of God to whom he entrusts a revelation concerning the coming of his Son.

Mary and Martha

Luke's picture of Mary sitting at Jesus' feet in the posture of a disciple[21] has been called perhaps the "strongest and clearest affirmation on the part of Jesus that the intellectual and 'spiritual' life was just as proper to women as to men."[22] It is generally agreed that Jesus went far beyond the rabbis of his day in permitting this woman to assume the role of a disciple. This is certainly implied by Luke in portraying her as sitting "at the Lord's feet listening to what he said."[23] Such a posture is described in the rabbinical literature (e.g., "Let thy house be a meeting-house for the Sages and sit amid the dust of their feet and drink in their words with thirst"),[24] and Paul said that he was instructed "at the feet of Gamaliel" (KJV).[25] It is clear that this is more than a posture of worship, as people so commonly think.

There is no evidence that Mary (or Martha) accompanied Jesus on his travels as other women did, but this does not preclude their being disciples. While the disciples of rabbis in the early centuries of this era did sometimes travel with their teachers, this was not a condition of learning. Paul seems to have understood the new freedom Jesus gave women, since he himself went beyond the usual rabbinic restrictions and permitted women to learn.[26] The fact that he wanted the women to learn *quietly* is so often stressed that it may be overlooked that he took the large step of *permitting* learning, against the customs of his day.

The account of Mary and Martha is, however, much more than just an example of a woman learning. It is full of vivid description and personal interaction. First of all, it was Martha who welcomed Jesus as a guest. There is not a word about Lazarus, who, according to John 11, also lived there. In that chapter of John, it is Martha who takes initiative rather than Mary, a characteristic that appears here also. The picture of Mary sitting and learning at Jesus' feet is followed by a graphic description of Martha's agitation. Luke says that Martha was "distracted by all the preparations that had to be made. She came to him and asked, 'Lord, don't you care that my sister has left me to do the work by myself? Tell her to help me!' " (10:40).

Luke makes no effort to hide Martha's anger. The verb that Luke uses to describe her being distracted could very well be used to describe someone we would today consider a "workaholic." She was, literally, a driven woman. Her anger is understandable. No doubt many homes and many friendships have been strained by a person who feels compelled to be constantly active in Christian work to the neglect of ordinary family and household responsibilities. In this case, Martha did not even attempt to hide her feelings from Jesus, as one might expect she would do with a guest. Quite on the contrary, she opened the entire matter to him and asked him to intervene. Aída Besançon Spencer, in her vivid description of the scene, makes the following point:

Nevertheless, Martha's indignation was perfectly understandable in the light of her culture. A Jewish woman's primary role was that of homemaker. She was exempt from rabbinic training and received no merit from learning the law. Should not Martha's request that Mary help her in service *supersede* Mary's desire to learn?[27]

Jesus' response was to address Martha directly concerning her own attitude: "Martha, Martha, you are worried and upset about many things, but only one thing is needed. Mary has chosen what is better, and it will not be taken away from her" (10:41).

Martha at the Tomb of Lazarus

Jesus' conversation with Martha at the tomb of Lazarus[28] is remarkable not only for its content but because Martha's christological confession is virtually identical to that of Peter at Caesarea Philippi.[29] This is seen in a comparison of the Greek words:

> *su ei ho christos ho huios tou theou* (Martha)
> *su ei ho christos ho huios tou theou tou zontos* (Peter)[30]

In English this reads literally:

> "You are the Christ, the Son of God."
> "You are the Christ, the Son of God the living."

The importance of this must not be minimized. "In this scene the most important role of discipleship according to Johannine theology, that of proclamation of Jesus' true identity, is given to a woman."[31] An even stronger evaluation is this statement:

> By giving his audience a story in which a woman is the recipient of one of Jesus' most profound and direct statements about Himself, and in which a

27

woman makes a heartfelt and accurate response to Jesus' declarations, the Fourth Evangelist intimates that women have a right to be taught even the mysteries of the faith, and that they are capable of responding in faith with an accurate confession. In short, they are capable of being full-fledged disciples of Jesus.[32]

Martha seems to have a status as a spokesperson in John similar to that of Peter in the Synoptics. Certainly her role is greater than his in the fourth Gospel.

Mary's Anointing of Jesus at Bethany

One of the major themes in the Gospels is the lack of understanding and lack of faith of the disciples. The refusal of Peter to believe the first prediction of Jesus' passion, which came immediately after the great confession he gave at Caesarea Philippi of Jesus' deity and messiahship, illustrates this dramatically.[33] It was not until after the Resurrection that the disciples were able to understand that the Cross had to precede the crown. But one disciple did seem to understand. Six days before Jesus' final Passover, Jesus went to the familiar home at Bethany where Lazarus, Mary, and Martha lived. Martha (typically) served, and Lazarus was at the table. Mary took "about a pint of pure nard, an expensive perfume; she poured it on Jesus' feet and wiped his feet with her hair. And the house was filled with the fragrance of the perfume."[34] When Judas Iscariot complained that the perfume had not been sold and the money given to the poor, Jesus responded, "It was meant that she should save this perfume for the day of my burial." The wording in Matthew is even more specific: "She did it to prepare me for burial."[35] It is hard to escape the conclusion that this woman had a deeper understanding of the impending cross than did Jesus' male disciples.

The importance of what she did was underscored by Jesus himself when he said, "I tell you the truth, wherever this gospel is preached throughout the world, what she has done will also be told, in memory of her."[36] It is hard to imagine that any early Christian (or contemporary one, for that matter) would invent a saying that seems to direct attention away from Christ and to the woman. Obviously Jesus is the object of her ministration and the central figure in the narrative. But at this crucial point, Jesus directs attention to a woman. It is right, then, and in accordance with Jesus' own statement, that the retelling and rereading of this incident a few days before Jesus' crucifixion should direct our attention not only to him but also to her.

Women Who Traveled With Jesus

A number of women traveled with Jesus and "were helping to support them out of their own means."[37] A cursory reading of this passage could overlook the fact that there were many others traveling with Jesus besides the three named women: ". . . and also some women who had been cured of evil spirits and diseases: Mary (called Magdalene), from whom seven demons had come out; Joanna, the wife of Cuza, the manager of Herod's household; Susanna; and many others." The gender of "many others" in the Greek text is feminine, so there is no mistaking the fact that these were women. Luke further specifies that they "were helping to support them [presumably Jesus and his disciples] out of their own means." This is quite a different picture from that which most people have of the sheltered, dependent Palestinian women of the first century.

This fact is of extraordinary significance. In Judaism, women were exempt from learning the Torah. They might learn a great deal informally, as they did through synagogue teaching, but a woman would not on her own enter into an association with a rabbi to become his disciple. Further, women were not to be in close association with men, and it would be unheard of for women to travel with a rabbi. In addition, the idea of a woman assuming fiscal responsibility and having discretionary power over her own funds is an ideal that, in biblical literature, is found only in Proverbs 31.

It is not known how many of these women were married. One of them was, but presumably Mary Magdalene was not. This scene of traveling men and women, however, is a reminder of Jesus' words about the cost of discipleship. He said that everyone who has left houses or brothers or sisters or mother or father or children for his sake will receive many times as much in return. This statement is found in several locations in the Gospels.[38] In Luke's account the word "wife" occurs, but the word "husband" does not occur in any of the accounts. In another passage, Jesus spoke about those who make themselves eunuchs

for the sake of the kingdom.[39] Putting all of this together, it is clear that Jesus signaled the disruption of the close-knit interdependent family. From now on there would be those—initially, primarily men, but, already in Jesus' own lifetime, women as well—who were willing for at least some period of time to be away from that family structure.

While it may seem that the idea of celibacy, which is certainly involved here, is a restrictive mode of life, in Jesus' day it was quite the opposite. The expected norm was for men and women to be married and raise children. By teaching celibacy as a legitimate (though not a higher) mode of life, Jesus was freeing people from the responsibilities of marriage, freeing them to serve him. This was to have profound effects in the centuries to follow, with later generations exalting the idea of the celibate life. This is not to suppose that the married people—for example, Cuza's wife Joanna among the group of traveling women disciples—necessarily broke with their families in order to accompany Jesus on his itinerant ministry. This traveling group of women thus testifies to the advance in Jesus' ministry over Jewish limitations of women. The inclusion of this in Luke also testifies to his appreciation of Jesus' position in this regard.

Women to Whom Jesus Ministered

The Widow of Nain

Among the women Jesus helped in his earthly ministry, one whom Luke describes is a widow of the town called Nain. While the actual miracle was the raising of her son, the focus is on his mother. The son is described as "the only son of his mother, and she was a widow."[40] The word translated "only" is the same word that is translated "only begotten" in the King James Version of John 3:16. Interestingly, except for John 3:16 (though there also it applies in some sense), every time that word appears in the Greek New Testament or in the Septuagint, the Greek translation of the Old Testament, it refers to someone who was deeply loved and was either dead or in mortal danger. It adds a touch of pathos to this passage. The woman was left entirely alone when her son died.

In describing Jesus' pity for her, Luke notes that when the Lord saw her, his heart went out to her and he said, "Don't cry." This could hardly be a demeaning gesture, though it does appear as if Jesus was reproving her for her grief. (See excursus on Luke's view of women, page 49.) In the context, however, it is clear that Jesus was preparing her for the extraordinary event that would follow.

An additional factor in the understanding of this event is that Nain was around the other side of the mountain from Shunem, where Elisha had raised the son of the notable woman there. It seems inescapable that Luke's mention of this raising of a woman's son is intended to bring the other miracle to mind and to emphasize a theme found elsewhere in Luke, that Jesus came as a prophet (though more than that) in a manner that recalls the ministries of Elijah and Elisha.

The Woman Who Was a "Sinner"

The next women mentioned by Luke was a "sinner."[41] This means, in the vocabulary of the day, a person who lived a sinful life. After the woman had anointed Jesus' feet with her tears and perfume, the host, who was a Pharisee, reflected, "If this man were a prophet, he would know who is touching him and what kind of woman she is—that she is a sinner." The man was, of course, wrong on three counts. He assumed that Jesus was not a prophet, as Jesus apparently did not know who the woman was. He also assumed that had Jesus known that she was a sinner, he would not have allowed her to do what she did. Since Luke mentions that "he said this to himself," we know that the man assumed Jesus would not know his thoughts. Far from putting down women by singling out one who was sinful, Luke is contrasting the attitude of Jesus to such a woman with that of the Pharisee. (Ultimately, of course, there is a contrast between the Pharisee's attitude to Jesus and the forgiven woman's attitude.) Also the conclusion of the episode features the woman's faith—a faith that their host obviously lacked. The concluding focus, then, is not on her weakness or sinfulness but on her commendable faith.

A Woman With an Awkward Disability

Another woman whom Luke describes had been "crippled by a spirit for eighteen years. She was bent over and could not straighten up at all." Jesus declared her free from her infirmity and put his hands on her, and she straightened up immediately and praised God.[42]

There are two remarkable aspects in this account. One is that Jesus was willing to incur criticism for healing a woman on the Sabbath. The fact that she had been in this condition for eighteen years meant that there was no urgency about the healing. It was deliberately done on the Sabbath and can be seen as part of Jesus' program of setting the oppressed free.[43] In Luke's understanding this is a facet both of the true Sabbath and of the Jubilee year referred to in Luke 4:19.

The second remarkable aspect is the concluding statement of Jesus. After saying that Satan had kept her bound during those eighteen years, Jesus wiped out the indignity of those long years and bestowed dignity on her by calling her a "daughter of Abraham."[44] The idea of being a son of Abraham was common enough. Jesus used that term in reference to Zacchaeus a few chapters later in Luke. But Jesus with this one modification of the phrase— from "son" to "daughter"—raises this formerly pitiful woman to a new status. Ben Witherington says:

> In our context, we may note the specific contrast between the label "hypocrite" that Jesus places on the synagogue ruler and those who agree with him, and the title of daughter of Abraham He gives to the woman. Again we see a woman not only being used as a positive example as she praises God, and even given a positive title, but also being defended at the expense of the males and in particular the synagogue ruler who objects to Jesus' actions.[45]

The Widow and Her "Mite"

In his parable of the judge and the widow (cf. p. 44), Jesus portrays a widow, not to stress her weakness, though she was needy, but to show the result of her firm persistence. Another widow appears in the familiar narrative of the "widow's mite."[46] Although Luke here portrays a woman characterized by weakness, a woman existing at the poverty level and without the protection and support of a husband, she becomes an example of faithful stewardship. She is not presented as an object of sympathy but of admiration.

The Woman at the Well

The contrast between the learned Jewish rabbi Nicodemus, with whom Jesus conversed in John 3, and the Samaritan woman, with whom he conversed in John 4, is striking. Nicodemus is a male, a professional Bible scholar, and presumably of impeccable morality. But the immoral Samaritan woman unexpectedly also demonstrates an interest in matters of religion.

One of the major points of interest in this narrative is that Jesus spoke alone with a woman, in contrast to the rigorous care that the Jews usually took not to have any close contact with women. Second, Jesus shared a drinking cup with a Samaritan. Third, he entered into a theological discussion with her. Fourth, he uncovered her sin, but he did not reject her because of that. Fifth, he discussed worship with her, never implying that she could not be a suitable worshiper. Finally, the woman became a witness through

The Widow Giving Her Mite With the Blessing of Jesus. Sixth-Century Mosaic. S. Apollinare nuovo.   Alinari—Art Resource, New York.

whom many believed in Christ. There is no hint that her female sex in any way hindered Jesus' ministry to her.[47]

Of all the narratives recording Jesus' conversation with women, this one contains the most conversational content. The scene is a town called Sychar, which was located in an area that Jews avoided if at all possible. Relations between Jews and Samaritans had been troubled for years; there had even been bloodshed. It was customary for the Jews to cross the Jordan and proceed north or south on the east side of the river, recrossing after Samaria had been passed. In this case Jesus "had" to go through Samaria. We are not told why; some have suggested it was due to divine intention for the sake of

meeting this woman. Jesus' humanity is apparent as he, tired, sat down by the well.

Midday was not a normal time for women to draw water, and some have thought the Samaritan woman was trying to avoid observation by others because of her reputation. That reputation does not appear at the beginning of the account. Rather, there was a conversation about water. The woman referred to the hostility between Jews and Samaritans, and Jesus responded with a comment about the "gift of God and who it is that asks you for a drink." The conversation is rich with allusions. The woman's inability to understand about "living water" had nothing to do with her sex. It is doubtful that anyone would have understood

Jesus' symbolic language; certainly the learned Nicodemus, in the conversation recorded in the immediately preceding chapter, did not understand what Jesus meant by spiritual birth.

Interpreters have often commented on the gentleness with which Jesus spoke as he introduced the delicate matter of the woman's marital relationships. He led into a forthright comment that she had had five husbands and was not at the moment married to the man with whom she was living. Her calling Jesus a prophet and then introducing the matter about which of the conflicting claims by Jews and Samaritans concerning the legitimate place of worship was correct has often been considered a diversionary tactic. Whether it was or not, it is interesting that she introduced a theological matter and was not afraid to confront Jesus regarding his views as a Jew.

Jesus' response was to speak with her about the very heart of true religion, the worship of God in spirit and in truth. Jesus prefixed his comment with a description of the nature of God as spirit. The woman's response is surprising. While the Jews were expecting a Messiah, the Samaritans expected one they called a Taheb. They held that someone would come who corresponded to the prediction in Deuteronomy 18:18 (of a prophet like Moses). However, according to the Gospel of John, the woman spoke, not of the Taheb, but of the Messiah. The author simply inserts parenthetically "called Christ" by way of explanation. Jesus then identified himself as the Messiah.

The conversation was interrupted at that point by the return of the disciples. John significantly comments that they were "surprised to find him talking with a woman" but that "no one asked 'What do you want?' or 'Why are you talking with her?'" This points up the fact that Jesus once again broke with rabbinic attitude by conversing, this time alone, with a woman. It also implies that the disciples did not question Jesus' morals or wisdom in this respect.

The next part of the passage is highly important. To begin with, although the woman became a "missionary" to the townspeople, her message was not as clear as might appear on the surface of the text. The first part is clear: "Come, see a man who told me everything I ever did." She was quite open in her attitude to her past and present and also to the perception of Jesus. But the next words convey her uncertainty: "Could this be the Christ?" The question in the Greek (introduced by the particle, *mēti*) suggests considerable uncertainty. While one might like to celebrate this woman's bold confidence in Christ, something else is indicated that could be even more significant. Far from believing easily, or, to put it in crass terms, being gullible, as some might (wrongly) expect a woman to be, this woman was cautious about her conclusion. It is not that she was a doubter, for it is remarkable that any Samaritan would on the basis of one conversation even entertain the possibility that the speaker was the Jewish Messiah! She had ventured into the area of faith, willing to break with her own tradition but not rushing headlong and wide-eyed into something she did not understand.

Two early paintings of Jesus Christ and the Woman of Samaria. *Left:* In this painting (Cemetery of Calixtus, Rome), Jesus is pictured above the woman. *Above:* In this somewhat later painting (Catacomb Via Latina, Rome) Jesus and the woman are on the same level. Both are wearing an early version of the dalmatic, which symbolized status in the Christian community. Does this indicate changing perceptions of the woman in the early church?   Alinari—Art Resource, New York.

This caution did not lessen the import or effect of what she said. John reports, "Many of the Samaritans from that town believed in him because of the woman's testimony." This is similar to Jesus' words later, when, in the Upper Room after the Last Supper, he said to the Father, "I pray also for those who will believe in me through their [i.e., the apostles'] message."[48]

But what about the following words of the Samaritan people to the woman: "We no longer believe just because of what you said; now we have heard for ourselves, and we know that this man really is the Savior of the world"? Does this minimize the testimony of the woman? Raymond E. Brown comments on the people's remark: "Yet this is scarcely because of an inferiority she might have as a woman—it is the inferiority of any human witness compared to encountering Jesus himself."[49]

Peter's Mother-in-Law

Peter's mother-in-law had a fever while Jesus was visiting at Peter's home.[50] The seriousness of the illness is not stated. The incident occurs in Matthew, Mark, and Luke, with little modification. Matthew and Mark say that Jesus touched her, an act that was characteristic of Jesus. In this case, since she was a woman, it was a questionable act, according to the mores of that society, but there is no evidence that it was a matter of concern, perhaps because of the difference in age. (Although rabbis were known to take a sick person's hand if he was a man, "there are no examples of rabbis doing so for a woman, and certainly not on the Sabbath when the act could wait until after sundown.")[51] When she was healed, she immediately served Jesus and the others. In doing this she went beyond what was usually done by the "matron of the house."[52] All three Synoptic Gospels also mention this act of serving. It is surely not intended as a statement of subservience in any of the Gospels. It was an act of gratitude appropriate to the social situation of the day.

The Woman Taken in Adultery

It is difficult to know what the original biblical setting was for this episode. Most early texts do not have it where it presently is—John 7:53–8:11.[53] It could be said that even if it does not belong here, it does reflect an attitude of Jesus that rings true. The account is well known. A woman was caught in the act of adultery, and the religious leaders were about to stone her to death. Jesus wrote something on the ground (which the Scriptures do not disclose, but which curious people ever since have tried to reconstruct), after which he addressed the crowd: "If anyone of you is without sin, let him be the first to throw a stone at her." This, of course, does not mean that Jesus minimized the woman's sin. It is rather a statement that all have sinned and a statement also of God's mercy. In that society what a man could do and get away with could not be done with impunity by a woman. Jesus once again cut across the grain of his society. His double statement to the woman has been the subject of many sermons: "Then neither do I condemn you. Go now and leave your life of sin."

Jairus' Daughter and the Woman With a Hemorrhage

On one occasion, Jesus performed miracles on behalf of two women.[54] The narrative begins with a father, Jairus, pleading with Jesus to come to his daughter, who was dying. On the way, a woman with a hemorrhage pressed through the crowds and, seeking healing, touched the edge of Jesus' cloak. Jesus sensed that power had gone out of him, called out to ask who it was who touched him, and, when she approached, commended her faith.

Christ Healing the Woman With a Hemorrhage. Late third-century lunette. Crypt Arcosolium. From Art Resource, New York.

Meanwhile, Jairus' daughter had died. Jesus told the crowds that she was just sleeping, probably using that euphemism so that when he raised her the miracle would not bring him as much attention from those who were seeking a spectacular messiah. Jesus did raise the girl, after encour-

aging the father's faith. Incidentally, the girl's mother is not mentioned until the end, when there is a reference to the parents in the plural.

While the account is about two women, Jairus' daughter is, of course, passive. The two objects of attention are Jairus himself and the woman with the hemorrhage. Thus a man and a woman are paired together as people of faith. Actually, Jairus seems to have needed some encouragement and may not have been as strong as the woman. The reason Jesus singled her out was clearly not to embarrass her but to reveal and commend her faith. Jesus could have expressed distress over becoming ceremonially unclean, for that was understood to be the result of touching anyone with a physical discharge.[55] But he was obviously more concerned over the woman than over matters of ritual cleanliness. The woman with the hemorrhage was a member of a "marginal" group.[56] She was a woman, in this case unclean because of her hemorrhage, and there is no indication of her having any status such as being related to a prominent man might give her. She undoubtedly lived a lonely life. She stands in contrast to the ruler Jairus, a prominent person and community leader who had the social standing she lacked. Yet both exercise faith, and both are accepted by Jesus.

The Syrophoenician Woman

It is striking that "two of the longest conversations Jesus had with women were not with Jewish women who might have been expected to have some understanding of who he was and of the meaning of his message, but with a Samaritan and with the Syrophoenician woman from the region of Tyre."[57] It has been suggested that in Matthew the incident is the central point of a chiasm (a literary device with a sequence of elements that are repeated in reverse order).[58] However that may be viewed, it does occur, both in Matthew and in Mark, between the feeding of the five thousand and the feeding of the four thousand."[59] This sequence of events thus contrasts the feeding of thousands of people with the grateful acceptance by the Syrophoenician woman of (figuratively) a few "crumbs." The effect of this is to feature the lone figure of this woman of faith.

It may also be significant that in both Matthew and Mark this account is preceded by some teaching of Jesus on the subject of ritual cleanness. That may be significant because the woman involved was not only not Jewish but, according to Matthew, also a "Canaanite." This reference to the woman's descent from the pagan inhabitants of Palestine prior to the settling there of the Jewish people underscores the fact that she would have been considered ritually and personally unacceptable to the Jewish people. How this is so becomes evident in the reading of the story.

This incident took place in the vicinity of the city of Tyre and Sidon. Thus Jesus was in Gentile territory, outside of the borders of Galilee. The area, which is now in Syria, was known then as Phoenicia. This is why the woman is called a "Syrophoenician." Matthew introduces the action with a word designed to get the reader's attention: "Look!" (the Greek word *idou*, often translated, "Behold"). This woman came to Jesus and begged him to cast a demon out of her daughter. Matthew's version, which has more detail than Mark's, says that Jesus did not at first answer her but responded when the woman got on the disciples' nerves.

Jesus' response has disturbed many readers of this narrative. It seems rude and racist to tell her in effect that Jesus' mission was only to Jewish people and that it would be wrong to take the "bread" that belongs to them (whom he describes figuratively as children) and give it to dogs, a term by which the Jewish people described Gentiles such as this woman. "The woman's answer is masterly. 'Yes, Lord,' she agrees, 'for even the dogs under the table eat the children's crumbs.' Those two words 'for even' reveal immense wisdom and faith."[60] The woman did not argue with the theological premise of Jesus' messianic mission. Matthew records the fact that she had initially addressed Jesus as "Son of David." She then realized that this was not the basis on which she would receive help; instead, the Lord is merciful to all who call on him, regardless of their position in or outside of Judaism with its messianic privileges.

This woman showed herself to be perceptive, able to hold her own in conversation, and possessing a deep faith that not only achieved her desire but undoubtedly also won the admiration of Jesus. Her place in the Gospel account is well deserved.

The Women at the Cross

Matthew[61] and Mark[62] mention by name several women who were watching the events of the Crucifixion "from a distance." Luke[63] does not mention any names here, probably since he did so in chapter 8. Interestingly, Luke wrote that among those who knew him and "stood at a distance" were "the women who had followed him from Galilee."[64] John does not mention the distance at all; on the contrary, he says that the women, whom he names, were "near the cross."[65]

Matthew, Mark, and Luke all say that these women "followed" Jesus. The word "follow" is usually considered the equivalent of "be a disciple of," though that idea has been challenged.[66] The word that Luke uses conveys the idea of "follow along with" and is less likely to mean discipleship, though that is not ruled out. It could actually convey the idea of an even closer relationship. Still another difference is that Matthew and Mark say women were "ministering to" or "serving" Jesus, whereas Luke omits this idea. The reason that this, like the names of the women, is absent from Luke here is probably that in the passage studied above he already identified several women who "ministered" to Jesus (Luke 8:1–3). Mark speaks also of "many other women who came up with him to Jerusalem."[67] It is not known whether these were regular disciples or not.

What does it mean that these women "ministered" to Jesus? Is this term the equivalent of what is connoted by its use today? Could the women be called ministers? A semantic error can be avoided by noticing that whereas ministry in the contemporary sense is done *for* the Lord *to* other people, here it is *to* the Lord and his associates. It is an overstatement to say, "This was equivalent to calling the women . . . ministers."[68]

But having said that, there is no reason to think that the women ministered to Jesus any *less* than the men did. Nor is there any reason to think that the women did not minister to others after the resurrection of Christ. Nor should it be concluded that, when Luke says the women ministered "out of their substance," this was intended to introduce a restriction on the extent of their ministry. To be realistic about it, the way in which the women—or men— could minister to Jesus probably *was* largely in providing for his material and personal needs. It would be unrealistic and anachronistic to think that if Luke had not included the words "out of their own means," ministering would have meant something like our modern concept of ministry.

Women were not only at the cross; they also went to the tomb. Luke is careful to note that the women "saw the tomb and how his body was laid in it. Then they went home and prepared spices and perfumes. But they rested on the Sabbath in obedience to the commandment."[69] Several things are worth noting here. In spite of their grief, the fact that Jesus had been executed as a criminal, and the danger from the hostile crowds and officials that all the disciples felt, these women identified themselves as Jesus' followers and went to the tomb where the Roman soldiers were standing guard.

The preparing of spices for Jesus' body (a necessary provision for a corpse in that hot climate), was not only the ministry of women, as one might infer from a statement by Charles C. Ryrie—a statement to which Dorothy Pape takes strong exception.[70] Ryrie says that the ministry of women to Christ was to care for his physical needs and implies that it was only in response to such ministry that he allowed women to follow him. However, John tells us that Nicodemus accompanied Joseph of Arimathea to the tomb and "brought a mixture of myrrh and aloes, about seventy-five pounds."[71]

Women as Witnesses of the Resurrection

The narratives of the Resurrection events are among the most revealing in all of the Gospels, not only as to the character and role of women but also as to the perceptions of men concerning them.

All four Gospels open their accounts of the day of Resurrection with the early visit of the women to the tomb of Jesus (Matt. 28:1–8; Mark 16:1–8; Luke 24:1–8; John 20:1–10). John has a further section about Mary Magdalene (John 20:11–18). Mark 16:9–11 also mentions Mary Magdalene; the verses in Mark, however, are part of a section that most New Testament scholars consider to be a later addition to the original text. All four Gospels mention Mary Magdalene. She is already well known in the Gospel narration and was one of those who accompanied Jesus in Luke 8:1–3. She is the first person mentioned at the tomb, the one who lingered nearby, and the first one to see Jesus.

Another Mary (mentioned in Matthew, Mark, and Luke) is identified by Mark as the mother of James. Mark mentions Salome, and Luke mentions Joanna; the probability is that this is the same Joanna mentioned among the companions of Jesus in Luke 8:1–3. When Luke tells of the report these women gave to the other disciples, he says that there were other women with them who were also telling these things to the apostles. There is no way to tell how many women were involved altogether.

These women came as early as they could following the close of the Sabbath. It appears from a comparison of the Gospel narratives that they started out before dawn and reached the tomb as the sun was beginning to rise. The scene that greeted them— the empty tomb and the angels—is well known. Mark and Luke describe the women as alarmed and frightened. There is no hint that this response had anything to do with any alleged emotional difference between men and women. After all, it was the male disciples who had been terrified on the Mount of Transfiguration, and Zechariah had been startled and frightened by the angel in the temple in Luke 1.

Some interpreters of the Gospels have rightly emphasized the fact that the first proclamation of the resurrection of Christ was made to women. Assessments of the significance of this, however, vary. Gilbert Bilezikian comments, "It was the reward of the loyal female disciples, who had accompanied Jesus to the place of crucifixion and stayed with Him through the horror of His execution, to be intrusted by Him with the most powerful message that has ever impacted the world: 'He is risen.' "[72]

Mary Evans has a well-balanced

The Women at the Tomb. From the Christian Baptistry at Dura Europas. Third Century. From the Yale University Art Gallery, Dura Europas Collection.

statement. After disposing of what she considers the false alternatives of whether "the angels appeared to the women rather than the men as a reward for their greater love [which seems to be Bilezikian's position] or as a support for their weaker faith," she says, "it seems likely that the angels appeared to the women as the ones who were first at the tomb, and having corroborated the evidence there was no need for them to appear again."[73] Evans then notes that the women not only were "witnesses to the facts and receivers of the message" but also were commissioned to declare that message. "The women might have been the first," she writes, "to receive the message of the resurrection because they were first at the tomb; they were the first proclaimers of it by the direct command of the angels and of Christ himself."

It is surprising that there are books from the feminine perspective that include data from the Gospels but do not mention the women at the empty tomb. Even those that do mention

them do not discuss the significance of the role they play. Evan's statement strikes the right balance. The point is not simply that the women were there; it is rather that they were commissioned to tell. But immediately they encountered a problem, and this problem makes the commission all the more striking. Luke reports that when the other disciples heard the report of the women, "they did not believe the women, because their words seemed to them like nonsense" (Luke 24:11). Luke's record is not a put-down of the women, as some have supposed. On the contrary, if anything, it is a put-down of the men who failed to believe them. But it is not certain that the men disbelieved because the messengers were women. No one seemed disposed to believe the Resurrection facts at first. This makes the belief and boldness of the women all the more significant.

If there was a reluctance to believe even partly because the word came through women, that would not have been unusual. Paul, we may remember, fails to list the women as witnesses to the Resurrection (1 Cor. 15:3–8). This may be attributed to the fact that women were not accepted as legal witnesses.

The Penitent Mary Magdalene. This statue from Florence is one of several portrayals of her that overemphasize the aspect of sin and repentance. This is not, however, the way she is presented in the Gospels.   Alinari—Art Resource, New York.

John's added narration of the meeting between Jesus and Mary Magdalene is a moving account. She did not recognize Jesus. This could be because of the nature of the resurrection body of Jesus (if there was some variation in corporeal structure), or it may have simply been that she did not see his face at first. In any event his calling her by name resulted in immediate recognition. Her natural impulse was to cling to Jesus (the verb indicates more than just touching); but Jesus said that she should not hold on to him, because he had not yet ascended to the Father. It is not certain whether this refers to an immediate ascension followed by periodic appearances and then the final visible ascension or whether it refers to the single ascension we know of from Luke 24 and Acts 1. But this does not affect the fact that Jesus indicated to Mary that things were different and she must not try to hold on to him. It is a beautiful scene and consistent with what we know of Jesus' relationship with these faithful women.

Women in the Teaching of Jesus

Jesus did not teach explicitly on the subject of women. His attitudes, however, can be gleaned indirectly from comments on other subjects, such as divorce. They can also be gathered from noting some of the negative Jewish opinions and observing the absence of such ideas in the Gospels.

Jesus and Jewish Thought

In the Gospels, Jesus makes little reference to the belief systems of others, apart from those of the sectarian leaders with whom he had personal confrontation. How much background is necessary in order to portray him historically against his times is difficult to know. Jesus and his disciples were untrained in rabbinic thought,[74] so discussion of that subject will await the chapter on Paul. It is more likely that he read or heard of the teachings of another Jesus— Jesus ben Sira (Sirach). But whether he did or not, his own teachings and attitudes toward women are seen in clearer perspective when we know something of the teachings of that sage.

Ben Sira lived nearly two centuries before the time of Christ. He made a number of comments about women, strongly positive and strongly negative. The latter probably express his inner feelings more accurately.[75] As is true of other ancient writers, ben Sira seems to find a woman's virtues mainly in her relationship with her husband, not in qualities of her own. A passage that on the surface seems to celebrate the beauty and desirability of woman begins, "Any man will a woman accept" (i.e., a woman will accept any man—a statement that is hardly flattering to women). Structurally it is parallel to 36:18, "Every food does the stomach eat," and both are followed by "Yet one [food/woman] is more pleasant than another." In the opinion of ben Sira, therefore, a woman's beauty is not one of a number of virtues contributing to her dignity as a woman; rather, it is something that pleases her husband sexually and can also get her into trouble with other men.

It has often been observed that the compliments paid to women in Jewish literature around the time of Jesus and the early church relate to her role as wife, mother, and provider. This is true also in Sirach, but several considerations should be kept

in mind. One is that ben Sira does show appreciation for his wife's character.[76] Woman's virtue is not merely sexual or utilitarian; it is also intellectual and moral. Another consideration is that given the culture of his day, there was little opportunity for a woman to demonstrate her virtues and abilities outside of the family. Sirach is a vivid demonstration of this situation, and this in itself provides a valuable insight into the background of the Gospels. The cultural setting of ben Sira's comments also includes the fact that wives were viewed as a husband's possession: "He who acquires a wife gets his best possession."[77]

Ben Sira's portrayal of the bad wife is very negative. He pictures her as publicly disgracing, uncontrollable, drunken, adulterous, angry, impossible to live with, worthy of a curse, babbling, seductive, emasculating, unpleasant, sin-originating, outspoken, and worthy of divorce.[78]

The description "sin-originating" is particularly important. This is a theme found in later writings, including the works of the church fathers. Ben Sira says, "From a woman did sin originate, and because of her we all must die."[79] This view accords with later ideas both of rabbis and of the church fathers. A reference to Eve is also found in Paul, but the difference is that it is not her sin as such but her being deceived that Paul mentions.[80] Paul specifically says that it is because of Adam's sin, not Eve's, that we all die.[81] Jesus does not refer to Eve's sin or to her deception. It is clear in Genesis that man would dominate his wife following the Fall.[82] Whether the Fall left woman with an inordinate desire for, or dependence on, her husband or whether it made her competitive with her husband for leadership[83] does not seem to be an issue in the Gospels. Nothing appears in Jesus' teaching to compare with Paul's reference in 1 Timothy 2:12–14 to Eve's having been deceived.

In fairness to ben Sira, in his passage on the bad wife the subject is just that, "a bad wife," not "wives are bad."[84] And if he says that it is "better to dwell with a lion and a dragon than to dwell with an evil wife,"[85] this is reminiscent of "Better to live on a corner of the roof than share a house with a quarrelsome wife" (Prov. 21:9; 25:24). If we read in Sirach that it is "hard slavery and disgrace" for a woman to support her husband, that is not to say that ben Sira looks down on women in general because some support their husbands.[86] Rather, it reflects the ideals of the age. Even in Proverbs 31, the industrious wife has a distinguished husband.

All this shows that during the centuries immediately preceding the coming of Christ, there was a pervasive low view of women abroad in Palestine that is reflected even in a work such as Sirach, which at times shows real appreciation for a virtuous wife. How dark this picture was is a matter of disagreement among scholars.[87]

Women in Parables and Allusions

In contrast, no one attributes a low opinion of women to Jesus. One way to perceive Jesus' high view of women is to survey his parables. Jesus told parables portraying a remarkably wide variety of human situations. They pertain to such real-life circumstances as weddings, business, a mugging, finding and losing valuables, farming, baking, house construction, an unexpected guest, investments, and the courtroom. Naturally these reflect the social structures of Jesus' day. Thus males are found in such positions as those of judge, farmer, employer, shepherd, and religious leader among the Jews. If Jesus' parables were to be an effective means of communication, they had to reflect life in a recognizable way.

The Prodigal Son.[88] This parable has an all-male cast. It is about a father and an older and a younger brother. This is natural because it would have been a son rather than a daughter who would acquire a portion of the inheritance and seek his way in the world. Another son, rather than a sister, would have had cause for jealousy. It would have been a father, not a mother, who would give a portion of the inheritance, and the action of the father in running out to meet his son would have been more striking than similar action on the part of the mother. Further, and here theology is involved, Jesus taught about the heavenly Father, and in that respect, at least, it was appropriate to represent God by a human father.

The Lost Sheep and the Lost Coin.[89] In the other two parables of Luke 15, it was natural that the shepherd be a man. But when the opportunity was open to choose between the sexes for one who lost and found a coin, Jesus chose a woman. There is no reason why this was necessary, for it could just have easily been a man who lost a coin in the house. In fact, it is more striking that Jesus chose to make the character a woman in that she also, like the shepherd and the father of the lost son, represents God. In this case fatherhood is not involved, so the choice of a woman is possible.

The Persistent Widow.[90] The main characters in the parable of the unjust judge are a gruff judge and a disadvantaged widow. In spite of his resistance to her appeals, in the end she prevails. As noted above, this passage does not demean women as weak. On the contrary, it features a woman's persistence. Clearly the woman comes off better than the man in this parable. This is all the more striking if the man to a degree is analogous to God and the woman to the believer who petitions God. Possibly the judge says he is afraid that further delay on his part will cause the woman to give him a "black eye," since the verb usually translated "wear me out" actually means to strike someone under the eye. It therefore could mean literally and figuratively to give someone a black eye, just as we use the expression today.[91] If this is the case, the point may be that God, like the judge, will respond so that his reputation is not blackened. The thrust of the parable may be one of comparison (God, like the judge, will eventually respond) or contrast (God, unlike the judge, will show compassion).

Either interpretation arouses admiration for the widow. Although she is a relatively helpless member of society, she shows tremendous strength of character and a healthy aggressiveness in the pursuit of her rights. She emerges as a colorful character who wins the day.

The Wise and Foolish Bridesmaids.[92] These women are evenly divided between the wise and the foolish. There is no suggestion that women in general are foolish or that they are lacking in foresight or industry. What is significant here is that Jesus chooses to use a parable solely about women and that this parable is parallel to the following one about men in business. This is one of several instances where Jesus mentions men and women in balance. In some cases male and female are paired in Jesus' teaching.

The Pairing of Men and Women. There are some interesting cases of the pairing of men and women. A man plants a mustard seed and a woman uses leaven in Jesus' parables of the kingdom.[93] The Queen of the South appears in parallel to Jonah as witnesses in the future judgment in two allusions that Jesus makes to Old Testament narratives.[94] To say that the Queen of the South will "rise at the judgment with the men of this generation and condemn them" is a powerful statement about the significance of this woman. It is probably reading too much into the text, however, to say that she "would stand in judgment over men" and that "a woman will be given judgment over a whole generation of men and condemn them for their spiritual obduracy."[95] The fact is that while the word is frequently used in condemning, it need not imply that the individual functions as a judge passing sentence. Rather, as a major New Testament Greek lexicon puts it, "The conduct of one person, since it sets a standard, can result in the condemnation before God of another person whose conduct is inferior."[96] Therefore, although the other interpretation is incorrect, the correct understanding does not minimize the outstanding character and significance attributed to this woman.

An Eschatalogical Picture.[97] Jesus made a further reference to women, not this time in a parable or an Old Testament allusion, but as typical of the activity that would be interrupted by the return of the Son of Man. In the discourse of Luke 17, Jesus said that there would be two men sleeping in one bed (probably referring to the common arrangement of people sleeping all together on pallets on the floor of a house) and one would be taken and the other left (v. 34). In parallel to this he spoke of two women grinding their grain together, one being taken at the Lord's coming and the other left (v. 35). It is clear that Jesus wanted to use one illustration concerning men and another concerning women. For that purpose he chose a typical activity of women. The illustration of the men in bed portrays the fact that the Lord's return could be at night as well as in the daytime.[98] Therefore, one illustration was chosen from each time period. The suggestion that Jesus deliberately chose both men and women is supported by the fact that in the similar setting of Matthew 24:40–41, although Jesus speaks of two women grinding at the mill, as in Luke, the companion reference to men is a different one, in this case two men working in a field. The point is that even though Jesus uses different illustrations for men, he retains the same illustration of women, showing that this was a constant factor in repeated teachings on the subject.

Jesus and Social Change

Every time Jesus visited Jerusalem, he no doubt observed that women were permitted in the Gentile court of the temple and into the next one only if they were not in their period of impurity. Only Jewish males were permitted into the inner court. Women could not participate in the rites performed there, so entrance would have been useless anyway. There is no evidence that Jesus spoke out against this as unacceptable discrimination. This need not constitute approval of the distinction, for Jesus as an individual could do no more to change that situation than Paul could change the practice of slavery. It is true that Jesus did cast out the money changers, but their activity was an imposition on the established structure, not a part of it. Whether women were segregated in the synagogue and how much they may have participated in synagogue activities will be discussed in connection with Paul.

"Less lust and larger families" was the slogan with which Cicero had advised Julius Caesar to legislate reforms in the Roman Republic. This message, with its implied small print about the place of women, describes the secular situation in the decades prior to the birth of Christ. Laws were finally passed under Augustus in 19/18 B.C. to encourage large families by providing substantial benefits for having three or more children, and to stipulate severe penalties for adultery (banishment of the offending pair to different islands for life).

In such ways the superpower of Jesus' day was attempting to deal with matters of justice for women. As

45

might be expected, laws that seem to have been designed to help women were just as likely intended to benefit society as a whole (and consequently men as well).

Jesus, in contrast, showed little interest in direct action to modify the social conditions of women—or of men, for that matter. Yet his teaching on adultery and divorce, among other subjects, not only addressed moral issues in a radical way but in effect raised the level of women's dignity and security. The effect of Jesus' teaching on divorce, to continue this example, was not only to maintain a high level of personal morality but also to protect women from irresponsible tactics on the part of men who simply wanted freedom to pursue a new relationship. In contrast, some of the rabbis, notably Hillel and his followers, were permitting men to divorce their wives for minor and ridiculous reasons. Jesus put the matter squarely on a moral basis. In this respect, Judaism (except for the more conservative rabbi Shammai) had lagged behind the Romans in protecting the rights of the women.

The Male Apostolate

One of the questions most often asked by both traditionalists and feminists is why Jesus did not appoint any women apostles. Traditionalists use this fact as a challenge, and it is a problem feminists must face. First, if Jesus intended to declare women not only personally equal with men but also qualified for equal ministries, why did he not take the opportunity of making such a declaration by choosing at least one

woman among the Twelve? Would this not have been an opportunity not only for vividly demonstrating his position on the matter but also for pioneering social change? Second, traditionalists point out that no matter how many women may have been associated with Jesus, even in a discipleship relationship, the ultimate step was clearly not taken. Without listing pro and con authors, it should at least be generally observed that while more serious studies on such subjects as the priesthood of women may acknowledge the problem of an all-male apostleship, popular works surveying women in the New Testament tend simply to omit reference to this, thereby bypassing a troublesome fact.

To be equally honest, however, one should ask the question, "What would have happened if Jesus had appointed a female apostle?" First of all, from a practical standpoint, it would have been logistically difficult for a woman to travel alone as an itinerant missionary in the first-century world. Second, from a social viewpoint, a woman would not have been accepted as a religious teacher in most areas. This will become clear in the second chapter. There were women involved in religious cult leadership, but their image was that of emotion and frenzy. Third, women were not accepted as witnesses. The basic function of the apostle was to witness to the words, deeds, resurrection, and person of the Lord Jesus Christ. Because of the unacceptability of women as witnesses, Paul does not list them among the witnesses to the Resurrection (1 Cor. 15). Fourth, the apostles symbolically represented the twelve tribes of Israel. This is apparently why it was felt that a successor had to be appointed to take the place of Judas,[99] and even though Paul was shortly to have the ministry of apostleship conferred on him, that would not provide the visible completion of the body of Twelve in Jerusalem. If this symbolic group was to gain acceptance among Jews, it was unthinkable that one of them be a woman.

Were all or any of these considerations behind Jesus' decision not to appoint a female apostle? This question cannot be answered with certainty. But those who see the lack of women apostles as a proof that women should not have any authority in the church today will do well to ponder what implications there would have been had Jesus taken the other course of action.

Concluding Reflections

Jesus' attitudes to women are, therefore, seen only indirectly in his teaching. It is more in the Gospels' description of his positive relations with women in daily life that we learn his thoughts. Even without pronouncements on the subject, we are left in no doubt as to his position. Making a clear break with custom, Jesus had women learning from him as disciples and traveling with him in service. He engaged in theological dialogue with women. He helped women in need and in sin without demeaning them. He treated men and women alike with regard to their failings. He encouraged both men and women in their faith. He was absolutely pure in his relations with women. In his parables, which had to reflect life as it was in order to be

effective, he portrayed women accurately in their various social roles.

All this makes understandable the strong reaction of Dorothy Pape to the claim of Charles C. Ryrie that Jesus "limited [women's] activity by not choosing one of them for official work. Thus we may say . . . He limited the sphere of their activity by glorifying the domestic responsibilities with which they ministered to Him." Pape questions what "official work" may be and asks, "Where in the Gospels does Christ especially 'glorify' domestic work? The woman mixing bread does not seem any more 'glorified' than the farmer sowing seed or dressing vines."[100]

Jesus' attitude toward women is seen especially in his relationship to his own mother, Mary. He helped her to see that her ultimate relationship with him had to be one of obedient faith. At his death, he cared for her future needs by committing her to John's care.

The Gospels, reflecting Jesus' attitudes toward women, sometimes portray women in need. This is not done, however, with the purpose or effect of demeaning them. Women in the Gospels have dignity. In the Resurrection narratives, the women are described as the first at the tomb and as the first in the long and distinguished line of those who have born witness to the living Savior.

Dorothy Sayers has understood what all this means:

Perhaps it is no wonder that the women were first at the Cradle and last at the Cross. They had never known a man like this Man—there never has been such another. A prophet and teacher who never nagged at them, never flattered or coaxed or patronized;

who never made arch jokes about them, never treated them either as "The women, God help us!" or "The ladies, God bless them!"; who rebuked without querulousness and praised without condescension; who took their questions and arguments seriously; who never mapped out their sphere for them, never urged them to be feminine or jeered at them for being female; who had no axe to grind and no uneasy male dignity to defend; who took them as he found them and was completely unself-conscious.[101]

EXCURSUS ON
LUKE'S VIEW OF WOMEN

Students of the Gospels have long been accustomed to observing the prominence of women in the Gospel of Luke. Luke seems to have had an empathy for women, an understanding of their physical and spiritual needs that displays more sensitivity than is shown by the other Gospel writers. Recently, however, this fact has been viewed from a different perspective. Rather than commending Luke's sympathetic portrayal of women, some now consider it a patronizing putting down of women:

> Luke characteristically qualified every mention of women by a reference to some negative aspect of their character. Here he noted that these women had been healed of evil spirits and infirmities, especially Mary of Magdala from whom seven demons had been cast out. This is a literary device used throughout the gospel of Luke to present women as both weak and sinful.[102]

Such a viewpoint is not only contradicted by the preceding survey of women in Luke, but by the following observations:

1. When Luke includes incidents about *men* in sections that are *also* found in one or more of the other Gospels, he portrays their physical and moral needs as well, not minimizing their weaknesses in contrast to those of women. Luke includes incidents found in Matthew and Mark that show male weakness: he mentions a demon-possessed man (4:33). Jesus healed a male leper (5:12–14) and a paralyzed man who was in need of forgiveness (5:17–20). He calls Levi, a tax collector and "sinner" in 5:27–32, where Jesus says, "I have not come to call the righteous, but sinners to repentance." The centurian's servant near death is a male. The Gerasene demoniac in 8:26–39 is male, not female. It is a son, not a daughter, who is suffering from convulsions in 9:37–43. It is a man, not a woman, who is blind and helpless in 18:35–43. It is Peter, not a woman, who denies the Lord.

2. Luke presents several incidents about *men* that are *not* found in the other Gospels. In each case he brings to the fore their physical or moral weakness. Only Luke includes the special call of Peter. In this incident Peter called himself a sinful man (5:8). The Pharisee in 7:36–50 is clearly inferior in character to the woman who is called a sinner, and likewise the judge in the parable of 18:1–8 is inferior in character to the widow. Prostitutes (such as the woman in Luke 7 seems to have been) have always been a marked group in any society. For Luke to introduce this woman is not to brand women as morally inferior but to show God's grace and Jesus' love to even such a person. Likewise, widows were a distinct group in that society. It is no reflection on women to recognize the statistical reality of first-century mortality tables. The story of the unjust judge is not literary fiction to emphasize the weakness of a widow, but a parable that encourages the church to identify itself with the widow who perseveres against the injustice of an unjust judge. A widow, generally thought of as helpless, is here transformed into a character of strength, a model for the church.

Virgin of the Annunciation, a woodcut from the fifth or sixth century. If this is, as assumed, a portrayal of Mary, it is one of the earliest representations of the Virgin extant, and perhaps the earliest. Mary has remained the ideal Christian woman over the centuries.   From the Louvre.

3. Also in passages that have no counterpart in the other Gospels, Luke presents women as spiritually strong as well as portraying some of them, like men, in conditions of weakness and sin. Perhaps Elizabeth's childlessness (Luke 1:7) could be considered a weakness, but in verse 6, as noted earlier, Luke specifically commends Elizabeth equally with her husband, Zechariah, who was a priest of God.[103] Certainly Luke does not present the virgin Mary as weak or sinful; on the contrary, he features her piety and biblical knowledge. Mary of Bethany is shown in Luke 10 to be a disciple learning from a rabbi, hardly a portrayal of weakness or sinfulness. Other women presented only in Luke are portrayed as fiscally responsible and supportive of Christian ministry, as was noted above and as will also be seen in Luke's narrative in Acts.[104]

4. Although there are places in Luke where women are described in terms of weakness and moral need, this is true of all the Gospels. But such references are not derogatory. Men and women share these characteristics, and Christ came to meet the moral and physical needs of *all* people. Luke tells us that Jesus came "to seek and to save what was lost."[105] For Luke, sinfulness and weakness, though negative, are conditions of humankind that affords God opportunity to exercise his saving grace. It is true that several of the women who appear only in the Gospel of Luke have serious physical or moral defects. Only Luke's story of an anointing features a woman who is

said to be sinful. Only Luke mentions that Mary Magdalene had been demon-possessed. It is only in his Gospel that we read of the woman who had been "bound by Satan" and unable to stand up straight.[106] Examples like these are easily observed also in the other Gospels.

Matthew has a statement about "Rachel weeping for her children."[107] John tells of Jesus' conversation with the woman at the well, an example of a woman who was in deep moral need and who became a proclaimer of the Messiah to her own people. The illness of Peter's mother-in-law appears in several Gospels.[108] The dying daughter of Jairus and the woman with a hemorrhage likewise are found in all three Synoptics.[109] The details about the infamous Herodias and her role in the death of John the Baptist are in Matthew and Mark, though not in Luke.[110] The parable in which a debtor fears being sold along with his wife and children, a vivid picture of the times, appears only in Matthew.[111] The original setting of the story of the woman taken in adultery is uncertain; its present location is in John.[112] It is Matthew, not Luke, who reports that prostitutes enter the kingdom (and there they are paired with male tax collectors).[113] The story of the widow's mite occurs in both Mark and Luke.[114] Here again, although the woman is portrayed in a position of weakness, widowhood with its consequent poverty was a common state in that society, conveying nothing concerning the morality of the individual woman. Further, the widow here is featured in contrast to rich people. Women were also prominent in the passion narrative.

Human beings are thus seen in Luke and in all the other Gospels as essentially weak and sinful, and many of them became the recipients of God's saving grace. This includes men and women without discrimination.

Chapter 2

Acts and Epistles: Prophesying Daughters and Silenced Wives

Only a few years separated the career of the apostle Paul from that of Jesus, and only a few pages separate their teachings in the biblical text, but the differences between them are dramatic. Although Jesus faced a variety of opinions among his contemporaries, all of his conversations and confrontations took place within a few square miles in Palestine. And all the recorded ones, at least, occurred within a few years. Paul's ministry, in contrast, spanned two decades and carried him across the Roman Empire. Although the later Greek culture we know as Hellenism had penetrated Palestine, Jesus' environment was not comparable to that of a resident of cosmopolitan Corinth, Ephesus, or Rome.

It is not surprising, therefore, that the writings by Paul about women and the church introduce issues and approaches not found in the Gospel accounts of Jesus. One instance of this difference is the fact that the Roman laws on the rights of women were advancing over the traditions of the Jewish rabbis, and they affected the environment in which Paul, but not Jesus, preached. Another instance is the dominant figure of the Roman matron—the socially prominent, articulate, forceful kind of woman who appears in contemporary descriptions of Roman life. She was the "liberated" woman of her day and stood in strong contrast not only to the secluded women of earlier years in Rome and in ancient Greece but also to women in Palestine at the time of Jesus' ministry. The church had to come to terms with the society it was trying to penetrate.

Such differences signal the fact that there are several points of transition that call for attention in a survey of the history of the church in the apostolic age. An understanding of these transitions helps to resolve the tensions that the average reader feels in trying to resolve the ideal of "sons and daughters" prophesying (Acts 2:17) with the reality of the words in 1 Corinthians 14:34 about wives being silent in church.

The Political Transition:
From Greece to the
Roman Republic and Empire*

These transitions took place before the time of Christ, but they affected most of the communities mentioned in Acts, and most of these were significant to Paul. It is a commonplace that the conquests of Alexander carried Greek culture across the known world in the process known as "Hellenization." Successive political transitions were accompanied by a blending of cultures that was especially seen in religion. All of this affected women.

Greece

One might think that women in ancient Greece would have had a high standing in view of the fact that their pantheon included strong female deities as well as male deities. The celebrated goddesses, Athena and Artemis, immediately come to mind, along with Hera, Zeus' wife, who held considerable power. Yet, as students of the classics will recall vividly, the male deities did not limit their amorous activities to their female counterparts; Zeus himself had a reputation for fondling mortal women. One has to ask whether the stories of this use of women, known from myth and drama, did not affect the average man's attitude. Of course, the myths themselves were nothing more than products of human fantasy, and most reflected the way men would like to have seen the world. Either way one looks at it—human values shaping the myths, or the myths in turn affecting human behavior—women fared poorly.[1]

Whatever the reasons, women, especially wives, lived for the most part in seclusion in ancient Greece. However much they might have been honored in literature or drama, daily life was something else. Men in ancient Athens who found their wives boring and good for little else than housework and rearing children had recourse to the *heterae*, companions who could provide intelligent party conversation and other favors. Other women, both slave and freedwomen, whose talents were limited to prostitution, were also available. Wives had little to say about it. The situation of women varied somewhat from city to city. Women in Sparta, for example, were better nourished and more active than those in Athens. They were expected to bear children for warfare. In dress they were different also, wearing slit skirts that bared the thigh.[2] Nevertheless, the average woman in ancient Greece had a dismal existence, with little genuine sexual pleasure, to say nothing about respect and companionship. To be sure, there were notable women, such as Aspasia, the honored companion of the Athenian general Pericles, and Sappho, a renowned poet. Sappho is perhaps known less today for her poetry than for the fact that she was apparently lesbian (the term coming from the name of her island of Lesbos).

In spite of the activities of some outstanding women and some gains

---

*As with the previous chapter, in order to maintain the flow of historical narration, significant issues concerning the interpretation of the biblical texts will largely be reserved for appendix B.

by all, "Athenian law of all periods tended to regard the wife as a veritable child, having the legal status of a minor compared to her husband."[3] We ought to keep this somber fact in mind even when noting that women gradually gained more freedom in various areas. Women did play a large role in religion, including that of priestess; yet it has been demonstrated that although women were accepted as prophets, they were not accepted as teachers, a fact that may have some bearing on Paul's words about women and teaching.[4] Hellenistic civilization brought some changes, of course, but in the Graeco-Roman world of the last centuries before Christ these were not necessarily for the better. Women became more visible, especially in stage plots (comedy was increasingly popular) and in art, which was often sexually explicit.[5] The man who wanted a respectable female companion could find a courtesan,[6] but at the lower level of society, there were, as always, prostitutes.

The Roman Republic

Roman women during the pre-Christian centuries fared somewhat better than Grecian women, though women in the lower classes of Roman society had menial jobs and little respect. Many were slaves. Some were on the public dole. However, education for women was increasing, and the age difference between husbands and wives was decreasing. These trends brought men and women into a closer social relationship. Nevertheless, men preferred to keep their wives in relative seclusion.

Shortly after 200 B.C. Roman women

joined in protest of a law called the Oppian Law named after its proponent, C. Oppius) that prevented them from displaying their status in public by means of jewelry, fine clothes, and riding in carriages. Cato, the conservative Roman senator, spoke against repeal, complaining, among other things, that the Roman matrons "could not be kept at home by advice or modesty or their husbands' orders." They "dared even to approach and appeal to the consuls." Cato considered their actions "shameful."[7]

More of Cato later, but for now we should note that the forces for repeal won out despite his opinion. Susan Bell observes, however, "The modern sympathizer of women's emancipation might deplore the argument which the tribune Valerius put forward on behalf of the women of Rome almost as much as one might deplore Senator Cato's entrenched conservatism." Valerius' argument was: "Give the women their baubles. These will satisfy their trivial minds and keep them from interfering in more serious matters."[8]

The Roman Empire

The transition from the Roman Republic to the Roman Empire following the military victory of Augustus over Antony and Cleopatra in 31 B.C. facilitated the passage of laws long awaited. Among these, as noted in chapter 1, were provisions to ensure the growth and stability of families by imposing stiff penalties for adultery and rewarding large families. The institution of the family came under state protection. There is some question, however, as to how effective these laws were in actually improving

Roman morals.⁹ Moreover, women continued to be inferior to men *de facto*. Some received an elementary education and beyond, but marriage at an early age, usually around fourteen, prevented further education for many. Life expectancy for women was to what we today would consider middle age, so it was well to begin a family early. Marriage had differing effects on the status of a woman, depending on the status of her husband and on whether the legal arrangement of *manus* was adopted. The old custom by which a woman was transferred from the power (*manus*, "hand") of her father to the power of her new husband transferred control over her and, for the most part, over her possessions. But this practice diminished under the Roman Empire, and an increasing number of women married *sine* (without) rather than *cum* (with) *manu*. Eventually women studied subjects—such as rhetoric, philosophy, and law—that were previously the domain of men. They attended major social events and participated in sports formerly considered suitable for men only. By the end of the second century the satirist Juvenal would be finding this all too much.¹⁰

The Roman Matrons: Liberated Women

There were women in the early years of the Empire who gained a high degree of prestige and power. Some achieved this by marrying men prominent in politics or in the military. The wives of some of the Roman emperors during the period of the New Testament have been described as "sensational."¹¹ There were those who exercised great influence in public affairs. Influential women of the upper classes were known as the "Roman matrons."

After the establishment of the Empire under Augustus, women were allowed to accompany their husbands if the latter had to live for a time in the provinces (perhaps in some governmental post). Prior to that, the wives had to stay in Rome, where they not only could do little but were also suspected of having secret affairs. In fact, it was not unknown for a husband to divorce his wife on returning from an extended tour of duty just on the assumption that she had been unfaithful.¹²

The Roman matrons were criticized by some of the people. It is possible that some of them used their new freedom for unworthy ends. Nevertheless, most of them carried their status of freedom with dignity. Their situation was far better than that achieved by Greek women. They enjoyed a healthier relationship with their husbands, ate with them at table, managed their homes, engaged in informed discussion, and had freedom to be involved outside the home in social activities. In spite of some strong criticism to the contrary, most of them did not flaunt their freedom, and the "women's movement" of the early Roman Empire gained much attention and many supporters. Some of the moralistic philosophers, such as Musonius Rufus and Seneca, were outspoken on the subject of women's equality, though in a limited way.¹³ Musonius Rufus thought that women should at least study philosophy.

Certainly Paul and members of his

The Eucharist, a Second-Century Painting in the Catacomb of Priscilla. Such a painting is not unique, as there are memorial portrayals of idealized banquets with the departed person participating. If this is a representation of the Lord's Supper, as it appears to be, it is noteworthy that all the participants, including the apparent celebrant, are women. (See also the comments on the Eucharist in chapter 3, page 92.)   Alinari—Art Resource, New York.

congregations were aware of these outstanding women. For women to exercise leadership in church ministries would, therefore, not be as unusual in that society, as might be supposed. Priscilla, Phoebe, and Lydia were some of the notable women in the church. The early church apparently prospered through the travels of Christian women. Also, a woman in whose home the Christians met would probably have had a strong positive influence in the church, especially if her husband was not yet a believer and she functioned as a hostess and benefactress.

Outside Influences and Roman Conservatism

In general the movement was from a restricted to a more free role for women in the age of Augustus and during the ensuing decades of the Roman Empire. This was especially true of the higher classes. But even Augustus himself had his limits. Prior to his final conquest over Antony and Cleopatra, he taunted Antony for having been influenced by the "feminists" in Cleopatra's Egypt. In particular the religion of the goddess Isis promoted feminism. This was one of the so-called mystery religions that flooded into the western part of the Empire around the end of the Republic and the beginning of the Empire. The conservative Romans were wary of these religions, some of which indulged in excesses, such as public self-castration, and it is not surprising that they were viewed with disgust. This became a problem for the Christians, who had to distinguish themselves from such groups. Since Christianity came from the east—the source of many cults, entertainers, and immoral adventurers—this was not easy. It may be that some of Paul's restrictions on women were at least partly intended to make the distinction clear.

The rumors that Augustus (at that time he was still known by his name, Octavian) heard about the status of men and women in Egypt must have been frightening, if the following comments by the historian Diodorus Siculus were at all typical. Diodorus said that in Egypt

> it was ordained that the queen should have greater power and honour than the king and that among private persons the wife should enjoy authority over her husband, the husbands agreeing in the marriage contract that they will be obedient in all things to their wives.[14]

Octavian could hardly refrain from reacting to such a state of affairs. To be sure that his soldiers kept their values straight, he urged his troops, "Maintain the renown of your forefathers, to preserve your own proud traditions . . . to allow no woman to make herself equal to a man."[15]

It is worth noting the reference to preserving the honor of the forefathers. There is a traditionalism here,

not merely implied, but explicit. In spite of the strong legal developments of this period after the accession of Augustus, and in spite of the emergence of strong upper-class women, a moral conservatism continued. This conservative reaction has considerable importance for the study of Paul's injunctions to women, especially regarding public deportment and appropriate covering of the head. Paul wrote about keeping his "traditions." Although this is often thought of only in terms of doctrine, the word also reflected the perpetuation of traditional moral values. It was vitally important for Paul's congregations to keep his traditions and thus their reputations.

Laws and customs of the various nations in which Christians were living were not uniform. Egypt was more flexible than Rome regarding women, Rome was more flexible than Athens. All, it might be added, were more flexible than Judaism in some ways, but Judaism did accord women a dignity and some practical advantages, such as property rights, that its contemporaries did not. It is therefore not wise to generalize about the position of women in ancient society.

The Religious Transition: From Judaism to Christianity

At the same time that he was trying to adapt the more indifferent aspects of Christian attitudes and behavior to the conventions of his day, Paul was wrestling with how to apply the principles of women's equality before God and of his responsibility in ministry in confrontation with Judaism. In this, Paul was not merely dealing with ideology and conventional morality, but also with religious opinions that claimed the authority of centuries of tradition and were thought to have had their origin, like Scripture itself, in divine revelation. As observed in the previous chapter, Jewish writings contain both lofty statements about the worth of women and what might almost be called a backlash of opinion concerning "woman's place." But in addition to the opinions already surveyed, there are other traditions and laws that, if indicative of attitudes existing in Paul's day (even if not yet formulated as they came to be in the Talmud), are important to know. Paul's teachings, especially those in 1 Timothy 2, are customarily viewed against rabbinical teachings, and he is often thought to have reflected his own rabbinic education in his views. But it is notoriously difficult to be sure of what opinions now found in the Talmud were actually held at the time of Paul, let alone what would have actually influenced him. Nevertheless, it is common practice today to quote denigrating comments by the rabbis about women in order to show how bleak the picture was at that time. Some of these comments may reflect attitudes held in Paul's day, but as we study them, we should be cautious in our evaluation.

The Talmud

The Talmud does contain a number of laws pertaining to women. In fact, an entire section of the Talmud is devoted to women's matters. It is called *Nashim*, "Women." The subdivisions or tractates are on sisters-in-law (*Yebamoth*), marriage deeds (*Ke-*

tuboth), vows (*Nedarim*), the Nazirite vow (*Nazir*), a suspected adulteress (*Sotah*), bills of divorce (*Gittin*), and betrothals (*Kiddushin*). Even *Nazir*, hardly a female subject, includes laws regarding women; e.g., a woman cannot impose a Nazirite vow on her son or bring the hair-offering for her father's vow. According to Kiddushin 33b, women are exempt from laws that are positive (prescriptions rather than prohibitions) and "time-bound" (applicable only on certain days or occasions, as on the Sabbath or at Passover).[16] This principle was a flexible one, with many exceptions. It does, however, help one to see why there were certain restrictions on women.

Actually these were not necessarily restrictions as such. For example, if women were "exempt" from some duty, that exemption might have *relieved* them from fulfilling the duty, but it would not have *prevented* them from doing so. It is well known that women were exempt from the study of the Torah, the Jewish law. It is not as commonly known that they were also exempt from the reading of the Torah and from prayer. This does not mean that women were not permitted to pray, but that they were exempt from certain prayers on specific occasions. Even here, a time-bound prayer, such as one said after meals, may be a matter of general spiritual attitude, and so it is specifically permitted by the Talmud. It is debated whether the reason women cannot be counted toward the minimum number of people required to form a congregation is that their function would be essentially that of praying.[17] The suitability of a woman's reading the Torah in a synagogue service continues to be a subject for debate to this day.

Studying the Torah

As for the *study* of the Torah, rabbinic opinions were quite strong. It is often said that Judaism prohibited women from learning the Law. One saying is that whoever teaches his daughter the law teaches her nonsense (or, "lechery," or "obscenity").[18] This provides us with a specific saying that is variously interpreted and hence worth considering as an example. In the context, the discussion centers on the ordeal of bitter water to determine whether or not a woman had committed adultery (see also Num. 5). Ben Azzai says that it would be well for one to teach his daughter the Torah so that she would know whether she had acquired sufficient merit to sustain this ordeal. Ben Azzai was not an ordained rabbi, though a respected scholar.[19] Therefore, his opinion was not as valuable as that of the noted Rabbi Eliezer, a judgment supported by the fact that the ensuing discussion in the Talmud includes a comment on R. Eliezer's saying but not on ben Azzai's. Probably we can assume that R. Eliezer's view is the more representative of Jewish thought at the time.

On the other hand, it could be suggested that the reason there is a comment on R. Eliezer's saying, rather than on ben Azzai's, is that his comment relates to the nature of the Torah itself, containing language that could be interpreted as derogatory of it. (The comment is that the rabbi had not said the Torah *was* nonsense, but that to one's daughter it could be

as nonsense.) Biale points out that the use of the ordeal in the case of suspected adultery had long since ceased, so ben Azzai was not dealing with an actual situation, but rather was using this as a means of discussing the importance of a daughter's knowing the Torah.[20] Biale holds that even R. Eliezer would have accepted the appropriateness of teaching one's daughter some Torah for guidance in her daily life. We should also note that in the Mishnah, this discussion is immediately followed by a comment by R. Joshua that a woman "has more pleasure in one *kab* [a measure of liquid or dry substance] with lechery than in nine *kabs* with modesty."[21] Without expanding the discussion further, we can see something of the complexity of the issue. What is impossible to determine is how prevalent Eliezer's viewpoint was in the early part of the first century. We do know that women were not disciples of rabbis in a formal study of Torah.

There is one other source telling of R. Eliezer's opposition to teaching women anything of the Torah beyond the essentials for life. In the Jerusalem Talmud there is a story of a woman asking him a question about the Law—a question he refused to answer on the grounds that "a woman's wisdom is only in her spinning wheel." When his son, who, it appears from this passage, was supported by this woman, asked Eliezer why he had not answered her question, he replied, "Let the words of the Torah be burnt and not given to women!"[22] It is impossible to absolve Eliezer of having a low view of women. His words about women's wisdom being in the spinning wheel

is a perversion of Exodus 35:25—
"Every skilled woman [lit. "wise of
heart"] spun with her hands." Further examples showing that women
were often held in low esteem could
be accumulated. One often hears the
saying that a woman is a "pitcher full
of filth with its mouth full of blood,
yet all run after her."[23] Probably few
such sayings can be attested as from
the first century. Also they are balanced to a degree by kind words
about wives, somewhat like those in
ben Sira. A question may be raised
here, as with the sayings in Sirach, as
to whether they are examples of
genuine esteem for women as individuals or only as wives and mothers.
A celebrated example of a capable,
intelligent woman that is often cited
is that of Beruria, the wife of the
famed Rabbi Meir. However, she lived
in the early second century A.D., too
late to have served as a model for the
first generation of Christian women.
Her example is relevant to the early
church, though, for it signals the fact
that a strong theologically sophisticated woman could make her own
way within the Judeo-Christian tradition. She studied the Torah[24] and
even challenged Meir regarding interpretation.[25]

Thanksgiving for Being a Male

The following prayer is well known
but not always well understood:
"Praised be God that he has not
created me a gentile; praised be God
that he has not created me a woman;
praised be God that he has not
created me an ignorant man." This is
not an isolated saying but occurs in
three traditions—the Tosephta (sayings of the Tannaitic rabbis, mainly in
the first two centuries A.D.),[26] the
Palestinian or Jerusalem Talmud,[27]
and the Babylonian Talmud.[28] Further, it is a prayer (which is by nature
an expression of deep feeling) of
something that is an ingrained part of
one's religion. The Talmud traces the
prayer back to the first century—
again, a claim that cannot be proved
but must at least be considered. It is
essential to realize that the reason for
this prayer is that Gentiles, women,
and ignorant men cannot learn the
Torah. The person who thus prays is
not necessarily prejudiced against
the groups cited, but is grateful that
he himself can learn the Law. The
locus of the problem is therefore not
in the prayer itself, but in the previously determined "exemption" of
women from this responsibility.

Marriage Laws

As for marriage laws, the Talmud
protected women in some ways, but
in other ways it tolerated male domination. As had been the case in
earlier Roman times, a woman was
under the authority of her father
until marriage, at which time she was
"acquired" by her husband. The marriage relationship held some insecurities for the woman. Although she
was expected to belong fully to her
husband, he could belong partly to
her and partly to others (". . . become
betrothed to a half of me . . .").[29] It is
disputed, however, whether such po-
lygyny (plurality of wives) was typical.[30] The life of a Jewish wife was, of
course, largely spent in caring for
husband and children. According to
the more liberal view of Rabbi Hillel,
minor failures in carrying out her
duties could constitute grounds for

divorce. Some later rabbis even considered bad breath or the size of her bosom to be a factor.[31] Technically only the man could both initiate and carry through a divorce, but there were ways for women to effect the termination of an impossible marriage.[32]

Touching and Ritual Uncleanness

One aspect of the relations between men and women that is especially important with regard to the Gospels is that of touching. In spite of the freedom that women were increasingly granted in the Talmudic period, it was still considered improper for a man to touch a woman or even to exchange glances.[33] Of course, the periods of a woman's uncleanness were to be observed rigorously from early biblical times (Lev. 15:16–24). A new mother was unclean for seven days and then needed purification rites after thirty-three days (cf. Luke 2:22), or after a longer period if the child was a girl. Any discharge was considered unclean. All of this is relevant to Jesus' close association with women and the fact that he touched women who were ceremonially unclean (including the dead body of Jairus' daughter, since a corpse was considered unclean). In the Book of Acts, Peter spoke to Tabitha (Dorcas), but did not touch her until she was resuscitated.

Evidence From Synagogues

The preceding rabbinic opinions seem to be somewhat balanced by evidence that the title "head of the synagogue" and other terms of honor were applied to women in certain inscriptions.[34] But some issues revolving around this evidence are not yet satisfactorily resolved. One is whether the titles were merely honorific, not signifying actual office; another is whether a title was given to a woman only because of the status of her husband; and a third is whether the occurrence of titles ascribed to children minimized the significance of those ascribed to women.[35]

A more positive result regarding the status of women has come from archaeological studies of the structure of ancient synagogues. It was previously assumed that there were separate women's galleries in the synagogues. Actually there are only three synagogues that seem likely to have come from the first century: those at Masada, on the Herodion, and at Gamla.[36] None of these has a women's gallery. There is a stairway in the synagogue at Capernaum, but this comes from a much later date, and it is doubtful that it led to a women's gallery. The evidence therefore does not point to a strict separation of women and men in ancient synagogues.[37]

Philo's Viewpoint

There are yet other sources of information as to how Jewish people felt about women. One of these is the Alexandrian philosopher Philo. The status of women was, in general, much higher in Hellenistic Egypt than it had been in classical Greece and also much higher than it was in communities visited by Paul. Women in Alexandria during the Hellenistic period enjoyed dignity and freedom, and those of the aristocracy were esteemed by men. On several sections of a frieze women were depicted engaged in various activities, including teaching.[38] Respectable women were allowed to participate in religious ceremonies.

In this environment one might have expected that Philo would be outstanding in celebrating the worth and dignity of woman. On the contrary, he was essentially negative. He thought that the virtuous women of the Old Testament were anomalies; he did not think of women as intellectual. They should not frequent "market places and council halls and law-courts and gatherings and meetings"; in short, they should avoid places "with full scope for discussion and action," for they are "best suited to the indoor life which never strays from the house."[39] Furthermore, "the female sex is irrational and akin to bestial passions, fear, sorrow, pleasure and desire, from which ensue incurable weaknesses and indescribable diseases."[40] He also believed that "because of softness [a woman] easily gives way and is taken in by plausible falsehoods which resemble the truth."[41] This same attitude toward women's untrustworthiness is found in Josephus. In a section on witnesses, Josephus said, "From women let no evidence be accepted, because of the levity and temerity of their sex."[42]

The Spiritual Transition: From the Pre-Christian Era to the Age of the Holy Spirit

The definite transition from the pre-Christian era to the age of the Holy Spirit is fundamental in the theology of the New Testament. Volumes have been written on the Holy Spirit in the New Testament era, but, until recently, only a few pages have been written on the implications of the coming of the Spirit for Christian women.

Women at Pentecost

The emphasis that is rightly given to the ascension of Christ, the coming of the Holy Spirit, and the rapid growth of the church in the first chapters of Acts has tended to divert attention from the remarkable role of women in that narrative. The first notice we have that a new age was dawning is the mention of women participating in prayer with the men. "They all joined together constantly in prayer, along with the women and Mary the mother of Jesus, and with his brothers" (Acts 1:14). These women are probably mentioned specifically for the same reason that Jesus' brothers are cited: they had not been accustomed to doing so before. There is no reason to think that the women were not still with this group when the Holy Spirit came upon them. In fact, Acts 2:1 specifies that they were "all together in one place," and, as we will observe immediately below, women are mentioned in the prophecy of this event. Absolutely no distinction is made between men and women in the act of praying.

The Age of the Spirit: Prophesying Men and Women

The next mention of women is of prime importance. Neglecting to grasp its implications can skew all attempts to understand the New Testament perspective on women. It is foundational for a proper comprehension of the present age (or dispensation) of God's grace. Peter's explanation of the Pentecost experience has at its very core the affirmation that God has poured out his Spirit on "all people" (not just on a few prophets or prophetesses, as in the Old Testament period). As he continues, the statement "Your sons and daughters will prophesy" receives reinforcement in the words "Even on my servants, both men and women, I will pour out my Spirit in those days, and they will prophesy" (Acts 2:17–18). It is hard to conceive of any formulation that would state more clearly that the gift of God's Spirit and the ensuing prophetic ministry in the church was now bestowed fully and equally on women as well as men. There is a double force here: (1) a prophetic text in the Old Testament (Joel 2:28–32) emphasizes the role of women, and (2) Peter, filled with the Holy Spirit and therefore under God's direction, chose this text to describe and explain the inception of the age of the Spirit.

The function of this quotation in Acts may be compared with that of the quotation from Isaiah 61:1–2 at the beginning of Jesus' ministry. In the fourth chapter of Luke's Gospel, the first part of his two-volume work, he describes Jesus' initial preaching in the synagogue of his home town, Nazareth. Jesus quoted the words "The Spirit of the Lord is on me . . . " and then proceeded to describe his own anticipated ministry to the socially disadvantaged in terms of Isaiah's prophecy (Luke 4:18–19). This becomes the programmatic state-ment of Jesus' ministry. Likewise, Luke makes a reference to an Old Testament passage about the Spirit of God at the beginning of his second volume. The rest of Acts demonstrates the fulfillment of this prophecy, including the pouring out of God's Spirit on women and their consequent ministry of prophecy. Just as the ministry of Jesus provided evidence of the fulfillment of the prophecy of Isaiah and the truth about the Lord Jesus Christ, so the ministry of men and women in Acts provides evidence of the fulfillment of the prophecy of Joel and the truth of God's plan for the church.

If it is suggested that not all of Joel's prophecy was fulfilled at that time, two comments will clarify the matter. One is that even if that is so concerning Joel 2:28–32, certainly the opening words, if anything, apply to the event at hand. The formula "This is what was spoken" is reminiscent of the formulas used in the Dead Sea Scrolls—e.g., the Habakkuk Commentary—where the authors were accustomed to say, "This" (the event at hand) "is that" (the event predicted in the Old Testament). It is inconceivable that the immediately ensuing words do not apply. Second, the concluding words, "And everyone who calls on the name of the Lord will be saved," certainly apply to the present age. Therefore it must be acknowledged that the full and equal participation of women in the Spirit-led ministry of prophecy is a mark of the church age.

If it is suggested further that this was a temporary gift, again two observations may be made. First, it would be strange for the explicit characteristic of the present age to be temporary. Second, the passage usually appealed to as proof that prophecy has ceased, 1 Corinthians 13:8 ("But where there are prophecies, they will cease. . . .") clearly relates, not to the present time, but to the future. The threefold condition described in verses 10–12 of that chapter for the cessation of prophecy does not yet exist: (1) "when perfection comes," (2) "then we shall see face to face," and (3) "then I shall know fully." Perhaps one reason that some interpreters have difficulty in acknowledging the presence of prophecy in the church is that they restrict the meaning of the word *prophecy* to the infallible form of prophecy that characterized the inspired work of the so-called writing prophets found in the Old Testament Scriptures. But in the New Testament there is a broader meaning to both "prophecy" and "prophet" as we will discover below.

"Neither Male nor Female"
(Galatians 3:28)

Galatians 3:28 stands, in the opinion of many, as the most significant single statement of Paul on women: "There is neither Jew nor Greek, slave nor free, male nor female, for you are all one in Christ Jesus." This bold statement takes its place in a passage in which Paul is describing the transition from the days of Israel's existence under the law. That law was like the slave in a household who was responsible for the children and saw to it that they did their school lessons. The law was "put in charge to lead us to Christ that we might be justified by faith. Now that faith has

come, we are no longer under the supervision of the law" (vv. 24–25). Not only so, but in this new day of faith, we have a new relationship with God, as sons to a father (v. 26). The language here emphasizes the difference between the old age of the law and the new age of faith. Now we are "baptized with Christ" (v. 27). Having thus expressed our union with Christ, Paul proceeds to make his famous statement about our union with each other. But it is a relationship that goes even beyond union: it is a relationship in which differences disappear: "There is neither . . . male nor female." More precisely, the Greek text has "neither . . . nor" in reference to Jews and Greeks, slaves and masters, but "neither . . . *and*" in reference to males and females, in an apparent allusion to Genesis 1:27, which says that God created us "male and female." Perhaps there is an implication here that Christ has not only delivered women from the curse but has also brought them into a new relationship in the new creation—a relationship that transcends that of the original creation.

Perspectives will, of course, differ on how Galatians 3:28 relates to Paul's other teachings. For some it is so sweeping that any restrictions Paul places elsewhere on women's ministry must be somehow explained so as to eliminate any suggestion of an essential differentiation between the sexes. For others this statement is limited to mean that salvation is available to all irrespective of sex. The reason offered for this latter view is that the context in Galatians deals with justification. The fact is that the immediate context is a contrast between law and gospel. Verses 23–25 describe the chronological sequence of law followed by faith, by which we are justified. "Now that faith has come, we are no longer under . . . the law" (v. 25). Instead of that, "you are all sons of God through faith in Christ Jesus" (v. 26). This is a new relationship to God, and it is accompanied, as verse 28 states, by a new relationship of believers to one another. The idea of "newness," which the text has described so far, first in terms of chronological succession and then in terms of relationship, is also described in the terminology of baptism and of being "clothed with Christ." We know from Ephesians 4:20–24 and Colossians 3:9–11 that this is the language of conversion and new life. In the Colossians passage Paul continues with words similar to those in Galatians 3:28: "Here there is no Greek or Jew, circumcised or uncircumcised, barbarian, Scythian, slave or free" (Col. 3:11).

We can see the implication of this when we read the exhortations that follow. These relate to mutual forbearance and love (vv. 12–14). Obviously when someone has put on the new "clothing" of Christ, the obliteration of differences in Christ affects not only position but also practice. This should lead us to a proper interpretation and application of Galatians 3:28. The point of this passage is not so much that there is equality as that there is no difference: "There is . . . neither male nor female." As we have now seen, such an affirmation has definite, practical consequences in Christian social relationships.

The Geographical Transition: From Palestine to the "Ends of the Earth"

The Book of Acts is a book of transitions. Several major stages are evident in the progress of the gospel from Jerusalem to Rome. One is the spread of the church from Aramaic-speaking Jewish believers to Greek-speaking Jewish believers. This is apparent in Acts 6:1, where Greek-speaking widows were being neglected by the Aramaic-speaking Christians. These women, the widows, were important enough in the community to have their needs drawn to the attention of the apostles. But the group selected to care for them consisted entirely of men. Was this because only men were considered able to handle the matter or because it was not customary for women to be involved in the distribution of funds in that community, or was it because women would be the beneficiaries of the distribution and therefore it was thought best that they not participate in that work? It is impossible to know with certainty.

It is when the gospel advanced to Samaria that women were mentioned for the first time in the recounting of those who were converted. Acts 8:12 speaks of "both men and women." In Peter's wider travels along the Mediterranean coast, where there had been a strong non-Jewish population for centuries, he came to Lydda (Acts 9:32). There he heard of a woman "disciple" in Joppa. The giving of her name in both Aramaic (Tabitha) and Greek (Dorcas), shows that the society was bilingual and hence bicultural. Tabitha had died and because of her reputation for "always doing good and helping the poor," she was deeply mourned. Peter was called, and the woman was brought back to life, with the result that "many people believed in the Lord" (v. 42).

There is one more brief scene involving Peter when he was released from prison in Jerusalem. On his release he went to the home where the Christians were praying, and Luke notes that it was a Greek servant girl by the name of Rhoda who met and recognized him at the door (Acts 12:13–14).

Bust of Aqmat, Daughter of Hagago; Palmyra, Late Second Century. Christianity was reaching out to prominent women like this.   From the British Museum.

Into the Gentile World: Prominent Greek Women

Peter was also involved in the next transition: the taking of the gospel to the Gentile world. Although the Ethi-opian servant had become a believer in Jesus before this, it was the conversion of the centurion Cornelius and a large number of other Gentiles (Acts 10:1–11:18) that, by its accompanying vision to Peter and its more public occurrence, clearly marked a new dimension to the preaching of the gospel. The stage was now set for Paul's mission to the Gentiles.

With the opening of the Gentile world to the gospel, we find that Luke makes more frequent reference to women. This seems to be significant. In the Jerusalem scenes, apart from Pentecost itself, women were not prominent. The Hellenistic widows were in need, for example, but the ministration to them was specifically put in the hands of men. Now the circumstances were changing. Not only are more women mentioned, but their social status often seems to be higher than was true in the Palestinian scene. Luke specifies that women of status were turning to Christ. It is hard to reconcile this attention to prominent women with the claim by some feminists that Luke minimizes the ministry of women in the church. (Cf. the discussion on women in Luke's Gospel in the excursus to chapter 1.) It has been observed that he fails to mention them to the extent that Paul does in his letters (as, for example, in Romans 16).[43] Why does Luke feature women and downplay them at the same time? One reason why relatively little is said of Paul's female associates may be that Luke mentions mainly those who were actually traveling from one place to another with Paul (e.g., Barnabas, Silas, Timothy, Titus, and the group in Acts 20:4–6). He does mention Priscilla in reference to her and Aquila's traveling with Paul (Acts 18:18) and their subsequent teaching of Apollos (v. 26). In regard to the teaching of Apollos, it has been said that the leading part played by Priscilla "is in perfect accord with the manners of that country. In Athens or in an Ionian city it would have been impossible."[44]

The Case of the Prejudiced Scribe

Actually, Luke's citation of important women was apparently too much for one later scribe as he was copying the text of Acts. In Acts 17:4, where Luke speaks of "a large number of God-fearing Greeks and not a few prominent women," this scribe changed the text to read, "a large number of the Greeks, and not a few of the wives of the principal men." In verse 12 of the same chapter, Luke wrote that the new believers included "a number of prominent Greek women and many Greek men." But the scribe put down, "many of the Greeks and men and women of honorable estate." He also completely dropped the reference to the woman Damaris, who responded to Paul's Areopagus speech (v. 34). In Acts 18:26 he reversed the names of Priscilla and Aquila, so the woman's name would not appear first.[45]

Two women who were unquestionably of strong spiritual character played a role in the progress of the church across Asia Minor, but their names do not appear in the Book of Acts. When Paul arrived in Lystra, he met a man who was to have an important share in the ministry. Timothy was highly commended by the Christians in that area. His father was a Greek, but his mother was "a

Jewess and a believer."[46] It is not until Paul's second letter to Timothy that their names appear, along with a comment on their faith: "I have been reminded of your sincere faith, which first lived in your grandmother Lois and in your mother Eunice."[47] In the same letter Paul remarks that Timothy knew the Scriptures from his infancy.[48] Credit for this early training must go to his mother and grandmother, since Timothy would not have learned the Jewish Bible from his Greek father. Even though his father could have been a Jewish proselyte or God-fearer (a Gentile who agreed with basic Jewish teachings), since there is no reference to his name or his faith, in contrast to the strong statements about his mother and grandmother, it must be concluded that these women were solely responsible for the home teaching of the Jewish Scriptures.

To Philippi in Macedonia: Lydia the Business Woman

When Paul arrived in the major Macedonian city of Philippi, he met two contrasting figures. The first was a business woman, whose name may have been derived from the name of the area, Lydia, which in previous years had been the province to which her city, Thiatyra, was attached. The dye industry and the production of dyed cloth for which Thiatyra was famous were of great commercial importance. It is obvious that Lydia was a woman of means and influence. Lydia heard Paul at a Jewish gathering for prayer. She was a "God-fearer"—that is, a person who, though Gentile, attended Jewish services and accepted the basic Jewish teachings about the one true God. She took the initiative to invite Paul to her house and, after Paul's prison experience and release, she again brought him there. At that time she also had a group of Christian believers there (Acts 16:40). Lydia was a major figure in the apostolic church, and in this chapter of Acts she towered over the other woman, a demon-possessed slave girl whose clairvoyant abilities were being used for profit by her owners. Although the demon was exorcised by Paul, the girl has been lost in the succeeding chain of events; we do not know whether she also was converted. This girl and Lydia represent extreme positions of women in that society. Christianity sought to help each of them.

On to Greece: Damaris

The next major transition in Acts is from Macedonia to Greece itself. Paul's address before the Areopagus council in Athens is well known. Several people became believers on that occasion, including the woman Damaris (Acts 17:34), who has already been mentioned. The fact that she was converted through Paul's address at the Areopagus may indicate that she was of some prominence. At least she attended the meeting of that council. She may have been both intellectually curious and religiously sensitive. It may be that she heard Paul speak in the marketplace and desired to learn more of his teaching. The little we know is tantalizing.

Priscilla and Aquila at Corinth

From Athens Paul went on to the important commercial city of Cor-

inth. There he met a Jewish couple who had been expelled from Rome under an edict of Emperor Claudius. Priscilla's name is mentioned first in Acts 18, a phenomenon that cannot be accidental or meaningless (vv. 18, 26). Her importance in a survey of women in the church, however, stems especially from the particular instance of her teaching Apollos. It is important to assess the significance of this correctly, especially because some years later Paul was to write Timothy that he did not permit women to teach or to arrogate authority to themselves over men (1 Tim. 2:12). Those who hold that Scripture cannot contradict itself generally assume that the teaching referred to in that passage and the teaching that took place here in Acts 18:26 are of different sorts. Some hold that in 1 Timothy Paul taught that women were easily deceived and therefore should teach only other women or children, not men. It is crucial, therefore, to observe the narrative about Priscilla, Aquila, and Apollos accurately, as well as the teaching in 1 Timothy 2:12. What, then, was the nature of Priscilla's teaching here?

Apollos was "a learned man, with a thorough knowledge of the Scriptures" (Acts 18:24). He had been "instructed in the way of the Lord, " he spoke "with great fervor," and he "taught about Jesus accurately." He was therefore an intelligent, well-educated, and able teacher. The teaching was apparently done jointly by Priscilla and Aquila and, if the order of the names implies what it seems to, it was not Aquila who took the lead, as might be expected, but his wife. This was not simply a matter of witnessing, but rather of explaining God's truth. Because Apollos had known "only the baptism of John," Priscilla and Aquila "explained to him the way of God more adequately," and after his instruction he "vigorously refuted the Jews in public debate, proving from the Scriptures that Jesus was the Christ."

Why was this ministry on Priscilla's part not inappropriate? Was it because the teaching was done privately, not in the church?[49] It is hard to see how location changes the essential nature of communicating doctrine. Likewise, the fact that she did not occupy a ministerial office is hardly a factor (unless one interprets 1 Timothy 2:12 as relating to teaching specifically as a function of elders), since the concept of religious "office" as we know it today is post-apostolic. The New Testament emphasizes what is internal, rather than what is external, so one would expect that Priscilla's right to teach Apollos had to do with her own spiritual character and knowledge of biblical doctrine, rather than with location or ecclesiastical recognition. Further appraisal must wait for the discussions on 1 Timothy 2 later in this chapter and in appendix B.

Some women in Paul's day had considerable influence, and intellectual forces such as Stoicism were improving their situation. We have seen that women in Rome were beginning to engage more in social events. But as Christian missionaries pressed their way through the cities and countrysides mentioned in the Book of Acts, they no doubt met only a few women who were really active in public life in any official sense.

Women did not vote, did not serve as *iudices*, were not senators or magistrates or holders of major priesthoods. They did not, as a rule, speak in the courts . . . [One who did] seems to have provoked a praetorian ruling that no woman should usurp the masculine role of advocate. As a rule, women took no part in public life. . . . Women might, then, have considerable influence and interests outside their homes and families, but they were acting from within their families to affect a social system managed by men: their influence was not to be publicly acknowledged.[50]

It is not hard to picture Priscilla fitting this role as she and Aquila privately explained the Word to Apollos.

Priscilla's role in teaching is clear from Luke's narrative and has earned her a secure and important place in the history of women in the church. Any discussion about the justification for her teaching must not draw attention away from the fact that she must have had remarkable characteristics to qualify as a teacher of someone as capable and theologically educated as Apollos. Why were she and Aquila to do this, rather than someone else? Why is she usually named before her husband? Was she more outgoing than Aquila? Was she better educated theologically, more perceptive, more articulate than he? One thing is certain: she must have had outstanding spiritual qualities to be allowed by God to instruct such a potential leader as Apollos.

Caesarea on the Mediterranean: Prophesying Daughters

Before the apostle Paul returned for the final time to Jerusalem, he stayed for a while in the city of Caesarea, on the coast of Palestine. His host, Philip the evangelist, had four daughters who had the gift of prophecy (Acts 21:9). They were literally "prophesying daughters" and were proof of the validity of Pentecost and the fulfillment of Joel's prediction about the gift of prophecy to the daughters of Israel. Did they exercise this gift in the church service? Of course, prophecy was not limited to this setting. In the same passage we read that Agabus came and spoke to Paul in a clearly informal situation. But the same Agabus on a previous occasion spoke in what seems to have been a church meeting, as suggested by the fact that he "stood up" to speak and that at the conclusion a decision was made by the disciples (Acts 11:28–29). Also 1 Corinthians 11 indicates that women were prophesying in the church. Paul seems to have approved of that practice ("I praise you," v. 2; contrast v. 17), though he needed to correct them in regard to their head covering.

There was nothing unusual about women prophesying in the early church. Some commentators have suggested that this charismatic activity of women was due to the carnal state of the Corinthian church. It is indeed likely that the church was overenthusiastic and that some of their activities had gotten out of hand, needing the directives of Paul to bring them to order. But it must not be overlooked that the activities of the women (and men) at Corinth and those of Philip's daughters were in accord with the prophetic declaration of Joel about prophesying daughters.

What was the relation of prophesy-

ing to teaching in these New Testament instances? Did the four daughters of Philip and the other "prophesying daughters" actually teach? Paul distinguished between prophets and teachers (1 Cor. 12:28). At the same time, learning did take place when people prophesied and believers were edified (14:5, 19, 26, 31).

Women in Paul's Letters

During the swift geographical expansion of the church, Paul was busy keeping in touch with previously established congregations. His letters reveal that women were active with him in this mission. The same Paul who had previously persecuted women along with men (Acts 8:3; 9:1–2) now welcomed them as his coworkers. In writing to the church at Philippi he encouraged the church to help the women who had "contended at [his] side in the cause of the gospel."[51] The word "contended" implies hard work that involved some conflict in the battle to release people from the power of the evil one. He referred also to women who were hostesses of churches that met in their homes. One of these women was Nympha, who lived at Colosse. Paul requested in his letter to the Colossians, "Give my greetings . . . to Nympha and the church in her house."[52]

Another house church was that of Philemon. Apphia was not the main person addressed there, but she was mentioned in Paul's greeting: "To Philemon . . . to Apphia our sister . . . to Archippus . . . and to the church that meets in your home." The role of Chloe (1 Cor. 1:11) is uncertain, though the NIV interprets the literal

Greek "those of Chloe" as meaning "those from Chloe's household." Twice Paul referred to the church that met in the home of Priscilla and Aquila, with Aquila's name coming first in the latter passage, in contrast to the Romans passage and all but the first mention of the pair in Acts.[53]

Romans 16

It is the last chapter of Romans that contains the most references to women who were associated with Paul in his ministry. Peter Richardson has noted that the proportion of women, ten out of twenty-nine people mentioned, is "startling."[54] He also notes that there is a balance in the opening sequence: two women, two men, one woman, one man. But even more striking is that "the range of specific roles is greater for women than for men. Further, in the opinion of an increasing number of scholars, two of the highest offices or roles are ascribed to women: deacon (Phoebe) and apostle (if Junias is a woman, Junia).

Phoebe. Paul mentioned Phoebe first of all, describing her as a "servant of the church." The word *diakonos* ("servant") is that from which "deacon" is derived. It could mean (1) "servant"; (2) "minister," in the sense of one who ministers the gospel; or (3) "deacon," in the sense of 1 Timothy 3:8–13. If the expression "their women" in verse 11 of the latter passage means women deacons rather than merely the wives of deacons, as is possible, there would be little doubt that women deacons are referred to in Romans 16. Even without that consideration, unless one assumes that a woman was not permitted to be a deacon, that would be a natural understanding of the term as applied to Phoebe. While the verbal form of the word *diakoneō* was used to mean serving in general, in the Pauline Epistles the noun form, *diakonos*, usually indicated a person with a distinctive Christian ministry. In its meaning of "minister" it appears more frequently than many may realize. In 1 Corinthians 3:5; 2 Corinthians 3:6; Ephesians 3:7; Colossians 1:23, 25; and 1 Timothy 4:6 it clearly means someone who ministers the gospel. Although it probably does not have this sense in the case of Phoebe, as she is called a "*diakonos* of the church," it is helpful to recognize the potential force of the word, so that we will not automatically think of it only in terms of hidden service.

Portrait of a Woman With Tablet and Stylus, Pompeii. This appears to be a fine, educated woman of the general period of the New Testament. Alinari— Art Resource, New York.

The next word used to describe her, *prostatis*, belongs to a word group that has a strong connotation of leadership and authority.[55] It also refers to a benefactor who offers protection. If it were used in the masculine form here, there would be no question but that it would mean one who exercises leadership. A common translation is "helper," which is too weak. The term in ancient Greek sources was even used for divine beings.[56] The situation is described by E. A. Judge:

> The better attested reading [*prostatis*], "protectress," suffered from appearing to assign Phoebe a much higher social status than might have been anticipated, and from the fact that no other individual woman could be found referred to by this term anywhere in ancient Greek. Its common use was for a patron-goddess.[57]

Judge goes on to say that the "missing link has now appeared" in a partially published papyrus dating from 142 B.C. In a legal document a woman is said to be the *prostatis* of her fatherless son. It means perhaps that she has the formal responsibility of being his guardian (*epitropos*), but possibly the broader term has been used because of the anomaly of a woman's being in this position. Paul is thus "acknowledging his dependence on Phoebe."

Priscilla and Mary. The next woman Paul commended in Romans 16 is Priscilla, well known from Acts 18. He describes her and her husband as "fellow workers." There is no indication that Paul considered her to be any less a worker than Aquila. Both of them "risked their lives" for Paul (v. 4). Paul also mentioned a woman named Mary, who "worked very hard" (v. 6).

Junia. Andronicus and Junia are the next people whom Paul commended. The name Junia is almost certainly feminine—"almost" would not be necessary were the name in the nominative form in Greek. As it stands, it is a direct object, and the nominative form has to be assumed. But since Junia as a Latin female name would be the feminine counterpart of Junius, as Julia is the feminine counterpart of Julius (a masculine name known from Latin literature), there is every reason to assume that Paul refers to a woman. No contrary evidence has been found by the date of this writing. Neither is there any evidence from the Latin literature of a longer name of which this is an abridgement. John Chrysostom and Jerome referred to this person as a woman; in fact, it was not until the late thirteenth or early fourteenth century that a commentator referred to her as a man.[58] The eminent New Testament scholar C. E. B. Cranfield concludes that "it is surely right to assume that the person referred to is a woman."[59]

But does Paul say that Junia was outstanding *among* the apostles, or *to* them—i.e., in their opinion? The Greek syntax implies the former. There is, however, another difficulty. Rarely in the New Testament is the word used of a specific person apart from the twelve apostles and Paul. In Acts 1:23–26 Luke says that Matthias was chosen to replace Judas. Also in Acts 14:14 Barnabas is called an apostle. Beyond that, except for general references, such as to false apostles, no individual is so named. It is difficult to know, therefore, just how to take this use with regard to Junia. On the one hand, it is improper to jump to the conclusion that she had the "office" of an apostle. On the other hand, it would not be right to assert that she could not have had some distinctive role deserving of the appellation "apostle."

Other Women. In Romans 16 Paul also mentioned Mary, Tryphena, and Tryphosa—women who "worked hard"(vv. 6, 12); Persis, "another woman who has worked very hard in the Lord" (v. 12); the mother of Rufus, "who has been a mother to me, too" (v. 13); and Julia and the sister of Nereus (v. 15). The ten women mentioned in this group of Paul's associates stand as a testimony to the participation of women in the ministries of the church.

Single and Married Women

In 1 Corinthians 7 Paul addressed some delicate matters. The details of his instructions are beyond what can be discussed here, but some overall observations can be made. One is that Paul addressed men and women in balance, and in similar balance he evaluated the single and married states. In a remarkable statement, he declares that "the wife's body does not belong to her alone, but also to her husband. In the same way, the husband's body does not belong to him alone but also to his wife" (v. 4). The clear implication is that any sexual activity is to be by mutual consent. Men in Paul's day may have felt that they "owned" their wives and could deal with them in any way they chose. But Paul's balance, coupled, it might be added, with the Golden Rule, protected the wife from unilateral advances on the part of her husband.

Paul advises those with an unbe-

lieving spouse that their children were not unclean, for, contrary to the common idea that contact with evil ritually defiles, one's own Christianity "sanctifies" the children and the spouse (v. 14). The so-called "Pauline privilege" allowed a believing partner to permit his or her spouse to leave; the believer was not guilty in such an event (vv. 15–17). Virgins were not to be anxious; it was all right for them to stay as they were. A man who had a virgin (possibly one to whom he was engaged; others have proposed that the reference is to the virgin's father or even, improbably, to one in a "spiritual" partnership) might proceed with marriage arrangements, if that seems good. In all of this, there is no preferential treatment given to men. In every relationship a person is to be pure and considerate.

The "Elect Lady" in 2 John

The apostle John apparently wrote his second letter to a woman. The address reads: "To the chosen [or elect] lady and her children." John's mention of her as the recipient of his second letter is parallel to his mention of Gaius in the third. Although some have held that the term *lady* refers to the church itself, this is hard to square with the alternation between singular pronouns (vv. 4, 5, 13) and various plural forms (vv. 6, 7, 8, 10, 12). The plural probably refers to the lady's "children" (v. 1), who presumably were the congregation who met in her house (cf. v. 10). The word translated "lady" is *kyria*, the feminine form of *kyrios*, "lord" or "sir." Several women noted above had churches in their homes. This lady seems to have been in the same position. If all these women had the same function as Phoebe—that is, as a *prostatis*—they may well have been far more than merely hostesses in their relationship to the Christians who gathered in their homes.[60]

It is evident that as the church grew and extended into the Roman world, women were active and prominent. But this expansion required extreme care. The very freedom Christian women had was a potential obstacle to the acceptance of the gospel. It was therefore necessary for the Christian missionaries to take into account the ideological differences among the various sectors of society they were trying to reach.

The Ideological Transition: From Freedom to Conformity

As Paul ventured into city after city, each with its individual history and its heritage of customs and ethical conventions, it was necessary for him not only to contextualize the gospel but also to ensure that nothing in his presentation would unnecessarily alienate his audience. He expressed his principles in that regard in 1 Corinthians 9:19–23: "Though I am free and belong to no man, I make myself a slave to everyone, to win as many as possible." This meant, "To the Jews I became like a Jew" and applied also "to those under the law . . . to those not having the law . . . to the weak." In short, Paul said, "I have become all things to all men so that by all possible means I might save some." Clearly this meant working hard to empathize with people with whose theology and principles he disagreed. It meant some significant adjustments in his own lifestyle so as to avoid giving offense. He had to find ways to maintain his stand on principles and yet show that he understood the sources and expressions of other people's principles.

Conventional Secular Morality

Ancient society, like our own, had its conventional morality. Paul realized that the way he would express certain moral principles was not necessarily the way others would. And there was no uniformity in that respect in the Graeco-Roman world. Women were indeed receiving (and taking) more liberties in spite of lingering inequalities. But there was evidence of a backlash among some of the conservative Roman moralists. As noted above, the first-century A.D. historian Livy wrote of the conflict that took place in a previous century when some laws (the "Oppian" laws) restricting expenditures for women's luxuries were repealed. Some conservatives wished to have these laws continued. The following is from his description of the scene that had taken place in 195 B.C.: "The matrons, whom neither counsel nor shame nor their husbands' orders could keep at home, blockaded every street in the city and every entrance to the Forum." The famous Cato then said:

> If each man of us, fellow citizens, had established that the right and authority of the husband should be held over the mother of his own family, we should have less difficulty with women in general; now, at home our freedom is conquered by male fury, here in the Forum it is bruised and trampled upon, and, because we have not contained the individuals, we fear the lot. . . . I should have said, "What kind

of behavior is this? Running around in public, blocking streets, and speaking to other women's husbands! Could you not have asked your husbands the same thing at home?"[61]

Cato issued a warning in the same speech that reveals a fear that lasted far beyond his own time: "As soon as they begin to be your equals, they will have become your superiors."

There were laws pertaining to women in various societies, and of course the marital laws would have been universally understood to place women in submission. It is possible that Paul is using the word "law" in 1 Corinthians 14:34 ("women . . . must be in submission, as the law says") to refer to these laws. Although it is usually maintained that "law" here refers to the Old Testament, no specific text can be found. Some think it refers to rabbinic law, but others object because Paul never elsewhere uses the term in that way. More to the point, this would have given status to a Jewish legal structure Paul opposed. Given a unique context that does not deal with the doctrine of salvation, there is no reason why Paul could not have used the term "law" in a unique way. Since he was concerned with the submission of women, it is not surprising if he refers to marital law, which, in any form the Corinthians knew it, Jewish or pagan, would support his point. He did not have to subscribe to all the implications of such submission in order to argue that women should not act in church in a way that offends common moral sensibilities.

Plutarch, who lived shortly after the time of Paul, displayed a strongly moralistic tone:

Theano, in putting her cloak about her, exposed her arm. Somebody exclaimed, "A lovely arm." "But not for the public," said she. Not only the arm of the virtuous woman, but her speech as well, ought to be not for the public, and she ought to be modest and guarded about saying anything in the hearing of outsiders, since it is an exposure of herself; for in her talk can be seen her feelings, character, and disposition.[62]

Plutarch continued in the next section to say that a woman "ought to do her talking either to her husband or through her husband." He says further that if women "subordinate themselves to their husbands, they are commended . . . and control ought to be exercised by the man over the woman . . . as the soul controls the body." This quotation may provide a clue as to why Paul was so concerned about women speaking publicly and about their attire when they did so (1 Cor. 11:1–16; 14:34). Plutarch also said that "it is a matter of pride to hear a wife say, 'Husband, thou unto me art guide, philosopher, and teacher of the noblest and divinest lessons.' "[63] It was therefore considered appropriate for a woman to look to her husband for teaching. Although Roman women were more free to appear in public with their husbands, moral convention, according to this same passage in Plutarch, dictated what might be considered the ultimate put-down: in the company of others "the wife was expected to support her husband and not disagree with him."[64] These opinions come from an articulate writer who lived in Greece, where values were somewhat more conservative than those at Rome. Paul, of course, was writing to a church in a Greek city when he wrote to the Corinthians.

For Paul to restrain women from speaking under certain circumstances would therefore avoid offending the moralistic Romans and Greeks. At the same time he would avoid offending conservative Jewish people who would have approved of ben Sira's dictum: "A silent wife is a gift from the Lord; her restraint is more than money can buy."[65]

Woman at an Initiation to a Mystery Religion, Pompeii. This wall painting is from the Villa of the Mysteries. Many of the women—as well as men—in Paul's day were attracted by the Oriental cults with their impressive ceremonies. Alinore—Art Resource, New York.

Apprehensions Concerning Women

As in earlier years, women of New Testament times were active in religion. Their activities encompassed many types of religious cults and ceremonies, from the vestal virgins in Rome to the adherents of the various eastern cults on the fringes of the Empire. Standards of morality varied greatly: the vestal virgins were held in high honor for their fidelity (on which the fortune of the entire Empire was understood to depend) while, at the other extreme, the religion of the goddess Isis spawned both temple prostitution among some and sexual purity among others at the same time. Frenzied or immoral women in the religious cults of Corinth may also have had something to do with the restrictions Paul placed on believing women in 1 Corinthians 11 and 14. Several scholars have thought that Paul was trying to maintain the distinction between the sexes in chapter 11. One explanation for this may be that he was strongly opposed to homosexuality; another may be that he wanted to counter the sex reversal practiced in some pagan religious initiations. Richard and Catherine Kroeger shed some light on this:

> At certain religious events women also shaved their heads, and men assumed veils or long flowing hair and golden hairnets . . . by the first century of our era a shaven head on a woman and long tresses on a man were viewed as sexual inversions. . . . Sex reversal was also a significant factor in the worship of Aphrodite (the Roman Venus), whose temple dominated the Corinthian acropolis.[66]

They continue by quoting Epictetus to show that even pagan philosophers opposed such confusion of the sexes. Whatever else is involved in 1 Corinthians 11 (and certainly the order of headship is foundational), the passage on women's head covering, or hair bound up properly,[67] stands as a strong repudiation of sex reversal and homosexuality. To repudiate or to obliterate the identity God has bestowed on us as sexual beings is a disgrace."[68] With respect to 1 Corinthians 14, the Kroegers produce evidence they believe is relevant to Paul's instructions about women's silence, showing the "religious pandemonium" that characterized the frenzied worship of the first-century world, including Corinth.[69]

Reference was made earlier to Augustus' call to observe tradition. E. A. Judge has shown that there is a strong call in 1 Corinthians 11, as well as elsewhere in Paul's writings, to observe conventions and "traditions," these being not so much legal or theological traditions as those connected with moral teachings.[70] There is a heavy use of the language of convention in this passage, and Paul's final plea at the end of the section on the veiling of women uses the word "custom" rather than "command," "law," or the like.[71] This same passage contains various words having to do with honor and shame, concepts that have to do with the perception of Christian standards by the outside world. Even the word "glory" relates to this, as does the concept of doing things in an "orderly" way.[72] H. C. Kee has shown how strong a motif the concept of shame is in Scripture.[73]

In short, 1 Corinthians 11 cannot be interpreted in a vacuum. The language is too loaded with significant terms of conventional morality to ignore the world in which the first-century churches existed. Paul knew that the appearance and behavior of women in the church would be a symbol to the watching world.

But his arrangements for women would appeal to Jewish people as well. They were appalled at pagan immorality, and Christians dared not appear to partake of this. Richardson referred to this:

> In order not to sever all relationships with the Jewish community, Paul advises some concessions. . . . He wishes to keep himself and the Corinthians sufficiently within Jewish norms to maintain a distinction from the prevailing Greco-Roman behavior. . . . Too much sexual freedom would create problems for the church's mission to Jews and associate it with the Hellenistic mystery religions.[74]

Paul's Strategy: Freedom With Restraint

What all this means is that Paul faced a critical question in his missionary strategy. He had stated his principle of the unity of men and women in Christ when he wrote Galatians 3:28. He had also written the Galatians about his authority as an apostle and about his freedom from the Jewish law. But in 1 Corinthians he seemed to reverse himself. He was willing, he said, to become like a person under that law in order to win them to Christ.[75] That meant both an abrogation of his personal freedom and a modification of his attitude to Jewish legalists. It was a self-limiting concession, not a reversal of conviction. In the same way, for Christian women to avoid offending Jewish and pagan moralists, they needed to be veiled (or appropriately coiffured) when they spoke in the public assembly, and under certain conditions they were not to speak at all.

But this was not mere social accommodation, nor was it an abandonment theology or of conviction. Quite to the contrary, it was in complete accord with Paul's conviction that the man was the head of the woman and should not be "shamed" by her. It was also in accord with his missiological principles. Therefore, his instructions were solidly based on three sets of convictions: (1) there must be a proper relationship between wives and husbands; (2) one must have a sensitivity to the moral conventions of others, especially those whom one desires to win to Christ; and (3) personal freedom under grace must be respected.

Maintaining his principle of freedom while exercising restraint presented a difficult challenge for Paul. How could he maintain his own convictions about women being one with men in Christ and at the same time avoid offending the people he sought to win for Christ? It is significant that shortly after he explained his approach in 1 Corinthians 9, he came to the matter of women's attire and coiffure in chapter 11. This provides us with an example of how to deal with ideologies, values, and conventions in differing cultures. The abiding value of 1 Corinthians 11 is not in the specific apparel women wear but in the means by which we (1) express our sensitivity to the ethical conventions of others and (2) communicate our own biblical, ethical values.

One obvious clue that this is what Paul was doing is the proliferation of words in that chapter that have to do with honor and shame. There are also some clues in the following chapters, including the passage in chapter 14 on women's silence. In fact, the concluding words to the latter chapter about doing things "in a fitting and orderly way" leap out at the reader who is familiar with the vocabulary of first-century ethical convention.

In chapter 11, Paul wrote to people in Corinth and in other cities where there were churches who were familiar with certain conservative attitudes to women, on the one hand, and with certain pagan aberrations, on the other. These included the shrieking of women in the temple cult and the exchange of sex roles in some of the pagan cult rituals. To meet the first requirement of sensitivity in those who seek to communicate the gospel message within a given culture, Paul honored the ethical conventions about women's modesty by prescribing veils (or having the hair bound up). The same recommendation also accomplished the second requirement: to communicate his own ethical values about the distinction between men and women and the responsibility of a woman not to shame her "head"—i.e., her husband. By having a modest appearance, the Christian woman was able to maintain her distinction as a woman, honor her husband, and avoid offending Jew and Gentile moralists (for whom a woman's speaking may have been difficult enough, let alone her appearing in what was considered immoral attire).

Moral sensibilities were also protected by women when they were careful about when and how they spoke in church. It was one thing to prophesy; it was something else to enter into discussion, ask probing questions, and presume to evaluate the words of a prophet. Therefore, 1 Corinthians 14:34–35 would have been understandable "in all the congregations" (v. 33). Just as those speaking in tongues were to desist if there was no interpreter (v. 28), and those prophesying were to cease if the Spirit gave a word of prophecy to another (v. 30), so there was a time when women were to be silent as well (vv. 34–35). Since most women in that society were married, and since it would have been awkward for single women to speak when wives were to be silent, it is probable that all women were under the same restrictions.

Such restrictions did not cancel the privilege of women to prophesy, nor did it abrogate Paul's principle of equality expressed so vividly in Galatians 3:28. Paul was able, therefore, to allow freedom to the "prophesying daughters" and at the same time to impose restrictions for the sake of reaching people for Christ and maintaining ethical standards.

The freedom Paul gave women was apparently to pray and to prophesy, provided they had the appropriate headcovering (possibly coiffure— their hair should be bound up modestly). In 1 Corinthians 11:10 Paul says that women "ought to have a sign of authority on their head." Although this was formerly understood to mean that they were *under* authority, with translators adding the words "sign of" before the word "authority," recent research has brought this into question. Many scholars now think that the Greek phrase means that women *have* a

certain authority or right. This may be the right to speak in public.

The approach suggested here is just one of several that biblical scholars have proposed. This issue, along with such crucial matters as the meaning of headship (1 Cor. 11) and the structure of the passage on women's silence (1 Cor. 14) must wait until Appendix B, where full citations will be given.

"Household" Relationships

Non-Christians no doubt had varied opinions concerning the scattered groups of Christians meeting in homes across the Roman Empire. To some they might have been thought of as another voluntary association such as the clubs, guilds, and voluntary religious groups. Perhaps they reminded people of the mystery cults meeting secretly in small groups. To others they might have had some of the characteristics of a Jewish synagogue. Since they had a community life with at least some organization and government, they could be compared in some ways to a small municipal community. Because they studied the Scriptures assiduously, they also could be described as a scholastic community.

But there was also a point of comparison with another known social unit: the household. The Christians functioned as a family. Very likely the owner of the home where they met had a certain prominence as the host or hostess. Households could be small, but they could also be very large, as was the case with pagan Roman households that included a number of slaves. The various members of the household need-

Procession in Honor of Isis, Rome. Isis was a favorite goddess at the time of the New Testament. Note that, in contrast to Christian practice, the men have head coverings, whereas the women do not. This frieze is in the Vatican Museum.   Alinari—Art Resource, New York.

ed to have guidelines for their mutual relationships. Several New Testament passages provide such guidelines, for example: "Wives, submit to your husbands, as to the Lord. For the husband is head of the wife as Christ is the head of the church. . . . Husbands, love your wives, just as Christ loved the church and gave himself up for her. . . . Children, obey your parents in the Lord. . . . Fathers, do not exasperate your children. . . . Slaves, obey your earthly masters. . . . Masters, treat your slaves in the same way" (Eph. 5:22–6:9; cf. Col. 3:18–4:1). "Wives, in the same way be submissive to your husbands, so that, if any of them do not believe the word, they may be won over without words by the behavior of their wives" (1 Peter 3:1).

A first-century reader would have recognized these words as being a part of the familiar "domestic code." Scholars today call the various series of ethical injunctions found in and outside of the New Testament by the German name *Haustafeln*, "household tables [of rules]." These go back to the time of Aristotle.[76]

In the New Testament, these codes are found in the writings of both Peter and Paul. There are typically three pairs of instructions: to husband and wife, to father and child, and to slave and master. This form appears clearly in Ephesians 5:21–6:9 and in Colossians 3:18–4:1.

The reference in each of these to the submission of wives has been troublesome to feminists. Was Paul subordinating wives to husbands, and did Peter follow this same line of thought with regard to the marriage of a Christian wife and an unconverted husband? Or did Paul not intend to make this an absolute command for women, but rather simply to include her submission as one way in which Christians are to submit to each other? In Ephesians 5 there is first the injunction to mutual submission (v. 21) and then the application to women—without even repeating the word "submit" in the original text. This has often been taken to mean that all Christians are to submit to all other Christians, even husbands to wives (by their loving self-sacrifice—the extreme act of submitting one's own good to that of another). In the same way, fathers express this quality by not provoking their children, and masters by not threatening their slaves.

Objections to this interpretation include the fact that the parallel passage in Colossians does not begin with a command to mutual submission. That is not an insurmountable problem, especially if Paul wrote the two epistles at virtually the same time and had the same general circumstance in mind. Nevertheless, the form of the Colossian passage must not be glossed over. It is also said that it is impossible for everyone to submit to everyone else. This assumes that submission means obedience, that this is what the Greek word always means, and that two people cannot obey each other.

But, some maintain, it is noteworthy that although Paul tells slaves and children to obey, he does not use that word with wives. Likewise, in 1 Peter, although Sarah is said to have expressed her submission to Abraham by obeying him and calling him "lord" (or "master"), that certainly does not mean that submission is expressed in every culture by obedience and calling one's husband "lord." Few would insist on the second part of Sarah's submission.

Feminists argue that there is a voluntary submission that *can* be mutual, because it is an attitude, an ideal. There is, they say, nothing impossible about mutual deference. In fact, they might argue, it is no more impossible than it is for each Christian honestly to consider every other Christian better than himself or herself, something Paul also commanded in Philippians 2:3.

Yet another approach to the matter of the submission of wives is to note that such an injunction was not particularly Christian, since such submission had long been expected in most ancient societies. The new and Christian element, the argument would run, was the *way* in which this submission was to be expressed—i.e., as to the Lord himself and on the analogy of Christ and the church.

Recently scholars, most notably David L. Balch, have given more attention to the social circumstances of Peter's injunction to wives. If Christians were under scrutiny and in danger of severe persecution, as the First Epistle of Peter makes clear; if the Romans were uneasy about new religions (recalling, for example, the "feminism" of the religion of Isis from Egypt); and if the domestic code was a common way of expressing relational values, Peter's injunction to wives takes on new significance.[77] It follows injunctions to submit to the government (2:13) and to masters (2:18). It begins with an adverb, "likewise," or "in the same way" (3:1), which reappears in verse 7: "Husbands, in the same way be considerate as you live with your wives." It would have been unthinkable—and suicidal, if this code of moral values is part of the defense Christians can make to governing authorities (cf. "be prepared to give an answer" in v. 15)—to say, "Husbands be submissive to your wives." But it could be argued that if Ephesians teaches a kind of mutual submission, this exhortation to husbands not to exercise a pagan heartless domination over their wives fits in well.

Whether or not the Christian domestic code was, as Balch has argued, a useful tool in averting Roman persecution (see appendix B for alternatives), the text itself gives a reason for the wives' submission: to bring about the conversion of their husbands. This attention to submissive relationships in view of unbelievers who were observing the Christians has a parallel in Titus 2:3–10. Wives were "to be subject to their husbands, so that no one [would] malign the word of God." Young men were to be self-controlled and have integrity of character so opponents might be ashamed because they had nothing bad to say about the Christian community. Slaves were to be subject to their masters and show that they could be fully trusted so that "in every way" they would "make the teaching about God our Savior attractive." Feminists suggest that just as slaves were told to be obedient for the sake of Christian witness even though slavery was destined for abolition, so wives were to be submissive for the same reason, though arguably their submission was not intended by either Peter or Paul to be permanent. Traditionalists, however, could respond that in neither Colossians nor Ephesians does Paul specifically relate his teaching to Christian witness as is done in 1 Peter and Titus.

In summary, Paul moved from convictions regarding freedom in Christ in Galatians to apparent conformity to conventional morality in Corinthi-

ans and perhaps in Titus, with a parallel in 1 Peter. These conventions were not immoral or unethical but, in fact, were compatible with Old Testament teachings. Interpreters differ as to how much of the teachings about head covering, silence, and submission was part of this conformity to moral convention for the sake of an unimpeachable Christian testimony and how much embodied timeless commands. Was the principle, for example, of not dishonoring one's head intended to be applied today in head coverings or in some other way? What would Peter or Paul say?

The Chronological Transition: Approaching the End of the Apostolic Era

After the events narrated in the Book of Acts, Paul was apparently set free and resumed his travels. But once again he was arrested and imprisoned. During this latter imprisonment, around A.D. 65, he wrote the Pastoral Epistles, 1 and 2 Timothy, and Titus. Although the apostle John was, as far as the facts can be established, still to live for some years, the first great wave of missionary advance was ending. Sadly, false teachers were already penetrating the church. Paul needed to maintain order in the churches and assure the continuity of sound teaching. He sent letters to Timothy in Ephesus and to Titus in Crete for this very purpose.

Several important kinds of instructions are in these letters. There is a concern, first of all, for doctrine to guard against false teaching. Second, Paul insisted that Timothy and Titus maintain a moral teaching and personal way of life that would be in accord with their teaching. Third, he established a continuity of doctrine and pastoral protection of the "flock" by providing clear qualifications for elders and deacons. In this context Paul touched on several topics, including activities of men and women in the church services and the enrollment of widows for support.

Paul's instructions about prayer (1 Tim. 2:8–10) can be viewed in two ways. Either he taught that the men were to pray and the women to adorn themselves modestly or he taught that the men were to pray in an appropriate manner, lifting holy hands, and the women also were to pray in an appropriate manner, not displayng extravagance. The verb "to pray" does not occur in the clause about women. However, the fact that the verb "adorn," which is in the proper form to be the main verb, does not occur in the same early position as the verb "pray" does in the first clause, but appears later in the clause, raises the question as to whether it really is the main verb. Also, Paul says "likewise," or "in a similar manner," which could mean that the women were doing the same thing as the men. So opinions are divided as to whether Paul was including or excluding women in his statement about public prayer.

Far more difficult is the next paragraph beginning with the words "A woman should learn in quietness" (v. 11). The word "quietness" (sometimes rendered "silence," though its adjective form appears immediately above in verse 2 with the clear meaning of "quiet") reappears at the end of verse 12. This shows two things: women are indeed to learn, a remark-

able advance over Jewish reserve on that point, and they are to learn in a quiet spirit.

Paul then stated that he did not permit a woman to teach or to assume undue authority over a man. Traditionally, the passage has been understood to enjoin the permanent restriction of women from teaching and from any kind of church authority. One problem with this viewpoint is that the word Paul used for having authority is not the normal one. In fact, it is an extremely rare verb that had, along with the noun form, a history of bizarre meanings, such as murder, suicide, and sexually related actions. At the time this book is being written there is still need for an accurate, exhaustive study of this verb.[78] One thing does seem certain already: it had a meaning much stronger than the normal verb for exercising authority, *exousiazō*. Around the time of the New Testament it seems to have indicated the act of originating (not likely here, unless it means the heretical *idea* of woman originating man) or of taking undue, possibly prime or sole, authority to oneself. Since the principle of Christian ministry is service rather than domination (cf. Mark 10:42–45), many now believe that whatever the verb means, it should not prevent women from being active in Christian ministry in its biblical sense.

What Paul meant by "teaching" also requires careful consideration. It meant more than providing instruction for edification, which the prophets also did. First Corinthians 14:31 says the purpose of prophesying is that "everyone may be instructed and encouraged." Teachers were highly honored, especially in Judaism. In ancient Greece women were considered fit for prophesying but not for teaching.[79] Prior to the completion and accessibility of the New Testament, Christian teachers conveyed the apostolic tradition of the teachings of Jesus. They were considered witnesses to the truth, and it should be kept in mind that women were not accepted as witnesses.

The story of Eve's deception was widely used against women's trustworthiness. Some hold that Paul cited it as an explanation of his position. Others hold that Paul's reference to Genesis implies that his withholding of permission in this passage was timeless and universal. Teachers were very important in the early days of the church, but as time went on, and as the number of converts increased and the Scriptures became more readily available, one reads more of the catechists than of the teachers.

There are, therefore, several approaches that can be taken to 1 Timothy 2:12. One is to take the verbs about teaching and authority simply in their modern sense. Another is to press research further into the first-century meaning of these two key verbs that describe what women were not to do. A third (not mutually exclusive of the others) is to ask what it was about women that made them unsuitable for doing whatever the verbs signified.

One fact is clear: Christian women at the time Paul wrote were in a spiritual transition. Formerly in Judaism or paganism, and formerly under the "curse" that followed the sin of Adam, women were not only dominated by their husbands (as Genesis 3:16 said would happen) but also stamped with the deception of Eve; they were hardly ready to be teachers in the church. If, as appears from 2 Timothy 3:6, some of the women were not only learning error but were "weak-willed," "loaded down with sins," and "swayed by all kinds of evil desires"—victimized by the false teachers—it is not surprising if extreme caution was needed in dealing with the question of allowing women to teach.

Aída Besançon Spencer has suggested that the Christian women were only beginning to emerge from the bondage of the "curse" and required time to mature and to prove their "faith, love and holiness with propriety" (1 Tim. 2:15).[80] This was therefore a major transition for women, the significance of which must not be underestimated. The coming of the Spirit and the dawn of the new age of the church meant a new spiritual ministry for women. Spencer's view, if it is correct, means that as the apostolic age drew to a close, Christian women were only beginning to be ready for ministry in the church. This is a thought-provoking interpretation that, along with other views, including the matter of Eve's deception, will be discussed in appendix B.

Widows

Less attention is usually given to Paul's instructions about widows in 1 Timothy 5 than to the matter of women's teaching in chapter 2. Yet these instructions were of great importance, especially as widows became increasingly recognized in the early church as an order of ministering women. As for widows in the New

Testament period, Kelly says, "Such glimpses as we obtain from Acts (vi.1; ix.39ff.) reveal that at the earliest stage the community treated the widows in its midst as an important responsibility, and that they for their part were grouped together as a body occupied in deeds of kindness to the poor."[81] He goes on to note that in this "surprisingly long section" in 1 Timothy there are "definite conditions of entry" and also "definite duties" for the widows to perform. In the following chapter we will discuss the development of this body of ministering women.

Deaconesses

Did Paul refer to deaconesses in 1 Timothy 3:11? After listing the qualifications for elders, Paul says, "Deacons likewise . . . " and then "Women likewise. . . ." The question is which of the two meanings of the word *gynē*, "woman" or "wife," was in Paul's mind. Because the statement concerning women immediately follows the instructions to deacons, some take it to refer to the deacons' wives. One problem with this assumption is that there is no parallel instruction for wives of the elders. Hanson's argument that the elders' wives would be older and better known seems weak.[82] Another problem is that there is no definite article before the word, as one would have expected if it referred to the wives of the men who were just mentioned.[83] In favor of its referring to a distinct group of serving women is the verbal structure seen in the phrases quoted above, "likewise . . . ," "likewise. . . ." This seems to introduce a certain group of women in parallel with the deacons.

As Hanson notes, most modern commentators think it means "women" rather than "wives."[84] This judgment seems sound, though Hanson himself disagrees, as do many others. But one other factor should be introduced: there was no special Greek word for "deaconess." A separate order known as deaconesses developed toward the third century in the Eastern church. In the meantime, however, women were serving in that capacity. In a great number of instances, women deacons were the wives of male deacons. It could well be that this was the situation in Paul's day. If this is true, the ambiguities are fully understandable. The women were serving as deacons, but most, if not all of them, were the wives of deacons.

Summary

The significance of the events in the apostolic era, including the coexistence of prophesying daughters and silenced wives, can be understood more clearly in the context of the six types of transition: political, religious, spiritual, geographical, ideological, and chronological. Interpreters sometimes treat the biblical texts as though they were written in isolation from the momentous events and ideas that were swirling around them. Others appear to seize on cultural factors and make Scripture relative. But Scripture is not culturally relative—it is culturally *relevant*. It speaks to culture. The transitions described here were powerful and affected both the lives of women and others' perceptions of them. Through it all, Jesus demonstrated a pure, noble, and consistent attitude toward women, not moved by the opinions of others. Paul steered a careful course through the changing cultural seas. And all the while, women were taking their place in the young church. Paul, in spite of the restrictions he felt were necessary, gave these women important opportunities to minister. Whether the developments of the next several centuries constituted an advance or a decline in this respect is a question to keep in mind in moving now into the next period.

Chapter 3

The Rise of the Church and the Downfall of Rome: Martyrs and Sex Objects

A Lost Tradition is the intriguing title given a 1981 book on women writers of the early-church period.[1] In a sense the tradition, not only of their writings, but also of most of the women themselves who served their Lord courageously during the same period has been lost. It is mainly because of the modern discussions over women's ordination, especially among Catholics, that the specific activities of women in subapostolic and patristic times have become a matter of intense interest and research.[2] Yet there were some earlier writers who sought to direct attention to women who had been outstanding during the first centuries of the church's advance against pagan darkness. In 1959 Edith Deen, who had previously written *All the Women of the Bible*, published a book entitled, *Great Women of the Christian Faith*.[3] She had drawn on other works, especially an 1851 book, *Women of Christianity*, by Julia Kavanagh.[4] The major early figures whom she chose to include for their

spiritual contribution were Perpetua, Helena, Macrina, Nonna, Marcella, Monica, Anthusa, and Paula. She adds vignettes of other women, such as Thecla, (a dubious choice because the main source of information is the Apocryphal Acts), Flavia Domitilla, Cecelia, Olympias, Fabiola, Pulcheria, and Genevieve.

Along with the paucity of references to women in the textbooks, another frustration awaits the student of church history. Those passages in early church literature that do relate to women deal in large measure with such matters as the desirability of celibacy and "spiritual marriage," rather than with the actual accomplishments of women—whether virgins, married women, or widows—in the cause of Christ.

The occupation of the church fathers with the marital status of women was closely linked with their opinions of the women's moral status. Their comments are not in some cases very different from some comments made by rabbis of their

89

day. But just as the rabbis expressed divergent opinions, so the Fathers failed to reach any consistent viewpoint. As Elizabeth Clark puts it:

> The most fitting word with which to describe the Church Fathers' attitude toward women is ambivalence. Women were God's creation, his good gift to men—and the curse of the world. They were weak in both mind and character—and displayed dauntless courage, undertook prodigious feats of scholarship. Vain, deceitful, brimming with lust—they led men to Christ, fled sexual encounter, wavered not at the executioner's threats, adorned themselves with sackcloth and ashes.[5]

It is not easy to present a fair picture of the perceptions that men had of women during the patristic period because of the danger of selectivity. This is the same danger observed earlier in connection with rabbinical materials, evidence from the Graeco-Roman world, and even from the Bible itself. Not only are there changing perceptions among the Fathers, but apparent discrepancies within the works of the same person. These may be reconciled logically, but one suspects that they represent an inner conflict, perhaps between theology and experience. Also the descriptions that exist (especially those in the Apocryphal Acts) are not necessarily reliable accounts of real women, but rather perceptions of what the ideal Christian woman should be. Conversely, as can be seen in the quotation from Clark above, what the Fathers wrote is not necessarily a true reflection of the kind of Christian woman they actually knew.

Agnes Cunningham points out the difficulty faced by those who would seek some standard for women's ministries today by reference to the early church:

> The reason for this problem is not the failure of women to participate actively and extensively in the ministry of the Church. On the contrary, even limited historical evidence witnesses to the fact that the ministry of women flourished during the first six hundred years of Christianity. Rather, serious investigation points increasingly to the evidence that no uniform practice or policy regarding the admission of women to ministry prevailed universally during the early Christian centuries.[6]

Sister Cunningham continues by noting that each church had a measure of autonomy that, along with the perceptions of the bishop and the way the apostolic tradition was followed, determined different courses of action in different locations.

But in spite of such divergences and the questionable nature of some of the early accounts, there is much that is reliable and instructive. There can no longer be any question as to whether women were active in various church ministries in the early church. There also seems to be virtually no question that women did not serve as priests in the contemporary sense of the term. A Protestant explanation for this is that there was no separate class of priests in the earliest years of the church, but even Roman Catholic writers acknowledge the omission of women from sacerdotal ministry.[7] There were, however, distinctive ministries for widows and virgins. It appears that at times these women were considered part of the clergy, though ordination was another matter.

It has also been questioned whether widows and virgins always formed two separate orders of ministry or whether the latter grew out of the former (which is thought to have its roots in Paul's rules for widows in 1 Timothy 5:3–10). The tendency now is to see them as two distinct orders, though not always existing side by side.[8] Widows were called "the altar of God," a designation that shows how they were respected for their spiritual ministries.[9] Ignatius spoke of the "virgins called widows," a reference to the fact that there were widows who spurned the idea of remarriage and lived separately in service to God.[10] Recent study has produced the hypothesis that the Apocryphal Acts represents a reaction on the part of widows whose ministries were repressed.[11]

Whatever the actual situation may have been in that respect, there is a strong suspicion that what many consider a promising situation in the early church, reflected in the prominence of women in the list of Paul's associates in Romans 16, continued for some time but did not survive in the church's records.

What kind of service did women perform in the earliest centuries? The diaconate provided an open avenue of service, particularly in the Eastern church. This included both the ministry of women married to church officials and those who may be called "women deacons," who served along with male deacons in personal and liturgical ministry.[12] Agnes Cunningham has suggested two kinds of ministry that drew women in the early church. One was the ministry of love, through which women could embody the *agapē* that was charac-

teristic of all believers but which women especially had opportunity to express in the social situations of that era. The other she calls "ministries of commitment." These were demonstrated in martyrdom, then in the orders of widows and virgins, and ultimately in the commitment to monastic living.

History shows what women *did*; some of the ancient writers show how they were *perceived*. Women were sometimes thought to be deceived, lascivious, and incapable, but they were also lauded as mothers, martyrs, intelligent students and teachers of Scripture, and—as some men acknowledged—as cherished friends. The profile of these two contrasting portraits will be clearly delineated in this chapter.

The Testimony of Archaeology: Women in the Shadows

There is evidence from the papyri and inscriptions of the first several centuries that women did hold ecclesiastical office. The 1976 issue of *New Documents Illustrating the New Testament* lists two instances of a woman being called a *diakonos* (=deacon?) and two instances of the use of a form of *presbytis*. It is not certain whether the latter term simply means "elderly woman." There is also a citation of a "fourth-century Christian letter which mentions twice (5, 12) a woman called [Kyrian tēn didaskalon]."[13] This might be translated "Madame teacher." A suggestion by E. A. Judge places this at the time when there was an attempt to separate women from men "for the purposes of prayer and instruction." The conclusion of the compiler of this material is that "these texts provide a continuity of evidence for women as office-holders in the Church (note *diakonos* at Rom. 16.1)."[14]

A fresco from the catacombs of Rome pictures a group, apparently all women, in the celebration of the Eucharist. (See illustration on page 57.) "The arrangement of the hair . . . in comparison with datable coins depicting emperors' wives, has been an important factor in dating this fresco to the end of the first century, A.D."[15] It is suggested that this portrays a "eucharistic" vigil, held in the catacombs on the anniversary of the death of a Christian. The figure on the left end, wearing a long woman's skirt (in contrast to the knee-length garment worn by men at this period), has her hands outstretched, breaking the bread. The fresco is therefore known as the "Fractio Panis" or Eucharist. The significance of this lies in the portrayal of a woman performing an act that is usually considered to have been reserved for a man, and, by many, to be the prerogative of an ordained minister or priest. On the other hand, there are other portrayals of feasting, and it could be argued that all these are simply portrayals of the present happy circumstance of the departed.

From Instruction to Persecution

As the church fathers ranged over the Scriptures, they found many passages about women to include in their church instruction. The teachings they formulated touched on such topics as morality, marriage, household duties, and church ministries. Meanwhile the women were proving their dedication in the face of persecution.

Clement of Rome

The letter to the Corinthians, known as 1 Clement, written by Clement of Rome around the last decade of the first century, commends the Corinthians:

And to the women you gave instruction that they should do all things with a blameless and seemly and pure conscience, yielding a dutiful affection to their husbands. And you taught them to remain in the rule of obedience and to manage their households with seemliness, in all circumspection.[16]

In this early opinion, the words "dutiful affection" and "rule of obedience" seem to clash with the teaching that "women manage their households." The word "dutiful" could be translated less harshly as "proper" or "fitting," but the Greek word often does convey the idea of duty.

In the same epistle there is admiration for the women who suffered cruel martyrdom: "Through jealousy women were persecuted as Danaides and Dircae, suffering terrible and unholy indignities; they steadfastly finished the course of faith and received a noble reward, weak in the body though they were."[17] In this way women in the first generations following the apostles took their place in the company of those who suffered for their faith. Whatever position Clement and others may have taken regarding women's ministry, there is no question as to their admiration for their sisters.

Polycarp

Polycarp, writing around the middle of the second century, encouraged wives, as Clement did, to a committed marital life: "[Teach] your wives [to walk] in the faith given to them, and in love and purity tenderly loving their own husbands in all truth, and loving all [others] equally in all chastity."[18] This expresses the theme of purity in marriage that will become increasingly prominent in the Fathers. In the same work Polycarp also provides an early reference to widows: "Teach the widows to be discreet as respects the faith of the Lord. . . ." This is the passage noted above where they are called "the altar of God." It was already clear in the Pastoral Epistles that widows needed to be helped and guided as a special class of people in the Christian society.[19]

Susanna. This third-century painting is from the Catacomb of Peter and Marcellino, Rome. It portrays a typical female *orans* or praying woman. Note the veil, which is common in these portrayals of women. From Fratelli Alinari, Rome. Permission from Art Resource, New York.

Ignatius

Although some of the material in the writings of Ignatius may be a later interpolation, most of the work attributed to him was undoubtedly written during his trip to Rome, where he was executed—sometime near the beginning of the second century. Ignatius told Polycarp that he should not neglect widows and that he should not despise either male or female slaves.[20] He also urged husbands and wives to fulfill their duties, encouraging celibacy for those who could "continue in purity." Marriage should not be a means to fulfill one's lust.[21]

This did not mean, however, that women were to be given equal opportunities for service. When urging the appointment of someone for a special mission, Ignatius specifies that it be a man.[22] Nevertheless, Ignatius had a characteristic that is pleasing to find in various writings of the Fathers: a cordial and gracious attitude to Christian women. In his letter to Polycarp he specifies that greetings should be given "in particular [to] the wife of Epitropus, with all her house and children."[23]

Blandina

Martyrdom in the early centuries was not simply the death of a Christian at the hands of unbelievers; it was an execution specifically brought on by the Christian's steadfast and clear testimony to the faith. Nor was martyrdom described only in dark, grieving words. The martyrs were privileged; they were honored. They showed courage and dependence on God for endurance. Martyrdom was, of course, not a happy occasion, but it was a victorious one.

The story of Blandina, who was martyred in 177, is known through the writings of Eusebius. In 325 Euse-bius produced the revised edition of his *Ecclesiastical History*; thus this account of a second-century martyr-dom is seen through the eyes of a fourth-century churchman.

The dating of Blandina's martyr-dom depends on a reference in Euse-bius to "the seventeenth year of the Emperor Antoninus Verus." This is the other name of Marcus Aurelius. His seventeenth year was 177.

Eusebius, after telling something of the background and the hostility of both crowds and officials against the Christians, provides a vivid descrip-tion. He says that Blandina was proof that God uses and honors "things which are obscure and contemptible among men." Did he consider her womanhood part of her contempti-bility?[24] The narration continues:

For while we were all afraid . . . Blandi-na was filled with such power that she was released and rescued from those who took turns in torturing her in every way from morning until evening, and . . . they marveled that she still remained alive, seeing that her whole body was broken and opened . . . but the blessed woman, like a noble ath-lete, kept gaining in vigor in her confes-sion and found comfort and rest and freedom from pain from what was done to her by saying, "I am a Christian woman and nothing wicked happens among us."

Eusebius continues his description of the martyrdom of Blandina and others by telling of another woman, Biblias, who had renounced the faith. She reaffirmed her commitment to Christ and was included among the martyrs. Meanwhile Blandina was taken to the amphitheater. While other Christians were beaten and burned, Blandina was hung on a stake, where she was exposed to wild beasts. Eusebius describes the scene:

She seemed to be hanging in the shape of a cross, and by her continuous prayer gave great zeal to the comba-tants, while they looked on during the contest, and with their outward eyes saw in the form of their sister him who was crucified for them, to persuade those who believe on him that all who suffer for the glory of Christ have forever fellowship with the living God. [Blandina was taken down again, be-cause the wild beasts did not touch her, but eventually brought back and was killed by a bull.] And so she too was sacrificed, and the heathen them-selves confessed that never before among them had a woman suffered so much and so long.[25]

Deaconesses Interrogated by Governor Pliny

Undoubtedly there are many other women who likewise suffered during this period. We know of two such, not from Christian writings, but from the correspondence between Pliny, governor of Bithynia, and Trajan in the year 111. Pliny wrote Trajan about two women slaves whom he arrested because they were Christians. He said, "I have judged it necessary to obtain information by torture from two serving women called by them 'deaconesses.'"[26] Why was it that Pliny tortured women slaves in order to get information about the Chris-tians? Did he think they would yield under questioning? Was it that they were the only Christians known to Pliny who had remained faithful dur-ing the persecution? Could it have been that these women were the only church leaders whom Pliny knew?

He called them "serving women." The Latin word *ancillae* normally means "slaves." In the opinion of Jean Daniélou it "seems to denote some kind of inferior office."[27] It could also have been used to describe people Pliny thought were doing servile work. The word *ministrae* seems to be the equivalent here of the Greek *diakonos*. It came to be used for deaconesses. Wilson-Kastner has this explanation: "Although one must keep in mind that the terminology for various Christian offices was not fixed firmly by this period, at the same time one ought not to minimize the fact that these women clearly did have a recognized function with the local church."[28] Gryson, noticing that the word *ancilla* is followed by *ministrae*, thinks that *ancilla* may simply describe these women's "social condition."[29]

The Curious Case of Flavia Domitilla

The women interrogated by Pliny were slaves. But socially prominent free women were also becoming Christians. This is seen already at the time of Acts, when "many of the Jews believed, as did a number of prominent Greek women and many Greek men" (Acts 17:12). A perplexing question is whether the Roman matron Flavia Domitilla was a Christian. Her grandmother was the wife of Emperor Vespasian. Since her mother was Vespasian's daughter, Flavia Domitilla was the niece of Vespasian's son, Emperor Domitian. She married a cousin of Domitian, the consul Titus Flavius Clement.

She was banished to the island of Pandateria. The reason for this exile was the charge that she had lapsed into "Jewish customs" and into "atheism." This has been interpreted to mean that she was a Christian or, at least, a Christian sympathizer. On the surface it sounds as though she were Jewish; the charge of atheism, however, was often leveled at Christians, who did not have the status that Jews did in the Empire.[30]

Irenaeus on Eve and Mary

In about 178 Irenaeus became bishop of Lyons. He is known for his great work against heresies, in which he attacked Gnosticism and the Montantists. While arguing against the Gnostics, Irenaeus drew a parallel between Eve and Mary, emphasizing the physical reality of the Incarnation. He referred to the sin of Eve, but did so mildly compared to some of the later writings of the Fathers. Whereas Mary was obedient, Eve was disobedient. She and Adam did not understand about the procreation of children. In a manner similar to the comparison between Adam and Christ in Romans 5, Irenaeus asserted that Eve by her disobedience was the "cause of death both for herself and the whole human race," while Mary through her obedience was the cause of salvation, again both for herself and for the whole human race.[31]

Irenaeus was not the only ancient churchman to blame Eve, nor was he the only one to laud Mary. In both respects, there was a tendency to extremes.

The Shepherd of Hermas

The Shepherd of Hermas, written sometime around 120, regarded women as symbols of "holy spirits" in his imaginative description of the church.[32] In his opinion, however, women are also symbolic of evil. In a more earthy section of his work, Hermas referred to the matter of divorce and claimed there was no possibility of remarriage even for the innocent person. Significantly, in spite of the custom in the ancient world to give more freedom to the man than to the woman in a divorce situation, Hermas declared, "Men and women are to be treated in exactly the same way."[33] Like a number of other church leaders in the early centuries, Hermas was against remarriage on the death of one's spouse. His language is mild compared to later writings: "If they remain unmarried, they gain honor and glory with the Lord."[34]

Hermas mentions widows as those who minister and also who need the supportive ministry of others.[35] In a totally different vein he tells of a vision in which a woman named "Graptē" is supposed to exhort widows and orphans. It is not known whether this is a well-known personage in the ancient church, or even an actual person.[36]

The Purity of Christian Women

The Christian apologists portrayed Christian men and women living in a purity that contrasted with pagan practices. Tatian, writing in the latter part of the second century, contrasted the luridness of Greek art, which was characterized by strong sexual suggestiveness, with the purity of Christian women.[37] In the same vein another Christian apologist, Athenagoras, extolled Christian morals,

saying that even lustful looks are prohibited.[38] He wrote on behalf of celibacy, saying that it brings one nearer to God. Like the Shepherd of Hermas, he was against remarriage and called it "a specious adultery."[39]

Justin Martyr on Ministering Women

Some of the evidence for the ministries of women comes in oblique ways. Justin Martyr's *Dialogue With Trypho* provides just such an indirect testimony. A chapter about the bestowal of the Holy Spirit on Christ commences with the observation that "it is possible to see among us women and men who possess gifts of the Spirit of God. . . ."[40] There is no further comment on this, and we are left with the bare observation that such was the case.

Clement of Alexandria

The first example of an apparent ambivalence between two views on marriage occurs in Clement of Alexandria. Writing around the end of the second century, Clement expressed himself almost harshly against certain tendencies that he saw mainly in women, such as the wearing of luxurious clothes, immodesty, the use of cosmetics, the wearing of jewelry and especially gold ornaments, and the wearing of fashionable shoes. He attributed the desire to own more clothes than are necessary to the "weakness of women."

He also spoke disparagingly of "diaphanous materials" and dresses of any kind that excite lust by revealing the female figure.[41] He inveighed further against rings, women's going to church without being entirely covered (face included), and women's having short hair rather than long hair bound up. Men should "turn away from the sight of women. For it is sin not only to touch but to look."[42]

As for marriage, Clement adopted the position that marriage is for procreation; it is not right for everyone.[43] While men and women have the same human nature, and women are able to do such things as manage the house and take care of the flocks, the husband is the head of the wife.[44] A person who is a "gnostic" (not in the heretical sense, but one who has true spiritual knowledge) should be able to resist the approaches of a beautiful woman as Joseph did in Egypt. True marriage is free of inordinate affection.[45]

Yet at the same time Clement rejected gnostic celibacy, citing 1 Corinthians 7 in support of his position.[46] In opposition to gnostic ideas, he defended marriage as good. He did so in a passage that "may sound like a lukewarm defense of its subject to the contemporary reader, [but] is in fact the strongest for the goodness of marriage to be found in the writings of the first three Christian centuries."[47] Clement thought that when Paul said one should "marry rather than burn," he was referring to a second marriage.[48] He attacked the wife sharing advocated by some gnostics. In short, he supported two standards of ethics without contradicting himself, because these two standards did not suit only one kind of people.[49]

Clement argued both that women have a different nature from that of men (they get pregnant; they are under the "ruling power" of the husband as head) and that they have the same nature as regards virtue. He referred to a woman in Greek tragedy who acted "manfully"; to Judith, who prevailed over Holofernes "though a woman"; and to Leaena of Attica, who endured torture in a "manful" manner. Clement thus paid women a backhanded compliment.[50]

Heretical Sects

It is a curious fact that women were prominent in the life and literature of fringe groups. The Naasenes claimed to have received their teachings from James, the brother of Jesus, mediated by a woman named Marianne. Epiphanius said that the Nicolaitans had a work they ascribed to a woman they thought was Noah's wife, called Noria.[51] The Apocryphal literature names not only Thecla, in the *Acts of Paul and Thecla*, but also Marianne, alleged to have been the sister of Philip, and a number of other women who were said to be prophetesses.[52] The New Testament itself had spoken scathingly of "that woman Jezebel, who calls herself a prophetess" (Rev. 2:20). But does this mean that only deviant sects had prophetesses, or, conversely, that prophetesses were always heretical?

The answer is clearly negative, since the canonical Book of Acts mentions that Philip the evangelist had four daughters who prophesied (Acts 21:9). Why then were prophetesses apparently more active in heretical groups than in the orthodox stream of the church? One can only speculate, but the following facts may have a bearing on the question. In order for the deviant groups to gain adherents it was necessary for them to demonstrate their superiority over the established church. This was done, in part, by claiming truth the orthodox Christians did not possess or emphasize. Such "truth" had to come from a divine source, and the expected mode would be prophecy. By their nature, these groups were individualistic and lacked the established church's corporate structure (such as it was by that time). The way was open for individual prophetic activity, which in these groups included the participation of women. It could also be suggested that because women were increasingly restricted in the developing church structure, some of the more strong-minded or impulsive ones would gravitate to groups that allowed them more expression.

Gnosticism

Whatever the case may have been with the other sects, in Gnosticism the female presence was prominent in its very theology. While the question could be asked as to why their theology became so feminized, for purposes of the present survey it is more important to observe that the existence of a feminine principle at the heart of their system could hardly fail to raise the female consciousness in their society. Much research has been done in this area, especially by Elaine Pagels. In a chapter entitled "God the Father/God the Mother,"[53] she assembles a curious assortment of texts. They are not monolithic, but evidence a diversity of attitudes toward sexual differentiation. One of these reveals an assumption that for women to enter the kingdom of heaven they must, as Pagels puts it, "assimilate themselves to men."[54]

Simon Peter said to them [the disciples]: "Let Mary leave us, for women are not worthy of Life." Jesus said, "I myself shall lead her, in order to make her male, so that she too may become a living spirit, resembling you males. For every woman who will make herself male will enter the Kingdom of Heaven."[55]

Some of the data are assembled in an article by Louis A. Brighton: "The Ordination of Women: A Twentieth-Century Gnostic Heresy?"[56] Brighton amasses a number of the gnostic texts on women and on the feminine principle in God to prove that the idea of the ordination of women is heretical, presumably because it echoes gnostic ideals. While his conclusion may go beyond the facts, he offers a convenient summary of data, found also in Pagels and, in their original context, in the *Nag Hammadi Library*. These include the following:

In *The Dialogue of the Savior* Jesus is said to have selected three disciples to receive his sayings: Matthew, Judas, and Mary Magdalene (called Mariam). Mary Magdalene is a "revealer," who knows all things.[57] In the *Gospel of Mary*, she is not only a "comforter" but also a "revealer." On the sayings of Jesus she is an authority equal to any of the other disciples.[58]

In addition to such recastings of Jesus' disciples, there is the figure of Helena, who was the associate of Simon Magus and whom he called "the first thought of my mind."[59] Another woman, Philoumene, will be noted below.

When Irenaeus thundered against the Gnostics, he took pains to describe their alleged heavenly beings in detail. The reconstructions of the

Christian apologists are, of course, always likely to suffer from misinformation on their part, but at the very least they provide insight into the perceptions of the Fathers concerning Gnostic teaching and practice. Among the supraterrestrial female beings he mentioned were Ennoea (also called Charis or Sige),[60] Sophia,[61] and Achamoth.[62] Irenaeus claimed that the Gnostic Marcus profaned the consecrated cups with the blood of the female being Charis.[63] He also mentioned that Marcus was particularly devoted to women.[64]

But lest it seem that women were automatically drawn away by heresies, it is worth noting that Irenaeus spoke of faithful devout women who were not deceived and who withdrew from Marcus.

Equally important is Irenaeus' observation that these women knew that the gift of prophecy was bestowed directly by God, not by someone like Marcus.[65] This shows both that the gift of prophecy was expected by the orthodox in that era of the church and that there were women who had great discernment. Nevertheless, there were also "silly women," like the deacon Asiatic's wife, a beautiful woman who fell victim to Marcus "in mind and body."[66]

At the heart of all of this is the theological discussion among the Gnostics themselves (again according to Irenaeus) as to the feminine element in Bythus, who was generally thought to be the supreme being among the Gnostic hierarchy. Some considered "him" to be sexless, while others thought he was both masculine and feminine, "assigning to him the nature of a hermaphrodite."[67]

The feminine principle in Gnostic thought was expressed frequently and under a variety of names, including "Mother," "Sound," "Thought of the Father," "Image of the Invisible Spirit," "Perfect Mind," "First and Last," "Thunder," "Whore," "Mother of All," "Virginal Berbelon," and the "Ineffable Mother who presides over heaven."[68]

How does this complex of Gnostic ideology—of which only a part is reproduced here—fit into the whole picture of women in the early church? It has become increasingly common for students of the religious literature and history of the early Christian centuries (including the New Testament itself) to view this from a social perspective. Commenting on the Gnostic views and the diversity within the Christian church (e.g., Paul's teachings in comparison with the prominence of prophetesses in Montanism), Pagels remarks:

> Such contradictory attitudes towards women reflect a time of social transition, as well as a diversity of cultural influences. . . . In Greece and Asia Minor women participated with men in religious cults. . . . In Egypt women had attained . . . a relatively advanced state of emancipation. . . . In Rome, forms of education had changed . . . [women were active publicly in business and social activities]. . . .
>
> Yet despite all of this, and despite the previous public activity of Christian women, the majority of Christian churches in the second century, like the majority of the middle class, opposed the move toward equality.[69]

Montanists

In contrast to some of the heretical sects that developed a competing system of theology over against orthodoxy, Montanism was flourishing as an attempt to bring in a new spiritual and visionary order emphasizing the Second Coming; this order was established to counter the formalism of the church. Along with Montanus himself were two prophetesses, Maximilla and Priscilla. They were accused of leaving their husbands to follow Montanus. These prophetesses announced the imminent return of Christ and the advent of the New Jerusalem.

Maximilla declared, "After me, there will be no prophetess anymore, but the end will come."[70]

Montanism itself was condemned by the church, but the extant pronouncements of the Montanist prophetesses, though they are somewhat mystical, do not contain outright denials of basic doctrine. These women spoke in the name of God but did not claim to be divine themselves. On the contrary, they sought to call the church to Christ and to an expectation of his return. Opinions have differed on whether their adherence to a deviant sect invalidated their belief that God had called them to prophesy. But throughout the centuries there have been women who were willing, even under criticism, to commit themselves to ministries they thought—rightly or wrongly—were the call of God. Some, suffering not merely criticism but also persecution, even committed themselves to martyrdom. The views of Tertullian, the most famous Montanist, will be discussed later.

Understanding the Conflict

There are at least three ways to view the conflict between the ortho-

dox and the sectarian practices regarding women. One is that the orthodox biblical position forbade the public ministry of women, with much of the prophetic and other leadership activity of women being thought of as simply out of order. Another view is that the more orthodox churches were in reality opposing the activity of women in heretical sects such as Gnosticism and Montanism largely because they opposed the sects themselves. A third view is that in keeping with the social movements of the day, as Pagels says, perhaps Christianity moved upward in the social scale, from lower-class status, in which women had been needed in ministry (a theory Pagels ascribes to Morton Smith), to the middle class, where women were still restricted in that society. In this last view, we should also note that Christianity was not completely at home in the upper classes in which, certainly in Roman as well as in other societies, women had long since gained status and freedom. Perhaps all three of these views are in some degree valid.

Perpetua

Approximately twenty-five years after the death of Maximilla another women died, perhaps the best-known martyr among early Christian women. Vibia Perpetua, a woman who had been born into a wealthy family was taken captive during the persecution under Septimius Severus around 202/3, along with her slave, Felicitas, and several men. Knowledge of the tragic events comes from a unique source, a firsthand account coupled with a third-person narrative by an eyewitness. There is also a first-person narration by Saturus, one of the men who was martyred with Perpetua.

The account by Perpetua (and the eyewitness) is one of only a few writings by a woman from the early-church period. It is a touching and poignant story, encompassing far more than just the details of her arrest and martyrdom. The reader is drawn in sympathy to her father who could not understand or identify with her Christian determination to obey God rather than the state. His anxiety far exceeded hers. The response of Perpetua's slave, Felicitas, provides an exemplary story in itself.

Even granting the tendency for legends to develop at this period, Perpetua's story seems to be essentially historical. An abbreviation of the original Latin version was used in church services, and a translation was made into Greek as well. A basilica was dedicated to Perpetua in Carthage. The anniversary date of her martyrdom was included in the Roman church calendar, and St. Augustine preached sermons about her. There are other pieces of evidence as well to show not only that the early church assumed the historical fact of her martyrdom but also that Christians esteemed her very highly.

After an introduction by a later editor, the account proceeds with a description of her arrest; her father's attempt, first with considerable hostility, to dissuade her from her testimony; then Perpetua's concern for her child; and finally her peace in the situation. When her father heard that she was to be tried, he came again, this time with a more kindly attitude, to dissuade her: "These were things my father said out of love, kissing my hands and throwing himself at my feet. With tears he called me not daughter, but woman. I was very upset because of my father's condition. He was the only member of my family who would find no reason for joy in my suffering."[71] Perpetua continues to tell her experiences, which include visions. One of them is of contending with the devil himself. She tells the experience of Felicitas, who was pregnant when she was arrested. One month before her baby was due she became concerned lest her martyrdom be delayed because it was not permitted to execute a pregnant woman. She prayed, and immediately went into labor; after considerable pain she gave birth to a daughter. The conclusion of the story is worth quoting in full:

The day of their victory dawned, and with joyful countenances they marched from the prison to the arena as though on their way to heaven. If there was any trembling it was from joy, not fear. Perpetua followed with a quick step as a true spouse of Christ, the darling of God, her brightly flashing eyes quelling the gaze of the crowd. Felicitas too, joyful because she had safely survived childbirth and was now able to participate in the contest with the wild animals, passed from one shedding of blood to another; from midwife to gladiator, about to be purified after child-birth by a second baptism. . . . For the young women the devil had readied a mad cow, an animal not usually used at these games, but selected so that the women's sex would be matched with that of the animal. After being stripped and enmeshed in nets, the women were led into the arena. How horrified the people were as they saw that one was a young girl and the other, her breasts dripping with milk, had just recently given birth to a child. Consequently both were recalled and dressed in loosely fitting gowns. Perpetua was tossed first and fell on her back. She sat up, and being more concerned with her sense of modesty than with her pain, covered her thighs with her gown which had been torn down one side. Then finding her hair-clip which had fallen out, she pinned back her loose hair, thinking it not proper for a martyr to suffer with disheveled hair; it might seem that she was mourning in her hour of triumph. Then she stood up. Noticing that Felicitas was badly bruised, she went to her, reaching out her hands and helping her to her feet. . . . And when the crowd demanded that the prisoners be brought out into the open so that they might feast their eyes on death by the sword, they voluntarily arose and moved where the crowd wanted them. Before doing so they kissed each other so that their martyrdom would be completely perfected by the rite of the kiss of peace. The others, without making any movement or sound, were killed by the sword . . . but Perpetua, in order to feel some of the pain, groaning as she was struck between the ribs, took the gladiator's trembling hand and guided it to her throat. Perhaps it was that so great a woman, feared as she was by the unclean spirit, could not have been slain had she herself not willed it.[72]

The Apocryphal Acts

The so-called Apocryphal Acts were patterned after the ancient romance, literary elements of which are also found in the canonical Book of Acts. The literary form in itself has no bearing on the historicity of the book. In the case of the Apocryphal Acts, however, pious imagination took over. The ancient reader enjoyed hearing stories about travel, and especially about dangers and shipwreck.

The absence of the romantic and female element in the canonical Book of Acts is adequately "remedied" in the unhistorical story we know as the *Acts of Paul and Thecla*. The woman Thecla sacrificed everything to follow the apostle Paul. She cut her hair and traveled around looking like a man. Paul commissioned her as an apostle. As might be expected, she became a model in later years for Christian women who desired to live a life of asceticism and sacrificial devotion to the Lord. The significance of Thecla lies not, as with Perpetua, in an actual devotion to the point of dying for the sake of the Lord, but rather in the ideal that characterized the thinking of many women of that time. As noted earlier, there is a theory that the Apocryphal Acts represents a reaction to the oppression on the part of the church against the activities of the orders of widows.

Tertullian

Tertullian's writings come mainly from the period 196 to 212. He grew up in a cultured pagan environment in the North African city of Carthage. After he became a Christian, he developed strong views about morality and eventually became a Montanist. Tertullian has been the object of much recent study.[73]

Tertullian's strong views have resulted in some equally strong reactions on the part of modern students of human social behavior. Gryson says, "Tertullian could not find words vehement enough to stigmatize the abusive pretensions of women in the heretical sects he opposed." And Tertullian did not oppose women only for their heresies, for, Gryson adds, he "did not tolerate women pretending to teach or to discuss."[74]

Women's Guilt for Sin

Perhaps the best known and most explosive of Tertullian's statements about women is found in his work *On the Apparel of Women*. He addressed this work to "best beloved sisters." Christian women, he admonished, should dress humbly and walk around "as Eve," in an attitude of mourning and repentance

> in order that by every garb of penitence she might the more fully expiate that which she derives from Eve—the ignominy, I mean, of the first sin, and odium [attaching to her as the cause] of human perdition. . . . In pains and in anxiety dost thou bear, woman; and toward thine husband [is] thy inclination, and he lords it over thee. . . . And do you not know that you are [each] an Eve? The sentence of God on this sex of yours lives in this age; the guilt must of necessity live too.

The words that follow are among the most notorious comments on women:

> *You* are the devil's gateway; *you* are the unsealer of that [forbidden] tree; *you* are the first deserter of the divine law; *you* are she who persuaded him whom the devil was not valiant enough to attack. *You* destroyed so easily God's image, man. On account of *your* desert [i.e., punishment], that is, death—even the Son of God had to die.[75]

It is easy for a modern writer, addressing readers who have become sensitized to the hurts caused by sexual slurs, to quote this passage for its shock value. Because of the controversial nature of Tertullian's writings, it is important to understand his reasoning. As Manges observes, "Historical work in an area such as the history of sexuality in the Church should be constructed on a foundation of individual analysis of each figure who contributes to that history. Rapid surveys which pull out provoking quotations from an entire series of writers will not do the job."[76] Tertullian worked from the same biblical premises as other church fathers and confronted an essentially similar pagan environment as they (although care must be exercised against oversimplification here). The strength of his comments was due largely to his revulsion against pagan sexual excesses.

Women's Modesty

Tertullian's repugnance toward the sexual excesses of pagan women appears also in a passage where he insists that it is not enough to avoid fornication. Women should also avoid "the studied graces of form and brilliance."[77] It is clear from the context that his attribution of evil to women stems from his observation of pagan immorality and reflections of that immorality even among Christian women, and not simply from a low view of women.

Tertullian's outrage over the immodest dress of unmarried women in his culture comes out all the more strongly in his work *On the Veiling of Virgins*: "The virgins of men go about, in opposition to the virgins of God, with front quite bare, excited to a rash audacity.... Are therefore chaste virgins to be, for the sake of these marketable creatures, dragged into the church, blushing at being recognized in public, quaking at being unveiled, as though they had been invited as it were to rape?"[78]

Celibacy and Marriage

Celibacy, especially the virginity of women, was important to Tertullian, as it increasingly was to the other church fathers. Veiling was important also. In particular he said, "Let virgins alone be veiled, and this when they are coming to be married, and not until they have recognized their destined husband."[79] If people want to know a specific divine law regarding veiling, there is one in Paul's words, "Does not even nature teach you...?"[80] A woman should have her head covered because, among other reasons, "She has the burden of her own humility to bear."[81]

Although Tertullian addressed married women as "women of the second (degrees of) modesty, who have fallen into wedlock," he wrote positively of marriage in his treatise to his wife; even so, of course, celibacy is preferable.[82] Tertullian did oppose remarriage, however.[83]

Tertullian's concept of marriage and celibacy becomes clearer in his treatise, On Exhortation to Chastity. He described three classes of virgins. The first class is those who are virgins from birth; the second, those who are virgins from their second birth—i.e., from their baptism; and third, those who are monogamous "when after the inception of a marriage once contracted, there is therefore a renunciation of sexual connec-

tion." This he called the glory of "moderation."[84] The principles illustrated by the excerpts quoted here are continued in other treatises of Tertullian, such as On Monogamy and On Modesty.

Another summary of his views on marriage is found in his response to Marcion: "We do not reject marriage, but simply refrain from it."[85]

Throughout his treatises, Tertullian frequently refers to Scripture. Much as he or any of the other fathers was a child of his age, imbued from childhood with a patriarchal attitude, this perspective was consistent with their understanding of Scripture. Tertullian's view of women—whether it concerned veiling, the sin of Eve, or whatever—was not in tension with, but rather stemmed from, his theology. We may have trouble with the idea that every woman today is guilty of Eve's sin, but it was perfectly logical and theologically sound to Tertullian. Further, Tertullian must be understood as a strong opponent of both the immorality he saw in the pagan culture of his day and the heretical ideas he saw in the Gnostics and especially in Marcion. If it seems strange that he urged continency within marriage, for him that was a sensible and biblical response to Marcion's opposition to marriage itself.

Tertullian's view that marriage should not be a sexual convenience was spelled out in even more detail in later church fathers. There are, according to Ernest Manges, three "theological incentives" in Tertullian that lay behind his "notable preoccupation with sexuality." One is the Christian witness before pagan contemporaries. A second is the eschatological viewpoint that the end of time was near. The third is Tertullian's view of soteriology, that salvation is partially dependent on the moral behavior of the Christian.[86]

Manges summarizes Tertullian: "If sexual pleasure even in marriage can lead to lust, then it is better to abstain from such pleasure by controlling and restricting marriage."[87]

Headship: Authority or Source?

Tertullian's discussion of 1 Corinthians 11 deals with the sense in which Paul used the word *head.* He begins with Paul's affirmation that Christ is the head of man and indicates that this is the Christ who is the "author" of man. This is a comment of significance for those who emphasize the meaning of "source" for *head.* But Tertullian goes on to support his reference to Christ as "author" (*auctor*) by stating that he has "authority" (*auctoritas*) and then observing that "authority can belong to no other than the author." Turning to the relation of woman to man, Tertullian states that the reason she needs to have "power" on her head is that she was taken out of man and was made for his sake. This seems to reinforce the impression that Tertullian thinks of headship primarily in terms of source.[88]

Teaching and Baptizing

Tertullian (a Montanist) held that women should be silent in the church but should be permitted to prophesy when veiled.[89] Not only should women be veiled and silent, they should also not be too bold even to learn, much less teach and bap-

tize. After asserting that laymen have the right to baptize, Tertullian resisted any "woman of pertness, who has usurped the power to teach." "For how credible would it seem that he who has not permitted a *woman* even to *learn* with over boldness, should give a *female* the power of *teaching* and of *baptizing*! 'Let them be silent,' he says, 'and at home consult their own husbands.' "[90]

The Mystic Marriage of St. Catherine, by Parmigiano. Notice the spiked wheel. It is customary in paintings of St. Catherine to portray the wheel on which she was tortured.   National Gallery of Art, Washington, D.C. Used by permission.

Application of Restrictions to Single Women

One issue of biblical interpretation is whether Paul's injunctions regarding women's silence, veiling, and teaching were intended for single as well as married women. Tertullian had no question about this, because "the precepts of ecclesiastical discipline concerning *women* have an eye to the *virgin*."[91] With regard to virgins and headship, Tertullian held that "if 'the man is head of the women,' of course (he is) of the *virgin* too, from whom comes the *woman* who has married; unless the *virgin* is a third generic class, some monstrosity with a head of its own."[92]

Prophets and Prophetesses

A problem that has surfaced from time to time in the history of the church is the appearance of those who claim to be prophets or prophetesses but whose teachings seem to be against the teachings of Scripture. This was a particular problem at the time of Tertullian. When Tertullian became a Montanist, he had to come to grips with the role prophetesses had played in the beginning of that movement. While he continued to oppose allowing women in ecclesiastic leadership, he did uphold the right the apostle Paul gave to women to prophesy.[93] But he could not tolerate all he heard from women. He opposed "a certain virgin [called] Philoumene an angel of deceit, transformed into an angel of light, by whose miracles and illusions Apelles was led [when] he introduced his new heresy."[94] Tertullian makes no effort to conceal his disdain for this prophetess, saying that "afterwards [she] became an enormous prostitute."[95] Tertullian also objects to the boldness of heretical women who are bold enough to teach, to dispute, to enact exorcisms, to undertake cure— it may be even to baptize. Their ordinations are carelessly adminis-

tered, capricious, changeable."[96] Tertullian brings his charges to a climax with a statement that is significant for its concept of ministry as well as for the role of women: "For even on laymen do they impose the functions of priesthood."

Phoebe and Others in Origen's Commentaries

If Tertullian had problems with women in ministry, Origen (the Alexandrian scholar who was prominent in the first part of the third century) spoke out even more strongly, especially against the Montanist prophetesses. In his comments on 1 Corinthians 14:34–35 (about women being silent), he said this about Philip's four daughters who prophesied:

> . . . at least they did not speak in the assemblies; for we do not find this fact in the Acts of the Apostles. . . . There is no evidence that Deborah delivered speeches to the people . . . Huldah did not speak to the people, but only to a man, who consulted her at home . . . Anna [Luke 2:36–38] . . . did not speak publicly. Even if it is granted to a woman to prophesy and to show the sign of prophecy, she is nevertheless not permitted to speak in an assembly . . . . Certainly, women should "teach what is good," but men should not sit and listen to a woman . . . even if she says admirable things, or even saintly things, that is of little consequence, since they come from the mouth of a woman.[97]

Origen's understanding of the ministry of Phoebe (Rom. 16:1–2) also reveals something of the feelings about women in his own time as well as contributing to our understanding of the diaconate in his day. He begins, "This text teaches with the authority of the Apostle that even women are instituted deacons in the church."[98] The reader immediately learns that *even* women can be deacons. But more than that, it takes the "authority of the Apostle" (Paul) to validate this practice. This suggests that even by the early part of the third century deaconesses were not commonly accepted in Egypt.

Origen continues by saying that Phoebe's ministry was one of assisting people and exercising hospitality. The example with which he compared her was Abraham's nephew Lot. Phoebe was pious and helpful, and she "deserved to assist and to serve the Apostle himself." He therefore defines Phoebe completely in terms of service.

The following comment illustrates how Origen's opinion of Phoebe is viewed by a present-day feminist biblical scholar, Elisabeth Schüssler Fiorenza:

> Those women whom the patriarchal writers could not erase from historical consciousness they declared frauds or heretics or interpreted from a patriarchal perspective. Origen, for example, acknowledges Phoebe, but reduces her to an assistant and servant of Paul and argues that women who do good works can be accepted as deaconesses.[99]

Origen is known for his allegorical interpretation of Scripture. It is not surprising, therefore, that he developed a symbolism of woman as representing the church in his commentary on the Song of Solomon. "The appellations of Bride and Bridegroom denote either the church in her relation to Christ, or the soul in her union with God the Word."[100]

Prophetesses, Virgins, and Widows in Hippolytus

One of Origen's contemporaries, Hippolytus of Rome, whom Origen heard preach in that city, is known for his *Refutation of All Heresies* and *Apostolic Traditions*. The *Refutation* contains comments on the prophetesses Priscilla and Maximilla mentioned above. Hippolytus' opinion comes through sharply:

> They have been deceived by women, a certain one named Priscilla and one named Maximilla, whom they considered to be prophetesses, into whom they say the Comforter, the Holy Spirit has come. And before these, they similarly believed a certain Montanus to be a prophet . . . they also glorify these women above the apostles and every spiritual gift, so that some among them have come so far as to dare to say that there is something more in them than in Christ. These people . . . bring in new observances by way of fasts and holidays, diets of dry food and radishes, alleging that they have been taught to do so by these women.[101]

Virgins and Widows

Although virgins ultimately constituted an order in the church, Hippolytus asserted that "a virgin does not receive the laying on of hands; it is her choice alone that makes her a virgin."[102] He was equally opposed to the ordination of widows.

Like virgins, widows constituted a special ministering group in the early church. Hippolytus asserted:

> When a widow is appointed she is not ordained but she shall be chosen by name. But if she lost her husband a long time previously, let her be appointed. But if she lately lost her

husband, let her not be trusted. And even if she is aged let her be tested for a time for often the passions grow with him who gives place for them in himself. Let the widow be instituted by word only and let her be reckoned among the [enrolled] widows. But she shall not be ordained because she does not offer the oblation nor has she a liturgical ministry. But ordination is for the clergy, on account of their ministry. But the widow is appointed for prayer, and this is a function of all Christians.[103]

In regard to widows, as Hippolytus saw it, one whose husband had been dead for a time could be "appointed" to the group of enrolled ministering widows. The Greek verb Hippolytus originally used (we have only a translation) was apparently *kathistēmi*, a common word that could be used also in secular situations of appointment. But a widow was not, in his opinion, to be "ordained." The Greek word for "ordained" was probably *cheirotoneō*. It was formerly used to indicate any designation (originally by stretching out one's hand to point or to vote) but came to be used in an ecclesiastical sense for ordination to the clergy. By contrast, virgins were not even appointed.[104]

Ordination

This passage is of obvious importance not only for Hippolytus' opinion concerning widows but also for his perception of ordination. Among the issues discussed both in ancient times and today regarding ordination are: (1) whether celebrating the eucharist is a special priestly function different from ordinary ministries, (2) whether it therefore requires ordination, (3) if so, whether people in

other ministries should or should not have the same ordination, and (4) whether women may have ordination for either an ordinary or a liturgical ministry. For those whose decisions are molded by church tradition, this opinion of Hippolytus is of considerable significance. In his judgment, ordination was clearly for the clergy, who performed a liturgical ministry that widows did not. Women were appointed for prayer, a "function for all Christians." It is this kind of issue that makes the question of women's ordination so complex.

A Christian Concubine

A controversy that Hippolytus had with Callistus yielded a curious fact. In a biography that the former wrote of the latter, there is a reference to a Christian woman named Marcia. She was a concubine of the emperor around the year A.D. 225. She used her influence in the emperor's court to win the freedom of Callistus and other imprisoned Christians. This is reminiscent of the role of Esther in the pagan court of her day.[105]

Other Prominent Christian Women

Church historians have found evidence of socially prominent women of the fourth century who were Christians. When Emperor Diocletian launched his persecution against the Christians, he made his own wife and daughter offer pagan sacrifices. This suggests that they were Christians. Prior to the toleration of Christianity under Constantine, Constantine's father had a daughter who was named Anastasia. Only those favorable to Christianity would have bestowed such a name. Flavius Ianuarinus, who was Roman consul for the year 328, had a Christian wife, Marcia Romana Celsa. The sarcophagus he made for her pictured the raising of Lazarus. Eustorgius, a man known as an Epicurian, left clues on his grave and on that of his wife that she had Christian morals. Julian the apostate grumbled about those whose wives gave money to the poor. Such a wife would "carry everything out of his house to the Galileans."[106] W. H. C. Frend cites an ancient complaint about women who tried to persuade their husbands not to go to the pagan altars. He quotes Libanius as saying that "when a man gets home, his wife and her tears and the night . . . draw him away from the altars."[107]

Cyprian on Virgins

Cyprian (who lived during the first half of the third century) was bishop of Carthage. He wrote extensively about virgins. The virgin was mystically married to Christ and was required to live in absolute purity. She was to dress modestly, something Cyprian also advised for all women. His instructions concerning virgins came at a time when they were increasingly recognized as a separate group of women devoted to the service of Christ. However, at that time they were not living a communal life in convents.[108]

Didascalia Apostolorum

Also in the third century a compilation of instructions on church order was developed, probably in the Syrian church, called the *Didascalia Apostolorum*. This work was later modified and included in the *Apostolic Constitutions*.

Women Not to Teach

Chapter three of the *Didascalia* is very clear on the opinion that a woman should be subject to her husband. She should reverence, please, and give her life in ministry to him. She should be modest so as not to attract other men. Elisabeth Schüssler Fiorenza cites this writing as an example of third- and fourth-century "patriarchal reaction against female leadership." It "maintains that women are not appointed by Jesus to teach and to proclaim Christ."[109]

Although the *Didascalia* mentions several women, including Mary Magdalene, as disciples, it maintains that the Lord "did not send them to instruct the people with us. For if it were required that women should teach, our Master Himself would have commanded these to give instruction with us." The rule that the *Didascalia* gives, based on Jesus' action, is, "We do not allow women to teach [*didaskein*] in the Church, but only to pray."[110]

Widows and Deaconesses

In spite of these restrictions on women's ministry, the *Didascalia* did encourage an order of widows and also, according to some, provides the "earliest reliable witness to the existence of an office of deaconess."[111] This judgment has not gone unchallenged, for some see earlier evidence, beginning with Romans 16:1 and perhaps 1 Timothy 3:11. Much of the ministry of a deaconess (or woman deacon, to distinguish her from one who was the wife of a church official) was to other women, not to men: "But let a woman rather be devoted to the ministry of women, and a male deacon to the ministry of men."[112] Yet the same passage, in speaking of their spiritual ministry, mentions the example of the women who served Jesus. Nevertheless, the role of the deaconesses was clearly to assist women at the baptism and to minister to women who were sick.[113] Gryson observes that while the Didascalia in various places describes male deacons as closely associated with the bishop, nothing like that is said of women deacons.[114]

The actual term *deaconess*, was not used until the third century. Ministries were being carried out, especially by widows, but not by a separate, named ecclesial order. But once such an order was recognized, it spread quickly throughout the eastern part of the Empire. The reason for the church's fostering this was perhaps not so much to fill a need for service, as this was already being met, as it was a means of order and control.[115]

"It is a fact," says van der Meer, that deaconesses, and later the "abbesses of the canonesses' foundations . . . did much in the ecclesiastical and cultic area which is now forbidden to women. The real problem is whether they received an actual sacramental consecration."[116]

It would certainly be interesting if it were established that the ancient Church had actually seen deaconesses as incumbents in a hierarchical office. . . . It would be a clear proof that the church had already overcome its low interpretation of women. But it is not decisive. For no matter how high the position of deaconesses can be fixed, the fact still remains that no one among the orthodox Catholics at that time had the remotest idea that a woman could be ordained a priest.[117]

Nevertheless, it should be noted that at least by the time of the Council of Chalcedon (A.D. 451), the technical term for ordination, *cheirotonēa*, was clearly used for deaconesses.[118]

Regarding widows, the *Didascalia* specifies that those who were enrolled should be over fifty years of age. They should be "meek and quiet and gentle . . . and . . . not be talkative." The widows' ministry should largely be one of prayer. "It is in this context that the *Didascalia* speaks against women teaching." Widows are to be "obedient to the bishop and the deacons" and not even "lay hand on and pray over anyone without the command of the bishop or the deacon."[119] Hippolytus of Rome thought, as we observed earlier, that some widows, those whose husbands had been dead for some time, should be "appointed" (but not ordained). Gryson, after surveying the material in the *Didascalia*, asks whether the widows in the Syrian community were "members of the clergy or of the laity." He continues, "On the one hand, they were the object of a special call from God, and they occupied a "place" or "rank" apart from lay people. But, on the other hand, there is no evidence that they were in some way positively associated with the bishops, presbyters, and deacons, so that they too were considered members of the clergy."[120] Gryson also notes that the widows described in the *Didascalia* "had also at least two things in common with the nuns of the following centuries: the vow of continence and the duty of prayer."

Women and Priesthood

Dionysius, who was bishop of Alexandria around 247–264, gave clear expression to one of the reasons women have been barred from priesthood: not only should women not be touched during "the time of their separation" [i.e., menstruation], but a woman is not to "approach the holy table or touch the body or blood of the Lord" (i.e., in the sacrament). The reason is that during her period she is not perfectly pure in soul and body.[121] This restriction finds precedence in the legislation of Leviticus 15:19–24, where the woman's periodic discharge is mentioned as one of the bodily emissions that result in defilement. Actually the emission of males had the same result. Theoretically a male could opt for celibacy, though that does not necessarily preclude an emission. But a woman has no way short of age to prevent her discharge. In this connection E. Margaret Howe cites the incident in the *Protevangelium of James* when the temple priests pondered how to handle the situation when Mary, Jesus' mother, became twelve years of age and, with the onset of her period, would pollute the temple.[122] Was this condition truly a problem the church fathers could not overcome, or did it offer a convenient "pious" support for restrictions established for other reasons?

The Beginnings of Monasticism

A significant development took place during the first part of the fourth century. Pachomius, who had constructed a monastic community for men, proceeded to do the same for women. We read about this from the later writings of Palladius: "With these men there was also a monastery of about 400 women. . . . The women were across the river, with the men on the opposite side." Apart from the necessity of transporting the body of a virgin who had died, no one "except for the priest and the deacon, crosses over to the women's monastery, and this happens only on Sundays."[123]

The ideal of the celibate, virgin life developed rapidly during the fourth century. "From the middle of the third century," writes LaPorte, "there was a special rank or dignity for virgins. It paralleled, and progressively substituted for, the rank of widows in the exercise of contemplative life."[124] LaPorte observes that there were many widows who were living in poverty and therefore not drawn to the contemplative life. The virgins, however, increasingly lived in communities (at this time in private homes, not, as later, in convents). They lived an ascetic life with vigils and fasting. Their ideal was to be like the angels, not marrying and totally given to the contemplation and praise of God.[125]

A Curious Argument for Virginity

A reason for virginity was offered in the *Banquet of the Ten Virgins*. This early fourth-century work by Methodius was written in a similar way to Plato's famous *Symposium*. These virgins discuss among themselves the virtues of the celibate life and, in a section of considerable theological

Procession of Virgins (Saints Agatha, Pelagia, Euphemia, and Agnes). This mosaic is from S. Apollinari nuovo, Ravenna. From Fratelli Alinari, Rome. Permission from Art Resource, New York.

and apologetic interest, the matter of polygamy in the Old Testament. In early New Testament times, the argument runs,

> the race of mankind was still very small in numbers; and it was necessary that it should be increased in number and then brought to perfection. Therefore the men of old times thought it nothing unseemly to take their own sisters for wives until the law coming separated them. . . . For the world was still unfilled with men, it was child, and it was necessary that it should be filled with these, and so grow to manhood.

As time went on, God intended that such kinds of marriage should cease, and also that polygamy itself should cease. Methodius then introduces an argument used by the church fathers to justify celibacy: overpopulation. "But when hereafter it [the world] was colonized from end to end, the race of man spreading to a boundless extent, God no longer allowed man to remain in the same ways. . . ."[126] So, the argument ran, marriage to a sibling and polygamy were permitted by God in order to populate the earth. However, when the world reached its saturation point (which, according to the Fathers, had already taken place in their day!) celibacy became the ideal, and virgins could "advance nearer to heaven, until, having obtained to the very greatest and most exalted lesson of virginity, they should reach to perfection."[127] Christ was the supreme example, having been born of a virgin and being celibate himself.

The World of Eusebius

It was about this time that Eusebius of Caesarea was writing his *Ecclesiastical History*. His narration of the martyrdom of Blandina in A.D. 177 was related earlier. There were also in his day a number of women whose Christian character, witness, and martyrdom he celebrated.

Women Under Adversity

One of the believers martyred during the persecution under the Roman emperor Decius was a woman by the name of Quinta. She was taken to the idol temple where they tried to force her to worship. When she turned away in disgust, "they bound her by the feet and dragged her through the whole city over the rough pavement, so that she was bruised by the big stones, beating her all the while." They stoned her to death and then attacked the homes of other believers.[128]

They then seized an elderly virgin, Appollonia. Pictures of her, like the one in this chapter, include a pair of pliers because her persecutors broke out all of her teeth. When they lighted a pyre to torture her, she jumped into the flames and ended her life a martyr.[129]

Others who were tortured at that time included Ammonarion, a holy virgin who was "tortured very vigorously" but held firm. Another was Mercuria, a highly revered, elderly woman. Yet another was Dionysia who had many children but "did not love them above the Lord."[130]

Eusebius described another martyr as "a certain holy person, admirable for strength of soul yet in body a woman," who was noted "for wealth, mirth and sound judgment." She had two beautiful unmarried daughters. They attracted the amorous attention of soldiers. To preserve their purity they escaped and jumped into a river where they drowned.[131] Still another woman avoided violation by committing suicide with a sword. In one terrible incident an entire Christian town was set on fire by soldiers; all perished, including women and children.

Potamiaena, who had faithfully maintained her virginity against the advances of lovers, faced a further struggle when brought to court. The judge, Aquila, "imposed severe punishments on her entire body and finally threatened to hand her over to the gladiators for bodily abuse." Her courageous response caused her to be put to death.

A soldier by the name of Basilides was kind to Potamiaena, and she offered to intercede to the Lord for him. Then "boiling pitch was poured slowly and gradually upon the various parts of the body from the tips of her toes even to her head." Not long after that Basilides confessed to having become a Christian. He said that Potamiaena had appeared to him three days after her martyrdom, assuring him that she had interceded for him and that the Lord had heard.[132]

After a summary of the horrible tortures endured by the Christian men, Eusebius says, "And the women, on the other hand, showed themselves no less manly than the men, inspired by the teaching of the divine word: some, undergoing the same contests as the men, won equal rewards for their valour; and others, when they were being dragged away to dishonor, yielded up their souls to death rather than their bodies to seduction."[133] He goes on to describe a Christian woman who was "most famous and distinguished among those at Alexandria," whose name, Dorothea, we know from a later account by Rufinus. The price she paid for resistance to the advances of a tyrant named Maximin was to be exiled and to lose all of her property.[134] Another woman similarly threatened by a tyrant at Rome asked to be excused to make herself more attractive. When she was alone, she killed herself with a sword.[135]

Eusebius tells of a woman who came to believe and gave up a sinful life. Her husband, however, did not follow her in the faith. She tried her best to persuade him to change, but to no avail. Finally, "in order not to become a party to his injustices and impieties while remaining in wedlock and sharing in his board and bed, she gave him what among you is called a bill of divorce and was separated." Her husband, instead of being glad that she had given up her former partying and worse, brought charges against her, accusing her of being a Christian.[136] Such a story is not intended, of course, to justify the woman's divorce proceedings but to portray her strength of conviction and willingness to make any sacrifice necessary for the Lord.

Women Against the Mainstream

Eusebius' opinion of other women did not always match his opinion of Blandina and the others just described. He tells of the "possessed maiden" Philoumene who influenced Appelles.[137] He also writes of the Montanist prophetesses, Priscilla and Maximilla.[138] Citing another work by Miltiades, Eusebius mentions the names of Ammia and Quadratus among others prophesying in the New Testament period.

Apparently, during this period of flourishing prophetic activity, women as well as men were prophesying, and some apologetic was needed to defend both. We are beginning to see a pattern that is discernible at different stages of church history. Alongside the "mainline" churches are groups that feel the church is not fulfilling its proper function in a spiritual way. These groups find support in prophetic activity among themselves. Among such groups it is not unusual to find women prophesying. This pattern will become more apparent in the late-nineteenth and twentieth centuries.

Naturally, perspectives differ on the validity of the prophetic activity, especially through the women. Eusebius relates the charge "that these first prophetesses themselves deserted their husbands from the moment that they were filled with the spirit."[139] In that day and since, such criticisms have flowed easily from churches in the mainstream, picking up deviations in theology or practice among the prophets and prophetesses. Conversely, groups such as the Montanists have tended to criticize the formality and deadness of the more orthodox churches. In their opinion God is not speaking through the official church channels, but he chooses ordinary men, and—here is the point—especially women, to mediate his Word.

Other Women Martyrs

A number of stories about women martyrs similar to those in Eusebius are vividly narrated in the compendium of martyrology known as *Foxe's Book of Martyrs*.[140] Although the sources are often obscure, the instances related are linked with one or another of the major persecutions during the reigns of Roman emperors.

When a widow named Symphrosa refused to sacrifice to the heathen deities, she was tortured and killed. Under orders from Emperor Trajan (A.D. 98–117), "she was scourged while she was hung up by the hair of her head," and afterward she was weighed down by a large stone and thrown into a river. Anthia, "a godly woman," was beheaded with her son, a bishop. During the reign of Marcus Aurelius (A.D. 161–180), Felicitas, "an illustrious Roman lady of a considerable family and great virtues" refused to forsake her faith and was beheaded. Her seven sons were also tortured and killed.[141]

The persecutions under Decius (A.D. 249–251) claimed the lives of many faithful Christians. One was Denisa, who, at the age of sixteen, took a firm stand against sacrificing to idols. Although the soldiers admired her, the

proconsul of Asia had her beheaded. There were a number of stories about women of considerable beauty who refused the advances of pagan men. One of these was Agatha, a woman of Sicily. Her refusal to yield to the governor "changed his desire into resentment." When he learned that she was a Christian, he "ordered her to be scourged, burnt with hot irons, and torn with sharp hooks." After all of this was done to her, she was "laid upon live coals, intermingled with glass" and taken back to prison, where she died.[142]

Saint Apollonia by Piero della Francesca, Assistant to Umbrian (c. 1470). St. Apollonia is typically pictured with pliers representing the tool with which her teeth were broken off during her martyrdom. National Gallery of Art, Washington, D.C. Samuel H. Kress collection, 1952.

During the same period a young woman in Antioch, Theodora, was condemned to a brothel when she refused to sacrifice to idols. A Christian man visited her, changed clothes with her, and in this way helped her escape. However, fearing for his safety, she told the authorities, with the result that both of them were killed. A number of other virgins were martyred during the Decian persecution.[143]

Emperor Diocletian (A.D. 284–305) is also known for his persecution of Christians. It was during his reign that a woman named Zoe, the wife of a prison guard, cared for some martyrs who had been tied to posts, their feet pierced with nails. Although they were eventually killed by spears, she was moved and impressed by their testimony and became a Christian herself. When she refused to sacrifice to the god Mars, they hung her on a tree, lighted straw underneath her, and then threw her into a river with a large stone tied around her neck. Another Christian woman, Faith, was broiled on a gridiron and then beheaded in 287.[144]

One woman maintained her faith at the expense of her child—a seven-year-old who professed his faith in Christ as the only true God. When they whipped him, his mother reproved him for asking for water. The more she encouraged him to faithfulness, the more he was tortured. Other stories tell of Suzanna, of Justina, and of Eulalia, who was burned to death in 303.[145]

Many women were tortured by Galerius, the adopted son of Diocletian. These included a young woman named Victoria and three sisters—Chionia, Agape, and Irene. Irene was shamefully exposed in public, she and her sisters were burned to death in 304. In the same year Anastasia, Mouris, and Thea were martyred.

Another woman, Maura, tried to persuade her husband, Timothy, to sacrifice to idols. When he refused, she turned back to God, after which they were crucified near each other. A child of Julitta, a descendent of a royal family in Lyconia, confessed faith in Christ and was killed. She followed him in death after boiling pitch had been poured on her feet and her sides torn with hooks. Names of women who suffered during those days could be multiplied.[146]

Epiphanius: Women Are Mediocre

In the process of these charges and countercharges, some highly offensive comments were made. Epiphanius (c. 315–403) rigorously opposed what he considered to be heresies. "His weaknesses included an unenlightened zeal for orthodoxy and an inability to understand the points of view of others."[147] Perhaps this explains the following comment on women: "In very truth, women are a feeble race, untrustworthy and of mediocre intelligence. Once again we see that the Devil knows how to make women spew forth ridiculous teachings, as he has just succeeded in doing in the case of Quintilla Maximilla and Priscilla."[148]

Ironically, among Epiphanius' contemporaries were some remarkable women who could have taken the witness stand against his accusations. These included Proba; Marcella; Paula; the notable mother and daughter, Melania the Elder and Melania the Younger (or Junior); and Olympias.

Some Outstanding Women of the Fourth Century

Proba

Proba is known for an outstanding literary work, the date of which is difficult to establish but very likely was around 351, when Epiphanius was in his mid-thirties. Her work is known as a cento, which is a literary (or a musical) composition that is composed of sections of other works. In this case Proba drew on the famous first-century B.C. poet Virgil to write a vivid description of Creation and the Incarnation. It is a moving literary experience, especially for one who is familiar with ancient Latin literature, to see how she "baptized" secular and pagan vocabulary and pressed it into the service of Christianity. She had an educated and keen mind. Here are some examples:

Then the almighty Father whose
    sway over the universe is su-
    preme
removed the darksome air and dis-
    pelled the shades
and divided the world into two,
giving half to light and half to
    night. . . .

Of a sudden, as He pondered His
    will took shape:
Rich clay He took up and shaped it,
molding fertile earth from the first
    months of the year.
And now, unexpectedly, the novel
    form of a man came forth.
The brightness of his great holiness,
    beautiful beyond all else,
like unto God in face and body,
    whose mind and soul
God in His greatness directs and
    moves towards deeds of mo-
    ment.
Now another is sought for this one;

but none dares comes forth to be
    called His comrade in sover-
    eignty.
Without delay God brings restful
    slumber to the young man's
    limbs;
    his eyes sink into blissful sleep.
It is a marvelous story—a maiden
    shone forth in brightest light,
beautiful of face and breast
already ripe for husband, in age
    right for marriage.

And concerning the incarnation of Christ:

because Thy Son descended from
    high heaven
and time brought to us with our
    hopes at last
succour and the coming of God
    whom for the first time
a woman bearing the guises and
    habit of a virgin—marvelous to
    say—
brought forth a child not of our
    race or blood.
And now the promised day was at
    hand when first
He showed His hallowed face, the
    first of a holy race
sent for a kingdom, and virtue came
    in His body
one with God, the very image of His
    beloved Sire.[149]

Marcella

Another great mind among the women of this period was Marcella. She was born around the year 322 and was highly esteemed by Jerome. The following description of her by Jerome is interesting, not only for its portrayal of a remarkable woman, but also for its description of how a woman in that day could effectively teach God's truth without being considered a teacher:

And because my name was then especially esteemed in the study of the Scriptures, she never came without asking something about Scripture, nor did she immediately accept my explanation as satisfactory, but she proposed questions from the opposite viewpoint, not for the sake of being contentious, but so that, by asking, she might learn solutions for points she perceived could be raised in objection. What virtue I found in her, what cleverness, what holiness, what purity, I am afraid to say, lest I exceed what belief finds credible. I will say only this, that whatever in us was gathered by long study and by lengthy meditation was almost changed into nature; this she tasted, this she learned, this she possessed. Thus, after my departure, if an argument arose about some evidence from Scripture, the question was pursued with her as the judge.[150]

The next sentences deal with the matter of a woman teaching:

And because she was so discreet and knew about what the philosophers call in Greek *to prepon*, that is, "how to behave appropriately," when she was thus questioned, she used to reply as if what she said was not her own, even if the views were her own, but came either from me or from another man, in order to confess that about the matter she was teaching, she herself had been a pupil. For she knew the saying of the Apostle, "I do not, however, permit a woman to teach" (I Tim. 2:12) lest she seem to inflict an injury on the male sex and on those priests who were inquiring about obscure and doubtful points.[151]

In other words, Marcella, with Jerome's concurrence, ascribed her theological opinions to him so that she would not seem to be taking over the position of a teacher.

A later passage in the same tribute shows something further of her character as well as of her brilliance: "She was in the front line in condemning the heretics; she brought forth witnesses who earlier had been taught by them and later were set straight from their heretical error. She showed how many of them had been deceived. . . . She called upon the heretics in frequent letters to defend themselves."[152]

Paula

Paula was a member of the Roman aristocracy. She was widowed and was left with five children. One of these children died an unfortunate death after turning to asceticism too soon after a serious illness. Her relatives reacted angrily against Jerome, who, with Paula, had been pleased with the daughter's decision. Another one of Paula's daughters was Eustochium. Jerome wrote a treatise to her on virginity, as well as, later on, a memorial to her mother.

Paula left the other children, and, taking Eustochium, went with Jerome to begin a new life of devotion. They went to Palestine and visited the holy places there. After a trip to Egypt, they returned to Bethlehem, where they decided to develop a monastery for women; one already existed there for men. Ultimately, Eustochium led the women's monastery after the death of her mother. Here are some of Jerome's appreciative comments on Paula:

What poor man, as he lay dying, was not wrapped in blankets given by Paula? What bedridden person was not supported with money from her purse? Not mindful of home, of children, of servants, of possessions, of anything that pertains to the world, she was eager to proceed alone. She was slow at speaking and quick at listening. She had memorized the Scriptures; she urged me that she, along with her daughter, might read through the Old and New Testaments, guided by my discussion. If at any passage I was at a loss and frankly confessed that I was ignorant, she by no means wanted to rest content with my reply, but by fresh questions would force me to say which of the many possible meanings seemed to me the most likely.

Paula and her daughter also learned Hebrew, speaking it without a Latin accent.[153]

In the same epistle Jerome describes the rule of the women's monastery under the gentle and wise leadership of Paula. This was a significant step in the development of communal life under the spiritual leadership of competent women. Increasingly, women of ability were to find opportunity to serve their Lord, not in the church at large, but in the community of ascetics. Naturally, there are different perspectives on this development. One might celebrate such a ministry of women to women and collectively to the needy. On the other hand one might regret the loss of such spiritual and theological ability to the church at large. Further, it is becoming apparent that the ascetic life was in one sense a release to women. The restrictions in marriage, and indeed the strong feeling that marriage itself was not for any reason other than procreation, meant that it was virtually hopeless for women of spiritual ability to live a happy married life of fulfillment and at the same time to serve their Lord.

Melania the Elder

Melania the Elder was born a few years before Paula but outlived her. She is called the Elder, not because she was an ecclesiastical elder but to distinguish her from her daughter, commonly known as Melania the Younger. Like some of the other women of importance in the history of Christianity, she was born into a prominent family. After losing her husband and two of her children, she devoted herself to the Lord as a Christian ascetic. During a time of persecution after the death of Athanasius, she used her resources to help the ecclesiastical leaders who had been exiled. She disguised herself but was arrested anyway; she was released, however, when she made her social position known.[154]

The following description was written in A.D. 419–420:

> She was very learned and a lover of literature. She turned night into day by going through every writing of the ancient commentators, three million lines of Origen, and 250,000 lines of Gregory Stephen, Pierius, Basil, and other excellent men. And she did not merely glance through them casually, but laboring over them, she read each work seven or eight times. Therefore she was able to be freed from "knowledge falsely called" (I Tim. 6:20) and to take flight by the influence of the books, making herself a spiritual bird, passing over to Christ in good hopes.[155]

Another writer, possibly Melania's cousin Paulinus of Nola, said of her, "What a woman she is, if it is permissible to call such a manly Christian a woman!"[156] It is easy to see from this and from other comments recorded in our survey that some virtues were typed as masculine. Palladius quotes Melania in her old age saying as she reflects on a long life of self-discipline: "Look I am sixty years old and neither my feet nor my face nor any of my members, except for the tips of my fingers, has touched water. . . . I have not yet made concessions to my bodily desires nor have I used a couch for resting nor have I ever made a journey on a litter."[157]

Melania the Younger

Melania's daughter, Melania the Younger, was married, but after her children died she and her husband, Pinian, took a vow of chastity. They built monasteries for both men and women on the Mount of Olives. She made an intensive study of the Bible and of the lives of the desert Fathers. Although Pinian had been in charge of the monastery for men, after his death Melania the Younger was left alone in charge of the entire complex. In addition, she taught a group of women in theology so they could refute Nestorianism.[158]

Olympias

"The most holy and admirable Olympias," as Palladius called her, followed in the footsteps of Malania's "resolution in her reverence and in her footsteps." She also was of noble birth. She was married only a few days, and it was said that she died a virgin. "She contended eagerly in no minor contests for the sake of the truth, taught many women, held solemn conversations with priests, honored the bishops, and was deemed worthy to be a confessor on behalf of

truth. . . ."[159] We learn more of her from an anonymous fifth-century work, which tells us that "by the divine will she was ordained deaconess of the holy cathedral of God and she built a monastery at an angle south of it."[160] The "holy cathedral" mentioned in the text was in Constantinople, where she lived. Note that this evidence of a deaconess does not come from the western church, but from the eastern.[161]

Macrina

The name of Macrina is not as well known as those of the so-called Cappadocian Fathers—Basil of Caesarea, his brother Gregory of Nyssa, and Basil's close friend Gregory of Nazianzus. Even so, it was because of Macrina, who was Basil's sister, that he became dedicated to Christian ministry. Gregory said of Macrina: "It was a woman who was the subject of our discourse, if indeed you can say 'a woman' for I do not know if it is appropriate to call her by a name taken from nature when she surpassed that nature." Gregory and Macrina's brother Basil had been in a school for rhetorical training. Macrina "detected that he was enormously puffed up with pride over his rhetorical abilities; he despised all the worthy people and exalted himself in self-importance above the illustrious men of the province. Yet she drew him with such speed to the goal of philosophy that he renounced worldly renown."[162] Gregory's further descriptions of the various ministries of Macrina included the founding of a monastery for women near one that Basil had founded for men.

Basil wrote on the problem of

"fallen virgins." If widows who sinned caused a problem to the early church, virgins did so even more seriously. According to Basil, since a virgin is a "spouse of Christ," deviation constitutes adultery. He acknowledges that some who were enrolled among the virgins did not become so of their own choice, but because of the ambitions of their families.[163]

Gregory of Nyssa also wrote about virgins. Virginity is celestial, he said; it transcends this life, and, unlike marriage, is "stronger than the power of death."[164]

Fourth-Century Compilations of Church Order

From time to time rules were drawn up, sometimes pseudonymously, to govern the increasingly complex affairs of the church. Some of these incorporated or imitated earlier works.

The Ecclesiastical Canons of the Apostles

This is also known as The Apostolic Church Order, not to be confused with Hippolytus' Apostolic Tradition, or with the Apostolic Constitutions of the late fourth century. Gryson cites a passage in which Jesus' disciples are reported to have discussed the matter of women's ministry. Andrew observed that it would be good "if we established ministries for women." Peter responded that some progress had been made in this, but that there remained the matter of "the oblation of the Body and Blood"—i.e., the celebration of the Eucharist. John objected that Jesus did not permit

women to "stand with us." Gryson interprets this to mean officiating, since otherwise they would be sitting. Mary and Martha get into the discussion (though not to press for this ministry), and finally James declares that women's place was to minister to other women in need.[165]

A fourth-century work, the Canons of Hippolytus, was modeled on the earlier writing of Hippolytus. One important opinion it expresses is that "the appointed widows should not be ordained. . . . Let them not be given ordination, but prayed over, since ordination is for men."[166]

The Apostolic Constitutions

In the late fourth century a work on ecclesiastical practices was compiled. It drew on earlier works such as the Didascalia and the Apostolic Tradition of Hippolytus, referred to earlier. This probably represents the thought of some eastern Christians, but it never had official status in the eastern church. Therefore, as we survey some of the teachings of the Constitutions, we need to bear in mind that this is personal opinion, though undoubtedly it represented the thinking of many. Among the various instructions are a number concerning widows and deaconesses. Some of the instructions concerning widows are similar to those found elsewhere, including the age at which they are to be recognized (in this case sixty years) and standards of character. Other statements, however, are strongly restrictive, as will be noted below.

Instructions are given for the ordination of deaconesses. The bishop was to lay hands on her in the presence of the presbytery and deacons and other deaconesses. A prayer is given on behalf of the one ordained to the office of a deaconess.[167] Virgins, however, are not to be ordained, "for we have no such command from the Lord."[168] Other instructions include these: Wives are to be obedient to their husbands on the basis of 1 Corinthians 11:3.[169] Widows are to "mind nothing but to pray and to answer basic questions concerning the faith, but of the remaining doctrines not answer anything rashly, lest by saying anything unlearnedly she should make the word to be blasphemed."[170]

> We do not permit our "women to teach in the church," but only to pray and hear those that teach; for our Master and Lord, Jesus Himself, when He sent us the twelve to make disciples of the people and of the nations, did nowhere send out women to preach, although He did not want [i.e., lack] such. . . . For "if the head of the wife be the man," it is not reasonable that the rest of the body should govern the head.[171]

There are both virgins and widows who live for themselves, not for the Lord. A good widow will be modest and not greedy and will be found "sitting at home."[172]

The following passage is clear as to its line of argument, and probably expresses the convictions of many churchmen today:

> Now as to women's baptizing, we let you know that there is no small peril to those that undertake it . . . it is dangerous, or rather wicked and impious. For if the "man be the head of the woman," and he be originally ordained for the priesthood, it is not just to abrogate the order of the creation.[173]

The argument continues with a reference to the creation of woman from man, who is therefore to rule her. She is not to teach, so cannot possibly be a priest. The reason is that

> this is one of the ignorant practices of the Gentile atheism, to ordain women priests to the female deities, not one of the constitutions of Christ. For if baptism were to be administered by women, certainly our Lord would have been baptized by His own mother, and not by John.[174]

The laity are not allowed to perform any of the offices of the priesthood either. They cannot offer the Eucharist or baptize or lay on hands in ordination or pronounce the blessing. The obvious point here is that women can never rise higher than the level of the laymen. In a later book of the *Constitutions* there is a severe statement about remaining in one's appropriate rank. In support of this, allusion is made to the statement of 1 Corinthians 14:33, that God is not the God of confusion. The "subordinate persons" should not "tyrannically assume to themselves the functions belonging to their superiors. . . ."[175]

No one but a bishop or a presbyter was allowed to baptize, and not even presbyters were allowed to ordain. This shows the extent to which ecclesiastical structure had been developed. This obviously worked against the ministry of women.[176] Then, as in most segments of Christendom today, the issue of ordination was crucial. The devoted ministry of women in many capacities was certainly recognized by many writers of the early church period. There was much that women, especially deaconesses and women in the orders of widows and virgins, could do. The dividing line, however, was ordination to the liturgical aspect of ministry. Did the "Yes, but ... " that aggravates Christian feminists today have the same effect then?

Monica and Augustine

Augustine's mother, Monica, seems to have been influential at every major turn of his career. He attributed his conversion to her piety. His father was not a Christian and did not become one until just before his death. Augustine said of him, "His was the drunken joy in which this world becomes forgetful of Thee, its Creator, and loves Thy creature in place of Thee." In contrast, his mother "experienced a rising feeling of holy fear and trembling for me; though I was not yet one of the faithful, she nevertheless feared the crooked ways in which they walk who turn their back and not their face to Thee."[177]

The story of Augustine's conversion has often been told. During a time of deep emotional tensions, Augustine heard someone saying, "Take it, read it!" repeatedly. He took this to mean that he should read a book, and so he took the Book of Romans and read the first verse that he came upon. It was Paul's injunction in Romans 13 to forsake debauchery and make no provision for the lusts of the flesh. This changed his life. When he told his mother what had happened, "she was exultant, triumphant, and she blessed Thee. . . . She saw that much more in regard to me had been granted her

by Thee than she was wont to ask with her unhappy and tearful laments."[178]

Monica was also influential in Augustine's rejection of the Manichaean heresy. In this connection he describes her as "womanly in her dress but virile in her faith, mature in her serenity, motherly in her love, Christian in her piety."[179]

Augustine wrote an extensive passage in his *Confessions* about her death. It is a moving narrative. In a slightly mystical manner he praised her spirituality by saying, "Such a person was she, under the influence of Thy teaching as an inner Teacher in the school of her breast."[180] Augustine freely confessed that his knowledge of Christ came through her teachings and his spiritual life through her prayers.

The views of Augustine, whose major literary work was produced in the first quarter of the fifth century, are fairly well known. Augustine did not condemn marriage; on the contrary, one of his treatises is called *On the Good of Marriage*. There are, however, some modifications to this. Eve was created to be man's helper "specifically for the production of children."[181]

This sounds something like the teaching of Ambrose, who had been bishop of Milan in the last quarter of the fourth century. He felt that woman was a good helper, in that her purpose was to generate human nature.[182]

According to Augustine, marriage would have produced children without lust if Adam had not sinned. He described in rather explicit terms how man could have placed his "seed" into his wife without any passion being involved.[183] Of course, life completely without sex would have been even better. "Thus a good Christian is found to love in one woman the creature of God whom he desires to be molded again and renewed, but to hate in her the corruptible and mortal sexual connection, i.e., to love in her what is human, to hate in her what pertains to a wife."[184]

Saint Lucy by Francesco del Ferrarese Cossa (c. 1470). St. Lucy is typically portrayed with a pair of eyes, because, according to tradition, she gouged out her eyes and sent them to a young man who was attracted to her because of the beauty of her eyes. She made this sacrifice to deter him from inordinate desire for her.   National Gallery of Art, Washington, D.C. Samuel H. Kress collection, 1939.

Rosemary Ruether, referring to Augustine's view that the relationship of woman to man is similar to that of body to spirit, and to his conclusion that only the man possess the full image of God, calls this "perhaps the ultimate core of misogynism."[185]

John Chrysostom

If Augustine's views can be so described, those of John Chrysostom are more extreme—in both directions. He has some tender comments in his homily on Ephesians 5:22–24, but contemporary feminists will be quick to point out this statement: "The wife is a second authority; let not her then demand equality, for she is under the head; nor let him despise her as being in subjection, for she is the body; and if the head despises the body, it will itself also perish."[186]

Although Chrysostom attempts to argue for an "equality of honor" between Adam and Eve, he makes a point of Paul's comment on man being the image of God, while woman is (only) the glory of man.[187] The man is "skilled at the greater things" but he is "downright inept and useless in the performance of the less important ones, so that the woman's service is necessary. . . . God maintained the order of each sex by dividing the business of human life into two parts and assigned the more necessary and beneficial aspects to the man and the less important, inferior matters to the woman."[188]

Authority and Teaching

Chrysostom did not think that a woman should exercise authority: "She asserted her authority once and asserted it badly." Neither should she teach: "Therefore let her descend from the professor's chair!"[189]

Eve

In his homily on 1 Timothy, Chrysostom states that Paul "wishes the man to be preeminent in every way." After all, the woman had her chance. Eve "taught the man once, upset everything, and made him liable to disobedience. Therefore God subjected her, since she used her rule, or rather, her equality of honor, badly." But what about the question of deceivability? Was not Adam also deceived? Yes, but "it is not same thing to be deceived by a fellow human being, of the same kind as we, as to be deceived by an animal. . . . [Adam] sinned not because he was blinded by desire, but merely by his wife's persuasion."

Eve's deception affects all women, because "the female is weak and vain, and here this is said of the whole sex. For he does not say, 'Eve was deceived,' but 'the woman,' which is the common name of the sex, not her particular name." And how do women have salvation? "through having children."[190]

Priscilla

Those who mainatin that women may not teach must explain Priscilla's instruction of Apollos in Acts 18:24–28. The way Chrysostom explained it is that Priscilla was more pious than Aquila. She was not like the worldly women of Chrysostom's day. Also, if a man is "an unbeliever, wandering in error, Paul [in 1 Timothy 2:12] does not deprive her of the power of a teacher." "In a word, then, when Paul says, 'I do not permit a woman to teach,' he is talking about public instruction that involves arguing in front of people and about the teaching that befits the priesthood. But he does not rule out her exhorting and giving advice in private."[191] Actually, says Chrysostom, if a man is ashamed to be taught by a woman, he should repent on his own![192]

As if that were not enough, Chrysostom compares one's going to a woman for instruction to his going to the "irrational animals of the lower kind" like the ant of Proverbs 6:6.[193]

Mary and Junia

Amazingly, in view of such comments, Chrysostom celebrated the outstanding women whom Paul mentioned in Romans 16. Regarding Mary, whose hard work Paul commended in verse 6, Chrysostom said that Christians are both honored and shamed by having her among us. Men are put to shame "in that we men are left so far behind" by such women. He also wrote glowingly of Junia (whom he understood to be a woman), whose devotion made her worthy to be called an apostle.[194]

Virgins

Like other church fathers, Chrysostom has extensive comments about virgins. He also was upset over those who abused the position of virgin. Certain ideals had been developing, especially as set forth in the work of Methodius, as to what virgins should be. These were not yet uniform, but Chrysostom knew what he did not consider appropriate.[195] Chrysostom, we should note, also favored the office of deaconess and encouraged the work of deaconesses.[196]

Marriage

And what is the justification for marriage according to Chrysostom? "So there is one excuse for marriage, namely, avoiding fornication."[197] Even the wedding ceremony and the festivities surrounding it can be a means of evil:

"What," someone asks. "Are you criticizing marriage? Speak up!" By no means—I am not *that* crazy! But I do criticize the baggage wickedly dragged along in the wake of marriage: the make-up, the eye-shadow, and all the superfluities of this sort. Indeed, from that day she will receive many lovers and these even before she receives her bridegroom-to-be. . . . Then see what happens next. Not only during the day, but also in the evening, drunken men . . . are supplied to gape at the beauty of the girl's face. . . . Nothing is decent, everything is full of indecency. Will not the bride have a lovely lesson in discretion, seeing and hearing such things?

All of this, he says, is the devil's work against marriage, that "fortified outpost stationed against sexual immorality.[198]

We should note that Chrysostom does argue that men and women are equal to the extent that there is just one sexual standard for both.[199] Not all church fathers honored that standard. Chrysostom also had strong words for husbands:

You see the rule of obedience? Well, hear also the rule of love. Do you wish your wife to obey you, as the Church obeys Christ? Then take care for her, as Christ did for the Church; and even if you must give your life for her, or be cut in a thousand pieces, or whatever you must undergo and suffer, shrink not from it; and even if you suffer all this, you have not yet done anything that Christ did; for you do this being already joined in marriage to her, but He suffered for a Bride who rejected and hated Him. . . . A slave a man may perhaps bind by terror . . . but the partner of your life, the mother of your children, the subject of all your joy, you ought to bind not by terror and threats, but by love and gentle considerations."[200]

If Augustine thought that children could be produced through marriage without any sexual passion, Chrysostom thought that it was "even more probable that God could make humans aside from marriage, just as he created the first people without marriage. . . ."[201]

One practice that flourished in the early church in spite of a definite lack of approval, was "spiritual marriage"—a man and woman living in the same home together but without sexual relations. Chrysostom opposed this practice, for he was concerned about its impropriety.[202] Tertullian had said that a "second marriage must be said to be nothing else than a kind of fornication."[203] Chrysostom agreed with that, implying that those who marry after the death of a spouse show where their minds have been![204]

Women as Friends

In concluding this chapter, we may recall that in spite of severe statements of the church fathers about women's intelligence and morals, some of them, at least, had a high esteem for, and even a warm friendship with, certain women. In a fascinating work[205] Elizabeth Clark suggests several factors that produced this phenomenon. One of these is especially pertinent here. It is that there was a contrast between women in general, whom they pictured as "light-minded, vain, unintelligent, and even treacherous," and the particular women with whom they had close fellowship. These individual women were seen as beginning, at least, to transcend their femaleness. Clark supports this with a reference to recent anthropological studies on liminality or the transition from one state to another.[206]

Without making too facile a comparison on the basis of a complex explanation, one may venture to suggest that Paul envisioned Christian women as transcending, in the Lord, the conventional limitations of their sex in anticipation of the world to come. If this were the case, his arguments for restriction of ministries would have been addressed to specific circumstances that in his judgment would require conventional morals, but with full realization that in Christ such distinctions were transcended. This would accord with the restrictions in 1 Corinthians that are followed by the transition words, "Nevertheless, in the Lord. . . ."

Concluding Observations

The early church has left a rich heritage of faithful women. Some were martyrs, resisting violation not only of their chastity but also of their pure faith. Others found that the alternative to martyrdom was not necessarily an easy life. There were restrictions that not all accepted. Women in general tended to be branded as sexually loose. Some writers were so preoccupied with

women in their physical sexual role that it might be said that women were sometimes viewed as sex objects.

At the same time, it is too easy to judge the church fathers; a better understanding of their times can help us understand their concerns. Tertullian is an example. Those who read modern authors who write about women in the early church quickly realize how strong their own perspectives are.

The writers quoted here have provided a curious juxtaposition of opinions on marriage, sex, celibacy, church offices, and a number of related topics. It is important to note that all of these opinions were claimed by their proponents to have been based on Scripture.

It should also be kept in mind that the men who denied women access to liturgical ministries did so on the basis of views concerning ordination, the Eucharist, and celibacy that many today (Catholics among them) challenge. Those who hold "traditional" views need to know what that tradition included. The biblical hermeneutics and ecclesiastical assumptions of the church fathers require careful attention. The issues are both important and complex.

During the period just surveyed, the Roman Empire tolerated and then adopted Christianity. Christian ethics were affecting society. For example—to cite a matter that involved women—adultery with slaves was not prohibited. The Roman Empire itself was on the verge of collapse. But the ministry of women would continue, mainly within monastic walls.

Chapter 4

Medieval Catholicism: Nuns, "Heretics," and Mystics

Who was the medieval church-woman, and does she have any relevance for Christian women of the twentieth century? This a difficult question to answer. If one were to read only certain theologians, it would appear as though the medieval woman was some sort of inferior species with no serious function to carry out within the confines of organized Christianity. On the other hand, the record of medieval history abounds with stories of women who spent their lives in Christian ministry. There are a number of factors that account for this apparent discrepancy. Above all, medieval Christianity was not static. As society changed over the centuries and as Christianity adapted to new cultures, major changes occurred. Likewise, there was always a significant gap between prescribed church polity and the actual practice of the church. And closely related to that was the gap between two major traditions that have always coexisted in Christianity—the organized institutional church and the decentralized "spirit-led" fringe movements, the former characterized by a patriarchalism and the later by egalitarianism.

Another complicating element in understanding the role of women in medieval Christianity relates to the credibility of the sources. Much of the primary source material is in the form of hagiography—fictionalized biography dealing with the lives of the saints. But despite its inherent weaknesses, hagiography gives the reader the medieval concept of the ideal saint—if not the real one. And there is much historical reality to be found in the pages of hagiography. There is enough at least to aid the historian in making some broad generalizations about the period and about the individuals who wielded the greatest spiritual influences in society.

One such generalization regarding medieval churchwomen relates to the nature of their ministry in the church. Indeed there were limitations, but women sought to avoid these limitations and attain power through nonconventional means. Holy living, charismatic phenomena, and emotional ecstacy all became a means of gaining recognition in a church that placed enormous emphasis on hierarchical office holding. For women more than men, it seems, this charismatic element often became the standard for advancement in the church—or at least for recognition within the community of believers.

Was this in any sense demeaning for women? A cursory glance might give that impression. In the words of one historian:

> . . . there is a suspicion among twentieth-century Christians that the female holy ones were not quite as equal as their brothers. . . . It would seem that just as medieval businesswomen in the textile trade specialized in embroidery and small cloths, so the female saints exemplified a piety extravagant or sentimental, marred by erotic, amorous imagery, removed from the normative rigor and clarity of the Scholastic luminaries.[1]

While it is true that women may appear to be more emotional and given to spiritual fantasies, it does not necessarily follow that this was an inferior mode of religious expression or that it was regarded as such by the medieval world. Indeed, it is argued by some that Christianity was more "feminized" during this period than it has been since and that women were responsible for this by placing more stress on the emotional side and less on the intellectual. Eleanor McLaughlin writes:

> . . . these holy women exemplified a human nature and a vision of divine nature that gave more weight to affectivity, love, and the integration of love and intellect. . . . This more "feminized" human nature was not seen as "feminine" by men and women of the pre-Reformation Church but rather as Christian, typical and in the image of God, who was Mother as well as Father, Love more than Intellect.[2]

Female Status in the Early Medieval Church

Although the medieval world was greatly influenced by women, there was a strong underlying current that envisaged women as inferior—endowed with less spiritual insight than men and incapable of the highest forms of Christian ministry. Just how chauvinistic the medieval churchmen were is difficult to determine. Indeed, there are significant differences of opinion on this matter. According to one author, "men debated whether women had a soul, and the question found its way to the agenda of the Council at Macon (585), attended by 59 bishops. By a majority of just one vote, they did answer in the affirmative."[3] Such a charge, however, is not supported by the historical record, and is inconsistent with what is known from early sources to be the church's position on women. That women were incapable of knowing God and not included in his plan of salvation was never a position espoused by the Roman Catholic Church. If there were certain churchmen who believed women were so inferior spiritually as to be "soulless," they were not publicizing their views and they were not representative of the church as a whole.

That is not to say, however, that

the church's perspective on women had become less demeaning and restrictive than it had been in the early centuries of the church. Women continued to be widely viewed as perpetrators of sin. The Council of Tours in 567 blamed women for luring men into sin, comparing them to serpents who make themselves more alluring by shedding their skins. A synod convened at Auxerre at about the same time "asserted that women by nature were impure." That synod decreed women could not receive the communion bread with their naked hand, or partake at all in the Eucharist during their menstrual period. It also "denied women the right to sing in church, causing church choirs to rely on male eunuchs to sing in the high-pitched voices."[4]

How strictly such decrees were observed is unknown, but it is certain that they were not universally followed. According to Will Durant, congregational singing, popularized in the East, spread to the West: "The men alternated with the women in antiphonal song, and joined with them in the Alleluia." In the late fourth century, Ambrose of Milan introduced antiphonal singing into many of the churches in his diocese and wrote, "Psalms are sweet for every age, and becoming to either sex."[5]

Whether or not women should be permitted to participate in congregational singing seems to have troubled the early medieval churchmen less than whether or not to place restrictions on them during their time of menstruation and immediately following childbirth. In 601 Augustine of Canterbury (who had been sent to England as a missionary some years earlier) wrote to Pope Gregory I, inquiring about various church policies and practices. Among his questions were some that related to these very restrictions. The true character of Gregory shows through in his response. He argued that it would be illogical not to baptize a pregnant woman—denying the gift of grace through baptism to one whose very condition was evidence of God's gift of fertility. As to whether an "unclean" woman should be allowed to enter a church and partake of the sacrament, Gregory reminded Augustine of the woman (with an apparent menstrual problem) who touched the hem of Christ's garment. Thus it was not sin for such women to partake, he concluded, and therefore they should not be prohibited from doing so.[6]

Gregory's pronouncement did not settle the matter, however. Several decades later Theodore, who was then bishop of Canterbury, reverted to the old practice of restricting women following pregnancy and while menstruating, and such restrictions continued during the medieval period in England and on the Continent as well.[7] It is important to keep in mind, though, that the rules and regulations on the books did not necessarily mirror the actual practices. How many women simply ignored the restrictions will never be known. In church music and in virtually every other area of the church relating to women, there was always a gap between the ideal and the reality—between the proscriptions and theological opinions and the actual involvement of women in the church. Writes Susan Stuard, "Historians dealing with women have grown increasingly wary of accepting restrictive laws and misogynous interpretations of women's position at face value."[8]

Ministry in the Local Church

Women's ministries during the Middle Ages are generally associated with nunneries rather than with local churches. There were opportunities, however, in the early medieval period for women to serve in parish ministry. In some instances such female ministry created heated controversy. This occurred in the Frankish church during the early years of the sixth century, when two priests, Loovocatus and Catihernus, were censured by three local bishops for working with female assistants. These priests conducted an itinerant ministry of celebrating the Mass in villages where there was no parish priest, and it was the responsibility of the women to act as "cohostesses." In the eyes of the bishops, the female involvement contaminated the holy Eucharist, and it therefore had to be discontinued.[9]

Whether these women had a specific title such as deaconess is not known, but the function of deaconess was still open to women during this period. At least two deaconesses, Radegund and Helaria, were consecrated by Frankish bishops during the early years of the sixth century. From the earliest times, the office of deaconess had been viewed as a necessary one. It was reserved for widows, and until the Council of Chalcedon in 451 lowered the age requirement by twenty years, deaconesses were required to be sixty years of age. Most of these widows had previously been married to bishops or lesser clergy, and upon entering the diaconate, they committed themselves to singleness lest they be "anathematized." Their duties mainly involved caring for the sick and the needy and helping with female baptisms.[10]

The deaconesses, like the deacons, were consecrated or "ordained" by prayer and the laying on of hands in the presence of the other clergy. This was not accomplished without hearing a justification of female ministry. The ordination prayer that was commonly used may have been worded purposely to counteract those who would object to a woman's leadership role in the church:

> Eternal God, Father of our Lord Jesus Christ, Creator of man and woman, who didst fill Miriam and Deborah and Hannah and Huldah with the Spirit, and didst not disdain to suffer thine only-begotten Son to be born of a woman; who also in the tabernacle and the temple didst appoint women keepers of thine holy gates: look down now upon this thine handmaid who is designated to the office of deacon, and grant her the Holy Ghost, and cleanse her from all filthiness of the flesh and of the spirit, that she may worthily execute the work intrusted to her, to thine honor and to the praise of thine Anointed; to whom with thee and the Holy Ghost be honor and adoration forever. Amen.[11]

By the sixth century, such consecrations were becoming less and less common in the Western church. In the Eastern church, however, the ministry of deaconess, which began in the apostolic period, lasted more than a millennium. For a period during the sixth century, the cathedral at Constantinople had under its supervision forty deaconesses, out of a total of more than five hundred church officers—all offices except that of deaconess being for males only. In the West, however, the circumstances were entirely different. Church councils during the sixth century gradually lowered the status of these women until the position of deaconess was virtually nonexistent. Initially the women were denied consecration, and in this way they were prevented from assuming a clerical role. The office of deaconess was "wholly abolished" in 533 when the synod of Orleans decreed that "no woman shall henceforth receive the *benedictio diaconalis*, on account of the weakness of this sex."[12]

Along with the restrictions on widows came restrictions on clerical wives. In 538, the Council of Orleans forbade married clerics to sleep with their wives. This legislation not only separated wives from their husbands in their marriage relationship, but also deprived them of ministry. Such restrictions did not apply to the Celtic church, which was independent of Rome during this period. Columban, one of the greatest Irish churchmen "did not harbor prejudices against women. Instead of emphasizing their impurity, he recognized their spiritual equality." And it was this attitude that led to the later development of double monasteries.[13]

Early Medieval Monasticism

It was the institution of monasticism, far more than the local church, that offered women the real opportunities for "professional" ministry during the Middle Ages. Despite its many shortcomings, monasticism was an important outlet for women who desired to commit their lives to full-time spiritual endeavors, especially after the fifth century, when communal monasticism began to flourish. Monasticism for women began in the West in 512 when Bishop Caesarius of Arles established a convent that was ruled by his sister Caesaria. Only virgins or widows were permitted to join the convent, and they were required to make a lifetime commitment, renouncing all claims to material wealth. The purpose of this convent seems to have been primarily focused on personal spirituality, for the women were admonished by Ceasarius to dwell in their cells, "seeking in earnest prayer the presence of the Son of God," that they might "be of the number of holy virgins devoted to God, who wait with tapers alight and a calm conscience, calling upon the Lord."[14]

While some nunneries accommodated as many as three hundred women, the vast majority were much smaller and were generally privately owned and operated. By the seventh century their numbers vastly increased, as it became a status symbol for wealthy families to found their own convents. "This type of institution usually remained quite small," according to Suzanne Wemple, "representing no more than an extended household, that is, an aristocratic house turned into a family cult center."[15]

The Benedictine monasteries, organized under the rule of Benedict, were the first to be organized on a wide scale. The first of these were strictly for men, but around the year 530, Benedict of Nursia, with the help of his twin sister, Scholastica, founded a convent for women. These women, like their male counterparts, took a vow of chastity, poverty, and obedience. Scholastica was an adept administrator, and soon there were Benedictine convents dotting the continent, with the number of nuns rivaling the number of monks. The Benedictine convents, like the monasteries, were structured around strict rules that affected every waking hour of the nun's life. Spiritual functions were intermixed with manual labors to provide a degree of variety, but they allowed for virtually no deviation from the regulated daily pattern.[16]

Dissatisfaction With Convent Life

The lofty ideals and standards set for women's monasteries frequently did not correspond with reality. Many of the convents were built in pagan areas, and the caliber of women attracted to them was not high. It was difficult for many of these women to submit to the strict rules of the convent, and on occasion they broke out in open revolt. Such a revolt occurred at the Frankish convent at Poitiers in the late sixth century. Gregory, Bishop of Tours, has left an interesting account of the turmoil that erupted there. One of the nuns, Chrodield, and forty followers rebelled against the abbess.

> The vexations [writes Gregory] sown by the devil . . . daily increased in troublesomeness. For Chrodield, having collected about her . . . a band of murderers, wrongdoers, law-breakers, and vagrants of all kinds, dwelt in open

revolt and ordered her followers to break into the nunnery at night and forcibly bear off the abbess. . . . The armed bands rushed in, ran about the monastery by the light of a torch in search of the abbess, and . . . carried off the prioress whom they mistook for the abbess in the darkness.

When they realized they had the wrong woman, they returned and "secured the real abbess, dragged her away, and placed her in custody near the basilica of St. Hilary." They then went back and "plundered the monastery of all its contents."[17]

The local bishops and church leaders stayed away from Poitiers for fear of their lives, but finally Count Macco came to the rescue and with his private army attacked Chrodield and her followers, causing "some to be beaten down, others struck down by spears, and those who made most strenuous opposition to be cut down by the sword." The women were excommunicated for a period of time, but many repented and returned to the nunnery. Chrodield, however, remained a rebel, living out her days in a villa supplied by the king. Lina Eckenstein wrote:

> The revolt of the nuns at Poitiers, which for two years defied the efforts of church men and laymen, is the more noteworthy in that it does not stand alone. Within a year we find a similar outbreak threatening the nunnery at Tours where a certain Berthegund, similarly disappointed of [not] becoming abbess, collected malefactors and others about her and resorted to violent measures."[18]

The Prestige of Female Monasticism

The rebellion of nuns at various convents not only indicates a dissatisfaction with a particular style of monasticism, but also demonstrates the potential for personality conflict within such tightly controlled communities. Maintaining peace was largely in the hands of the abbess. A strong abbess who was confident in her position of authority and who was able to inspire loyalty from those under her was often able to wield power that extended far beyond the boundaries of her own community.

One might assume that the abbess was in charge of women only, but that was frequently not the case. Double (coed) monasteries were common until the eighth century, and they were very often ruled by an abbess. In England between the seventh and ninth centuries they were, in fact, almost always under the control of a woman. Such was the case of the Abbey at Wimborne where the great abbess Lioba was sent as a young child. It was a double monastery, and Mother Tetta ruled both the men and women "with consummate prudence and discretion." Lioba moved on for her formal religious education to another double monastery, headed by Abbess Eathelberga, and later when she accepted the call of Boniface to serve in Germany, she herself was in charge of a double monastery at Tauberbischofsheim. In 787 at the Second Council of Nice, the double monasteries were outlawed, but later on, during the twelfth century, they began to make a comeback.[19]

The abbess was not only a ruler, but also an educator at some of these "coed" monasteries. The seventh-century abbess Hilda trained a number of men who later served in high positions in the church—one of them being Bosa, the archbishop of York. In light of her ability as an educator, it is not surprising that Hilda actively recruited students for her monastery. Among them was Caedmon, "the most celebrated of the vernacular poets of Northumbria." He accepted the invitation, and began studying the Scriptures, and soon he was turning biblical stories into poetic verse.[20]

All things considered, monasticism had a great deal to offer women and continued to appeal to those who gladly renounced marriage for the privilege of devoting their lives in service to God. But the "call" to asceticism did not usually arise out of a vacuum. Recruiting new converts to the contemplative life was the medieval concept of personal evangelism, and both men and women were at times the objects of intense propaganda campaigns. In many areas of Europe, nominal conversion to Christianity had occurred en masse as a result of military or political ploys. Monasticism, then, became a more personalized commitment to God on a higher level. Irish missionaries in particular put out the call to asceticism, sometimes almost glamorizing the ascetic lifestyle. Women were a vital part of Irish monasticism, particularly in the realm of missions, and missions and monasticism were inseparably linked.

Missions

Boniface, who was one of the most distinguished missionaries of the Middle Ages, becoming known as the "Apostle to Germany," was a strong advocate of women's involvement in missions. He quickly realized that the spread of monasticism and church planting necessitated the gifts and labors of both men and women. Thus he requested that nuns from the abbey at Wimborne leave the security of their cloistered walls and come to Saxony to serve among the warring pagan tribesmen. But in some respects his deep involvement in monasticism was a setback to women. He unified the monasteries under the Benedictine Rule, which placed them under episcopal authority. As a result, nuns were "deprived of the last vestiges of quasi-clerical functions, which women had continued to exercise after the abolition of the female diaconate in the sixth century."[21]

In his request for women to serve as missionaries, Boniface specifically asked for his cousin Lioba, "whose reputation for holiness and virtuous teaching," he wrote, "had penetrated across wide lands and filled the hearts of many with praise of her." She, along with five other nuns (and six monks from Malmesbury), agreed to go, and they all journeyed to the continent in 748 to begin their very difficult ministries. Boniface was well aware of the horrors facing these women in Germany. He wrote of two kings who "have shown their evil disposition and have sinned in a criminal way against the teaching of the gospels" by persisting "in the seduction of nuns." Soon after she arrived, Lioba was appointed abbess of Bischofsheim, and from there she helped in the establishment of new convents. Indeed, there was "hardly a convent of nuns in that part which had not one of her disciples as abbess." Yet, despite her power and influence, she did not enjoy the independence that her male counterparts did. The abbesses were directly accountable to the bishops, while some of the abbots were able to develop monasteries that were virtually independent of the church hierarchy.[22]

As an abbess, Lioba found her life filled with richness and variety. Her position, according to Edith Deen, "was not merely that of a ruler, but of a teacher and expositor, and she . . . became so learned in the Scriptures and so wise in counsel that bishops often discussed church matters with her." She was respected not only for her knowledge of Scripture, but also for being a "skilled classicist" and one who was well read "in the works of the Church Fathers, in canon law and in the decisions of all the councils."[23]

Yet with all her learning and scholarship, she was a mystic who believed she was endowed with certain charismatic gifts. It was this sense of charismatic authority—a feeling of being personally chosen by God to carry out a special mission that propelled Lioba on. Her success as a missionary-abbess was viewed as a direct result of her holiness and evidence of her ability to make direct contact with God in prayer. And if, indeed, her prayers were so powerful in the establishment of convents and training young women in ministry, why could they not be put to use in the practical matters that so affected life in the wilds of Germany? It seemed only natural, then, that during a violent thunderstorm she was aroused by a frightened crowd of villagers, pleading with her to entreat God in their behalf. According to Lioba's hagiographer, she rose up from prayer and, as if challenged to a contest, flung off the cloak which she was wearing and boldly opened the doors of the church . . . she made a sign of the cross, opposing to the fury of the storm the name of the High God. . . . Suddenly God came to their aid. The sound of thunder died away, the winds changed direction and dispersed the heavy clouds, the darkness rolled back and the sun shone, bringing calm and peace.[24]

Throughout her lifetime Lioba was credited with numerous other miracles—all of which could be considered routine activity for the Medieval saint—and very effective missionary strategy.

The emotional, charismatic element that frequently characterized the faith of medieval women was essential to their role in the church. According to Eleanor McLaughlin, "holiness and power were as charisma granted to individual women which relieved them, as it were, of the disabilities of their sex." So respected was Lioba that she was permitted to pray at Boniface's monastery at Fulda, "a privilege never granted to any woman either before or since."[25]

The Decline of Female Monasticism

As significant as Lioba was, she was clearly an exception to the rule during this period. The eighth-century Carolingian churchmen went to great lengths to insure the cloistering of nuns. Council after council imposed rules to restrict their movement. Moreover, the egalitarianism of the double monasteries that had thrived especially in England, faded as

monks were removed from many of these monasteries. The effect of such restrictions, according to Suzanne Wemple, "considerably tempered women's enthusiasm for monastic life in the ninth century."[26]

Interestingly, it was monastic reform that led to a further setback for women in the church. The power and influence that women enjoyed during the early centuries of monasticism in the West declined sharply in the ninth century, paralleling the gradual decline of Benedictine monasticism that had flourished in the first centuries of the medieval period. From then on there were repeated reform efforts. One of the most successful of these efforts was the Cluniac reform, which began at the abbey at Cluny in central France. This was a "firmly masculine monastic reform movement," and women lost position and prestige in the process. "The opportunities for women in the higher echelons of Benedictine monasticism declined," and "no new abbacies for women were created, in contrast to the large number that were created for men." The Gregorian reform movement in the late eleventh century further limited the options for women in monasticism. "The reform demolished the double monasteries of the earlier era and quite effectively walled women's houses off from the institutional hierarchy of the church."[27]

Nonmonastic Ministry

With the decline in monasticism, one would expect an increase in other religious endeavors, but the opportunities for women in ministry outside the convent were very limited during the Middle Ages. In most instances, such ministry was entirely independent of the church and without its sanction or approval. In fact, many women joined religious sects, where they found freedom to pursue a ministry outside the convent. For those women who remained within the established church, however, it was more difficult to pursue a ministry outside the convent. In the ninth century, Theoda of Mainz illustrates this. "She claimed to know, as though it had been divinely revealed to her, the exact day on which the world would be consumed and other secrets known to God alone. She preached that the last day of the final year was close upon us," wrote a contemporary observer. "Whence many of both sexes were filled with fear and went to her, offering gifts and commending themselves to her prayers." Not surprisingly, her ministry was "creating no small turmoil for the parish of Bishop Salomon," for many people under his jurisdiction had "turned from doctrines of the church . . . to follow her as though she were a teacher sent from heaven." But despite her popularity, she was powerless in the face of the church. On the threat of being "publicly flogged," she "gave up the ministry of preaching."[28]

In rare instances independent women preachers were actually sanctioned by the Roman Catholic Church, though they were expected to keep within prescribed boundaries. Saint Liutberga, another ninth-century preacher, is an example. According to Suzanne Wemple, "her humility and submissiveness to the hierarchy had been carefully scrutinized before she was allowed to practice an individualistic form of religious life." Moreover, she willingly confined her ministry to women's work. "She gave instruction to women of the neighborhood in the art of working with wool. Only as her fame grew did she begin to preach and prophesy to those who came to visit her cell."[29]

Crusades

For laywomen during the Middle Ages, religious holidays, fairs, pilgrimages, and saint worship combined to make the faith an active and integral part of daily life. Time-honored superstitions, combined with a strong belief in God's intervention in the routine affairs of living, made religion far more than a lofty creed. Nor was the afterlife forgotten. Indeed, the fear of purgatory, as much as anything else, turned Christianity into a religion of works. This prompted an effort to expiate sins in a wide variety of church-sanctioned activities, including participation in the Crusades. These "holy" wars to regain the Holy Land became the Christian response to the Muslim advance.

Surprisingly, there were large numbers of women involved in these military campaigns. For those who were inclined toward adventure, joining the Crusades was a perfect way to demonstrate religious zeal. Women eagerly joined the motley swarms headed for the Holy Land to do battle with the infidels. The most pitiful of these civilian armies were known as the Children's Crusades. Although accompanied by men and women, these boys and girls were easy prey for vile profiteers, and thousands, it is estimated, either died or were sold into slavery.[30]

Most of the women who joined in the Crusades were accompanied by their husbands, but apparently enough went on their own to warrant a regulation that required them to obtain their husband's consent.

It is laid down that the husband may take the cross without his wife's consent. . . . And yet the wife is not entirely deprived of her right, since she can follow him. . . . Moreover there would be more danger to the wife's chastity as a result of wandering from country to country, than to the husband's and less profit to the Church. Wherefore the wife cannot take this vow without her husband's consent.[31]

Clergy Wives

Wives of members of the clergy are rarely mentioned in a treatment of medieval church ministry, except in regulations to keep them separated from their husbands. That is because, as a rule, those who committed themselves to "professional" church ministry during the Middle Ages also committed themselves to celibacy. There were, however, exceptions— particularly in the tenth century when Nicolaitanism was widely practiced. Nicolaitanism, a term taken from *The Revelation of John*, referred to clergy who were married or had mistresses—not differentiating between the two. Interestingly, when the church initiated a crackdown, a frequent objection of the married men was that wives were necessary for their sustenance. The priests at Vercelli responded that "unless they were maintained by the hands of their women they would succumb to hunger and nakedness." And later in the century when the bishop of Vero-

na sought to enforce celibacy in his diocese, he found "the excuse of almost everyone was 'this can in no wise be because of our poverty.' "[32] It is unlikely that these working wives had any meaningful part of the ministry, but they certainly were viewed as a financial asset to their impoverished husbands.

Papess Johanna

The influence of medieval churchwomen was most evident in the convents where they rose to the position of abbess and often wielded substantial power—political as well as spiritual. But beyond the position of abbess, how high could a medieval woman rise in the church? Could she attain to the office of bishop or to the papacy itself? Indeed, one of the most fascinating footnotes of medieval history is the story of the Papess Johanna, who wore "the triple crown" for more than two years in the period between Pope Leo IV (847) and Benedict III (855). Because of her sex she was forced to disguise herself while a student in Athens and later while teaching theology in Rome. She went by the name Johannes Anglicus, and took the name John VIII when she was "elevated to the papal dignity." But her reign as pope came to an abrupt and tragic end. Her life was terminated suddenly "in the open street during a solemn procession from the Vatican to the Lateran." Or, did she die soon after giving "birth to a child as she was taking part in a procession to the Lateran"? Or was she "tied to the hoof of a horse, dragged outside of the city and stoned to death by the people"? Or was the whole story of her life and death a mere myth? Probably the latter is closest to the truth. "The story is undoubtedly a mere fiction," writes Schaff, "and is so regarded by nearly all modern historians."[33]

This mysterious saga of the scholarly Papess Johanna apparently originated with the Dominicans and was widely accepted as truth during the late medieval period—so much so that a bust of this mythical female pope was actually displayed alongside the busts of other popes during the early fifteenth century, and the myth was cited as fact at the Council of Constance in a statement against the popes. But why would anyone invent such a bizarre story? Perhaps as a satire of a number of popes perceived to have been controlled by ambitious women, or a satire on Pope John VIII, who was believed to be weak and ineffective. At any rate, the story was an interesting conversation piece for some two centuries, and it served as an argument for Torrecremata, a staunch defender of papal authority (no matter what the character of the man was), who insisted that if the church could permit a woman to be a pope, it could also permit a heretic to be a pope.[34]

That a woman could have become pope in the Middle Ages or any other period in history is utterly absurd. The Roman Catholic Church was deeply committed to a position of male domination in spiritual matters. Women had a place in the church, but that place was clearly defined as one that carried with it no official authority. By their own leadership ability and charismatic influence, women on occasion overcame this disability, but whatever role they attained almost always remained within the confines of monasticism.

Convent Life

The cloistering of nuns and the general decline of female monasticism that began in the eighth and ninth centuries continued on in the succeeding centuries. According to R. W. Southern, "in the great period of monastic foundation from the early tenth to the early twelfth century the position of women in the monastic life suffered a sharp decline."[35] But despite this continued setback, the convent continued to be the most viable option for women who desired a life commitment to religious ministry.

Who were the nuns of the medieval period? They were vastly different in social standing from nuns of the modern age. The majority of them were of high social status, coming from the ranks of the nobility. Later, during the High Middle Ages, some came from the ranks of the gentry and merchant classes, but rarely did any come from below that level. Why? "The chief barrier in admission to a nunnery was money rather than class," write Frances and Joseph Gies. "Although canon law and monastic rule strictly condemned accepting fees from postulants, nunneries from earliest times evaded the ruling by requiring parents to provide girls with dowries of lands, rents, or cash, sometimes even clothes and furniture."[36]

Frequently the decision to send girls to a convent was made by the parents when their daughters were very young. For Edburga, a tenth-century nun, the decision had been made when she was only three years old. Still a toddler, growing up in a royal family in England, Edburga

An Illustration Depicting the Medieval Officers of a Nunnery. The abbess is depicted with her crozier, the cellaress with her keys, and the sacristan at the bell ropes. At the bottom, ordinary nuns are in procession.   British Library, MS Add. 39843, f. 6v.

allegedly had a part in the decision. "Her father set before her both religious objects (Bible, chalice, and paten) and secular (jewels, gold, and silver) in an attempt to decide the future course of her life." Without hesitation she reached out for the religious objects, and with that sign, her exuberant father placed her in a convent under the care of Abbess Etheldreda.[37]

Were nuns, many of whom were placed in convents as youngsters, truly happy with their lot in life? There is ample evidence that even in the convents with the most relaxed standards and lifestyles, some of the women felt trapped. According to

Durant, by 1300 in the older orders, such as the Cistercians, "most of the nuns came from the upper classes, and nunneries were too often the repository of women for whom their male relations had no room or taste." This was not a new problem to the late Middle Ages. Indeed as early as the middle of the fifth century the emperor decreed it unlawful for parents to lighten their burden of family responsibilities by sending their daughters off to the nunnery. "Many parents," according to Susan Bell, "put their young daughters into nunneries for life in order to avoid having to provide (often crippling) dowries," though lesser dowries were sometimes required by the convents.[38]

Life in a medieval convent was routine. Duties ranged from cleaning and cooking to designing vestments for priests and copying manuscripts. Usually each nun was assigned a particular duty. The chambermaid cleaned and mended clothing and bedding. The Fratress repaired furniture and did housekeeping. The cellaress was in charge of meal preparation. The almoness was responsible for the almsgiving. The novice mistress served as the teacher for new recruits. The sacrist designed and mended vestments and altar clothes, and the chantress was in charge of church services. But a duly certified male cleric (usually a priest) was brought in from the outside to say the masses and hear confessions. Of course, the daily vigils and prayers were accomplished without a male chaplain, and so were the special days that were set aside for nothing but prayer and fasting.[39]

Convents and orders varied considerably in the freedom that women were permitted. The Carthusian and Cistercian orders required the nuns to observe strict silence unless speaking was deemed absolutely necessary. Although some nuns were involved in charity work, the strict cloistering of women limited such activities. Some convents specialized in education—providing the only higher education available to young women, though most had only a few boarding students.[40]

Not only were women restricted in monasticism by the regulations foisted on them by the church, but also in the actual openings available to them in monastic life. While on the one hand there was intense recruitment of women during certain periods of time, at other times the women who desired the monastic life far outnumbered the spaces available. In the central Middle Ages only a small number of new convents were founded, but in the twelfth and thirteenth centuries there was a significant increase in women's monasteries. Yet, despite that upsurge, men far outnumbered women in monasticism. In the early thirteenth century there were more than six hundred Augustinian and Benedictine monasteries for men in England alone, while the women's houses numbered fewer than one hundred and fifty. In population totals there were about fourteen thousand men and only three thousand women in the monasteries. By the beginning of the fourteenth century there were some seven hundred Cistercian convents in Europe. But while such numbers are impressive, the total number of nuns was far less than the total number of monks and priests.[41]

The increasing restrictions that

women confronted in the church apparently did not diminish their zeal for ministry. There was an "explosion of female piety," Eleanor McLaughlin writes, and the religious orders were deluged with requests for membership.[42] The Cistercians were able to accommodate only a third of the women who were desirous of joining them, and the order sought to further limit their numbers by stricter regulations—enclosing the houses and banning visitors. Still women pleaded to join. "But the Cistercian general chapter made the point most forcibly that there was little place for more women in its order and that they were accepted only with extreme reluctance."[43]

When women were barred from joining certain religious orders, they quickly found new outlets for their services, many of which were only reluctantly sanctioned by the church. These outlets included new religious orders that began springing up in the twelfth century, some of which seemed to have a special appeal for women. The Fontevrault, a twelfth-century community, is an example. It was one of the double monasteries that sprang up after the ban placed on them during the Gregorian reform was lifted. Its founder, Robert of Abrissel, was a popular itinerant preacher of the day whose ministry attracted a large following of women, and the community served as an outlet for their expressions of piety. Although the order was founded by a man, an abbess ruled over both the men and the women of the community. This female leadership was not just by happenstance, but was purposely arranged to symbolize the Virgin Mary's authority over Jesus

and later John, when at the cross he became as it were her adopted son. The men and women lived in separate residences but shared the same chapel. This order continued on until the end of the eighteenth century when the last abbess died.[44]

This concept of a double monastery was, according to Eleanor McLaughlin "a radical innovation, at least on the theological level, for never before had there been an explicit acceptance of a woman's preeminent spiritual authority." Inherent in the system was the belief that the female was the "weaker and more delicate sex, for whom the life of contemplation and psalmody is appropriate." The monks, on the other hand, were more suited to an active role involving service and manual labor. "Thus the women's cloister dedicated to the Virgin Mary and the monk's cloister to John the Evangelist represent these reciprocal roles, in which the male is servant and subordinate to the nuns, who rule."[45]

Another order started by a charismatic twelfth-century preacher was known as the Premonstratensian order. Founded by Norbert of Xanten, it attracted some ten thousand women to its numerous double monasteries. But the heyday of this massive outpouring of female volunteerism was short-lived. Because of his alleged concern for the welfare of the women, Pope Innocent issued a bull in 1198 forbidding the acceptance of any more women in the order.[46]

Abbesses

Whatever the restrictions on female monasticism were at any particular time, the actual lifestyle at a particular convent was determined to a large extent by the abbess. In many instances she had as much power as did her male counterpart. Despite the church's best efforts to place tight reins on nunneries, the abbess often ruled her community according to her own prescribed standards. This was possible because "monasticism from its very beginning," according to Lina Eckenstein, "lay outside the established order of the Church." It was this factor, more than any other that allowed women a meaningful place in the religious life of the Middle Ages. Susan Bell maintains that "nuns could and did achieve complete equality with men during the Middle Ages, particularly between the sixth and twelfth centuries."[47]

Whether there was actually "complete equality" between the sexes in monasticism is a matter for debate, but certainly monasticism offered women a place of prominence that could not be found elsewhere in the church. Indeed, in rare instances abbesses wielded power comparable to that of the local bishop. Lioba's mentor, Mother Tetta, for example, was said to be "so powerful in her ability to lead her community that no man dared enter her monastery; even bishops were forbidden." The power of the abbess was reinforced by the religious symbolism that was and is so pervasive in Catholicism. "Like the bishops and abbots, they wore the mitre and cross and carried the staff." During the installation service of the abbess of St. Cecilla in Cologne, "each member of the clergy under her jurisdiction passed before her, prostrating himself and kissing her hand."[48] The abbess of Las Huelgas in Spain served as "dame, superior, prelate, legitimate administrator, spiritual and temporal," not only of her own monastery but also of the "convents, churches, and hermitages" under her jurisdiction."[49] Even if she did not wield ecclesiastical power, it was common for the head of the convent to act as a business administrator with wide-ranging duties closely tied to the local economy and politics. This is illustrated in Chaucer's *Tales*. Here the prioress is "a woman of proud breeding and large responsibilities, administering a spacious domain as the source of her convent's revenues."[50]

The position of abbess was the highest to which a woman could attain. It was clearly above that of prioress—women who also ruled convents, but who were usually subject to an abbot.[51] The abbess not only ruled a large community of nuns (and frequently monks as well), but also had jurisdiction over vast territories that often included villages and towns. And this jurisdiction in a number of instances did not involve merely civil matters. According to Joan Morris, "the abbess of a religious order was an ordained person even though those under her were not so," and they "were exempt from the jurisdiction of a bishop and directly dependent on the Holy See."[52] Morris argues in her book *The Lady Was a Bishop* that the long history of women with clerical ordination has been purposely hidden in an effort to hold women back.

Whatever credentials an abbess possessed, the recognition accorded her depended initially on her social rank (very often from royalty) but to an even greater extent it depended on the local church and political authorities and, of course, on her own charisma and assertiveness. If these conditions and attributes were in her favor, she might serve as the king's or the pope's local representative—involving herself is such secular responsibilities as raising armies or sitting in on assemblies.[53]

No matter how high her social rank was, it was not uncommon for an abbess to have to fight for her authority. This was the case at the abbey at Jouarre in the twelfth century and following. At one time the local bishop requested and received jurisdiction over the abbey, and Abbess Eustache dutifully recognized his authority and vowed obedience to him in an installation ceremony over which he presided. Her successor, Agnes I, however, refused to follow suit. Although she had the support of the local clerics and residents, Pope Innocent II sided with the bishop and excommunicated Agnes and all those under her, both clergy and laity. Eventually, however, this decision was reversed when Abbess Agnes II journeyed to Rome with a delegation of supporters and documents disproving the bishop's authority over her.

So significant was the power of the abbess over a monastic community that the community often collectively seemed to take on the personality of the abbess. Her interests became the interests of the community. If education and the arts were her priorities, so with the nuns under her. Or if she was a mystic, it was likely that the entire community would have a mystical aura.

Education and the Arts

During the Middle Ages, many convents became centers of female education—often providing the only schooling that was available to women. As women were barred from the universities, monasticism afforded the only opportunity for education beyond that which might be given in the home. The academic standards of the convents deteriorated, however, as the medieval period progressed. One of the primary reasons for this deterioration was the effects of mysticism. According to Lina Eckenstein, "devotional interests were cultivated to the exclusion of everything else." Earlier in the period it was not uncommon for women in convents to read and write in Latin and to quote from the classics and the church fathers, but as time passed such scholarship declined.[54]

For many medieval women, the seclusion and solitude of the convent was an ideal environment to express their literary and artistic talents. It is not surprising, then, that Hroswitha, Germany's first poet and playwright, was a nun. Her literary genius is best demonstrated in her six Latin comedies. Why would a nun write comedies? In her words, it was to make "a faint sound to the praise of God." She deplored the Latin comedy of the day, and thus her mission was to offer her own Christian version.[55]

Hroswitha's "faint sound" was surprisingly open about physical sexual desires, and she presented an interesting perspective of men from a woman's viewpoint—particularly in light of the standard view of woman as the evil temptress. In *Dulcetius*, one of her dramas, Emperor Diocletian orders three saintly virgins to deny their faith. Their refusal leads to imprisonment, which is followed by a ludicrous ordeal with Dulcetius, an army general. He is enamored of their beauty; so he locks them in the kitchen, scheming to seduce them later that night. His plan runs awry, however, when he is overcome by a strange sensation. He enters the kitchen but is utterly confused.

> Befuddled, he begins to caress the pots and pans, while the girls watch through a crack in the wall. "Why, the fool is out of his mind, he fancies he has got hold of us," reports one of them. "Now he presses the kettle to his heart, now he clasps the pots and pans and presses his lips to them. . . . His face, his hands, his clothes are all black and sooty; the soot which clings to him makes him look like an Ethiopian." One of her companions comments, "Very fitting that he should be so in body, since the devil has possession of his mind."[56]

Despite her brilliance, Hroswitha was ever conscious of the perceived inferiority of her sex. In a letter to three men to whom she had sent her dramas for criticism, she wrote:

> I cannot sufficiently admire your great condescension . . . for your kindness towards me; you, who have been trained in the study of philosophy and have perfected yourselves in the pursuit of knowledge, have held my writings, those of a lowly woman, worthy of admiration. . . . You have declared that there is in me a certain knowledge of that learning (*scientiam artium*) the essence of which is beyond my woman's understanding.[57]

There are other notable examples of literary and artistic self-expression that blossomed out of medieval nunneries. The masterpiece produced by Herrad, a twelfth-century abbess who headed a convent in Alsace, is an example. She, with the assistance of her nuns, compiled the "Garden of Delights," a massive encyclopedia that contained all the knowledge that a well-educated medieval nun would ever need to know. Through lengthy texts and hundreds of colorful illustrations, "the book instilled a broad spectrum of history, religion, philosophy, and science, and it simultaneously taught Latin to her German readers in the most painless manner."[58] The volume also tells a great deal about the particular nunnery Herrad ruled. The atmosphere was stimulating. Enthusiasm was high. Liberty reigned. The sixty nuns and lay sisters wore stylish clothes with brightly colored veils. For them life was certainly more challenging than it was for most women of the Middle Ages.[59]

Music was another area of artistic endeavor that sometimes flourished in the convent. Indeed some abbeys became famous for their music—foremost among them, the abbey of Las Huelgas. Under Abbess Berenguela during the thirteenth century, there were more than one hundred nuns and some forty children in the choir, which was trained to sing the highly complicated compositions for which the abbey was known. "But the greatest testimony of their musical erudition," writes Joan Morris, "is to be seen in the *Codex Musical de Las Huelgas*, a manuscript whose complexity indicates that the musicians had contact with conservatories throughout Europe.[60]

The freedom granted nuns at cer-

domine deus salutis mee

A Choir of Franciscan Poor Clare Nuns. From a fifteenth-century psalter, British Library MS Cott. Dom 'AXVII, f. 74v.

tain convents was a threat to some church officials. At the beginning of the fourteenth century Boniface VIII sought to tighten his control by issuing a papal bull requiring nuns to remain secluded in their convents. This certainly indicates that there was widespread disregard for the previous clerical decrees to keep the nuns cloistered. At least one group of nuns openly defied the directive— hurling the document at the bishop who delivered it to them. How widely the bull was heeded is impossible to ascertain, but no doubt there were many other convents where it was simply ignored. As Will Durant points out, "The prioress in Chaucer's Tales had no business there, for the Church had forbidden nuns to go on pilgrimage."[61]

Spiritual Life at Convents

The spiritual quality of the convents naturally varied, depending on the leadership provided by the abbess and on the type of women who were in residence. Becoming a truly spiritual person was the primary purpose of monastic life, and the activities of the convent were centered around this goal. Personal and corporate worship was a strictly regulated aspect in the daily routine of most medieval convents. Confession and communion were generally scheduled on a regular basis, varying according to the monastic rule. The Rule of St. Clare, for example, specified that confession would be made twelve times a year, and communion taken seven times a year on special holidays.[62]

The style of the spiritual life in the convents varied considerably. There were a number of ways to attain a reputation for spirituality or saintliness. Often it was associated with charity and menial service rendered to others, with vigils and prayers, and with various forms of penitence. The road to perfection for some medieval holywomen involved sleeping on boards, wearing a hair shirt, walking barefoot in the snow, or putting stones in their shoes. Even flagellation was taken up by some of these would-be saints. "Countless are the stories," writes Rudolph Bell, "of young girls who whipped themselves until the blood ran."[63] Bell's most recent book, entitled *Holy Anorexia*, details the lives of medieval female "saints" who starved (or nearly starved) themselves to death in order to demonstrate their dedication to God.[64] But an even more significant factor than asceticism involved charismatic qualities of an individual—the proclivity to receive visions and revelations or the ability to perform miracles.

For a nun to attain sainthood generally meant that she must have manifested throughout her life a combination of the above characteristics. St. Edburga of Winchester, a tenth-century nun, is an example. Although a royal princess, she was known for her humble and pious deeds such as cleaning the shoes of other nuns and keeping private vigils during the night while the other nuns slept. Her miracles included one spectacular story of a woman's sight being restored after she was directed in a vision to bathe her eyes in the water in which Edburga washed herself.[65]

Toward the end of the Middle Ages the female candidates for sainthood steadily increased. The thirteenth century saw a remarkable upsurge in female piety, the percentage of women saints nearly doubling that of the previous century. By the fifteenth century, some 28 percent of the designated saints were female.[66]

Thirteenth-century Italy was particularly known for its female saints. There monastic communities were usually located in towns where the residents mixed freely with the townspeople, performing sacrificial deeds of all kinds. These nuns, unlike their sisters of an earlier age and elsewhere in Europe, often were of humble origin. Margaret of Cortona is a prime example of the thirteenth-century Italian female saint. She was born into a peasant family around 1247. She was a member of the Franciscan Third Order. According to Donald Weinstein and Rudolph Bell, "Margaret was a protector of the poor and sick and took special care of pregnant women, founding hospitals and houses of refuge."[67]

While humility, deeds of charity, and keeping vigils were important to medieval spirituality, it was the charismatic element that gained the most publicity, and it was in Germany where such phenomena were most in evidence. Here female monasticism was frequently associated with fervent mysticism and visionary experiences—quite unlike the monasticism of England and France (representing a higher percentage of noble-women), which was known for its education and intellectual achievements.[68]

German Mysticism

"The German nunneries," writes Will Durant, "tended to be havens of intense mysticism." But it was not only in Germany that female mystics proliferated. Beginning in the thirteenth century, women mystics outnumbered men, and "their ecstasies were more frequent and more often accompanied by paramystical phenomena." Directly related to their mysticism was the emphasis they placed on the humanity of Jesus. This involved a fascination with the baby Jesus and also a near-obsession with his death—"devotion to the sacred heart and to the wounds of Jesus."[69]

One of the most powerful abbesses and well-known visionaries of the entire medieval period was Hildegard (1098–1179), who ruled the Benedictine convent of Disebodenberg, located on the Rhine. She corresponded with two emperors, four popes, and many other high church officials, and was regarded as "the most prominent woman in the church of her day."[70] As with other women, her power was derived more from the charismatic qualities she possessed than from education, family, or rank. She claimed to have been directed by a Divine Light—a power that guided her in writing, counseling, and teaching. "From my infancy," she wrote, "my soul has always beheld this Light. . . . The brightness which I see is not limited by space and is more brilliant than the luminous air round

the sun."[71] Unlike other visionaries, she claimed that she never fell into trances: "The visions which I saw, I did not perceive in dreams or sleeping, nor in delirium, nor with the corporeal ears and eyes of the outer man; but watchful and intent in mind I received them according to the will of God."[72]

Hildegard of Bingen. This woman is receiving a revelation through "a great flash of light from heaven." From a contemporary manuscript of Scivias. Hessische Landesbibliothek. Wiesbaden, f. I.

Like other churchwomen, Hildegard pleaded for reform within the church. She despaired over the corruption and immorality of the clergy, and she admonished her audiences to look to the Scriptures as their authority and to Christ, not the priests, for salvation.[73] And she was an outspoken evangelist. She pleaded for sinners to repent, lest they suffer the agony that was so vividly depicted to her in visions:

> I saw a well deep and broad, full of boiling pitch and sulphur, and around it were wasps and scorpions. . . . Near a pond of clear water I saw a great fire. In this some souls were burned and others were girdled with snakes. . . . And I saw a great fire, black, red, and white, and in it horrible fiery vipers spitting flame; and there the vipers tortured the souls of those who had been slaves of the sin of uncharitableness. . . . And I saw a thickest darkness, in which the souls of the disobedient lay on a fiery pavement and were bitten by sharp-toothed worms."[74]

It was the convent at Hefla where German mysticism of the thirteenth century was most pronounced. It was here that "reports of visions and inner experiences or meditations form the largest single body of women's mystical writing in the period." The mystical character of this community developed under the forty-year leadership of Gertrude of Hackeborn. The preponderance of mystical writing, however, came from three other women: Gertrude of Hefla (also knowns as Gertrude the Great), Mechtild of Hackeborn, and Mechtild of Magdeburg. They all served as ordinary nuns—their reputations being built on their revelations and visions.[75]

These nuns believed that they served as special conduits from God to man, and in this capacity they revealed specific messages to individuals and groups. As their popularity increased, they served not only their own convent but also outsiders, including a wide range of male clerics.

"They provided information about what practices Christ wished performed and about the state of souls in the afterlife." They were convinced that "Christ himself guaranteed the efficacy of their prayers, particularly for removing souls from purgatory." Gertrude of Hefla was known particularly for her specific revelations concerning souls in purgatory, and she did not hesitate to give precise data on the number of souls released for any given amount of prayer or service.[76]

The content of Gertrude's visions, as well as those of the other nuns of Hefla, varied, but there were common characteristics. The themes were frequently pessimistic—particularly the themes of the dying Son and the damning Father. Sometimes the vision provided justification for a specific activity or belief. In several of Gertrude's visions she claimed for herself and other nuns the explicit instruction to preach—an activity that the church frowned on for women. One particular nun was commanded in a vision to "imitate Jesus especially in his nights of prayer, his preaching in villages by word and example, and his service of neighbor."[77]

So, as the decades passed, the convent at Hefla maintained its steady flow of visions and revelations—churning them out as fast as they could be recorded. And if ordinary visions became mundane for some, there were always more spectacular miracles to seek. Indeed, Gertrude's meditation on the dying Savior became such an obsession that she received the "stigmata"— nail scars in her hands and feet. They were not visible to others, but they were allegedly real to her.

Although Hefla was known for its extreme mysticism, women's monasteries in general were fertile soil for visions and revelations. What was the cause of this? Were women by their very nature more emotionally inclined, and thus more prone to mystical experiences? This issue has been hotly debated by historians and behaviorists alike. Caroline Bynum, a church historian, argues strongly against those who contend that there is "some kind of inherent female 'emotionalism.' " In her view, "these answers will not do. If women become mystics because they are intrinsically more emotional, imaginative, religious, or hysterical than men, why did it take centuries for this to emerge?"[78]

Bynum suggests that the visionary experiences women had frequently transported them into priestly roles that they were denied in real life, and it gave them "direct authorization to act as mediators to others."[79] So in that sense they were seeking to overcome (whether consciously or subconsciously) their inferior position in the church. Other historians, including I. M. Lewis in his book *Ecstatic Religion* have come to similar conclusions. Lewis maintains that such mysticism was a reaction to social oppression. Whatever the cause, this trend of women's predominance in mysticism continued within the framework of the Roman Catholic tradition, and later in radical Protestantism.

Although many nuns gained wide acclaim for their visions and revelations, others met with ridicule and threats from the church authorities. Even Hildegard, despite her fame and popularity, was denounced by some of her contemporaries as being "demon-possessed."[80]

Women in Seclusion—Anchoresses

Monastic life varied not only from community to community but also from one individual to another. So impelled were some women to be secluded from the world that even the strictly cloistered communities were unsatisfactory to them. For these women, living in solitude was the best means of maintaining a truly contemplative life. In the early centuries of the church, many such anchoresses, like the male hermits, lived in the desert, near others for protection but entirely away from civilization. How many women opted for such a lifestyle will never be known, but Bishop Palladius (d. 425), who spent a number of years as a desert monk in Egypt, claimed that there were as many as twenty thousand female ascetics in the desert—outnumbering the men by a ratio of two to one.[81]

The decline of desert asceticism did not signal the end of the hermit lifestyle. As Christianity pushed northward, it was only natural that ascetics would move indoors, and thus various communities of anchoresses and hermits developed—often attached to cathedrals or churches. The accommodations usually consisted of unfurnished cells, often built into the exterior walls of the building, where the ascetic could have complete privacy. Women were more commonly found in these cells than their male counterparts, who often took up their abode in the forest or in caves. The most famous of these communities was located in England at Whitby and was headed by Hilda.[82]

One of the most celebrated anchoresses of the medieval period was a fourteenth-century English mystic, Julian of Norwich. Virtually nothing is known of her life, except that she presumably lived in a small cell built into the wall of the St. Julian's church at Norwich and that she allegedly lived to be one hundred. Her fame was a result of her series of sixteen revelations, recorded in *Revelations of Divine Love*. These revelations began when she was thirty years old. By her own account, she was in her teens when she began living a contemplative life. Although she prefaced her revelations by describing herself as "a simple, unlettered creature" who was "lewd, feeble and frail," there is ample reason to believe that she was familiar with the writings of other mystics as well as those of theologians and was more learned than she was prepared to admit. One probable explanation for her self-effacement relates to her sex:

> These protestations are ... anticipating the criticisms of her book which she expects from hostile men, who will say that she is disobeying Paul's precept that women must not preach. She tells them ... that she is not preaching, that she is no more than the witness to the graces of enlightenment which she has received.[83]

It was not only her "preaching" that raised questions in the minds of her critics, but also her message. More than a half millennium before the modern feminist movement arose, she was offering her hearers a feminine image of God. Her writings contain many phrases such as "god is oure mother," "oure savyoure is oure very moder," "very moder Jhesu," and "oure moder, Christ."[84]

Christina of Sweden.   From Franz Blei. *Fascinating Women: Sacred & Profane* (New York: Simon and Schuster, 1928).

For Julian, living the life of a hermit was by choice—her own personal preference of how she could best serve God. For others, however, such living was an escape. Christina, a twelfth-century Anglo-Saxon mystic, is an example of the latter. From her earliest childhood it was her desire to enter a convent, and at the age of thirteen she made a vow of virginity—a vow that was strongly opposed by her parents, who desperately wanted to see their daughter married. Indeed they were so determined to have her marry that they encouraged Burthred, her most persistent suitor, to enter her room while she slept. Through "providential intervention," Christina was wide awake and prepared to fend him off. But her parents were persistent. By bribing clerics, she was forced to face their arguments. Again she prevailed. In one instance, she "defeated the Bishop in the ensuing contest of prooftexting." Finally she escaped by disguising herself as a boy, fleeing to a remote area to live with Roger, a religious hermit, with whom she was able to share her spiritual pilgrimage without fear of breaking her vow.[85]

Christina was a visionary, who spent much of her time in meditation and prayer—often ecstatic in nature. But she was more than that. She involved herself in the lives of others, including the unconverted and worldly abbot of St. Albans. Through her influence, his life changed dramatically, and over the years she discipled him in the way of holiness.[86]

Women Abroad—Pilgrims

In sharp contrast to the holy woman secluded in her cell was the holy woman who demonstrated her piety by making pilgrimages from one holy shrine to another. One of the most noted pilgrims of the late medieval period was Margery Kempe, whom Edith Deen describes as a "wandering evangelist." She spent most of twenty years traveling, mainly on foot, as far South as the Holy Land and as far North as Norway. As a wife and a mother of fourteen children, she began to have visions and became convinced that Christ wanted her to live in celibacy and devote the remainder of her life to the pursuit of holiness. As she traveled she not only worshiped at the sacred shrines but also met with churchmen and theologians, often detailing her visions and experiences with them, seeking to assuage "her constant fear of diabolical delusions." Her travels required separating from her husband, but for her the separation was more than a matter of convenience. She was convinced that she could not maintain a perfectly holy marriage to Christ if she was continuing to have sexual relations with her husband. "By a carefully executed scheme of divine manipulation, Margery follows Christ's lead and strikes a bargain with her husband," and eventually convinces him to join her and "mutually enter a pact of chastity before the bishop."[87]

Although she was regarded as mentally unbalanced and a fanatic by many in her own day and since, her love for Christ made a deep impression on many she encountered, including Julian of Norwich, from whom she sought counsel. She left a record of her spiritual and geographical journeys in her autobiography, *The Book of Margery Kempe*.

New Religious Orders

By the beginning of the thirteenth century, monasticism had peaked. The Cistercians, an offshoot of the Benedictines, had seen phenomenal growth during the twelfth century, despite a tightening of regulations, but monasteries in their traditional form were beginning to be replaced by new religious orders consisting of friars who were actively involved in the cities and towns. The Dominicans and the Franciscans were the most prominent of these orders, the former emphasizing education and Roman Catholic orthodoxy, and the latter stressing the importance of self-sacrifice and service.

What was the response of these new orders to women? Both were amazingly open to female ministry in the early years. Indeed, Dominic founded a nunnery at Prouille before he founded the Dominican order—using it in his effort to stamp out heresy in southern France by educating young women who would have otherwise been educated by the Cathars. He founded other convents as well. However, his position regarding women changed over the years, and at the time of his death he was warning his followers against any association with women. Women would have been virtually excluded from that order after his death had they not, with the aid of Pope Innocent IV "launched a massive counteroffensive."[88] The Cistercians also sought to prohibit additional nunneries in the thirteenth century, but to no avail. Like the other orders, they could not stem the tide of pious women yearning to serve God.[89]

Were there valid reasons for the effort to exclude women from these religious orders? Perhaps there were. The women, unlike the men, were generally cloistered, and it was therefore necessary for several friars to serve each such convent—performing the duties that required contact with the outside world, and thus preventing them from fulfilling their call to preach. This problem is closely tied to the more general economic problem of maintaining a convent of unproductive nuns. The friars were out in the world, sustaining themselves through alms. But probably the major objection to women in the religious orders was the view of the

woman as temptress and the fear that any association with her would inevitably bring about the downfall of an institution dedicated to the service of God. This view has endured throughout Christian history and was accepted as valid by leaders of the new religious orders of the thirteenth century. The Dominicans, known for their preaching expertise, rarely mentioned women, except in the context of their sensuality. McLaughlin writes, "The typical thirteenth-century preacher harped on the danger of women, stringing out his biblical exemplars—Eve, Jezebel, Delilah, Bathsheba, Salome."[90]

Although the Cistercians, Dominicans, Franciscans, and other such orders did not close the door completely to women, they did on occasion impose very strict regulations on them. The emphasis was more and more on the strict isolation of women from society—particularly men. "For example, elaborate curtains were erected lest a dying nun see the priest who administered last rites," and "in double monasteries the sisters were not allowed to sing the offices lest their song . . . arouse male passion." Seclusion for women was confirmed by Pope Boniface VIII in 1293 when he issued a bull restricting nuns from leaving the convent unless they had the local bishop's permission.[91]

The Poor Clares

Despite the opposition they faced, women did play an important role in these new religious orders. The female arm of the Franciscans was founded in 1212 by Clare of Sciffi. Clare was only a teenager when she first heard Francis of Assisi preach. His message was compelling, and with his assistance she fled the security and wealth of her noble family and took a vow to live her life in the service of Christ. Soon afterward the order of Poor Clares (or Clarisses) was officially organized, and she headed that order for some forty years.[92]

The Young Clare Speaking With Francis. From a painting in the basilica of St. Clare, Assisi, photo by Alinari-Giraudon.

Unlike the Franciscans, who mixed freely in society, preaching in the cities and towns, the Poor Clares spent most of their lives behind the locked gates of their monasteries. Clare, in fact, according to her contemporary hagiographer, never left Saint Damian's monastery during her forty-two years of ministry. Although this statement is refuted by others, it nevertheless indicates a very cloistered lifestyle. Indeed such a lifestyle

was central to their purpose for existing. In a letter from Pope Gregory in 1228 to "the abbess Clare, and to the cloistered religious of the monastery of San Damiano," he reminded them of their calling:

> Remember that of your own free will you have followed the divine call, that you have enclosed yourselves in these poor cells to the end that being free from the tumult of the world, and preserved from the snares of earthly vanity, you may unite yourselves by a pure and holy love to the heavenly Bridegroom, Whom you have preferred to all others until He shall introduce you into His eternal dwellings.[93]

But if the Poor Clares could not match the efforts of their Franciscan brothers in public ministry, they could and did match them in their vow of poverty that both orders were committed to uphold above all other rules. Poverty became a virtual obsession to the noble-born Clare—an obsession that was borne out in her letters:

> O blessed poverty who givest eternal riches to those who love and embrace her! O holy poverty, it is enough to desire thee and to share in thee for God to promise us the Kingdom of Heaven, eternal glory and a life of rest and blessedness! O beloved poverty whom our Lord Jesus Christ found worthy of His love, He to whom heaven and earth and all creation are eternally subject![94]

The respect accorded Clare was due in part to her association with Francis of Assisi, but she earned a name for herself in her own right, and this is borne out in the hagiography penned after her death. One particular account depicts Clare as a humble woman receiving the highest honor that could be accorded her. And, typically, it ends with a miracle. The story took place in 1228 at Saint Damian's and the guest of honor was Pope Gregory IX.

> St. Clare had the table laid, and set loaves of bread thereon that the Holy Father might bless them. . . . St. Clare knelt down with great reverence, and besought him to be pleased to bless the bread. . . . The holy Father answered: "Sister Clare, most faithful one, I desire that thou bless this bread, and make over it the sign of the most holy cross of Christ, to which thou hast wholly devoted thyself." And St. Clare said: "Most Holy Father, forgive me, but I should merit great reproof if, in the presence of the Vicar of Christ, I, who am a poor, vile woman, should presume to give such benediction." And the Pope answered: "To the end that this be not imputed to thy presumption, but to the merit of obedience, I command thee, by holy obedience, that thou . . . bless this bread in the name of God." Then St. Clare, even as a true daughter of obedience, devoutly blessed the bread with the sign of the most holy cross. Marvelous to tell! Forthwith on all those loaves the sign of the cross appeared figured most beautifully. . . . And the Holy Father, when he saw this miracle, partook of the bread and departed, thanking God and leaving his blessing with St. Clare.[95]

Personality Cults

In remarkable distinction from the anchoresses and the cloistered Poor Clares were certain independent women who spent their lives seeking to affect change in society—women who were recognized by bishops and popes for their influence and power, and around whom often developed personality cults.

Catherine of Siena

The most famous of all medieval churchwomen was Catherine of Siena, a fourteenth-century mystic. As with all medieval saints, it is difficult to sort fact from fantasy in seeking to discover her true character, but, unlike some, she left behind a wealth of information in personal letters and writings. Many biographies have been written on her life—the most thoughtful and balanced (and readable) account being De La Bedoyere's *Catherine: Saint of Siena*.[96] He shows Catherine to be one of the strangest of all the Roman Catholic saints and, at the same time, one of the most influential.

From early childhood, Catherine sensed that God had a special ministry for her. At the age of seven she made a vow of virginity (the age a child could legally consent to marriage). Like Christina, she met with strong family resistance and at the age of twelve cut off her flowing hair to repel the man to whom she had been matched. Though raised in a congested household (she being the twenty-third of twenty-five children), she managed to steal time for contemplation, and she had numerous visionary experiences during her childhood and young adult life. One of the most enduring of these visions came to Catherine during a pre-Lenten carnival—at a time when she was undergoing doubts about her commitment to celibacy. She was

> tormented by demons who paraded before her the earthly and womanly pleasures she was giving up. . . . The

Sienese were in the streets eating, drinking, playing at love, and mocking their betters. In her dark cell Catherine heard the carnival riot while her demons continued to torture her. Suddenly Christ appeared with his mother and a host of saints. Placing a gold ring on her finger, he took Catherine as his bride. The ultimate mystic joy was hers.[97]

Such ecstatic trances served to deepen her commitment to God—a commitment that during her teenage years was manifested in extreme asceticism that included shunning food and sleep, long periods of silence, severe flagellation, and wearing a painfully course undergarment and an iron chain. Although she later joined the Third Order of St. Dominic (with a membership in Siena of some one hundred women), her lifestyle changed very little. She began playing a more public role, but she always remained on the fringe of that movement. She was very often the subject of local gossip and ridicule, and her activities were closely scrutinized as she moved with relative ease from the secluded chamber in her family home to the disease-ridden, vermin-infested streets of Siena.[98]

Catherine's extreme asceticism and her sometimes shocking ways of displaying her love and concern for others were directly related to the role she perceived God had given her—that of being in essence a sin-bearer for those who, unlike herself, could not or would not be responsible for their own sins. This role is unmistakably laid out in one of her written prayers:

Lord, whatever you say must be right. . . . If so many take the wrong road, it's they themselves who are to blame. It's because they obstinately follow their own wills. But I know what I'll do. I'll gather together all our sins, all our faults, all our human miseries, and I'll make a great bunch of them all and carry them all on my shoulders, and I'll carry the hateful burden to the foot of the throne of your infinite mercy."[99]

Catherine of Siena, Painted by Caracci. From *Light and Life for Women* 32:4 (April 1902): 193.

It would surely seem that attempting to carry the sins of mankind on her shoulders would lead to despair and utter helplessness. But amazingly this was not the case. According to De La Bedoyere, Catherine displayed "a combination of delight in sacrifice with delight in life," and "a geniality, charm, playfulness of manner." This attitude was no doubt prompted by the overwhelming love and concern that she felt for the helpless victims to whom she ministered and the joy she derived from her spiritual ecstacies. Yet, there were moments of dejection and doubt as well. "At times she doubted whether even her celestial visions were God-sent or Devil-sent."[100]

There are many stories about Catherine's selfless sacrifice toward others—the most gruesome of which have been the most publicized. One of these stories depicts her with a dying woman—Catherine gently swabbing the pus-filled sores, but nearly overcome by the sickening stench. But then in an instant, Catherine was guilt-stricken by her revulsion. In a demonstration of love and identity with this wretched creature, she picked up the bowl of pus she had drained from the foul sores and drank it, later claiming that it delighted her taste buds as nothing else ever had.[101] During the plague of 1374 that ravaged Siena, Schaff writes that "she was indefatigable by day and night, healed those of whom the physicians despaired, and she even raised the dead."[102]

The sick and dying were not the only ones to feel the loving touch of Catherine's sacrificial service. In one instance she came to the aid of an accused criminal. The accused was a nobleman charged with defaming the city fathers and had been sentenced to death. Before he met Catherine, he was abusive and violent, but her visits soon transformed him. In a letter to one of her dedicated followers, Catherine described the ordeal of his execution, which was turned into a virtual celebration:

> I was there at the place of execution, waiting and praying. . . . At length he came, like a meek lamb. When he saw me, he laughed and asked me to make the sign of the Cross over him. When I had done so, I said: "Kneel down now, my sweetest brother. To the nuptials! In a moment you will have entered into life eternal." He knelt down gently and I bent over him and held him as he lowered his head, reminding him of the blood of the Lamb. His lips murmured nothing but the names, Jesus and Catherine. I closed my eyes accepting in the Divine Goodness the sacrifice, and as he was speaking I received his head into my hands.[103]

As touching as these acts of mercy were, Catherine's prestige lies more in her involvement in church affairs than in her humanitarian labors. This more than anything else separates her from the vast majority of medieval saints, whose reputations are often based on flimsy accounts of miracle working. She was deeply troubled by the lowered status and corruption of the papacy since its relocation to Avignon and was convinced that there would be no real reform until the pope moved back to Rome. She was also deeply concerned about the Florentines and others of her own countrymen who demonstrated open defiance of the pope. These were terrible wrongs that had to be corrected. But that meant gaining influence at the highest levels of the politically powerful and strictly male-dominated Roman Catholic church. It would have been a difficult feat for any woman, and thus the accomplishments of Catherine stand as truly amazing when one considers her lack of social status, her obscure background, and her utter lack of renown in ecclesiastical circles.

The event that stands above all

others in Catherine's life is her march to Avignon with an entourage of some twenty dedicated followers. Her purpose was to convince the pope to depart from that "Babylon of the West," and return to Rome. Obtaining an audience with Pope Gregory XI was not a simple matter, and other complications soon developed. The Florentine delegation, whom Catherine was unofficially representing, was delayed in their coming and refused to recognize her when they finally did arrive. Although the pope treated her with respect, his advisors did not; in fact they insisted that this strange woman be examined—a routine precaution to prevent the pope from being influenced by a heretic or a witch. She passed the test and had further interviews with the pope, during which time she debated with him over the feasibility of launching another crusade. Gregory argued that it was necessary first to establish peace among the Christians, while Catherine insisted that a crusade would be the critical factor in bringing unity to the seriously divided Christians.[104]

Just how successful was Catherine in her mission to Avignon? Gregory did return the papal seat to Rome, but what part did Catherine's prodding play in the decision to do so? M. Robert Fawtier, a French scholar who has done the most extensive research on her life, contends that her role in persuading the pope to return to Rome has been greatly inflated. De La Bedoyere, on the other hand, claims that she "greatly impressed" the pope and "proved to be a determining factor" in prompting the "vacillating Pope to take the actual step of returning to Rome."[105]

Whatever her role was, she was greatly disappointed when the pope died soon after his return to Rome. But her dreams were not tied to the fate of one man. Catherine immediately made contact with the new pope, Urban VI, who, in the face of intense opposition and disloyalty, welcomed all the support he could muster. Urban's sole claim to the papal throne, however, was short-lived. The election of Clement VII by dissidents reestablished the papacy in Avignon. The Great Schism had begun. Catherine's impassioned support of Urban VI is evident in her letters to him, and she did not hesitate to blast the election of Clement VII: "I have learnt that the devils incarnate have elected not the Christ on earth, but have cause to be born an anti-Christ against you, the Christ on earth."[106]

The Great Schism that divided the Western church continued for four decades. The fighting among churchmen continued unabated, though Catherine had sought desperately to end it, and the crusade that she had so strongly pressed for was never launched. Thus despite her efforts, she failed to make any significant impact on the church at large. That "she dominated Pope Gregory and, to a lesser extent, Urban VI," or even that "she was held in high regard in Florence," as Eleanor McLaughlin maintains[107] is certainly not an obvious conclusion from the historical record.

To be sure, if the greatness of Catherine of Siena, is tallied by her political prowess, she would not necessarily receive high marks by historians. The greatness of this woman, however, is seen more in her failures than in her success. She did not reform the church or even the papacy, but her voluminous correspondence to accomplish that end stands as a permanent monument to one lowly individual's fight against corruption and immorality. "A person might well argue," De La Bedoyere writes, "that if things in the Church were as bad as Catherine makes out, it was indeed high time that men spoke out. But the fact remains that they did not."[108]

Unlike the churchmen of her day, she had nothing to lose—except her life. And her bold denunciations could never be construed to signify disloyalty to the church. Her scathing indictments were accompanied by affirmations of love and concern. She maintained a balanced approach, and her admonitions could be applied to spiritual leaders in any age. On one occasion she scolded the pope for turning his back on "the abundance of many iniquities committed by those who are fed and pastured in the garden of the Holy Church," and then she went on to say, "Since He has given you authority and you have assumed it, you should use your virtue and power; and if you are not willing to use it, it would be better for you to resign what you have assumed; more honor to God and health to your soul would it be."[109]

Catherine of Siena died in 1380 before she had reached the age of thirty-three. Many came to mourn the passing of a life that had been so brief—yet so full. She truly was a saint in the eyes of her countrymen—a role model for generations of Christian women. "She was excelled by none in her own age," writes

Schaff, "in passionate effort to save her people and help spread righteousness. Hers was the voice of the prophet, crying in the wilderness, 'Prepare ye the way of the Lord.' "[110] In 1461 when she was canonized by Pope Pius II, he characterized her ministry by saying that "none ever approached her without going away better."[111]

Brigitta

Catherine was not the only fourteenth-century female reformer who made her presence known to popes and political rulers. Brigitta of Sweden was also on the scene, ministering to the poor and hurling insults at the popes. She did not begin her work as a reformer until after her husband died. Then as a middle-aged widow she journeyed to Rome, where she lost no time in taking a stand against the corruption and political vice she saw all around her. When Pope Urban announced his intention to return to the papal residence in Avignon, she promptly predicted his death as a result. Her prophecy was not fulfilled, but that did not silence her. She continued her scathing indictments against the church hierarchy. She bemoaned how far the papacy had drifted since the time of the apostle Peter, who "was appointed pastor and minister of Christ's sheep." But now, "the pope scatters them and lacerates them. He is worse than Lucifer, more unjust than Pilate, more cruel than Judas." But Brigitta did not limit her diatribes to third-person accounts. In a letter to Pope Gregory she wrote, "In thy curia arrogant pride rules, insatiable cupidity and execrable luxury. It is the very deepest gulf of horrible simony. Thou seizest and tearest from the Lord innumerable sheep."[112]

Women in Sects

Part of the fear of permitting women freedom in ruling monasteries or forming their own orders was based on the belief that women were more prone to become snarled in heresies than were men. There was concern that the prophecies and visions so frequently attested to by women would lead to beliefs not sanctioned by the church—or, even worse, would lessen the authority of the church. Was this fear warranted? Were women more likely than men to be snared by heretical sects, or were they more like to initiate heretical doctrines? The main problem in answering those questions lies in the church's definition of "heresy." Indeed while some women were elevated to sainthood for their alleged miracles and acts of charity, others whose doctrine was just as orthodox (or perhaps more so) were denounced as heretics. There was often a fine line between heresy and orthodoxy.

The Beguines

A striking example of a movement that began to be considered heretical is that of the Beguines, a religious order of women that spread across Europe during the twelfth and thirteenth centuries, without the sanction of the papacy. This, according to Caroline Bynum, was "probably the first 'women's movement' in western history." It was a mass groundswell of goodwill, initiated and carried out by women, few of whom came from wealthy aristocratic families. "The women renounced their goods and lived a semi-conventual life, but took no vows and followed none of the approved monastic rules." Their organization was simple, without a complex hierarchical structure.[113]

Unlike most of the other women's orders, they were not cloistered and they spent much of their time feeding the hungry and caring for the sick. Doctrinally, many of these groups were as orthodox as other medieval orders. Others, however, apparently were caught up in the heresy of the Free Spirit—a mystical antinomianism that found its way into many of the sects of the Middle Ages. Some Beguines were accused of this heresy, though most avowedly denied it. They were condemned by the Synod of Cologne in 1260, and in 1312 by the Council of Vienne. Among the charges against them were their failure to confess to a priest, their lack of worshipful respect for the host, and their perfectionist and antinomian tendencies (their alleged belief that an individual could attain perfection in this life, and then could indulge in illicit sex and vice without committing sin).[114]

That they supposedly held to such antinomian heresy was bad enough, but added to that were charges of gross sexual immorality. Such accusations were rarely substantiated and may have been prompted by the threat these women were to the established church. But there were other accusations that were easily substantiated—that they were translating the Bible, preaching, and acting as self-appointed theologians—

and these were equally serious, and perhaps more so, to medieval theologians.

> The Franciscan Gilbert of Tournai . . . claimed that certain beguines had translated the Bible into the Gallic idiom, that they were reading their vernacular commentaries not only in conventicles, but openly in public squares, and that he himself had seen one of the Bibles which church officials had exhibited in Paris in order to display the many heresies and errors contained therein.[115]

Although the nature of these heresies is not specified, "he no doubt . . . thought that the Beguines' greatest crime was simply daring to translate and discuss the Bible even though they were mere laypeople."[116]

Outside the Roman Catholic church during the Middle Ages there were many other sects in which women found a spiritual refuge. Indeed, many such groups allowed women more opportunities for meaningful ministry than did the institutionalized church. Women had leadership positions and in many instances were involved in preaching and teaching. Whether the sects actually offered women a greater share of the ministry over the long term, however, is a matter of debate. Eleanor McLaughlin argues that "before the sixteenth century, it was in the Church, not in sects, that women found the most enduring and powerful roles."[117] Although she concedes that the sects permitted women great freedom and opportunities for ministry in their early years of development, she rightly points out that these roles gradually diminished as the sect officially organized. Yet, the equality that women were accorded in religious groups outside the church—even if it did not extend for generation after generation—cannot be ignored as a significant factor in attracting women in such large numbers.

The Waldensians

During the Middle Ages, membership in a sect automatically characterized an individual as a heretic. And unrepentant heretics were not treated kindly by religious authorities, whether they were women or men. In 1212 there was a crackdown against the "heretics" in Strassburg, eighty of whom were burned at the stake, twenty-three of them being women. It is presumed that many if not all of these were Waldensians—a religious group that denied the authority of the Roman Catholic church while emphasizing the authority of Scripture and the need for all to study it. The group was known for its lay preachers and evangelists (one of whom was its founder and leader Peter Waldo), and their activities were proof to the inquisitors of the group's heretical nature. And what is worse, "the Waldenses went still further in shocking old-time custom and claimed the right to preach for women as well as for men." Indeed, laypersons were permitted to administer communion and baptism, and apparently that included women. At least a charge was made to that effect, and there was no denial of it. Whether the women were permitted to minister in such a way to both men and women or were limited strictly to their own sex is unknown. Nevertheless, they participated more fully than did those women who remained under the umbrella of the Roman Catholic Church.[118]

The Cathari

The persecution against the Waldensians, though severe, was mild in comparison to that waged against the Cathari (also known as Albigensians), whose heaviest concentration was in southern France. Unlike the Waldensians, the Cathari were a truly heretical sect holding to a Manichean form of dualism. The most important rite of the Cathari was the *consolamentum*, which involved the laying on of hands and guaranteed the recipient absolution of past and future sins. Women, as well as men, performed this rite. Women were given positions of authority, while at the same time normal husband-wife sexual relationships were denounced, and women were viewed as the instigators of sin. Philip Schaff illustrates this:

> A strange account of the fall of the angels was current in Southern France. Satan ascended to heaven and waited in vain thirty-two years for admittance. He was then noticed and admitted by the porter. Hidden from the Father, he remained among the angels a year before he began to use his art to deceive. He asked them whether they had no other glory or pleasure besides what he saw. When they replied they had not, he asked whether they would not like to descend to his world and kingdom, promising to give them gifts, fields, vineyards, springs, meadows, fruits, gold, silver, and women. Then he began to praise woman and the pleasures of the flesh. When they inquired more particularly about the women, the devil said he would descend and bring one back with him. This he did.

> The woman was decked in jewels and gold and beautiful of form. The angels were inflamed with passion, and Satan seeing this, took her and left heaven. The angels followed. The exodus continued for nine days and nights, when God closed up the fissure which had been made.[119]

Early in the thirteenth century Pope Innocent III announced a crusade against the Cathari. In the words of Philip Schaff:

> The same reward was promised to those who took the cross against the Cathari [Albigensians] and Waldenses, as to those who went across the seas to fight the intruder upon the Holy Sepulchre. There was no mercy. Two emissaries of the pope reported the carnage as the crusaders entered Beziers: "Divine vengeance raged wonderfully against the city. . . . Ours spared neither sex nor condition. The whole city was sacked, and the slaughter was very great."[120]

The Taborites

No matter how "orthodox" a sect might be, the very fact that it did not recognize papal authority or was not recognized by the pope made it the target of fierce opposition. This was true of the Taborites in the early fourteenth century. They were known as "the most radical branch of the Hussite movement." Although viewed as a heretical cult by the Roman Catholic church, the Taborites "were fundamentalists in the tradition of John Wycliffe and wished to confine doctrine to what was explicitly stated in the Bible."[121] In light of this, it is all the more interesting that they permitted women to be preachers.

Theologians and Women

Despite the impressive roles played by women in the medieval church and the tributes paid them by their contemporaries, theologians in many instances perpetuated a view that held women back in church-related ministries. While this may have been due in part to the active role women played in sects outside the church, it seems to have been prompted more by simply a low view of the female sex. Women such as Catherine of Siena rose above the place accorded her sex, but others no doubt were constrained by it.

Thomas Aquinas

Thomas Aquinas, a thirteenth-century theologian, did a considerable amount of writing on the subject of women, invariably in a derogatory manner. According to Durant:

> he follows the climactic egotism of Aristotle in supposing that nature, like a medieval patriarch, always wishes to produce a male, and that woman is something defective and accidental (*deficiens et occasionatum*); she is a male gone awry (*mas occasionatum*); probably she is the result of some weakness in the father's generative power, or of some external factor, like a damp south wind.[122]

Aquinas argued that a woman is dominated by her sexual appetite, whereas a man is ruled by reason; and a woman is dependent on the man for everything in life, whereas he depends on her for procreation only. For these reasons and others women were unsuited for any meaningful role in the church or society. Indeed, women were beneath slaves in some respects:

A Thirteenth-Century Depiction of the Expulsion of Adam and Eve From the Garden of Eden. Eve was blamed for the expulsion.   British Library, MS Stowe 17, f. 29.

> The woman is subject to the man, on account of the weakness of her nature, both of mind and of body. . . . Man is the beginning of woman and her end, just as God is the beginning and end of every creature. . . . Woman is in subjection according to the law of nature, but a slave is not. . . . Children ought to love their father more than their mother.[123]

Because of her subjection, woman is not fit for ordination, Aquinas argued. It is interesting that his case against the ordination of women included arguments in their favor. He pointed out that women had been prophets (he viewed the prophetic office as higher than that of priest), that women could possess some "perfection" even as men, and that ordination pertained to the soul and the soul has no sex. Unlike Aquinas, the other thirteenth-century Catholic theologians who dealt with the ordination of women did not give opposing arguments.

Bonaventura argued against the ordination of women on the basis of their biological makeup—particularly because the one who performs the sacrament must be in the image of God, and only the male sex qualifies. John Duns Scotus, another thirteenth-century commentator, took essentially the same position but concluded that a woman is incapable of being ordained, solely because it is not the will of Christ. He conceded that there would be benefits in ordaining women, but that such benefits could not be considered, since Christ had willed otherwise.[124]

The restrictions placed on women by the theologians corresponded closely to canon law. Women were denied the right to baptize or to take communion to the sick. In fact, they were not even permitted to touch the consecrated vessels or cloths used for communion. The *Nova Quaedam*, issued by the powerful thirteenth-century pope Innocent III, prohibited abbesses "from giving a blessing to their nuns, hearing confessions, reading the Gospel, or preaching in public."[125] Although neither the commentaries of the theologians nor canon law corresponded strictly with the actual situation, there was nevertheless a concerted effort in the high Middle Ages to further restrict the ministry of women in the church.

Bonaventura

Not all late medieval theologians so consistently demeaned women as did Aquinas. Bonaventura, a leading Schoolman and the "prince of the mystics" of the thirteenth century, has been singled out as one who deeply appreciated the characteristics of "the devout feminine sex." According to Sister Emma Healy, he argued that "the soul of woman—no matter what restrictions or inhibitions philosophers might offer—is the perfect equal of the soul of man. And hence, woman is man's equal in nature, grace, and glory." Yet, even he could say that Aristotle "has spoken truly" that "woman is an embarrassment to man, a beast in his quarters, a continual worry, a never-ending trouble, a daily annoyance, the destruction of the household, a hindrance to solitude, the undoing of a virtuous man, an oppressive burden, an insatiable bee, man's property and possession."[126]

The Limits of Sexism

The low view of women in the Middle Ages was no doubt a factor that brought sexual harassment on women. Whether it was verbally demeaning them or physically abusing them, such harassment reached into the highest echelons of the church. Throughout the entire period women not only struggled for a meaningful place in the church, but also fought against the vicious slander inflicted on their sex as a whole. These outrageous attacks were more pronounced in the late medieval period—at the very time that some Renaissance humanists were beginning to look on women as their equals.

Witchcraft

Perhaps the most infamous diatribe against women of this period is included in the *Witches' Hammer*, written by two Dominican Inquisitors and published in 1486. The subject matter of the book is witchcraft, but, not surprisingly, women are an essential theme. In the words of Philip Schaff, "Of all parts of this manual, none is quite so infamous as the author's vile estimate of woman. . . . She deceives, because she was formed from Adam's rib and that was crooked." One full chapter deals with women's inferiority and her willing cohabitation with demons. Few men, say the authors, would consent to such vile sexual relations, while women offer themselves freely in such degradation. The very word to describe woman, *femina*, according to the authors is derived from *fe* and *minus* or *fides minus*, interpreted as "less in faith."[127]

Was the *Witches' Hammer* unique in the literature of the late Middle Ages? According to Schaff it was not. He points to a number of writings that denigrate women, and asserts that "it was the common representation of the writers of the outgoing century of the Medieval Age that God permits the intervention of Satan's malefic agency through the marriage bed more than through any other medium." Only a century earlier, a Roman Catholic bishop, writing from Avignon had "enumerated 102 faults common to women, one of these their cohabitation with the denizens of hell." How did he know? "It was practiced, he says, in a convent of nuns and vain was his effort to put a stop to it."[128]

Were the accusations against medieval women true? Were women more inclined toward superstition and demonic rituals of all kinds? Perhaps they were. While Berthold of Regensburg may have been overstating the case, there is no doubt some truth in his contention that women were deeply involved in the popular superstitions and folk magic of the day. He accused them of casting "spells for getting a husband, spells for the marriage, spells before the child is born, spells before the christening." His conclusion was typical: "It is a marvel that men lose not their wits for the monstrous witchcrafts that women practice on them."[129]

The belief that women practiced spells and cohabited with demons—acts that were viewed as solid evidence of their being witches—made them the brunt of vicious accusations that often resulted in trials and executions. Women were many times more likely to be executed for witchcraft than were men. And how did their proclivity for witchcraft affect their eternal state? Berthold of Regensburg believed that many more women would be in hell than men because of their witchery.[130] Indeed, the witchcraft frenzy of the late Middle Ages was one of the most sexist atrocities to have occurred in all of history.

Sexual Harassment

There were other forms of physical harassment besides that of imprisonment and execution. One very well-known account that has generally been treated as a love story would more correctly be categorized as a classic case of teacher-student sexual harassment. It is the case of Peter Abelard (1079–1142), the most brilliant theologian and philosopher of his age, and Heloise, a beautiful and intelligent young woman who had studied for a time at the convent of Argenteuil. She was in her early teens when they met—Abelard being more than twice her age. Through his reputation as a scholar and renowned teacher, he obtained permission from her uncle to be allowed to come to his home and tutor her. How much tutoring was accomplished is unknown, but apparently more kisses and caresses were given than instruction. Indeed, Heloise became pregnant by Abelard and gave birth to a son.[131]

In an effort to pacify her uncle, Abelard reluctantly agreed to marry Heloise, but he insisted that it would have to be kept secret so as not to mar his reputation. But even a secret marriage was not his style. He wrote, "Who intent upon sacred and philosophical reflections could endure the squalling of children, the lullabies of nurses and the noisy crowd of men and women! Who would stand the disagreeable and constant dirt of little children!"[132]

Abelard later claimed that they had been married secretly, but Heloise denied it. She apparently cared enough about him not to want to harm his career. Yet she was well aware that their relationship had been lacking in true affection. In a letter to him she wrote: "Thy passion drew thee to me rather than thy friendship, and the heat of desire rather than love." Heloise returned to the convent of Argenteuil, and Abelard to his scholarly activities, but he did not go unpunished. How else could an enraged uncle avenge such a deed except by hiring ruffians to attack him at night and carrying out the insidious crime of castration? Following this, Abelard entered the monastery of St. Dennis, and several years later, when his position of authority allowed it, he selected Heloise to be in charge of the nuns at the Paraclete, a chapel that he had built in Champagne.[133]

From her letters it is apparent that her love for him did not die easily. In one letter she confessed that she "was allured to the asperity of monastic conversion . . . not by religious devotion, but by thy command alone," adding that she could not expect a reward "from God for the love of Whom it is well known that I did not do anything."[134] Yet she saw great success in this position, while Abelard faced charges of heresy and continued to generate controversy wherever he went. Despite the scandal, Abelard is recognized as one of the greatest of the philosopher- theologians of the Middle Ages, and Heloise is remembered as his mistress, though she was one "of the last of the great abbesses" of medieval monasticism.[135]

Perhaps an even more despicable case of sexual harassment involved Elizabeth of Hungary (1207–31), who married at the age of fourteen and was widowed some years later. She dedicated herself to charitable works for a time in Wartburg, but then she came under the influence of Konrad of Marburg, the infamous German inquisitor. "Scarcely any scene in Christian history," writes Schaff, "exhibits such wanton and pitiless cruelty to a spiritual ward as he displayed to the tender young woman who yielded him obedience." He separated her from her children and every day reprimanded her severely and forced her to do menial labor. One day, on a charge of disobedience, she was ordered beaten by one of Konrad's aids, and soon thereafter, she died of her wounds.[136] Why Elizabeth submitted to such treatment can be understood only in the context of the medieval status of women and the unquestioned authority the Roman Catholic church had on its subjects.

There were many other instances of sexual harassment throughout the medieval period. In fact, the situation was so serious in England that Theodore, the Archbishop of Canterbury, and Egbert, the Bishop of York, issued an injunction forbidding bishops, priests, and abbots from seducing nuns.[137]

Apparently the women in convents were not always the innocent victims of aggressive males. The nuns of St. Fara's Convent, according to the bishop of Chartres (d. 1115), were involved in prostitution, and so were the nuns in many of the French convents, if Abelard is to be believed. A century later, in 1246, the bishop of Rouen "gave a generally favorable report of the religious groups in his diocese, but told of one nunnery in which, out of thirty-three nuns and three lay sisters, eight were guilty, or suspected, of fornication, and 'the prioress is drunk almost any night.' "[138]

Veneration of Mary

One of the most paradoxical aspects of medieval thought in regard to women was the veneration given the Virgin Mary, while ordinary women—particularly those outside aristocratic circles—were looked down on. Although women were often viewed as the source of evil, it was Mary who was the mediator between God and man, and it was she who, with divine authority, took on the devil, rebuking and even punishing him. The cult of Mary paralleled the medieval aristocratic concept of chivalry, and only in that light can it be properly understood. The poetry, the songs, the cathedrals, and even the scholarly writing of this period all reflected on the great reverence there was for her on all levels of society. Stories of her miraculous deeds of kindness abounded. One woman who had been dead for a year was reported to have suddenly reappeared, claiming to have been released from purgatory in answer to her prayers to the Virgin.[139] But as important as these stories and other expressions of veneration were, "the worship of the Virgin Mary entered into the very soul of medieval piety and reached its height in the doctrine of her immaculate conception." One after another—from Anselm to Aquinas—the medieval theologians argued that Mary was conceived without sin and remained sinless throughout her lifetime. There were points of difference, however. Some argued that she was conceived sinless; others, that she somehow attained her sinlessness while yet in the womb. Along with the belief in her sinlessness was the belief in her perpetual virginity. Aquinas stated the popular position succinctly: "As a virgin she conceived, as a virgin gave birth, and she remains a virgin forever." But if the proclamation of the immaculate conception by the church's greatest scholars and theologians was insufficient for some, credibility was added by the saints and mystics, not the least of whom were women. Brigitta of Sweden verified the doctrine through a vision, and Catherine of Siena gave it a new slant by claiming direct revelation that confirmed that Mary was not perfected until three hours after she was conceived. In the end, it was the position of Duns Scotus—that Mary was sinless from the instant of her conception—that prevailed and became part of church dogma in 1854 under the papacy of Pius IX.[140]

Another issue relating to Mary's supposed sinlessness centered on the birth of Christ—whether he was born naturally or in a supernatural manner. The "closed uterus" theory developed to support the belief that Jesus could not have been born through the natural, "unclean" process of childbirth. There were those who took an opposing view, but by the thirteenth century it was generally believed that "Mary's womb remained closed" and that the birth process was entirely unique and thus supernatural.[141]

What the overall effect of the cult of Mary had on women is difficult to determine. Will Durant suggests that "the worship of Mary transformed Catholicism from a religion of terror . . . into a religion of mercy and love."[142] It thus "feminized" both the church and society as a whole. Besides that, it provided a fantasizing outlet for men who had renounced romantic love and marriage in order to commit themselves to the church. For many of them there was an intense erotic delight in loving her

who was described as "the most beautiful of all virgins."[143] But the perfection associated with Mary established an impossible standard for all others of her sex. She was larger than life—the ideal female and the perfect lover, and other women were just women.

Summary

So, overall, how did women fare in the medieval church? Certainly not as badly as women in other societies during that period. And in many ways, the church came to the aid of women. Durant points out that civil law was more hostile to women than was canon law—though both had a clear antiwoman bias.

> Both codes permitted wife-beating, and it was quite a forward step when, in the thirteenth century, the "Laws and Customs of Beauvais" bade a man beat his wife "only in reason." Civil law ruled that the word of women could not be admitted in court, "because of their frailty"; it required only half as high a fine for an offense against a woman as for the same offense against a man.[144]

There were instances in which the woman's place was lowered with the advent of Christianity. This apparently was true in Scandanavia. Under paganism, "she was the mother not of sin but of strong brave men; she had one-third—after twenty years of marriage, one half—right in all wealth acquired by her husband; she was consulted by him in his business arrangements, and mingled freely with men in her home."[145] How much Christianity was able to alter that situation is uncertain, but certainly such liberty was not promoted by the church.

All in all, despite the degrading statements about women by medieval theologians, the charges of witchcraft, and the impossible ideal of the Virgin Mary, medieval women as a whole were not forced into a position of second-class citizens. "The aristocratic ideal of chivalry and the Church's ideal of feminine submissiveness were indeed ideals. In her daily life the average medieval woman neither stood on a pedestal above men nor groveled submissively below them but was treated as a 'married friend.' "[146] The same could be said for the "sisters" in the church. In many ways they stood as equals to their clerical "brothers."

Perhaps the most pronounced shortcoming of women in the church during the medieval period was their lack of true ministry. This period of church history had a high proportion of women in "professional" ministry. Yet the effectiveness of this ministry is questionable. One has to wonder how many women—Christian and pagan—could have benefited from the warmth and concern of another woman who could not only give spiritual counsel, but also give advice and assistance to alleviate some of the grueling problems of life. But instead, the nuns were by and large cloistered in their convents and many had virtually no ministry to the outside world. Not that they alone should be faulted. The majority of male clerics, who far outnumbered the women, also remained cloistered and were often of little real service to mankind. It was a failure of the church at large. The work of charity and the commitment to evangelism that so distinguished the Christians in the early centuries was no longer a primary function of the church. But wherever the blame is placed, the ministry of women in the Middle Ages was frequently of little effectiveness and profit. Although written in a spirit of humility, Clare's frequent description of herself as "the useless servant of the monastery of Saint Damian's"[147] could perhaps be taken at face value, and unfortunately that description is fitting of many medieval church women.

Chapter 5

Reformation Protestantism: Daring Noblewomen and Godly Wives

The sixteenth century was an era of upheaval in the Christian church. The contagious spirit of doubt and inquiry that engaged the minds of the Renaissance thinkers spilled over into the church. Indeed the sixteenth century produced a new breed of churchmen—innovators who were quick to challenge traditions and church dogma. In the process, very few facets of church life were left untouched by the ecclesiastical and theological changes that took place. These included the institution of marriage and the role of women in the church.

The question of what effect the Protestant Reformation had on women is a very significant one in regard to the history of changing perspectives on women in the church. Did the Reformation serve to liberate women or did it intensify their repression? How did the attitudes of the Reformers differ from those of their Catholic counterparts and from the leaders of the Radical Reformation? These are issues that

historians have long wrestled with. To some extent the debate has been colored by denominational factors. Catholics are more likely to emphasize the negative influence the Reformers had on women, and Protestants are more likely to emphasize the positive.

As significant as the Reformation was in influencing attitudes toward women, it is important to keep in mind that *La Quelle des Femmes* (the dispute about women) arose before the Reformation. Certain Renaissance humanists had taken issue with the medieval view of female inferiority. Erasmus is an example. Although not outspoken on the subject, he, like many humanists, had a much higher view of women than did medieval theologians. According to Natalie Davis, he "sensed the depths of resentment accumulating in women whose efforts to think about doctrine were not taken seriously by the clergy."[1] Likewise, his views on marriage and divorce, and the education of women is devoid of the sexual bias that was so prevalent in the medieval world.[2]

One of the most outspoken Renaissance humanists to hold to a feminist position was Agrippa of Nettesheim. A resident of Geneva in the 1520s, he argued that women in no way are inherently inferior to men, and that indeed women are in some respects superior to men. Jane D. Douglass sums up his line of reasoning:

> women are even superior in some ways . . . having been made directly by God in paradise with the angels whereas Adam was created outside paradise in a field with the animals. Eve's superiority is shown by her name, which means life, whereas the name Adam means earth. As the last of all that God created, Eve is the crowning achievement of God, the most perfect work of God. Original sin is to be traced to Adam, not Eve; and Christ, to save sinful humanity, was made human by means of a woman, not a man, in the more lowly male sex from which sin came forth.[3]

Renaissance women—primarily the upper-class women—had an influence on public opinion during the fifteenth and sixteenth centuries. They availed themselves of educational opportunities that had previously been limited to the convent. "A certain kind of woman, the court lady, suddenly advanced to a less submissive and less confined role."[4] So there was a growing sense of women's equality developing in scholarly circles prior to the Reformation.

During the sixteenth century, according to Charmarie Blaisdell, both humanists and Reformers were "departing, albeit cautiously, from the traditional misogynist themes: woman is cursed by the sin of Eve, crooked because she is made from a rib, bestial because of consorting with serpents, concupiscent and crafty because of her biology."[5] Indeed the theology of the Reformers excluded any understanding of women as a "necessary evil" and endowed them with a sense of worth that had not been as evident in the writings of medieval theologians. "The Protestant cry against the cloister brought a revitalized emphasis upon the dignity and spirituality of marriage," write Julia O'Faolain and Lauro Martines. "Quite obviously women stood to gain from this change."[6] Thus while abandoning the option of ministry through monasticism—the only real opportunity for women to serve in the church—the Reformers bolstered women's status in society. But even in doing that, they so often betrayed their prejudice against the female sex—a carry-over from medieval thought that was not easily laid to rest.

The Reformers' View of Women

The role of women in the church was not an issue that figured significantly in the writing or preaching of the Reformers, and when it did surface, it generally related to the matter of celibacy among clergy. Although Martin Luther had proclaimed the priesthood of all believers, it apparently did not occur to him or to his fellow Reformers what the ramifications could actually mean for the church. Whether women themselves could hold the clerical office was not even seriously considered. Society offered women very few opportunities for leadership roles, and the Reformers were clearly not anxious to be innovators in this area.

Martin Luther

In his sermons and commentaries Luther spoke often about women and their purpose in life as wives and mothers: "As a creature of God, a woman is to be looked upon with reverence. For she was created to be around the man, to care for children and to bring them up in an honest and godly way, and to be subject to the man."[7] In many instances his comments about women were a reaction to what he perceived the Roman Catholic view of marriage to be: "They deter their children from marriage but entice them into priesthood and nunnery, citing the trials and troubles of married life. Thus do they bring their own children home to the devil, as we daily observe; they provide them with ease for the body and hell for the soul."[8]

Although Luther had high regard for women who willingly fulfilled their domestic duties, he was a man of his times and held some very biased opinions about women—particularly regarding their supposed frailty and their limitations outside the domestic sphere. "Take women from their housewifery," he quipped, "and they are good for nothing." And on another occasion he said, "If women get tired and die of bearing, there is no harm in that; let them die as long as they bear; they are made for that."[9] In describing the differences between men and women, he observed, "Men have broad shoulders and narrow hips, and accordingly they possess intelligence. Women have narrow shoulders and broad hips. Women ought to stay at home; the way they were created indicates this, for they have broad hips and a wide fundament to sit upon, keep house and bear and raise children."[10]

Yet, according to Ian Siggins,

within his severely limited horizons, there is no doubt he intended to enhance the respect accorded women, especially by contrast with the contemporary fashion among academic humanists of waxing eloquent about female pulchritude while scornfully and contemptuously ridiculing women as worthless. He repeatedly attacked those who disdained women as inferior or as necessary evils for blaspheming the creation of God, who made women and men equally human and noble, and equally bearers of the image of God. When his biblical text provided him an image of a strong woman, his exposition took on a special liveliness.

And though Luther disdained the medieval veneration of the Virgin Mary, he granted her "all honor, all blessedness, and a unique place in all humankind, amongst whom she has no equal."[11]

Likewise, Luther had a progressive view of female education. He encouraged parents to give their children (daughters as well as sons) formal schooling so that they could be trained in religion, arts, languages, and history by "well-trained schoolmasters and schoolmistresses," so that they could "draw the proper inferences and in the fear of God take their own place in the stream of human events."[12] His position contrasted significantly with that of Calvin who "exhibited little interest in instruction for girls beyond the catechism." German Reformers, taking their cue from Luther, appealed to city councils to provide public education for both sexes—a far-sighted gesture for the sixteenth century. Although the response by the city councils was limited, "the very existence of public schools for girls in the 1520s placed Germany far ahead of England, where humanists had done so much for women of the upper classes."[13]

Nevertheless Luther basically considered women to be inferior. This is seen clearly in his commentary on Genesis. In reference to the creation account in 1:27—"Male and female he created them"—Luther wrote:

> Moses here places the man and the woman together in order that no one might think that the woman was to be excluded from the glory of the future life. The woman certainly differs from the man, for she is weaker in body and intellect [than he]. Nevertheless, Eve was an excellent creature and equal to Adam so far as the divine image, that is, righteousness, wisdom and eternal salvation, is concerned. Still, she was only a woman. As the sun is much more glorious than the moon (though also the moon is glorious), so the woman was [created] inferior to the man both in honor and dignity, though she, too, was a very excellent work of God. So also today the woman is a partaker of eternal life, as the apostle writes (1 Pet. 3:7) that she is a coheir of [divine] grace. Therefore the woman should not be excluded from any honor which human beings enjoy, even though she is the weaker vessel.[14]

A little later on in his commentary, Luther seems to reverse himself on the issue of female inferiority at creation, asserting that any such inferiority came only after the Fall. In reference to Genesis 2:18, he states:

> As Adam was created by premeditated counsel, so also Eve. Therefore also the woman, who is necessary for the preservation of the human, belongs the [eternal] life for which Adam waited. Had the woman not been deceived by the serpent, she would have been equal to Adam in all things. That she is now subjected to the man is a punishment which was inflicted upon her after and because of her sin, just as she has also sorrows and troubles, such as labor in travail and the like. Therefore Eve was not as women are today. She was far more excellent so that she was behind Adam in no bodily or spiritual gift."[15]

In practical matters Luther's advice to women was often entirely devoid of any sex bias. Indeed, his position allowed for women to have an amazing degree of freedom in the marriage relationship, even to the extent that their so-called rights in certain instances took precedence over actions of very questionable morality. For example, in his well-known tract "The Babylonian Captivity of the Church," published in 1520, he prescribed radical measures that no doubt seemed as shocking to some of his fellow Reformers as they did to Catholic churchmen. He cited a case of "a woman, wed to an impotent man." Because "she is desirous of having children or is unable to remain continent," Luther outlines two possible courses of action: (1) "to procure a divorce from her husband in order to marry another," and, if her husband refuses, (2) "to have intercourse with another, say her husband's brother, but to keep this marriage secret and to ascribe the children to the so-called putative father." She must, however, obtain the consent of her husband, "who is not really her husband, but only a dweller under the same roof with her." Luther was well aware of the questionable morality of this arrangement:

The question is: Is such a woman saved and in a saved state? I answer: Certainly, because in this case an error, ignorance of the man's impotence, impedes the marriage; and the tyranny of the laws permits no divorce. But the woman is free through the divine law, and cannot be compelled to remain continent. Therefore the man ought to concede her right, and give up to somebody else the wife who is his only in outward appearance.[16]

As to the role of women in public ministry, Luther opened up the possibility for this by suggesting that if no men were available, it might "be necessary for the women to preach." Thus "he conceded that women might exercise the preacher's office" in places such as convents where the male presence was restricted. For normal situations, however, he believed the Pauline injunctions against women's teaching prevailed.[17] Only men "should be allowed to preach, to baptize, to absolve, and to administer the sacraments. . . . The Holy Spirit has excepted women, children, and incompetent people from this function, but chooses (except in emergencies) only competent males to fill this office."[18] One aspect of ministry for women that was a carry-over from medieval Catholicism involved the baptism of babies whose death was imminent. "Lutheran church orders made special provision for midwives to be instructed in baptismal procedure."[19]

John Calvin

Calvin's relationship with women generally had far more to do with political ties than either personal spiritual matters or matters involving their sex. He corresponded with some twenty women during his lifetime—most of them being of French nobility. It was his respect for their power and influence that prompted his correspondence, as was the case with many men with whom he corresponded. His homeland was France, and he was deeply involved in the Reformed movement there, though for most of his adult life he lived in Geneva. He was well aware of the pressures many of these noblewomen faced as supporters of the Huguenots, and thus his letters were filled with exhortations to stand strong in the face of opposition.[20]

Calvin's view of women in the church is not altogether clear, and a controversy has developed among historians over this issue. Most historians have seen him as a traditionalist who would deny women equality in the church. Such is the stand of Willis DeBoer, who contends that Calvin upheld the traditional view of women's subordination to men—a position he believes is clearly taught in Calvin's commentaries. On the other side is Jane Dempsey Douglass, who leans more heavily on the *Institutes.*[21]

According to Douglass, Calvin did "something quite new in systematic theology of his day [in the *Institutes*] by shifting Paul's advice on women's silence in the church from the context of eternal, divine law to the context of Christian freedom, of human law which is open to change."

She further believes that "he certainly makes clear that no eternal law of God requires women's silence in church, and that customs which serve the edification of the church in one era can well be changed in another if they cease to serve the edification of the church."[22]

In his 1559 final edition of the *Institutes* Calvin wrote, "The statement ... in which only the man is called by Paul the image and glory of God and woman is excluded from this degree of honor is clearly to be restricted, as the context shows, to the political order." According to Douglass, "'Political' here is to be understood as the realm of human governance, the realm of human rather than divine law."[23]

In his commentaries, Calvin came to similar conclusions. He was convinced that "common sense dictates that the rule of women is defective and unseemly"; nevertheless in dealing with Paul's restrictions on women in 1 Corinthians 14:34, he stated, "The discerning reader should come to the decision that the things which Paul is dealing with here are indifferent, i.e., neither good nor bad; and that none of them is forbidden unless it works against decorum and edification."[24]

If indeed these writings indicate a liberalized view of women, how does one explain Calvin's strong position on male authority? According to Douglass,

Calvin's personal judgment seems to be that Geneva in the sixteenth century would be as scandalized by women in public roles of authority in either church or state as Paul imagined the first-century society would be. Since Calvin regarded major social upheaval as a great danger to civilization, he was unwilling to recommend revolutionary social change of any sort unless required by the Word of God. Given his concern for the consciences of his brothers, who indeed would have been greatly offended by women in authority, he seems generally content to teach the subordination of women both in church and society as a style of decorum approved by the Bible.[25]

Why might Calvin have been more liberal in his views toward women than other Reformers were? Douglass conjectures that through his relationships with prominent women (many of whom supported his efforts), he "could have learned what Luther and Melanchthon could not teach him about women's subordination as part of human governance, historically conditioned and therefore open to change."[26] She also suggests that he may have been influenced by the French humanists.

But was Calvin actually more open-minded toward women in ministry? To rank Calvin with the French humanists in his view of women seems to be begging the issue. Although he did view women's role as a matter of order and decorum, which indeed has the potential for revolutionary change for women, his own reflections on women at times appear as derogatory as any of the late medieval or Reformation theologians. His comments on the women witnesses of the resurrection of Christ are an example. Rather than viewing that as a high honor bestowed on Jesus' faithful female followers, Calvin viewed it as a stinging rebuke to the disciples for their lack of faith:

I consider this was done by way of reproach, because they had been so tardy and sluggish to believe. And, indeed, they deserve not only to have *women* for their teachers, but even oxen and asses; since the Son of God had been so long and laboriously employed in teaching, and yet they had made so little, or hardly any progress.... Yet it pleased the Lord, by means of those weak and contemptible vessels, to give a display of his power.[27]

John Knox

John Knox, the powerful voice of the Scottish Reformation, was an outspoken opponent of placing women in leadership positions. His intolerance stemmed in part from personal animosity against two Catholic rulers, Mary Tudor ("Bloody Mary"), queen of England, and Mary Guise, queen regent in Scotland. He and other Protestants suffered considerably under their rule, and thus his attacks on them are understandable. But he did not limit his condemnation to them. In a lengthy tract entitled "The First Blast Against the Monstrous Regiment of Women," which first appeared anonymously in 1558, he railed against any women who would assume a position of authority in government.

Years earlier he had questioned "whether a Female can preside over and rule a kingdom by divine right," and concluded "if women take upon them the office which God hath assigned to men, they shall not escape the Divine malediction." The book expanded Knox's position on the subject and, not surprisingly, offended many people. Even John Calvin, who had privately told Knox that "the Government of Women ... was a deviation from the original and proper order of nature," and that "it

was to be ranked, no less than slavery, among the punishments consequent upon the fall of man," was distressed by the publication. He wrote, "When I was informed of it ... I sufficiently shewed my displeasure ... but ... I thought that the evil which could not now be corrected should rather be buried in oblivion than made a matter of agitation."[28]

The first painfully long sentence of the tract sets up Knox's defense for what he surely realized would be a controversial position:

> Wonder it is, that amongst so many pregnant wittes as the Ile of Greate Britany hath produced, so many godlie and zealous preachers as England did sometime norishe, and amongst so many learned, and men of grave judgement, as this day by Jesabel are exiled, none is found so stowte of courage, so faithful to God, nor loving to their native countrie, that they dare admonish the inhabitantes of that Ile, how abominable before God is the Empire or Rule of a wicked woman, yea, of a traiteresse and bastard; and what may a people or nation, left destitute of a lawfull head, do by the authoritie of Goddes Word in electing and appointing common rulers and magistrates.[29]

In supporting his position, Knox used scriptural injunctions regarding women, particularly those of the apostle Paul, but he went far beyond Scripture in arguing that women were "weake, fraile, impatient, feeble and foolishe," in addition to being "unconstant, variable, cruell and lacking the spirit of counsel and regiment." In reflecting on creation, he reasoned that "woman in her greatest perfection was made to serve and obey man."[30]

In spite of these strong statements,

Knox had close relationships with women and admitted his dependence on them in spiritual matters. This was especially true with Anne Locke, an outspoken Protestant woman in London who became a close personal friend and confidant. Knox praised her for nourishing and confirming him in the faith, and he confided on one occasion that he was in desperate need of her spiritual counsel.[31]

Anabaptist View of Women

Although Anabaptists were known for allowing women to have a broader role in the church than they were permitted by the followers of Luther and Calvin, most of them held a very traditional view toward women in regard to both marriage and ministry. Indeed, in some instances the Anabaptist emphasis on the patriarchalism in the Old Testament "reinforced the already common tendency to subordinate the wife."[32] And there were many among the "radicals" who feared the growing influence of women in their midst. According to John Cairncross, certain of the Anabaptist groups required the "complete subordination of women to men." The husband was "absolute master in the home," and wives were expected to "address their husbands as Lord, reflecting their dependence on him—analogous with man's dependence on God."[33]

Bernard Rottman, a radical Anabaptist leader, holds the distinction of writing "the first known apology for polygamy in Europe,"—a book entitled *The Restitution of Sound Christian Doctrine*. Here he argued that "women have been wearing the trousers for too long. It is time for man to assert his God-given superiority."[34] This superiority, he believed, was best demonstrated through the practice of polygamy.

Menno Simons much more closely represents the Anabaptist tradition than Rottman, and his position on women closely parallels that of the mainstream Reformers. "His most revolutionary thought in this area, according to Joyce Irwin, seems to have been the denial of a husband's right to beat his wife."[35] His words to women, on the other hand, were very traditional.

Remain within your houses and gates unless you have something of importance to regulate, such as to make purchases, to provide in temporal needs, to hear the Word of the Lord, or to receive the holy sacraments, etc. Attend faithfully to your charge, to your children, house, and family. . . .[36]

Why then were Anabaptists known for their women preachers? According to Joyce Irwin, "Radical Protestantism . . . enabled women to preach and prophesy, not through a willing approval of such activities but through theological loopholes." She maintains that in the "sects where spiritual illumination might be expected to come in the form of visions and direct revelations, there was no basis for denying women such experiences." Thus she concludes that "the male radicals might not have approved of female preachers or prophets, but their theology had left the door ajar."[37]

The Female Response

Early Protestant women were well aware of their unequal status in the church, and on rare occasions they spoke or wrote publicly on the issue. Marie Dentiere of Geneva wrote a short work entitled "Defense of Women" in which she underscores the role of important women in Scripture, while at the same time reminding her readers that it was a man who betrayed Christ, and it was men who devised false creeds and heresies. Dentiere did not hesitate to go on and present a contemporary application:

If God then has given graces to some good women, revealing to them by his holy scriptures something holy and good, will they not dare to write, speak, or declare it one to another? . . . Ah! It would be too audacious to wish to stop them from doing it. As for us, it would be too foolish to hide the talent which God has given us.[38]

If indeed the Reformers' view of women uplifted them in their role in the home and society, as Protestant historians have argued, did it have the same effect in the church? What did the Protestants have to offer women who desired ministry? This is truly a crucial issue regarding women in church history. Did the Reformation open the door for women to serve God, or were they more repressed under Protestantism than they had been under medieval Catholicism?

Generally Catholic scholars have emphasized the repression of female ministry under Protestantism, while Protestant scholars have questioned the value of monasticism and underscored the lay ministries of Protestant women. Roland Bainton, in his three volumes on women of the Reformation, singles out various women who made an impact on early Protestantism. His work lends credence to the idea that women did play a significant role in the movement.[39] Yet, while the Reformation offered men an opportunity to have meaningful full-time ministries, it offered women only the traditional role of wife and mother. Even lay ministries were severely curtailed. In her study of the women of Zwickau during the Reformation, Susan Karant-Nunn found that the Fraternity of Calends, which offered laywomen (and men) opportunities for religious ministry, was banned by the Reformers.[40] Indeed, it could be argued that at no time in church history had the opportunity for women in ministry been so limited, and on the surface that would appear to have been the case. Nevertheless, women rose above their prescribed station in Protestantism and left an indelible mark on church life. Particularly notable were women whose monastic heritage paved the way for a ministry in Reformed circles.

Katherine von Bora

Among those monastic women was Katherine von Bora (1499–1550), the daughter of a poor aristocratic family from Saxony. She was one of forty nuns at the Cistercian Convent of Nimbschem, where seclusion from the world was strictly enforced. Even relatives who visited were separated by a latticed window from the nuns who were accompanied by an abbess. "The regulations forbade friendships between the nuns. . . . Silence was the rule, as it had been in Luther's monastery at Erfurt, and the nuns were required to walk with lowered heads and slow steps."[41]

Katherine von Bora Luther, a Portrait. From Georges Hirth, *Bilder aus der Lutherzeit* (Munich and Leipzig, 1883), 19.

In spite of the strict supervision, Luther's writings apparently managed to penetrate the walls of the convent. For some of the nuns the new ideas offered hope for a new life outside the cloister. Indeed, in 1523 Katherine and eleven other nuns secretly made arrangements to escape. Their struggle in accomplishing that end illustrates the problem nuns faced in many parts of Germany and elsewhere in Europe. Their convent was located in an area controlled by Duke George, a staunch enemy of the Reformation—a man who treated "kidnapping" nuns as a capital offense. These women sent word to Luther of their plight, and, despite the personal risk involved, he made arrangements for their escape. The story is familiar. He arranged to have a merchant who sold smoked herring to the convent make the delivery late at night and on his return trip to bring out the nuns instead of the empty herring barrels.[42]

It was an ingenious coup, but it only added to the many frustrations already confronting Luther. What to do with the nuns was the most immediate problem facing him. Some were able to return to their families, but the rest would need more than just temporary lodging. The problem was addressed by a cynical student in Wittenburg who reported, "A wagon load of vestal virgins has just come to town all more eager for marriage than for life. May God give them husbands lest worse befall."[43]

Husbands were found for the nuns, except for Katherine von Bora, and after unsuccessfully attempting to pair her with another man, Luther, who had previously resolved to remain single, consented to marry her—to the dismay and disappointment of some of his close associates. Luther's marriage, however, did not seem to affect his relationship with his close friends, several of whom observed the marriage ritual itself— one of the many indignities that a sixteenth-century female had to endure between infancy and death. Luther's biographer Richard Friedenthal describes the ordeal:

> On the evening of 13 June 1525, according to the custom of the day, he appeared with his bride before a number of his friends as witnesses. The Pomeranian [Johann] Bugenhagen blessed the couple, who consummated the marriage in front of the witnesses, [Justus] Jonas reported the next day: "Luther has taken Katharina von Bora to wife. I was present yesterday and saw the couple on their marriage bed. As I watched this spectacle I could not hold back my tears."[44]

At times Luther may have questioned that hasty decision. Katie was a strong-willed, independent, feisty redhead, who at the age of twenty-six was prepared for a far more egalitarian marriage than was the sixteenth-century norm. Although he praised her on occasion for being a submissive wife, he conceded that at times he played the role of a "willing servant" to his "lord Kathe."[45] Indeed, Luther is said to have remarked on one occasion, "The only way to get an obedient wife is to hew her out of stone." Yet the marriage was a good one, and Luther's love for Katie was unquestioned.

Their marriage not surprisingly was harshly criticized by Catholics (some being convinced that the offspring of their union would certainly be the Antichrist). Some Protestants as well criticized the event, fearing it had scandalized the whole Reformed cause. Melanchthon reportedly despised Katie, remarking prior to the marriage, "Marry, yes, but for heaven's sake not that one."[46]

Even more than her husband, Katie was singled out as a subject of scorn. A pamphlet published two years after their marriage denounced her in scathing terms:

> Woe to you, poor fallen woman, not only because you have passed from light to darkness, from the cloistered holy religion into a damnable, shameful life, but also that you have gone from the grace to the disfavor of God, in that you have left the cloister in lay clothes and have gone to Wittenberg like a chorus girl. You are said to have lived with Luther in sin. Then you have married him, forsaking Christ your bridegroom. You have broken your vow and by your example have reduced many godly young women in the cloisters to a pitiable state of body and of soul, despised of all men.[47]

Other nuns who fled the convent faced similar indictments. Their faith was no doubt tested as it had never been before, and many may have at times secretly longed for the life they left behind.

It is difficult to assess the influence of Katie Luther. She ever lived in the shadow of her larger-than-life husband. What her role in the Reformation would have been had she not been his wife is pure conjecture. But as the mistress of the first Protestant parsonage, she served with distinction. Indeed, she should be viewed as a model "preacher's wife" for all times. She was a gracious hostess to hundreds of house guests over the years, not only seeing that their physical needs were cared for, but also making them feel welcome. She often joined Luther as he talked with refugees and students who had come for counsel, and her congeniality and wit were a source of encouragement. Yet she was not tied to the parsonage. Besides managing their home in Wittenberg, she operated a small farm at Zuhlsdorf, and on occasion she was away from Wittenberg for days or weeks at a time. Indeed she was highly versatile—a fact that Luther himself acknowledged in his letters to her when he spoke of her as his "gracious Miss Katharina Luther of Bora and Zuhlsdorf" and as the "preacher, brewer, gardener, and all things else."[48]

Ursula of Munsterberg

Another nun to leave German monasticism in favor of Protestantism was Ursula of Munsterberg (c. 1491–1534), who, like most other nuns, had entered the monastery as a child. She was unhappy with the rigors of monasticism—despising most the rude awakenings in the predawn hours for vigils. Likewise, the fasting took a toll on her already-weak constitution, and she derived no spiritual benefit from it. This attitude no doubt contributed to her openness to Reformation doctrine—particularly after some of Luther's books were smuggled into the convent. She was certainly not alone in her inclination toward "heresy," however. Of the nearly eighty nuns in the convent, fewer than twenty remained unaffected by the new teaching. This had occurred in part because of the freedom permitted the nuns in the convent at Munsterberg. Yet, Ursula felt imprisoned, and on the night of October 6, 1528, she and two other nuns quietly left, never to return.[49]

In the months that followed, her escape became a matter of political controversy in Germany. Duke George wanted her back in his domain, fearing that her profane example might cause other "sisters . . . to embrace a godless life." Elector John supported her, though he insisted that he "had no hand in her escape." For her part, Ursula refused to be intimidated and published a tract defending her actions. In it she clearly enunciated her theological shift in belief:

> The only hope lies in faith. By baptism we have been received into the kingdom of Christ. To say that the monastic vow is a second baptism and washes away sins, as we have heard from the pulpit, is blasphemy against God, as if the blood of Christ were not enough to wash away all sins. We are married to Christ and to seek to be saved through another is adultery. The three monastic vows are the work of men's hands. There is only one way to relieve our consciences and that is to make a clean break. We have suffered such torments of spirit that we could no longer hold on.[50]

Katherine Zell

One of the most outspoken women of the Reformation was Katherine Zell (c. 1497–1562), the wife of Matthew Zell, a Catholic priest turned Lutheran preacher. Her avid interest in spiritual matters began early in life—a decade before Luther posted his famous theses. "Ever since I was ten years old I have been a student and sort of church mother, much given to attending sermons. I have loved and frequented the company of learned men, and I conversed much with them, not about dancing, masquerades, and worldly pleasures but about the kingdom of God."[51]

Matthew Zell's marriage, like Luther's, was highly controversial, and in 1524, the bishop suspended the clerical privileges of all married priests. The bishop's action infuriated Katherine, who was well aware of the lifestyle of the celibate clergy, who were often accused of seducing young women and girls. She defended her own role by arguing that marriage to a priest was a ministry that uplifted the moral degradation of the clergy, and she accused the church of having financial considerations in preventing such marriages.[52]

Katherine was not intimidated by being a woman. In fact, she lashed out against her opponents who wanted her voice silenced: "You remind me that the Apostle Paul told women to be silent in church. I would remind you of the word of this same apostle that in Christ there is no longer male nor female and of the prophecy of Joel: 'I will pour forth my spirit on all flesh and your sons and your *daughters* will prophecy.'" She forcefully made her case and refused to be silenced, but she did not pursue her argument to the point of proclaiming equality for women in the church. Indeed, she was careful to couch her statement in humility—though with more than a touch of sarcasm: "I do not pretend to be John the Baptist rebuking the Pharisees. I do not claim to be Nathan upbraiding David. I aspire only to be Balaam's ass, castigating his master."[53]

Katherine's primary ministry involved hospitality and service to Protestant refugees and travelers, many of whom were well-known Reformers of the day. She thoroughly enjoyed her illustrious guests and offered them much more than food and lodging. She "conversed with them on theology so intelligently that they ranked her above many doctors."[54]

During one three-week period she provided room and board in the parsonage at Strasbourg for some sixty homeless victims of religious persecution. "Her zeal is incredible for Christ's lowliest and afflicted," a Protestant leader wrote of her. But even in this selfless task she became embroiled in controversy. She did not limit her kindness to those with whom she agreed on theological points, stating emphatically that "anyone who acknowledges Christ as the true Son of God and the sole Savior of mankind is welcome at my board." This included the radical Schwenckfeld and certain of the Anabaptists. On one occasion she berated a Lutheran leader for his bigotry: "Why do you rail at Schwenckfeld? You talk as if you would have him burned like the poor Servetus at Geneva. . . . You behave as if you had been brought up by savages in a jungle. The Anabaptists are pursued as by a hunter with dogs chasing wild boars. Yet the Anabaptists accept Christ in all the essentials as we do."[55] In her view the need for unity was of greater import than the ideal of doctrinal conformity—a view that disturbed many of her male contemporaries.

Other things about Katherine disturbed her contemporaries as well. She was apparently so much a threat to the Protestant establishment in Strasbourg that she felt obligated to speak at her husband's funeral assuring her listeners that she did not seek to become "Doctor Katrina," as rumor had it. "I am not usurping the office of preacher or apostle," she insisted. "I am like the dear Mary Magdalene, who with no thought of being an apostle, came to tell the disciples that she had encountered the risen Lord."[56]

Some years later she was again forced to defend her ministry—this time against charges of disturbing the peace:

A disturber of the peace am I? Yes indeed, of my own peace. Do you call this disturbing the peace that instead of spending my time in frivolous amusements I have visited the plague infested and carried out the dead? I have visited those in prison and under sentence of death. Often for three days and three nights I have neither eaten nor slept. I have never mounted the pulpit, but I have done more than any minister in visiting those in misery. Is this disturbing the peace of the church?[57]

Katherine Zell, Singing Hymns in the Home.   From Georges Hirth, *Les Grands Illustrateurs* (Munich: Knorr & Hirth, 2nd ed., n.d.), 1:41.

Katherine's ministry involved more than charitable work for the needy. She also compiled hymns and published them in pamphlet form in an effort to more effectively focus the minds of laypeople on God. Her motivation illustrates the depth of her own spiritual maturity:

When I read these hymns I felt that the writer had the whole Bible in his heart. This is not just a hymn book but a lesson book of prayer and praise. When so many filthy songs are on the lips of men and women and even children I think it well that folk should with lusty zeal and clear voice sing the songs of their salvation. God is glad when the craftsman at his bench, the maid at the sink, the farmer at the plough, the dresser at the vines, the mother at the cradle break forth in hymns of prayer, praise and instruction."[58]

One of her final acts of selfless service was conducting a funeral service for a woman disciple of Schwenckfeld. A Lutheran minister had agreed to conduct the funeral but only with the stipulation that he publicly renounce her for denying the faith. Her husband refused and instead called upon Katherine, now old and feeble, to conduct a graveside service at dawn, so as to avoid the authorities. Later the city council voted that if she recovered from her illness they would duly reprimand her. She did not recover.[59]

Katherine Zell stood out among the Reformers' wives in her very active ministry, but she was certainly not unique in seeing herself as a partner with her husband in the ministry. The role of a minister's wife very early in the Reformation was associated with expectations far above and beyond that of an ordinary layman's wife. Because of these expectations and the peculiar problems related to their ministries, there was a certain amount of networking among them. Wibrandis, wife of the German reformer Oecolampadius, corresponded with a number of other ministers' wives, including Anna Zwingli, Elisabeth Butzer, and Agnes Capito. They saw themselves as women of God in the tradition of biblical heroines. Indeed, Agnes Capito sent Wibrandis a prayer book that featured the great women in Scripture.[60]

Argula von Grumback

Although women were restricted in entering ministries on their own, their identity was not exclusively limited to that of being clerical wives.

Some women—particularly highborn women—made a significant impact on the Reformation in their own right. This was especially true in France and to a lesser extent in Germany. In some instances the influence of these women involved little more than being a "thorn in the flesh" to Catholic leaders, but even in this capacity their presence was often deeply felt. This was true of Argula von Grumback (c. 1492–1563). She had a claim to Bavarian nobility both by birth and by marriage, and her education and critical mind allowed her to become a force to be reckoned with.

She first came to the attention of the Catholic leaders when she wrote a letter in support of a young instructor and colleague of John Eck who had been forced to recant his "Lutheran" theology. She sought to buttress her position by assuring the "honorable, worthy, highborn, erudite, noble, stalwart Rector and all the Faculty of the University of Ingolstadt" that her words were "not a woman's ranting, but the Word of God." Such a defense, however, did not make her letter any more palatable to her Catholic opponents. According to one, she was "an insolent daughter of Eve, a heretical bitch and confounded rogue."[61]

What kind of heresy could her letter have contained for her to have merited such a scathing attack? Actually, her letter, interspersed with Scripture references, was well reasoned and mild compared to much of the rhetoric of the Reformation period. Her emotionally charged first sentence is followed by penetrating questions and pithy answers:

When I heard what you had done to Arsacius Seehofer under terror of imprisonment and the stake, my heart trembled and my bones quaked. What have Luther and Melanchthon taught save the Word of God? You have condemned them. You have not refuted them. . . . You seek to destroy all of Luther's works. In that case you will have to destroy the New Testament, which he has translated. . . . Even if Luther should recant, what he has said would still be the Word of God.[62]

So convinced was Argula of her position that she challenged these learned university administrators and professors to a debate, offering to base the debate on a translation of the Bible published some decades earlier. What kind of woman was it who would make such a challenge? Was she a feminist demanding an equal place for women in the church? Apparently not. Indeed, she did not presume that her bold activities should be the norm for women: "I am not unacquainted with the word of Paul that women should be silent in church . . . but, when no man will or can speak, I am driven by the word of the Lord when he said, 'He who confesses me on earth, him will I confess and he who denies me, him will I deny.' "[63] It is interesting to note, however, that Seehofer, the young instructor she was defending, was accused of being a heretic in part because he had allegedly argued that women and laypeople in general were not excluded from being theologians—a profession always presumed to be exclusively for males.[64]

Incredible as it may seem, considering the spirit of the times, Argula was permitted to present her position in 1523 in Nurnberg before the diet of the Empire. It was hardly a victory, though. The princes were unmoved by her appeal and were apparently far more interested in indulging their appetites in food and drink. "I am distressed," she wrote, "that our princes take the Word of God no more seriously than a cow does a game of chess."[65]

Argula suffered for her courageous stand—not so much from the authorities as from her own husband. To her cousin she wrote, "I hear you have heard that my husband has locked me up. Not that, but he does much persecute Christ in me. At this point I cannot obey him." She did not take this disobedience lightly. And truly there was reason for her husband to be upset with her stand, for she also wrote "I understand that my husband will be deposed from his office. I can't help it. God will feed my children as he feeds the birds and will clothe them as the lilies of the field."[66] Indeed it was a heavy price that this woman of faith paid for her Christian witness. She was not, however, without recognition—and from the highest quarters. Luther spoke of her in glowing terms. In a letter to a friend he wrote:

> The Duke of Bavaria rages above measure, killing, crushing and persecuting the gospel with all his might. That most noble woman, Argula von Stauffer, is there making a valiant fight with great spirit, boldness of speech and knowledge of Christ. She deserves that all pray for Christ's victory in her. . . . Her husband, who treats her tyrannically, has been deposed from his prefecture. What he will do you can imagine. She alone, among these monsters, carries on with firm faith, though, she admits, not without inner trem-

bling. She is a singular instrument of Christ.[67]

Yet despite such encouragement and support, Argula continued to suffer for her faith. In fact at the age of seventy she was still being hounded by Bavarian authorities. The Duke had incarcerated the "old Staufferin" for the second time—and for good reason. In the words of Roland Bainton, she "had incited the people to disobedience by circulating books contrary to the Catholic religion. She had seduced them from the services of the church and had conducted private conventicles in her home. She had gone to the cemetery and had officiated at funerals."[68] Because of her age and health she was released, and later that year she died.

Marguerite of Navarre and Jeanne d'Albert

It was in France that noblewomen had the most profound influence on the Reformation. Without the benefit of their political might, the Huguenots would have been far less successful in establishing a solid base for the Reformed faith during most of the sixteenth century. The first powerful French noblewoman to take up the cause of reform was Marguerite of Navarre (1492–1549), the sister of King Francis I. She had been influenced by Jacques Lefevre, a biblical scholar whose commentary on the Pauline epistles espoused the doctrine of justification by faith several years before Luther posted his theses in Wittenburg.[69] Despite such influence, Marguerite remained at heart a Catholic. Although she was sympathetic to Reformed theology and denounced persecution of the

Huguenots, she often took the side of the Catholics. Neither side fully trusted her. "Our greatest hope is in the Queen of Navarre," wrote Calvin, "but we cannot place on her too great reliance."[70]

Although Marguerite could hardly be categorized as a feminist, she was well aware of the power of her sex as a noblewoman, and she was not afraid to address women's issues in her writing. An example of this is found in her novel *Heptameron*. In the midst of a discussion of the virtues of women, one of her female characters responds to a derogatory remark by saying:

> You would like to follow . . . the opinion of wicked men who take a passage of Scripture for themselves and leave behind the one which is the opposite of it. If you have read St. Paul all the way to the end, you will find that he recommends himself to the ladies who have worked very hard with him in the Gospel.[71]

It was her mysticism that most separated Marguerite from the Reformers. In many ways her ideology more closely resembled that of the mystics of the Catholic Reformation than that of the theologians of the Protestant Reformation. Although some of her poetry bore the markings of Reformation doctrine—particularly in their titles ("Justification by Faith," "The Primacy of Scripture," and "The Doctrine of Election")—her theology was experience-oriented, and her mysticism at times bordered on heresy. According to Bainton, she believed she would "be made divine" and she called herself "the mother of God." She "felt herself to be a bearer of God. At the same time she was the sister and the bride of Christ."[72]

It was Jeanne d'Albert (1528-1572), the daughter of Marguerite, who is best remembered among the French noblewomen for taking a strong stand in support of the Reformed cause. She made a public profession of her Protestant faith on Christmas Day in 1560—a decision that was influenced by Beza, Calvin's successor at Geneva. "His visit to her court at Nerac in the summer of 1560 was certainly an important factor in her announced conversion later that year, and thereafter she always sought his advice in important matters such as the choice of a tutor for her son or the means of stamping out 'idolatry' in her domains."[73]

According to Bainton, her conversion seemed to be simply "the conviction that Calvin's teaching was God's teaching as set forth in the Bible." As the queen of Navarre, she wielded a powerful influence over French politics, but her efforts to establish the Reformed faith permanently among her countrymen were thwarted by her husband. Her unreserved support of the Huguenots created marital disharmony, and for a time her husband kept her locked up and threatened divorce in order to prevent her from giving further aid to the Protestants. Their eight-year-old son, Henry, was torn between them in a bitter custody battle. Jeanne forbade him to ever attend Mass, while his father forced him to study under Catholic tutors.[74]

In addition to opposition from her royal family, Jeanne met strong resistance from church officials. Her cousin, Cardinal d'Armagnac accused her of "being misled by evil counselors who seek to plant a new religion" and of inciting "subjects to

Jeanne D'Albret. She is pictured here riding out to battle to give support to the Huguenot Army.

take up arms against kings and princes." Her response shows the depth of her religious convictions: "I am not planting a new religion but restoring an old one." And regarding her "evil counselors," she retorted, "I follow Beza, Calvin and others only in so far as they follow Scripture."[75]

Unlike her mother, Jeanne did not seek to establish an atmosphere of religious toleration. Rather, she imposed restrictions on the Roman Catholics that served to deepen the tensions between the two sides. In 1566, she issued decrees that curtailed Roman Catholicism in the region of Navarre. Her aim was mainly to restrict the use of the crucifix and other religious paraphernalia that she believed constituted idolatry; she did so in order to prevent the judgment of God on her domain. Revolts broke out, and bloody battles between Catholic and Protestant forces ensued. When the Huguenot general was killed, Jeanne rode out and rallied the troops—a move that contributed to a military victory. Partly because of her powerful influence, the Huguenot faith continued to grow in France. But hard times lay ahead. She died in 1572, and later that year Protestants were slaughtered en masse in what became known as the St. Bartholomew's Day Massacre. Although her son Henry IV was raised in the Protestant faith, after he ascended the throne he yielded to Catholic demands and switched his religious allegiance. Yet, he is remembered for signing the Edict of Nantes, which granted religious toleration to the Huguenots for most of a century.[76]

Renée of Ferrara

Another noblewoman who served the cause of the Reformation well was Renée of Ferrara (1510–1575). She was the daughter of King Louis XII of France, and as a young woman she agreed to an arranged marriage to an Italian prince in an effort to forge a political alliance. Influenced by Marguerite of Navarre, she quickly became a Protestant sympathizer. "Her court at Ferrara became a known refuge for both French and Italian religious fugitives and a center for secret Protestant preaching."[77] Like Marguerite and Jeanne, she was courted by prominent Reformers. Calvin corresponded with her for nearly three decades, and he assigned one of his most trusted preachers, Morel, to serve as her private pastor at her court at Montargis.[78]

Like Argula, she was harassed by her husband, who complained that she had been "seduced by some Lutheran rascals" and had "refused to go to confession and Mass, and when one of her servants was dying, she refused him extreme unction."[79] Her husband called on the Jesuits for help in bringing her back into line, and as a result she was "forced to attend Mass openly and publicly."[80] That she submitted to the pressures was a bitter disappointment to Calvin and other French Reformers, and they sought more diligently to persuade her to commit herself to the side of reform. She continued, however, to waver, "caught between the forces of French Protestantism and Jesuit militancy," but outwardly bowing to the pressure of the Catholic officials.[81]

In some respects Renée was similar to Katherine Zell who manifested a spirit of toleration far broader than the Reformers were known for. After she returned to France, she was harshly criticized for her refusal to dispose of the "nest of heretics" in her domain, but she stood her ground and instituted freedom of religion and offered charitable services not only to Huguenots but also to needy Catholics—including some impoverished monks. She renounced Morel and other Reformers for the vengeance they wrought on their enemies—"sacking of the shops of the Catholics." She pled with Calvin to use his influence to stop the carnage: "Monsieur Calvin, I am distressed that you do not know how the half in this realm behave. They even exhort the simple to kill and strangle. This is not the rule of Christ. I say this out of the great affection which I hold for the Reformed religion."[82]

Although she was recognized as a very influential woman of the Reformation, Renée was unable to have the meaningful role she desired in the church. Morel wrote to Calvin concerning this issue: "Renée wants to attend the meetings of the synod. . . . But if Paul thought that women should be silent in church, how much more should they not participate in the making of decisions! How will the Papists and the Anabaptists scoff to see us run by women!" Renée also wrote to Calvin, pointing out Morel's inconsistency—his selectivity in permitting certain women a role in church affairs while denying other women the right to have any part in the leadership of the church. She wrote, "At first he invited me to attend the consistory of elders chosen by himself. Then he told me that women should not attend, although the Queen of Navarre, the wife of the Admiral [Coligny] and the queen herself attend such assemblies. But I did not press the point."[83]

Women of the English Reformation

In England the Reformation was even more politicized than it was in France, and powerful female rulers played a significant role in both sides of the long struggle. Mary Tudor, the daughter of Henry VIII, sought to bring the church back under the domination of Rome and to rid the country of "heresy"—a policy that resulted in the martyrdom of Thomas Cranmer, Hugh Latimer, and Nicholas Ridley. She died in 1558 and was succeeded by her sister Elizabeth, who steered the church away from Rome to a position more closely identified with Protestantism, while at the same time persecuting those religious groups who refused to conform to the prescribed patterns of worship.

But while the faith of the monarchs was often politicized, the faith of the commoners sometimes manifested deep religious conviction. Both women and men were forced to face the bitter consequences of following their personal convictions in religious matters. Joyce Lewes is an example. She was converted after witnessing the deep faith of Lawrence Saunders while he was being burned at the stake—a sentence pronounced on him during the reign of Queen Mary for not attending Mass. His gripping testimony prompted

Mrs. Lewes to question her own participation in the rituals of the Mass and soon after that she demonstrated her disapproval by refusing to face the altar during the ceremonies and subsequently avoiding Mass altogether. For these acts of religious defiance she was sent to prison for a year, after which she was burned at the stake. According to John Foxe, the torture was mercifully brief: "When the fire was lighted, she neither struggled nor stirred, but only lifted up her hands toward heaven, and was dead very speedily; for the under-sheriff, at the request of her friends, had provided such a quantity of dry wood and straw that she was very quickly despatched out of this evil world."[84]

The Martyrdom of Joice Lewes in Lichfield in 1557. From Walter Walsh, *The Women Martyrs of the Reformation* (London: Religious Tract Society, n.d.).

Foxe records the suffering of several other women who held firm to their faith in the face of severe persecution during the reign of Queen Mary. In one instance in Smithfield, England, three women—Catherine Hut, Joan Hornes, and Elizabeth Thackvill—were charged with adhering to the Reformed "heresy." Because they refused to recant they were thrown into prison and were finally executed. They were tied to one stake and burned together. Another instance involved the burning of a blind woman, one Joan Waste of Derby. So eager was she to learn the Scriptures after her conversion to the Reformed faith that she purchased a copy of the New Testament and hired an old man to come and read it to her daily. She memorized large portions of it, and for this crime and for refusing to attend Mass she was imprisoned and later burned at the stake, in August 1556.[85]

The most famous of the female martyrs during the Reformation in England is Anne Askew (c. 1521–46). She was in her mid-twenties when she was burned at the stake in 1546 during the reign of Henry VIII. Her personal testimony of the torture she endured has been preserved, and it sheds light on the active—though often secretive—role women played in the English Reformation. Her first arrest and imprisonment came to an end after her relatives made an appeal for her release and, according to Foxe, after she "was persuaded to sign a paper, upon which had been written a formal promise to return to the Romish church." There is some debate concerning the latter point, but at any rate, she was shortly arrested again and brought before an

examiner who interrogated her concerning others involved in her "sect." "They asked me of lady Suffolk, lady Sussex, lady Hertford, lady Denny, and lady Fitzwilliams. To this I answered, 'If I should pronounce anything against them, I would not be able to prove it.' "[86]

Ann Askew Pleading Her Innocence Before the Lord Chancellor. From Walter Walsh. *The Women Martyrs of the Reformation* (London: Religious Tract Society, n.d.).

From there the line of questioning moved to the issue of the gifts of food and money she had received while in prison—the implication being that they had come from women supporters who belonged to her "sect." Her answers were vague and resulted in torture and finally death.

Then did they put me on the rack, because I confessed no ladies or gentlewomen to be of my opinion, and thereon they kept me a long time, and because I lay still and did not cry, my lord chancellor and Mr. Rich took pains to rack me with their own hands till I was nigh dead. . . . Then was I brought to a house and laid in a bed, with as weary and painful bones as ever had patient Job. My lord chancellor sent me word, if I would change my opinions I should want for nothing; if I would not, I should forthwith to Newgate, and so be burned. I sent him again word, that I would rather die than break my faith.[87]

This passive acceptance of persecution was only one side of Askew's response. Indeed, while she was undergoing examination by authorities, she exhibited a bold and at times audacious manner. She defended herself with Scripture, citing the stoning of Stephen as an analogy to her own persecution. And she had a ready answer when she did not wish to respond: "I answered I would not throwe pearles amonge swine." She was caustic in her criticism of Catholicism: "I said that I had rather to reade five leaves in the Bible, than to hear five Masses in the temple . . . because the one did greater edify me and the other nothing at all."[88]

It was clear that the authorities did not wish to go through with the death sentence of Anne Askew, for even on the day of her burning letters were brought to her, offering her a pardon if she would recant. They realized all too well that her unbending faith in the face of torture and death only served the cause of the Reformers. Women were active on both sides of the religious struggle during the Reformation in England. When Catholicism was outlawed un-

der the reign of Elizabeth, the authorities discovered very quickly that exterminating a religion was a complicated ordeal and that "one of the greatest obstacles . . . lay in the wives of the gentry who harbored the priests."[89]

Women in Sectarian Movements

Traditionally, most historians have maintained that women had considerably more freedom for ministry in the radical sects than in the institutionalized churches. This, they contend, was due in part to the fact that the sects generally had a "preponderance of women." Roland Bainton, among others, holds this position and suggests that this may be due to the fact that the sects "placed more stress on piety than on dogma" and that this stance was congenial to women.[90] In recent years, however, this thesis has been challenged. Certain scholars have argued that there is no evidence that the sects contained a larger percentage of women than did established churches. Yet there is abundant evidence that women were permitted a wider range of ministry in the various sects. Indeed, women preachers were not uncommon among the sects.

Anabaptists

Among the Anabaptists the "sisters" were "referred to as being on the same level as the brethren," according to George Williams, in his massive work entitled *The Radical Reformation*. Speaking of the Anabaptists, he states, "Nowhere else in the Reformation Era were women so nearly the peers and companions in

The Martyrdom of Anneken Heyndricks, an Anabaptist. From *Martyrs' Mirror*.

the faith, and mates in missionary enterprise and readiness for martyrdom, as among those for whom believers' baptism was an equalizing covenant." Williams further contends that "the extension of the priesthood of the Christophorus laity to women constituted a major breach in patriarchalism and a momentous step in the western emancipation of women." He also points out that "besides numerous patronesses, protectresses, and martyrs, the Radical Reformation acknowledged several prophetesses, at least two women apostles, and one redemptress (William Postel's Venetian virgin)."[91]

It was inevitable that controversy would rage over the issue of women in positions of spiritual authority.

Criticism came from all sides, from both within and without the ranks of the Anabaptists. Sometimes this criticism was fostered by the bizarre charismatic ministry and conduct of the women leaders themselves. Johannes Kessler, a Reformer of St. Gall, made no attempt to disguise his disdain for one Margarita Hattinger, an Anabaptist who "came to the point that she said she was God." According to Kessler, she "asserted that whoever prays is sinning," and "she undertook to say things that no one could understand, as if she were so deeply immersed in God that no one but she in God could understand her tongue and speech."[92]

Kessler related another scornful account of one Magdalena Muller, who allegedly professed to be Christ. She had two disciples, Frena and Barbara, whose religious fervor was considered as scandalous as her own. On one occasion, according to Kessler, one of them "began to speak with a frightful voice and to shake and foam at the mouth," while rebuking the other for her sin.

> After she had spoken these words with great fury, Barbara fell down and cried wailingly in a loud voice . . . her body swelling up, her face burning as bright as a rose, sweating drop after drop. So her belt and all her clothes were undone so that she wouldn't suffocate. After she had lain there two hours, she came to herself again.[93]

This sort of behavior continued, and apparently many people believed the women to be insane. Whatever their condition was, Kessler and others used the bizarre episodes to discredit women in ministry.

Zwickau Prophets

Among the Zwickau Prophets there were a number of women who were recognized as religious leaders— especially "in the wake of the Muntzerian and Storchian outbursts." Indeed, there were a number of prominent women who had been "infected" with heresy. One of those was Soff Teucher, who apparently ignored the city council's admonitions to stop preaching and conducting private religious meetings. In 1521 the council gave this order: "She and her husband are to be sent for and told that the wife is henceforth to cease her doings." Yet eight years later after repeated efforts to silence her, the council was still being frustrated by her tenacity. Her name and

description was listed along with other female troublemakers: "Soff Teucher, who can never keep quiet, her influence must also be removed."[94]

Polish Brethren

Women were also prominent among the Polish Brethren, a sixteenth-century utopian community that emphasized pacifism and unitarianism. According to the testimony of critics, in this group women enjoyed equal rights with men. Roman Catholics held the community up as an example of decadent Protestantism, where women were "unstable, flitting like Salome from opinion to opinion." Bona Sforza, the queen of Poland, abhorred the spread of such heresy, lamenting that "every crucifix in Cracow has been smashed . . . and even women, I hear, are preaching. While my husband was alive I would have taught them what it is to preach. I'm a Christian queen and I won't stand for any of this nonsense."[95]

Francisca Hernandez

Reformation sects developed not only on the fringe of Protestantism, but also on the fringe of Catholicism, and even though representatives of such "heresies" often differed very little from individuals in good standing in the church, their independence and individualized "leading of the Spirit" made them targets for official condemnation, persecution, and martyrdom. Many such individuals were women who, like the Beguines of an earlier age, believed they could follow their own consciences and be faithful to the Catholic church at the same time. But that was often idle fantasy. Yet there was often a fine line between those who were condemned to death and those who were canonized. It came as a shock to many of these women when they suddenly realized they were suspected of heresy.

Francisca Hernandez was one such woman. A Catholic laywoman, she was known for her healing miracles. Many Franciscan friars held her in high regard, including one Francisco Ortiz, a popular preacher of his day. Like others, he sought out Francisca for healing. Bainton describes his apparent desperation: "During a period of four years he had been so tormented by erotic dreams and frequent emissions that he made an attempt at suicide. Word reached him that through her miraculous power others had been delivered from a like affliction"—apparently a not uncommon malady among celibate friars.[96]

Francisca initially shunned his efforts to see her, but he persisted and was given an audience. "In the very first conversation she divined all my thoughts. I recognized by a marvelous light that to seek and find God I had no need of any greater truth than that which fell from her lips and that this was the pure grain and substance of the gospel." Indeed, he became convinced that this unlettered woman understood the Scriptures more clearly than did the best theologians. So grateful was Ortiz for being delivered from his "debilitating temptations" that he paid her the highest tribute he could conceive: "She can be compared to the Mother of God."[97]

When word of this "miracle" reached Catholic authorities, there was immediate suspicion of Francisca, and no doubt some concern that a woman—a mere laywoman— would be the recipient of such honor and praise. The Inquisition stepped in and Francisca was imprisoned. Soon after that Ortiz, too, was thrown into a dungeon. The precise crimes they were accused of were not specified, but it was intimated that the alleged cure may have been affected by their having had sexual relations. It was a trumped-up charge that had been used by the Inquisition against many other female "heretics"—and perhaps a charge Francisca feared when she initially refused to see Ortiz. In the end, with no reliable witnesses to counteract their testimony of their innocence, both were released, though Ortiz was placed under a form of probation at a monastery and Francisca was kept under surveillance.[98]

Many women who were brought before the Inquisition fared far worse than did Francisca. Maria Cazalla was one. She was a Spanish mystic and an admirer of Erasmus, who was a brilliant Renaissance humanist and a critic of the church whose books were banned by Catholic authorities. "I hold what Erasmus holds," she asserted, "because Erasmus holds what Holy Mother Church holds." The inquisitors pressed her for further clarification of her views, asking her if she had been critical of the church's holy days, if she had downplayed the importance of the sacraments, and what she thought of Luther. Although she sought desperately to avoid incriminating herself, the inquisitors were not satisfied with her answers. They suspected

Maria Cazalla, a Sixteenth-Century Woman Undergoing Water Torture. From S. G. Pozhniskii, *Istornia Inhvizitsii*, 1914 (in Russian), 54.

that she was denying her beliefs to avoid condemnation. That in itself would not have been so serious had she not also been accused of preaching—preaching at private meetings without church authorization. So, the obvious solution in the minds of the inquisitors was to torture her.[99]

They first tortured her by stripping her and then "tying cords around the thighs and arms with a belt around the waist from which in front cords went up over the shoulders and down to the belt in the back. Tourniquets dug the cords into the flesh at any point of the body." Still she refused to admit to heresy. They then gave her the water torture, by forcing water into her mouth and nostrils until she nearly suffocated. But it was to no avail. Without the hard evidence they needed to give the death sentence, the inquisitors freed her with the stipulation that she do public penance, limit her travel, and pay a large fine.[100] Although she was one of the fortunate ones who faced the inquisitors' tortures and lived to tell about it, it is safe to say that her own experience was a deterrent to other Catholic women who were inclined to function in a spiritual capacity outside the official sanction of the church.

Deterrent or not, Catholic women continued to be involved in ministry, and when their ministry did not conform to the prescribed standard established by the Inquisition, their very lives were in danger. According to Bainton, the number of women brought before the Inquisition was on a par with the number of men. Many of these, however, were simply laypeople who were accused of supporting or sympathizing with the Protestant cause.

Women in Catholicism

The Protestant Reformation involved far more than the struggle to

Reformation Woman Enduring Torture by the Wheel.
From S. G. Pozhniskii, *Istornia Inhvizitsii,* 1914 (in Russian), 580.

worship God freely in accordance with a Reformed theological position. It also involved an effort to eradicate Roman Catholicism—either by persuasion or by coercion. In some instances Protestant women were actively involved in this effort—particularly in persuading nuns to leave the convent. A Catholic nun from Geneva wrote in the early decades of the sixteenth century of two Protestant women who came to a local convent uninvited. One of them was Marie Dentiere, a former abbess who became a Protestant pastor's wife. She allegedly "meddled with preaching . . . perverting people of devotion." On another occasion Claudine Levet came to the convent under the protection of a group of Protestant men who defended her ministry, saying she was enlightened by God, a fact demonstrated by her preaching and teaching that had brought many people to the truth of the gospel. From another contemporary account, it be-

comes clear that Madame Levet did not confine her preaching to nuns in the convent. She explained the Scriptures at public gatherings where men as well as women were among her listeners.[101]

The Reformers themselves were also actively involved in persuading nuns to forsake the convents. Calvin corresponded with a number of women, including nuns. One of the nuns to whom he wrote was Abbess Philippe Chasteigner, who after her conversion in 1557 fled to Geneva with eight of her nuns from the monastery of St. Jean de Bonneval.[102]

The widespread voluntary exodus of nuns from their convents clearly confirms that many nuns welcomed the new ideas associated with the Reformation. With the onslaught of publishing initiated by the Gutenburg Revolution, Protestant books—particularly Luther's—were found in the most unlikely places, including Roman Catholic convents and monasteries. Behind those seemingly inpenetrable walls individuals were being transformed by the biblical injunction "The just shall live by faith" and other long-ignored truths of the New Testament. Many laywomen, too, welcomed the Protestant Reformation. Because of the Protestant emphasis on personalized faith, there was a corresponding emphasis on female literacy—a "conviction that women . . . should be able to read the Bible and other devotional literature."[103] This may have been a fulfilling alternative to the popular religious superstition that was so much a part of female spirituality in the Middle Ages.

This popular superstition was often a critical issue for women—especially laywomen—who were pressured to convert to Protestantism. Women, more than men, seemed to rely on prayer to the saints—particularly to Saint Margaret, "the patroness of women in childbirth," and Saint Anne, "the patroness of widows," who, like Saint Margaret, also protected women in childbirth or women who were suffering from menstrual problems.[104] Under Protestantism, however, dependence on the saints was denounced.

Pressure for Catholic laywomen to convert to Protestantism came in some instances from their husbands. Sister Jeanne de Jussie, a nun from the Order of St. Claire who lived in Geneva, recorded a number of instances of "good Catholic women" whose husbands had become Protestant "heretics." One woman allegedly died of a broken heart when she realized that her infant had been baptized by William Farel, the famous Genevan Reformer. Sister Jeanne described many of these women as "more than martyrs" because they had to endure physical and mental abuse from their husbands and from Protestant authorities. In one instance when three women refused to participate in the Reformed Easter service, they were locked together in a room only to escape and sneak away to a Catholic Mass. On other occasions Sister Jeanne claimed that it was the Catholic women who fought the most bravely to preserve artwork and relics that were being vandalized by the Protestants.[105]

During the mid-sixteenth century when Protestants were at war with Catholics in Switzerland, Catholic women joined their husbands in the battles. According to Sister Jeanne de Jussie:

> The wives of the Christians assembled, saying that if it happens that our husbands fight against those infidels, let us also make war and kill their heretic wives, so that the race may be exterminated. In this assembly of women there were a good seven hundred children of twelve to fifteen years of age, firmly decided to do a good deed with their mothers: the women carried stones in their laps, and most of the children carried little rapiers . . . others stones in their breast, hat and bonnet.[106]

Nuns During the Reformation

Virtually every aspect of church life was profoundly affected by the sudden emergence of the Protestant Reformation. Women in ministry were no exception. The medieval church had offered education and careers for women comparable to no other institution in society. Although monasticism had its obvious limitations, women in large numbers found fulfillment through its varied opportunities and lifestyles. By the sixteenth century, monasticism was rapidly declining, and with the advent of the Reformation, the institution was challenged as never before. It was viewed as corrupt, and monks and nuns were admonished to forsake its evil influence.

While many nuns such as Katherine von Bora willingly joined the Protestant cause, others wavered, unsure of what to do in the face of mounting pressures. But most clung tenaciously to their Catholic faith, stoically suffering the consequences. While the Protestants had no such organized tool of repression comparable to the Inquisition, they were not without their own means of harassing and brutalizing individuals and groups who did not quickly convert to the prescribed patterns of belief and action. Indeed, one of the unfortunate results of the Reformation was the often brutal displacement of nuns—the forced removal of them from their convents. In the words of Melanchthon, "The preachers scream, swear, and storm, and do everything in their power to rouse the hatred of the masses against the poor nuns; they openly say that, as words were of no avail, recourse should be had to force."[107]

In some instances the Reformers showed more charity than in others, but too often the end result was the same. In Zwickau, Germany, for example, the city council forced the nine elderly nuns of that town to sell their convent house and move into a boardinghouse, where they were put to work mending clothing. Although they had initially fought the move, they apparently conformed to the dictates of the council outwardly, fearing their punishment would be worse. A report to the city council stated that they were no longer following the rule of Saint Francis.[108]

Charitas Pirckheimer

One of the most interesting documents relating to Roman Catholic nuns during the Reformation is a memoir by Charitas Pirckheimer. Charitas was a German abbess who ruled a convent of St. Clara at Nurnberg during the turbulent decade following Luther's posting of his *Ninety-five Theses.* Unlike the nuns of Helfa a few centuries earlier, who were known for their mysticism, the nuns of St. Clara were known for their intellectual pursuits—so much so, that they were viewed with suspicion by their male monastic leaders. Indeed the Franciscan friars permitted Charitas to become abbess only under the condition that she discontinue her Latin correspondence with various intellectuals whose friendship she had enjoyed. Her brother denounced "those soft-footed men" who "have forbidden her to write Latin for the future," characterizing their actions as "roguery." But the love of learning was not stifled in the convent, and when Erasmus' New Testament appeared, the nuns avidly read it, and according to Charitas' brother, had more understanding of it than many scholarly men.[109]

Although Charitas was very close to her brother, she did not join him in his strong initial support of Luther. To the contrary, she deplored what was taking place in the church, and she strongly defended the role of women in monasticism against growing and virulent criticism. It was a very difficult time for nuns, as her account clearly illustrates:

> Many powerful and evil-minded persons came to see the friends they had in our cloister, and argued with them and told them of the new teaching, how the religious profession was a thing of evil and temptation in which it was not possible to keep holy, and that we were all of the devil. Some would take their children, sisters and relatives out of the cloister by force and by the help of admonitions and promises of which they doubtless would not have kept half. This arguing and disputing went on for a long time and was often accompanied by great anger and abuse. But since none of the nuns by God's grace was moved to go, the fault was laid on the Franciscans, and everyone said they encouraged us, so that it would be impossible to convince us of the new belief while we had them as preachers and confessors.[110]

The conflict was not resolved peacefully. Great pressure was put on Charitas to submit peacefully to the Reformers' insistence on her disbanding the convent in order to avoid bloodshed. This was meant not only for her own convent but also for many others, which, it was believed, would follow her example. The fear of bloodshed was real. The peasants' uprising was gaining momentum, and many were convinced that the nuns were easy targets for vengeful mobs. But more was at stake than safety. The new Protestant leaders were concerned about the spiritual well-being of the nuns as well, and if the nuns would not willingly listen to the followers of Luther, they would listen by force. Reformed preachers took the place of the Franciscan friars in the convent church. Despite this "spiritual poison," as Charitas described it, none of the nuns asked to leave. In other convents, however, the situation was different. Many of them disbanded for fear of being taken by force, and some of the nuns, with no other place to go, took refuge with Charitas. But even there they were not safe. In some instances family members brutally dragged young women out against their will.[111]

In the end it was Philip Melanchthon, not surprisingly, who helped bring about a peaceable solution. His presence was welcomed by Charitas. "I am glad to hear Melanchthon is coming," she wrote; "since I have heard he is an irreproachable, upright and justice-loving man, I do not suppose he can approve of what has been done here." He did not approve, and through his mediation, it was agreed that there would be one further effort to convince the nuns to leave the convent, and after that they would be left alone.[112]

Women of the Catholic Reformation

The name most closely associated with the Catholic Reformation is that of Ignatius of Loyola, the founder of the Society of Jesus, better known as the Jesuits. Ignatius has been criticized for his adamant refusal to found a female branch of the Society of Jesus, and sometimes his role is viewed as that of "fending off the attentions of these women, protecting his colleagues from their zealous desire to be associated too intimately with the Order."[113]

Ignatius, however, had a deep concern for women. It is true that his ministry was primarily to men, but with good reason. The Jesuits were highly visible and were the brunt of widespread criticism—some justified and some not. Ignatius was deeply concerned about the reputation of his society, and he was well aware that any involvement with women, even the founding of a female order, would be controversial. He continually warned his followers to avoid even the appearance of wrongdoing with the opposite sex. In a letter to Jesuits in Portugal, he wrote, "I would not enter upon spiritual conversations with women who are young or belong to the lower classes of the people, except in church or in places which are visible to all." But his fears also related to contact with upperclass women— particularly women who sought out Jesuits to be their confessors. Individual Jesuits, including the order's most illustrious missionary, Xavier, were on occasion accused of scandal involving women, and the House of St. Martha was said by some to be a Jesuit brothel.[114]

Yet, Ignatius' concern for women— particularly "fallen" women—was deeply felt and prompted him to donate money for the establishment of the House of St. Martha. Others before him had sought to establish convents where prostitutes were welcome if they were willing to devote their lives to service for God, but Ignatius wanted more of a "half-way" house where such women would stay until they were ready to go back into the world and live a moral life. Many of the prostitutes plying their trade were married, and it was his goal that they be reunited with their husbands, through the assistance of the religious house. Ignatius' chief concern was to reform prostitutes, not to fill up convents: "The unmarried women shall be quite free either to marry or to take the veil." According to Hugo Rahner, "the House of St. Martha flourished. Ignatius was proud of it. . . . At the end of 1543 there were already nearly eighty inmates; but in May 1545 there were only thirty-eight, for many had been sent forth, completely transformed, to lead respectable lives in the world."[115]

Women themselves were not entirely successful in founding religious orders during the Reformation period. Some sought to open the doors of the cloister and involve themselves in service to the poor and needy, but they confronted strong opposition from the church. Angela Merici initially received papal approval for her new order, the Ursulines, to minister in homes to women and children, but she and her nuns were later instructed to maintain full cloister. This was a lesson for other would-be founders of female religious orders. "The Daughters of Charity, founded by Vincent de Paul and Louise de Marillac, learned from this pattern and never became nuns." Instead, they carried out social services without formal vows and uniform dress. "Ironically, then," writes Denise Carmody, "the only religious women who could do active works of mercy were those who did not profess their religious status officially. So strong were the controls of the Catholic reform initiated at the Council of Trent in the sixteenth century that not until 1900 were nuns officially granted the right to an active life."[116]

Teresa of Avila

The best-known woman of the Roman Catholic Reformation was Teresa of Avila (1515–82), a Carmelite reformer and mystic. Like the beliefs of many other Spanish mystics, hers did not always conform to strict Catholic dogma, and, like so many others, she was viewed with deep suspicion by certain church officials. Even so, very shortly after her death her reputation for saintliness was elevated to the point that she was canonized.

Teresa had entered the convent of the Incarnation at the age of twenty and the following year took her vows as a Carmelite nun. Soon after this she became very ill, and, after she recovered, she credited St. Joseph with her miraculous healing. But although she was physically healed, she continued to struggle spiritually. Of her first ten years as a nun she wrote, "I went through a life of the greatest conflict. On the one hand, God called me; on the other, I followed the world." Throughout that time she had held herself up to an impossible standard. She felt so guilty after talking " 'even briefly with a visitor at the screen' (a barrier installed after the Council of Trent), she withdrew at once to her cell and 'lashed herself with the utmost cruelty.' " Another account tells how she whipped herself "until the walls of her cell dripped with gore." Her life changed suddenly after she read Augustine's *Confessions*. "When I started reading the *Confessions* it seemed to me that I was seeing my own self right there. When I got as far as his conversion and read how he heard that voice in the garden, it was just as if the Lord gave it to me, too."[117]

Following her conversion and more debilitating illnesses, Teresa began to experience ecstacies. These voices, visions, and levitations persisted during periods throughout her lifetime and contributed considerably to her reputation as a saint. Her first rapture came unexpectedly: "Having spent a day in prayer and begging the Lord to help me, I began the hymn [*Veni Creator*]; and while I was reciting it, a rapture came on me, so sudden that it snatched me out of myself.... It was the first time the Lord had given me the grace of raptures. I heard these words: 'Now I want you to talk no longer with men, but with angels.' "[118]

The admission of having visions and raptures was not entirely safe during the sixteenth century. The inquisitors eagerly sought out those they deemed to be heretics or possessed—some of whom resembled Teresa all too closely. Time had not yet forgotten the "notorious Magdalen of the Cross who, ten years before, had enthralled the royal family with her ecstacies and her reception of the stigmata before she was exposed."[119] Some of Teresa's friends believed that she was demon-possessed; they advised that she be exorcised, and her confessor instructed her to snap her fingers (apparently to bring her out of the trance) whenever she felt a rapture coming on. "Others advised her to spit."[120]

Unlike many visionaries, Teresa did not equate ecstatic experiences with sanctity. She believed that women were more prone to have visionary experiences, but warned that they should not seek them, lest they fall prey to "spiritual gluttony." She herself often viewed her raptures as "the recurrence of some troublesome disease, saying that she was praying to be delivered from them."[121]

Teresa's mysticism focused on communing with God through meditation. "Enter into yourself" was her motto, but her goal was not mere inward reflection, but bringing God inside oneself. Such deep communion, she believed, did not come automatically. After years of experimenting, she concluded that it could best be accomplished through four stages: "First the inner self must be stilled. Next comes concentration on spiritual meditation. The repose of the soul . . . and perfect union of the soul with God are the final stages. Its four degrees may be described as tranquillity, union, ecstasy and, finally, spiritual marriage."[122]

In her most well-known mystical trance, Teresa experienced her heart being pierced by a spear of divine love. Nevertheless, her mysticism had its practical side also. Loving God resulted in service for Him. She wrote, "Let everyone understand that real love of God does not consist in tear-shedding, nor in that sweetness and tenderness for which we usually long, just because they console us, but in serving God in justice, fortitude of soul and humility."[123]

Teresa's most enduring work was the reform and establishment of Carmelite houses all over Spain. She founded her first convent in Avila when she was in her mid-forties, after she had undergone an intense reli-gious experience. It was this experience that caused her to see the desperate need for reform within the church, and she believed that a reorganization and expansion of the Carmelites was the best way to accomplish this task. The Carmelites, like other Catholic religious orders, had deviated from their original purpose, and she sought to return the order to the austere and contemplative character that it had once known. So powerful was her appeal that she established fifteen additional houses in less than a twenty-year period, during which time she suffered two heart attacks.[124]

Like other Catholic women who sought to make changes in the church, Teresa met with strong opposition. Sega, the papal nuncio, came to Spain to investigate her activities and to make certain of her absolute allegiance to the church. The very fact that the religious houses needed reform reflected poorly on the church, and Sega was obviously threatened by Teresa's ministry. He described her as "a restless gadabout, disobedient, contumacious woman who promulgates pernicious doctrine under pretense of devotion." As to her reforming activities, he wrote, "She leaves her cloisters against the orders of her superiors contrary to the decrees of the Council of Trent. She is ambitious and teaches theology as if she were a doctor of the Church in spite of St. Paul's prohibition."[125]

Teresa's assessment of her work was quite different. She considered herself and her nuns to be in the very midst of the battle to rid the countryside of the "mischief and ravages those Lutherans had wrought in

France." Indeed, she wrote, "Had I a thousand lives, it seemed to me I would give them all to save a single one of the many souls which were going to perdition." Yet she recognized her handicap:

> Since I was only a woman, and a base one at that, . . . I resolved to do the little that was in me: namely, follow the evangelical precepts as fully as I could, and endeavor that those few nuns who were with me should do likewise, . . . dedicating ourselves to prayer for the preachers and learned men who are defending the Church.[126]

How did Teresa avoid torture and imprisonment after receiving such a reference from the pope's emissary? She hid. Her close associate, John of the Cross, was not so fortunate. He was confined in a dungeon for most of a year. But more than torture and imprisonment, Teresa feared that all her efforts for reform would be reversed by the Catholic authorities. In the end, however, the pope ruled in favor of Teresa by permitting her reformed convents to continue functioning.[127]

Teresa's commitment to God and to the reformation of the Catholic church is perhaps best summed up in a verse that she penned:

> Thine am I, I was born for thee,
> What wouldst thou, Master, make of
> me?
>
> Give me death or give me life
> Give health or give infirmity
>
> Give honor or give obliquy
> Give peace profound or daily strife,
> Weakness or strength add to my
> life;
> Yes, Lord, my answer still shall be
> What wilt Thou, Master, have of
> me?

> 'Tis Thou alone dost live in me.
> What wilt Thou I should do for
> thee?[128]

Jacoba Bartolini

Teresa was only one of many itinerant female "preachers" of the Catholic Reformation. Indeed, there were a number of them who enjoyed a wide reputation during the sixteenth century, but whose names have since become obscure. One such woman was Jacoba Bartolini. Her story has been preserved in the diary of the Portuguese priest Father da Camara:

> It was about the year 1544 that there arose in Italy a woman, a native of Bologna, who lived in the reputation of great spiritual gifts and holiness. After long exercise in the contemplative life, during which extraordinary things occurred, she withdrew to the mountains near Bologna, in order that, remote from the world she might give herself entirely to the life of perfection. There she converted many highway robbers, murderers, and other outcasts who came to her, and brought them to repentance, confession, and the Sacrament of the Altar, which was administered by some priests of irreproachable reputation who lived nearby for this purpose.[129]

This type of evangelistic ministry was in itself unique for a woman, but it is not the reason for her popularity. That was due largely to her claim of having "an open wound in her right side" from which blood flowed. This stigmatic condition outshone even that of the great Saint Francis, and according to Camara, "this wonder became so well known, that people flocked to see it."[130]

The story of Jacoba Bartolini illustrates the considerable religious influence that a woman was able to have during the Reformation period even though she was at the same time restricted by severe limitations. As was true during the Middle Ages, the source of a woman's power was usually her charismatic qualities, and the scope of her ministry was outside the institutionalized church. The security a woman was able to have depended heavily on her relationship with local clerics. In Jacoba's case, she was able to bolster the work of the nearby parishes. For women in sectarian movements, the situation was similar. They also depended on charismatic qualities to authenticate their public ministries. In Reformed circles, a woman's religious influence generally was more closely related to her social standing, and even then she confronted strict limitations.

What is significant about the Protestant Reformation in regard to women is that while there was a change in viewpoint toward women as wives and their worth as human beings, the theological perspective on their role in the church had changed very little from the perspective that pervaded the medieval Catholic church. The concept of the priesthood of believers raised the status of the laity in their direct responsibility to God, but it did not open the door for equality of men and women in the church. Women were excluded from leadership positions and office holding. Male clerics—were they Catholic, Reformed, or sectarian—held tenaciously to the traditional view that restricted their ministry.

A Century of Reaffirming Tradition

What did the Reformation era have to offer women in the church—women who desired meaningful ministry? On the spiritual level, it certainly was a period of time that offered women (like men) a fresh look at Scripture, with an emphasis on personal salvation through faith in Christ. But beyond the realm of personal faith, there was no significant place for women in religion. Public professional ministry was a male domain. Indeed, on that subject, tradition reigned. The Council of Trent reaffirmed tight restrictions on Catholic women who sought public ministry, and Protestants boldly condemned convent life—the only "professional" ministry that was available to women. Anabaptists permitted women to engage in charismatic ministries, but probably no more than medieval sectarian movements had.

Even the symbolism of womanhood suffered a reverse. In his book *The Woman Shall Conquer*, Don Sharkey laments "one of the most tragic events of history," which he defines as "the Protestant Revolt." It was then "that millions of people turned away from their heavenly Mother."[131]

It is true that the Mariology of the Middle Ages did not provide a realistic role model for women, but the deemphasis of the "heavenly Mother" does reflect the Reformation mindset.

Some would argue that the Protestants uplifted the view of woman as a human being. That may very well be true, but in doing so, they put woman "in her place." She would henceforth be regarded more highly for her domestic duties, but the stage was set for a spiritual climate that would discourage professional female ministry. Ministry would be redefined by the Reformers as marriage and motherhood. To be sure, women rose above their prescribed role. Through political, social, or personal prestige, they often wielded considerable power, but in religious matters their influence was achieved in spite of the Reformation mentality, certainly not because of it.

Chapter 6

Post-Reformation Sectarianism: Visionaries and "She-Preachers"

The seventeenth and eighteenth centuries saw many significant changes in religious life. The seventeenth had clearly demonstrated that the Reformation spirit could not be easily contained, and a continuing fragmentation of Christianity continued in the decades (and centuries) following the first generation of Reformers. The decentralization of Protestantism invited the proliferation of religious groups, and as the fervency of the established churches and sectarian movements waned, the stage was set for awakenings and revivals. While the vast majority of people during this period remained in the established churches, the fluidity of religious ideas offered an outlet for those who wanted more freedom in religious belief and activity. Among those so inclined were women, and it is during this period that significant numbers of women, for the first time in history, became involved in dissenting religious movements—many of which were viewed as radical and outside the sphere of respectability.

Here women were offered opportunities not available elsewhere in secular or religious life.

On the whole, however, the place of women in society and in the established churches changed little during the centuries following the Reformation. Although Elizabeth I of England had demonstrated how powerful and popular a female leader could be among her people, the attitudes toward women in general were slow to change. Elizabeth was succeeded by James I, and, according to Selma Williams, "The moment James had had the crown placed securely on his head, he gave notice that, in pointed contrast to Elizabeth, he would take every opportunity to trample women into permanent invisibility." He instituted harsher penalties for witchcraft, making the "crime" punishable by hanging. As a result, many times more such executions occurred during the early years of his reign than in the final years of Elizabeth's. To justify this slaughter, James reprinted *Daemonologie*, a tract he had written denouncing witchcraft as a pact with the Devil. He stated that witchcraft was particularly appealing to women because they were more susceptible to "the snares of the Devil as was ever well proved to be true by the Serpent's deceiving of Eve at the beginning." He concluded that there were twenty times as many female witches as there were male.[1]

Likewise, James I opposed efforts to upgrade female education, and when he was advised to have his daughter study Latin, he refused, claiming that "to make women learned and foxes tame had the same effect: to make them more cunning."[2]

This antifemale trend did not go unchallenged. When Joseph Swetnam published a tract in 1615, claiming that "women spring from the Devil" and entitled it *The Arraignment of Lewd, Idle, Froward, and Unconstant Women* (that being the short title), it was quickly answered by an angry woman who wrote a tract entitled *Esther hath hanged Haman; or, an answer to a lewd Pamphlet, entitled The Arraignment of Women. With the arraignment of lewd, idle, froward and unconstant men, and Husbands.* But despite such isolated attempts by women to defend their sex, post-Elizabethan English society continued to be very confining for women.[3]

The Church of England

The Church of England reflected this general attitude toward women in society. Indeed, the behavior of women in every aspect of their lives was closely monitored by the church. This is illustrated by a 1620 document disclosing that

the Bishop of London called together all his clergy about this town and told them he had express commandment from the King to will them to inveigh vehemently and bitterly in their sermons against the insolency of our women and their wearing of broad-brimmed hats, pointed doublets, their hair cut short or shorn, . . . adding withal that if pulpit admonitions will not reform them he would proceed by another course.[4]

Admonishing women to shun any appearance of worldliness could have been justified in spiritual terms, but there were other instances when women were flagrantly disregarded by church leaders. William Laud is an example. He was installed as archbishop of Canterbury in 1633, and, according to Selma Williams, he "lost no love or sympathy for women." He ignored the complaints of the pregnant Goody Taylor, who objected to the treacherous climb up the "lofty and bleak stairs" that was required to reach the elevated communion table. Even the support of some two dozen other women in the church failed to move the obstinate bishop, and women were forced to make the climb if they were to maintain their standing with God and with the church.[5]

Not surprisingly, active female involvement in the church, if not altogether banned, was generally viewed with contempt. Despite the lip service given to the "priesthood of the believers," the Reformers had not opened the doors of ministry to women. For the most part, they clung tenaciously to the prejudices that had become ingrained in society throughout the centuries. There were very few advocates of women in ministry—either among the Reformers or among the Anabaptists and other sectarians. This mind-set continued in the established state churches during the centuries following the Reformation. The Anglican church in England and the Lutheran and Reformed churches on the Continent remained closed to the idea of women in clerical ministry.

The seventeenth-century Anglican position relating to women in ministry is expressed by John Bewick in his work *An Antidote Against Lay-Preaching*, published in 1642. Although the book dealt with more than the issue of women in ministry, it was this issue that the author seemed most concerned about. In reference to the Joel 2 passage that speaks of daughters prophesying, Bewick wrote, "That kind of prophesying which consists in interpreting Scripture, thence deducing Doctrinall and Practicall conclusions for the Instruction of others, (I am sure) cannot bee meant in this place; because in that kind of prophesying the daughters of God have no part nor fellowship with the sons of God; for God hath excluded them."[6]

Lady Eleanor Davis

But despite such admonitions, the Church of England was not entirely free of "prophesying daughters." The country's most famous prophetess of this period was Lady Eleanor Davis, whose father was the Earl of Castlehaven. In 1625 she testified that she "heard early in the morning a Voice from Heaven, speaking as through a trumpet these words: 'There is nineteen years and a half to the Judgment Day.'" For twenty-five years she attracted attention to her prophesies through writing and speaking. Her commentary on *Daniel*, which prophesied a dire end for Archbishop Laud and Charles I, was one of her most controversial writings, and it resulted in a prison term and a heavy fine. She was a colorful character, described variously as insane, hysterical, and eccentric, and she did not limit her protests to written and oral prophesies. One of her more notorious acts was her unlawful entry into the Lichfield Cathedral, during which time she desecrated the alter hangings and then defiantly situated herself on the episcopal throne, "declaring she was the Primate of all England."[7]

Despite her reputation for the bizarre, Lady Eleanor published some forty widely circulated tracts and had multitudes of followers, including some in high places. One of those was Sir Edward Dering, a respected political figure; another was Peter du Moulin, an Anglican churchman, who at the time of her death spoke reverently of her as having been "favoured with some beam of divine knowledge of future things." Her family honored her at death with an epitaph that credited her with having "in a woman's body, a man's spirit."[8]

Jane Hawkins and Grace Cary

Another woman in the Church of England who created a controversy over her claims of divine guidance was Jane Hawkins. And although she was "a poor woman (and she but a pedlar)," she, too, had an impressive following. It was in 1629 that Hawkins, "having fallen into a rapture or ecstacy," began prophesying the doom of the Church of England. Known as the "rhyming preacheress," she attracted a crowd of some two hundred people who came to her bedside and marveled at her prophetic rhyming, which continued to flow out in a steady stream for three days and nights. Among those who witnessed this was the Reverend Tokey, his curate, and a "scholar," who copied thousands of verses that came through her revelations. The Bishop, however, was not similarly affected by her prophecies—perhaps in part because they predicted his own fall from office. He took action against Tokey and his curate and turned Hawkins over to the civil authorities. Later Tokey, no doubt under pressure to be reinstated, submitted a written statement alleging Hawkins was an impostor and that he himself had been unwise in supporting her.[9]

Grace Cary, another controversial woman, made the king himself her target, following him around and calling out to him to institute religious reform or God would pour out His wrath on the church. Keith Thomas has suggested that the educational and religious restrictions placed on women during this period may have prompted women to engage in prophetic ministries. It was the only avenue of public expression open to them.[10]

Mary Penington

Yet, as visible as they were, the Lady Eleanors and Grace Carys were not typical of women in the post-Reformation era. Women, like men, struggled with doctrinal issues and how to live the Christian life. Their search for God was often a painful one that often led them outside the boundaries of the sanctioned spirituality of the Church of England. One woman who illustrates the struggle for a meaningful faith is Mary Penington (1616–1682). As a young girl growing up in the Church of England, she had an unusual interest in spiritual matters. In fact, she later recalled an occasion during her childhood when she became so concerned about her prayer life after her maid read her a sermon entitled "Pray Continually," that she became very distraught. "When she had done reading, and all were gone out of the chamber, I shut the door, and in great distress I flung myself on the bed, and oppressedly cried out: 'Lord, what is prayer?' "[11]

Some time after this, while listening to a minister at a neighboring church, Mary related how her search to know God progressed: "When I came there, he prayed fervently (he was one called a Puritan) and with great power. Then I felt that was true prayer." Yet she herself was unable to pray, and that led to further agony: "I mourned solely because I kneeled down morning after morning, and night after night, and had not a word to say. My distress was so great, that I feared I should perish in the night, because I had not prayed." Mary continued going to the neighboring church and "refused to hear the priest" of her own parish. Soon she was able to pray, but was accused by her family of praying "with the spirit," rejecting "godly men's prayers," and of being "proud and schismatic."[12]

Following her marriage to a spiritually minded young man, Mary's life continued to stabilize, but her husband's death two years later left her alone with an infant daughter to raise in the faith. "I refused to have her sprinkled, which brought great reproach upon me; so I became a byword and a hissing among the people of my own rank in the world." Family members pleaded with her, and ministers were "sent to persuade" her. Harassed on every side, Mary's faith began to falter. "I was weary of prayers, and such like exercises, finding no peace therefrom; nor could I lift up my hands without doubting, nor call God Father. In this state, and for this cause, I gave over all manner of religious exercises in my family and in private, with much grief, for my delight was in being exercised about religion." She became involved in "many excesses and vanities; as foolish mirth, carding, dancing, singing, and frequenting of music meetings." Yet, "in the midst of all this," she confessed, "my heart was constantly sad."[13]

It was after her second marriage to a man in a "disconsolate condition" that Mary once again sought God. "And oh! the groans and cries in secret that were raised in me, that I might be visited of the Lord and come to the knowledge of His way." She and her husband later joined the Quakers, and it was among these people that she found true spiritual happiness. Speaking of her spiritual condition, she wrote: "Sweet is this state, though low; for in it I receive my daily bread, and enjoy that which He handeth forth continually; and live not, but as He breaketh the breath of life upon me every moment."[14]

The martyrdom of Catholic women under Cromwell's reign in 1649. From Myles O'Reilly et al., *Lives of the Irish Martyrs and Confessors* (New York: James Sheehy, 1881), 283.

Roman Catholicism

During the post-Reformation period, after the pope and Roman Catholicism had been officially rejected in England, Catholics—both men and women—suffered persecution at the hands of Protestants. Under Cromwell's reign particularly, Catholics were hounded from their homes, tortured, imprisoned, and in some instances put to death.

The attitudes of Roman Catholics toward women were in many ways similar to those of Anglicans. One of the reasons many Roman Catholic churchmen were fearful of female influence on religion was that they, like their medieval predecessors, believed women were easy prey to heresy, witchcraft, and demonism. "Women are easy to all persuasions," wrote Sebastian Michaelis, a seventeenth-century Frenchman, "because of the natural simplicity of their sex," causing them to be easy prey to the devil. Valderama, a Spanish Jesuit, agreed, claiming that women were "weaker, more curious, and more ignorant than men."[15]

Bendetta Carlini

One of the women who was accused of being "easy prey to the devil" was Bendetta Carlini, who became the first abbess of the Convent of the Mother of God in Pescia, Italy, in 1619. Her story has recently been told by Judith C. Brown in *Immodest Acts: The Life of a Lesbian Nun in Renaissance Italy*. This account is based largely on the record of ecclesiastical investigations into her life and visionary claims. The first investigation related to her ecstatic experiences, which resulted in a wedding ceremony (with Jesus taking her as his bride) performed in the convent in front of all the nuns. She was initially removed as the abbess, but following the investigation she was reinstated. A second investigation some three years later, however, found her guilty. The testimony in this instance came mainly from a nun who had shared a cell with Bendetta. She told of how she and Bendetta had indulged in a sexual relationship for three years—though she had been assured by Bendetta that it was her guardian angel Splenditello living within Bendetta who

was actually performing the sexual acts. Convinced that she was demon-possessed or deceived by the Devil, the investigators sentenced her to a life of solitary confinement within the convent—a prison sentence that lasted until her death, thirty-five years later.[16]

Mary Ward

Despite such accusations of demonic influence and such instances of indiscretion, there was a strong inclination among Catholic women to break out of their cloistered cells and become involved in the religious life of the community and in the affairs of the world. An example is Mary Ward, whose vision it was to give all English girls a good Catholic education. Not surprisingly, such a dream was not well received in Protestant England during the early seventeenth century. After being harassed by civil authorities, she fled to the Continent where she traveled extensively, establishing convents and schools for female education. But among Catholics there she encountered opposition as strong as she had met in England. Many Catholic clerics were highly suspicious of convent education that sought to prepare girls for a life in the world. She "was accused of wishing women to rival men in the ministry" whereas she had "in fact deliberately made the point that women could not and should not preach or administer the sacraments."[17]

Sor Juana Ines de la Cruz

Another woman who rose above the characterization of her sex and who faced strong opposition in the area of education was Sor Juana Ines de la Cruz (1651–95), of Mexico. As a teenager she joined a convent of Barefoot Carmelites but left after only a few months because she was unable to endure the schedule that allowed so little time for study. Two years later she entered the Convent of Saint Jerome, where she had ample time for study—particularly theology. For more than two decades she pored over theological and literary works, accumulating a library of some four thousand volumes—probably the largest in the New World—in Greek, Latin, Spanish, and Portuguese. She wrote theological poems and critiques of theological positions that she found untenable, but her major contribution was her translation of Jerome's works from Latin into Spanish.[18]

For all her dedication and effort, Sor Juana received nothing but scorn and opposition from her male counterparts. Following the publication of *Crisis of a Sermon*—a harmless little work that defended Augustine, Chrysostom, and Aquinas against the attacks of Antonio Vieyra, a Portuguese Jesuit—she was admonished by her bishop to turn away from her studies: "You have wasted much time in the study of philosophers and poets; now is the time to perfect your means and improve your occupation." Her reply, in the words of Anne Fremantle, "is one of the glories of early Latin-American Literature, and one of the most remarkable pieces of writing ever produced by a woman." She began by giving her own testimony:

From the first ray of the light of reason that reached me, my inclination to letters was so strong, that no censure from others, of which I had plenty, nor any personal outside repressions, nor any considerations of my own were enough to prevent my following the natural impulse God put into me. . . . I took orders because . . . the one consideration . . . was . . . to refuse any occupation that interfered with the liberty of my studies.[19]

From there she went on to make a noble defense of her rights as a female and of an individual's freedom to think independently: "Am I not as free to dissent from Vieyra's opinion as he is to dissent from mine? Is my understanding any less free than his? Is it a tenet of our holy Faith that we must believe with our eyes shut?"[20]

In recalling the struggles she encountered with church officials, she later wrote, "There was a rouse of emulations and persecutions, so many that I cannot even count. . . . I have been persecuted for my love of wisdom and literature. . . . I have been persecuted through hate and malevolence." When church authorities sought to curtail her studies, she defended her role and denounced the church's prohibition on women's studying theology.[21] At the age of forty, Sor Juana turned away from her theological studies. Her decision was not prompted by her opponents, but rather by a deep mystical experience. In her effort to attain a oneness with God, she apparently could not justify something that gave her so much personal pleasure. She gave away her library and spent her few remaining years in contemplation. Very soon after that she died of the plague that struck the convent of Saint Jerome.[22]

Madame Jeanne Guyon

A far more influential Roman Catholic woman during this period was the French mystic Madame Jeanne Guyon (1648–1717). Although faithful to the Roman Catholic Church, she, too, was condemned by church officials. She had a large following, however, and, like other Catholic mystics of this period, she had a significant influence on Protestants, among them John Wesley—especially in his early years. Of her Wesley wrote, "We may search many centuries before we find another woman who was such a pattern of true holiness."[23] She, along with François Fenelon and Miguel de Molinos, was a leading spirit in a seventeenth-century movement known as Quietism, which emphasized a passive contemplation over and above an active religion of works.

Soon after her marriage as a teenager to a wealthy middle-aged nobleman, she realized that true happiness could be found only in devotion to God. It was then that she turned her back on Parisian society life and began reading devotional books and helping the needy. After the death of her husband, she dedicated herself entirely to Christian ministry. Because she had two small children, it was a difficult decision—one that was prompted by a priest who admonished her to "do what our Lord has made you know he desired of you," after she had said her confession. She questioned his advice:

> I answered him, "My Father, I am a widow, who has little children four and six years of age. What else could God require of me but to rear them?" He said to me, "I known nothing of it. You know whether God had made you recognize that he wished something of you. If it is so, there is nothing which should hinder you from doing his will. One must leave one's children to do it."[24]

With that advice, she began her itinerant ministry through the towns of France and Switzerland sharing her insights on how to live a holy life.[25] Guyon's ministry was largely one of personal evangelism, challenging people to live a holy life by placing their faith in Christ. "She did not appear as a *preacher*," wrote her biographer. "Her efforts were private; and entirely consistent with the sense of decorum which adorns the female character."[26] She reached out to all segments of society, and the response was gratifying. Indeed, her ministry gives a glimpse of the deep piety among certain Catholics during the post-Reformation period. She was overwhelmed by the spiritual hunger she found in the town of Thonon:

> I have never in my life had so much consolation as in seeing in that little town so many good souls who vied with each other in giving themselves to God with their whole heart. There were young girls of twelve and thirteen years of age, who worked all day in silence in order to converse with God, and who had acquired a great habit of it. As they were poor girls, they joined in couples; and those who knew how to read, read out something to those who could not read. It was revival of the innocence of the early Christians.[27]

Another individual who was seeking spiritual consolation was an impoverished "laundress," the mother of five children, who by her own testimony "had formerly been without religion, and was a wicked person." Her husband "seemed to have nothing left mentally but his angry dispositions, and nothing left physically but just strength enough in his unparalyzed arm to beat his suffering wife." Despite her travail, she became "rich in faith"—so much so that many of the townspeople "were willing to receive instruction from her," believing "God . . . had taught her inwardly by the Holy Ghost." Her teaching and her extemporaneous prayers, however, soon attracted the attention of the church authorities. "They visited her; and, as her method of worship was somewhat out of Church order, they reproved her, and told her it was very bold in her to practice prayer in the manner she did. They said it was the business of priests to pray, and not of women. They commanded her to leave off prayer, in the methods in which she practiced it, and threatened her if she did not." Church officials continued to harass her, but she held steadfast in her faith.[28]

Guyon's ministry extended to the more educated in society as well. When she was ill and needed to consult a physician (a friar specializing in medicine), she did not let the opportunity pass without witnessing to her faith:

> I entered into conversation with him on the subject of religion. He acknowledged that he had known something of the power of religion, but that the religious life had been stifled by the multitude of his occupations. I endeavored to make him comprehend, that the love of God is not inconsistent with the duties of humanity. . . . The conversation was greatly blessed to him. And he became afterwards a decided Christian.[29]

Later she related, "This same worthy friar had occasion to bring to me some of his companions, and God took them all for himself."[30] Guyon, likewise, sought opportunities to conduct personal evangelism among the nobility. In Paris she "formed a little association of ladies of rank, among whom were the Duchess of Beauvilliers, the Duchess of Bethune, and the Countess of Guiche, with whom she met from time to time for religious objects." Through her dedication to the Lord, "some of the most distinguished ladies of the capital of France" began "recognizing the truths of religion, and rejoicing in the experimental power of piety."[31]

Nor did Guyon overlook the convents or monasteries in her evangelism. She was the first woman ever to enter the monastery of the Grande Chartreuse, previously off limits to the female sex. There "she proclaimed, not authoritatively or in any way inconsistent with female modesty and propriety, the indispensable necessity, not only of justification by faith, but of faith as the foundation of the whole inward Christian life." Her ministry at nunneries was equally significant. On one occasion she met with a nun contemplating suicide because of her inability to "obtain reconciliation with God." The solution to her problem, Guyon was convinced, was simply the gospel of Christ.

> I endeavoured to explain to her that . . . she must no longer rely upon observances, or trust to personal merits, but must trust in Christ and resign herself to Him alone. God was pleased to bless these efforts. . . . Submitting herself to God through Christ, and willing to leave all things in His hands

215

in faith, she entered at once into the peace of Paradise. She was so much changed, that she became the admiration of the Religious Community. God's presence was with her continually, and her spirit and power of prayer were wonderful.[32]

Besides her work of personal evangelism, Guyon wrote some forty books, including a seven-hundred-page autobiography and a twenty-volume commentary on Scripture. Most of her writing was done at night, though she claimed she did not actually write the volumes, but rather that God wrote them through her. In her book *Spiritual Torrents* she taught the concept of the silence of the soul. "To her the Torrents are souls that issue from God and have no repose until they have returned and lost themselves in Him, never again to find themselves. But they lose neither their nature nor their reality, only their former condition of separation."[33]

Much of Jeanne Guyon's autobiography tells of her sufferings while she was traveling around preaching holiness. These accounts include a variety of illnesses and close escapes from death, some of which are bizarre stories of self-inflicted pain. She put stones in her shoes; rolled in prickly, stinging nettles; sucked on bitter herbs; and pulled healthy teeth out of her mouth—all in an effort to achieve holiness. She was convinced that in her complete identification with God, she herself had actually ceased to exist—that her actions were really God's actions and that it was impossible for her to do anything but God's will. Although she herself practiced extreme asceticism, her efforts toward others were directed at

relieving their suffering. Countless healing miracles were associated with her ministry.[34]

It was her traveling preaching and healing ministry that brought her fame, but church leaders begrudged her increasing popularity. Her books were burned, her reputation was assailed, and finally she was arrested and sent to prison. The last two years of her seven-year imprisonment were spent in solitary confinement in the Bastille. But even following this long period of injustice, humiliation, and suffering, her response reflected her Quietist faith: "I found myself, I say, in a happiness equal to that of the Blessed . . . ; nothing here below affected me; and neither at present do I see anything in heaven or in earth which can trouble me as regards myself."[35]

English Puritans

The Puritans, like their Anglican cousins, strongly opposed public ministries for women, except perhaps in unusual circumstances that indicated God's special anointing. According to one Puritan divine, "it was permissible if women were 'extraordinarily called thereunto, and have certain signs of their calling.'" Women's inferior efforts to preach, according to a another Puritan writer brought shame on the ministerial profession—their participation making it "vile and despised."[36]

Nor should women seek to play the role of theologian. They were to rely entirely on their husbands in such matters. Such deep thought could render her mentally useless—so was the theory of Governor Winthrop of the Massachusetts Bay Colony. He used the example of Mistress Hopkins, whose insanity he blamed on the fact that "she spent too much time in reading and writing."[37] Writing about this same situation, Thomas Parker made the following assertion:

> Her husband, being very loving and tender of her, was loath to grieve her; but he saw his error, when it was too late. For if she had attended her household affairs and such things as belong to women, and not gone out of her way and calling to meddle in such things as are proper to men, whose minds are strong, etc., she had kept her wits, and might have improved them usefully and honorably in the place God had set her.[38]

One of the strongest attacks against women in public ministry came from a Thomas Edwards, a London Puritan minister whose tract entitled "Gangraena" was published in 1646. In this tract he describes a women's meeting that was attended by another minister: "In brief, there was such laughing, confusion, and disorder at the meeting, that the minister professed he never saw the like: he told me the confusions, horror, and disorder which he saw and heard there, was inexpressible, and so he left them, fearing lest the candles might have gone out and they have fallen to kill or mischief one another."[39]

Although women were not permitted to preach or play a significant roll in Puritan churches, they certainly were not excluded from Puritan religious life itself. Margo Todd wrote:

> The importance of women ... in Puritan theories of domestic conduct, as well as the exaltation of marriage

and the household, obviously belies the thesis that Protestantism reduced the significance of women when it banned veneration of the Virgin and the saints (many of whom were female) and gave the father a semi-priestly role upon which the wife was dependent. ... The Puritans viewed men and women as spiritually equal, and equality was to be manifest in the marriage relationship.[40]

This "equality," however, did not grant the women equal authority, as is illustrated in an excerpt from a Puritan sermon:

> The husband is also to understand, that as God created the woman, not of the head, and so equall in authoritie with her husband: so also he created her not of Adam's foote that she should be trodden downe and despised, but he took her out of the ribbe, that she might walke joyntly with him, under the conduct and government of her head.[41]

Some historians have concluded that because the Puritans exalted the role of wife and mother and permitted women freedom of conscience along with formal education, they should be credited to a large extent for the faint signs of female liberation that were seen in the post-Reformation era. While other historians would rightly argue that the Renaissance humanists were the originators of modern egalitarian ideas, it was in many respects the Puritans who turned theory into practice and thus influenced society as a whole. The more radical sects that permitted women equality in ministry had little influence on society in general as regards women, and it can be argued that what influence they did have had a negative effect.

Nonconformists and English Civil War Sects

If there were tight controls on women among Anglicans, Catholics, and Puritans, the same cannot be said for the sectarian movements (the radical wing of Puritanism) of the English Civil War era. This growing free church movement was comprised of numerous sects that began to appear on the scene in the late sixteenth and early seventeenth centuries. According to Keith Thomas, "They were known by a variety of names—Brownists, Independents, Baptists, Millenarians, Familists, Quakers, Seekers, Ranters—and they represented a wide diversity of theological opinion." They did, however, have some very important commonalities: "They believed in a pure Church, they made spiritual regeneration a condition of membership and insisted upon separation from a national church which contained ungodly elements."[42] And, like earlier sectarian groups, they entertained a much more open view of women in ministry.

The active role of women in sects in the mid-sixteenth century corresponds to a more active role women were taking in society in general. According to David Latt, "The events of the Civil Wars and the experiences of the Court in France during the Interregnum produced a liberalizing effect on attitudes about women's active participation in the important areas of public life." It was during this time that women started gaining recognition for literary achievements, though they continued to be ridiculed by a large and chauvinistic element in society that regarded them as "silly, pretentious, and misguided when they sought a more active or a more accomplished place for themselves in the world."[43]

English and Colonial Separatists

While there seems to have been an upsurge in female involvement in religious activities in the 1640s and 1650s, there is evidence that women were actively involved from the very early years of English nonconformity. The fear of religious schisms prompted London Aldermen and common councillors to send a petition to the House of Commons in 1646 reporting that in one parish alone there were "eleven private congregations and conventicles who deserted the parish churches and [had] tradesmen and women preachers." Within weeks, several women preachers were taken into custody and others were ordered to appear before the Committee of Examinations of the House of Commons.[44]

This was just one of many factors that disturbed Anglican churchmen. In 1568, an Anglican bishop claimed that a particular Separatist church in London was made up largely of women—and not only that, but lower-class women. In fact, there were a number of Separatist congregations where women made up a majority of the membership and some that were founded by women. An example is that of Dorothy Hazzard, the wife of an Anglican priest; she left her husband's parish church to help establish a Separatist congregation that met in her home until the rapidly growing group (which numbered over one hundred and fifty in three years) was forced to move on.

Such foundational work for women was generally accepted among the Separatists, but there were limitations to what a woman could do— particularly after the congregation was well established. Many Separatist congregations denied women a vote in church affairs and had strict regulations on women's ministries.[45]

Due to intense persecution in England, groups of Separatists fled to Holland, where it appears there was more leniency toward the ministry of women. Among the Separatists in Holland were the followers of Robert Browne, and in these circles there appeared to be a spirit of openness toward the ministry of women. The *Brownists' Conventicle* (1641) states:

And in this our thanksgiving let us remember all the blessed pastors and professors, whether at Amsterdam or elsewhere; as also for our she-fellow labourers, our holy and good blessed women, who are not only able to talk on any text, but search into the deep sense of the Scripture, and preach both in their families and elsewhere."[46]

While there was no official position among Separatists relating to the role of women in the church, the view of John Robinson (1575–1625), a Puritan pastor who fled to Holland with other Separatists to avoid persecution, is representative of the nonconformist mind-set. In a treatise justifying his separatist position, he wrote what might have been taken as a very radical statement: "And hereupon also it followeth necessarily, that one faithful man, yea or woman either, may as truly, and effectually loose, and bind, both in heaven, and earth, as all the ministers in the world." This "feminist" stance was quickly qualified, however, by specific restrictions on the female sex. "And for women, they are debarred by their sex, as from ordinary prophesying, so from any other dealing wherein they take authority over the man. I Cor. 14:34-35. I Tim. 2:11-12."[47] But women were clearly not barred entirely from speaking or sharing in the worship. In the view of Robinson:

They may make profession of faith or confession of sin, say Amen to the church's prayer, sing Psalms vocally, accuse a brother of sin, witness an accusation, or defend themselves being accused, yea in a case extraordinary, namely where no man will, I see not but a woman may reprove the Church, rather than suffer it to go on in apparent wickedness and communicate with it therein.[48]

Puritans and Separatists who emigrated to America and became known as Congregationalists tended to be more restrictive toward women than Robinson was. Separatists generally sought to avoid any hint of "radicalism" that might be associated with certain of the sects. That generally included women preachers and in many instances women's participation in church government. Some critics of Congregationalism were quick to point out the inconsistency of claiming a congregational form of government while denying a large segment (often a majority) of the congregation any voice in decision-making. They charged that such a system would inevitably lead to female participation and would not prevent female control.[49]

Richard Mather (1596–1669), a prominent Congregationalist in New England, sought to counter the critics by taking a hard line against women's participation in church affairs:

The rule is express and plain that women ought not to speak in the Church, but to be in silence. . . . And therefore they ought not to vote in Church matters, besides voting imports some kind of government, and authority and power: now it is not government and authority, but subjection and obedience which belongs unto women . . . and so is the practice of women amongst us.[50]

Yet there were occasional women "preachers" among the Separatists— though they apparently never served in established congregations. There were accounts of women preachers in the Netherlands as well as in the Massachusetts Bay Colony. Indeed, Robert Baillie (1599–1662) charged that certain of the Separatists "permitted women to be leaders to their whole Churches, and chief pastors in Church actions of the highest nature." As to specific examples, he cited only two: "We have good witness that a woman was the founder of Mr. Simpson's Church at Rotterdam; that a woman, and that none of the best, led away Mr. Cotton, and with him great numbers of the best note in New England, towards the vilest errours."[51]

Anne Hutchinson

The woman who allegedly led John Cotton and many others into "the vilest errours," was Anne Hutchinson (1591–1643), the most well-known woman "preacher" in colonial New England. Anne's controversial reputation preceded her to New England. In England she was known for her claims of personal revelations—"that she had never had any great thing done about her but it was revealed to her beforehand"—and for her outspoken criticism of certain Puritan ministers. It is not surprising that such traits were viewed with deep suspicion upon her arrival in the New World.[52] In fact, so much suspicion surrounded her that her church membership was delayed. She was not admitted to the church at Boston until she had been brought before a hearing conducted by the governor and other colonial fathers to examine her and determine whether she was fit to be numbered among the elect.[53]

In New England, Anne found a more open and tolerant spirit toward women—perhaps because, unlike Europe, where there were considerably more women than men, the ratio of men to women in New England was three to two, and the colonial fathers were anxious for more women to immigrate. Among other things,

wife beating was not allowed, nor were men permitted to treat their wives as servants; and both proscriptions were enforced on pain of jail or heavy fine. In church-related matters, too, women found greater liberties in the New World. Just before Anne's arrival, John Cotton and his supporters waged a successful battle against the long tradition requiring women to wear veils."[54]

Such liberties only encouraged Anne to exercise her gifts of teaching and leadership freely and openly and to take an active part in the community.

For all the commotion Anne created in Boston in the year after her arrival, one would think that she had sought to take over the pulpit in the

Boston church. In actuality, her activities were very mild—particularly by twentieth-century standards. Her ministry involved other women, and it began very slowly. Her first meetings were held once a week with about a half a dozen women. It was a social time as much as a time for learning practical household tips and for exchanging childcare advice, but even more it was a time to focus on spiritual matters and particularly on the Sunday sermon. Anne was a student of Scripture and she took it upon herself to explain the sermon in her own terms to the women in attendance. Such meetings were not uncommon among the Puritans—except when led by a woman.[55]

So popular were these meetings that soon the large numbers of women who attended could no longer fit in Anne's living room, and she had to hold extra meetings to accommodate them all. Her critics charged that she frequently had as many as sixty women in attendance. Almost immediately these gatherings were seen as a threat to male authority, but not all men held this view. In fact, her own pastor, John Cotton, whose sermons were the subject of her lectures, initially praised her:

> Shee did much good in our Town, in womans meeting at Childbirth- Travells, wherein shee was not onley skillful and helpfull, but readily fell into good discourse with the women about their spiritual estates. . . . By which means many of the women (and their husbands) were . . . brought to enquire more seriously after the Lord Jesus Christ."[56]

Although Anne's activities on the surface might have appeared to be noncontroversial, there was an element of radicalism involved that simply could not be tolerated by the colonial church fathers. Anne was a thinker who was not averse to criticizing other ministers and challenging other women to think for themselves. This was viewed as highly dangerous. According to the Reverend Thomas Weld, Anne's influence was similar to that of Eve's in the Garden of Eden. In his eyes, it was her meetings that "began to raise sedition amongst us, to the endangering of the commonwealth." The process began with the women, "the weaker to resist," who were "more flexible, tender, and ready to yield." That was serious enough, but worse still was that "as by an Eve" they might "catch their husbands also, which often proved too true amongst us."[57]

The fear that Anne would "catch their husbands" was a real concern for the Boston church leaders, not simply because women in general, by virtue of their female nature, were more prone to deceive, but because Anne in particular was spreading "heresy." In many ways she was an unlikely candidate for heresy. Unlike some Quaker women who would later honor Boston with their presence, she did not abandon her husband and family and come alone into the enemy camp without any political and religious connections. Anne was the wife of the highly respected and well-to-do William Hutchinson and was the mother of fifteen children, ten of whom came to the New World with their parents. In England, she had been an ardent supporter of John Cotton, sometimes hearing several of his sermons and lectures each week. Although his views were suspect in England, he had quickly become the leading religious figure in Boston. Nor was Anne without important colonial political connections. One of her most loyal followers was Henry Vane, who served for a short time as governor of the Bay Colony.[58]

Yet, despite her well-placed connections, Anne was banished from the Bay colony. Governor John Winthrop matter-of-factly summarized the account in his *Journal:*

> The court also sent for Mrs. Hutchinson, and charged her with divers matters, as her keeping two public lectures every week in her house, whereto sixty or eighty persons did usually resort, and for reproaching most of the ministers . . . for not preaching a covenant of free grace, and that they had not the seal of the spirit, nor were able ministers of the New Testament; which were clearly proved against her, though she sought to shift it off. And, after many speeches to and fro, at last she was so full as she could not contain, but vented her revelations; amongst which this was one, that she had it revealed to her, that she should come into New England, and should here be persecuted, and that God would ruin us and our posterity, and the whole state, for the same. So the court proceeded and banished her; but, because it was winter, they committed her to a private house, where she was well provided, and her own friends and the elders permitted to go to her, but none else.[59]

How could this middle-aged mother of fifteen be brought to trial, charged with subverting the townspeople, and banished from the colony? Was it because she was a woman—indeed a feminist—challenging the sex roles in society and in

the church? There is little evidence of this, despite what some modern feminists scholars would contend. It is true that she was charged with having "rather been a husband than a wife, a preacher than a hearer, and a magistrate than a subject" and that she was told her behavior was not "fitting of your sex."[60]

But the real case against her had little to do with her sex. The drama that held Boston spellbound during the fall of 1637 was not a plot against feminism but an open battle against "heresy," and the leading character who took her place on center stage before forty-nine inquisitors just happened to be a woman. The fact that she was a woman was used against her, but the central issues were doctrinal. And it is important to note that men were not immune from the very same charges. The Reverend John Cotton's theology had come into question since his arrival in Boston, and the Reverend John Wheelwright (Anne's brother-in-law) was disenfranchised and then banished from the colony before Anne received her sentence. His crime, like Anne's, was that he challenged the doctrine of original sin and criticized other colonial ministers of preaching a covenant of works rather than a covenant of grace.[61]

Anne's "heresy" was not particularly innovative, but according to Selma Williams,

> she offered her own version of the Renaissance-inspired Covenant of Grace: each person's actions to be guided by his or her own conscience and inner morality; each person to communicate directly with God, without need of outside supervision; life in the here-and-now to be stressed, afterlife deemphasized.[62]

Such "antinomianism" was not surprisingly a threat to the Boston colonial establishment. And in Anne's case, this covenant-of-grace theology was bolstered by her own revelations. She was accused of having "often boasted of the guidance of God's spirit and that her revelations are as true as the Scriptures."[63] How could such revelations be tolerated? "If they be allowed in one thing [they] must be admitted a rule in all things," admonished Governor Winthrop, "for they being above reason and Scripture, they are not subject to controll."[64] It was clear that Anne was a threat to any sort of religious uniformity in the Bay Colony.

Perhaps even more threatening than her theology and personal revelations was her popularity. According to Selma Williams, after only two years in Massachusetts, she "had the strongest constituency of any leader in the whole colony, and her Boston disciples were beginning to spread the word to the other thirteen towns." Men as well as women, in large numbers, were captivated by her. Her followers were known as "the Hutchinsonian party or simply the "Hutchinsonians."[65]

These factors were all taken into consideration when Anne was summoned to court in the fall of 1637 and when she was brought before the church in the spring of the following year and publicly excommunicated. That this was a case of sex discrimination is a difficult position to sustain, and such a position to a degree denies the actual threat Anne was to the establishment apart from her sex. She was a very influential religious leader who was challenging the authority of Scripture and, maybe more

importantly to the colonial Boston churchmen, the very core of the Puritan Calvinistic covenant theology.

Following her banishment, Anne and her family moved first to Rhode Island and then, after the death of her husband in 1642, to Long Island. To the relief of the Boston establishment, Anne left no cohesive movement behind, but she was not soon forgotten. Her detractors kept her name alive as a warning to others who might seek to follow the same course that she had followed. They went to great lengths to blacken her name. Following a painful miscarriage that she underwent while she was still under house arrest, a minister wrote that she had actually brought forth "30 monstrous births or thereabouts, at once, some of them bigger, some lesser, some of one shape, some of another; few of any perfect shape, none at all of them (as farre as I could ever learne) of humane shape."[66]

If the specter of giving birth to monsters was not warning enough, the news that reached Boston in September of 1643 certainly was. Anne and her children had been killed by Indians in their home on Long Island. The Reverend Thomas Weld had a ready and fitting explanation for the tragedy:

> I never heard that the Indians in those parts did ever before this, commit the like outrage upon any one family, or families, and therefore God's hand is the more apparently seene herein, to pick out this woeful woman, to make her and those belonging to her, an unheard of heavy example. . . . Thus the Lord heard our groanes to heaven, and freed us from this great and sore affliction."[67]

Although Hutchinson's "heresy" was not an issue of women's rights per se, there clearly was an element of sexism involved in the lengthy controversy that was perpetuated even after her death. The stories of monster births were reminiscent of accusations made against other female "heretics" in history who were maliciously linked with witchcraft or demonic activity. Writes Donald Mathews, "The Antinomian debate was not, therefore, just a disagreement about theology, but a dispute concerning a social order maintained by strict rules of behavior associated with sex."[68]

Baptists

Another group of nonconformists were the English Baptists, who were sometimes difficult to distinguish from other English Separatists. John Smyth, "founder of the first identifiable Baptist church of modern history," recognized the place of women in church ministry. In 1609, he wrote, "the Church hath power to Elect, approve & ordeyne her owne Elders, also: to elect, approve, & ordeyne her owne Deacons both men & women."[69]

Women preachers were not uncommon among the early Baptist congregations. They were unordained lay preachers, as were many of their male counterparts. Antonia Fraser writes that "women probably first began to preach in Holland in the 1630s in the Baptist churches, whose congregations had always included a large number of their sex."[70]

According to some contemporary observers, the Baptists, more than certain other Separatist sects, were open to the ministry of women. One such preacher was a Mrs. Attaway, (who is at times referred to as a Brownist) a "lace woman," whom a contemporary Puritan critic referred to as "the mistress of all the she-preachers in Coleman St."—that being the most prominent General Baptist Church in London. Thomas Lamb was the pastor and he apparently gave his blessing to her Tuesday afternoon meetings, which she began conducting in 1645. She was a vivacious woman, attracting large crowds who were frequently derided by sober churchmen for "laughing" and "lightness." Regarding one of her meetings, it was reported that "there came a world of people, to the number of a thousand."[71]

More commonly women preached in their own homes. Anne Hempstall, accused of preaching to "bibbing Gossips," opened her home in Holborn, as did Mary Bilbrowe, the wife of a bricklayer from St. Giles-in-the-Fields.[72] But despite such opportunities for ministry, "it is clear that even among the Baptists," writes Constance Coltman, "the number of women preachers was very small."[73]

Opposition to female preachers often consisted of ridicule and scorn, but that alone was generally not enough to silence them. Further action was frequently taken, and the first step usually involved reporting the indiscretion to authorities. A report given to the Right Hon. Lord Conway, dated July 25, 1653, illustrates how offended certain individuals were with women in public ministry:

> Here is starting up an audacious virago (or feminine tub-preacher) who

last Sunday held forth about two hours together within our late Queen's Mass Chapel at Somerset House in the Strand, and has done so there and elsewhere, divers Sabbath days of late, who claps her Bible and thumps the pulpit cushion with almost as much confidence (I should have said impudence) as honest Hugh Peters himself.[74]

The most significant role that women played in Baptist circles was in their foundational work in the development of churches. Many Baptist churches would not have survived without the active participation of women in the initial stages. Two well-known examples of such churches are John Smyth's Baptist church, which sought religious freedom in the Netherlands, and the Baptist church at Bedford, where John Bunyan later served. The latter was started in 1650 by eight women and four men.[75]

Fifth Monarchists

Another movement that was known for permitting women to have an active role in ministry was the radical millenarian group, known as the Fifth Monarchists. This group appeared in England in the mid-sixteenth century. This was a small but highly visible sect that expected to usher in the reign of Christ as the fifth monarchy (the previous four having been the Assyrian, Persian, Macedonian, and Roman empires). Under the rule of Christ, this new kingdom would eliminate class and sex barriers. Women would enjoy complete equality. This hope for the imminent future attracted women to the movement and encouraged them

to seek equality within the movement. They were supported in this effort by John Rogers, the founder and leader of the movement. He argued that "in the Church all the members, even sisters as well as brothers, have a right to all Church-affairs; and may not only implicitly but explicitly vote and offer or object, etc." In defending this position, Rogers used not only biblical arguments, but also personal observations. He pointed to the "excellencies and abilities of some women surpassing men for piety and judgment," qualities that to him were justification enough for women "to have equal liberty with them in Church-affairs."[76]

Despite Rogers' strong support of women's equality in the church and their "public liberty" to preach, women among the Fifth Monarchists, like women in other sects, faced opposition. Some, claiming divine revelation, publicly prophesied, but generally full equality in leadership positions was denied them.[77]

One woman who did attain a place of recognition among the Fifth Monarchists was Mary Cary who wrote tracts in support of the movement. Though she referred to herself as a "minister," she apparently did not have a congregation. She was rather a prophetess and practical theologian of sorts for the movement. She gave specific prophetic utterances as well as advice for everyday living. Among other things she denounced those in the movement who followed "fickle, nice, phantastical and foolish" fashions, making them "unsuitable to their high calling! as if they had not things of a higher nature to minde." She was quick to speak her mind even when she did not agree with male leaders of the movement. Like Katherine Zell and other women of the Reformation, she spoke out for religious toleration. According to B. S. Capp, she "wished to tolerate papists and atheists, but this was condemned by Rogers, and by Canne."[78]

Another Fifth Monarchist woman to gain prominence was Anna Trapnel, "the most celebrated visionary" in the movement. Indeed, she believed that education and normal means of learning were unnecessary because "Christ's Scholars . . . are perfected with learning from above." On one occasion in 1654, she "fell into a trance lasting many days, during which time she uttered a torrent of divinely-inspired verse, prophesying that the Lord would 'batter' Cromwell and his friends." Her utterances did not sit well with the religious establishment, and she was arrested for subversive activities. Like Mary Cary, she advocated toleration of other religious groups, and went so far as to speak to joint meetings held with Quakers, though the leaders of the respective movements shunned any such ecumenism.[79]

French Prophets

Another sect that appeared in France in the seventeenth and eighteenth centuries was known as the Cevenols or Camisards. The term *French Prophets* was the designation given to them after they fled from France to England because of persecution. They were characterized by "enthusiasm" and prophetic gifts, and the basis for ministry was the Spirit's empowering. Women thus conducted ministries alongside men.[80]

Early in his ministry John Wesley had an interesting experience with a female member of this sect. He wrote in his *Journal* that he

went to a house where was one of those commonly called French prophets. After a time, she came in. She seemed about four or five and twenty, of an agreeable speech and behaviour. She asked, Why we came? I said, "to try the spirits, whether they be of God." Presently after she leaned back in her chair, and seemed to have strong workings in her breast, with deep sighings intermixed. Her head, and hands, and, by turns, every part of her body, seemed also to be in a kind of convulsive motion. This continued about ten minutes, till (at six) she began to speak (though the workings, sighings and contortions of her body, were so intermixed with her words, that she seldom spoke half a sentence together) with a clear, strong voice, "Father, thy will, thy will be done. Thus saith the Lord, If any of you that is a father, his child ask bread, will he give him a stone? If he ask a fish, will he give him a scorpion? Ask bread of me, my children and I will give you bread. I will not, will not give you a scorpion. By this judge of what ye shall now hear."[81]

In her role as a prophetess, the young woman spoke "as in the person of God, and mostly in scripture words." She prophesied the imminent return of Christ and challenged her listeners to evangelize the world in preparation for his return. "She added, with many enforcements, that we must watch and pray, and take up our cross, and be still before God." Some who were with Wesley were impressed with her, convinced that "she spoke by the spirit of God."

Wesley himself, however, was skeptical, believing "the motion might be either hysterical or artificial. And the same words, any person of a good understanding and well versed in the scriptures might have spoken." His final judgment was to "let the matter alone; knowing this, that 'if it be not of God, it will come to nought.' "[82]

Quakers

Among the Civil War sects, it was the Quakers, or the Society of Friends, that most obviously demonstrated egalitarianism between the sexes. In fact, in the very early years rumors spread that this new sect was made up entirely of women. As with the other nonconformist groups, religion was personal and intense, and an individual's relationship or communion with God—in this case the "inner light"—was not restricted by sex barriers.[83]

George Fox, the founder of the Quakers, strongly defended the full involvement of women in ministry. In a doctrinal tract entitled "The Woman Learning in Silence, or the Mystery of the Woman's Subjection to her Husband," he clearly spelled out his views on female ministry, making frequent reference to the various Old and New Testament passages pertaining to women. Despite the title, which would indicate a restrictive role for women, Fox challenged those who would limit a woman's ministry. To those who emphasized the apostle Paul's restrictions, he responded by quoting the prophecy in the book of Joel that was repeated in the book of Acts and adding:

Here the prophet Joel was not against the daughters prophesying, nor the apostles were not against it, but said, "despise not prophesying" and saith the Lord ... "Touch not mine anointed, and do my prophets no harm." So you that persecute the daughters on whom the spirit of the Lord is poured, and believe them not, you are them that despise prophesying, and so have broken the apostles' command. ... So be ashamed for ever, and let all your mouths be stopped for ever, that despise the spirit of prophecy in the daughters, and do cast them into prison, and do hinder the women-labourers in the gospel.[84]

Fox's first convert was Elizabeth Hooton, a Baptist preacher prior to her "convincement." Her life vividly illustrates the courageous spirit among Quaker women. As a Quaker she believed all men and women were equal before God, and thus she did not hesitate to challenge a priest on doctrinal matters or to refuse to kneel before King Charles II. Such behavior was not looked upon lightly, and on several occasions she was beaten and imprisoned in England, but she still refused to curtail her activities. Following the visit of her fellow Quaker Mary Fisher to Boston, during which time she was publicly whipped, Hooton herself booked passage. The Boston authorities refused to allow the ship to dock, so Hooton and her companion were taken to Virginia. "From there the two resolute women, advanced in years and unaccustomed to the perils of the wilderness, proceeded to walk toward New England." They eventually were able to secure passage on a small boat, and arrived in Boston, only to be "banished a two days' journey into the wilderness escorted by armed men on horseback."[85]

With no other alternative, Hooton returned to England, denouncing the Boston religious establishment—the "Independents who fled from the bishops formerly, which have behaved themselves worse than the bishops did to them by many degries." But she was so determined to make her mark on the Bay Colony that she personally petitioned the king for a land permit in Boston so that she could build a home and thus have a Quaker in residence right in the middle of the enemy camp. Although the king granted her request, the Boston authorities paid no heed, and arrested her as soon as she arrived. She was once again beaten severely and banished from the town. To her, it was just another trial of her faith to endure: "So they put me on a horse & carried me into ye wildernesse many miles, where was many wild beasts both beares & wolves & many deep waters where I waded through . . . but ye Lord delivered me."[86] She later journeyed to Jamaica, where she served as a missionary.

Another Quaker woman who displayed the courage of her convictions in the face of Bostonian bigotry was Mary Dyer. She and her husband immigrated to the Bay Colony in the 1630s, at which time they were considered fully orthodox and were received into membership in the Boston church. Soon after that, however, Mary became acquainted with Anne Hutchinson, and from that time on her life was never the same. She was described by Governor Winthrop as "a very proper and fair woman . . . notoriously infected with Mrs. Hutch-

inson's errors, and very censorious and troublesome (she being a very proud spirit, and much addicted to revelations)." So loyal was she to Anne Hutchinson, that on the day Anne was excommunicated from the Boston church, Mary made a public protest by leaving her seat and walking out of the church with her.[87]

It was while she was visiting in England in 1652 that she joined with the Quakers. She returned to Massachusetts a few years later publicly professing her faith, despite laws forbidding Quakers entry into the colony. On two occasions she was banished from the colony, but she returned each time and continued to testify of her faith publicly. In 1659 she was convicted by the General Court in Boston and sentenced to be hanged along with two Quaker men. The magistrates, however, could not bring themselves to hang a woman— even in Boston—and, after receiving an appeal from her family, they stayed her sentence. But they waited until the very last moment to do so: "She stept up the Ladder and had her Coats tied about her feet, and the Rope put about her neck, with her face covered, and as the Hangman was ready to turn her off, they cryed out to stop, for she was reprieved."[88]

Most individuals would have greeted such a stay of sentence with at least a sigh of relief, but not Mary Dyer: "She was not forward to come down, but stood still saying she was there willing to suffer as her Brethren did; unlesse they would null their wicked Law, she had no freedom to accept their reprieve."[89]

Mary was not given the choice of rejecting the reprieve. She was brought down from the gallows and forced to leave the town. But she was determined that the "wicked law" be repealed, and so she returned to Boston the following spring—presumably believing that sacrificing her life would indeed change the law. Again she was sentenced to die, and on May 31, 1660, she was hanged in Boston. An observation made by General Atherton, one of her strongest opponents, was a fitting epitaph: "Mary Dyer did hang as a flag for others to take example by."[90]

Mary had believed that her death would create such an outcry among the people of New England that the magistrates would be forced to repeal their "wicked law." Her death did stir up controversy, but not enough to prevent the beatings of Elizabeth Hooten and her companion in Boston not long after Mary's death and certainly not enough to stave off the impending "witch" executions that would send shock waves through Salem only three decades later.

The courage of the early Quaker women was a significant factor in determining their place within the movement. But the opposition they faced, particularly from outside the organization, indicated a need to articulate the biblical basis for an active female role in ministry.

It was Margaret Fell (1614–1702) who did more than any Quaker woman to raise the status of women in that organization. When she was first introduced to the Friends, she was in her late thirties, the mother of nine children, and the wife of Judge Thomas Fell, the patriarch of Swarthmore Hall. She and eight of her children soon joined the Friends. Thomas remained outside the movement, but he did not prevent his wife

from opening their spacious home for Quaker meetings and refugee lodging.[91] Following her husband's death, Margaret became more active in the movement. Her persuasive writing combined with her own personal example had a profound influence on the society. She traveled widely among Quaker groups and obtained a personal audience with Charles II, seeking to persuade him to demonstrate greater leniency with Quakers who were being persecuted. She herself was brought to trial along with Fox for conducting religious meetings at Swarthmore Hall and for refusing to take the Oath of Allegiance. She was found guilty and was imprisoned for four years; two years after her release she was arrested and tried again.[92]

A fascinating report by Margaret Fell of a court trial in 1664 tells of the terrible prison conditions the Quakers were subjected to. As Fell was stepping down from the witness stand, the judge recalled her and questioned her about a letter she had previously written to him. In that letter she had complained, "Your prisons . . . are bad and [it] rains in, and are not fit for people to lie in." She acknowledged the complaint, and then made a bold impromptu challenge to the judge: "If you were to lie in it yourselves you would think it hard, but your mind is only in cruelty to commit others, as William Kirby here hath done, who hath committed ten of our friends, and put them in a cold room where there was nothing but bare boards to lie on."[93]

In 1669, after eleven years of widowhood, Margaret married George Fox. It was a marriage of common interest but little togetherness. "They lived missionary lives, preaching and traveling, were more often separated than not, and were frequently, though never together, in prison."[94] She was ten years older than he and lived for more than another decade after he died.

The most enduring legacy that Fell left to the Quakers was her writing. She was an outstanding apologist for the movement during the early years, and her policy positions became an integral part of Quaker belief. In 1660, she wrote a "Declaration and an Information," that officially set forth the Quaker position on pacifism. She also responded in print to critics of Quakerism, seeking to show that the movement was not a bizarre or seditious sect that was dangerous to society. But the writing that is most often associated with her is *Women's Speaking Justified by the Scriptures*, first published in 1666. Here again her influence on Quaker belief was enormous. Fox himself had written against restricting women in ministry a decade earlier, but he "had not fully developed the argument in favor of women preaching; that remained for Margaret Fell to do."[95]

Fell's pamphlet, which is fewer than twenty pages in length, is packed full of Scripture references from Genesis to Revelation relating to women in ministry. If there is any theme that is carried through her argument justifying women's speaking, it is that the "Spirit is poured upon all flesh, both Sons and Daughters." This was the Magna Carta for Quaker women—the biblical promise that women were equal to men in witness through the power and authority of the indwelling Spirit—and

Fell was quick to take the offensive against the "dark priests, that are so mad against women's speaking." For her there was no room for accommodation. The opposition to women in ministry came from nowhere other than hell itself:

> But all this opposing and gain-saying of women's speaking, hath arisen out of the bottomless pit, and the spirit of darkness that hath spoken for these many hundred years together in this night of apostacy, since the revelations have ceased and been hid, and so that spirit hath limited and bound all up within its bond and compass, and so would suffer none to speak, but such as that spirit of darkness, approved of, man or woman.[96]

Among the many passages that Margaret quoted to defend the female role in spiritual matters was Genesis 21. Here she emphasized God's command to Abraham: "In all that Sarah hath said to thee, hearken to her voice." What Sarah had to say to Abraham, Fell argued, was in the realm of spiritual matters, and this she maintained should be seen as a natural way for God to instruct his people.[97]

As much as Margaret Fell argued for the right of women to preach and speak at public meetings, such activity involved only a small percentage of Quaker women. But another activity—attending women's meetings—did involve all the women and was almost as controversial as preaching. Despite the fact that these women were involved in the traditional female activities involving deeds of charity, the very fact that they were meeting without the supervision of a man drew heavy criticism. Fox rebuked his critics (including fellow

VVomens   Speaking   *355*

Juſtified, Proved and Allowed of by the

SCRIPTURES,

All ſuch as ſpeak by the Spirit and Power of the

LORD IESUS,

And how WOMEN were the firſt that preached
the Tidings of the Reſurrection of JESuS,
and were ſent by CHRIST'S Own
Command, before He aſcended
to the Father, John
20. 17.

---

*And it ſhall come to paſs, in the laſt dayes, ſaith the Lord, I
will pour out of my Spirit upon all Pleſh; your Sons and Daughters ſhall Propheſie,* Acts 2. 27. Joel 2.28.

*It is written in the Prophets, They ſhall be all taught of God,
ſaith Chriſt,* John 6.45.

*And all thy Children ſhall be taught of the Lord, and great ſhall
be the Peace of thy Children,* Iſa. 54. 13.

*And they ſhall teach no more every man his Neighbour, and every
man his Brother, ſaying, Know the Lord; for they ſhall all
know me, from the leaſt to the greateſt of them, ſaith the Lord.*
J:r. 31. 34.

London, Printed in the Year, 1667.

The Title Page of Margaret Fell's Defense of
Women in Ministry, *Women's Speaking Justified*
(London, 1667).

Quakers): "And now, you that stumble at women's meetings, had not your women many vain meetings before they were convinced, and you were not then offended at them, when they met to satisfy the flesh. . . . And why should they not now meet in their conversion, in the Lord's power and spirit, to do his business. . . ?"[98]

Fell's writings and concerns extended far beyond the women's issue. She felt a personal responsibility to keep the movement pure, and this

231

concern deepened after Fox's death. During the final years of the seventeenth century she was enveloped in a controversy over the legalism that had penetrated the Society of Friends. She denounced the inroads of this "silly poor gospel." She lamented that the quarterly meetings were no longer a time for people "to be admonished and instructed in the truth," but rather had turned into a forum for "private persons to take upon them to make orders, and say this must be done and the other must not be done." "Away with these whimsical narrow imaginations," she wrote, "and let the Spirit of God which he hath given us lead us and guide us: and let us stand fast in that liberty wherewith Christ hath made us free."[99]

Few segments of society have faced more intense religious persecution than did Quaker women of the seventeenth century. Their struggle to live peaceably in a bigoted society was continually frustrated by the two marks that condemned them—their sectarianism and their sex. Women who dared to preach were not only criticized and reproved with Bible verses but were also slandered, and this slander was often riveted with sexual slurs. At one time when a complaint that two women had been preaching was brought before the mayor of Cambridge, England, in 1653, he ordered the women to appear before him. "He asked their names [and] their husbands' names. They told him: they had no husband but Jesus Christ and [that] he sent them. Upon this the Mayor grew angry, called them whores and issued his warrant to the constable to whip them at the Market-Cross till the blood ran down their bodies," an order that was forthwith carried out.[100]

This kind of sexism, however, was not directed only to Quaker women. Palela Volkman has found in her research that women who joined any of the sects in the late seventeenth century were more likely than men to be viewed as highly emotional, immoral, or even insane.[101]

It was to be expected that there would be opposition to women in ministry from outside the Society of Friends and other sects. But there was opposition from within as well. According to Keith Thomas, the effort to make the woman's role an equal one met with "serious opposition from within the Society of Friends itself. The Women's Meetings developed only slowly and even at the beginning of the eighteenth century women did not really enjoy completely equal status. . . ."[102]

Charismatic Phenomena

One of the strong objections to sectarianism in the post-Reformation era was the *charismata* and emotional fervor so often attached to it. Such behavior and activity resulted in ridicule as much as it did in amazement. One Suzannah Pearson allegedly attempted to bring a deceased man back to life. Jane Holmes was said to have some sort of religious fever that turned her into "a wild eyrie spirit, which . . . kicked against reproof, and would not come to judgment." Another, Sarah Wight, allegedly fasted for fifty-three days. Still others, like Anna Trapnel, "were gifted with an almost endless capacity for the composition of ecstatic religious verse."[103]

Were women of this period more prone to ecstatic religious experiences than men? It would be difficult to make such a determination, but it is clear from the record of history that charismatic religion was not exclusively a woman's domain. Men also reported visions and trances, and, like women, used such experiences to authenticate their ministry. But women generally received more attention. Critics emphasized their ecstasies to discredit them in ministry or conversely to discredit ecstatic religion.

American Pietism and Revivalism

The attitude toward women on the American scene by the time of the First Great Awakening had changed considerably since the seventeenth century when Anne Hutchinson and Quaker women were banished from the Bay Colony and the cause of Mistress Hopkins' insanity was judged to be her interest in intellectual subjects. Cotton Mather, an eighteenth-century Puritan divine, represents this change in thinking. He made a point of counteracting sexism in the church and society. He was certainly no feminist, but he accorded far more respect to women than did most of his Puritan forebears. He lamented that "whole Volumes have been written, to disgrace the Sex," and thus part of his mission was to correct that falsehood and to teach women how they "may recover [their] Impaired Reputations." One such work was his *Ornaments for the Daughters of Zion*, in which he wrote, "If any Men are so wicked (and some Sects of men have been so) as to deny your being rational Creatures, the best Means to confute them, will be by proving your selves religious ones."[104]

Not only did Mather lament that volumes had been written against women, but also that the contributions of women had been virtually ignored. "He explored the theme of women's invisibility centuries before it was recognized as a problem for historians." In a booklet entitled *Bethiah*, he featured the "People, who make no Noise at all in the World; People hardly Known to be in the World; Persons of the Female Sex." Recognition of women was also demonstrated in his preaching—particularly in funeral sermons eulogizing women. It was partly due to his vantage point as a minister that Mather so highly respected women. He could not overlook the fact, as perhaps other ministers had, that the majority of his most faithful parishioners were women. He warned single women that "it were better to have no Husband, than to have such a Buzzard as could be caught by any Cassandras." Yet, his position on marriage and ministry was very traditional.[105]

It is in that sense that his views had an impact on American revivalism. Women would be seen as a necessary ingredient for revival, but their presence—though not invisible—would remain behind the scenes. There were exceptions, however, when women were permitted to have a more visible public ministry—particularly when they were perceived to have divine sanction. An example is the case of Mary Reed of New Hampshire, who in 1742 claimed, along with others, to see visions. Nicholas Gilman, the local minister, acknowledged the spiritual validity of the experiences by adding "a word of Exhortation to the People" after Reed had "declared in Publick the close of Her last Vision."[106]

Jonathan and Sarah Edwards

The influence of Cotton Mather and others paved the way for Jonathan Edwards and other revivalists of the First Great Awakening who were conscious of the indispensible role women played in community-wide evangelistic efforts. No doubt because of this factor, revivalism like sectarianism, generally offered women a more meaningful role than did the established churches. Like his Puritan forebears, Jonathan Edwards found no place for women in a public preaching or teaching ministry. Yet he did seem more open to the idea of women's expressing themselves on spiritual and theological issues than many of his New England predecessors had. This can be seen in the ministry of Sarah Edwards, his wife. Although Sarah did not aspire to a ministry role beyond that of pastor's wife, her role in the Great Awakening has been characterized as "hardly inferior to that occupied by her husband."[107] Indeed, she had a profound influence on her husband that tempered his fear of religious ecstasy. "Mrs Edwards was a mystic devotee, and it was her religious experience which convinced her husband against his will that intimate communion with the Divine could possibly overpower the human body."[108]

Sarah Edwards had been inclined toward spiritual values since her childhood. When she was thirteen, Edwards, who would wait several years to marry her, already recognized the depth of her faith. He wrote that God

> comes to her and fills her mind with exceeding sweet delight, and that she hardly cares for anything, except to meditate on him. . . . She is of a wonderful sweetness, calmness and universal benevolence of mind; especially after this Great God has manifested himself to her mind. She will sometimes go about from place to place, singing sweetly; and seems to be always full of joy and pleasure; . . . She loves to be alone, walking in the fields and groves, and seems to have some one invisible always conversing with her."[109]

Like most revivalists, Edwards found that the majority of converts were female. Many of them were in their teens or even younger. In fact, on one occasion he related the story of a four-year-old girl's conversion. She went into a closet where she pleaded with God for salvation: "she continued exceedingly crying, and wreathing her body to and fro, like one in anguish of spirit . . . till at length she suddenly ceased crying and began to smile. . . . From this time there appeared a very remarkable abiding change in the child."[110]

In his pastoral and revival ministry, Edwards made no distinction between men and women and their involvement in personal evangelism. Indeed, he urged women to speak boldly of their faith:

> 'Tis beautiful in private Christians, though they are women and children, to be bold in professing the faith of Christ, and in the practice of all religion, and in owning God's hand in the work of his power and grace, without any fear of men, though they should be

reproached as fools and madmen, and frowned upon by great men, and cast off by parents and all the world. But for private Christians, women and others, to instruct, rebuke and exhort, with a like sort of boldness as becomes a minister when preaching, is not beautiful.[111]

Dinah Hardenbergh

Among the Reformed Pietists in the Middle Colonies were some women who played an active role—perhaps most notably Dinah Hardenbergh (1725–1807). She was first married to John Frelinghuysen, a minister who, like his well-known father, Theodore, served in the Raritan Valley. John died only a few years after they were married, and she then married a young student (thirteen years her junior) who had come to study under her late husband. "Both husband and wife were forceful leaders in the church, sharing piety and learning. They supported each other in the work of the ministry. Between her husband's morning and afternoon services, Dinah would gather with the women to further expound the texts and elaborate on matters of doctrine."[112]

One of Dinah's priorities in the ministry was to be an example in 'sanctification." She corresponded regularly with people concerning spiritual matters, and she kept a spiritual diary that strengthened her own spiritual life and helped her minister more effectively to others. Her diary reflects the depth of pietist spirituality and describes her own experience of sanctification:

It was the beginning of the year 1747. Midnight had passed; and I continued in earnest wrestlings, and drew near with a renewed dedication of myself to God, yielding myself unreservedly to Him and His ways and His service and His people. It was my inmost desire that I might receive larger measures of the renewing grace of the Holy Ghost— that my old and sinful nature might be more fully broken, the depravity of my heart subdued and the precious image of the Lord Jesus be more fully transferred to and impressed upon me, and all things became more and more new.[113]

In her later years, Dinah's ministry extended far beyond that of women's work. Her counsel was eagerly sought by ministers. "She wrote to them humbly, yet as a bishop in her concern for the church. . . . She was a pastor to pastors."[114]

The Wesleyan Revival

The evangelical revival in England that corresponded with the First Great Awakening in the Colonies gave birth to a "sectarian" movement that resembled in some ways the earlier Civil War sects. Although early Methodism was loyal to the Church of England, it focused on the individual's personal relationship with God and sent out its own itinerant preachers to unify the movement. Women played a vital part in organizing the movement on a grassroots level, particularly as class organizers and leaders, and as time passed their ministry became more and more public and official. Yet the influence of women in general in Wesleyanism was behind the scenes and was far greater than their positions of leadership would indicate.

235

Susanna Wesley

The first woman who had a major impact on the movement was, of course, Susanna Wesley, the mother of John and Charles. She left a profound spiritual influence on her children. Yet, she was outside the Wesleyan movement, and, in fact, had chosen as a young woman to turn away from the nonconformist teachings of her parents. Indeed, she was a remarkably independent young woman. "Before she was thirteen years of age she had carefully sifted the tenets of her father's belief. She had weighed them in the balance against the doctrines of the Established Church and had decided in favor of the Church."[115]

Susanna Wesley Prior to Her Marriage to the Reverend Samuel Wesley. From *John Wesley the Methodist: A Plain Account of His Life and Work* by a Methodist Preacher (New York: Methodist Book Concern, 1903), 17.

Susanna's proclivity for independent thinking did not subside with her marriage to Samuel Wesley. With a spirit of independence like hers, he had turned away from the views of his father, who was a Dissenting minister, but that, it seems, was where their similarities ended. Susanna was an aggressive, organized, and strong-willed woman who was patient with her children and tolerant of other people's views. Samuel, on the other hand, lacked that iron will, had difficulty getting along with people, was inept in money management and business affairs, and was often stubborn and intolerant in his interpersonal relationships. This last trait manifested itself in his parish and the community as well as in the home. As an Anglican priest, Samuel continually encountered difficulties with his parishioners. He "was a strict disciplinarian where his parishioners were concerned. He minced no words in his preaching, and tact was never one of his virtues." It is no exaggeration to say that his presence was deeply resented in the community. He and his family were harassed by his own parishioners. "They burned his flax crop, taunted the Wesley children, pried the hinges off the rectory doors. They stabbed his cows so that they gave no milk and once even tried to cut off the legs of the house dog." During the local elections of 1705, the situation became even worse. The Wesley home was surrounded by angry armed townspeople. Soon after that Samuel was arrested for failure to pay a debt to one of his parishioners and was confined to debtors prison.[116]

Even before this humiliating incident, however, Samuel had been away from his parish for an extended period of time. His departure was occasioned by a family dispute—specifically a political disagreement between him and Susanna. Susanna, who viewed the Stuarts as the only legitimate line of royalty, considered William of Orange a usurper of the throne. This personal political conviction suddenly became ensnarled with the issue of wifely submission when Susanna refused one evening to say "Amen" to her husband's prayer for King William III. In Samuel's mind, his wife had overstepped her bounds—a defiance that required drastic action. "We must part," he demanded, "for if we have two Kings, we must have two beds."[117]

Susanna later recalled the incident. After calling her to his study, "he immediately kneeled down and imprecated the divine vengeance upon himself and all his posterity if ever he touched me more or came into a bed with me before I had begged God's pardon and his, for not saying amen to the prayer for the King." Following that Samuel left home, and after that Susanna wrote a letter expressing her concern for the children who had been abandoned by their father, but confessed her true feelings about the situation: "I am more easy in the thoughts of parting because I think we are not likely to live happily together." Furthermore, she was firmly convinced that the fault lay with him not herself: "I have unsuccessfully represented to him the unlawfulness and unreasonableness of his Oath; that the Man in that case has no more power over his own body than the Woman over hers; that since I am willing to let him quietly enjoy his opinions, he ought

not to deprive me of my little liberty of conscience."[118]

Samuel returned home after the death of King William III. The political difference that had separated them had been removed, and it was during that period of reconciliation that John Wesley was conceived. The practical and philosophical differences between them, however, continued throughout their married life. One very significant disagreement came years later when John had written to them expressing his desire to become ordained and get involved in the ministry. Samuel advised him to do further study first. Susanna strongly disagreed. "Mr. Wesley differs with me, and would engage you, I believe, in critical learning. . . . I earnestly pray God avert that great evil from you of engaging in trifling studies to the neglect of such as are absolutely necessary. I dare advise nothing; God Almighty direct and bless you."[119]

Susanna's influence went far beyond her family and the home. In later years, John referred to her as "a preacher of righteousness"—and for good reason. He quoted a letter she had written to Samuel when he was away during the winter of 1711–12. While she recognized that because she was a woman and "also mistress of a large family . . . , the superior charge of souls" was his responsibility, yet in his absence she felt obligated to serve as a spiritual guide. Initially her involvement was confined to her own family and the children in her neighborhood, but that quickly changed—though not through a concerted effort on her part: "Other people's coming and joining with us was merely accidental. One lad told his parents: They first desired to be admitted; then others that heard of it, begged leave also: So our company increased to about thirty; and it seldom exceeded forty last winter." Her initial passivity, however, turned into a zealous passion to affect spiritual growth among the people who had sought her out. And what about the sex barriers? "Though I am not a man, nor a Minister, yet if my heart were sincerely devoted to God, and I was inspired with a true zeal for his glory, I might do somewhat more than I do."[120]

Still Susanna, aware of a woman's place, kept the meetings confined to her home, but she could not prevent the spontaneous growth that followed. "With those few neighbours that then came to me, I discoursed more freely and affectionately. I chose the best and most awakening sermons we have. And I spent somewhat more time with them in such exercises, without being careful about the success of my undertaking. Since this, our company increased every night; for I dare deny none that ask admittance." This defensive tone was apparently necessary. As a woman, she had to make it clear that she was not overtly seeking a congregation to listen to her renditions of "awakening sermons." Growth continued to the point where she could say: "Last Sunday I believe we had above two hundred. And yet many went away, for want of room to stand."[121]

Perhaps it is not surprising that Samuel questioned his wife's activities. He certainly had never experienced such popularity among his parishioners. At any rate, Susanna felt obliged to answer his concerns for his own reputation with strong convictions of her own:

I cannot conceive why any should reflect upon you, because your wife endeavours to draw people to church, and to restrain them from profaning the Lord's day, by reading to them, and other persuasions. For my part, I value no censure upon this account. . . . As to its looking particular, I grant it does. And so does almost any thing that is serious, or that may in any way advance the glory of God, or the salvation of souls.[122]

Yet, she had her own reservations "because of [her] sex." "I doubt if it is proper for me to present the prayers of the people to God. Last Sunday I would fain have dismissed them before prayers; but they begged so earnestly to stay, I durst not deny them." Indeed, she would have gladly had a man read the sermon, but none were literate enough to do so. Clearly she, like so many women before and after her, was not making a stand for women's rights, but rather simply felt compelled to preach the gospel.[123]

Mrs. Turner

Another woman who had a significant influence on Methodism even before the movement was born was a certain Mrs. Turner. It was this woman who served as a catalyst for the conversion of Charles Wesley on May 21, 1738, just three days before John's heart-warming experience at Aldersgate Street. Charles recorded in his journal that Mrs. Turner challenged him with the words, "In the name of Jesus of Nazareth arise, and believe, and thou shalt be healed of all thy infirmities." Although Charles was initially taken aback by the apparent audacity of this woman, he heeded her words and later "became convinced that indeed God had used her to effect his own conversion."[124]

Lady Salina Huntingdon. From J. Wesley Bready, *This Freedom — Whence?* (New York: American Tract Society, 1942), 65.

Lady Selina, Countess of Huntingdon

Still another area of influence of women in early Methodism related to patronage and protection, and the most noted example of this was Lady Selina, Countess of Huntingdon. Her wealth and influence helped establish Methodists on a secure footing and provided a measure of safety to itinerant preachers who were often hounded by officials. "When Welsh Methodists found themselves harried, arrested, and heavily fined for what were called 'illegal' religious meetings, it was through her that an investigation was undertaken that resulted in the return of the fines and full liberty for the Methodists' preaching."[125]

One of the greatest contributions Lady Selina made to Methodism was her sponsorship of itinerant Methodist preachers. She opened her estates to various preachers, including both Wesley and Whitefield, and then invited her friends among the nobility to attend the meetings. She also sponsored the Trevecca School for training preachers. These young preachers often became part of what was known as the "Huntingdon Connection," by their ministry in chapels that were provided by her. Indeed, during the decades of the 1760s and 1770s she built more than twenty chapels for her preachers.[126]

As the chief administrator of the "connection," Lady Selina served essentially as a bishop. She was in charge of the pastoral training, pastoral assignments, and finances and was the general overseer of the work, often traveling from chapel to chapel to ensure continuity in the ministry. She was a student of the Bible and very aware of doctrinal issues, and she did not hesitate to take a strong stand when she believed the issue warranted it, such as in the case of the Calvinist-Arminian struggle that plagued Methodism for decades. She took a strong Calvinistic stand with Whitefield and others and removed the Arminians from her college at Trevecca. Yet, she worked very hard to keep the peace with Wesley and the Arminian faction.[127]

John Wesley

Despite the dependency of John Wesley and other Methodist leaders on Lady Selina and other wealthy women, Wesley initially took a very conservative stand on the place of women in ministry. In a letter to Thomas Whitehead written in 1748, he spelled out some of the differences "between Quakerism and Christianity," denouncing the Quaker practice of allowing women to preach to a church assembly.[128]

This hard-line position was beginning to weaken, however, by 1754, when he published his *Explanatory Notes Upon the New Testament*. In commenting on 1 Corinthians, he qualified the admonition that "women be silent in the churches" with a significant loophole—"unless they are under an extraordinary impulse of the Spirit."[129]

Wesley had a very practical bent, and his initial reservations about women preaching were modified when he observed the effectiveness of their ministry. The change, however, came slowly. Women had always been permitted to speak in small informal groups—bands or classes, but as those groups grew—sometimes as a direct result of an effective female leader, the situation became more complicated. He was forced to grapple with some practical issues— one in particular that has often arisen in church history, namely, what constitutes the difference between 'exhorting" or "testifying" and "preaching"?

One reason that women played such an important role in early Methodism was that they, according to Earl Kent Brown, "made up a majority of the early Methodists—perhaps a rather substantial majority. Moreover, Mr. Wesley's letters to those women strongly urged that they be active within the societies." The encouragement of women to be active on a lay level not surprisingly was an

impetus for them to seek even more responsible roles. This inevitably involved a public ministry that called for public speaking—a daring act for an eighteenth-century woman. Women often went to great lengths to make their public speaking as unoffensive as possible.

> To avoid giving possible offense, some, like Margaret Davidson, were careful never to "presume to stand up as an exhorter, lest any should take an occasion to say I assumed the character of a preacher, which might have hurt the cause of God." Similarly, Mary Bosanquet Fletcher customarily did her speaking from the steps leading to the pulpit in the society chapels rather than from the pulpit itself.[130]

Wesley's reserved permission for women to minister in public forums was accompanied by advice that was aimed to make their presence more tolerable. To Sarah Mallet he wrote: "Never scream. Never speak above the natural pitch of your voice; it is disgustful to the hearers. It gives them pain not pleasure." In 1761 when he received word from Sarah Crosby that crowds approaching two hundred people were coming out to her class meetings and wanting her to speak to them, he suggested that she preface her comments with the statement, " 'You lay me under a great difficulty. The Methodists do not allow of women preachers; neither do I take upon me any such character. But I will just nakedly tell you what is in my heart.' This will in great measure obviate the grand objection." Interestingly, only months later, he encouraged a woman to speak, without such an introduction: "If a few more persons come in when you are meeting . . . enlarge for a few minutes . . . with a short exhortation."[131]

So, as practical considerations took precedence, the rule that applied to women allowed them to "exhort" but not to "preach." This is clearly seen in Wesley's advice to Sarah Crosby in 1769:

> In public you may properly enough intermix *short exhortations* with prayer; but keep as far from what is called preaching as you can: therefore never take a text; never speak in a continued discourse without some break, about four or five minutes. Tell the people, "We shall have another *prayer-meeting* at such a time and place."[132]

Despite such warnings, women did "preach" from texts. Sarah Mallet is an example, and her own testimony reveals her style: "My way of preaching from the first is to take a text and divide it, and speak from the different heads." So, as women continued to "preach" sometimes from texts and often in front of large groups, Wesley's position continued to evolve— partly as a reaction to the criticism he and the women leaders were confronting. By the 1770s his line of defense had changed:

> I think the strength of the cause rests there—on your having an *extraordinary* call. So I am persuaded has every one of our lay preachers. . . . The whole work of God called Methodism is an extraordinary dispensation of His providence. Therefore I do not wonder if several things occur therein which do not fall under the ordinary rules of discipline. St. Paul's ordinary rule was, "I permit not a woman to speak in the congregation." Yet in extraordinary cases he made a few exceptions; at Corinth in particular.[133]

The "Call" to Ministry

The emotionalism that was often characteristic of Methodism allowed for phenomena that could be termed an "extraordinary call," and indeed women justified their ministry by what they perceived to be a response to God's supernatural direction in their lives. Generally this would consist of no more than what might be considered a traditional "call" to the ministry—a personal sense of God singling out an individual for his service. On occasion, however, the "call" to women, as with men, had a more sensational twist. Sarah Mallet is an example. She considered herself "no friend of women's preaching," despite the fact that from an early age she sensed God was calling her to preach. Finally, "she began to have 'fits,' or trances, during which she would see herself before congregations, praying and preaching. Over the course of several years, Mallet experienced about eighteen such episodes, until she finally told God she would preach.[134]

Such charismatic "calls" were ridiculed by churchmen. One such "call" was described in a tract entitled "A Discoverie of Six women preachers." The anonymous author shows his obvious contempt for one Anne Hempstall, a Baptist, who "called an assembly of her bibbing gossips together, whose thoughts were bent more upon the strong water bottle, than upon the uses or doctrines which their holy sister intended to expound unto them." The author goes on to recreate Anne's testimony of a miraculous call: "Beloved sisters, this last night I dreamed a strange dream, moreover me thought I saw a vision, in which Anna the Prophetess was presented unto my view. . . .I could conceive no interpretation of my dream but this, that I should imitate godly Anna, by preaching unto you, as she prophesied to others."[135]

Although the accuracy of this testimony is questionable, what is most significant is the fact that in the eyes of many men, women were not even permitted to have a ministry to other women—even an evangelistic ministry, as this apparently was, if indeed the women who attended were more interested in drinking than hearing the Word of God.

The "call" was not the only defense for female Methodist preachers. Their success convinced many women that God was truly working through their labors, and Scripture itself was used as a defense of their position. In a letter to Wesley, one women preacher pointed to 1 Corinthians 11:5, which refers to women prophesying and praying, and insisted that the passages in the Epistles that seemed to place a ban on women's fulfilling that role referred to women's usurping authority over their husbands or meddling in church disciplinary affairs.[136]

Wesley eventually became so convinced of the rightness of women's ministry that he openly encouraged women to preach, despite the opposition he knew they would face. Sarah Mallet recalled that he had advised her "to let the voice of the people be to me the voice of God;—and where I was sent for, to go, for the Lord had called me thither." She was quick to point out, however, that "the voice of the people was not the voice of some preachers." How did she stand against the opposing preachers, then? "Mr. Wesley soon made this easy by sending me a note from the Conference."[137]

Sarah Crosby

Some of the early Methodist women actually became itinerant preachers. Sarah Crosby, the best known of these, traveled until her health no longer allowed it. Four meetings a day, the first beginning at 5 A.M., with many hours of travel in a carriage or on horseback in between, was not unusual. "In one year, itinerating out of Leeds, she traveled 960 miles, held 120 public services, led 600 classes and private meetings, and wrote 116 letters."[138]

For more than twenty years Crosby continued her itinerant work before she retired from active ministry. But even then her interest in Methodism and particularly women's work did not wane. While living in Leeds during the last decade of the eighteenth century, she headed several classes and bands, and she served as the matriarch of a group of women preachers, referred to as "the female brethren."[139]

Her success and the success of other women preachers was closely related to the support and backing of Wesley. Although Wesley believed in his later years that opposition to women in ministry had decreased, such was not the case. Indeed, the opportunities for woman to publicly minister quickly declined following his death. According to Earl Kent Brown, "Antifeminist prejudice hardened in the decades following Mr. Wesley's death, and nineteenth-century Methodism would be far less liberal on this matter than Mr. Wesley had been."[140]

Continental Pietism

There is little evidence that indicates that any women had leadership roles in German Pietism. Unlike Wesleyanism, German Pietism never made a clean break from the state church, and the leaders placed great stress on education and ordination credentials. Women may have had a very important behind-the-scenes role, but apparently they had no public ministry.

Moravians

The Moravians, led by Count Nicolaus Ludwig von Zinzendorf, were made up of refugees from different parts of Europe and of different theological backgrounds and were more mystical and sectarian than were the German Pietists. Here again, the men were firmly in control of leadership positions, but women, nevertheless, had an extraordinary influence—particularly in the area of doctrine and practice. A case in point is that of Anna Nitchmann, who later became Zinzendorf's second wife. Even before she became his wife she had a powerful ideological influence on him and the movement in the area of mysticism. Indeed, it was a fanatical mysticism that led to grave problems in the sect. She herself had developed a gruesome obsession with the death of Christ, and years before her marriage to the Count, she wrote a circular letter to a number of Moravian churches that included such expressions as, "Like a poor little worm, I desire to withdraw myself into his wounds."[141]

So contagious was her brand of mysticism that an "Order of Little Fools" was organized, and Zinzendorf encouraged the Moravians to behave like children and to imagine themselves as "little fish swimming in the bed of blood" or "little bees who suck the wounds of Christ." This morbid form of mysticism had a negative fall-out on the movement. The more introspective the Moravians became in their personal identification with Christ's suffering and death, the less they cared about evangelistic and humanitarian efforts. They regarded their mystical ecstasy rather than Christian ministry as evidence of true spirituality, and the world-wide Moravian missionary endeavor suffered. After a time, however, Zinzendorf recognized that the church had become "greatly degenerated," and he steered his followers back to a more stable course.[142]

Two Centuries of Losses and Gains

The seventeenth and eighteenth centuries provided women with more opportunities for ministry than they had previously enjoyed, but only if they were willing to defy male leadership in the institutionalized churches or be associated with sectarian movements and endure the scorn of respectable society. During this period, perhaps more than any previous period in history, women claimed divine sanction on their ministry. Indeed, *charismata* played an important part in giving many of these women a wide hearing and also in giving them self-confidence. There was a boldness and audacity that so often characterized female ministry during this period. Women "preachers" in both the Protestant and Catholic traditions during the post-Reformation period claimed supernatural and direct authority from God with little or no regard for the established church. Unlike Protestant women of the Reformation, who generally behaved in a manner that was more socially suitable for women, sectarian Protestant women—particularly Quakers—openly defied their opponents. Indeed, they sought out opportunities to challenge authorities and proclaim their right to preach.

But even when women such as Margaret Fell sought to open the door for women through carefully reasoned scriptural arguments, there was no room for debate in theological circles. Women were admonished to keep silent in the churches, and the vast majority did.

Women themselves, it should be pointed out, often objected to the idea of other women's involvement in public ministry, and they often de-preciated their own abilities and talents on the basis of sex. Elizabeth Warren, a well-known author of the mid-sixteenth century, is an example. She betrayed her feelings of low self-esteem in her efforts to downplay the validity of her writing. Conscious of her "mentall and sex-deficiency," which made her more susceptible to heresy, she "urged obedience to all whom God had placed in lawful authority."[143]

Yet, there were encouraging signs for women, especially with the advent of Methodism and the visibility of prominent society women and itinerant female preachers. But even in the case of Methodism, women's ministry was not looked on as natural. It was regarded an "extraordinary" measure that God allowed for launching a particular movement. And, whatever gains that were made quickly evaporated as Methodism became more a part of institutionalized Christianity.

Chapter 7

Trans-Atlantic Reform and Revivalism: Social Workers and Lay Evangelists

When Victor Hugo declared that "the nineteenth century is woman's century," he was well aware of the progress women were making in religious endeavors. Indeed, the nineteenth century brought significant advances for Western women in every area of life. Women began speaking out and organizing and assuming leadership positions as never before in history, and the church above all other institutions became a center for such activity. "It is among the distinguished glories of the commencement of the Nineteenth Century," wrote an editor of the *Assembly's Digest* of the Presbyterian Church in 1800, "that pious females are more extensively associated and more actively useful in promoting evangelical and benevolent objects than in any former period of the world."[1]

Frontier Revivalism

The Puritans in England and colonial America had elevated the woman in her position as wife and mother, but had taken a strong stand against a public ministry for women—such as that of Anne Hutchinson and the Quaker women preachers—and some had even suggested that Mistress Hopkins went insane because she thought too much about deep theological and philosophical matters. But that began to change as American religion loosened up as a result of religious revivals and sectarian movements. "Revivalistic religion," writes, Lawrence Foster, "has always provided both men and women—but especially women—with greater outlets for self-expression and innovation than have the established churches."[2] Women were viewed as having a very important place in the Great Awakening—not as revivalists, but by their attendance at religious services and their involvement in women's prayer meetings. When he was conducting meetings in South Carolina in 1795, Francis Asbury recorded in his diary, "Our few male members do not attend preaching; and I fear there is hardly one who walks with God: the women and Africans attend our meetings, and some few strangers also." Some years later when he was holding religious services in New England, he referred to a meeting in Marblehead where the "audience, chiefly female, nearly filled the room."[3] He was certainly not alone among itinerant evangelists who frequently preached to crowds made up mainly of women.

Without female involvement, the Great Awakenings might never have transpired. Indeed, it was widely believed in early America that women by nature were more religious than men and that they were destined by God to be the keepers of religion. When Benjamin Rush praised women for their religious faithfulness, claiming that "the female breast is the natural soil of Christianity," he was representing a widely held view. Women were expected to maintain a spirit of domestic piety and to instill spiritual values in the home and in the community—a role they willingly accepted.

That women were more religiously inclined is born out by church membership records, which indicate that women joined at a somewhat higher rate than men during periods of revival and at a substantially higher rate during the periods between revivals. Many of the local revivals in early America were the apparent result of women's prayer meetings.

> Conscious that as church members they were within the covenant of grace and confident that God answered the prayers of His people, devout women responded to the general apathy with concerted weekly prayers for a revival. Their prayers helped precipitate re-

vivals in that expectations of success made the prayer meeting members especially sensitive to others' spiritual state.[4]

Although women rarely led revivals, the frontier revivals of the Second Great Awakening offered women an even greater opportunity than they had had previously to actively participate on a lay level in revivalism. "Perhaps the most common female revival effort was the prayer meeting. By the 1820s, its evangelical efforts were so accepted that a Presbyterian magazine could suggest that God showers down grace in direct proportion to women's prayers."[5]

For women on the frontier, religious revivals and camp meetings provided an outlet for much-needed social interaction. "Women in particular," writes William McLoughlin, "were drawn to camp meetings, for they bore the heaviest burdens of pain, sickness, sorrow, unremitting labor, and old age." In these meetings they "found a place outside the home where they could gather, express their fears and hopes, and join in song and prayer with other women."[6]

Indeed, in many instances women were the most active participants in the revivals. They freely gave way to their emotions—much to the chagrin of the more sedate observers. Frances Trollope, the widely read nineteenth-century English observer of the American scene, was shocked by what she saw at a revival being conducted at a large Presbyterian church. In response to the hell-fire sermon, "frightened young girls, sobbing and trembling, made their way to the 'anxious benches.'" Men walked the isles whipping up emotions, and the girls "became hysterical, falling on their knees and crying 'Oh Lord!' 'Oh Lord Jesus!' and 'Help me, Jesus!' " To the English woman it was a horrifying spectacle.

> It was not simply a matter of the lower orders indulging in emotion, she reminded her readers; the congregations in general were very well dressed. She concluded that these excesses were the direct result of boredom. With no card games, no billiards, and no theater, the women of Cincinnati had to find release somewhere.[7]

It was during the last years of the eighteenth century and the early decades of the nineteenth century, when the Second Great Awakening was making an indelible impact on churches and families, that female lay ministries began to flourish. Women desired to carry their religious influence beyond the realm of their families and to make a difference in society.

Lay Ministries

As important as revivals and prayer groups became for religiously inclined women, they were not enough to satisfy those who desired a more active and public ministry. Women began seeking lay ministries both inside and outside the church, but whatever the ministries entailed, they were generally closely tied to the womanly sphere. Indeed, according to Page Miller, "the evolving recognition of mothers as the primary spiritual nurturers of children and the idealization of the hearth eventually provided the rationale for women's new public role."[8] The vast majority of women did not desire paid professional religious careers; they wanted to serve God, and they were fully satisfied if they could minister in a meaningful volunteer capacity.

Benevolent Societies

During the early nineteenth century, there was a tremendous increase in women's involvement in lay ministries—a literal overflowing of volunteer service that had not before existed on such a broad scale. Ford Brown humorously describes this society craze that began in England in the early nineteenth century as part of a broad-based reform movement:

> There were societies for putting down gin-mills and Sunday fairs and closing cook-shops on Sundays, for sending Bibles, homilies and Prayer Books everywhere and for keeping country girls at home. There were societies for educating infants, and adults, and juveniles, and orphans, and female orphans, and adult orphans, and nearly everybody else, according to the formularies of the Established Church or not according to them but always according to some religious formularies. There were societies for the deaf and dumb, for the insane, for the blind, for the ruptured, for the scrofulous, for the club-footed, for the penitent syphilitic and for the impenitent syphilitic; for legitimate children and illegitimate children, for chimney sweepers' apprentices and against Tom Paine and Shelley; in aid of juvenile prostitutes and against juvenile mendicants; for distressed respectable widows, for poor pious clergymen in the country, for poor females in the maritime districts, for distressed foreigners, for small debtors, for prisoners, for female emigrees, for the deserving poor, for respectable married women

and disreputable unmarried women, for sick people in hospitals and sick people out of hospitals and for simple ordinary sick strangers.[9]

The vast majority of the societies were founded or directed by women or at least were supported largely by women, and they were very often tied to religious ideals, if not directly to an organized church. Women were very active in such ministries to the sick, poor, orphans, prostitutes, and prisoners. In America the city reform movement among women began early in the nineteenth century. Home mission societies of various kinds developed alongside mission support groups. Collecting money for missionaries was too passive for many women who wanted to be where the action was.

Of the vast army of women who volunteered to serve the downtrodden in society, an amazing number were recruited from the mission homes themselves. Seth Cook Rees cited many such cases from the late nineteenth century in his book *Miracles in the Slums; or, Thrilling Stories of those Rescued from the Cesspools of Iniquity, and Touching Incidents in the Lives of the Unfortunate.* The following are only a few of the trophies of the missionaries to people in the slums: Orpha, who "fell prey to a professional procurer, . . . became a slum missionary and an ordained deaconess." Little H——, who "had been taken to men's rooms and forced to drink," was later "sanctified and went to Bible School in order to prepare to become a slum missionary." Miss M—— "was put in jail for grand larceny" and later "became a missionary in the New York City

slums." Lucy "was ruined by her employer who turned out to be a bartender and was put in a Negro sporting house." After she was rescued, "she began teaching a Sunday School class of nineteen scholars." Dicie, who was "a drunkard, cigarette fiend, and user of morphine, cocaine, and other druges," later "became a slum missionary." "Little Ella," who was "sold as a prostitute for $5.00," later "became a Quaker and started preaching." Christine, a pregnant teenager who "was forever hopelessly ruined," was "called to be a slum missionary" and "went to Bible school for training." And Bernie, who "after trying suicide . . . decided to have a man without marriage . . . was saved, sanctified" and "became assistant matron of the Home."[10]

Women's social work was certainly not focused only on women and girls. In England women were heavily involved in evangelistic and humanitarian outreach to working-class men. One of the most effective of these ministries was begun in the 1840s by Catherine Marsh. She reached out to railroad laborers, and many were converted through her efforts. She detailed her experiences in a book entitled *English Hearts and English Hands*, published in 1858, in which she challenged others to show more concern for the workingmen of the nation.

When . . . labourers either in fields or factories are within your reach, meet them with a frank and genial friendliness. Alleviate their discomforts as far as lies in your power. Provide some little innocent pleasure—a tea party for instance—from time to time, for their hard-worked existence. Above all, seek to secure to them their Sabbaths;

and hold forth to them the Word of Life. Give them Bibles or Testaments. . . .[11]

In the 1860s, Louisa Daniell organized missions to servicemen at various military bases, providing them with recreational facilities, home-cooked food, and Bible study materials.[12]

The Sunday School Movement

It was out of the reform movement that Sunday schools emerged. In the earliest years, they were often focused on the lower elements of society and were hardly distinguishable from other social and humanitarian efforts. Yet they proved to be highly controversial. Many churchmen feared that they would interfere with the professional teaching ministry of the church. These leaders were appalled at the idea of lay people—particularly women—teaching the Bible. As Martin Marty has observed, the early Sunday school movement was "often opposed by ministers not simply because it was new or was a threat to established ways of doing things but because it was often in the hands of women."[13]

Yet without women, the movement would never have flourished. Robert Raikes, considered the founder of the Sunday-school movement, began his work in the 1780s with four women, who held weekly Bible classes for children. According to Ian Bradley, "the most active agents in the conversion of the working classes to vital religion seem to have been the females. Most of the teachers in Sunday schools and ragged schools were women."[14] There is little evidence that women heeded the voices of

opposition, perhaps partly because they saw the value in their work and realized how much their ministry was appreciated by their pupils. Lord Shaftesbury, writes Bradley,

> was alarmed to find a young woman in her mid-twenties in charge of a class of men in a ragged school in a particularly rough area of London, but the Superintendent told him that what worried him was not that they would molest her but "that some day a man might drop in who, not knowing the habits of this place, might lift a finger against her, for if he did so, he would never leave the room alive."[15]

Hannah More, an early leader of Sunday-school work in England, also faced opposition. "She and her sisters, who fostered schools among the poor, were condemned and their teachers persecuted by curates of the church, until she appealed to the bishop, gaining no redress beyond a diplomatic letter." According to More, "the aim of the curates was not merely to ruin the teachers employed but to strike at the principles of all my schools and to stigmatize them as seminaries of fanaticism, vice and sedition." Altogether, she and her co-workers organized schools that accommodated some twenty thousand children.[16]

The early Sunday-school movement in America also was deeply influenced by women. Two women—Joanna Bethune and her mother, Isabella Graham—started a class for poor children in 1803, after Joanna had visited Scotland and surveyed the Sunday-school work there. In the years that followed there were various similar classes started by women in New York and Philadelphia. More than a decade later, after hearing enthusiastic reports of Sunday schools being organized by Robert Raikes and his followers in England, Joanna and her husband determined that it was time for the work to be organized on a broad scale in America. Initially her husband sought to interest some other Christian businessmen to become involved, but, unsuccessful at that, he encouraged his wife to take the initiative with some of her female friends.[17]

Although she had been actively involved in teaching Sunday schools, Joanna had not thought of herself as the organizer of a large movement, but she accepted the challenge. In a letter to a friend she told how she had talked up the Sunday-school idea and passed out literature, "in hopes the gentlemen would come forward in the business, but after waiting a number of weeks, I conversed with several of my own sex, who expressed a wish to unite with me in a Female Sunday-School Union." She called a meeting in January 1816 at the Wall Street Church. Several hundred women from a number of denominations attended. After Bethune's very impassioned message, "there was not a dry eye in the room, and tears flowed copiously down the cheeks of many." Out of that meeting came The Female Union for the Promotion of Sabbath Schools.[18]

Classes started the following week, and by July of that year there were two hundred and fifty teachers and more than three thousand pupils. This launched Bethune into an administrative position with responsibilities rarely granted women of this period. According to Page Miller, "she supervised a large budget, estab-

lished policy, oversaw the publication of the curriculum, and coordinated an enormous staff." Yet, like most women, she depreciated her own value. In the Society's fifth annual report, she wrote, "Of myself, I feel utterly unable to think a good thought—far less to fulfill the duties of the responsible situation you have assigned me."[19]

Like the women in England, the American women involved in Sunday schools frequently faced strong opposition. Fearing that "these women will be in the pulpit next," some pastors and church boards denied the use of their facilities for Sunday-school work.[20] Although the men had initially been unwilling to form a Sunday-school organization, they apparently did not want to be outdone by the women. One week after the women's organizational meeting, the men met, with Joanna's husband presiding. They founded the New York Sunday School Union, of which the Female Society soon became an auxiliary. Although the men were now in control, the women continued to be the backbone of the organization, with the vast majority of teaching staff being female. The following year, the American Sunday School Union was officially organized.[21]

In the decades that followed the organization of American Sunday schools, women continued to fill the ranks as teachers. Their prominence in the movement was evident at the Women's Christian Temperance Union convention of 1889. When the Sunday-school workers were asked to stand, Frances Willard observed that out of the 466 delegates, only a few remained seated.[22]

Why did the women simply hand over the reins of leadership to men? Most of them apparently had no desire to be in leadership positions and were glad the men took over. Edwin Rice, who wrote a history of the American Sunday School Union on its one-hundredth anniversary, made the following observation:

> In view of the prominent service which women rendered to this movement in its teaching force and in contributing so largely to the preparation of its literature, it seems remarkable that they did not become more conspicuous in some organized capacity in the work of extending and improving Sunday schools. Possibly it may have been because woman's day had not yet arrived. In most of the churches it was not popular for women to speak in public or to attempt to interpret the Sacred Word. . . . Women accepted the humbler but no less important sphere of instructing the race in its formative period and giving the young some knowledge of the rudiments of religion. . . . It would seem a distinct loss, however, that the American Sunday-School Union should miss the opportunity of fostering and encouraging an organization of women in the work in which they might have become such valuable auxiliaries.[23]

The rapid growth rate of the Sunday-school movement in England and North America was not duplicated in Continental Europe. The movement faced opposition from Protestant state churches as well as from Roman Catholicism, but where it did take hold, women were generally at the forefront. Sweden is an example. There it was initiated in the 1850s by Lady Ehrenborg, who had become a Sunday school enthusiast after visiting London. Under her leadership, the movement grew "with greater rapidity . . . than in any other continental country." By the early twentieth century there were nearly twenty-five thousand teachers and more than three-hundred thousand pupils.[24]

Charles Finney and the Women's Issue

Although the public lay ministry of women was sometimes very controversial, in other instances it was strongly encouraged. The behind-the-scenes work of women in the Sunday-school movement, humanitarian services, and in support missions was an enormous asset to the church, and it did not go unnoticed. Yet there was always an underlying fear that women would assume roles unsuited to their sex. A controversy over this issue flared up during the Second Great Awakening—particularly in reference to the revivalistic work of Charles Grandison Finney. He was perceived by many as being too eager to use the services of women. This was evident at a conference he attended in New Lebanon, New York, in 1826, at which time the issue of "the propriety of women taking any part in social meetings" arose. According to Finney, "Dr. [Lyman] Beecher brought up that objection, and argued it at length, insisting upon it, that the practice was unscriptural and inadmissible."[25] Asa Nettleton, another well-known revival and church leader from the East, also strongly opposed women's participation in mixed groups.

Why, with such active involvement of women in lay ministries, was there so much controversy over women's involvement in revivals? One reason relates to the "promiscuous" meetings—women speaking where men were present. As a general rule, women in early America had observed the ban on their speaking in church and revival meetings. There were exceptions among sectarian groups, however, particularly in situations where male leadership was lacking, but most "respectable" churches adhered to the rule of silence for women. It is not surprising, then, that Charles G. Finney, the most popular revivalist of the early nineteenth century, created an uproar when he permitted women to pray and testify in public meetings. He was not the first revivalist to do so, however. As early as 1825 Theodore Weld had challenged women to speak and pray—a challenge that did not go unheeded. During a meeting one night "seven females, a number of them the most influential Christians in the city, confessed their sin in being restrained by their sex and prayed publickly in succession."[26]

Was Finney breaking new ground in his attitude toward women, or was he just trying to maintain the status quo? This is an important issue. Some evangelical feminist historians in recent years have tried to make the case that the real roots of feminism are among the nineteenth-century Evangelicals. Donald Dayton, Lucille Sider Dayton, Nancy Hardesty, and others have emphasized this. According to Donald Dayton, "it was in the American revivalism of Charles G. Finney that such tendencies [egalitarianism] began to have wide cultural impact and were transformed into the practice of full ordination for women and a form of Christian and biblical feminism."[27]

It should be pointed out, however, that Finney himself did not advocate the ordination of women. He was a traditionalist at heart. Like other revivalists of this period, he depended heavily on the support of women. His *Memoirs* attest to that fact. The women's door-to-door visitation and prayer meetings paved the way for his revivals. Likewise, he argued that "the church that silences the women is shorn of half its power" and supported certain feminist causes, but he did not encourage women to seek leadership positions on an equal basis with men. According to Antoinette Brown, who studied under Finney at Oberlin, he "thought that exceptional women might be called on to become religious teachers."[28] Indeed, Finney believed that the primary sphere for women was the home, and he advised them to avoid speaking if they encountered opposition.[29]

Finney's first wife, Lydia, reflected her husband's thinking in opposing women in public ministry. According to Brown, when Mrs. Finney heard that she "intended to study theology," she "appealed to me not to do so, at least not to become a public speaker or a minister." Among her "stereotyped arguments" was her warning: "You will never feel yourself wise enough to go directly against the opinions of all the great men of the past."[30]

Finney's second wife, Elizabeth, took a very active role in his revival ministry, but her speaking was generally limited to female audiences.[31] But women had previously been involved in such activities. So, what Finney seems to have been doing is reacting against the conservative Calvinists in the East who were seeking to tighten up controls on women. He himself admitted as much. In his book *Revivals of Religion*, under a section entitled "Women's prayer meetings," he wrote: "Within the last few years women's prayer meetings have been extensively opposed." He goes on to argue that such meetings were valid, but his writing certainly does imply that a reaction had set in against women, and that he was opposing it.[32]

Professional "Women's" Ministries

As opportunities for women in lay ministries proliferated, the door slowly opened for women to become involved in professional ministry. At first the only "approved" ministries were ones that were strictly in the women's sphere—such activities as social work and writing, but eventually more and more women ventured into the male domain of evangelism and preaching.

The Deaconess Movement

Much of the humanitarian work that was conducted by benevolent societies was carried out independently of the churches, but this began to change as some churchmen saw the need for bringing these women and their activities under the umbrella of the church itself. This came in part with the reintroduction of the the diaconate in the early nineteenth century. Theodore Fliedner, a German Lutheran pastor, and his wife, Friederike, established a hospital in 1836 at Kaisersworth. After that they founded the Institution of Protestant Deaconesses, using the Roman Cath-

olic Sisters of Charity as their model. The Institution was complex, "replete with motherhouse, hospital, center for rehabilitating women prisoners, a training school for teachers, a girls' high school and laboratory, kindergarten, orphans home, home for female Protestant lunatics, home for lonely and invalid women, and a preparatory school for deaconesses." Within three decades, Kaisersworth was sponsoring more than four hundred deaconesses and served some one hundred outstations throughout the world.[33]

In England, the revival of the diaconate came with the founding of the Mildmay Deaconess Home in 1860 by William Pennefather and his wife. Pennefather was the Vicar of Christ Church in Barnet. After learning of the work of Fliedners at Kaisersworth, he founded a similar work in England. Soon after it was founded, Mrs. Pennefather wrote: "I have been gratified by having numerous applications for Bible-women, matrons, and female visitors of the poor. Our infant institution has not yet been able to supply the demand, but the fact of such a demand shows the necessity for our Missionary Training Home."[34]

According to Maude Royden, "The Mildmay Deaconess was at first neither ordained nor 'set apart' nor even 'admitted' by a bishop, and there were some complaints at her venturing to call herself a deaconess at all." The Deaconess Order was begun in the Church of England in 1862, but again, according to Royden, "even in this case no one seems to have known whether the deaconess was actually ordained into minor or merely 'set apart.' Nor has there been any very clear idea of the nature of her work, her obligations, or her vocation."[35] Further impetus to the revival of the diaconate in England came with the Anglo-Catholic movement and its concern for bringing back women's religious orders, but it was not until late in the century that deaconesses were widely accepted in English churches.[36]

Efforts to reinstitute the diaconate in America met with less success than they had in Europe. In the 1840s William A. Passavant, a Lutheran minister, established a hospital in Pittsburgh with the help of Fliedners, who sent some of their Kaisersworth-trained deaconesses to assist. At about the same time, an Episcopal priest from New York organized a diaconate for his denomination, but as with the Lutherans, it did not interest very many women nor the church at large. "Evidently the need for such communities," writes Janet James, "was not sufficient to overcome Protestant prejudice, for they attracted little support."[37] After 1870, the interest in the diaconate increased, and in the next three decades more than one hundred homes, representing many different Protestant denominations, were established in the United States.[38]

As a result of the dedication of Lucy Meyer, the Methodists opened a training school and deaconesses home in Chicago in 1887. It was a thriving school, largely because it trained women for many other professions besides that of deaconess. The New England Deaconess Home and Training School was founded two years later, but it remained very small. In 1906, seventeen years after its founding, its enrollment was less than thirty.[39]

Other deaconess homes were established as well, and in some Protestant circles enthusiasm for the concept ran high. Christian Golder, a medical doctor, wrote in 1903 of the need for women to do evangelism in the ghettos. He cited the findings of George W. Gray, superintendent of Methodist City Missions in Chicago. Dr. Gray had found that in one Chicago district of more than twenty thousand people there were "two hundred and seventy-two saloons, eighty-five wine-houses, seven opium and eight gambling dens, and not less than ninety-two houses of ill-fame," but only three churches. What was Golder's solution?

More than ever before are we in need to-day of female power. We need women who will give up the luxuries of life, who will forsake society and friends, and condescend to help this class of men. The only hope and possibility of elevating and saving this class of the population in our great cities lies in the unselfish and devoted activity of such women. . . . Here is the great and useful field for deaconesses. . . . The time will come when tens of thousands of deaconesses, in city and country, will sacrifice their lives in Christian love services.[40]

Despite such optimism the antagonism toward celibate Protestant "sisterhoods" remained. These sisterhoods smacked of Roman Catholicism, and some of the strongest sentiment against the Catholic concept of female religiosity came from the pen of evangelical women. The evangelical emphasis on female piety that was centered on the home and family was diametrically opposed to the Catholic ideal of celibacy and complete oneness with God. Such was the anti-Catholic sentiment that "many evangelical Protestants over-dramatized the threat and intentions of Rome." An example is Maria Monk, who in her book *Awful Disclosures of the Hotel Dieu Nunnery of Montreal* "described a nunnery's ghastly and elaborate system of infanticide, the Catholic solution to 'criminal inter-course' between priests and nuns."[41]

Writing and Publishing

Writing was a very significant area of women's lay ministries. Women were often able to have a more wide-ranging and less controversial minis-try through the pen than they would have been able to have in a public speaking ministry. Their writing gen-erally centered on spiritual themes. An example is Hester Ann Rogers, who became well-known to Method-ists in the early nineteenth century through her *Memiors* and *Letters.* "One preacher reported that in 1817 on his circuit alone he had sold fourteen copies of her *Life* and seven of her *Letters.*"

The story of Rogers' struggle to attain sanctification was one aspect of the book that appealed to the readers, and her writing had an im-pact on the doctrine of entire sanc-tification in Methodist circles. She described her prayer for that "bless-ing": "I thought, shall I now ask small blessings only of my God: Lord, cried I, make this the moment of my full salvation! Baptize me now with the Holy Ghost and the fire of pure love: Now 'make me a clean heart, and renew a right spirit within me.' Now enter thy temple, and cast out sin forever. Now cleanse the thoughts, desires and propensities of my heart, and let me perfectly love thee."[42]

Rogers was also deeply involved in lay evangelism, a fact that was noted in the sermon delivered at her fu-neral:

She . . . was a leader of classes and bands, and a mother in Israel to the young believers entrusted to her care. After her marriage, she became still more extensively useful. Mr. Rogers, on his entering into a Circuit, would only give a very few to her care, desiring her to complete the class out of the world: and soon, by her conversation and prayers, and attention to every soul within her reach, would the number spring up to thirty or forty; and then her almost cruel husband in this re-spect, for the glory of God, would transplant all the believers to other classes, and keep her thus continually working at the mine. In the city of Dublin only, Mr. Rogers himself con-fessed, some hundreds of those whom he received into the society were brought to Christ, or were awakened, by her gentle but incessant labors of love.[43]

Besides writing autobiographies and devotional works, women of the nineteenth century contributed heav-ily to the market of religious novels and tracts. Hannah More from Eng-land, was an innovator in the latter category. She determined to do battle singlehandedly with the promoters of atheism and political radicalism who were flourishing in the years after the French Revolution, and her method was through cheap religious leaflets. "It has occurred to me," she wrote, "to write a variety of things, some-where between vicious papers and hymns, for it is in vain to write what people will not read. . . . I propose printing striking conversions, Holy Lives, Happy Deaths, Providential Deliverances, Judgments on Breakers of Commandments etc." In 1795, she began publishing three tracts a month, and by the end of the first year she had sold over two million of them.[44]

One area of religious literature that was considered off limits for women in the nineteenth century was that which involved theological and doctrinal treatises. Yet women like Hester Ann Rogers managed to weave doctrinal views into their devotional works, and other women did the same in poetry and novels. Emily Dickinson is an example. "Most critics rank her with Ralph Waldo Emerson, Edgar Allan Poe, and Walt Whitman as the finest American poets of the country."[45] Among her many themes, she often expressed her frustration with God, who seemed so remote. She yearned for a close communion that seemed so difficult to realize:

> I know that he exists;
> Somewhere, in silence,
> He has hid his rare life
> From our gross eyes.

"Although sentimentalists and evangelicals would have called her impious," writes Amanda Porterfield, "Dickinson worshiped their God on her own terms. In the demands she made on God's justice and existence and in the independence she cultivated, she hunted for God with passion and played with him with wit."[46]

Another area of writing ministry for women involved hymns. According to Erik Routley, "hardly any hymnody by women comes from the 18th century or earlier."[47] But during the nineteenth century many women began writing hymns that are still sung in Protestant churches today. Among those whose work was widely recognized were Charlotte Elliott, Frances Havergal, and Fanny Crosby.

Charlotte Elliott, born in Clapham, England, is best known for "Just As I Am," a hymn frequently sung at the close of revival meetings. "This hymn," writes Kenneth Osbeck, "has touched more hearts and influenced more people for Christ than any other song ever written." It was written in 1836, as a reflection of her conversion experience fourteen years earlier. At that time (in 1822) she was bitter about her ill health, and Dr. Caesar Malan, a renowned Swiss evangelist, visited her home and encouraged her to come to Christ just as she was—with all her struggles and doubts. Although she remained an invalid the rest of her life, she was able to minister effectively through her hymn writing. In fact, "Just As I Am" was first published in a volume entitled *The Invalid's Hymn Book*, a collection of more than one hundred of her hymns.[48]

Frances Ridley Havergal (1836–79) was the daughter of an Anglican priest, who was himself a recognized poet and musician. Unlike many nineteenth-century hymn writers, she was trained in music. Yet her hymn writing was characterized by a mystical dependence on God, and she purportedly "never wrote a line without first praying over it." Indeed, "her entire life was characterized by spiritual saintliness."[49] An admiring critic wrote: "She devoted herself from her early adult years to private evangelism. Not all of us are sure that she might have not proved a somewhat overwhelming guest . . . , but one can only admire—even if one keeps a safe distance—her zeal and sincerity."[50] Three of her best-known hymns that reflect her evangelistic zeal are "I Gave My Life for Thee," "Take My Life and Let It Be," and "Lord, Speak to Me That I May Speak."

The best-known female hymn writer of all time, of course, was Fanny Crosby (1820–1915), the author of more than nine thousand hymns and gospel songs. Born into a poor family from New York state, she became blind as an infant. It was this handicap that prompted her to develop her creative genius, and she began composing poetry as a youngster. By the time she was in her early thirties, she was writing popular songs including, "Rosalie, the Prairie Flower," which earned some three thousand dollars in royalties—though Crosby received but a fraction of that.[51]

After teaching for a number of years at a school for the blind, she married one of her colleagues and after that devoted her time to composing hymns. Nearly all of her well-known hymns were written during the first ten years of her hymn-writing ministry—prior to 1876. They included such favorites as "Blessed Assurance," "Rescue the Perishing," "Pass Me Not, O Gentle Saviour," "Safe in the Arms of Jesus," "I Am Thine, O Lord," "All the Way My Saviour Leads Me," "Close to Thee," "Praise Him! Praise Him!" and "To God Be the Glory." Her biographer, Bernard Ruffin, writes:

In later years, with two or three possible exceptions, none of her hymns would equal in popularity those she wrote in the first decade of her career.

Why was this? Had she written herself out? Most likely, yes. Fanny Crosby had said everything that she had to say, and almost everything she would produce in the future was simply a paraphrase of something that she had written earlier.[52]

Although the vast majority of her thousands of hymns have been lost in obscurity, Crosby nevertheless has had an amazing influence on the church. What she could not have done in a public ministry, she was able to do behind the scenes. Preachers, theologians, and Bible scholars, who would not permit a woman to speak or teach in a worship service, week after week sang her hymns and profited by her ministry. And there were many other nineteenth-century women who also gave to the church some of its best-loved hymns. Although most of these women have long been forgotten, their ministry lives on. They include Elizabeth Clephane, "Beneath the Cross of Jesus"; A. Katherine Hankey, "I Love to Tell the Story"; Sarah F. Adams, "Nearer, My God, to Thee"; Emily E. S. Elliott, "Thou Didst Leave Thy Throne"; Anna Ross Cousin, "The Sands of Time Are Sinking"; Mrs. Cecil F. Alexander, "There Is a Green Hill Far Away"; Anna B. Warner, "Jesus Loves Me"; and Lina Berg, "Day by Day."

Pulpit Ministries

The nineteenth century, more than any century before it, was one of "women preachers." Most of these women were not ordained and did not have their own parish, but they nevertheless "preached," attaining wide recognition. They moved across denominational barriers and sometimes even in circles of high social standing. This indeed was a new phenomenon in religious life—one that prompted strong criticism from more traditional elements in the established churches.

The reason for the strong reaction by the conservatives against women in ministry was not only women's more pronounced visibility in lay ministries, but also their greater numbers in full-time public ministries. This reaction had set in among the Methodists the decade following John Wesley's death. In 1802 at the Irish Conference a resolution was passed affirming "that it is contrary both to Scripture and prudence that *women* should preach or should exhort in public; and we direct the Superintendents to refuse a Society Ticket to any woman in the Methodist Connections who preaches, or who exhorts in any public congregation." The Conference of 1803 eased the restrictions slightly by declaring that women might preach—but only to other women or in extreme cases when no male preachers were available.[53]

In spite of such efforts to silence them, women continued to become involved in ministry in greater numbers than ever before. But if it was not specifically nineteenth-century evangelicalism that allowed for such ministry, how did women attain the prominent roles in religious life that were particularly evident in the mid- to late-nineteenth century?

Although women played a larger role in religious life in the nineteenth century than they had previously, the manner in which they attained recognition had not changed. The nineteenth-century women "preachers" were generally in movements that could be considered sectarian. In England these groups included the Quakers, Primitive Methodists, and Bible Christians; and in America, the Quakers, Freewill Baptists, Free Methodists, as well as factions connected with the holiness and deeper-life movements. They also were involved in unorthodox sectarian movements. All of these movements emphasized direct communion with God, the leading of the Spirit, and the call to ministry over and above clerical counsel, church bylaws, and ordination. As was the case with the Anabaptists and other free church movements in history, the high priority placed on spiritual gifts left the door ajar for women in ministry.

Early Nineteenth-Century Itinerant Evangelists

In rare instances women themselves conducted revivals and served as itinerant evangelists. This was true in New England among the Freewill Baptists in the late eighteenth and early nineteenth centuries. The first of these women preachers was Mary Savage, who went to New Durham in 1791, and from there extended her ministry into surrounding villages where there were no churches. Although her ministry in that area lasted less than a year, she apparently made a significant impact on the movement: "The melting power of her exhortations was often irresistible, and so greatly was the effect with which she sometimes spoke at the Quarterly or Yearly Meeting, that a note of the fact was entered upon the book of records."[54]

Another female Freewill Baptist preacher was Sally Parsons, who conducted itinerant work during the 1790s in New England. "For several years she traveled considerably, and was very useful in the feeble churches." Indeed, so useful did the Yearly Meeting in New Durham, in 1797, regard her ministry that enough money was raised to purchase a horse, bridle, and saddle for her personal use. She continued her active preaching ministry for four more years until she married. Yet, as supportive as the Freewill Baptists were of her ministry, she, like other aspiring women, was not ordained and did not serve in an established church. A report from an Elders' Conference held in 1801 not only indicates that women held a small minority of ministry positions, but also reveals that they were on the lowest rung of the ladder:

> The number present was fifty-three—eight ministers, fifteen ruling elders, ten deacons, and twenty unordained preachers and exhorters, three of the latter being females. They were seated in the order above named, ministers occupying the front seats, ruling elders the second range, deacons the third, and in the rear sat the unordained speakers.[55]

The most successful of the early Freewill Baptist female preachers was Clarissa Danforth, who, according to I. D. Stewart, was "the sensation preacher of this decade" (1810–20). In 1817 she spent several months in a region of Vermont "where almost every church was visited in mercy, and large accesssions were made. . . . Crowds went to hear the woman preach, and many returned with hearts fixed to seek the Lord. In one of those meetings, the high sheriff of Danville was one of her first converts. In 1818 Clarissa began an evangelistic ministry in Rhode Island that "resulted in many revivals, and the organization of several churches." She easily crossed over denominational lines, and "almost all houses of worship in that region were opened for her, and ministers and people in multitudes flocked to hear." In less than a year after she arrived in Rhode Island, "the great revival commenced in Smithfield . . . and continued with great power for sixteen months, and extended into all parts of the State, and into all societies." In 1821 she returned to preach in her hometown of Wethersfield, Vermont, "where not less than one hundred were converted." Soon after that she married, and, as was the case with Parsons, her active public ministry came to an end.[56]

The "Call" to Ministry

As had been true in previous centuries, the "call" was a very important factor in justifying a woman's role in Christian ministry. Women often testified of their reservations about entering a man's domain, but that they finally relented and obeyed the voice of God. Jerena Lee, the first widely traveled woman preacher of the African Methodist Episcopal Church, testified to such an experience:

> Between four and five years after my sanctification, on a certain time, an impressive silence fell upon me, and I stood as if some one was about to speak to me, yet I had no such thought in my heart.—But to my utter surprise there seemed to sound a voice which I

thought I distinctly heard, and most certainly understood, which said to me "Go preach the gospel!" I immediately replied aloud, "No one will believe me." Again I listened, and again the same voice seemed to say—"Preach the Gospel; I will put words in your mouth. . . ."[57]

Lee initially feared that it was Satan who had spoken to her. So distraught was she that she went to the Reverend Richard Allen, "the preacher in charge of the African Society," and told him of her call to preach the gospel. "As to women preaching, he said that our Discipline knew nothing at all about it—that it did not call for women preachers." She initially accepted the verdict without protest, and almost a sense of relief. "This I was glad to hear, because it removed the fear of the cross—but no sooner did that feeling cross my mind, than I found that a love of souls had in a measure departed from me; that holy energy which burned within me, as a fire, began to be smothered."[58]

Another woman who related her reluctance to obey God's call to preach was Salome Lincoln, whose "mind was first exercised on the subject of preaching, about the year 1823." She was certain it was the leading of the Lord, "but O, my soul shrunk from the work! I thought I could never move forward; and soon lost the enjoyment of religion." But while the Spirit of God was saying, 'Go, go," Satan cried out, "Woman, woman!" "It is no wonder," wrote her biographer, "that at the midnight hour, while she wept and prayed till her pillow was wet with tears; she should sometimes exclaim, 'Lord, I pray thee, have me excused!' " Despite her strong sense of calling,

Lincoln did not begin preaching until 1827, and then only because there was no one else to take the service: "A large number of young persons were present, and not one among them that had ever professed religion. I sat a few moments trembling under the cross: and then fell upon my knees and commenced praying. While in prayer, the power of God was manifested—and the fear of man taken away. I then arose and began to speak."[59]

After that beginning, Lincoln began preaching three or four sermons a week, while supporting herself by working in a factory. Her ministry was confined largely to Reformed Methodist churches and nondenominational meetings. She sometimes confronted opposition, on one occasion having a school house locked so that she could not hold her service. Most of the time, however, her preaching was regarded as better than no preaching at all, and some of her admirers went so far as Elder Benton to suggest that "she possessed an uncommon mind for one of her sex."[60]

Mary Cole, who began her preaching and healing ministry in Missouri in the 1880s, was attending a camp meeting when she received her call, which was in the form of a question: "Will you consecrate yourself to go out as a life-worker for me?" Immediately, however, "the devil" prompted her to make excuses and degrade her own ability. Further discouragement came from her Methodist class leader who told her, "You are a pretty looking thing to be called to preach." And during her early years of ministry she "met with considerable opposition to woman's preaching." But the compelling nature of her call sustained her even when her enemies went to great lengths to discredit her. "Falsehoods were told about me that should have shamed the devil himself. One rumor was that I was one of the famous outlaws, known as the 'James boys,' disguised as a woman."[61]

Virtually every woman who conducted a public professional ministry during the nineteenth century testified of a special call from God, and some of these women had very prominent public ministries. Among their numbers was the great triumvirate Phoebe Palmer, Hannah Whitall Smith, and Catherine Booth—whose lives and ministries had much in common. All of them were members of husband-wife teams, with the women more prominent or equally prominent in each case. They all had several children, and they all were very much a part of the Holiness–Deeper Life movement, which emphasized sanctification as a distinct second work of grace.

Phoebe Palmer

Phoebe Palmer (1807–74), often referred to as the "Mother of the Holiness Movement," was the most influential woman in nineteenth-century Methodism. She lived in New York City with her husband, a physician, and began her ministry in the 1830s with her Tuesday Meeting for the Promotion of Holiness, which she continued for some twenty years. These were very significant meetings. "Hundreds of Methodist preachers, including at least two bishops and three who were later to hold that office, were sanctified under Mrs.

Palmer's influence. The *Guide to Holiness*, printed in Boston, publicized her work and served as well to unite and inspire the clergymen great and small who shared her concern." She was described by a well-known minister as "the Priscilla who had taught many an Apollos the way of God more perfectly."[62]

Phoebe Palmer, a Well-known Nineteenth-Century Holiness Teacher and Evangelist. Made from nineteenth-century prints by Deane K. Dayton for Donald W. Dayton, *Discovering an Evangelical Heritage* (New York: Harper & Row, 1976).

The well-publicized success of Phoebe Palmer's informal prayer meetings inspired other women to conduct the same type of ministry, and dozens of such meetings sprang up all over the country. "These intimate little gatherings," according to Timothy Smith, "brought together the most earnest Christians of all evangelical sects under the leadership of women. . . ." Indeed, Palmer had a significant influence also outside Methodist circles, particularly among Congregationalists, Episcopalians, Baptists, and Quakers.[63]

There was a very practical side to Phoebe Palmer's concept of Christianity, and, according to Smith, her "pioneer work in social welfare projects illustrates the part which urban evangelization played in the origins of the Christian social movement." She played an influential role in establishing the Hedding Church, a city mission work under the auspices of the Methodist Ladies Home Missionary Society. This mission project represented the early beginnings of the later settlement houses. For more than a decade during the 1840s and 1850s she served as an officer of The New York Female Assistance Society for the Relief and Religious Instruction of the Sick Poor. She also distributed tracts in the slums of New York City and conducted prison visitation at the Tombs, and in doing so she became acutely aware of the material needs of the poor. Likewise, she founded the Five Points Mission, her "crowning achievement." It was a mission project in New York that housed some twenty poor families and provided schooling and religious training as well. This mission project represented the early beginnings of the later settlement houses.[64]

Phoebe Palmer did not confine her ministry to informal prayer gatherings and social work. Her "all-consuming desire" was not to be a great evangelist or philanthropist, but to be, in her words, a "Bible Christian."[65] She was a student of the Bible and as such did not hesitate to challenge church doctrine if she believed it to be nonbiblical. Yet, she was influenced deeply by her denominational heritage. There was a strong "holiness" emphasis associated with her Tuesday meetings. She acknowledged her indebtedness to John Wesley's theology of entire sanctification, and in the early years of her ministry, there was little apparent difference between her views and his. By the late 1840s, however, she was proposing a radically new concept that made the Wesleyan doctrine of entire sanctification compatible with American revivalism.

Wesley's emphasis on the disciplined life that led to an eventual attainment of this "perfect love" was, in her mind, an unnecessary prolongation of a "blessing" that was available the moment a Christian consecrated everything to God and claimed this promise of "perfect love." All an individual needed to do was to become a "living sacrifice on the altar of Jesus Christ." This "altar" theology, though highly controversial, made a lasting imprint on the doctrine of sanctification among various perfectionist groups.[66]

In 1858 Walter Palmer, Phoebe's husband, purchased the *Guide to Holiness* and under Phoebe's editorship, the circulation grew from thirteen thousand subscriptions to thirty thousand. Besides her editing duties, Phoebe traveled with her husband, conducting evangelistic meetings during the summer months. As the demand for their ministry increased, Walter Palmer curtailed his homeopathic medical activities and teamed up with Phoebe in full-time evangelistic ministry. Although she did not believe it was right for women to "preach," she was able in good conscience to give "lengthy exhortations in connection with her husband's sermons" (her meetings drawing the largest crowds).[67]

Phoebe's own position on women in ministry was traditional. She strongly defended that position in her book *Promise of the Father*. Even though she wrote her book after hearing the "anguished testimony of a woman who felt compelled to speak and yet was rebuked by the elders of her church," she did not view the religious leadership of women to be the norm. Reflecting on the leadership of Deborah and Huldah in the Old Testament, she wrote that

> it is in the order of God that women may occasionally be brought out of the ordinary sphere of action and occupy in either church or state positions of high responsibility; and if, in the orderings of providence, it so occur, the God of providence will enable her to meet the emergency with becoming dignity, wisdom, and womanly grace.[68]

In the fall of 1857 she and her husband traveled to Canada where they attracted crowds of several thousand people. According to Timothy Smith, an afternoon prayer meeting in Hamilton, Ontario, became a ten-day revival in which four hundred people were converted and many "sanctified." The next winter they traveled from town to town in New York, where they were welcomed not only by Methodists, but also by Congregationalists, Presbyterians, and Baptists. Concerning these revival campaigns, Phoebe wrote, "Never have we witnessed such triumphs of the cross as during the

past summer and fall. I think . . . not less than two thousand have been gathered into the fold at various meetings we have attended. Hundreds of believers have been sanctified wholly, and hundreds have received baptisms of the Holy Ghost, beyond any former experience."[69]

The holiness revival in America spread to England through the writings of Finney, Palmer, and other Americans, and in 1859 Phoebe Palmer and her husband made a four-year visit to England, "which created a minor sensation in English Methodism." According to Timothy Smith, they "preached for weeks to packed houses at Leeds, Sheffield, Manchester, Birmingham, and dozens of other places."[70] At the time of her death, she was credited with having brought some 25,000 people to Christ for salvation.

For all her activity and influence within the ranks of Methodism, Phoebe Palmer's situation did not reflect the role of women in the denomination at large. She was not the norm, and her influence on the position of women in the church was nominal. Her holiness emphasis, distinguished by her own "altar" theology, further alienated her from many Methodists. She was outside the mainstream of Methodism, and she and others viewed her ministry as unique—not the norm for women. So despite her recognition and popularity, Methodist women had gained little, if any, ground on account of her example. This may have been due in part to her own insistence on a secondary role for women in ministry. Yet, while denying an equal role for women in the church, she served as a role model for other women both inside and outside the ranks of Methodism.

Catherine Booth and the Salvation Army

It was criticism of Phoebe Palmer's preaching in England in 1859 that thrust Catherine Booth (1829–90) into a public defense of women in ministry. This came in the form of a pamphlet entitled *Female Ministry; Or, Woman's Right to Preach the Gospel.* Here she not only emphasized the biblical precedent for women in ministry, but the personal leading of the Spirit: "If she have the necessary gifts, and feels herself called by the Spirit to preach, there is not a single word in the whole book of God to restrain her, but many, very many, to urge and encourage her." She believed that the attitude toward women was based more on her contemporary culture than on biblical tradition: "Oh, that the ministers of religion would search the original records of God's Word in order to discover whether the general notions of society are not wrong on this subject, and whether God really intended woman to bury her gifts and talents, as she now does."[71]

As the wife of a Methodist minister, she had not herself preached when she wrote her defense, but the following year on Whit Sunday as her husband William finished his sermon, she stood up in front of a crowd of more than a thousand packed into Bethesda Chapel and began to speak. Catherine later recalled her inner feelings that morning: "It seemed as if a voice said to me, 'Now if you were to go and testify, you know I would bless it to your own soul as well as to the souls of the people.' I gasped and said in my soul . . . 'I cannot do it.' and then the devil said, 'Besides, you are not prepared to speak. You will look like a fool and have nothing to say.' " Her first words when she rose to speak were, "I want to say a word. . . ." William was as surprised as anyone when she made her sudden announcement, but he quickly recovered, and when she had finished, he announced that she would preach that evening.[72]

Catherine Booth, Co-founder of the Salvation Army. Made from nineteenth-century prints by Deane K. Dayton for Donald W. Dayton, *Discovering an Evangelical Heritage* (New York: Harper & Row, 1976).

Catherine's only regret was that she had waited so long. Earlier when giving temperance lectures, she wrote to her parents: "I only wish I had begun years ago. Had I been fortunate enough to have been brought up amongst the Primitives [Methodists], I believe I should have been preaching now. . . . Indeed, I felt quite at home on the platform, far more so than I do in the kitchen!"[73]

Although Catherine Booth was, in her own words, "one of the most timid and bashful disciples the Lord Jesus ever saved," she was well-prepared for her public ministry.[74] She had been active in the temperance movement and was well versed in Scripture. She had been a Bible student from the time she was a child. By the time she was twelve she had read the Bible through eight times. Unlike Palmer, she was a committed feminist. She insisted before she was married that she and her husband would have an egalitarian marriage. Whether they actually did is difficult to determine, but by nineteenth-century standards, she enjoyed freedom accorded few married women, and William apparently was not threatened by the potential competition of her ministry. Soon after her pulpit debut, William became ill, and his slow recovery opened the door for her own preaching ministry. For a time he was so ill that she took over his entire circuit. Soon after that, dissatisfied with their lack of independence, the Booths broke their ties with the Methodist connection, and began working together in a revivalistic ministry. Then, in 1865, they moved to West London. "William began preaching to the poor East Enders, walking eight miles there and back each Sunday, while Catherine attracted large crowds to her meetings in London's affluent West End."[75]

She was a dynamic and forceful speaker, as is seen in a sermon that she delivered in 1880 to the congregation at the West End. On the subject of evangelism she was dogmatic: "Oh! people say, you must be very careful, very judicious. You must not thrust religion down people's throats." To that opinion, she responded vehemently: "Then I say, you will never get it down. What! am I to wait till an unconverted Godless man *wants* to be saved before I try to save him?" She did not shy away from controversy. In fact, she viewed discord as a sign of true Christianity. "Opposition! It is a bad sign for the Christianity of this day that it provokes so little opposition. If there was no other evidence of it being wrong I should know it from that."[76]

Catherine did not limit her ministry to the West End. She was also involved in city mission work, and it was through this common interest with her husband that the Salvation Army was born. "Reclaiming" women from a life of prostitution was a significant part of the mission work. Most of these women were of the "poorer class," but a surprisingly substantial number came from the upper class—enough for Catherine Booth to report: "At this moment one of our most pressing needs is a temporary home for the reception of the lady portion of them, until we can fit them for some useful occupation."[77]

From the very beginning, the Salvation Army welcomed the service of women. Clause 14 of the Foundation Deed submitted in 1875 specified that

nothing shall authorize the conference to take any course whereby the right of females to be employed as evangelists or class leaders shall be impeded or destroyed or which shall render females ineligible for any office or deny to them the right to speak and vote at all or any official meetings of which they may be members.[78]

In 1878, only three years after clause 14 was formulated, forty-one of the total ninety-one Salvation Army officers in the field were women. Indeed, many of these "women" were mere girls—"Hallelujah lassies," as they were termed. A London journalist reported the work of two of these girls:

> I was amazed. I found two delicate girls, one hardly able to write a letter, the other not yet nineteen, ministering to a crowded congregation which they had themselves collected out of the street, and building up an aggressive church militant out of the human refuse which other churches regarded with blank despair. In the first six months . . . a corps or a church was formed of nearly two hundred members.

Another young girl, Eliza Shirley, was promoted to the rank of lieutenant at the age of sixteen. When her family emigrated to America, she and her mother rented a factory warehouse in Philadelphia and began an evangelistic outreach there. Handbills were posted with the message:

> Blood and fire! The Salvation Army
>   Two Hallelujah females
> will speak and sing for Jesus
>   in the old chair factory
> at Sixth and Oxford Streets
> Oct. 5th at 11 a.m. 3m. 8m.
> All are invited to attend.

The first service brought out twelve people, but a few weeks later, "every bench in the factory was filled . . . every foot of standing room was taken."[79]

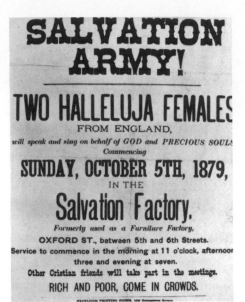

Salvation Army Poster Advertising Women Preachers. From Salvation Army Archives.

When the Booths decided to officially inaugurate the work of the Salvation Army in America, Commissioner Railton was sent with "the Splendid Seven," a team of seven women. There was no condescending to them on account of their sex, as is illustrated in the farewell prayer offered by an Army officer: "Lord, these ladies are going to America to preach the gospel. If they are fully given up to Thee, be with them and bless them and grant them success. But if they are not faithful, drown 'em, Lord, drown 'em!" They did succeed, and they served as an example along with many others that prompted William Booth to say, "My best men are women."[80]

In spite of the humanitarian work that the Salvation Army conducted in the poorest urban districts, the organization met bitter opposition from virtually every sector of society. From rowdies and thugs to sophisticated high churchmen, the Army was the subject of scorn. In the streets, the ridicule frequently turned to violence, and in 1882 there were more than six hundred reported assaults on Army volunteers, more than a third of the victims being women— one dying of her wounds.[81]

Six of the "Splendid Seven" Who Immigrated to America in 1880.   From Salvation Army Archives.

Catherine trained her own children for ministry in the Salvation Army, where they all served faithfully. The training began when they were young, and getting them "saved" was her first priority. In response to another mother's question, "How have you managed to get your children converted so early?" she responded, "*I have been beforehand with the devil. I have not allowed my children* to become pre-occupied with the things of the world before I have got the seed of the Kingdom well in."[82]

Catherine Booth lived through the stormy decade of the 1880s, but was ill much of the time and died of cancer in 1890 at the age of sixty-one. Her last years had been devoted to preaching and to rescue-mission work, especially that involving young teenage prostitutes. But as important as her work was with the Salvation Army, her public ministry was perhaps even more significant. Of her thirty years of preaching in England, Norman Murdoch writes, "Many agree, no man of her era exceeded her in popularity or spiritual results, including her husband."[83]

Hannah Whitall Smith and the Deeper Life Movement

Hannah Whitall Smith (1832–1911) was raised in a Quaker home and, like Phoebe Palmer, gave a new slant to the holiness movement—a slant that reflected her Quaker background and one that gave the movement a form of passivism or Quietism. Her book, *The Christian's Secret of a Happy Life*, published in 1875, became a best seller almost immediately and still remains a popular devotional classic, having sold more than two million copies. Here she emphasized the passiveness of the Christian as clay in the potter's hands: "In order for a lump of clay to be made into a beautiful vessel, it must be entirely abandoned to the potter, and must lie passive in his hands."[84]

The argument that women are more emotionally inclined than men and therefore gravitated to ecstatic religious movements is not supported by the heavy female involvement in the holiness movement. The movement, at least as it penetrated the urban middle class, was not characterized by ecstatic religion, nor were the female leaders of the movement so characterized. Hannah Smith's testimony is particularly interesting in this regard. She had desperately sought for an ecstatic religious experience after her husband experienced great emotion and ecstasy at a camp-meeting revival. She tried desperately to achieve the same experience (and even went to the altar with a stack of handkerchiefs, thinking she would be overcome with tears), but nothing happened. For years she sought the experience. Later she wrote that she believed it was her husband's emotional nature that allowed him to have the experience, and she conceded that she was still "a dry old stick."[85]

As the years passed, she began to question the validity of emotional experiences and actually to renounce them:

> I have discovered by careful investigation that spiritualists have wonderful emotional experiences quite as often as Christians. I am convinced, too, that there are emotions common to highly exalted mental states, no matter what the cause of this exaltation, whose origin is purely physical or psychical and have nothing to do with God's Spirit. Since such experiences can be of the body and not of the spirit at all, I fear many people are sadly deceived by them into thinking they must necessarily be from God and *must* be tokens of His especial favor, when the individuals concerned know nothing whatever of the reality of being filled with the Spirit."[86]

The unemotional character of her religious experience was similar to that of Sarah Lankford, who with her sister Phoebe Palmer had initiated the Tuesday Meetings. "All was calm and stillness," she wrote. "I had none of the expected emotions. I arose from my knees fully determined to rest in God."[87]

Despite the recognition that came from her writing, Hannah Smith was at times a liability to her husband's ministry. Certain of her theological positions were very controversial. In the 1870s after her husband had been invited to conduct meetings in England, it surfaced that Hannah held to universalism. There were loud protests, but they went ahead with the tour, and Hannah won the hearts of vast numbers of English Evangelicals and was dubbed "the angel of the churches." "It is most remarkable," writes Melvin Dieter, "that in spite of a longstanding commitment to a universalist view of the restitution of all things," she was used widely in the churches.[88]

In spite of the Smiths' popularity, their public ministry was short-lived, and it was not Hannah's heresy that created the problem. It was Robert's. By the mid-1870s he was deeply embroiled in controversy over a scandal, and his career came to an end at an international higher-life convention in the resort city of Brighton, England. Robert and Hannah were the featured speakers and were viewed by many as the leaders of the movement. But suddenly it was announced that his meetings were canceled and that he was returning to America for health reasons. Despite the efforts of the convention leaders to suppress the details, rumors of sexual misconduct with a young woman circulated. But even more disturbing were the reports of his antinomian views. A contemporary charged that he was teaching that "those who are in Christ are no longer subject to the law of God, as the rule of their conduct; that they are lifted to a higher sphere of life, and walk in a freedom unknown to those who are strangers to the exalted experience of the new and better life."[89]

Hannah Smith appeared occasionally on public platforms following the scandal, but Robert, for most of the remaining quarter century of his life, remained in semi-seclusion. In 1895, when she was in her early sixties, she returned to England to speak as part of a promotional effort for churchwomen. The London *Echo* described it as an "invasion" of one hundred and seventy-five chapels by women preachers. Hannah described the event as follows:

> One of the most interesting things that took place during our week of meetings was on Sunday the 16th. The newspaper extract . . . describes it, and also describes me as I appear to English eyes—'active though elderly.' It was a wonderful thing to get an entrance for women into so many places of worship in London, and the funny thing was that when our supply of women failed and we offered men, nobody would have them! No wonder.[90]

Single Women on the Circuit

While Palmer, Smith, and Booth all depended on their husbands to be the real "preacher" in the family, other women made it on their own.

The widow Margaret ("Maggie") Van Cott, "was on the sawdust trail for thirty years." Her early ministry consisted of traditional women's work—prayer meetings, charity, and tract distribution, but her reputation as a spell-binding speaker eventually launched her into a wider ministry that included men as well as women. Yet she had serious reservations about entering a male profession. Spurned by a man in her audience and plagued by "self-doubts," she was at first reluctant to accept actual preaching invitations. Women preachers were unheard of in Methodist circles. The invitations continued coming, however, and in 1868 she applied first for an Exhorter's License and then for a Local Preacher's License, and in 1869 she became the first woman in the United States to be licensed to preach by the Methodist Episcopal Church.[91]

In the early 1870s, Van Cott conducted a revival in Evanston, Illinois, where Frances Willard was serving at the women's college. After preaching and singing, "she placed her kind hands on every head as she was going around that large circle" and "asked a blessing on all. The revival that followed was the most memorable ever known in Evanston, and all my girls but two . . . became members of the church."[92]

During a one-year period at the height of her career, Van Cott delivered some four hundred sermons and brought more than seventeen hundred people into the membership of the Methodist church. So influential was she that her ministry was compared to that of one of her contemporaries—evangelist Dwight L. Moody.[93]

Amanda Smith, Nineteenth-Century Black Holiness Evangelist. Made from nineteenth-century prints by Deane K. Dayton for Donald W. Dayton, *Discovering an Evangelical Heritage* (New York: Harper & Row, 1976).

Amanda Smith

Another woman to gain recognition as a preacher and revivalist in Methodist circles was the black scrub woman Amanda Smith (1837–1915). She was born a slave in Maryland and grew up experiencing hard work and intense religious emotion. "Red hot" camp meeting revivalism often provided her only leisure-time activity. She was married twice. Her first husband abandoned her, and her second husband died. After that she heard a distinct call from God to preach. In the words of Elliott Wright, "She was an unusual sight in post-Civil War America—a black woman evangelist, an ex-slave, traversing North and South preaching to all races and then spending fourteen years ... evangelizing in England,

India and Africa." She too was part of the holiness movement.[94]

Amanda's ministry was deeply influenced by the modeling of her mother and grandmother, who, not unlike countless other slave women in the antebellum South, overcame the drudgery of their day-to-day toil by sharing their faith and religious experience with others—often their mistresses and their families. When "the spirit of the Lord got hold of my young mistress," Amanda wrote, "my mother was awfully glad that the Lord had answered her and grandmother's prayer. As I have heard my mother tell this story she has wept as though it had just been a few days ago." So strong was the influence of these slave women that the young mistress "wanted to go to the colored people's church." Her family "would not have that. So they kept her from going. Then they separated my mother and her. They thought maybe mother might talk to her, and keep up the excitement. . . . About a quarter of a mile away was the great dairy, and Miss Celie used to slip over there when she got a chance and have a good time praying with mother and grandmother."[95]

Like white women in ministry, Amanda faced opposition on account of her sex. In 1870, when the African Methodist Episcopal Church held its first general conference south of the Mason-Dixon line in Nashville, Amanda was determined to attend. Since women were not permitted to be delegates, she was looked on with suspicion: "I was eyed with critical suspicion as being there to agitate the question of the ordination of women. All about, in the little groups that would be gathered talking, could be heard, 'Who is she?' 'Preacher woman,'" was the answer. Amanda was not a feminist or an agitator for women's ordination. "The thought of ordination had never once entered my mind, for I had received my ordination from Him, Who said, 'Ye have not chosen Me, but I have chosen you, and ordained you, that you might go and bring forth fruit.'"[96]

The opposition that she confronted came not only from her own people but from whites as well. When she was conducting itinerant evangelistic work in England and in India, she was trailed by Plymouth brethren who verbally attacked her ministry. After her work in England in 1878, she wrote, "The work seemed to be signally blessed of God. But the good Plymouth brethren did not see it at all, because I was a woman; not that I was a black woman, but a woman. . . . They would try, in a nice way, to get me into an argument; but I always avoided anything of the kind; for it is like bodily exercise which profiteth little." Later in India she was again confronted by "the good Plymouth brethren" who "were much disturbed because I was a woman. . . . so they had nice articles in the daily papers; then they wrote me kind letters, and bombarded me with Scriptural texts against women preaching."[97]

When she was in India, she met Bishop James Thoburn, a missionary and strong advocate of women's ministries. He later wrote of that encounter:

The penetrating power of discernment which she possessed in so large degree impressed me more and more the longer I knew her, indeed, through my association with her I learned many valuable lessons, more that has been of actual value to me as a preacher of Christian truth, than from any other person I ever met.[98]

Women's Temperance Movements

During the nineteenth century women were very active in temperance movements—movements that were closely allied with religious values. In fact, some of the greatest opportunities for women in ministry came through the temperance cause. The most well known of these movements was the Woman's Christian Temperance Movement (WCTU), but most of the early organizations were headed by men, and women were not allowed in leadership positions. Their support was sought after, but their public presence was shunned. This attitude toward women was demonstrated again at the World's Temperance Convention in New York City in 1853. Antoinette Brown was a duly elected delegate from her local society, but when she tried to speak, she met with strong opposition: "There was a great furor, and I stood on the platform for three hours except when someone brought me a chair, and I did not have a chance to open my mouth. So much stamping and pounding with canes that [the] air was full of dust. . . . Regular hubbub." Horace Greeley sarcastically reported accomplishments of the convention in the *Tribune: "First Day*—Crowding a woman off the platform. *Second Day*—Gagging her. *Third Day*—Voting that she shall stay gagged. Having thus disposed of the main question, we assume the incidentals will be finished this morning."[99]

The result of such treatment was the formation of women's temperance groups, which provided many Christian women with their first opportunities to be involved in organizational activity and public speaking. Mother Stewart, in her book *Memoirs of the Crusade: A Thrilling Account of the Great Uprising of the Women of Ohio in 1873, Against the Liquor Crime*, recounted the stories of many women who were suddenly thrust into the limelight. "God quickly made Captains and colonels and commanders out of timid women, who had never known their powers till God called them out."[100]

Some of the women who acquired their public exposure through temperance activism went on into other spheres of ministry. This was true of Mary Lathrap, the wife of a Michigan physician. Her first public speaking was reciting a temperance poem, and she later became active in the state WCTU. But through the years, "the call to preach Christ's Gospel" never left her. Her temperance speaking opened the door for preaching, and she eventually became a licensed Methodist peacher. She was a popular evangelist who had the support of Methodist bishop Simpson and other church leaders. Unlike some of her male contemporaries, she apparently was not an emotional "hell-fire and brimstone" preacher. Wrote Frances Willard, "I have often seen her hold the earnest attention of six or seven thousand people, many of them standing, for over an hour, by her clear logic, original thought, and her deep earnestness in putting forth the Truth."[101]

Frances Willard, the Foremost Nineteenth-Century Temperance Leader. From Anna Gordon, *The Beautiful Life of Frances E. Willard* (Chicago: Woman's Temperance Publishing Association, 1898). Frontispiece.

Frances Willard

One of the best-known female temperance leaders of the nineteenth century was Frances Willard (1839–98), who was active in founding and directing the WCTU, the largest nineteenth-century women's organization. Her life and ministry illustrates how closely the temperance movement was aligned to religious activities. In spite of intense opposition, temperance work offered the only viable public ministry for many women of the nineteenth century. Frequently the religious activity associated with the WCTU involved evangelistic outreach to men. The WCTU department of evangelistic work sponsored Bible readings and gospel work in prisons and in police stations and among railroad employees, soldiers, sailors, and lumbermen. A national superintendent, a woman in each case, was in charge of each of these areas of ministry. She was aided by state and territorial assistants, who were responsible to coordinate the workers on the local level. "These," wrote Frances Willard, "make an aggregate of several thousands of women who are regularly studying and expounding God's Word to the multitude, to say nothing of the army in home and foreign missionary work, and who are engaged in church evangelism." This vast army of women functioned outside the church, "not because they wish to be so," but because the church "is afraid of her own gentle, earnest-hearted daughters."[102]

Willard herself was converted at a Methodist revival meeting when she was in her early twenties and soon after joined the Methodist church, with the commitment of "seeking to lead others to Christ." Then five years later, under the preaching of Phoebe and Walter Palmer, she experienced "entire sanctification"—a "second blessing" that she later admitted she had lost. Her deep religious faith, however, continued to influence her ministry. Regarding her temperance work, she wrote, "[Only] as I come close to God and through Christ's blood am made a new creature, am I ready for this work so blessed and so high."[103] Willard's work was not limited to the United States. Indeed, the WCTU was probably the first large women's organization to spread world-wide on a large scale. By the 1880s, the White Ribbon Missionaries were organizing chapters in Asia, Africa, South America and elsewhere in the world.[104]

Closely connected with her work for temperance was her support of women's suffrage, for she believed that laws supporting prohibition would be enacted only if women had the ballot. As with her temperance work she claimed the direct leading of God: "While alone on my knees one Sabbath, in the capital of the Crusade state, as I lifted my heart to God, crying, 'What wouldst Thou have me to do?' There was borne in upon my mind, as I believe from loftier regions, this declaration, 'You are to speak for woman's ballot as a weapon for protection for her home.'"[105]

Following her years of service with the WCTU, Willard, despite her lack of biblical education, was invited to work with evangelist Dwight L. Moody during his Boston campaign. She conducted afternoon Bible lectures and spoke at women's meetings. There was open opposition to her work, and when Moody invited her to preach at a Sunday afternoon meeting, she expressed her concern that it would "hinder the work among these conservatives." Her tenure with the Moody revival campaigns was short lived—due in part to differences of opinion with Moody regarding her association with the women in temperance groups who held to unorthodox religious beliefs. Yet, she was able to say: "I deem it one of the choicest seals of my calling that Dwight L. Moody should have invited me to cast in my little lot with his great one as an evangelist."[106]

By the 1880s, Willard was openly demanding an equal role for women in the church. She had moved far beyond the sentiments of Phoebe Palmer and other women who saw themselves as anomalies hiding behind the authority of their husbands. In her book *Woman in the Pulpit,* she presented a strong defense of female ministry. She also confessed to her own calling in life and encouraged other women not to be intimidated as she had been: "Let me, as a loyal daughter of the church, urge upon younger women who feel a call, as I once did, to preach the unsearchable riches of Christ."[107]

Years earlier in a letter to Mrs. D. L. Moody, Willard expressed her sentiments succinctly:

> All my life I have been devoted to the advancement of women in education and opportunity. I firmly believe God has a work for them to do as evangelists, as bearers of Christ's message to the ungospeled, to the prayer-meeting, to the church generally and the world at large, such as most people have not dreamed. It is therefore my dearest wish to help break down the barriers of prejudice that keep them silent. I cannot think that meetings in which "the brethren" only are called upon, are one half as effective as those where all are freely invited, and I can but believe that "women's meetings," as such, are a relic of an outworn *regime.* Never did I hold one of these meetings without a protest in my soul against it. As in the day of Pentecost, so now, let men and women in perfectly impartial fashion participate in all services conducted in His name in whom there is neither bond nor free, male nor female, but all are one."[108]

Carry Nation

On the extremist fringe of the temperance movement was another well-known temperance activist, Carry Nation, whose fame was based largely on her "smashing" of saloons. This type of activity was a result of what she described as a "divine call": "One day . . . I opened the Bible with a prayer for light, and saw these words: 'Arise, shine, for thy light is come and the glory of the Lord is risen upon thee.'" But she also claimed very specific divine guidance:

> When I arrived near home . . . I said: "Oh, Lord, if it is Thy will for me to go to Kiowa tonight, have Price, (my horse,) pass this open gate," which I knew he would never do unless God ordered it. I gave him the reins and when I got opposite the open gate my horse jumped forward as if some one had struck him a blow."[109]

Carry Nation, Holding the Hatchet She Used to "Smash" Saloons.   From Carry A. Nation, *The Use and Need of the Life of Carry Nation.* (Topeka: Stevens, 1909).

The next morning, she was awakened to a "murmuring, musical" voice saying, "Go to Kiowa," and "I'll stand by you." What was God leading her to Kiowa for? To "smash" a saloon. "I threw as hard, and as fast as I could, smashing mirrors and bottles and glasses and it was astonishing how quickly this was done. These men seemed terrified, threw up their hands and backed up in the corner. My strength was that of a giant. I felt invincible. God was certainly standing by me."[110]

As with Willard, she viewed her work as a Christian ministry. She was a jail evangelist for the WCTU in Medicine Lodge, Kansas, and her "smashing" was very often accompanied by an evangelistic message. On many occasions, as was the case in Topeka, she and her "sisters" stated their purpose before entering the saloon. "We asked to go in to hold gospel services as was our intention before destroying this den of vice, for we wanted God to save their souls, and to give us ability and opportunity to destroy this soul damning business."[111]

Sects and Women

As in other periods of history, there was a tendency for women who desired meaningful opportunities for ministry to gravitate to sects. In these developing fringe movements they were generally accorded more respect by their male counterparts than were the women in the institutionalized church where male domination was firmly rooted. Sectarianism provided opportunities for women to actually found or lead movements, though more often they served simply as equal partners in evangelism—a smart strategy for any developing sect that needed all the willing laborers that could be recruited to propagate the new creeds or doctrinal emphases.

Were women more inclined than men to found sects or cults? Some have argued that they were, but the historical evidence does not support such a contention. Throughout the history of the Christian church the vast majority of sectarian movements have been led by men. That women held more prominent positions in sects and cults indicates only that such movements permitted them such freedom—not, as Walter Martin and others have suggested, that the prominence of women proves they are more prone to be deceived than men.[112]

Mother Ann Lee

Among the eighteenth- and nineteenth-century sects and cults that have been founded or led by women, the Shakers, Christian Science, and Seventh-Day Adventism stand out. But even in these movements, the role of women was controversial, and when the leaders passed from the scene—particularly in Christian Science and Seventh-Day Adventism—male domination became firmly entrenched.

In the case of the Shakers, the leadership of Mother Ann Lee was virtually deified by many of her followers. According to a prominent Shaker, writing in 1780, "Some of them say, that the woman called the mother [Ann Lee], has the fullness of the God Head, bodily dwelling in her, and that she is the queen of heaven, Christ's wife: And that all God's elect must be born through her; yea, that Christ through her is born the second time." But that evaluation was not universally accepted, and some Shakers challenged her leadership position on the basis of the apostle Paul's writings regarding women. After her death, Joseph Meacham assumed leadership of the movement. It was his desire that women share an equal role in the ministry, and he even appointed Lucy Wright as a co-leader to head up the women's work, but not without opposition from the men and reluctance on the part of many women to assume equal roles.[113]

Unlike certain other utopian communities that advocated some form of "free love" or polygamy, the Shakers distinguished themselves by their insistence on celibacy. This factor as much as any other incurred the wrath of outsiders. The movement was led not only by a woman, but by a woman who was denying the very basis of female worth that was so intricately tied in with being a wife and mother.

Mary Baker Eddy and Christian Science

Unlike Mother Ann Lee, who was the spiritual head of socialistic communities, Mary Baker Eddy (1821–1910), the founder of Christian Science, was the spiritual leader of a pseudo-Christian movement that became a wealthy and respectable middle-class church. Rebelling against her Calvinistic upbringing, Mary developed a religious ideology that served her personally and appealed to masses of nineteenth-century Americans seeking a philosophy that would ease their bodies as well as their souls. Although her move-

ment was termed "Christian" Science, she veered sharply from the traditional orthodoxy of Christianity, and thus her life and movement are not strictly within the scope of Christendom. It is noteworthy, however, that despite her strong leadership, the movement was dominated by strong male leadership after her death.

Ellen G. White and Seventh-day Adventism

One of the most influential women in American Christianity in the nineteenth century was Ellen G. White (1827–1915). She was the prophetess of Seventh-day Adventism. According to her husband, she received literally thousands of visions, revelations, or "testimonies" throughout her long life, and it was the "inspired" writings that resulted from these visions that confirmed many of the new doctrines as well as the social and health regulations of the early Seventh-day Adventists. Although she was much criticized by people inside as well as outside the movement, she managed to maintain a powerful influence over the movement until the time of her death during World War I, and she was held in even higher esteem in the years following her death. In the late 1970s and early 1980s, with the publication of a number of articles and books questioning her honesty and originality, her place of prominence in the movement was strongly challenged, but even in the face of solid evidence that indicates she used other writings as a basis for her "testimonies" that were said to have come directly from God, the Seventh-day Adventists were unwilling to abandon her.

Ellen Harmon and her twin sister Elizabeth were born near Portland, Maine, where they grew up in the oftimes emotional atmosphere of revivals and camp meetings. Ellen herself underwent highly charged religious experiences during her youth, and at the age of seventeen she received her first "vision." This revelation confirmed to her that the Adventist people who had believed William Miller's prediction that the Lord would return on October 22, 1844, were on the path to heaven. Other visions that followed soon after confirmed to her the necessity of worshiping on the Sabbath and the doctrine of the "investigative judgment" that began when Christ moved from one apartment of the sanctuary in heaven to another on October 22, 1944, to begin the final phase of his atonement.[114] Although such views had been held by some Adventists prior to her esctatic trances, her claims of supernatural confirmation bolstered their place in the movement.

By the end of the first decade of the twentieth century, Ellen White had more than one hundred and thirty thousand followers. During her lifetime, Seventh-day Adventism had spread out all over the world. At the time of her death, according to Ronald Numbers,

> only one other woman—Mary Baker Eddy—had contributed more to the religious life of America. . . . Though she never thought highly of the founder of Christian Science, whom she regarded as little better than a spiritualist, she had much in common with her. Both women were born in New England in the 1820s. As children they both experienced debilitating ill-

nesses, which curtailed their formal schooling; as young women they suffered from uncontrollable spells that left them unconscious for frighteningly long periods of time. They both sought cures in Grahamism and hydropathy. . . . Both . . . claimed divine inspiration, and both succeeded in establishing distinctive churches. But despite their many similarities, the two women had basically different goals: Ellen White longed for a mansion in heaven, Mary Baker Eddy wanted hers here on earth.[115]

Roman Catholic Women

During the nineteenth century, when American Catholicism was faced with the monumental challenges of ministering to its millions of immigrant members, the number of nuns increased from fewer than forty to more than forty thousand. Sister Mary Ewens writes:

> If adequate means could be found to measure the relative importance of personal influences, it might well be shown that sisters' efforts were far more effective than those of bishops or priests in the Church's attempts to meet these challenges. . . . They outnumbered male church workers in the last half of the century in almost every diocese . . . and there were almost four times as many nuns as priests by the century's close.[116]

Elizabeth Bayley Seton

One of the most renowned Roman Catholic women in the nineteenth century was Elizabeth Bayley Seton, who founded the American Sisters of Charity in 1808 and served as Mother Superior from 1809 until her death in 1821. She was the mother of five children, and did not convert to

Roman Catholicism until after her husband died, when her children were yet small. During the early years, the new religious order made its home in a log house in Emmitsburg, Maryland. In the years that followed, orphanages and schools were established in Philadelphia and New York, and less than a decade after her death the first Catholic hospital in America was established by the Sisters of Charity.[117]

Seton rejected her Episcopalian upbringing to become a Roman Catholic, partly because of her attraction to the ritual, but it was the personality of the Virgin Mary that most influenced her in her decision. Mary became a real person to her: "I felt really I had a Mother—which you know my foolish heart so often lamented to have in early days." She later reflected how from her earliest days she had "looked . . . to the clouds for my mother," but found no one. But after finding Mary, it seemed as if I had found more than her. . . . So I cried myself to sleep on her heart."[118]

Male Opposition

Like their Protestant counterparts, Roman Catholic nuns struggled for a place of their own in a church dominated by men. This was particularly evident in the ministry of Mother Theodore Guerin, who emigrated from France to America in 1840 with her Sisters of Providence. Soon after settling on a farm in Indiana, she encountered the first of her many clashes with Bishop de la Hailandiere of Vincennes. Over the years he "repeatedly interfered in their internal affairs, reassigning sisters to different convents, closing and opening missions without consulting them, intercepting their mail, refusing them the sacraments, and forcing them to accept candidates they regarded as unsuitable." The situation finally improved when Mother Guerin threatened to move her sisters to another diocese.[119]

Catholic nuns in the nineteenth century also faced strong opposition from outside their faith in the form of anti-Catholic bigotry. They were assaulted both verbally and physically. Novelists and tract-writers sought to destroy their reputation, and mobs sought to "harry them out of the land." One of the most infamous incidents of physical persecution occurred in 1834 when an Ursuline convent in Massachusetts was destroyed by fire. "The mob looted the buildings and desecrated the chapel, even digging up the bodies of the sisters in the cemetery, before burning the convent and academy."[120]

Many of the Catholic sisterhoods in America were established by European nuns, a fact that did not improve their image among certain segments of nativistic Americans. One such order was the School Sisters of Notre Dame, headed by Mother Theresa Gerhardinger, who emigrated from Germany in 1847 to work among German immigrants in Pennsylvania. Her letters back home indicate that there was a lack of pastoral care among Roman Catholics: "How pitiful is the plight of the poor Germans. Entire families grow up and die without being baptized or instructed in their religion, especially those who live in the primeval forests." But even with such obvious needs for more help, the sisters met with rebuff from their own church leaders. Theresa feared the bishop would not permit them to stay: "He is afraid of jealousy and disharmony on the part of the sisters he requested from Ireland. Since he himself is Irish, these sisters are his favorites and darlings. He has entrusted the hospital, the orphanage and the English-speaking schools to them."[121]

Women in the Pastorate

Despite the influential positions women had as lay workers, organization heads, evangelists, sect leaders, and nuns, there were very few of them filling pulpits as pastors. Even as late as 1888, when Willard published her classic, *Woman in the Pulpit*, there were only an estimated twenty women in the United States serving as pastors. That figure did not include the some five hundred women evangelists or the Quaker women "preachers," whose numbers were estimated to be around three hundred and fifty. Nor did it include the female Salvation Army officers. The denominations known to have ordained women were the Methodist, Congregational, Baptist, Universalist, and Unitarian. Ordination for women was frequently a hard-fought battle, though many women refused to become involved in the fray themselves. A friend of Frances Willard who had served for fifteen years as a Methodist pastor illustrates this attitude. When asked to justify her ministry, she responded: "I have gone forth, never allowing myself to be drawn into an argument on the subject, and never saying a word in personal defense, but I knew all the time the Lord would send somebody to take care of the defense."[122]

Besides the standard biblical arguments that were used against ordaining women, it was frequently said that women pastors would not be able to care adequately for their homes and families. It was this issue as much as any other on which women felt obliged to defend their calling. One woman pastor wrote, "After twenty-five years' experience as pastor and preacher, I am convinced that there is no work outside the home circle upon which women can so consistently and properly enter as that of the Christian ministry." Such a ministry was not without sacrifice, however, as she went on to relate, "I never take vacations, and, excepting a very few Sundays when my children were born, have really lost no time; and yet I think it is conceded by my neighbors that my children are as well cared for as theirs, at any rate." Another woman pastor, frustrated by the grim forecasts regarding ministry and motherhood, wrote, "At the end of their profound arguments and fearful prophesying, I will still point to my five blessed boys, and meekly inquire, 'Have they gone to ruin?' "[123]

Antoinette Brown

Although many women preachers sought to stay out of the limelight and avoid arguments over their controversial role, Antoinette Brown, the first ordained woman preacher in America, did not fit that mold. When she was six years old, her parents were converted to "militant" Christianity through the revivalistic preaching of Charles G. Finney. She

Antoinette L. Brown, the First American Woman to Receive Full Ministerial Ordination. Made from nineteenth-century prints by Deane K. Dayton for Donald W. Dayton, *Discovering an Evangelical Heritage* (New York: Harper & Row, 1976).

quickly found herself at home in that religious atmosphere and began leading congregational singing and even did some preaching. Her family all "agreed that dear little Antoinette would grow up to be a minister's wife"; but she had different plans. She enrolled at Oberlin, only to be denied entrance into the theological department, and she continued to meet opposition at every turn throughout the course of her education. "Oberlin's Ladies' Board, stern watchdog of female morality, refused to let her earn money by teaching in the preparatory department." Without a fierce determination and an iron will, she never could have survived:

I was reasoned with, pleaded with, and besought even with tears . . . not to combat a beneficent order tending to promote harmony . . . in the family and in the commonwealth. Established, ordained masculine headship everywhere was held to be indispensable to morality, and grounded in the inmost fitness of things.[124]

Despite the resistance she faced, Brown completed the theological program at Oberlin in 1850, though without a degree and without ordination. (It was not until 1878, nearly three decades after she graduated that the college awarded her a degree. Later, in 1908, Oberlin awarded her an honorary D.D.) From 1850 to 1852 she was on the lecture circuit, speaking out for women's rights and filling the pulpit occasionally in churches where her preaching was not viewed as offensive. In 1853 she was offered an attractive salary and benefit package by Horace Greeley and Charles Dana to begin a pulpit ministry in New York City, but she turned it down, believing she was unprepared for such heavy responsibilities. That same year, however, she accepted a call to a small-town Congregational church "without steeple or bell." In response to her move, the New York *Independent*, a nondenominational religious circular "announced that any woman who would be ordained was an infidel and any church which would ordain her an infidel church. It neglected to print Antoinette's reply, only commenting that Miss Brown disclaimed being an infidel."[125]

Soon after her arrival at the little Congregational church in South Butler, New York, Brown was ordained—a ceremony that made her "the first fully ordained woman in a recognized American denomination."[126] Paradoxically, she went outside her own denomination for a minister to preach her ordination sermon—a minister in a denomination that did not ordain women. The Reverend Luther Lee, a firm supporter of women in ministry and a leading Wesleyan Methodist preacher used the occasion to defend the concept of women in the pulpit. Indeed, after offering a litany of New Testament examples of women in public ministry, he emphatically concluded, "I have now proved that there were a class of females in the Primitive Church called prophetesses, that is, there were female prophets, and those prophets were preachers or public teachers of religion."[127]

Brown's ministry at the little Congregational church was frustrating and lasted less than a year. She was "at her own request dismissed from her connection." There were several reasons for this: "She could not preach eternal damnation. She had refused to condemn and ostracize an unmarried girl whose baby had died, or to preach a sermon on infant damnation on that occasion. She had refused to force a dying boy into conversion, as his parents had demanded, by terrifying him with threats of hell-fire."[128]

After leaving the church, Brown went to New York where she labored as a volunteer in the tenement districts and prisons. Her heart went out to the impoverished slum-dwellers, and, through articles in Horace Greeley's New York *Tribune*, she rebuked the "polished, enlightened, civilized, Christianized society" for its "black shadow"—its failure to come to the aid of the oppressed. In 1856, Brown married Samuel Blackwell, a man with whom she had much in common. "They were believers in woman's rights, abolition, temperance, but most important they were highly religious and, at the time they met, both losing their orthodoxy."[129]

For the next two decades childbearing and domestic duties kept Brown out of the public sphere, but she still found time to write books, both fiction and nonfiction, often dealing with women's rights or religious issues. In 1878 she made it known that she was again available to accept a pastorate—this time as a Unitarian—but it was not until after her husband's death in 1901 that she was able to return to the ministry. She founded All Souls' Unitarian Church in Elizabeth, New Jersey, where she ministered until her death in 1921.[130]

Olympia Brown

Even in the Unitarian and Universalist churches, women preachers faced opposition. Olympia Brown, whose ordination in 1864 in Weymouth, Massachusetts, was the first such ceremony for a female universalist minister, met with strong disapproval when she first began studying theology with a pulpit ministry in mind. And the resistance continued after her ordination. After performing her first marriage ceremony, the issue was raised as to whether the marriage was indeed legal, since the ceremony had been conducted by a female. Apparently the question was not in jest, for it made its way to the Massachusetts State Legislature, where it was referred to the judiciary committee. After serious deliberations, the matter was settled. The marriage was declared legal.[131]

Mainline Denominations

It is an important fact of history that the institutionalized churches most strongly opposed women in ministry. This is particularly evident in the Protestant churches in America. While the sectarian movements often encouraged active women's involvement, the mainline denominations resisted it.

Methodists

The Methodists, more than any other denomination in the nineteenth century, were profoundly affected by women. The first American Methodist woman to make an impact on the movement was Barbara Heck, though her importance has frequently been overdrawn. She is often credited with being the inspiration behind American Methodism. According to Arthur Jennings, it all began when she discovered a group of men (apparently some of them Methodist immigrants) playing cards. "Her Methodist zeal flamed up at this sight and she seized the cards and threw them into the fire, also exhorting the men to repent of their sins and seek salvation. She went immediately to the home of her cousin [Philip Embury] and urged him to no longer hold his peace, but at once begin to preach the Word."[132] Thus began the first Methodist congregation in America. Her ministry was a behind-the-scenes organizational effort, as public preaching was considered a male domain. Some Methodist women were licensed to preach in the last half of the nineteenth century, but most women who actively "preached" among the Methodists, such as Phoebe Palmer, did so on a lay level.

In 1880, eight years prior to the publication of her book, *Woman in the Pulpit*, Frances Willard attended the Methodist General Conference. One of the issues on the agenda was the role of women in the church, and during the conference a motion was made to allow her to speak on the subject. The motion created an uproar, and even though it passed, Willard declined to speak in the face of such controversy. The Conference did vote to allow women to hold lay leadership positions as class leaders and Sunday-school superintendents but took a step backwards by discontinuing to license women as local preachers and denied Anna Howard Shaw's and Anna Oliver's requests for full ordination.[133]

The Methodists continued to debate the issue in 1888, at which time they approved deaconesses for ministry in the local church but voted down other measures favoring women's participation. This time Frances Willard was back "as one of the first five duly elected female local lay delegates" and as a woman who had experienced eight years of consciousness-raising. She was prepared to voice her concerns as an official delegate, but "after another lengthy and vicious debate, this time led by her rejected suitor, now bishop, Charles Fowler, the women were denied seats." So distraught was she that she contemplated leaving the Methodist church and starting a church of her own—a threat that was never carried out. It was not until 1904 that Methodist Episcopal women gained laity rights.[134]

Although Amanda Smith made

speaking trips through the South, the Southern Methodist General Conference was even slower than its counterpart in the North in extending to women meaningful opportunities for ministry. "At the Southern Methodist General Conference of 1898, women were authorized to be Sunday school superintendents," and the Woman's Board of Home Missions was given "virtual autonomy" in its affairs. "Its independence was short-lived, however. In 1910 the Conference placed the women's groups under control of the church's mission board and defeated a movement to give women laity rights, declaring that such a step ran counter to 'the view our people hold in regard to women's place in the church and in society. . . .' "[135]

Presbyterians

It was almost unheard-of for Presbyterian women to preach, and when they did, it created an uproar. This was true of Sarah Smiley of Brooklyn, New York, in 1874. When word reached the Presbytery that "a woman has preached in one of our churches, on Sabbath, at a regular service," it was resolved that "strict regard" should be taken to a General Assembly decision of 1837:

"Meetings of pious women by themselves, for conversation and prayer," we entirely approve. But let not the inspired prohibition of the great Apostle, as found in his Epistles to the Corinthians and to Timothy, be violated. To teach and to exhort, or to lead in prayer in public and promiscuous assemblies is clearly forbidden to women in the holy oracles.[136]

Although her sermons were described as "weighty, solemn, Scriptural, orthodox, tender, and melted some men to tears whom I have never seen so much moved before," Smiley was forbidden to preach to Presbyterians.[137]

The Presbyterians were probably the strictest major denominational group of the nineteenth century. Albert Barnes, professor at Princeton Theological Seminary, spoke for many of his fellow Presbyterians when he stated that Paul's command for women to be silent was a "positive, explicit, and universal rule. There is no ambiguity in the expressions and there can be no difference of opinion in regard to their meaning."[138]

Most women in the Presbyterian churches went along with the restrictions on their speaking, but the situation slowly began to change as they became more involved in missions and social causes. Some began to speak out for more opportunity for ministry and for voting rights. Some even appealed for the ordination of women, but "as the nineteenth century ended, there was little doubt that Presbyterian judicatories were 'not yet ready to settle' the issue of women's rights to ministerial ordination." A few women such as Edith Peake and Louisa Woolsey ministered in Presbyterian churches as evangelists, but not without strong opposition.[139]

The Lutheran Churches

Lutherans also remained closed to the idea of women in ministry throughout the nineteenth century. Women's public activity of any kind was seen as a threat to the home and to the traditional values of the church. The Missouri Synod is an example. Its most important German organ, *Der Lutheraner*, urged Lutherans to vote down women's suffrage. Likewise, in 1894 the Synod's

official English newspaper, the *Lutheran Witness*, described the catastrophe female suffrage would produce. "Many women," it predicted, "will be so busy about voting and political office that the home and children will have no attraction for them, and American mothers and children, like Christian charity, will be a rarity."[140]

Birth control also became an issue that was closely associated with feminism, and churchmen feared it as is seen in an article in the *Lutheran Witness* in 1898: "The new woman has cast the church aside, because it teaches subordination of the wife to the husband, and enjoins domestic duties from which the 'tastes' of the new woman revolts. The new woman hates children, and is madly exerting her ingenuity in frustrating the ends of matrimony." An editor further denounced women who "gave speeches and essays and high moral instruction to the world instead of giving children."[141]

Baptists

While the Freewill Baptists and other splinter groups opened their doors early to the ministry of women, the larger Baptist groups were much more restrictive in their view of women. The Southern Baptists illustrate this. The constitution of that church, which was formulated in 1845, did not specify the role for women—particularly as to whether women could be members of the convention and thus have voting rights as delegates. It was not settled until 1885, when Arkansas sent two female messengers as delegates to the national convention. After prolonged wrangling, the convention voted 202 to 112 not to seat the women. Fear of female domination was expressed by one delegate who predicted that if the vote passed, the Convention "would be flooded with them next year." Another honestly confessed, "I love the ladies, but I dread them worse." It was not until 1918 that the Convention permitted women to officially take part as delegates.[142]

The reactionary views of Southern Baptists toward women were expressed frequently in church literature, and such views were slow in dying. An article that opposed coeducation appeared in the *Biblical Recorder* in 1868; it took issue with the "erroneous opinion that the mental powers of the sexes are equal." The author maintained that women were the weaker vessel in body and in mind. Some women even joined in the effort to demean their own sex. A Mrs. James Hime of Georgia praised the 1885 Convention decision to bar women as delegates because she believed it was the duty of the men to "see that no heads inferior to their own" should be permitted to supervise "the vast network of missions."[143]

The issue of women speaking in mixed groups was even more controversial for the Southern Baptists. An article in the *Biblical Recorder* in 1892, expressed the sentiment of the vast majority of the members. It spoke of the troublesome fads in society, among which was "the determined effort to bring women to the front as public lecturers, or speakers before mixed assemblies, or as ordained preachers of the gospel." Although the author conceded that "we have a few pastors and laymen South, even in the Baptist churches" who support this "unscriptural and dangerous innovation," he called upon the stalwarts of the faith to "once for all, let it be known *everywhere* that our people South, as a rule, are unalterably opposed to this thing."[144]

Small Evangelical and Holiness Sects

The numbers of women in ministry increased each decade of the nineteenth century, not because the institutionalized church became more open to the idea of female ministry, but because of the birth and the growth of evangelical sectarian groups. Groups such as the Quakers contributed to this increase, but the greatest influence on this trend was the formation of new denominations—many of which were holiness groups that broke away from mainline Methodism. The holiness movement had begun as an effort in the Methodist church to revive Wesley's teaching, and it remained a part of that denomination until the late nineteenth century when a number of new denominations were formed as a result of "come-outism"—those who left the Methodist church to get back to a more primitive form of Christianity or to get back to Wesley's original teachings.

Quakers

The fierce opposition that the Quakers had faced among the Puri-

tans of Colonial New England gradually subsided, and by the nineteenth century, Quaker meeting houses were springing up in the West largely as a result of the efforts of itinerant preachers—many of them women. One of the most prominent of these female evangelists was Eliza Gurney, who began her traveling ministry after her husband's death in 1847. She was part of an evangelical trend in the Society of Friends that deemphasized the "inner light" and stressed Bible study and preaching, and much of her own itinerant ministry involved the organizing of Bible classes.[145]

The most famous female Quaker preacher of the nineteenth century was Lucretia Mott. This mother of six became a Quaker minister at the age of twenty-eight in the early 1820s. It was a turbulent period for the Quakers, when some were clamoring for a return of their primitive Quietism and others were calling for an evangelical awakening. She became involved with a Hicksite wing that emphasized the "inner light" and experience over Scripture, but she was ever disenchanted with the "intolerance and sectarianism she found within that community."[146]

Mott was a leading abolitionist and feminist, and as such she was keenly aware of the discrimination that existed even among the Quakers. "Although recognized as the spiritual equals of men, women were not accorded equality in areas of the church governance. For example, women did not have equal power with men to disown, that is to expel, members, or to make discipline." It was for the institutionalized church, however, that Mott had the harshest criticism. "At a time when evangelical religion was gaining increasing support from women, Mott pointed out that priestcraft was the greatest obstacle in changing the female condition." In 1848 she was a leading spokeswoman at the Seneca Falls women's-rights convention and was largely responsible for drafting the Seneca Falls Declaration of Sentiments, which declared that "the speedy success of our cause depends upon the zealous and untiring efforts of both men and women, for the overthrow of the monopoly of the pulpit."[147]

Wesleyan Methodists

Even though the founder of the Wesleyan Methodists, Orange Scott, opposed efforts of abolitionists to broaden their struggle to include women's rights, there were some very significant connections between early Wesleyan Methodists and the feminist movement. The Seneca Falls women's rights convention in 1848 was held in a Wesleyan Methodist Church, and Luther Lee, an early Wesleyan Methodist leader, strongly supported women's ministries and was willing to do so publicly in 1853 by giving the ordination address for Antoinette Brown. His speech was a strong defense of full equality for women in the church.[148]

It was not until the General Conference in 1864 that the ordination of women actually became an issue with the Wesleyan Methodists, sparked by the ordination of a woman elder by the Illinois Conference. The delegates voted down a resolution to deny women preaching licenses, and the whole women's issue was deemed a matter for local conferences. There was strong opposition, however, and in 1887, late in the General Conference proceedings after many delegates had left, a resolution passed denying women ordination. Four years later, the decision was reversed, and again it was left up to local conferences whether or not to allow female ordination to the ministry.[149]

Free Methodists

Although the Free Methodist Church, which was founded in 1860, did not ordain women, it allowed women to preach and conduct evangelistic ministries. B. T. Roberts, the founder of this denomination, however, was a staunch supporter of women in ministry and sought very hard to rally support for a resolution permitting the ordination of women in 1890. Although he was unable to obtain the necessary votes, he continued the battle, and in the following year published a book justifying his position from a biblical standpoint. In his book, *Ordaining Women*, published in 1891, he argued the equality of women from Genesis to Paul's Epistles, maintaining that women were fully equal to men in ministry as well as marriage. "The Gospel of Jesus Christ . . . knows no distinction of race, condition, or sex," he asserted; "therefore no person evidently called of God to the Gospel ministry, and duly qualified for it, should be refused ordination on account of race, condition or sex."[150]

Roberts also spoke in revolutionary terms regarding women's place in the home, presenting a model for an egalitarian marriage:

The greatest domestic happiness always exists where husband and wife live together on terms of equality. Two men, having individual interests, united only by business ties, daily associate as partners for years, without either of them being in subjection to the other. They consider each other as equals. Then, cannot a man and woman, united in conjugal love, the strongest tie that can unite two human beings having the same interests, live together in the same manner?[151]

Three years after Roberts' publication of *Ordaining Women*, another Free Methodist leader, W. A. Sellow, published *Why Not?* Despite his defense, however, a resolution to ordain women failed again that same year in 1894. The struggle continued into the following decade and by 1907 the consensus of opinion had changed enough to permit the ordination of female deacons. It was not until 1974 that women's ordination was placed on an equal par with men's.[152]

The Brethren Church

One of the most progressive evangelical sects regarding women in the nineteenth century was the Brethren church, which split off from the German Baptist Brethren in the early 1880s. "They moved quickly to grant women the privilege and responsibility of church leadership. . . . By 1894 both the General Conference and most of the district conferences had passed resolutions favoring the equality of men and women in the church or the inclusion of women in the ranks of pastors and missionaries." The first woman ordained by the movement was Mary M. Sterling, who received her credentials in 1890. After

that she conducted itinerant evangelistic work, which included a tour of West Virginia and Pennsylvania in 1894, during which time "she preached 207 sermons in 187 days, receiving 27 additions to the church, 18 of whom she herself baptized." She was well received, despite her sex, and in that same year she was asked to give the Sunday morning sermon at the General Conference meetings.[153]

The Christian and Missionary Alliance

In 1887 A. B. Simpson, a Presbyterian minister who had established himself and his family in New York City, founded the Christian and Missionary Alliance (then known simply as the Christian Alliance). His "attitude toward women," according to Leslie Andrews,

> must be viewed against the backdrop of his consuming passion to evangelize a lost world before the return of the King. He did not seek to placate those whose ecclesiastical agendas were, in his opinion, secondary to the task of world evangelization. If women furthered the primary mission of the Church to reach lost souls for Christ, then he enthusiastically endorsed their ministry to achieve that objective.[154]

Simpson was criticized for his open policy for women in ministry, but he was quick to defend his position. After a series of meetings in Atlanta, he responded to attacks by saying the matter was an issue "which God has already settled, not only in His Word, but in His providence, by the seal which He is placing in this very day, in every part of the world, upon the public work of consecrated Christian women." He concluded by chiding the pastor who led the attack: "Dear brother, let the Lord manage the women. He can do it better than you, and you turn your batteries against the common enemy."[155]

Simpson's theology also reflected his attitude toward the female sex. A chapter title in one of his books was "The Motherhood of God." Here he rejected the common belief that God was of the male gender and confessed his appreciation for the feminine qualities of God.

> The heart of Christ is not only the heart of man, but has in it all the tenderness and gentleness of women. . . . He combined in Himself the nature both of man and woman even as the first man Adam had the woman within his own being before she was separately formed from his very body.[156]

In reference to the Holy Spirit, Simpson wrote: "As our heavenly Mother, the Comforter assumes our nurture, training, teaching, and the whole direction of our life."[157] He encouraged women to become involved in his own ministry, as is evident by the testimony of Carrie Judd Montgomery. As a young woman she conducted a faith-healing ministry in Buffalo, New York, and when she visited New York City, Simpson invited her to become involved in his large "convention" ministry, which he conducted in New York as well as in other cities around the country. On one occasion when she had cut her afternoon message short, he invited her to return that evening to speak to a much larger crowd. He later invited her to join him full-time in the ministry, but she declined, believing God wanted her to continue her own work in Buffalo.[158]

The Church of God (Anderson, Indiana)

The Church of God (Anderson, Indiana) was founded by Daniel S. Warner and his wife in 1881. At the urging of his wife, Warner had experienced "entire sanctification," and after that they saw a need for a new movement—a "great holiness reform." From the very beginning, women were prominent in ministry, as was indicated in a publication in 1902, entitled *Familiar Names and Faces*. Some 25 percent of the movement's leaders were female. According to John Smith, historian of the movement, "Forty years before the time of woman's suffrage on a national level, a great company of women were preaching, singing, writing, and helping to determine the policies in this religious reform movement."[159]

Church of God (Cleveland, Tennessee)

The issue of women in ministry arose early in the history of the Church of God (Cleveland, Tennessee) as it did in other holiness denominations, in part because "considerably more women than men were being reached and won to the Church." When the subject of ordination was brought before the Fourth Annual Assembly in 1909, it was determined that women could preach and hold ministerial certificates but could not be ordained, "e.g., women preachers may not perform marriages, baptize, conduct business conferences, administer the sacrament, or 'usurp authority over the man.' " They were, however, permitted to evangelize and plant churches, "and numerous local churches came into being through the tears and labors of consecrated handmaidens of the Lord."[160] Indeed, the pattern of the Church of God (Cleveland, Tennessee) was similar to other sectarian movements in church history. Women were necessary to carry out the foundational work of church development, but once the movement was organized, men quickly took over the leadership positions.

The Belton Sanctificationists

While the holiness movement offered women greater opportunities for ministries, it did not generally espouse feminism per se. There were exceptions, however, and one of the most curious was the radical group of women who formed a community in Belton, Texas, and became known as the Belton Sanctificationists. The group started after Martha McWhirter "experienced a kind of pentecostal baptism." Following this experience she

> professed sanctification, and taught the doctrine in a way that led her to antagonize strongly the views of her successive pastors, but not to break openly with the church. Her ministry developed independently from the local church, and her convictions were most effectively set forth in a ladies' weekly prayer-meeting which was held from house to house in the town for some years succeeding her "sanctification." This finally merged into a meeting of her followers alone.[161]

By 1879 the women followers had separated into a self-sustaining communistic organization that operated a hotel, a farm, and cottage industries. Some of the women were widowed, and others were divorced or separated from their husbands. Initially they held to a strong view of Wesleyan perfectionism and "had regular and frequent devotional exercises," but by the early 1890s, though they claimed to be "living the Bible," they no longer had "formal worship of any kind." They did, however, continue "discussion among themselves of their religious experience, which," according to a contemporary observer, "they try to interpret so that it will serve to guide them. They frequently obtain this guidance from dreams. . . ."[162]

The Women's Century—an Overview

As the new denominations of the Holiness-Pentecostal movement were opening doors for women at the close of the nineteenth century, little headway was being made by women in the larger Christian bodies. This was due in part to a reaction against the feminist movement. Groups such as the Belton Sanctificationists brought disrepute to women in religious leadership, but even more significant were the radical feminists whose embittered protests hurt the cause of many women who simply wanted to have a ministry in the church. A powerful example of this was the publication of Elizabeth Cady Stanton's *Woman's Bible*. "The inspiration of the Bible itself was being called into question," and "no self-respecting . . . churchman or woman, the argument went, would want to associate himself or herself with such crass antibiblicalism."[163] When it was suggested that her Bible was the work of the devil, she responded, "This is a grave mistake. His Satanic majesty was not invited to join the Revising Committee, which consists of women alone."[164]

Yet the nineteenth century had indeed been a century for women in the church. Women had made great gains in organizational work, particularly in regard to home and foreign missions and humanitarian endeavors. Equally significant was the prominent role women played in sectarian movements that flourished in the nineteenth century. But by the end of the century, women had made very little official headway in the established churches. The vast majority of institutionalized churches barred them from ordination and from equal status on the lay level as well.

Chapter 8

Foreign Missions:
Jungle Pioneers
and Urban Church Planters

The one area of church ministry above all others that captured the imaginations of women during the late nineteenth and early twentieth centuries was that of foreign missions. The missionary profession offered women unparalleled opportunity for meaningful ministry. Women freely preached, evangelized, planted churches, trained nationals, established schools, and conducted humanitarian work. Their lack of clerical ordination had little effect on their ministries, and they were far out of reach of critics back home. Some would-be critics took comfort in the fact that most women missionaries were involved in "women's work" and those who were preaching to mixed or all-male groups were not seriously breaching any Pauline injunctions anyway, since their hearers were only "natives." So, for women who wanted a meaningful professional ministry, foreign missions provided the opportunity, though not without a struggle—a struggle that began on the home front.

Foreign missions offered far more than a meaningful Christian profession for thousands of women in the church. It was a cause—a movement that drew millions of women into its sphere. Indeed, it was "substantially larger than any of the other mass woman's movements of the nineteenth century" and outstripped in size both the Laymen's Missionary Movement and the Student Volunteer Movement. "By 1915 there were more than three million women on the membership rolls of some forty denominational female missionary societies."[1]

In spite of the fact that there were vast numbers of women involved in foreign missions, both at home and abroad, and that women had a powerful impact on the modern missionary movement, little mention is made of their contributions in the history-of-mission texts. "As so frequently happens in the writing of history," Patricia Hill points out, "the women have simply disappeared."[2] Kenneth Latourette's massive seven-volume history makes very little mention of women, though four of those volumes are devoted to the modern period. Stephen Neill, likewise, virtually ignores the work of women in his classic *History of Christian Missions.* Robert H. Glover's *Progress of Worldwide Missions*, revised and enlarged by J. Herbert Kane, makes mention of several notable women, but slights them in comparison to male missionaries. For example, Henry M. Stanley, an explorer-"missionary" to Africa, although he can hardly be considered a missionary at all, is given more coverage than Mary Slessor, who did extensive missionary pioneer work in Nigeria for nearly forty years. And David Brainerd, who spent five years in a less-than-successful attempt to evangelize the American Indians, is given more coverage than Amy Carmichael, who spent fifty years overseas in a fruitful ministry in India. Lottie Moon, a pioneer missionary to China, is not mentioned at all. An exception to this neglect of women is the recently published history-of-missions text, *From Jerusalem to Irian Jaya*, which chronicles the contributions of both male and female missionaries throughout missions history and devotes a separate chapter to the women's missionary movement of the modern period.[3]

Mission Support Societies

The first organized involvement of women in missions began in the early nineteenth century and entailed mission support societies. In 1800 Mary Webb organized the Boston Female Society for Missionary Purposes, which her biographer has termed "the first woman's missionary society in the world."[4] Although her own denomination was Baptist, the group, like many that would follow, began as a nondenominational movement—in this instance made up of Baptists and Congregationalists. (In 1829 the organization split into two separate groups, each supporting its respective denomination.) For more than fifty years, this tiny woman, who was confined to a wheelchair, served as secretary-treasurer of the organization and generated support for both home and foreign missions.

Two years after Webb's group was formed, women in Boston and all over New England rallied behind Mehitible Simpkins and formed "mite" societies, the proceeds of which went into the treasury of the Massachusetts Missionary Society. "Women were already giving their pennies for missions, and the Cent Society brought forth a flood of copper coins. . . . It caught the feminine imagination; Mrs. Simpkins was deluged by pennies."[5]

The early mission-support groups were welcomed by church leaders and generally were not viewed as a threat to male authority because they were organized as auxiliary societies and the disbursement of funds remained under the control of denominational or mission leaders. "By the 1820s," writes R. Pierce Beaver, "women were generally conceded the right to organize for fund raising, for prayer, and for educating themselves and their children with respect to mission."[6] With the approval, and in many cases the encouragement, of men, female mission support societies flourished during the first half of the nineteenth century, as did a wide assortment of home-missionary benevolent societies.

Missionary Wives

Long before women's support societies were officially organized, women had been actively involved in missionary work. Since the dawn of modern missions during the mid-eighteenth century when the Moravians, inspired by Count Nickolas von Zinzendorf, spread out across the world, they served with their husbands in a great evangelistic effort. But these women were considered merely wives of missionaries—not missionaries in their own right. So also was the case with missionary wives in the generations that followed. "Although the wife was considered indispensable, she got little official recognition. It was her husband who was appointed 'missionary' and handed the instructions. She was long designated only 'assistant missionary.'"[7]

Indeed, in many instances such a woman *was* merely a wife—going to the mission field only because she was constrained to follow her husband. She was a participant in the unhappy saga of leaving her family and homeland behind for the sake of her husband's ministry, living in deprivation, and dying young of childbearing. Jane Hunter cites a survey that showed "seventeen percent of the American Board women who were married when they went to the field indicated that it was for their husbands alone that they were in China. Women married long before they set sail were more likely to be in this category."[8] Dorothy Carey, whose lot it was to be married to William Carey, the "Father of Modern Missions," is an example of this.

Dorothy Carey

When William Carey suddenly announced in 1792 that he had volunteered himself to the newly formed Baptist Missionary Society to go to India for the rest of his life as a missionary, Dorothy was devastated. She had three young children and was pregnant with the fourth. Although she was illiterate (as were many lower-class English women of her day), she was well aware of the privations and disease her family would face—if they were fortunate enough to survive the dangerous sea voyage around the Cape of Good Hope. She had willingly served with William in his tiny Baptist parishes and shared the family's meager sustenance with others who were even less fortunate. But the proposition that she uproot her family and risk their lives in an unproven missionary venture for which she felt no "calling" seemed utterly absurd. She refused to go.

Nearly a century later Margaret Simpson was confronted with a similar situation when her husband (A. B. Simpson, who later founded the Christian and Missionary Alliance) shared with her his visionary call to China. As the mother of six children, she viewed the idea as preposterous, though she was careful not to discredit his call: "I was not then ready for such a sacrifice. I wrote him that it was all right—he might go to China himself—I would remain home and support and care for the children. I knew that would settle him for a while."[9] It did. Simpson served the cause of foreign missions on the home field, no doubt more effectively than he could have overseas.

Dorothy Carey's refusal to go did not elicit the same reaction. William left without her, taking only Felix, their oldest son. Before he actually departed England, however, his partner was detained by creditors, and the mission was delayed several months. In the meantime, Dorothy gave birth to her fourth child and was persuaded to accompany her husband to India. Her tenure as a missionary wife is one of the tragic footnotes of missions history. From the beginning she was intensely dissatisfied with missionary life, and William complained in a letter that she did "not see the importance of the mission" and was "continually exclaiming against" him.[10] And no wonder. The family situation progressively worsened. One after another, members of the family were stricken with tropical fevers or dysentery, and in the fall of 1794 five-year-old Peter died.[11]

The strain proved to be too much for Dorothy. Following Peter's death, little is mentioned of her, except for the occasional references to her "insanity." In 1901 William explained the situation to his sister: "Mrs Carey is obliged to be constantly confined; she has long gotten worse and worse, but fear both of my own life and hers and the desire of the police of the place, obliged me to agree to her confinement."[12]

Mary Morrison and Mary Livingstone

The outstanding accomplishments of William Carey are clouded by the distressing state of his marriage and family life, but he certainly was not alone among great missionaries in having a wife who was unable to cope with her lot in life. Mary Morrison, wife of Robert Morrison, a pioneer missionary to China, also suffered severe mental strain on the mission field. Robert wrote of "her feeble mind" being "much harassed," adding that she "walks in darkness and has no light."[13] Mary Livingstone, wife of David Livingstone, the famous explorer-missionary to Africa, likewise succumbed to depression. Unable to endure the rigors of African exploration with little children and frequent pregnancies, Mary returned to England with the children. There "she was not only homeless and friendless but was often living on the edge of poverty in cheap lodgings," and it was rumored she had lapsed into spiritual darkness and was drowning her misery in alcohol.[14]

Priscilla Studd

It was not uncommon for missionary wives, such as Mary Livingstone, to be abandoned by their husbands. Priscilla Studd is another example. As the wife of the famed British cricket player and student volunteer, C. T. Studd, she served faithfully as a missionary to China until her health was broken and the family was forced to return to England. But that did not end her husband's missionary career. He later left her with a debilitating heart condition and set out for Africa, where he served as a missionary without her for nearly two decades until his death.[15]

What was the solution to this conflict between missions and marriage? William Carey's advice was direct: "Pray be very careful what stamp missionaries' wives are of."

Hudson Taylor also addressed the issue, and admonished potential male candidates: "It is most important that married missionaries should be *double* missionaries. . . . Unless you intend your wife to be a true missionary, not merely a wife, home-maker, and friend, *do not join us*."[16]

The Worth of Missionary Wives

Indeed there were vast numbers of missionary wives who were "true missionaries," according to the Taylor definition. Rufus Anderson, one of the most noted mission leaders and strategists of the nineteenth century, paid high tribute to the worth of the missionary wife. He was wary of sending single women overseas, but he believed the missionary wife to be indispensable. They served as a "symbol of peace" and "often proved safeguards to their husbands"; he also believed they were a necessary personal ingredient in their husbands' success. Beyond that, it was the duty of missionary wives to "exert much influence in the department of education," and he cited several exemplary cases:

At the Sandwich Islands more than a dozen of the married female missionaries are regular instructors of female schools, some of which are numerously attended and by women as well as children. In Ceylon the late Mrs. Winslow exerted an admirable influence over a charity boarding-school of native females. And Mrs. Thomson who died not long since in Jerusalem, having been a successful teacher of a female seminary in this country, carried all her zeal in behalf of female education with her to Palestine, and no doubt would soon have presided over a flourishing school of females in that land, had not a mysterious Providence seen fit so early to remove her. There are now two female schools in Syria, one of Arab girls taught by a married female, the other of Druse girls on Mount Lebanon taught by the exemplary widow of a missionary not long since deceased.[17]

Ann Judson

The most noted of these married women was Ann Hasseltine Judson. The antithesis of Dorothy Carey, she was looked up to as a role model for all Christian young women. In the decades following her death in 1826, dozens of biographies and biographical sketches were published about her. She was the wife of Adoniram Judson, America's highly acclaimed "first" foreign missionary, and as such she played her part well. Indeed, before she married Judson, she had committed herself to serve God, and she maintained that her decision to go to India was not determined by her love for a man—"an attachment to an earthly object." Rather, she insisted that she was prompted by an "obligation to God . . . with a full conviction of its being a call. . . ."[18]

Ann was sent out to be much more than a missionary's wife. She was commissioned with the call to ministry in mind. In his farewell address, the Rev. Jonathan Allen gave her and Harriet Newell, her female colleague, a very specific charge:

It will be your business, my dear children, to teach these women, to whom your husbands can have but little or no access. Go then, and do all in your power, to enlighten their minds, and bring them to the knowledge of truth. Go, and if possible, raise their character to the dignity of rational beings, and to the rank of Christians in a Christian land. Teach them to realize that they are not an inferior race of creatures; but stand upon a par with men. . . .[19]

Ann Hasseltine Judson, Missionary to Burma and Wife of Adoniram Judson. From James D. Knowles, *Memoirs of Mrs. Ann H. Judson* (Boston: Lincoln and Edmands, 1829). Frontispiece.

As a missionary, Ann served with no lack of dedication but with the same drawbacks that confronted virtually all married women missionaries in the nineteenth century. Despite her best efforts to do translation work and conduct classes for women, she was severely hampered by illness and particularly by childbearing. Her greatest contributions to the cause of women and missions was her inspirational writing—her gripping stories of life on the mission field and the struggles she faced, particularly when her husband was confined for nearly two years in a Burmese death prison. She also wrote heartrending accounts of child marriages, female infanticide, and the trials of the Burmese women, who were kept under subjection by the "tyrannic rod" of their husbands: "The wife receives the appellation of *my servant*, or *my dog*, and is allowed to partake of what her lordly husband is pleased to give at the *conclusion* of his repast!"[20]

But worse than the ill-treatment of these women was their "imbecility." They were "taught nothing" and spent their days in "listless idleness." It was for this cause that Ann made her appeal to women back home:

> Shall we, my beloved friends, suffer minds like these to lie dormant, to wither in ignorance and delusion, to grope their way to eternal ruin, without an effort on our part, to raise, to refine, to elevate, and point to that Saviour who has died equally for them as for us? . . . Let us make a united effort, let us call on all, old and young, in the circle of our acquaintance, to join us in attempting to meliorate the situation, to instruct, to enlighten and save females in the Eastern world.[21]

The High Death Rate of Missionary Wives

Ann Judson served for thirteen years in Burma before she died— thirteen years more than her colleague, Harriet Newell, served. Harriet and her infant daughter died while sailing on the Isle of France before she had a chance to conduct mission work. Following Ann's death, Adoniram Judson married twice more (as had William Carey). Both his second and third wives served courageously as missionaries, wives, and mothers, and both died prematurely from the physical strain of missionary life. Their circumstances were not unusual, and in light of that, it is no wonder that there were cries of outrage against women's involvement in missions. When Emily, Judson's third wife left for Burma in 1846, the *Boston Evening Transcript* strongly protested: "This is another case of *infatuation* which would almost seem to be for an untimely death. We really think there should be a law against the wholesale sacrifice of life which is continually chronicled amongst those who imagine they are 'called' to labor in unhealthy climes as the wives of missionaries."[22]

Despite such warnings, married women continued to flood onto the mission field. They worked alongside or independently of their husbands, they had babies, and they died young. William Dean, a missionary to China in the mid-nineteenth century, who had lost two wives himself, was convinced that missionary women died young because they too often attempted to go beyond their wifely duties and minister outside the home. "Thus attempting to do what they cannot perform, they sacrifice health and life in the vain endeavor, and what is more, neglect the duties of their sacred calling and domestic relations." The missionary wife, he further lamented, is plagued by "the secret thought that she is not accomplishing what the public expect, though that expectation may be unreasonable, which is the worm at the root of her joys, and which withers her happiness and her health."[23]

Some missionary wives took to heart the warnings about the rigors of the mission field and went out of their way to take precautions. Lillias Underwood, who served with her husband in Korea for twenty-eight years, was warned when she sailed as a bride to the Orient in 1889 that she would return in a coffin. Despite that warning she and her husband ventured into the interior, "where no white woman had ever been." But she was not seeking to play the role of a martyr. Indeed, so concerned about her welfare was her husband that she felt "far too much babyfied for a hardy missionary." He arranged for her to travel in grand style.

> Under a bamboo roof covered with oiled and painted paper, she sat Turkish fashion on cushions with a hot-water bottle and footmuff at her feet, and a shawl draped round the inside of the blue muslin 'walls' to keep out the draughts. When the front curtain was buttoned down she was out of the range of curious eyes. Four coolies alternated in carrying the chair in pairs, three miles at a time, so that the travelers were able to make thirty or more miles a day.

It was such pampering that permitted Underwood to keep up her hectic pace of evangelistic and medical work for nearly three decades. But despite her precautions, when she left the field she was "in very feeble health."[24]

Except in port cities and international settlements where life frequently moved at a leisurely pace, it was generally the norm for missionary wives to maintain a heavy work schedule in addition to their domestic duties. During her eleven-year marriage to Adoniram Judson, Sarah Boardman gave birth to eight children and kept up a grueling schedule of work. According to Joan Brumberg,

Maria Taylor, Wife of J. Hudson Taylor, Founder of
the China Inland Mission.

this remarkable woman "had schools to superintend, Bible classes and prayer meetings to organize, and a new maternal association for educating Burmese mothers to supervise. In addition, she was doing translation work in Burmese and Talain, while learning Peguan. . . ."[25]

Maria and Jennie Taylor

Maria and Jennie Taylor, the two wives of J. Hudson Taylor, also distinguished themselves in their missionary endeavors. Maria was actively involved in the founding of the China Inland Mission, and on the field she took charge of mission matters when her husband was absent. She was so influential that some of the other missionaries regarded her as the "backbone of the Mission." Indeed, it was said that her husband "never took a step without consulting her."[26] Taylor's second wife, Jennie, was even more deeply involved in the work of the mission. In 1878, when Taylor was ill in London and a famine was ravaging North China, Jennie left him and the seven children (two of her own, four of Maria's, and an adopted daughter) and returned to China to head up the relief program. "After that, it was easier for Mr. Taylor to let other women join the front ranks, when his own wife had led the way."[27]

Inequality of Missionary Wives

As much as she was revered for her sacrifice and service, a missionary wife was rarely regarded her husband's equal. She was viewed as a "weaker vessel," whose ministry and life was sometimes cut short through ill health and childbearing. Daniel Eddy, in his book *Heroines of the Missionary Enterprise*, published in the mid-nineteenth century, represents this line of thinking: "Almost all the heroines who have gone forth from the churches of America, to dot heathen soil with their lowly graves, have been attended by some stronger arm than that of weak, defenseless woman."[28] An example of the discrimination that the "defenseless woman" faced is the situation Dr. Ida Scudder's mother confronted when she and her husband first made plans to go to India as missionaries. She was denied mission-board support because she was regarded a poor risk—too frail to withstand the unhealthy environment of India. She went anyway—her husband accepting the responsibility for her support. For sixty-three years she continued her ministry, outliving her husband by a quarter of a century.[29]

"Female Missionary Agencies"

Despite their great contribution to missions, missionary wives could not do the job alone. Domestic duties continually interfered with their ministries. "They glimpsed the promise of what might be achieved in women's work for women and children," writes R. Pierce Beaver, "but they longed for colleagues who would have more freedom and who could devote themselves solely to such activity."[30] It was in part because of the pleas for help of married women on the field that the door was opened to single women in missions.

Because of the domestic responsibilities that consumed the time of married women missionaries, single women were needed just to keep women's work on an equal par with men's work. But as time went on, many women argued that women's work was the most basic and important work in missions. According to Patricia Hill, "converting women was, in their view, more important than reaching heathen men in realizing the ultimate goal of Christianizing whole cultures." Methodist women justified their strong emphasis on women's work on the basis that women brought enduring stability to religion: "A man's church will last for one generation. Mothers are the conservators of religion, bringing up their children in their own faith."[31]

It was with this view in mind that the women's missionary movement was initiated. This was a post–Civil War movement confined largely to North America that was organized and directed by women for the purpose of sending women to the foreign field to evangelize women. The support societies had served a purpose, but were not specifically meeting the needs of women. By the eve of the Civil War these "women's Associations were in a sad state of decline, because of the lack of central direction in education and promotion, and, one suspects, because the women had no influence in policy which their funds implemented."[32] But even as interest in support organizations waned, interest in foreign missions increased. As reports of the downtrodden lives of Asian and African women were circulated in the West, women took up the cause to ameliorate their condition through a combined religious and social effort.

The Heavenly Mission Bestowed Upon Women to Reach out to Their Sisters and Brothers in Other Lands. From Daniel C. Eddy, *Daughters of the Cross: or, Woman's Mission* (Boston: Dayton and Wentworth, 1855).

According to the early twentieth-century missions historian, Edwin

Bliss, women's work began in India. He wrote:

> Not merely the seclusion in the zenana, but the terrible suffering occasioned by the customs of child-marriage, the suttee, and the position of widows, made their condition almost more pitiable than that of women in Africa or China. It was for them that the first women's societies were organized, and work for them has been from the beginning an integral part of missionary effort.[33]

This effort actually began decades before the Civil War on a very limited basis, but it was not until after the war that single women in large numbers began flooding onto the mission field.

According to Bliss, the first single woman to be commissioned to serve on the foreign field was M. A. Cooke, who responded to a plea from the British and Foreign Bible Society, to establish a school in Calcutta for Hindu girls. Soon after she arrived in India, while she was still in language study, she visited a boys' school to observe their curriculum and teaching methods. There she watched in anguish as the Indian teacher drove away a young girl who was begging to enroll at the school so that she could learn to read. The following day, Miss Cooke returned with her interpreter, and immediately gathered together fifteen girls who likewise had been denied education, and there she formed her first mission school.[34]

David Abeel

The request for single women to enter foreign missions was made in some instances by men. Most noted of these farsighted mission strategists was the Reverend David Abeel, a missionary to China who was ordained by the Reformed Church in America. In 1834, while he was in London en route to the United States, he admonished his English acquaintances to establish a "female agency" to sponsor single women. He viewed such an innovation as the only option, considering the unresponsiveness of the existing mission boards. As a result of Abeel's personal pleas and his published pamphlet "Appeal to Christian Ladies in Behalf of Christian Education in China and Adjacent Countries," The Society for Promoting Female Education in the East was formed, and within a few years women were supervising schools in several locations in the Far East.[35] Abeel effectively stirred the emotions of his women hearers—particularly by the burning plea he brought from the Chinese women, "O bring us some female men."[36]

Sarah Doremus

On returning to America, Abeel presented the same message to women in his denomination, and in doing so "he found a ready and able co-worker in one of the most remarkable laywomen in the whole history of American Protestantism"—Sarah Doremus, an active member of the South Reformed Church in New York City. She was eager to organize a "female agency," as her British cousins had done, but her dream was frustrated by Rufus Anderson, foreign secretary of the American Board of Commissioners for Foreign Missions. Anderson was well known for his opposition to single women in missions, and since Doremus was active-

ly involved in the support work of that mission, she deferred to his wishes.[37]

Doremus continued laboring for the cause of missions, and finally, in 1860, at a time when vocal opposition was lessening, she organized the Women's Union Missionary Society, an interdenominational mission board that functioned out of her home and under her direction until her death in 1877.[38] Other "female agencies" were founded in the 1860s as the needs on the foreign field were more widely published and as resistance at home decreased. One significant factor that affected the latter was the resignation of Rufus Anderson as foreign secretary for the American Board. His successor was N. G. Clark, a man who quickly established his reputation as a strong advocate of women in missions.[39]

By 1894 there were thirty-three women's foreign mission boards from which some one thousand women had been sponsored as teachers, doctors, evangelists, and relief workers.[40] No longer were single women faced with rejection when they selflessly offered themselves in this most difficult of vocations. They had many options in mission societies and mission fields, and they took courage in their numbers. Indeed, so many single women joined the ranks of missionaries that they began to pose a threat to men. "The flocking of women into the field in the 1880s and 1890s," according to Jane Hunter, "led some general board officials to feel the need to remind women of their place." An example of that was the admonition given by a Baptist mission leader in 1888:

Women's work in the foreign field must be careful to recognize the leadership of man in ordering the affairs of the kingdom of God. We must not allow the major vote of the better sex, nor the ability and efficiency of so many of our female helpers, nor even the exceptional faculty for leadership and organization which some of them have displayed in their work, to discredit the natural and predestined headship of man in Missions, as well as in the Church of God: and "the head of woman is the man."[41]

Feminism and Foreign Missions

Single women were in many instances a threat to their male counterparts on the mission field. When denominational boards began accepting single women, the women frequently worked alongside married men, and tensions sometimes arose over work assignments. This was the situation in China in which Lottie Moon found herself. She had come to China in 1873 as a Southern Baptist missionary with the intention of going "out among the millions" as an evangelist, but instead was assigned to teach in a girls' school. Relegating women to such roles was in her view, "the greatest folly of modern missions." "Can we wonder," she lamented, "at the mortal weariness and disgust, the sense of wasted powers and the conviction that her life is a failure, that comes over a woman when, instead of the ever broadening activities she had planned, she finds herself tied down to the petty work of teaching a few girls."[42]

Lottie Moon's dissatisfaction with the role delegated to women on the mission field was not an isolated case. Other women discovered that their assignments were not as fulfilling as they had anticipated they would be. Bishop James Thoburn, a Methodist missionary to India, pleaded with his sister Isabella to come and serve as a teacher in a girls' school. She went, but for months after she arrived she dutifully served as his personal secretary. When she finally refused to continue, he realized the injustice of his actions. "He understood for the first time that 'a Christian woman sent out to the field was a Christian missionary, and that her time was as precious, her work as important, and her rights as sacred as those of the more conventional missionaries of the other sex.' "[43]

Was Isabella Thoburn a feminist in her refusal to be her brother's secretary? There is a strong difference of opinion today as to whether the women's missionary movement was a feminist movement. R. Pierce Beaver subtitled his book on the subject, "A History of the First Feminist Movement in North America," and he seeks throughout that volume to prove that women's active involvement in foreign missions was spurred on by a feminist impulse. On the other side of the issue is Elisabeth Elliot: "Today strident female voices are raised, shrilly and ad nauseam, to remind us that women are equal with men. But such a question has never even arisen in connection with the history of Christian missions. In fact, for many years, far from being excluded, women constituted the majority of foreign missionaries."[44]

Elliot assumes that because women were in the majority they never raised their voices for equality. Not only is the logic faulty, but so is the conclusion. There were many women missionaries who raised their voices for sexual equality, not the least of whom was Lottie Moon, the "patron saint of Southern Baptist missions." "What women want who come to China," she wrote, "is free opportunity to do the largest possible work. . . . What women have a right to demand is perfect equality." Again, she wrote, "Simple justice demands that women should have equal rights with men in mission meetings and in the conduct of their work." Moon, however, did not make such statements without receiving criticism—even from her own sex. She had to deal with the Elisabeth Elliots of her own day. One Mrs. Arthur Smith, wife of a Congregational missionary, suggested that Lottie was mentally unbalanced for craving such "lawless prancing all over the mission lot." Mrs. Smith's idea of a proper role for the female missionary was to attend "with a quivering lip" her own children.[45]

But while women missionaries such as Lottie Moon spoke out against sex discrimination, it is overstating the case, as Beaver does, to claim that the women missionary movement was a feminist movement. Indeed, Beaver's own evidence time and again points in the opposite direction. He states that in 1860, "the women revolted and formed the first women's board," but his own historical data indicates that women's boards developed only slowly after years of delay because of male opposition, and he concedes that in the South long after 1860, "churchwomen were delayed in organization, hampered in action, and restricted in developing programs because of the long-lingering opposition of men to the public appearance and action of women."[46]

From their private correspondence and published articles, it would seem that the vast majority of women missionaries were motivated by a deep sense of commitment to God far more than by any desire to attain personal recognition or power. "For feminism to have gained a foothold among the women's missionary community," writes Jane Hunter, "would have entailed the replacement of the underlying premise of women's mission work, self-denial, with its opposite, self-advocacy."[47]

When female missionaries insisted on equality, it was generally in the context of ministry, for they believed they were being denied the opportunity to serve God most effectively. In their relationship with men, they were usually careful not to overstep their prescribed bounds. Mrs. Ethan Curtis assured her audience of this in a paper read at the Woman's Board of Missions in Brooklyn in 1891: "Nowhere do we oppose man. Our first object is to be his ready and willing assistant."[48]

Even Lottie Moon accepted the prohibition against "preaching" to men. Yet she was convinced that in order to get "any tangible, visible results" she would have "in some way to reach the men of the community." She solved the dilemma by stirring up enough interest in her women's meetings to rouse the men's curiosity to the point that they could not resist coming to hear. But she made it clear that her "preaching" was to the women. How could she help it if "the men crowded silently behind them and studied along with them. . . . Even Paul would not have objected."[49]

Other women went out of their way to avoid creating any offense on account of their sex. Isabella Thoburn accepted her first invitation to speak at a Sunday service while she was on furlough, only on the condition that she be allowed to answer questions from the front row pew rather than "preaching" from behind the pulpit. After that she more readily accepted invitations to speak, but was always very cautious not to do anything that would appear inappropriate.[50] On the mission field, however, she had far greater liberties, in part because her ministry was mainly to women. In fact, she went so far as to advocate women administering baptisms and the Lord's Supper "to the inmates of the zenanas, for one generation at least." Such suggestions were viewed as radical, however, by most churchmen, and for the most part women of the zenanas remained unbaptized.[51]

In her study of nineteenth-century Presbyterian women missionaries to the American Indians, Leecy Barnett did not find any correlation between the women's missionary movement and feminism: "In the more than 1000 letters read for this study no woman mentioned sympathy for or involvement in the women's rights movement." On the contrary, she found that women missionaries perceived the role of women on the mission field to be quite different from that of men. Jeannie Dickson requested men to come to help in the work at the Dakota mission: "We have some kind of work to do that women cannot do or ought not to do." When her request was not met, she complained that she had "to take a man's position in everything." Other women went out of their way to dissociate themselves from feminism. Referring to herself, Sue McBeth, a single missionary working among Nez Perce Indians, wrote to her superior: "Dr. Lowrie must not think for a moment that she is what is called a 'Women's Rights Woman.'. . . She has no affinity for such. Has more 'rights' now than she can make good use of—and aims to try to be with God's help a true woman." Yet, McBeth trained and supervised Indian pastors and preached herself.[52]

Singleness as a Way of Life

The vast majority of single Protestant missionaries who ventured forth to distant shores had no commitment to singleness. They were single for one simple reason. There were not enough male missionaries to go around. The ratio of women to men on the mission field in many areas during the early twentieth century was as high as 2:1. In many instances single women turned down marriage proposals because the suitor was not deemed suitable for or was not interested in missionary work or because his Christian ideals did not match hers.

This was true in the case of Lottie Moon, who endured depressing bouts of loneliness in China and yet turned down a marriage proposal from Crawford Toy, a Confederate army chaplain, who had courted her before she left for China while she was living at her family plantation in Virginia. Missionary life appealed to him, and marriage appealed to her, but his Christian ideals did not match hers. He was a Darwinian evolutionist, and evolution was a view Moon considered untenable and important enough to prohibit their future life together. Toy later became a professor of Hebrew and Semitic languages at Harvard University. Years later when she was questioned as to whether she had ever been in love, Moon responded: "Yes, but God had first claim on my life, and since the two conflicted, there could be no question about the result."[53]

While most of the single missionaries had no vow or commitment to singleness, the female agencies that sent them out did. It was a very serious matter for a single woman missionary, whose travel and support was financed by a mission committed to single women, to marry on the field. "The whole women's missionary movement," writes Beaver, "was built upon a celibate order of life-career missionaries maintained on a subsistence level. Women missionaries were expected to serve for life without ever getting married." In the event that a single missionary did marry or otherwise forsake her commission during her first term, "she was required, by a signed pledge, to return her travel and outfit allowance and sometimes her salary."[54]

The closest resemblance to taking vows of celibacy among Protestant female missionaries, next to that of a signed pledge, was membership in the community known as the Sisters of the Common Life, founded by Amy Carmichael in India. Carmichael was probably the most famous single woman missionary to leave the shores of England in the modern missionary period. Her thirty-five

books detailing her more than fifty years in India were widely read in Christian circles in England as well as America. She, like so many of her female colleagues, struggled with singleness. But during her early missionary service in Japan she came to terms with that struggle, as she later related:

Amy Carmichael, Missionary to India and Author of Numerous Missions Books. Courtesy of Donhavur Fellowship.

On this day many years ago I went away alone to a cave in the mountain called Arima. I had feelings of fear about the future. That was why I went there—to be alone with God. The devil kept on whispering, "It is all right now, but what about afterwards? You are going to be very lonely." And he painted pictures of loneliness—I can see them still. And I turned to my God in a kind of desperation and said,

"Lord, what can I do? How can I go on to the end?" And he said, "None of them that trust in Me shall be desolate." That word has been with me ever since.[55]

In India, Carmichael became deeply involved in children's work, most specifically in rescuing girls from temple prostitution. She established a home and school for these children. It became known as Dohnavur Fellowship. This all-consuming ministry became her life, and the staff and children were her family. She soon became convinced that the single life was the only alternative for those in the Fellowship, and this became the basis for the Sisters of the Common Life. Women joined the association voluntarily, and they were not bound by vows; however, they were forced to leave should they ever marry. The concept worked, and by 1952 the "family" numbered nine hundred.[56]

Roman Catholic Sisterhoods

The concept of celibate sisterhoods is generally associated with Roman Catholicism—though not necessarily with missions. Yet, throughout the medieval period and following, nuns had served the cause of Roman Catholic missions by establishing convents in non-Christianized areas. Indeed, nuns were encouraged to become involved in the missionary task under Boniface, the eighth-century "Apostle to Germany." But it was not until the sixteenth century that Catholic women again became actively involved in the missionary enterprise in their own right. They sailed from Spain to Mexico, where they established convents in several areas in the New World.[57]

Ursuline Nuns in Canada

In the seventeenth century Ursuline nuns from France sailed to Canada to teach Indian girls and establish convents. They were funded by the wealthy Madame de la Peltrie, who wanted to be a nun herself but stood to lose her inheritance if she did not marry according to her father's wishes. She needed the money to finance the mission, so she publicly went through with a bogus marriage, collected her inheritance, and secured passage for the New World. She was accompanied by six Catholic sisters, including Mary of the Incarnation, a nun from the convent in Tours who had previously testified of a vision depicting the need for mission work in Canada and of a double calling from the Virgin Mary and from St. Joseph. These single women, unlike so many Protestant women of a later date, were welcomed by their male colleagues, especially the Jesuits, who were already established in Canada. They founded a large convent, and the Indian girls were taught proper womanly behavior. According to a Jesuit observer, they "reared their pupils in so chaste a horror of the other sex, that a little girl, whom a man had playfully taken by the hand, ran crying to a bowl of water to wash off the unhallowed influence."[58]

Anne-Marie Javouhey

One of the most far-reaching missionary endeavors by Roman Catholic sisters was the work involving the

Sisters of St. Joseph, founded in 1805 by Anne-Marie Javouhey (1779–1851). "Roman Catholic historians attribute the first renewal of African missions in the nineteenth century to the faith and enterprise" of this remarkable woman.[59] She was born and raised in France, and at the age of nineteen she became a nun. In 1800, soon after she entered the convent, she received a visionary call to be a missionary. She later testified that she awoke from her sleep hearing voices and seeing her room strangely illuminated. She looked around and saw children from different races and cultures. In the midst of them was a nun who spoke directly to her: "These are the children God has given you. He wishes you to form a new congregation to take care of them. I am Teresa. I will be your protectress." With those words, the vision was finished, and Javouhey was left to contemplate its implications for her future.[60]

Without papal authority, but with this powerful "call," she founded the Sisters of St. Joseph, and the first missionary nuns were commissioned to an island in the Indian Ocean. In 1822, after the sisterhood was firmly established, she herself became a missionary to Africa. There she found the work and the people much to her liking: "I love the black peoples very much. They are good simple folk. Their only malice they get from us. It would not be difficult to convince them by example. They readily imitate what they see the whites doing."[61]

Javouhey was a humanitarian and an activist. Hospitals, educational institutions, and agricultural colonies were all part of her expanding minis-tries. The agricultural colonies were formed to help overcome the injustice she witnessed in the colonists' treatment of blacks, and she prohibited any form of race discrimination. Likewise she was eager to establish a native clergy, and for this purpose she founded a seminary for Africans in France.

After a number of years in Africa, Javouhey returned to her homeland to administer her growing mission society. She soon had her blue-robed sisters stationed all over the world— in Guiana, Martinique, Guadeloupe, New Foundland, Madagascar, the South Pacific, and India. She personally was responsible for overseeing the work and was referred to by a sea captain as "my most seasoned sailor." King Louis Philippe paid her his highest tribute by saying, "She is a great man." Yet she, like her Protestant counterparts, struggled against the male ego. This struggle erupted in the 1840s and was the most painful ordeal of her life. It was then that the bishop over her French diocese claimed authority over the Sisters of St. Joseph—his rationale being that he was her religious superior and therefore rightfully ought to control the order. She refused to turn over the leadership to him, and he retaliated by ordering her priest in Guiana to refuse her communion. "With anguish she watched her girls, her sister nuns approach the communion table from which she was excluded." She urged her nuns to pray for the bishop, and when he died in 1851, she said with no apparent hint of sarcasm: "The good Monsignor has preceded me. This is as it should be. All honor to whom honor is due." She died shortly after that, leaving some nine hundred nuns scattered throughout the world. The number of women in the order of the Sisters of St. Joseph have since reached as high as 3,500, and there are more than two hundred branches of this group world-wide.[62]

Women in Pioneering and Preaching Ministries

If feminism did not prompt women to enter foreign missions, surely the desire for meaningful ministry did. Except for certain sectarian movements, western Protestantism offered women virtually nothing in the area of professional Christian ministry on the home front. Individual women such as Phoebe Palmer had distinguished themselves as laywomen in Christian circles, but their example had done little to open the door for women in career ministries. It was an age prior to the advent of multistaffed churches and parachurch ministries, and the major field of Christian ministry, the pastorate, was closed—with rare exceptions—to women.

In the view of some mission leaders, women's work was a category all by itself. E. R. Pitman, in his late nineteenth-century volume, *Lady Missionaries in Many Lands*, wrote in this vein:

The Mission Field demands various classes of workers—each using different instrumentalities. Preachers, translators, teachers, native pastors, printers, catechists, and handicraftsmen—all are needed. But beside these come another class, not one whit less important, namely, *Female Missionaries*.[63]

Mary Slessor

In actuality, women served in virtually every capacity that men did on the mission field. In many instances single women "manned" remote mission stations in areas where men with families were reluctant to go. It was inevitable in such situations that their ministry would encompass more clerical duties than would have been the case if male missionaries had been accessible. Mary Slessor is a prime example. She was a Scottish Presbyterian mill worker who served for thirty-eight years in the interior of Calabar (present-day Nigeria), where tropical diseases had prevented her male predecessors from establishing a foothold. She had come to Africa at the age of twenty-seven in 1876, having been influenced by the death of her hero, David Livingstone, and like him, she spent her life in pioneer missionary work. She functioned as an evangelist and circuit preacher, paving the way for male missionaries who would follow her. Indeed, "she was convinced that pioneer work was best accomplished by women, who, she believed, were less threatening to unreached tribes than men."[64]

Slessor's life illustrates the satisfaction single women found in foreign missions. She adapted easily to the African lifestyle, caring little about fashion, hygiene, eating habits, or time schedules. Although she was often lonely, she broke a marriage engagement with a young missionary with whom she had fallen in love, because his health could not withstand the rigors of tropical Africa. Her affections were poured out to her adopted African children and those to whom she ministered, and near the end of her life she was able to say that she was "a witness to the perfect joy and satisfaction of a single life."[65]

Mary Slessor, Pioneer Missionary to Calabar, West Africa.

Malla Moe

Another pioneer missionary to Africa who conducted a wide variety of church work was Malla Moe, an American who served in South Africa for fifty-four years with the Scandinavian Alliance Mission (since renamed the Evangelical Alliance Mission), founded by Fredrik Franson, a strong supporter of women in ministry. Like other single women on the field, she conducted a ministry that would never have been permitted at home. During her second term, "Malla was . . . able to plunge into preaching as never before. Her pulpit was more

often a stone under the great open sky than a table in a chapel. Her vestments were the same plain dresses and coats day after day, her altar the thick bush or a grass mat in a hut," and "her sermons were simple."

"People are tired of polished meetings and polished sermons," she wrote home. "They are hungry. It makes no difference how simple the message if only God is in it." When she was in charge of a meeting . . . and if she thought the preacher was getting dry or tiresome or long-winded, she would interrupt him. . . . This happened at Bethel so often it was the rule rather than the exception."[66]

But she served not only as a preacher, but also more or less as a bishop. Much of her time was spent in travel, doing evangelistic work and overseeing the work of her converts. Yet, despite this active ministry in Africa, she was not permitted to speak in the state churches when she visited Norway on her furlough. Officials of the church "reminded her to read Paul's instruction that 'women should keep silence in the church.' "[67]

The treatment accorded Malla Moe was typical. Despite their wide-ranging ministries on the field, single women missionaries faced strong opposition when they returned home to share their experiences in the churches. This attitude toward them may have been due in part to the increasing power the women's missionary movement attained during the last decades of the nineteenth century and the early years of the twentieth. Many men feared that women were using missions to build their own religious stronghold outside of the church's authority. And indeed they were right. In the late nineteenth century, women such as Mrs. Mary Nind and Miss S. B. Loring, for whom professional ministries in the church were closed, served as paid agents for the mission societies. Nind, a Methodist, crisscrossed the western states from Minnesota to Oregon, stirring up enthusiasm for missions,

> traveling over the unbroken prairie and through the wilderness, in wagon, or cart, or sleigh, in summer and winter, by day and by night, by freight train or day coach (never in a Pullman, for the Lord's money was too precious for such luxuries), compassing as many as 5,000 miles in a single year.[68]

Loring, a Presbyterian, also maintained a rigorous schedule, traveling through Pennsylvania and Ohio. In less than a year after she assumed her position she had conducted nearly two hundred meetings and helped in the organization of nearly fifty new societies.[69]

National Organizations and Leadership

On the national level, women such as Helen Barrett Montgomery and Lucy Peabody provided dynamic leadership for the women's missionary movement that resulted in rapid growth in strength and numbers. They encouraged ecumenical unity among mission societies and made the movement a force to be reckoned with. One of their most lasting endeavors was their missions educational work through the Central Committee for the United Study of Foreign Missions. "It was the first interdenominational project of the women's boards and it was to be a lasting and significant one. In thirty-eight years the committee published more than four million textbooks that fostered knowledge and support of Christian missions around the world."[70]

Helen Barrett Montgomery

Besides her organizational work with the women's missionary movement, Helen Barrett Montgomery was a prolific writer and a thought-provoking missiologist. Many of her works were published by the Central Committee, her first being *Christus Redemptor: An Outline Study of the Island World of the Pacific.* This book, unlike so many written by missionary enthusiasts, was a straightforward account of the problems wrought by western imperialism. The solution to this "unmitigated curse," she believed was Christian missions:

> The strongest reason why the conscience of Europe and America ought to continue and immensely strengthen its missionary forces in the island world is because we owe it to these people to make the largest, most costly and statesmanlike reparation for the ills inflicted on them by unworthy representatives of our race and by our still unchristianized governments.[71]

She could not separate evangelism from social work, and this was evident in her strong influence on the women's missionary movement—a movement that placed high priority on humanitarian causes.

Montgomery's classic *Western Women in Eastern Lands*, chronicled the fifty-year history of the women's missionary movement from 1860 to 1910. She focused on the successful evangelistic endeavors and the progress that had been made in liberating women from their restrictive cultures:

> It is indeed a wonderful story. . . . We began in weakness, we stand in power. In 1861 there was a single missionary in the field, Miss Marston, in Burma; in 1909, there were 4710 unmarried women in the field, 1948 of them from the United States. In 1861 there was one organized woman's society in our country; in 1910 there were forty-four. Then the supporters numbered a few hundreds; today there are at least two million. Then the amount contributed was $2000; last year four million dollars was raised. The development on the field has been as remarkable as that at home. Beginning with a single teacher, there are at the opening of the Jubilee year 800 teachers, 140 physicians, 380 evangelists, 79 trained nurses, 5783 Bible women and native helpers. Among the 2100 schools there are 260 boarding and high schools. There are 75 hospitals and 78 dispensaries. . . . It is an achievement of which women may well be proud. but it is only a feeble beginning of what they can do and will do, when the movement is on its feet.[72]

Female Missionary Power and Influence

The increase in numbers of women on the foreign field did not necessarily correspond with a similar increase in power. "The single missionary," according to Valentin H. Rabe, "remained for decades a second-class citizen of the mission station."[73] Yet in comparison to her sisters serving in the church at home the single woman missionary was allowed an

unprecedented amount of freedom in her ministry, and her influence on mission-board policy and decision making gradually increased. This was evident in India prior to the turn of the century.

> The rapid development of woman's work, which is doing so much to hasten the day of redemption to truth and righteousness, appears in the fact that while at the first Conference at Allahabad, 1872–3, the sex was altogether unrepresented, at the second held ten years later, at Calcutta, there were 181 women, to 249 men among the members. However, though two had been appointed to prepare papers, it was not thought proper to have them presented by female lips. But ten years later still, at Bombay, where only 263 men were in attendance, and 276 women, the latter were admitted to full equality in every particular.

By 1890 India had a total of more than seven hundred foreign "female agents" and more than three thousand native "female agents."[74]

Female Mission Society Mergers

In spite of the impressive results of the women's mission societies, by the late nineteenth and early twentieth centuries, there were loud voices calling for the merger of women's missionary societies with the general boards. Since the general boards were accepting single women as candidates, it was argued that the women's societies were no longer needed. One influential voice calling for a "mingling of men and women" in mission societies was A. T. Pierson, a well-known missionary statesman and the editor of *Missionary Review of the World.* Unlike most of his

The Women's Missionary Jubilee Committee. Helen Barrett is seated in the center. From *Missionary Review of the World* 24:6 (June 1911): 401.

colleagues who supported mergers, however, Pierson advocated an equal role for women, not barring them from the position of board director "at the helm of affairs." "If Priscilla be the equal of Aquila," he wrote, "let her take rank with him, and if by superiority Priscilla outranks Aquila, let us not fear to put her name first."[75]

Pierson's egalitarianism was not contagious, and, as one might have expected, there were strong protests against the idea of mergers, particularly from women who feared they would lose the limited power they had struggled so long to attain. Helen Barrett Montgomery had convincingly argued against such mergers at the Ecumenical Conference of 1900, and at that time there was widespread support for her position. By 1910,

however, at the World Missionary Conference in Edinburgh, opinion was beginning to change, and in the decades that followed, one denomination after another (often after heated battles) opted for a merger.[76]

Golden Jubilee Celebration

Any negative signals that came out of the Edinburgh Conference regarding the women's missionary movement were overshadowed by the fifty-year Jubilee celebration held later that year. Two-day conferences featuring special speakers and luncheons were held in forty-eight cities across the country. In many instances women were turned away for lack of space. In Buffalo, tickets were sold out a week ahead of time, and in Pittsburgh nearly 5,000 attended the

Jubilee activities. Lucy Peabody and Helen Barrett Montgomery were the main organizers and speakers. Indeed, Montgomery addressed some two hundred meetings in an eight-week period, and her Jubilee book, *Western Women in Eastern Lands* sold some fifty thousand copies.[77]

The enthusiasm that the Jubilee generated was not enough to bring back the glorious age of women's missions. "The hoopla surrounding the woman's missionary Jubilee," comments Patricia Hill, "obscured the first disturbing signs that the woman's foreign movement was deteriorating at the auxiliary level." Although the women had been duly reminded that the celebration should "glorify God, and nowhere degenerate into mere glorification of woman's work," according to Hill, it "did glorify woman's work; at its worst it degenerated into an orgy of self-congratulation."[78]

Denominational Mission Societies

In the decade following the Jubilee some of the women's societies continued to grow. Of all the denominational mission societies, the Methodist was the largest, "not only in absolute numbers but also in the percentage of church members recruited." Between 1895 and 1920, its membership grew from some 150,000 to more than a half million. It was also one of the most independent of the denominational women's missionary organizations, with virtual total control over the disbursement of funds.[79]

In most instances, the denominational women's missionary societies had very little real power besides that of increasing the female missionary force abroad. The Women's Foreign Missionary Society of the Presbyterian Church (North) is an example. Unlike the Methodist women, they had no control over their funds. The situation was similar to that of the American Baptist's women's missionary society.[80]

Because of fear that women might misuse their power, the Southern Baptist Convention did not authorize a women's board until long after such organizations had been formed in other denominations. "Many of the men," writes Leon McBeth, "opposed the women's work precisely because they perceived it to be related to or at least similar to the women's rights movement." The matter was considered a "difficult and delicate problem," and Baptists were warned in 1882 that "a false step now might entail fatal embarrassments for years to come." In 1888, with the support of influential Southern Baptist leaders such as H. A. Tupper and the tireless work of Annie Armstrong, the Woman's Missionary Union was officially organized.[81]

But even Tupper was wary of allowing women too much authority over the disbursement of funds, and he frequently clashed with Annie Armstrong over such matters. On one occasion Armstrong, according to her biographer, wrote to Tupper's assistant with an idea, suggesting "that he present it to Tupper and the Board as his plan and not hers. She felt that men were not receptive to plans coming from women." On another occasion, when she proposed a project for the Womens Missionary Union, Tupper responded: "The best thing, in the matter of foreign mis-

Six of the Founders of the Woman's Foreign Missionary Society of the Methodist Episcopal Church. From *Missionary Review of the World* 17:7 (July 1905): 186.

sions the men and women of the country can do in my judgment is to raise money for the Board and let the Board appropriate it."[82] Indeed, the stated purpose of the Union was to help women "to be more efficient in collecting money and disseminating information of mission subjects"— hardly a militant feminist agenda. And the tone of comments made by organizing leaders was most conciliatory. Fannie Stout spoke for many women:

> Much will depend on the spirit which we show. The brethren are our guardians—and when they realize what we want to do, that we do not wish to wander in any dangerous ways, but are only trying to follow them as our leaders and trying to carry into practice what they have taught us from the pulpit and press, their anxieties will cease.[83]

Despite it's slow start, the Baptist Missionary Union became one of the most effective denominational missionary societies in Protestant circles. This was in part because of the far-reaching influence of Lottie Moon. From China she wrote articles and letters urging women to do more for the cause of missions. In 1887, a year before the Woman's Missionary Union was formed, she wrote: "Until the women of our Southern Baptist churches are thoroughly aroused, we shall continue to go on in our present hand-to-mouth system. . . . I am convinced that one of the chief reasons our Southern Baptist women do so little is the lack of organization."[84]

The following year, Moon called for a special Christmas offering from the women of the Southern Baptist churches. The amount collected exceeded the goal and was sufficient to support three additional women missionaries. Moon responded enthusiastically:

What I hope to see is a band of ardent, enthusiastic, and experienced Christian women occupying a line of stations extending from P'ing-tu on the north and from Chinkiang on the south, making a succession of stations uniting the two. . . . A mighty wave of enthusiasm for women's Work for Women must be stirred.[85]

The Christmas offering increased in the years that followed, but by far the greatest stimulus to its growth was the death of Moon. She had pleaded for relief funds for famine-stricken Tengchow and was grieved that the response was so paltry. She personally had done all she could to alleviate the suffering and was herself unable to eat among the masses of starving Chinese. She died of starvation and related complications, appropriately, on Christmas Eve of 1912. In the following decades the Lottie Moon Christmas Offering grew from hundreds of thousands to millions of dollars annually.

By the early decades of the twentieth century, most women's mission organizations were once again under at least partial control of men. Yet there was a spirit of independence that was summed up in a Scripture verse and used as a slogan by the Woman's Missionary Society of the North Carolina Methodist Conference in 1920: "Behold, I have set before thee an open door, and no man can shut it."[86]

British Women and Missions

It was on the American scene that the greatest enthusiasm for missions was generated by women, but across the Atlantic their British cousins were effectively conducting overseas ministries as well. Indeed, English women had been the first to become independently involved in foreign missions. The Society for Promoting Female Education in the East was founded in 1834, and the Church of Scotland Ladies' Association for Foreign Missions, three years later. In 1852 the Zenana Bible and Medical Mission and a few decades later the Church of England Zenana Missionary Society developed out of that organization. Before these missions were formed, the Church Missionary Society (Anglican) had sent out single women, but in 1873, more than a half a century after the first woman had been commissioned, the Society "counted among its agents only eleven such women." The last decade of the nineteenth century, however, witnessed a dramatic increase in single women. Between 1883 and 1893 the number of single women increased from fifteen to one hundred and thirty-four, and in 1894, the number reached one hundred and sixty. Less than a decade later, in 1901, that figure exceeded three hundred.[87]

English women spread out all over the world in their missionary endeavors, but according to Augustus Buckland "Africa was one of the earliest lands in which the fruits of work, distinctively woman's, were gathered." It was there that Mary Moffat, with her husband Robert, served for some fifty years with the

An Assortment of Turn-of-the-Century British and American Women's Missionary Magazines. From *Missionary Review of the World* 17:7 (July 1905): 403.

London Missionary Society and where Mary Slessor had worked so effectively for nearly four decades. It was there also that Bishop Alfred Tucker in 1894 escorted a party of English women into Uganda to establish mission work. Earlier that year he had sent out a strong appeal for single women, and the *Intelligencer* made public his views: "It is Bishop Tucker's distinct opinion that . . . we must no longer delay in sending up Christian women. . . . In the present circumstances of Africa women must be ready . . . to go with the distinct and solemn purpose of remaining single for a few years for the Lord's sake."[88]

Along with the gains in women's missionary work were the losses, and the most tragic loss of women in nineteenth-century English missions occurred in China in 1895. The massacre at Ku-Cheng claimed the lives of seven women and one man. A *Times* telegram from Shanghai told the gruesome story:

> Mr. and Mrs. Steward, Miss N. Saunders, and Miss Lena Irish were burnt in the house. Miss Hessie Newcombe was speared and thrown down a precipice. Miss Marshall's throat was cut. Miss Gordon was speared in the head. Miss Topsy Saunders was speared in the brain. Miss Lena Steward died from shock.[89]

"Faith" Missions

It was on British soil that the concept of "faith" missions was first developed. While faith was considered a necessary ingredient for any mission endeavor, J. Hudson Taylor particularly stressed it in regard to finances in his development of the China Inland Mission. Instead of receiving a salary, missionaries were to depend on God by faith for their needs. Other missions followed suit, particularly in North America, and by the end of the nineteenth century there were many "faith" mission societies reaching into every "unreached" corner of the earth.

It is unfortunate that some of the most scholarly mission histories produced in recent years have virtually ignored the faith-missions movement. Kenneth Scott Latourette and Stephen Neill are examples, as are historians of women's missionary work. R. Pierce Beaver says very little about faith missions in his *American Protestant Women in World Mission*, and monographs offer little more.

Jane Hunter's *Gospel of Gentility: American Women Missionaries in Turn-of-the-Century China* mentions the China Inland mission only in a footnote. Patricia Hill, in her book, *The World Their Household: The American Woman's Foreign Mission Movement and Cultural Transformation, 1870–1920*, does not even give it that much coverage. She argues that after the first two decades of the twentieth century women lost interest in missions. She maintains that "foreign missions no longer particularly gripped the imagination of large numbers of laywomen in postwar America" and that young women looked for careers in religious education rather than in missions.[90]

While such a generalization applies to the women's missionary societies and many of the denominational boards, it does not take into account the burgeoning faith-mission boards that began emerging in the late nineteenth century and continued to increase in size and number well past the mid-twentieth century. Partly because of their financial policy, faith-mission boards did not attract the same "quality" of candidates as did boards that guaranteed salaries. Uneducated and unordained men and women often filled their ranks.

The China Inland Mission

Beginning with J. Hudson Taylor and the China Inland Mission, founded in 1865, single women were eagerly welcomed by the "faith" missions. In fact, in the first mission party that sailed to China sponsored by that newly formed mission, seven of the fifteen new recruits were single women (the remainder being married couples). On the field single women were often stationed far in the interior and were responsible for evangelism and church planting in large regions, with no immediate male supervision. A fascinating sketch relating to Taylor and the China Inland mission, written by Julius Richter, appeared in the *Missionary Review of the World* in 1898. This sketch vividly illustrates the negative reaction to Taylor's policy regarding women:

> Hudson Taylor makes extraordinarily ample use of the services of unmarried ladies; whole districts of the Chinese mission field are exclusively under the management of mission sisters. I took the liberty of suggesting how unbecoming and repellent to our German ideas was this free employment of single mission sisters in the midst of entirely heathen districts.[91]

Taylor responded by suggesting that Richter view the situation from a Chinese standpoint instead of through "German or European eyes." He pointed out that the single women were required to be accompanied by a "married Chinese catechist," and this provided her with fully adequate protection, and offered an important advantage in the evangelistic work:

> The native catechist never comes to true inward independence at a station where he works under a European missionary; he feels himself to be only the dependent journeyman of the other, and is hardly noticed by the Chinese in presence of the overwhelming superiority of the European. It is quite otherwise when he is associated with a missionary-sister; then the whole work of teaching and preaching and representing the mission to outsiders devolves upon him; he counts as

the head of the mission, and must act independently. But at the same time he is under the control of the mission sister, who is with him to advise and instruct him, and to report about him. The sister herself has a sufficient sphere of activity in the female part of the heathen population and the Christian Church, and if sometimes men also listen to her Bible lessons, no offense is given. Of course, a great deal of tact is necessary for the sister and the catechist to maintain their mutual position.[92]

Later "Faith" Missions

Taylor was not alone among faith mission leaders in his staunch support of women. Fredrik Franson, the founder of The Evangelical Alliance Mission (TEAM), under which Malla Moe had served, eagerly welcomed women into the ranks. In other faith missions—including the Christian and Missionary Alliance, the Sudan Interior Mission, the Africa Inland Mission, the Gospel Missionary Union, and the Worldwide Evangelization Crusade—women also made up a high percentage of the recruits and sometimes administered vast regions with no immediate male supervision. Such was the case in Morocco in the 1930s, when Maude Cary and three other single women of the Gospel Missionary Union, were left in charge of the mission stations. The male missionaries had all left the field before the country was closed to missionaries at the outbreak of World War II, and the mission had no other choice but to turn the responsibilities over to women.[93]

C. T. Studd, the founder of the Heart of Africa Mission, which later became known as the Worldwide

Evangelization Crusade, depended heavily on single women in his missionary endeavors in Africa. A great revival occurred in the mission in 1925, and among the results was an increased dedication of the missionaries, particularly women, to advance the gospel:

> Single women go on long evangelizing treks among the villages, where there is a shortage of men; in one district, the worst cannibal in the region, who was reputed to have "a hundred black men inside him," was led to Christ by a single woman missionary who visited his village. Two of the most thriving stations with congregations from five hundred to sometimes as many as fifteen hundred are "manned" by single women only. In some places where there have been only two workers, they have sacrificed human companionship and voluntarily separated in order that one may go farther afield and evangelize a new area, although the usual plan of the Mission is to place them in couples.[94]

Eliza Davis George

In spite of the openness of faith mission leaders toward women and the support of men such as Pierson who advocated women in leadership positions in missions, very few were permitted such opportunities apart from the female missionary societies. The Maude Carys won their status only by default. One notable exception, however, was Eliza Davis George, who directed the Elizabeth Native Interior Mission. She was a Southern Baptist who had the distinction of being "the first black woman from Texas to go to Africa as a missionary." In 1945, when she was sixty-five years old and had served for thirty-two years as a Southern Baptist missionary in Liberia, that denomination insisted that she retire. Unwilling to comply, she returned to Africa, supported by "Eliza Davis George Clubs," and developed her new mission. The purpose of the mission was to train nationals for evangelism and church planting, and though it remained small and plagued with financial problems, it made an important contribution to the work of Christian missions in Liberia. In 1961 the directorship of the mission was transferred to a male national, but she continued in leadership until she was in her nineties.[95]

Mission Specializations

Combined with the growing faith-mission movement was an increasing emphasis on various mission specializations such as medicine, translation and linguistics, radio, and aviation. And it was often through such specialized ministries that women were given the highest recognition for their service on the mission field.

Medical Missions

Medicine was a specialization in which women particularly excelled. Women doctors, from Clara Swain to Helen Roseveare, made an indelible mark on missions. Their humanitarian service could not have been carried out by anyone else—particularly in Asia in the early years of missionary medicine. This impact was noted in a missions periodical in 1910: "In Christianizing foreign lands, the woman physician is an absolute necessity. No other human being has her privileges in the harem, the zenana, or the humblest home."[96]

Clara Swain holds the distinction of being the first female missionary medical doctor. She went to India in 1870 and treated some fifteen hundred patients that first year. A decade later she was treating more than seven thousand patients a year. Yet, she, like most other medical missionaries, considered herself primarily an evangelist.[97]

Swain's contribution to medicine for women in India was widely recognized, but even more so was the service of Dr. Ida Scudder, the first woman in a long tradition of Scudder missionary medical doctors to India. But the fact that her father and grandfather had been missionary doctors in India did not make the profession appealing to her. In fact, as a young person she had determined that India was the last place she wanted to spend her life. On a visit back to India to help care for her mother who was ill, her vision changed. Her "call" to medical missions came one night after two Hindus and a Muslim had come to her parents' home requesting help for their wives who were giving birth, but refusing her father's help because custom forbade contact with the opposite sex.

It was a traumatic night for Ida. She wrote:

I could not sleep that night—it was too terrible. Within the very touch of my hand were three young girls dying because there was no woman to help them. I spent much of the night in anguish and prayer. I did not want to spend my life in India. My friends were begging me to return to the joyous opportunities of a young girl in America. I went to bed in the early morning after praying much for guidance. I think that was the first time I ever met God face to face, and all that time it seemed that He was calling me into this work. Early in the morning I heard the "tom tom" beating in the village and it struck terror in my heart, for it was a death message. I sent our servant, and he came back saying that all of them had died during the night. Again I shut myself in my room and thought very seriously about the condition of the Indian women and after much thought and prayer, I went to my father and mother and told them that I must go home and study medicine, and come back to India to help such women.[98]

Scudder returned to the United States to begin her medical studies in 1895, and after graduating from Cornell Medical College, she left for India with her medical degree and a ten-thousand-dollar check donated by a wealthy supporter to be used to start a hospital. Soon after she arrived, construction began on a women's medical complex in Vellore that developed a reputation for being one of the best medical training centers on the entire subcontinent. Large sums of money were needed to finance such a large undertaking, and Scudder had a great flare for fund raising, particularly among women's missionary societies in the United States. But that fund raising and the ongoing ministry of the Vellore medical complex became the center of one of the most heated controversies in the history of the women's missionary movement. With new government stipulations imposed on medical programs following Indian independence, Scudder believed that it was necessary to merge with other mission medical facilities—men's hospitals and training centers that were run by male medical missionaries. She was convinced that the alternative to a merger was to be shut down.[99]

Unconvinced by her reasoning were two women, Hilda Olson and Lucy Peabody, who had been her staunchest supporters and most enthusiastic fund raisers. They found it unthinkable to share with men the medical facilities that had been built by the sacrificial gifts of women in America for women in India. Lucy Peabody wrote to Scudder:

> You must tell us where you stand before we can go out for more appeals. Some people say you favor this cooperation with the men. If you and the majority of the board go with the coeducational work and desire to turn *our* plant and endowment over to the men who have not done one single thing to help, of course the charter can be legally changed, and the board can give up and move out and let the men take charge.[100]

Olson, who likewise served on the governing board of the Vellore Medical Compound, also responded bitterly to the proposal: "Vellore is as you say, God's work, but I would like to add God's work for *women*. Every dollar would have to be given back to the givers."[101]

After years of wrangling and debate, the board voted for the merger, and Peabody and Olson angrily resigned their positions. It was a very difficult time for Ida and a low point for the women's missionary movement. There was no easy solution to the problem, and it seems that Scudder, in her determination to save her medical complex, failed to appreciate the position of her female colleagues.

Peabody and Olson had learned from experience that mergers of women's missions with general boards invariably resulted in male control. They had worked too hard for women in India to let the cause be lost without taking a stand for what they believed to be right.

Another missionary medical doctor frequently surrounded by controversy was Helen Roseveare, who went to the Congo in the 1950s with high ideals and came back after her first furlough discouraged and ready give up missionary work. Her difficulties related to her role as a medical doctor and a woman in a mission in which all the leadership positions belonged to men. Her brilliant mind and strong personality were threatening to her male colleagues—so much so that the hospital she had built from the ground up at an old leprosy camp at Nebobongo was removed from her control and placed under the authority of a junior medical missionary who had just arrived on the field. This was a devastating ordeal for Roseveare:

> In her terms, he'd just taken over Nebobongo—*her* place, which she'd built up out of nothing, out of her dreams, out of her heart, out of the money she'd raised. This was the place where she'd dug the water holes, cleared the ditches, fired the bricks. She had acknowledged the facts that you could not have two people in charge, that he was a man, and that in Africa a man was the superior being, so she handed over the keys. Then she found she couldn't take it. Perhaps she had been her own boss too long. But now she had lost everything. She had always taken Bible class; Dr. Harris took it now. Dr. Harris organized the nurses, and Helen had always done

that. Everything that had been hers was now his.[102]

Roseveare perceived her problem to be a result of her singleness and believed that the obvious solution was marriage. On furlough she set her sights on a young doctor and tried desperately to win him. She restyled her hair, bought a new wardrobe, and even resigned from the mission in an effort to win his favor. "In the end, I jolly near mucked up the whole furlough," she later wrote. "I couldn't find a husband in the mission, so I got out of the mission. God let me go a long way, and I made an awful mess. Then God graciously pulled me back and the mission graciously accepted me back."[103]

In 1960 Roseveare returned to the Congo to continue her medical work but was frustrated in her efforts by the Simba Revolution. All whites were viewed as enemies, and she was no exception. Soldiers entered her bungalow one night and brutally beat and raped her, and later she was taken into captivity where again she was raped repeatedly. After her release she returned home to England, believing her missionary career was over, but after the revolution she was needed more than ever and was unable to turn her back on the pleas from African Christians for her to return. Her final term in Africa was not the successful climax to her missionary career that she had hoped for. Independence had made Africans more suspicious of white missionaries, and the uncompromising demands she made on her nursing students created animosity among them. And the fact that she was a woman only seemed to complicate the situation. As her term was coming to a close, she planned a celebration to include her farewell and her replacement's welcome. But it was not a happy ending for her, as she later recalled: "At the last moment the whole thing fell to bits. The student body went on strike. I ended up having to resign the college where I'd been the director twenty years."[104]

Roseveare's attitude toward missions and life in general could have been one of bitterness, but instead she was humbled by the experience and went on to share her insights on medical missions and singleness in conference lectures and books.[105]

Translation and Linguistics

In other mission specializations also, women assumed prominent roles. Linguistics and Bible translation, once a male domain, became a major area of women's missionary work in the mid-twentieth century. Yet it was a field that single women penetrated only slowly. When Eunice Pike and Florence Hansen enrolled at the Summer Institute of Linguistics in 1936 to prepare for ministry with the Wycliffe Bible Translators to go to the Mazatec Indians in Mexico, they were given less than an enthusiastic welcome. They "did not impress Legters [the co-founder of the mission] as appropriate pioneer material. This, he felt, was a job for rugged men. He had not encouraged women to join the crusade—but these two had turned up."[106]

There were other grim warnings that these young women had to contend with, as Pike later related:

Some people had reminded Mr. Townsend that Latin American women never traveled alone, never lived alone, and were always well chaperoned. With genuine concern for Florrie and me, they had said that any attempt on our part to live in an Indian village would be misunderstood by the people and could only end in disaster.[107]

Despite such reservations, Pike and Hansen became the first single women to be accepted by Wycliffe, and Pike continued on in the work for decades.

There were a number of reasons why it was believed that women would be unsuitable for the task of tribal translation work. The problem of finding a suitable female informant was one, but that proved to be far less difficult than had been anticipated, and in many cases women used male informants without creating scandal in the local culture. Another problem that was raised in reference to women concerned the danger they would be exposed to in remote tribes. This fear also proved to be unfounded. Indeed, women were generally exposed to less danger than were men. A prime example is the case of Loretta Anderson and Doris Cox. They began their work in 1950 among the headhunting Shapras in the Peruvian jungle, and within a few years many in the tribe had turned away from headhunting and witchcraft and accepted Christianity. Years later, Tariri, the chief of the tribe, confessed to Cam Townsend, the mission leader, "If you had sent men, we would have killed them on sight. Or if a couple, I'd have killed the man and taken the woman for myself. But what could a great chief do with two harmless girls who insisted on calling him brother?"[108]

Another female Wycliffe Bible translator to make a friendly contact with a hostile tribe was Rachel Saint, who, with Elisabeth Elliot, entered the Auca tribe less than three years after her brother Nate and Elisabeth's husband, Jim, and three others had been slain by them. It was through these women that many of the Aucas turned to Christianity.[109]

Another advantage that single women had over their married colleagues was that they had more time to devote to the arduous task of language learning, and there have been many success stories as a result. In 1956, after nine years of language work with the Tzeltal tribe in Mexico, Marianna Slocum distributed copies of her newly translated New Testament to the tribespeople and soon thereafter left with her partner, a nurse, to do translation work in another tribe. They left behind not only the New Testament, but also Old Testament stories, hymns, and primers, and more importantly an indigenous church that had developed during their years of residence. In 1965, eight years after beginning their work with another group of Tzeltal Indians, the Bachajon New Testament was completed.

"How much does it cost?" was the oft-repeated question as the Indians stood in line. Seventeen and a half pesos was, of course, the answer to the question they had in mind, but the actual answer could never be given in pesos. Loneliness, illness, unfriendliness, primitive living conditions, and the sacrifice of marriage and family all made up the cost of the Bachajon New Testament. It was a heavy price, but one Marianna gladly paid. And when her work with the Bachajon people was over, she and Florence started all over again in the Andes Mountains of Colombia.[110]

Gospel Recordings

Another area of mission specialization pioneered by a woman involved the taping and reproduction of gospel messages into tribal languages that had not yet been reached by Bible translators and linguists. The organization that grew out of this ministry became known as Gospel Recordings, founded in 1941, by Joy Ridderhof, a single missionary to Honduras who had left the field because of poor health. It was in her attic apartment in California, while recuperating from her illness, that she conceived of the idea of sending messages back to Honduras on records. Her first efforts were so successful that missionaries from other areas requested her services. Eventually she and her staff members were traveling all over the world locating bilingual tribespeople to record short Christian messages for people who had never before heard the gospel. In the eyes of critics, it was superficial evangelism at best, but the testimonies of conversion in remote tribes all over the world that the mail brought in was all that was needed to convince Ridderhof that the ministry was a valid one.[111]

Missionary Aviation

The area of mission specialization that has been the most closed to women has been that of aviation, and yet even that specialization was initiated largely through the efforts of a woman pilot, Elizabeth Greene. She had served in the Air Force during the early months of World War II, but her heart was not in the military service. She viewed her training as preparation for future service in missionary aviation, a specialization that was only in the very early developmental stages. It was during the war that Greene wrote an article for a Christian magazine, presenting the need for missionary aviation. The article was spotted by a Navy pilot who promptly contacted Green, asking her to join him and some other pilots in founding an organization that later became known as Mission Aviation Fellowship. Her flying service with that organization included terms in Mexico, Africa, and Irian Jaya. Despite her impressive record of flying experience, she faced sex discrimination in her ministry, and she perpetuated that attitude in her own philosophy of missionary aviation by defending MAF's initial policy of refusing female applicants.[112]

New Mission Strategies

One of the last fields of missions for Western women to penetrate has been that of missiology, a field that is still heavily dominated by men. This is true in part because women have not had held high positions on mission boards and in mission schools of higher learning, but it is also due to the fact that women have simply not taken the initiative in this area. In the early years of the twentieth century, Helen Barrett Montgomery published works relating to mission strategy, as did Jean Kenyon Mackenzie. They "called on evangelical Christians to participate in the modernization of other cultures and to adapt the techniques of business management to the science of missions."[113] Their writings made a significant impact on mission board policy, but with the demise of the women's missionary movement, few women have offered their experience, knowledge, and creativity to develop new mission strategies.

One of those rare women was Constance Padwick (1886–1968), who served for three decades among the Muslims in Egypt and Palestine and then served the remaining decade of her missionary career in Sudan and Turkey. She was a prolific writer, and as a missionary it was her passion to provide attractive Christian literature for Muslims. She recognized the necessity of first having an understanding of Islamic culture and faith, and that prompted her to write *Muslim Devotions*, a work that resulted from more than twenty years of collecting and studying popular devotional books from various parts of the Middle East. She wrote dozens of articles and books throughout her missionary career, her most widely acclaimed being *Temple Gairdner of Cairo*, a biography of her colleague and a great missionary statesman.[114] In many ways, Padwick was missiologically ahead of her time. She insisted that the missionary have an understanding of Islamic thought. She argued that there were "two religious languages" that separated Christianity from Islam, and that the missionary's failure to understand the Islamic language was "one of the real problems of evangelization."[115]

Among those few who have entered the field of missiology in recent years are Marguerite Kraft, B. V. Subbamma, Ruth Siemens, and Elizabeth Brewster. Kraft, a former missionary to Nigeria and the wife of Charles Kraft, has made an important contribution to evangelism methodology in her work, *World view and the Communication of the Gospel: A Nigerian Case Study*. Here she challenges the missionary to gain an understanding of a particular culture's world view, and then to use that insight in a more effective communication of the Christian message. Like so many missionary women before her, Kraft has not espoused a feminist ideology in her concept of mission: "I do not see it my responsibility as an outsider to 'free' women up to be like me. If that change comes through the study of Scripture and the leading of the Holy Spirit, that is fine. But it is not my Christian responsibility to upset the society by redefining the roles."[116]

Subbamma, an Indian national who did her graduate work at the Fuller School of Mission, has stirred debate through her controversial approach to Hindu evangelism. As a caste Hindu, who was converted to Christianity in her youth, she had accepted the Western approach to evangelism that required a mixing of castes in Christian circles. She has since abandoned that position and in her book, *New Patterns for Discipling Hindus*,[117] has called for a respect for Indian culture, including the caste system.

Ruth Siemens' contribution to missiology lies largely in the concept of "tentmaking" missions—missions conducted by laypeople who have secular employment in crosscultural settings. She herself served as an elementary and high-school teacher in Peru, during which time she was actively involved in evangelistic work.

Since that time she has written articles and given papers on the subject and has founded Global Opportunities, a mission directly involved in placing missionary-minded Christians in secular employment overseas.

Elizabeth Brewster teamed up with her husband, the late E. Thomas Brewster, in strategic mission endeavors, and, like other missiologists, they stirred up controversy. Their textbook *Language Acquisition Made Practical* (LAMP) has been viewed by some as a highly creative and innovative solution to the difficulties of language study, and as impractical by others. Likewise their work on the subject of bonding has created strong differences of opinion. They expect participants in their crosscultural missionary projects to meet four conditions: willingness to live with a national family, limiting personal belongings to less than fifty pounds, using only local public transportation, and learning the language by developing personal relationships. They warn those who follow their philosophy of bonding that there may be serious problems to deal with. "The bonded missionary is invariably viewed with suspicion by nonbonded colleagues. At best they may think him to be a maverick, at worst a traitor."[118]

There are many less well-known women in recent years who have developed missiological principles in their day-to-day work on the mission field. An example is Ann Croft. As a schoolteacher in Nigeria, Croft had not anticipated being heavily involved in crosscultural evangelism, but through a deep friendship with one of her students, she developed an effective ministry with the Fulani people, who were largely Muslim. Realizing the importance of cattle to the Fulani people, she devoted her time to upgrading veterinary services, showing the people in a unique way that their concerns were hers. She also made a special effort to make Scripture relate to their culture. "In the Bible she found numerous references to nomadic cattle-herding peoples who played special roles in biblical history." Through the cooperation of a mission organization, she involved the Fulani in an evangelistic conference, which proved to be the turning point. "At the end of the evangelistic conference, the chief of the area said to Ann that he wanted his people to become part of the Christian community."[119]

A Backward Glance

The accomplishments of women during nearly two centuries of foreign missions has been without precedent in the history of Christianity. At no other time were women permitted so much latitude in Christian ministry. Their work ranged from evangelism and church planting to translating Scripture and teaching in seminaries. Ironically, the opportunities were available to them, not because Bible scholars had come to new conclusions as they exegeted Scripture, but rather because of geographical and cultural factors. For most of the women, however, the rationale for their permission to serve did not matter. Their motivation was, as it always had been, simply to serve God, and for that they were willing to sacrifice marriage, family, and the comforts of their homeland. And in doing so, they made a profound impact on the growth of world Christianity.

Yet, despite their contributions, women were frequently viewed as God's second best. Their work was acceptable only because there were not enough men to fill the ranks as missionaries. Some men certainly expressed such views, and women, too, often had a low estimate of their worth. Gladys Aylward, the famous unmarried woman missionary to China, confessed her insecurities as a woman in these words:

> I wasn't God's first choice for what I've done for China. There was somebody else.... I don't know who it was—God's first choice. It must have been a man—a wonderful man. A well-educated man. I don't know what happened. Perhaps he died. Perhaps he wasn't willing.... And God looked down ... and saw Gladys Aylward.[120]

Chapter 9

The Non-Western Church: Lowly Bible Women and Renowned Educators

From the Western perspective, Christianity in the Third World is often viewed in light of the missionary enterprise. American and European missionaries are cast as the leading characters while nationals play supporting roles or serve as stand-ins in a drama that is western in everything but the setting. Such a portrayal distorts the true picture of the non-Western church. Although the grandiose schemes of paternalistic missionaries often overshadowed the faltering efforts of nationals, most of the real success of church growth in the Third World has been accomplished by nationals—a high percentage of whom have been women. The work of evangelism and church planting in certain areas relied almost exclusively on women, some of whom were illiterate and had to rely on their own personal testimony, memorizing portions of Scripture in their determination to spread the gospel.

This story of national involvement in evangelism and church leadership has yet to be told. Both men and women of the Third World have been shortchanged in the historical account. *The Church and Women in the Third World,* edited by John and Ellen Webster, focuses on some specific aspects of women nationals in church leadership but does not provide the overview that is so sorely needed. Outstanding leaders have been featured in biographies, but there is no well-documented historical account that ties the story together. Moreover, many of the missionary accounts of nationals give a distorted and self-serving portrait.

Indeed, as important as women nationals were in spreading and exemplifying the faith in their homes and community, they no doubt fell far short of the portrayal of them made by some missionary women in stories and biographical accounts. Like the Western missionaries themselves, nationals suffered from a distorted reputation of super-sainthood. A realistic picture, it was feared, would reflect negatively on the super-saint missionary on whose ministry the saintly converts depended. Margaret Burton, for example, described Oriental Christian women as "attractive, intelligent, refined, spiritual, kind, truthful, helpful, energetic, ambitious in good ways."[1]

In actuality, there were often problems between women missionaries and women nationals—neither being the super-saints they were described to be. Speaking of Chinese women, Shirley Garrett writes:

> In the flesh . . . she was quite human, and some of her real characteristics were at odds with the cheerful picture the church presented to the public. She was superstitious, believing stubbornly in magic, native gods, and the spells and portents of wind and water and often sullenly resisting attempts to convert her. She was capable of hate and vengefulness, often using threats of suicide to get her own way.[2]

Conversion to Christianity certainly brought about significant behavioral changes, but serious problems remained. Bible women on occasion rebelled against the authority of the missionaries, and on more than one occasion girls went on strike in mission schools.[3]

The Effect of Christianity on Third-World Women

The most powerful argument in support of women missionaries before they were accepted in their own right was that they would be the means of uplifting pagan women who were subjected to the tyranny of religious and cultural strictures against their sex. In many instances Christianity, indeed, offered women freedom and opportunity for public service that was denied them in other religions. This was true, for example, of women who were converted from various tribal religions of the Pacific Islands. "In most Oceanic societies," writes Charles Forman, "women were not normally accepted as participants in religious ritual. Hence, the presence of women in Christian services marked a significant change for most island women."[4]

An even more significant influence that women missionaries had in ameliorating the social and legal injustices against women in the Third World involved such areas as education, marriage, widowhood, and home life. In India, as elsewhere in developing nations, "the first battle was a legal one, to clear away space enough in the tangled jungle of oppression for the women to stand on while they fought for better conditions." According to Helen Barrett Montgomery, "in this hard-fought fight missionary women were the leaders, and the arousers of a public sense of shame." Legislation permitting the remarriage of widows and restricting "the hideous evils of marriage consummated between adult men and little children were only passed because of the irrefutable testimony of medical women missionaries."[5]

The Influence of Christianity on Education

It was in the sphere of education perhaps more than any other that women in the Third World were influenced by women's missionary work. In 1910 Montgomery wrote, "The educated woman in India is still

A Bible Woman of Ceylon Teaching Women and Children. From Helen Barrett Montgomery, *Western Women in Eastern Lands* (New York: Macmillan, 1910), 21.

a very rare bird." She quoted *The Indian Social Reformer* of 1897, which indicated that some six out of every one thousand women were deemed literate and that fewer than ten girls per thousand were then being educated. It was the women missionaries who were taking the lead in female education, and as a result "the greater number of the new women of India [were] Christian"—a fact that concerned some Hindus. An early twentieth-century writer reflected this concern in *The Hindu*, a religious paper: "While the educated Indian has not yet got beyond the talking stage in the matter of female instruction, the Christian missionary has honeycombed the country with girls' schools."[6]

Some of the most anti-Christian Hindus had nothing but praise for what Christianity had done for women and were critical of their own religious traditions in the education of women. J. W. Pickett, who served as a missionary to India for many years, wrote of this attitude among Hindus:

A member of the often militantly anti-Christian Arya Samaj said to the writer in a village in West Godavari that the greatest value the Christian movement has brought to Andhra Desa is freedom for the minds and souls of women. He added, "A degenerate Hinduism had enslaved our women. They were condemned to illiteracy, idolatry, superstition, suffering, drudgery and dullness. The lovely things of life were all kept from them. Through Christian Missions the folly and the wrong of this treatment of our women has been convincingly demonstrated."[7]

The Influence of Christianity on the Home

Christianity also affected the attitude toward women in the home, as is evidenced by a statement made by a Hindu in the Punjab: "Before these people became Christians they bought and sold wives like we buy and sell buffalos. Now they choose one woman and remain faithful to her as long as she lives." This opinion was supported by a survey conducted by Mrs. Graham Parker, a Presbyterian missionary to India. To the question "Do Christian men treat their wives differently?" 143 responded in the affirmative, and only 20 responded negatively. To the follow-up question, asking, "If so, how?" there were varied responses: "They help wives in their work." "They don't fight." "They don't abuse us in words or actions." "They let us have the money we earn." "They are kind and pray for us and our children." "They don't make us do what we know isn't right." "They forgive our faults." "They give their wives their rights." "In Christian homes husband and wife obey each other."[8]

This change was also true in Africa, where Christianity had a powerful impact on marriage customs and the home. Here, as elsewhere in the world, missionaries generally advocated freedom of choice for marriage partners rather than traditional arranged marriages. "This freedom contributed to respect for the woman in the marital relationship, to an emphasis on her value as a person rather than on the dominantly functional role which she played." Some observers have suggested that the dignity accorded women in Christianity was one of the major reasons so many women were attracted to the faith.[9]

Negative Influences of Christian Missions

Although there is considerable evidence indicating that Christianity has uplifted womanhood in the Third World, not all scholars agree on the specifics and to what extent the status of women has actually been raised. One problem is the reliability of the sources. Along with concrete evidence there are exaggerations that must be viewed with skepticism. Many reforms called for by missionaries were long overdue and no doubt would have been instituted without the influence of the missionary community. Likewise the personal influence that Western women had over nationals has no doubt been overdrawn. Jane Hunter, in her book on women missionaries in China, speaks of this: "Missionaries liked to exaggerate the extent to which unattached Chinese women depended on them for protection from angry fathers or husbands." She cites the case of China missionary Emily Hartwell, who wrote gripping accounts of how she rescued women from life-threatening family situations—one from a wicked mother-in-law, another from her "opium fiend father," and another from being sold to strangers by her parents.[10]

But not only is there evidence of exaggerated claims of missionaries, there is also evidence that would indicate that in certain instances the missionaries' influence lowered the status of women. That was true among certain tribes in Africa, according to David Barrett. He has pointed out that "in many African cultures, women have long held prominent positions. They have been traditionally dominant among the Swazi, Luapula and Lunda, to name only three.... Many societies are matrilineal; some are matriarchal." As such, "certain categories of women ... stood to lose much of their traditional status when missionary work began." This was true in the home as well as in the church, where "women were not permitted in the ministry nor in the hierarchy of its executive structure." In many instances, argues Barrett, "the rigidity of institutionalized churches ... was felt primarily by women," and "the missions appeared to be practicing an unjustified form of social control."[11]

In the minds of some Third World women, Western Christianity has taken more credit than it deserves for emancipating oppressed women of the world—especially in religious affairs. This sentiment was expressed by the moderator of a women's conference when she was introducing a speaker from the West: "Now don't tell us about your women's organizations, because we know all about them; and the one thing we do not want is to become second-class citizens as you have become in the church."[12]

Church Attendance and Participation

As was true in the Western church, women in the Third World church generally far outnumbered men. They typically responded more readily to the Christian message and, as Christians, were more steadfast in the faith than were their male counterparts. This has been particularly true in most African denominations that originated in the West. Yet, de-

spite their strong numerical superiority, women rarely filled leadership roles. "Their involvement in the politics of the church," according to Joyce Siwani, was "almost nonexistent." Assessing the situation in 1984, she continued, "They are relegated on the one hand to the level of children, whereas they are expected to keep the financial wheels of the structure running smoothly, on the other."[13]

The Effects of Polygamy

In spite of the fact that women rarely held leadership roles in the churches, they wielded a significant influence. Indeed, the characterization of women as the backbone of the church has probably been more true of the Third World church than it has been of the church in the West. There were a number of reasons for this pattern, one of which involved lifestyle and tribal rituals. Polygamy is an example. Concerning the situation in West Africa, Penelope Campbell writes, "Polygamy was a great hindrance only in converting men because, whereas a confirmed Christian man could not be a polygamist, wives of polygamists were allowed full participation." There were exceptions, however, to this practice. In Uganda, the church required women to leave a polygamous household and become a member of a Christian household before being admitted to the catechumenate. Although "the missionaries half realised that this put the women in an impossible position," they supported efforts to eradicate polygamy from the church.[14]

In many instances where the polygamous husband became Christian he was allowed to be baptized only if he sent away all but one of his wives. The fate of these women, according to David Barrett, "was tragic." They were "sent away under the stigma of disgrace," and "many found a livelihood in prostitution in the new cities."[15]

Moral Qualifications for Church Membership

Typically, however, women in polygamous situations fared much better in the church than did men. And there were other reasons for women outnumbering men in the churches.

Women were important in sustaining congregations and in establishing Protestant Christianity permanently in equatorial West Africa because they were better able than men to meet the strict standards of conduct required of church members. Quarrelling, drunkenness, and adultery are not sins limited to one sex, certainly, but men were much more exposed to these and other temptations, which could result in discipline or suspension.[16]

The "Female Factor" and Church Weakness

It was not only because of their numbers and dedication, but also because of their influence in the home that women were such a vital factor in the growth of the African church. Yet it was the "female factor," as much as anything else that kept the African church weak and dependent on the Western missionaries. Women were rarely permitted to hold church offices, so when men were not available or qualified, the churches simply functioned without indigenous lay leaders.[17]

Because of the restrictions on women in holding church offices and professional leadership positions, there was less effort extended toward female education. According to Mercy Amba Oduyoye, this was a serious problem among the Methodists in West Africa in the late nineteenth and early twentieth centuries. The teachers for girls' schools were frequently unqualified, and the primary subjects were sometimes no more than "singing" and "needlework." It is no wonder, then, that female nationals were often too poorly qualified to assume leadership positions in the church.[18]

Women's Meetings and Clubs

One of the important benefits Christianity offered Third World women was a cause around which to gather for social and religious purposes. In many areas, at the urging of women missionaries, a system of networking quickly developed among women that crossed tribal, territorial, and even caste barriers. Such a feeling of camaraderie among women of Africa and Asia was uncommon outside Christian circles during the nineteenth century and paved the way for broader-based women's movements.

An example of this kind of networking developed around the turn of the century in Portuguese West Africa, where an annual congress of Christian mothers was attended by hundreds of women. So eager were these native women for Christian fellowship that it was not uncommon for them to walk a hundred miles to participate. The program consisted of Bible studies as well as instruction on health, hygiene, and child care. Although such topics were clearly not designed to foster feminist ideology or to threaten the place of the husband in the family, the movement was referred to as a "revolt of the Mother," and women did gain an awareness of the problems and needs of their sex as they never had before.[19]

The "Red Blouse" Movement

Another such movement developed in Southern Rhodesia and in Bechuanaland (now Botswana)—a movement whose primary purpose was to teach concepts of Christian morality and home life to women whose only understanding of marriage and sexuality came from tribes that encouraged polygamy and promiscuity. It was a uniformed organization called the "Red Blouse" movement, and by the 1950s there were some six thousand members. Although it had been started by a woman missionary, it was led by national women who were trained a local Bible schools.[20]

Women's clubs were likewise very prominent in denominational churches, particularly in South Africa. According to Barrett,

> a large majority of the powerful Manyano groups (Union of Women, or Mothers) in South African churches are still linked with the mission churches. In the early 1950s, the Methodist Church of South Africa had some twenty thousand Mayano members, and the Anglican diocese of Johannesburg alone had some four thousand members.[21]

Women's Organizations Imported From the West

Some of the women's organizations were imported from the West. A case in point was the Young Women's Christian Association. This organization was planted by missionaries in Asia and filled a need that could not have been met by a church per se. The movement generally appealed to young and well-educated women. Its agenda was not as narrow as the agenda of many Christian women's organizations, and sometimes non-Christian women from other world religions were included. This was true of the YWCAs founded in Hiroshima and Nagasaki in the years following the bombings. Many of the women viewed the organization as a forum to promote the cause of world peace, while others argued that the purpose should be social interaction and entertainment.[22] Like the YMCAs, the YWCAs gradually became more and more involved in secular concerns, and some entirely lost their Christian distinctives.

Personal Evangelism

One of the most striking features related to the growth of Christianity in the Third World has been the spontaneous evangelistic outreach by converts—especially in regions where powerful religious traditions have made Christianity anathema. Countless are the stories of Christians risking their family ties, their wealth, and their very lives in an effort to share the gospel with those they knew best. The pressure to recant the faith was enormous. When persuasion failed, persecution often followed, and as a result some denied the faith. In many cases, however, family members and friends were eventually converted because of the persistent testimony and refusal to bend in the face of persecution. As important as "professional" and organized lay evangelism were, it was often personal family evangelism that had the greatest impact on the growth of Third World Christianity.

Christiana Tsai

A remarkable example of personal evangelism in the Third World is that of Christiana Tsai, whose story is told in her autobiography, *Queen of the Dark Chamber*. This high-born Chinese woman, whose father was the vice-governor of the province of Kiangsu, grew up in Nanking in the early twentieth century knowing only luxury and ease. Each child in her large extended family had two personal servants, and the family chef had fifteen assistants. The family was deeply religious and, like most Chinese families, clung tenaciously to the traditions of ancestral worship. New Year's Day marked the beginning of the festivities each year as the family made a processional to the Ancestral Hall.

> Paintings of our ancestors hung on the walls, and before each picture was a bowl, a cup, chopsticks and a spoon for that person's spirit to use. Long tables were covered with steaming food—whole roast pigs, ducks, chickens, fish, and so on—offerings for the spirits. We all knelt in order of rank and kowtowed, after which the servants brought yellow bags of paper money, one for each ancestor, and gave them to Father, who burned them one by one in a great brass urn, and threw a cupful of wine on the ashes in farewell. When the ceremony was over we all went to the great hall for the feast. We seldom slept at all on New Year's Eve. In the morning of the New Year the doors were all opened, a barrage of firecrackers was set off, and we were free to do what we liked for eighteen days, except that we must still worship our ancestors each day of that period.[23]

It was out of that religious setting that Tsai was converted to Christianity. As was the case with so many Asian girls, education was the first step in her pilgrimage toward Christianity. Although she had studied under private Buddhist instructors, she was eager to go beyond what their tutoring offered. She enrolled in a local mission school, vowing that she would never convert to Christianity, but so anxious was she to learn English that she joined an optional English Bible class. When she transferred to another mission school, she was required to attend religious services, but she did so with deep resentment.

> This only increased my resistance, and I made up my mind that I was not going to "eat" their Christianity, so I used to take a Chinese novel with me to chapel and read it as I knelt at the bench. I did not like the preaching. I thought it was unpleasant and openly opposed it. Another girl, a Miss Wu, from a high-class family similar to my own, hated this teaching too, and we . . . started to write a book denouncing all Christian teaching, insisting that Confucius and Buddha were our teachers and that we did not want Christ.[24]

The resistance, however, eventually wore down. "God used my love for English to draw me to Himself." Through reading the Bible and listening to preaching in English, she was converted to Christianity, and through her testimony and influence Miss Wu also became a Christian. Family persecution immediately followed for both girls. When Tsai's family insisted that she participate in an ancestral ceremony for her deceased father, she did so, prostrating herself on the ground surrounded by Buddhist monks, but not without painful feelings of guilt, and "a cloud of spiritual defeat hung over" her. Her response was to publicly confess her faith through baptism and church membership, but that further alienated her family. She was bitterly rebuked for disgracing the family, and one of her older brothers grabbed her Bible and hymnbook out of her hands and tore them up. Her mother was particularly devastated because she depended on her children to offer food and incense to her spirit after she died.[25]

Despite the hostility of her family members, they were converted to Christianity one by one through her testimony. For her mother, conversion to Christianity involved breaking a long-held opium-smoking habit, and that remarkable change sparked the interest of other family members. Soon after that, she, along with two of her sons and their wives and two cousins, was baptized. She then opened her home for a family and neighborhood prayer group, and others were converted. Indeed, so enthusiastic was she in her newfound faith that at the age of sixty she learned to read Chinese so that she could read the Bible for herself.[26]

After Tsai graduated from high school—an extraordinary accomplishment for a Chinese girl in the early twentieth century—she began teaching in a government school. Here she used her position and influence in bold evangelistic endeavors. She talked personally with students during class breaks and opened her home for group Bible studies. So effective were her efforts that out of her two hundred students, seventy-two professed faith in Christ. Not surprisingly, the reaction of parents was one of outrage, as was observed in a newspaper article: "The Government normal school has employed a music teacher and gotten a Christian evangelist instead, who is teaching all the girls to cry, 'God! God!' and making Christians of them. The parents are up in arms!" The new dean of the school, Miss Plum, searched the dormitories and confiscated the New Testaments that the girls had hidden in their mattresses and threatened expulsion to any students caught attending a Bible study. The faith of the students, however, was infectious, and eventually Miss Plum herself was converted to Christianity.[27]

Although Tsai worked closely with missionaries and the local church, she never sought to become a "professional" evangelist. She was most effective when she simply shared her personal testimony as a lay woman—a fact that was born out by the remarkable response from students, neighbors, and family members. She was convinced that it was not training or ability that led to success, but simply dedication to God—a philosophy that she summed up in relation to her ministry to her family:

So the brother who tore up my Bible and persecuted me in the early days at last confessed my Lord. In all, fifty-five of my relatives, adults and children, have become God's children and expressed their faith in Jesus. I have never been to college, or theological seminary, and I am not a Bible teacher; I have only been God's "hunting dog." I simply followed at the heels of my Master, and brought to His feet the quarry He sent me after.[28]

It is significant that the impact Tsai had on her family included the male members as well as the female. Indeed, in many cultures where women were accorded a low status generally in society, they have had an unprecedented influence in religious matters—particularly within the extended family. B. V. Subbamma wrote of this phenomenon in Andra, India: "Women believed in the Lord first and then won their husbands and other relatives to the Christian faith."[29]

Organized Lay Evangelism

The success that Christiana Tsai experienced in personal evangelism was not necessarily typical. More often women encountered setbacks and prolonged frustration in their attempts to evangelize family and friends. To facilitate their efforts they often formed support networks and often worked in teams. This has been particularly true in Africa. In the 1930s Methodist women in Nigeria, with the blessing of the male leadership in the church, developed a volunteer evangelistic outreach—so effective that it was reported at a missionary meeting that "Ijebu womanhood was coming into its own. . . ."

The women were deeply concerned for their "Mohammedan sisters," and expressed their enthusiasm in witnessing by saying the "mouth [is] not wide enough to tell of all the goodness of God." They organized street processions, city-wide rallies, open-air campaigns, and retreats, demonstrating effectively what could be done in the area of female lay evangelism.[30]

"Women of the Good News"

One of the most far-reaching women's evangelistic organizations to arise in twentieth century has been the "Women of the Good News," which began in Zaire in the early 1970s. It was the brain child of Virginia Jones, an American missionary, and Rebeka Eliya, a Zairian pastor's wife, who during their exile from the Congo at the time of the Simba Rebellion became familiar with a women's evangelistic movement, "Quali ti tene Njoni," which had been started by Grace Brethren missionaries in the Central African Republic. Their paths separated in 1965, but the dream of a woman's evangelistic movement did not die, and in 1970 they were reunited when Virginia and her husband were reassigned to Banda in Zaire. At that time, before the women had opportunity to make further plans, Rebeka announced that "Madamo Jones had come with a new women's program, "Ade Wene Pangbanga." The decision had been made, and Virginia immediately made preparations to translate the program into Pasande. Thus the movement began in the Zande district with some one hundred women eager to participate.[31]

From the unpretentious beginning in 1970 the movement grew rapidly. In the years that followed, through the combined efforts of women missionaries and women nationals, the program was translated into other tribal languages and the movement was initiated in several other areas of Zaire. After a decade of activity, the number of women involved in the movement had grown to over fifteen thousand, and by 1984, that figure had surpassed thirty thousand in the churches associated with the Africa Inland Mission. The total number of women involved, however, far exceeded that number. By the mid-1970s, the movement had crossed denominational lines, and there were thousands more connected with other missions and churches.[32]

The popularity of "Women of the Good News" was due in part to the social outlet it offered African women, but the primary focus was ministry—perhaps the most attractive feature of the program. In many African churches social custom excluded women from leadership positions, but this parachurch organization provided the unparalleled opportunities for organized ministries that were sanctioned, and indeed welcomed, by the church leadership. On the local level, women were organized in groups that met weekly for Bible studies conducted by several women on a rotating basis. Bible memory was also emphasized, with each member expected to complete a booklet of required memory verses. Each group was subdivided into as many as five smaller groups that carried out different outreach assignments: (1) visiting the sick (providing water, food, wood, and words of both witness and encouragement), (2) bringing the gospel to unbelievers, (3) ministering to those who had left the church fellowship, (4) maintaining the church building and grounds, and (5) visiting elderly people.[33]

Women also organized on a wider scale. A yearly three- to four-day district conference gave delegates the opportunity to be challenged with biblical messages and fresh ideas for ministry. In addition, two days each year were set aside as a Women's Day of Prayer and a Women's Rally Sunday, the latter to acquaint the local church with the ongoing ministry of the organization. Every two years, leadership training seminars were sponsored by the districts for key women who were selected by their local group to attend.[34] Besides the evangelistic and humanitarian outreach of Women of the Good News, there were other achievements that were equally significant, according to Virginia Jones. The organization "brought unity of its women to the entire church of over 1,000 congregations," and it gave "women a place of active involvement" in a structured environment. It also "provided an excellent training ground for women in leadership." In the years since its founding, women missionaries have been replaced by nationals in leadership positions, the former continuing to serve, but only in the capacity of consultants.[35]

Professional Evangelism and Church Planting

In the Third World, unlike the West, much of the evangelism and church planting has been conducted by an army of paid church "professionals"—namely male evangelists and Bible women. Most of these workers were faithful to their ministry, and contributed significantly to the evangelistic thrust among their own people. Yet their work was not entirely without controversy.

Bible Women as Missionary Assistants

The term "Bible women" was the common designation of Christian female nationals who were employed for a pittance by the indigenous church or by women missionaries to function as teachers, interpreters, Bible readers, and evangelists. Their impact on church growth was enormous. In her book *Western Women in Eastern Lands*, Helen Barrett Montgomery wrote, "The Bible woman has become an institution. Her work is indispensable; she multiplies the missionary's influence, goes before to prepare the way, and after to impress the truth. One of the humblest, she is at the same time one of the mightiest forces of the Cross in non-Christian lands."[36]

In Japan Bible women worked very closely with the female missionaries. According to Winburn Thomas, "she acquired a reputation of being a personal servant to the woman missionary, so closely did her efforts supplement those of the foreigner." Rosalind Goforth, who ministered in China at the turn of the twentieth century, developed this kind of a relationship with the women nationals she worked with during her tenure as a missionary. She was nearly always accompanied by a Bible woman who usually made the

initial contacts that would have been inappropriate for Goforth herself to make. She wrote of a Mrs. Wang as "my dear Bible woman, in whom I had complete confidence."[37]

Mrs. Lau, a Chinese Bible Woman.   From *Light and Life for Women* 31:2 (February 1901): 57.

Bible women were also employed by organizations to carry out evangelistic work. The British and Foreign Bible Society, for example, in 1913, had in its employ thirty-six Bible women hired specifically to distribute Bibles and literature. According to Kenneth Scott Latourette, this practice continued for many years not only with the BFBS but also with other Bible societies. Another area of ministry that depended heavily on Bible women was hospital evangelism. Edith Dreyer, who served with the China Inland Mission, told the story of an encounter in a packed hospital waiting room between "Patient No. 125" and a Bible woman. The two women debated the validity of Christianity before a hushed crowd until the patient's number was called. Although no apparent headway had been made during the waiting room encounter, the next morning the woman's son returned to the hospital with the message that his mother, who had "not slept all night . . . wants to walk in the Jesus Way." The Bible woman was summoned and accompanied the boy to his home.[38]

Independent Bible Women's Ministries

Although Bible women generally functioned as assistants to Western missionaries or were employed by organizations, they also served independently in certain ministries that were closed to Westerners. Margaret Burton, an American missionary of the early twentieth century, described this role in her book *Women Workers of the Orient*: "Often she may enter doors which do not yet swing open for the foreign missionary. She goes from zenana to zenana and house to house, teaching the women and girls to read, telling them the story of the Good Tidings. . . . Wholly new ideas and purposes spring up in the home where these humble, consecrated workers have patiently gone."[39]

Bible women often made enormous sacrifices to maintain their ministry. The hours were long, the work was difficult, and the pay was barely enough to subsist on. Likewise, there were family pressures that added to the sacrifice, especially in the Orient where family ties were deeply embedded in culture. Even when the Bible women were unmarried or widowed, there were often aged parents who expected care, and leaving them in order to conduct a ministry was sometimes the supreme sacrifice. There were physical dangers that Bible women encountered as well. Rosalind Goforth wrote of a Mrs. Chang, a Buddhist preacher turned Bible woman who was persecuted during the Boxer Rebellion. "During the terrible ordeal of 1900, she was faithful almost unto death, being strung up by her thumbs by the Boxers, but saved through the intervention of neighbors."[40]

A Bible Woman From India. From *Light and Life for Women* 32:5 (May 1902): 207.

The distinction between Bible women and women evangelists has never been clearly defined, but there were women nationals who, like western women missionaries, traveled with their own Bible women. An example is that of Phoebe Rowe, a Eurasian, whose mother was Indian and whose father was English. She was educated at Isabella Thoburn's school in Lucknow, and while she was there, she was outstanding in evangelistic endeavors. "In 1847 chiefly through her agency all the boarders in the school became Christian." After leaving the school, she became an itinerant evangelist, traveling with a native preacher and a Bible woman—the preacher to conduct the baptisms that resulted from her evangelistic messages, and the Bible woman to conduct work among the women, who were often segregated from the men.[41]

In Japan, Bible women played a crucial role in the development of the Christian church. According to Winburn Thomas, the Bible woman was the "female equivalent of a male evangelist," but because of the low position of women in Oriental society, her place in the church—especially in the early years—was not as secure as was that of the male evangelist. Yet as early as the 1880s there were nearly forty Bible women employed by seven different missions in Japan. Many others were supported by local churches. Writes Thomas, "Of many it was said that their services were no less indispensable than those of the pastors. Some of them became so well known that their names were household words."[42]

Elsewhere Bible women also made a significant contribution to evangelistic work. The Reverend James L. Barton wrote of the more than three hundred Bible women he became acquainted with during his travels in India and Ceylon at the turn of the twentieth century:

> Some of them are well educated, and are doing the work of missionaries as they go into the homes, carrying the light and peace of the gospel. Not a few of these able and devout workers have won places for themselves in the confidence, if not the affection, of almost the entire community. Many of them are women of deep faith, of much prayer, and as they remain in the work they grow bold in the service. The people show them honors, and recognize their power of leadership.[43]

Barton told of a religious meeting, made up largely of men, that he attended in Ceylon: "One native preacher spoke at that service, but the impassioned, earnest appeal which held that large, motley throng in complete silence, and with fixed attention, was the address of the Bible woman." He also told of "a great heathen festival" near Madura where Bible women pitched tents to live in while they spent the festival days preaching the gospel to the "heathen throng."[44]

Opposition to a Paid Indigenous Ministry

As important as Bible women were in the Third World church, their role was not without controversy, as was the case with male evangelists. Indeed, according to Dr. John L. Nevius, the nineteenth-century missiologist most credited for the rapid growth of the Korean church, one of the most serious flaws of the "Old System" of missionary work was the employment of "professional" evangelists.

Such a practice, he argued, not only took the most capable nationals out of their home environment where they would have been most effective, but also left the impression that evangelism was the job of paid professionals. This problem caused some to question the widespread use of Bible women. "Their very existence tended sometimes to cause the women of a church to say that evangelism was 'Biblewomen's work,' and not only to excuse themselves from it on these grounds but to despise it as a lowly occupation."[45]

Fatima Hanum, a Turkish Bible Woman. This woman was forced to flee Constantinople because of persecution. From *Light and Life for Women* (April 1902): 158.

Women's Evangelistic Ministry Among Men

Evangelism conducted by women in the Third World was generally focused on other women, but there were always exceptions—exceptions that sometimes dismayed missionaries who had argued that certain cultures simply did not allow the possibility of women influencing men in such a way. A striking example of this was told by J. W. Pickett in his book *Christ's Way to India's Heart*, published in the late 1930s:

Early in this study we sat one day with 400 others in a temporary structure erected at the expense of a group of prosperous Hindu farmers for a series of evangelistic meetings. The most prominent Hindu of the village was in the chair. He introduced as the preacher of the afternoon an aged widow. For thirty-five minutes that preacher held the attention of her audience. Her sermon, in a language which the writer does not understand, was said to be logical, forceful and eloquent. At its close, the chairman thanked her and remarked that times were changing when a Hindu audience would listen with interest, respect and profit to an address on religion delivered by a woman."[46]

Education

A natural outcome of the strong emphasis that Western women missionaries placed on female education in the Third World was the interest in education among Third World women themselves. Government officials frequently lured the young women who had been trained in mission schools into teaching roles in public education, but many became actively involved in Christian education for girls, and some founded successful schools of their own.

Pandita Ramabai

One of the most outstanding Christian educators of the Third World was Pandita Ramabai (1858–1922), the daughter of a wandering Hindu guru who took his family with him on his pilgrimages to temples and other sacred places in an endless effort to appease the gods. It was a life of misery for young Pandita, except for the fact that her father had broken Hindu tradition and encouraged his wife and daughters to become Sanskrit scholars. Indeed she credited her father for her own commitment to female education:

I am the child of a man who had to suffer a great deal on account of advocating Female Education, and who was compelled to discuss the subject, as well as to carry out his own views, amidst great opposition. . . . I consider it my duty, to the very end of my life, to maintain this cause, and to advocate the proper position of women in this land."[47]

Ramabai's heritage gave her an advantage over other Indian women and it led her into an intensive search for God. After her parents died, she and her brother continued their lives as religious pilgrims, which she later wrote about: "I cannot describe all the sufferings of this terrible time. My brother and I survived and wandered about, still visiting sacred places, bathing in rivers, and worshiping the gods and goddesses in order to get our desire. . . . After years of fruitless service we began to lose our faith in them."[48]

Disillusioned with their search for the truth, Pandita and her brother settled in Calcutta, and there she came in contact for the first time with Christianity. She began studying the Bible and at the same time accepted a challenge from some leading Hindu scholars, who recognized her brilliance, to lecture to high-caste women in their duties according to the Hindu scriptures. In her study she discovered that the various scriptures contradicted themselves in virtually every area except in their view of women. The various Hindu writings and their interpreters all agreed

that women of high and low caste, as a class, were bad, very bad, worse than demons, as unholy as untruth, and that they could not get Moksha as men. The only hope of their getting this much-desired liberation from Karma and its results . . . was the worship of their husbands. The husband is said to be the women's god; there is no other god for her.[49]

It was this discovery that launched Pandita on the path of reform. She was influenced by other reformers who were seeking to dismantle the caste system and other relics of Hindu tradition, but her focus was on women. She soon became known throughout India for her outspoken challenge to Hindu beliefs and her efforts to raise the status of women—particularly of widows whose misery exceeded that of married women. This concern was heightened after the death of her own husband of only nineteen months. From that time on she dedicated her efforts to reforming society so that her infant daughter would never have to endure the same degradation. She traveled from city to city, lecturing and forming chapters of a society she founded, *Arya Mahila Somaj*, which served the needs of oppressed women. It was during this time that she came in contact with a Baptist missionary and began her pilgrimage toward Christianity. For a time she joined the Brahmo Samaj cult, a syncretistic religion that combined Christianity with Hindu belief.[50]

In 1883 Ramabai visited England, where she lived with a friend, Sister Geraldine, who was a member of the Anglican Community of St. Mary the Virgin at Wantage. Although she had vowed before she left India, "Nothing will induce me to embrace Christianity," she found herself irresistibly drawn to Christ and the faith of the Bible. When the news of her baptism reached India, there were cries of outrage that India's foremost woman reformer would betray her people and her culture.[51]

For Ramabai, however, her new faith was not a betrayal of her cultural heritage, and her insistence on that created conflict with her friends in England. She abhorred the idea of being part of the Church of England. She considered herself simply a Christian and deeply resented the efforts of the Sisters to make her conform to their lifestyle. Indeed, she remained very independent in her Christianity as her fascinating letters to Sister Geraldine illustrate:

I am, it is true, a member of the Church of Christ, but I am not bound to accept every word that falls down from the lips of priests or bishops. . . . I have just with great efforts freed myself from the yoke of the Indian priestly tribe, so I am not at present willing to place myself under another similar yoke by accepting everything which comes from the priests as authorized command of the Most High."[52]

Ramabai's questions and doubts regarding Christianity and the various denominational positions were upsetting to her Anglican friends in England who believed that she had committed herself to the Anglican faith at the time of her baptism. Ramabai argued that it was not possible for her to fully understand her faith at the time of her baptism. Again to Sister Geraldine she wrote:

I regret that I have been the cause of making you feel yourself wrong for the part you acted in my baptism. I wish I knew that your Church required a person to be quite perfect in faith, doubting nothing in the Athanasian Creed, so that he had left nothing to be learnt and inquired into the Bible after his baptism.[53]

She was likewise accused by Sister Geraldine of "clinging to caste prejudice which ought to have been thrown to the winds when you embraced Christianity." One such prejudice was her refusal to eat puddings made from eggs. Ramabai responded, "You may, if you like trace my pride in pies and puddings. . . . I confess I am not free from all my caste prejudices, as you are pleased to call them. I like to be called a Hindu, for I am one, and also keep all the customs of my forefathers as far as I can." Then, with more than a hint of sarcasm, Ramabai turned the tables on Sister Geraldine, "How would an Englishwoman like being called proud and prejudiced if she were to go and live among the Hindus for a time but did not think it necessary to alter her customs when they were not hurtful or necessary to her neighbours?"[54]

Pandita Ramabai, a Great Christian Educator and Evangelist From India. From Helen S. Dyer, *Pandita Ramabai* (London: Pickering & Inglis, n.d.).

It was with that spirit of independence that Ramabai developed her educational ministry in India. She continued giving lectures and even accepted invitations to preach in Hindu temples, where she read from the Hindu scriptures and shared her Christian faith. For this she was heavily criticized by fellow Christians and Hindus alike, but at times she seemed to thrive on the controversy. To Sister Geraldine she wrote, "I am having a right good time in the storm of public indignation that is raging over my head."[55]

Initially, Ramabai insisted on an open-minded approach in the school at Poona that she founded for child widows. She was convinced that the only way to bring Christianity effectively to India was to avoid making it alien to the Indian culture and the Hindu scriptures. The Hindu scrip-

tures were available to the girls as was the Bible, and she did not seek to coerce them to convert to Christianity. In fact she insisted that the school be secular even though it was supported to a large extent by American Christians. She was critical of missionary schools, particularly the ones founded by Mary Carpenter, because they did not demonstrate proper respect for Indian culture and traditions. "These schools," she wrote, "were opened to women of every caste, and while they have undoubtedly been of use, they have not realized the hopes of their founder, partly because of the impossibility of keeping caste-rules in them."[56]

Such criticism was disturbing to many Christians, but even greater controversy arose later when a number of the girls in her own school requested Christian baptism. Hindu reformers accused her of proselytizing, and newspapers reported that she had misrepresented her secular stance, and as a result many families removed their daughters from the school. Soon after that, in 1898, she abandoned her secular policy and openly introduced the Bible and Christian principles in the school. The work expanded considerably in the years that followed, especially during a famine in 1900, when the needs for child widows magnified. She opened additional facilities, and there was a major spiritual breakthrough that was evidenced when more than a thousand girls professed faith in Christ.[57]

Despite her success, criticism of her work persisted, but Ramabai continued her open educational policy of living the Christian life before her students and responding to their enquiries, yet refusing to give into demands that the school would actively seek to evangelize its students as did other mission schools. In many ways her concept of how to bring Christianity to India was more acceptable to the people than that of many Western missionaries. Christianity had to be presented not in the form of Western denominations but as a faith that was compatible to the Indian culture and one that was focused on Christ and a very personalized faith rather than institutionalized dogma. This philosophy was seen in her deep longing for revival:

> I was led by the Lord to start a special prayer circle at the beginning of 1905. There were about seventy of us who met together each morning and prayed for the true conversion of all the Indian Christians, including ourselves, and for special outpouring of the Holy Spirit. . . . In six months from the time we began to pray in this manner, the Lord graciously sent a glorious Holy Ghost Revival among us, and also in many schools and churches in this country.[58]

Writing and Translation Work

Because of the high rate of illiteracy in the Third World, writing ministries for women were not common, but women who did write, often had opportunities for a far-reaching influence that would not otherwise have been available to them. This was true of Kazue Miki, the daughter of the president of Japan's Osaka Stock Exchange.

Kazue Miki

Born in the early years of the twentieth century, Kazue Miki enjoyed educational advantages that were not available to the majority of Oriental women. Through the ministry of missionary Irene Webster-Smith and her Sunrise Home, Kazue began attending Bible classes and soon made a profession of faith in Christ. Through her testimony during the months that followed, the members of her family forsook their Buddhist faith and also turned to Christianity. It had been a painful break for many of the family members, and the transition from one set of values to another was difficult. For Kazue, however, the struggle to live the Christian life was complicated by other factors. Her marriage to a professing Christian man turned into a virtual prison sentence when she was forced to live with her mother-in-law who bitterly resented her Christian faith. She was abused and locked in a closet until she became so ill that she had to be hospitalized, and not long afterward she died. Yet her ministry lived on. During her time of stress she kept a diary that was later published under the title *Kazue's Diary*. Its distribution throughout Japan, according to Russell Hitt, "was instrumental in leading many to a knowledge of Christ."[59]

Language Informants

Another area of ministry that Third World women became involved in was Bible translation. They frequently served as language informants for women missionaries. Although their language proficiency was generally

347

inferior to that of males in their tribe, it was they who, for reasons of cultural propriety, were chosen as informants. Eunice Pike, who served with Florence Hansen under Wycliffe Bible Translators in Mexico among the Mazatec Indians, found Marta to be invaluable in the tedious process of learning the Mazatec language.

> Marta sewed while she acted as informant, and with her mind on her sewing she repeated, without impatience or comment, anything we asked her. One time I thought I had been particularly boring. About two hundred times she had repeated a sentence, each time substituting a different noun for the subject. I had been listening to the repetitions, ready to record any variations in the tone of the sentence. I was tired, and I was sure that she must be. In the way of apology, and to show a bit of sympathy, I said, "I'm a big nuisance." Marta, without a change of expression, and without looking up from her sewing, polly-parroted back, "I'm a big nuisance."[60]

Securing a competent informant who could endure the hours of tedium has been one of the most difficult problems missionary translators have faced. Men were particularly vulnerable to boredom, because language work often took them away from more exciting activities. Women, on the other hand, would sew or do other sedentary work while doing their job as an informant. Marta was an exceptional informant, in that she not only exhibited patience but also a keen interest in the work. She

> seldom tired of repeating, and she especially enjoyed helping us to translate Bible stories. Her eyes shown as she saw each story develop. Eloisa, her sister, liked them too, and she listened

while sewing or cooking nearby, and added her suggestions whenever Marta hesitated. Although only sixteen years old, Eloisa herself developed into a very able informant, and when Marta was busy she frequently took over.[61]

Foreign Missions

Despite the rapid growth of the church in certain areas of the Third World, the vast majority of foreign missionaries continue to be from the West. This has not always been true—especially in the South Seas where evangelistic endeavors to unreached islands was accomplished largely by native evangelists. Women were actively involved, accompanying their husbands as full partners in the missionary enterprise. According to Charles Forman, "the great period for indigenous missionary wives was the last quarter of the nineteenth and first quarter of the twentieth centuries." More than a thousand men and women from Samoa Tonga, Fiji, and the Cook Islands volunteered for crosscultural ministries mainly in the Solomon Islands and New Guinea. The women went as missionary wives, but they "shared fully in the hard work involved. In places where women had little voice in society, missionary wives showed new possibilities." Like their European counterparts, many of these women died young in childbearing, but those who returned to their native islands "were treated as heroines," according to Forman, and their public speaking in the home churches set the example for other women and opened up new avenues of public service for women on the home front.[62]

Another area of the Pacific island

world that was evangelized in part by women from the non-Western church was Hawaii. According to Alice Chai, "Bible women were on board almost every ship that brought [Korean] immigrants to Hawaii." The story of one such evangelist has been recorded by her granddaughter:

> My Grandmother was 28 years old when she left Korea with her eight-year-old daughter in 1903. Her own family had thrown her out of the house because of her Christian beliefs. She was estranged from her husband. With no future in Korea, she decided to go to Hawaii as a "Bible woman." She helped so many of the immigrant women, counseling them and encouraging them. . . . In the church you could see her standing with the men. They respected her convictions. My family often said, "Grandmother should have been a man!"[63]

China Native Evangelistic Crusade

The difficulty in raising financial support and the evangelistic needs in the homeland have limited the number of Christians to go abroad. These obstacles have been overcome, however, through financial aid from the West and through utilizing creative opportunities. In the 1940s the China Native Evangelistic Crusade, directed by N. A. Jepson, an American, sent out "thirteen gospel bands made up of Chinese evangelists, Bible women, and students" to unreached areas of China. In one area, north of Tibet, which was closed to the gospel, evangelism and church planting was conducted by the wife of a government official. "While her husband fulfilled his official duties, Mrs. Lee witnessed and taught the Bible, and soon a church was established."[64]

Burmese Women's Mission Societies

The church in Burma has been one of the most missionary-minded churches in the Third World. Here women's missionary societies, patterned after those in the West have flourished for more than a century. By the turn of the century there were such organizations in each of the major language groups. The Burmese Baptist Women's Society was supporting five full-time women evangelists in the early 1950s, while the Karen Society was supporting home missionaries in Lower Burma and foreign missionaries in Thailand, and the Methodist Women's Society was carrying out similar work. "All the work of the organization," wrote Kathleen Bliss, "is done by the women themselves on a voluntary basis."[65]

Women's Home Missionary Society of India

In India, support for missions also ran high among women. There the National Missionary Society depended heavily on local women's organizations for support. In the hilly region of Assam, the Women's Home Missionary Society made regular offerings for missionary work. "Our women take up a collection which is a handful of rice set apart from each meal. This handful of rice at the end of the week comes to about two pounds. This is brought to church and later sold at a little cheaper rate for the support of our evangelists."[66]

Humanitarian Ministries

Humanitarian services were from the very beginning a vital part of women's missionary work in the Third World—a work that would have been far less effective without the selfless sacrifice of nationals. Health care, refugee work, orphanages, and homes for prostitutes were all areas of ministry that captured the imaginations of Third World women. Indeed, in the nineteenth and twentieth centuries non-Western Christian women patterned their social work after that of women in the West. Although their cultures were vastly different, many of their concerns were similar. For example, Christian women in Japan formed a Women's Christian Temperance Union, and a Mrs. Yajima, the president, was described as "a Japanese Frances Willard."[67]

Hilda Lazarus

Women's medical work in India was stimulated as much by Dr. Ida Scudder as any other individual, and her most enduring legacy was the development of a large medical training facility to train nationals in a Christian atmosphere. As an American, however, she was unable to function as effectively in dealing with the Indian government during the difficult period following independence as was a national, and thus in 1947 Dr. Hilda Lazarus assumed the responsibilities of principal and director of the Vellore Christian Medical College and Hospital. She held seven medical degrees and had previously served in the Indian army as a chief medical officer, but equally important was her strong Christian faith. Her two Brahmin grandfathers, despite intense opposition, had become Christians, and it was her vision to share that faith throughout India. As an administrator she was able to do what no foreigner would have been able to do. "She was not only an instrument and product of the new free India. She was its living embodiment. Her experience in government made her ideal for the task of piloting Vellore through this period of crisis."[68]

Kieko Yammamuro

An organization that specialized in humanitarian ministries overseas as it did in the West was the Salvation Army, and female officers often played a leading role. An example was Kieko Yammamuro, who helped lead the fight against prostitution in Japan in the early twentieth century. Young girls were frequently bought or kidnapped and forced to work as prostitutes in the notorious Yoshiwara district of the city, and through the publicity and work of the Salvation Army, which stirred up public opinion and government intervention, more than a thousand girls were rescued. For Kieko, freeing the girls was only the beginning of her ministry. She directed a Salvation Army home that offered the girls education and training in a Christian atmosphere and a chance to turn their lives around.[69]

Although she was weak physically and had a husband and children to care for, Kieko did not limit her ministry to the home for prostitutes. Indeed, her greater ministry was establishing a sanatorium for tuberculosis patients, for whom there was no room in the Salvation Army hospital. It was a task that seemed beyond her capabilities, but a challenge she could not ignore. She wrote of this struggle in her diary:

It seems too adventurous perhaps, but God is able. I have no one save the Holy Ghost to rely upon. My weak health and lack of ability seem to deny me success, but when I am weak, God is strong. Depending upon Him alone, I go forward to establish the Sanatorium. To be with the children makes me happy and perhaps some will call me neglectful of my duty as a mother. But though my eyes are wet with tears, I must go forward. O Lord, fill me with the Holy Ghost. Give me power to move the people. Amen.[70]

Dohnavur Fellowship

In India, Amy Carmichael depended almost entirely on women nationals to carry out the work of Dohnavur Fellowship in caring for the girls who were rescued from temple prostitution. In fact, many of the girls whom she rescued later became the leaders in the institution. In 1916, she and seven of these Indian girls formed the Sisterhood of the Common Life. It was a spiritual union, but it had very practical goals—to steer young women into a single-minded ministry that was not encumbered by family responsibilities. One of these faithful women was Arulai. Of her, Carmichael wrote, "She has shared in every part of the work from the beginning and knows everything from the inside. . . . Her faithful heart has never swerved from the most flawless loyalty." For nearly forty years she served alongside Carmichael, conducting meetings, teach-

ing classes, and preparing young women to enter the Sisterhood, which grew to over nine hundred by 1952.[71]

Protestant Sisterhoods

The sisterhood that Amy Carmichael developed on Indian soil was independent of church control and was focused on one particular social problem. There were other Protestant sisterhoods, however, that were tied to the church and that were involved in a wider range of social and religious activities. One of those was the Order for Women in the Church of South India, founded in 1952. The Church of South India was a union of Protestant churches that recognized soon after its formation the need for women to be officially incorporated into professional church ministry. In the early years there were more than a thousand such female professionals involved in evangelistic and humanitarian endeavors, but the number dropped to two hundred and twenty-four by 1978.[72]

One of the reasons for the decline of women in professional ministry was the lack of control women had over their ministries. The bishop of the diocese assigned them to specific duties—duties that were considered appropriate for women. By the mid-1960s, many women were concerned about their lack of financial security and were questioning their status in the church in relationship to men. During the 1970s, the issue was brought before the synod of the church and a recommendation was made by the Executive Committee to ordain women. The proposed changes were initially delayed because of a failure to obtain a two-thirds majority of the dioceses, but in 1982 the measure passed, and women were ordained along with men.[73]

One of the decisive points that influenced the decision to give women equality in the church was the cultural factor. Although the Theological Commission had published a biblical and theological defense of women's ordination, it was societal changes that were given the most weight when the final consideration was made. The commission argued that denying ordination to women was not compatible with the "new understanding of the dignity of womanhood" in India. Pragmatic concerns were also voiced. The report concluded that there were certain types of pastoral work "for which women pastors are better suited."[74]

Roman Catholic Sisterhoods

From early in the nineteenth century when Anne-Marie Javouhey began commissioning the Sisters of St. Joseph to Africa, Asia, and Latin America, there was a conscientious effort to train nationals to share equally in the work. As female religious orders spread from the West into the developing nations, more and more nationals became involved.

One internationally acclaimed sisterhood that has drawn heavily from the Third World for its sacrificial volunteers has been the Missionaries of Charity founded by Mother Teresa. Indeed, the mission was born in India in 1949 after Sister Teresa left the security of her religious community and, with the help of a few Bengali volunteers, began her life of ministering to the "poorest of the poor." The first woman to join the movement was Subashini Das, one of Sister Teresa's former students. With the needs so great in India, the practice of cloistering nuns seemed to make little sense to Sister Teresa and her followers. Their focus was on the streets where teeming millions were oppressed by the effects of poverty. "Young women flocked to the Missionaries of Charity. Soon teams of Sisters spread out into fifty Indian cities, opening free clinics, antileprosy clinics, free schools, and vocational training centers."[75]

In the decades that followed, the Missionaries of Charity spread out all over the world. By 1981, there were more than two hundred houses functioning throughout the world, most of which had been founded by small teams of Indian women. In that year Mother Teresa established teams in such diverse geographical locations as East Berlin, Egypt, and Macao, off the coast of China. Other Indian sisters went to Korea, Ethiopia, Bolivia, and Haiti.[76]

Charismatic Ministries

A significant area of ministry for women in non-Western churches, as had been the case in the Western church throughout church history, was that involving charismatic phenomena. Generally such charismatic ministry was more characteristic of the independent national churches than of the denominational and mission churches that were heavily influenced and sometimes controlled by Western missionaries. In fact, one major reason for the birth and growth of independent churches in

Africa was the fact that they offered women a wide range of meaningful opportunities for ministry.

Women have had a significant religious influence in South Africa, particularly among the Zionist and Apostolic churches during the first half of the twentieth century, where they held prominent positions as healers and prophetesses. Typically such a woman claimed authority from God, testifying of a personal "call" that came "in the form of dreams or visions and usually after a history of illness of which she was cured." That her ministry was authenticated by a call, however, did not presume that she would have supernatural abilities or knowledge. Indeed, many of these women began a long process of training that gave them a reputation of being the most well-versed Bible teachers in the churches. In some instances these women founded their own churches and functioned as the pastor. Some of these women were considered lay preachers, but others were ordained and fully qualified to administer the sacraments. In most cases, however, the ministries of these women were limited to women's organizations that operated in conjunction with an established church and its male pastor.[77]

Even though the independent women's organizations functioned outside the local church, they wielded a powerful influence on the church, and pastors were frequently "heavily dependent on the women for a host of personal services." Fundraising was a significant aspect of their organizational activity, and churches and pastors knew the value of being in their good graces. Other than providing needed funds for the church, the main activity of these organizations was caring for their own in time of sickness. Occasionally, the women leaders were employed by the churches as evangelists, but the main ministry of the prophetess or healer was to lead the women's meetings. Here they exercised considerable freedom of expression in their religious worship. One woman after another would be "taken by the Spirit," which was generally characterized by violent shaking and high-pitched chanting and exhortation.[78]

African Independent Movements

Many of the African independent movements were founded by women, and some of these attracted large followings. Mai (Mother) Chaza founded the City of God movement in 1952, and Alice Lenshina founded the Lumpa church two years later, each of which had followings of nearly one hundred thousand. The vast majority of such movements, however, were much smaller, some no more than a single congregation. The number of such female leaders has numbered in the hundreds in recent decades.[79]

Alice Lenshina, the head of the Lumpa church, was an unusual character, but in many ways she typified independent female leadership. She "gained her reputation as a Ngulu-possessed girl, with an unhappy married life, who suffered from fainting fits. She rebelled against the elders' verdict that her visions were not genuine, and that as a woman of the catechumen class she could not be allowed to preach." She was excommunicated from the church and after that formed her own movement.[80]

The St. John's Apostolic Church

located near Johannesburg was also founded by a charismatic woman— "Ma Nku, the vigorous, outgoing, immensely popular healer and prophetess." Although she has been described as "powerful, ebullient, one of those African women who can lead thousands and exercise authority as one born to it," she struggled in maintaining leadership in her church. Men served in the office of bishop, and after her bishop husband died, she endured years of conflict with the succeeding leaders of "her" church.[81]

Unlike many other Third World Christian women's organizations, the women leaders in these independent churches ministered especially to their own people—other Christian women. But even through that type of ministry they reached out. The enthusiastic and charismatic character of their meetings attracted outsiders, and the result in many instances was rapid numerical growth.

Charismatic Revival in Indonesia

There were other areas besides Africa where the charismatic ministry of women was a significant factor in the Christian community. Indonesia is an example, especially during the revival movements of the 1960s. It was then that Mother Li, an uneducated woman with eleven children, claimed a divine call to missionary work. Before going overseas, however, she began a charismatic prayer ministry among her own people. As leader of a prayer group, she focused her followers' attention on communion, claiming that God had given her the assurance that for a two-year period he would perform a miracle

during each communion service, such as changing water into wine. She also developed a ministry of reconciling pastors whose strife was wreaking havoc on their pastoral work, claiming God had given her direct authority to act as peacemaker. "Traveling continually by foot, Mother Li has journeyed from one end of the island to the other reconciling pastors and elders and other Christians to each other, as the Lord has directed her."[82]

Another Indonesian woman who had an influential charismatic ministry was simply known as Sarai. She began preaching on the same night that she received her visionary call. She began at six o'clock in the evening and continued on, as neighbors gathered, until three o'clock in the morning. "During her preaching the spirit of prophecy suddenly came over her, and she began to tell the people present what fetishes they had in their houses, and where they were hidden. Those concerned hurried away and fetching their amulets and charms, they brought them back to the meeting and threw them into a heap." She also became deeply involved in a healing ministry, traveling from village to village on the islands of Timor and Rote.[83]

Pastoral Ministries and Church Leadership

Although full equality for women in church ministries has been resisted in most areas of the non-Western world even more than it has been in the West, there were exceptions such as those that were seen in the Independent churches of South Africa and Rhodesia. In other instances, although women's equality in theory was fiercely opposed, women nevertheless played a key role in conducting the affairs of the church. By the mid-twentieth century the church in Manchuria, for example, had many Bible-school-trained women—some of whom had given up promising careers—who were actively conducting itinerant ministries.

They sometimes do all the work of a pastor except administer the Sacraments. Others have been responsible for superintending the work of the Church in a whole district, traveling round, staying in one place for several weeks, organizing women's meetings and preparing candidates for baptism."[84]

Women Pastors in Oceania

In most areas of the Third World women have had more difficulty being accepted in the pastoral ministry than in the West. Oceania is a case in point. The first female ordinations came in the mid-1970s, and they involved women who were trained for specialized ministries rather than for the pastorate. Because of strong opposition, the pastorate has for all practical purposes remained closed to women. Yet women have risen to the highest leadership positions in church organizations. In 1971 and again in 1977, women were chosen to serve in the position of general secretary for the Pacific Conference of Churches.[85]

Women Pastors in Japan

The situation was similar in Asia. In the early 1950s, Kathleen Bliss reported that "no Indian women are ordained even in those churches which ordain women to the ministry in the West. . . . Thus social custom may make it impossible for the question of women's ordination to be raised although there is no theological barrier." In rare instances, however, women overcame strict social barriers and held high positions in the church. That was the case in Tokyo, where Bliss reported that "a woman is the minister of one of the largest churches." More often, though, because of the large female majority in church membership, women "pastors" served the needs of the women parishioners. One way for women to overcome social barriers was to work closely with their husbands. In Japan, the pastor's wife developed considerable influence, and sometimes served with her husband in the pastoral duties of two churches.[86]

An example of a contemporary Japanese female ordained minister is Yoshimura Sensei, who in 1984 at the age of eighty was still teaching the women's Bible studies she had begun more than forty years earlier. After becoming a Christian as a young woman she felt called to become a minister, but seminary education and ordination for women were at that time strictly prohibited. She became actively involved in lay ministries but did not give up her dream, and finally in 1962, when she was fifty-two years old, enrolled at Tokyo Union Theologate, which by that time had more than twenty women students. After her ordination she continued her teaching at a Japanese Christian school.[87]

Li Tim Oi Ordained in Hong Kong

In some instances women were ordained by church leaders over objections from their parent denominations in the West. This occurred in 1944 when Anglican Bishop R. O. Hall from Hong Kong ordained Li Tim Oi as a priest. He justified the unprecedented move on the basis that there was a severe shortage of male priests, and his local synod supported him. Although she was qualified to serve, her ordination was ruled invalid by York and Canterbury, and she agreed to relinquish her position.[88]

United Congregational Church in South Africa

One unlikely place for a woman—especially a black woman—to gain recognition as a church leader has been South Africa. Most denominational churches have been very reluctant to ordain or permit them to serve in high office in the church. An extraordinary exception, however, was the 1981 election of Rev. M. Constable to the presidency of the United Congregational Church in South Africa. She entered office at a crucial time when the church was reformulating its stand on various aspects of apartheid.[89]

Roman Catholic Women Leaders

The position of Third World women in the Roman Catholic Church has in some significant instances exceeded that of Western women. This situation has resulted because of a shortage of male priests and has been most common in areas of Latin America. "The service women lend the church is reflected in the Latin American Conference of Religious," writes Ada Maria Isasi-Diaz. "Of 160,000 members about 130,000 are women. Due to the shortage of priests, the pastoral roles of many women members of religious communities go far beyond what they do in the U. S. In many areas women religious are indeed 'pastors'—their exclusion from the ministry of the sacraments is all that keeps them from functioning as priests."[90]

Some Latin countries were more dependent on "women religious" than others. During the 1970s in Chile, for example, there was only one priest for every four thousand baptized Catholics, while in the United States there was one per eight hundred. Because of this severe shortage of priests, some ten thousand lay women were trained as "Mother Catechists" to teach children the faith. But even more significant was the promotion of sisters to the position of "sister administrators."

> They took over those tasks traditionally reserved to clergy: planning and conducting paraliturgical ceremonies and carrying the entire burden of religious formation of adults and children—prebaptismal talks for parents, prematrimonial formation of couples, the formation of basic communities for Christian living, parochial administration, and a limited participation in the administration of the sacraments. By 1976 there were nearly 80 of these "sister administrators" in parishes all over Chile.[91]

B. V. Subbamma

One of the most influential women leaders in the Third World Christian church in recent decades has been B. V. Subbamma, who has become recognized in the field of missiology for her *New Patterns for Discipling Hindus*. Equally significant, however, has been her ministry among her own people. She has served as the principal of the Charlotte Swenson Memorial Bible Training School and as an evangelist, drawing crowds of men and women sometimes numbering several thousand.[92]

House Churches in China

Perhaps the most striking example of women in church in recent years has been in the church of China since the 1950s. After visiting China in 1981, Arthur Glasser stated that he was convinced that women were a key to the survival of Christianity under the Chinese Communist regime. "Fully 85% of the leaders of the house churches thriving in the People's Republic of China are women."[93]

Ecumenical Activities

One of the most outstanding Third-World women in ecumenical circles during the early twentieth century was Lilavati Singh from India who served as a teacher in, and later president of, the Isabella Thoburn College in Lucknow. In 1900 she visited the United States and gave an address at the Ecumenical Missionary Conference in New York, where she passionately presented the educational needs of women in India. "So profound was the impression that no one was surprised when ex-President Harrison said that if he had given a million dollars to evangelize India, and this wonderful woman were the only convert, he should feel that his money had been well expended." In 1907 Singh represented the Young Women's Christian Associations of India at a world conference of university students held in Tokyo. Helen Barrett Montgomery writes, "She probably made a profounder impression of spirituality and intellectual power than any other woman of the conference." The following year she traveled to England and the Continent to speak to student volunteer conferences. Her untimely death in 1909 while she was on a speaking tour in the United States was a profound loss to the cause of educational and ecumenical work among women in the Third World.[94]

Lilavati Singh, Acting President of Lucknow College. From Helen Barrett Montgomery. *Western Women in Eastern Lands* (New York: Macmillan, 1910), 186.

357

A Future Built on the Past

The success and acclaim that accompanied Singh's ministry was not the norm for Third World women. Some did rise above the cultural and sex barriers and were recognized for their service, but the vast multitude of women who gave their lives in Christian ministry have been buried in obscurity without even a mention of their names on the rolls of the church. Yet the legacy they left lives on and serves as a shining example to the West, and for that reason as much as any other, their story needs to be written. Indeed, the history of the church will never be complete until proper recognition is given to Christianity in the non-Western world.

What does the future hold for women in ministry in the non-Western world? Geographical and denominational factors will continue to have a significant bearing on the role they have in the churches, but there are signs of rapid change on every continent. Latin America is a prime example. "A few years ago," writes Elisabeth Isais, "a typical conscientious Latin American father would never allow his daughter to study medicine or law. . . . But today in Latin America women are increasingly surfacing as doctors, lawyers, diplomats, or administrators." The churches—particularly the Evangelicals—have been slower to welcome change than secular institutions, but even here the evolutionary transition is noticeable.

True, most capable women are still found in the weekly Ladies' Missionary Society, singing in the choir, or teaching Sunday school. But some are teaching in Bible institutes, directing large choirs, leading Christian education programs, and even pastoring churches. In Mexico one very large denomination is led by a soft-spoken little lady named Febe Flores."[95]

History has demonstrated the potent force women can be in world evangelism, and the future growth of the Christianity in the Third World depends to a large extent on how women are incorporated into the total life and ministry of the church. As significant as the Bible woman was a century ago, that lowly position does not adequately meet the needs of the contemporary non-Western woman who desires a career ministry in the church. Protestant and Roman Catholic women alike are seeking meaningful ministries that reflect their higher level of education and training and that will more effectively meet the needs of modern society.

Chapter 10

Modern Pentecostalism and Denominationalism: Tent-toting Evangelists and Ordained Ministers

The early years of the twentieth century brought little change in the position of women in the established mainline churches. In most instances women were denied leadership roles, and in churches where they were permitted to vote in conference sessions, they found themselves hopelessly outnumbered by men. Most women accepted their inferior status as society's and Scripture's place for them, and they willingly filled the roles that were described as women's work. In the sectarian movements, however, the case was significantly different. The holiness movement and the emerging Pentecostal movement, like sectarian movements of previous centuries, offered wide opportunities for women, and some of the most influential voices in the early twentieth century were those of females. Their authority they believed came directly from God. Indeed, it did not come from men, for the men in those churches were not necessarily any more eager to allow them positions of leadership than were men in the established churches. But at the very core of holiness and Pentecostal belief was the emphasis on the Spirit being poured out "on all flesh" (Acts 2:17 KJV).

The Pentecostal Movement

The Pentecostal movement has been a significant part of twentieth-century religion. Indeed, that movement ushered in the twentieth century, and the leading character was a woman. "It was after midnight and the first day of the twentieth century when Miss [Agnes] Ozman began 'speaking in the Chinese language' while a 'halo seemed to surround her head and face.'" Not only did she speak in another language, but she also said, "When I went to write I did not write in English, but made characters in another language." Her experience at the Bethel Bible School convinced its founder, Reverend Charles Fox Parham, that glossolalia (speaking in tongues) was "the only evidence of one's having received the

359

baptism with the Holy Ghost" and "that it should be a part of 'normal' Christian worship rather than a curious by-product of religious enthusiasm."[1] It was Parham's teachings that became the basis for the Azusa Street revival and for the subsequent Pentecostal movement that spread across the country and throughout the world.

Charismatic phenomena were not new to sectarian Christianity, but prior to the twentieth century they had been associated with a crisis experience of ecstasy. With the inception of Pentecostalism, however, tongues and healings were deemed to be part of Spirit-filled living; and for those with sufficient faith, language study and medical treatment were thought to be unnecessary. This new gospel spread rapidly in America in the early decades of the twentieth century, and one of the factors relating to its spread was "that very early in their history the Pentecostals recognized the vital role that women could play in a spiritual awakening. They utilized them as pastors, evangelists, and missionaries."[2]

Although most of the leaders of Pentecostalism were men—Parham, Seymour, G. B. Cashwell, Nickolas J. Holmes, J. H. King, C. H. Mason, A. J. Tomlinson, and others—women were not excluded from the ranks. Indeed, women were involved in every aspect of the movement as it moved from Topeka to Los Angeles and spread throughout the world. William J. Seymour is generally credited with leading the Azusa Street revival that broke out in Los Angeles in 1906, but with him was Lucy Farrar, "who had received the baptism of the Holy Spirit in Kansas."

According to a contemporary who participated in the meetings, "the teaching here came by a colored man, (Seymour), and a mulatto woman, (Lucy Farrar)."[3] Farrar, like so many of the other women who would enter the movement, eagerly took advantage of the Pentecostal emphasis on spiritual gifts over and above education and ordination and moved into the ranks of leadership.

Florence Crawford and the Apostolic Faith

One of the early Pentecostal leaders was Florence Crawford, who founded the Apostolic Faith church in Oregon. Prior to this she had attended the Azusa Street revival in 1906, and it was there that she experienced her "baptism." As she explained it:

> A sound like a rushing, mighty wind filled the room, and I was baptized with the Holy Ghost and fire. Rivers of joy and love divine flooded my soul. God also gave me the Bible evidence of receiving this experience in letting me speak in another language. . . . But the greatest joy in my heart was the knowledge that I received power to witness for Christ, power to tell others what great things God can do in a human life.[4]

At the same time that she underwent this ecstatic experience, Crawford claimed that she was healed of an assortment of physical problems: "Once diseased from the crown of my head to the soles of my feet, I now was made sound and well through the blood of Jesus. The Christ of Calvary touched my body and made me whole."[5]

According to her contemporaries,

Crawford was the first of the Azusa Street "converts" to take the message on the evangelistic circuit. She began in Los Angeles and then went on to Oregon, Washington, Minnesota, and Canada, before settling down in Portland in 1907, where she established her headquarters. There she founded an extensive city mission work, which included two auditoriums with a combined seating capacity of more than three thousand. The philosophy of the work was not to attain rapid growth, but, as she explained it, "Rather, its concern is with members who have 'prayed through' to that born-again experience which enables them to live a life of victory over sin and to keep themselves 'unspotted from the world.' "[6]

Being "unspotted from the world" included a mandate that "remarried divorcees separate before being admitted to church membership," as well as strict regulations regarding "worldly amusements" and also a straight-laced dress code for women, which permitted "no extreme fads, no facial makeup or bobbed hair." The Apostolic Faith was an exclusivist body, considering itself the only true church. Indeed, her followers were to be so "separated" that they were not even permitted to participate in religious functions with other Pentecostal groups.[7] Other women who helped spread the Azusa Street revival throughout the country were Mrs. Rachel Sizelove in Missouri and Marie Burgess in New York.[8]

Open Bible Standard Churches

Women were certainly not without opposition in the early Pentecostal movement. Even Crawford, who seemed so securely established in the Northwest, encountered antagonism from her male colleagues. Indeed, a group of male evangelists in the Apostolic Faith Movement split off to form the Bible Standard Mission in 1919. There were a number of reasons for this, including the strong stand Crawford took on personal and ecclesiastical separation. But another factor was that "a considerable number in this group were men of uncommon abilities and experience who, though not expressing it in writing, were chafing under what they thought was feminine domination."[9]

The antagonistic feelings toward Crawford and female ministry were brought with the men into the new Open Bible Mission. "One of the important items of controversy which had to be settled at the first conference after leaving the Apostolic Faith," writes Robert Mitchell, "was the question of ministerial credentials for women preachers." The record of debate that ensued during this first meeting and the effect it had on one Mrs. Harrison is a fascinating account in the history of women's struggle for equality in the church:

When the question came up, there were not enough men to talk the women down. Fred Hornshuh told Mrs. Harrison that women had led people astray in religion. He named Mary Baker Eddy, etc. However, Mrs. Harrison retorted by saying that ten times as many men had led people astray, and she quoted from church history all the men who had led people astray, and won her point. They then decided that women could preach, but were not to lead. She was ordained that night but they muzzled her and kept her quiet two years. She chafed under this. Finally, this bondage was broken. Harry Neat apologized to her at a public conference. Dr. Conlee asked her to preach in Lighthouse Temple.[10]

In spite of the opposition women faced, they conducted a significant portion of the evangelistic work in the movement, and women, particularly "single lady evangelists," started "small new works where men could not support a family." On the denominational level, however, "they were not placed in positions of executive leadership."[11]

Maria Woodward-Etter

One of the leading spirits of the Pentecostal revival in the early twentieth century was Maria Woodward-Etter, whose revivalistic ministry began in the 1890s in central Indiana, where many of her followers claimed miraculous healings and the gift of tongues. So significant was her career that Janet Wilson James suggests "her ministry may have been the origin of the worldwide pentecostal movement."[12]

Woodworth-Etter was born in Ohio in 1844, and it was through the Disciples of Christ that she was converted as a teenager. Almost immediately she felt called to the ministry, but the obstacles seemed insurmountable: "The Disciples did not believe that women had any right to work for Jesus. Had I told them my impression they would have made sport of me. I had never heard of women working in public except as missionaries, so I could see no openings—except, as I thought, if I ever married. . . ." She did marry and had six children (five of whom died in

childhood), but her dream of having a husband who would be a partner in the ministry did not come to fruition. Although others encouraged her to begin a revival ministry, Woodworth did not: "My husband was not willing for me to go, or to engage in the work any place." He did not prevent her from preaching locally, however. "I continued to keep house, and spent as much time in holding meetings as I could, to give my husband a chance to attend his work."[13]

So successful was this ministry that she was in great demand:

> The United Brethren wanted me to take charge of the Woman's Missionary Society, or take a circuit; the Bible Christians wanted me to unite with them, and take charge of three large churches; and the Methodists wanted me to take charge of one church. These were all within ten miles of home and I would have received a good salary. But I felt that my mission was that of an evangelist.[14]

Soon after this she joined the United Brethren Church, which gave its blessing to her preaching and church planting, and the following year her husband agreed to accompany her on an evangelistic tour. The ministry was hers, though, and virtually nothing is mentioned of him after that.[15]

In 1902 she married S. P. Etter, who became for her the perfect preacher's "wife":

> He takes the best care of me, in and out of the meetings. It makes no difference what I call on him to do. He will pray, and preach, and sing, and is very good around the altar. He does about all of my writings, and he also helps in getting out my books, and looks after the meeting, in and outside.[16]

Maria Woodworth-Etter, Turn-of-the-Century Healing Evangelist. From Maria Woodworth-Etter, *Signs and Wonders* (Tulsa: Harrison, 1916).

According to her own account, her ministry extended beyond the unchurched. Indeed, many of her "converts" were from the ranks of the clergy: "At Munice and Anderson I met twenty-one licensed ministers who were converted or anointed in our meetings for the work. Some are ministers in the Church of God, some in the M. E., U. B., Friends, Baptists, and Newlights."[17]

Woodworth-Etter functioned as more than simply a female evangelist. She organized churches and conducted baptisms. In fact, people traveled from long distances just to be baptized by her, "and they felt that they were well paid for the sacrifice they had made in coming so far." The most widely publicized aspect of her ministry, however, was her emphasis on charismatic gifts—most notably tongues and healing. Her own account of these "mighty miracles" and "signs and wonders" details hundreds of spectacular stories.[18]

An example is a service held in Moline, Illinois, in 1903:

> A woman brought her boy, six years old, full of tumors all over his body, the most awful sight you ever saw, so deformed. They were in his throat and in his windpipe, he had a bad cough with it, nearly choking him to death; he had been treated by twenty doctors. . . . From the first time we prayed for him he never suffered any more. . . . The people could see how fast the tumors were disappearing. . . . Scores of deaf people of all ages were healed. . . . Over two thousand came or were brought to the altar. We prayed for them, and most all were converted or reclaimed. Nearly all were healed from one to a dozen chronic diseases.[19]

Other charismatic "wonders" were in evidence as well: "many fell under the power of God and had wonderful visions. . . . Sinners were struck down like dead men and women. . . . One sister spoke in unknown tongues all night," and another sister, Sarah Nelson, testified of being raised from the dead.[20]

In 1912 and 1913, when she was approaching seventy years of age, she held her largest revivals, many of them in camp-meeting settings. One such series of meetings took place at Alexandria, Indiana, where as many as twenty-five thousand were estimated to have attended. Another, held in Montwait, Massachusetts, is described in her book Marvels and Miracles: "Thousands attended the meetings. The miracles were as great as in the days of Christ and the apostles. The fear of God came on the people as they saw the sick carried in, dying on beds, and then rise up and shout praises to God and walk and run. They saw them leap and dance."[21]

One of the most amazing aspects of Woodworth-Etter's ministry was the wide acceptance she enjoyed from ministers and leaders of many different denominations. She faced some opposition, but probably no more than a "miracle-working" male evangelist would have encountered. One description of her ministry came from the Reverend Stanley Smith, one of the "Cambridge Seven" who served as a missionary with the China Inland Mission for many years: "Mrs Etter is a woman who has had a ministry . . . unparalleled in the history of the Church." Of her book Acts of the Holy Ghost, he wrote, "It is a book I value next to the Bible. In special seasons of waiting on God I have found it helpful to have the New Testament on one side of me and Mrs. Etter's book on the other, this latter is a present-day record of 'the Acts' multiplied."[22]

The Assemblies of God

The Assemblies of God, the largest white Pentecostal denomination, offered women unparalleled opportunity for ministry during the early years of the twentieth century. But even in this denomination, certain restrictions were upheld, except in extraordinary circumstances. An editorial in the Evangel in 1915 reflected the church's position:

> We know of no Movement where women of ability and filled with the Holy Ghost have been more highly honored or given much more freedom than among us. She is given the right to be ordained, to preach, witness, give advice, act as evangelist, missionary, etc. The only thing not thrown unscripturally upon her weak shoulders is the making of her a Ruling Elder. . . . Even here we allow such liberty as not to interfere [sic] with special calls God in His sovereignty may give to women under exceptional circumstances.[23]

This open attitude toward women began to change, however, as a new generation of leaders emerged in the Assemblies of God. That view was expressed by the Reverend Robert A. Brown, the husband of a leading female preacher. He argued that his own wife "always refrained from 'acts of priesthood' " and that he did not like "to see women put on a white garment and try to look like angels, and go into the baptismal pool to baptize converts." Brown's position prevailed at the General Council in 1931, and it was resolved "that ordination certificates of women shall clearly state that women are ordained only as evangelists."[24]

Although the General Council reversed that decision in 1935, "it had become apparent," write Charles Barfoot and Gerald Sheppard, "that women would never have the freedom they once had during the earlier years of the movement."[25]

Aimee Semple McPherson and the Foursquare Gospel

Of all the women church leaders and evangelists of the twentieth century, Aimee Semple McPherson certainly ranks at the very top in the influence she wielded over others religiously. Indeed, she would take second place to very few male church leaders and evangelists. *Time* called her "the most spectacular U. S. evangelist since Billy Sunday." She was the founder and lifetime president of the Foursquare Gospel Church and the senior pastor of the famed Angelus Temple in Los Angeles.[26]

Soon after she was converted at a revival as a teenager, Aimee sensed a call to preach the gospel, but her immediate response to God was, "How can I, a daughter of the farm . . . ever hope to be a soul winner? Besides, only men are allowed to preach." She queried her mother about the ban on female preaching, to which her mother responded that women could "go to heathen lands as missionaries," an answer that left her even more puzzled. "If they are good enough to exhort the black, the brown, and the yellow man, why not the white?"[27]

Although that question remained unanswered, foreign missions was the only option for many young women who desired Christian ministry in the early twentieth century, and Aimee soon found herself bound for the mission field. She had married Robert Semple, the evangelist whose preaching prompted her conversion, and soon after their marriage in 1908, they sailed for Hong Kong. The mission term was cut short, however, after Semple's sudden death, and Aimee returned to the United States with her infant daughter.[28]

Back in the United States, Aimee married Harold McPherson and settled into the domestic duties of a housewife, but the strain was too much for her physically and mentally: "The doctors said I would lose my reason if something was not done. I became very ill in body and inside of one year two serious operations were performed." The cause of her problems, she concluded, was her failure to respond to God's call: "Through all these strenuous days . . . a voice kept hammering at the doorway of my heart. It shouted, 'Preach the Word! Do the work of an evangelist.'" She was convinced that there was no other alternative but to leave her husband and begin an evangelistic ministry. The decision, however, did not come easily: "Oh, don't you ever tell me that a woman cannot be called to preach the Gospel," she later wrote. "If any man ever went through one-hundredth part of the hell on earth that I lived in, those months when out of God's will and work, they would never say that again."[29]

With her two young children, a threadbare, patched, "push pole" tent, and a 1912 Packard, she began her itinerant ministry. Her husband "Mack" soon joined her, and in 1916 they traveled together down the Atlantic coast from New England to Florida. The following year she was back in New England, and encountered such enthusiastic and generous crowds in Boston that they were able to purchase a truck and hire a driver. The success, however, did not last. Within months they were in dire financial circumstances, and Mack insisted they return home, but Aimee refused. From then on their lives went separate directions, with Aimee traveling alone with her mother and her children.[30]

Aimee Semple McPherson, Nationally Known Evangelist and Founder of the International Church of the Foursquare Gospel. From the International Church of the Foursquare Gospel, Los Angeles.

Aimee's mother, Minnie Kennedy, served as her manager and press agent and soon scheduled city-wide "Holy Ghost Revivals" in large cities, including San Francisco and New York, where Aimee received national newspaper coverage and was described as seeking to "drive the Devil from New York." After that she traveled to cities throughout the United States and Canada, making eight trips across the continent between 1918 and 1923, and earning as much as two thousand dollars a week after expenses.[31]

In 1921, while she was conducting meetings in a half-vacant arena in San Diego, Aimee announced her first healing service. That was a turning point in her career. "Canes, Crutches Discarded Upon Prayers of Woman Preacher," blazed the headlines of the San Diego *Union*. That article provided free publicity that set the stage for her future ministry:

> Jamming the seats of Dreamland Arena, filling the aisles and overflowing the sidewalks into the streets, more than three thousand people came to hear Mrs. Aimee Semple McPherson, evangelist, pray for the sick and to see with their own eyes just what miracles were performed in the ring last night. After the altar call, the afflicted crowded to the ring by the score and sought the aid of Mrs. McPherson. The woman evangelist prayed for them, anointing them with oil.[32]

It was an eventful year for her. Mack filed for a divorce, construction began on the five-thousand seat Angelus Temple in Los Angeles, and the Foursquare Gospel was born, later to become the basis for her Pentecostal denomination.

Perhaps more than any preacher before or since, with the possible exception of Billy Sunday, Aimee had a flare for the dramatic. According to one report, "Sister, in football togs, carried the ball of the Foursquare Gospel for a touchdown, Jesus ran interference." In another service she played the part of a motorcycle cop: "She drove recklessly to the front of the auditorium, slammed on the brakes, blew a screech on a police whistle, raised a white gloved hand to the congregation, and shouted: 'Stop, you're going to hell!' "[33]

Aimee's most dramatic theatrical event, in the eyes of her critics and many others, was her alleged kidnapping in 1926. On May 18, the headlines of a Los Angeles paper read, "Evangelist McPherson Believed

Drowned!" and for weeks the newspapers were filled with rumors and conjecture about her sudden disappearance. Nearly six weeks after her disappearance, Aimee appeared from out of nowhere in the small desert town of Douglas, Arizona, claiming she had been kidnapped. Many reporters initially accepted her story at face value. The Los Angeles *Times* headlined the incident with "Aimee Tortured for Huge Ransom." But others were more skeptical, claiming she had been spotted in a hideaway with Kenneth Ormiston, her radio announcer. So serious were the accusations against her that she was brought to trial on the charge that the kidnapping story was a hoax, but she was acquitted and soon returned to her ministry. However, the scandal lingered. Her most recent biographer, Robert Barr, rejects outright the kidnapping version of her disappearance and maintains that indeed she did run off with Ormiston, but Aimee maintained the veracity of her story until her death and "officials of the Church of the Foursquare Gospel still insist, at least formally, that Aimee's kidnap story is true, apparently believing the church's future stands or falls on the issue."[34]

Although she had some serious financial problems in the decade that followed her alleged kidnapping, she continued her preaching and her popularity nationwide soared beyond what it had been before the scandal. But scandal continued to plague her. In 1931, she married David Hutton, who almost immediately was faced with a law suit from a previous lover. Less than two years later Hutton filed for divorce from Aimee. Only months later, however,

she was back on the revival circuit. She made a fifteen-thousand-mile, twenty-one-state tour, during which time she preached more than three hundred sermons in nearly fifty cities to crowds totaling a million.[35]

After her death in 1944, her legacy continued. Since that time, according to a recent report from the Foursquare Gospel Church, the number of churches in the denomination "has risen from four hundred to seven hundred eighty-three; foreign mission stations from two hundred to over two thousand."[36]

Unlike many female religious leaders, McPherson did not view herself as an anomaly. She was a staunch defender of not only her own preaching, but also that of other women:

> This is the only church, I am told, that is ordaining women preachers. The Assemblies of God are not ordaining women, to my knowledge. . . . Foursquaredom is the only work that has given such acknowledgment to women preachers, as well as men. Even the Pentecostal works, in some cases, have said, "No women preachers." But I am opening the door, and as long as Sister McPherson is alive, she is going to hold the door open and say, "Ladies, come!"[37]

Did female leadership of a denomination increase the percentage of women members? This is an issue that has been fiercely debated. John Nickol writes concerning Pentecostal women preachers, "Perhaps this accounts for the multitudes of women who were won to Pentecostalism in those early years." The answer is far less certain, however, when statistics from various Pentecostal churches are taken into account. According to a survey taken of four Pentecostal denominations in 1936, McPherson's Foursquare Gospel had the highest percentage of men—sixty-five men to every one hundred women. In the male-dominated Assemblies of God, there were fewer than fifty-nine men to every one hundred women; and in the small black Apostolic Overcoming Holy Church of God, there were fewer than thirty males for every one hundred females.[38]

Even though women far outnumbered men, the contention that women predominated in "enthusiastic" or ecstatic forms of religion is not necessarily supported by the above statistics, since women in the Anglican Church at times outnumbered men by as much as seven to one.[39]

Holiness Denominations

The holiness movement initiated by Phoebe Palmer and others during the mid-nineteenth century was unable to flourish in the Methodist or other mainline denominations. The opposition was intense, and as a result those who cherished the doctrine of entire sanctification separated themselves into new movements and denominations. Many of these movements began in the late nineteenth century and continued growing in the early decades of the twentieth century alongside, but often in opposition to, the Pentecostal movement.

Like the Pentecostal churches, the holiness denominations' emphasis on the Holy Spirit and spiritual gifts opened the way for female ministry. The Pilgrim Holiness Church, founded in 1897, is an example. Seth Rees, who served as president from 1897 to 1905, made his own view on the subject abundantly clear:

> Nothing but jealousy, prejudice, bigotry, and a stingy love for bossing in men have prevented woman's public recognition by the church. No church that is acquainted with the Holy Ghost will object to the public ministry of women. We know of scores of women who can preach the gospel with a clearness, a power, and an efficiency seldom equaled by men. Sisters, let the Holy Ghost fill, call and anoint you to preach the glorious Gospel of our Lord.[40]

Rees' wife Hulda exemplified his ideal of the female preacher. She began preaching at age sixteen and continued throughout the rest of her life, serving alongside her husband as a pastor and evangelist. Although she initially was "excessively timid" and dreaded standing before a congregation, she overcame her fear after she was "sanctified wholly" and she began preaching "in the power of the Spirit." She became well known in holiness circles and was often referred to as the "Pentecostal prophetess."[41]

Alma White and the Pillar of Fire

Another early-twentieth-century revivalist and church leader was Alma White, the founder of the tiny "Pillar of Fire" movement that was distinguished by its emphasis on the "holy dance." White was born in Kentucky in 1862, and immediately after her conversion as a teenager she felt God's call to ministry. Soon after that she set out on a two-thousand-mile trek to the territory of Montana to serve as a school teacher. Almost immediately she was embroiled in controversy with the school board because "for one hour each day she turned the school into a mission; and taught the children to pray, read the Bible, and commit sacred hymns to memory." Although "there was an uprising against her," she refused to back down, and in the end, with community support, new board members were elected, and she was allowed to continue her "mission" work.[42]

Although the Pillar of Fire movement was initially organized as the Pentecostal Union in 1902, it was a holiness church strictly in the Wesleyan tradition. "The existence of the Pillar of fire," according to J. Gordon Melton, "is due in part to the reluctance of the Methodist Episcopal Church to allow female ministers in its churches in the late nineteenth century." As a Methodist minister's wife, Alma White began preaching after she experienced the "baptism of the Holy Ghost." In the words of an admiring contemporary, "Her tongue was touched with a live coal from the altar; she began to preach the Gospel in her husband's church; and later preached in forty different localities in the State of Colorado, where the great Pillar of Fire movement that now belts the globe was launched out through her efforts; her converts multiplied until it was necessary to effect an organization to take care of them and train them for missionary work."[43]

White might have remained in the Methodist Church, but the publicity from all her success led to opposition from Methodist churchmen, and that prompted her to organize a movement of independent missions similar to Wesley's early societies. When

the organization became more structured, it took on the episcopal form of government, and White became its first bishop.[44]

Alma White, Founder of the Pillar of Fire Movement. From Alma White, *Looking Back from Beulah* (Bound Brook, N.J.: Pentecostal Union, 1910).

Like most other holiness leaders, White took a strong stand against the emerging Pentecostal movement. In fact, she had the reputation for being one of the most vitriolic opponents of the movement. She believed tongues speaking was nothing less than "satanic gibberish" and "demon worship." She was very critical of William Seymour. After he visited her at her headquarters in Denver, Colorado, she wrote, "I had met all kinds of religious fakirs and tramps, but I felt he excelled them all." She was equally critical of Aimee Semple McPherson, calling her a "necromancer, familiar with the black arts," and whose "words were the mutterings of a witch."[45]

White's denunciation of other religious leaders and groups was not limited to Pentecostalism. Soon after she began her work, she began publishing *The Good Citizen,* a vicious anti-Catholic paper. According to a contemporary, "its fearless editorials and striking cartoons have opened the eyes of many thousands to the corruption of the Roman Catholic Church and the efforts it is putting fourth [sic] to make America Catholic."[46] By the 1920s White's verbal warfare had caught the attention of the Ku Klux Klan, and she joined their efforts as a writer, crediting the Klan for serving as "God's agent in maintaining social and racial distinctions."[47] Several years earlier she had denounced the Azusa Street revival because of the race mixing it encouraged.[48]

Amid all the controversy that she was involved in, White endeavored to defend her role as a woman preacher. Although she believed that "men are better qualified for leaders than women," she was convinced that at Pentecost (in fulfillment of Joel's prophecy) women were permitted an equal place in the church alongside men: "Let Christ reign in the heart, and woman will take her place beside man and help to fight the battles of life, and not only be a helpmeet, but socially and mentally his equal." With the advent of her "New Testament Church," she believed that this was already beginning to take place: "Great has been the loss the Church has suffered from the lack of proper teaching on this subject, but the world is no longer in darkness, women are now exercising their blood-bought privilege in wielding the sword of the Spirit."[49]

Church of the Nazarene

The largest holiness church in the early twentieth century was the Church of the Nazarene, which was formed out of smaller holiness groups that broke away from the Methodist Church in the late nineteenth century. It, too, opened the doors of ministry to women. The founder, Phineas Bresee himself, ordained a woman preacher, and women were the founders and teachers of the first Bible institute for that denomination. As was the case with other sectarian movements, there was a shortage of ordained clergy, and thus laymen and women actively served as itinerant evangelists and lay pastors. The denomination's constitution, in fact, specifically granted women the right to preach, and Mrs. W. S. Knott became the first ordained Nazarene preacher.[50]

The holiness groups that had merged to form the Church of the Nazarene also depended heavily on women preachers. This was particularly true of a tiny denomination the New Testament Church of Christ that merged with the Nazarene Church in the early twentieth century. Like the Nazarene Church, it had left the Methodist Church over the issues of worldliness and entire sanctification. It had congregations in Texas and Tennessee and almost all of its pastors and itinerant evangelists were women.

The women who carried on this independent gospel work seem to have combined piety and practicality to a remarkable degree. Between revivals they maintained a normal and apparently stable family life, if the few surviving letters may be taken at face value. Their husbands joined happily in their meetings when they were near home and accepted periods of separation without much protest.[51]

There were those who opposed these women preachers, but at a business meeting in 1899, it was decided that women could be ordained; however, as the individual churches and the denomination grew, "a group of aggressive men were replacing the women evangelists as the real leaders. . . . By the time the annual council met at Jonesboro in October, 1901, the new men were clearly in charge."[52]

This move was part of a general feeling of opposition to women preachers. How did the women respond? Most testified that God had called them into ministry, and though they resisted the call, they found no peace until they obeyed. In 1905 one of them published a volume entitled *Women Preachers*, in which twelve of them wrote autobiographical accounts of their religious pilgrimages. They all insisted, according to Smith, that they had been "called" to ministry—first to foreign missions (where women were welcome), but that God had providentially led them into home missions and then pastoral work.[53]

The Salvation Army

One of the most influential "holiness" denominations of the twentieth century is the Salvation Army—the movement that incurred the wrath of H. A. Ironside in his widely circulated volume, published in 1912, *Holiness: The False and the True*. Following the turbulent decades of the late nineteenth century, the Army emerged in the twentieth century as a highly acclaimed Christian humanitarian organization. As was the pattern in other sectarian movements, the role of women declined as the Army acquired respectability.[54]

This trend was disguised, however, by the visibility of the Booth daughters, who served in high-level positions. Catherine served as a marshal in western Europe. Emma served as consul in India for eight years before she was transferred to the United States where she served as co-commander until her untimely accidental death in 1903. Lucy, the youngest of the Booth children, served as commander in various western European countries for more than thirty years and then became commander in South America. And Evangeline served as the commander in Canada for eight years, the commander in the United States for thirty years, and finally general of the organization for five years during the 1930s.[55]

Evangeline Booth was one of the most noted woman religious leaders of the twentieth century. She was her father's favorite, and when she was yet a teenager, he recognized her potential value to the Army. When opposition flared up somewhere in the ranks, she was often sent in as a trouble-shooter, and she quickly earned a reputation as a calm and effective navigator in turbulent waters. Indeed, General William Booth's immediate response to many explo-

Salvation Army Lassies at the Turn of the Century. These women invaded poverty-and vice-ridden areas.　From Harry Edward Neal, *The Hallelujah Army* (New York: Chilton, 1961).

sive situations was, "Send Eva." With charm and tact, she dispersed angry mobs and dissuaded arrogant magistrates.[56]

Although her sisters—Catherine Booth-Clibborn, Emma Booth-Tucker, and Lucy Booth-Hellberg—had married with their father's blessing, Evangeline confronted strong opposition. She wanted to marry a Salvation Army major, Thomas McKie, but when the young man requested permission from her father, the request was denied. Soon after that, perhaps as a consolation prize, McKie was promoted to commissioner and dispatched to Germany. Although Evangeline found time in her busy schedule to conduct wedding ceremonies, she herself remained single the remainder of her life.[57]

Wedding ceremonies were only one aspect of Evangeline's "ministerial" duties. As was the case with other Army officers, she was not ordained and did not serve a parish, but she filled the role of a minister and evangelist to the same extent that male officers did. She conducted camp meetings at such well-known retreats as Old Orchard, Maine, and Ocean Grove, New Jersey. Of these meetings her biographer writes: "Old-timers remember the tremendous 'battle for souls' in her meetings, with seldom less than a hundred seekers at the penitent form."[58]

Evangeline's promotion to commander in the United States in 1904 did not occur without controversy. "That the General had succumbed to a certain inclination to nepotism," writes Edward McKinley, "could no longer be denied." Yet Evangeline proved to be very successful in that position. Although she was "vain of her appearance . . . impetuous, given to emotional flourishes, and something of a poseur . . . she was at the same time a compassionate soul, thoughtful, full of little kindnesses, genuinely sympathetic with the poor and lonely in their sufferings, and a dedicated, fearless evangelical." Likewise, she manifested a powerful personal magnetism. She "could hold large audiences spellbound for hours" and was "adept at charming large fortunes for the Army out of rich men."[59]

Evangeline Booth With Her Father. From Brian Lunn, *Salvation Dynasty* (London: William Hodge, 1936), frontispiece.

Soon after she became general of the Salvation Army, Evangeline launched her "World for God" cam-paigns, which entailed travel, speaking, inspecting of stations, and initiating new centers of work throughout the world. One of her meetings in India drew a crowd of more than twenty thousand.

> General Evangeline spoke for an hour on "His Name Shall Be Called Wonderful." Although there was no available space for a penitent-form, at the General's invitation, 5,000 seekers lifted their voices in prayer, "the sound rising like the waves of a mighty sea."[60]

But as significant as her five-year term as general was, her lasting legacy was the power and popularity she brought to the Army in the United States. For thirty years her personality pervaded the Army on the American scene, and her tens of thousands of loyal followers revered her to the very end.[61]

Holiness-Pentecostal Denominational Restrictions

The Salvation Army was not unique among holiness sects in the decline of the leadership of women during the twentieth century. Janet James writes that

> where the sects coalesced into organized churches, women's leadership and influence dwindled. In denominational structures, church life was routinized; charisma randomly distributed no longer provided sufficient authority. The holiness Church of the Nazarene and the pentecostal Assemblies of God ruled that female evangelists could no longer administer the sacrament, and many lapsed into the secondary role of teachers and missionaries.[62]

In a similar vein sociologist Max Weber maintained that in virtually every new religious movement, female leadership declined as soon as the movement stabilized:

> Only in very rare cases does this practice continue beyond the first stage of a religious community's formation, when the pneumatic manifestations of charisma are valued as hallmarks of specifically religious exaltation. Thereafter, as routinization and regimentation of community relationships set in, a reaction takes place against pneumatic manifestations among women, which come to be regarded as dishonorable.[63]

Women and the Social Gospel

While women in sectarian movements were actively involved in virtually every level of ministry and were moving into influential leadership positions, women in the mainline denominations had less opportunity for meaningful roles in the church. Leadership positions were filled by men who had high praise for women as wives and mothers but were not eager to share their places of responsibility with them. This is evident particularly in the social-gospel movement. Women had been actively involved in the "social gospel" long before it was known by that term, and more recently historians have come to realize that the women's role in the movement has been virtually ignored. But as with so many other areas of church work, the women were activists, not administrators. Indeed, all of the nationally recognized leaders of the social-gospel movement were men. "Protestant churchmen," writes Mary A. Dougherty, "assumed full paternal responsibility for the social gospel in 1912, when it already had matured." John R. Commons assessed the situation even more critically when he charged that Christian men "have hired someone else to love [their neighbors]. They have left it to the women."[64]

During the 1920s, the social gospel came under fire from more conservative elements in the church, but this, according to Gladys Calkins, did not have a significant effect on the work the women were doing.

> Their approach to social issues was essentially pragmatic and not doctrinaire. Women were concerned about the welfare and needs of individuals; while this had made them sympathetic to the preaching of the Social Gospel, it had not left them dependent upon it. To try to bring a more abundant life to women and children in foreign lands, and to do what was needed in this country and in the community, was still their motive and purpose. The battle of Fundamentalism versus Liberalism might rage in the pulpits, and the Scopes trial make headlines in the newspapers, but these would not throw the women off course. There was too much that needed to be done.[65]

Unlike the reform movements of the nineteenth century, the social-gospel movement did not concern itself with women's rights. Indeed, according to Janet James, "the last phase of what might be called the social action revival was the Men and Religion Forward Movement, which by preaching a muscular Christianity sought to bring men back into the mainline churches and restore the balance of the sexes." And as far as women were concerned, their primary place was in the home. "Walter Rauschenbusch declared that Christianity had already achieved the ideal family."[66]

Walter Rauschenbusch

Walter Rauschenbusch (1861–1916), a Baptist minister who is considered the "Father of the Social Gospel in America," demonstrated no particular zeal to open up more leadership opportunities for women in the church. In his view, "most women feel that their life gets its full meaning and dignity only when they can have and make a home." Yet he expected women to use their nurturing qualities outside the home, and this is where their sphere was crucial to the social gospel:

> The mother instinct is but a narrow thing if a woman forgets all other children and loves only her own. Her experiences as a mother have done their work on her soul only if they have broadened her intelligence and sympathy for all child-life. When a woman is through raising her own brood, she should graduate to the high school of motherhood and care for all children within her reach.[67]

As to a women's leadership role in the church or religious organizations, Rauschenbusch believed there was an underlying danger. Although he praised women for their sensitivity, he believed that this very attribute could "warp her judgment and make her less safe for teaching and administration." He pointed to Christian Science and Theosophy, and queried, "Is there any connection between the characteristics of these two religions and their feminine habitus?" He also lamented the fact that the churches had become "overwhelmingly feminine." As such, he was opposed to efforts to broaden women's responsibilities. "Regarding the teaching and administration of the church, Rauschenbusch found women's judgment less safe than that of men. He implied that due to the peculiarities of 'womanly character' it would not be wise to invest women with too much responsibility."[68]

Washington Gladden

Washington Gladden (1836–1918), a liberal Congregational pastor and theologian who was also closely identified with the social gospel, supported many aspects of the women's movement, including suffrage. Yet in reference to church ministries, he held a traditional line. Although he argued that "there seems to be no longer any good reason why women may not do any kind of work in the church that thy are fitted to do," he indicated that they were fitted mainly for social work and fund raising, and in doing so making the pastor's duties "easy and delightful." Because his concept of women's work in the church seemed to be very limited, Rebecca Garber concludes that he probably was "not favorable to women preaching and teaching or sharing the leadership responsibility with men."[69]

Lyman Abbott

Lyman Abbott (1835–1922), another social-gospel leader and the pastor of Brooklyn's prestigious Plymouth Congregational Church, also perpetuated the cult of motherhood. In his book *The Home Builder* he "sentimentally portrayed the ideal woman from her youth to her death as she existed within the context of her home and family. . . . She asked little for herself, but was willing to give all of herself for her family. She was a wife and mother, and she was most definitely not a feminist."[70] Abbott's concept of the proper wifely role was to be cultivated even before a woman was married, as is evident in his descriptions of a bride's thoughts on her upcoming marriage:

> She wishes, not to submit a reluctant will to his, but to make his will her own. She wishes a sovereign and is glad to have found him—no! to have been found by him. She laughs at the virgin reformers who have never known the mystery of love and are protesting against the subjection of women.[71]

Women in Mainline Denominations

In 1927 a study entitled "The Relative Place of Women in the Church in the United States" was conducted by a joint committee representing the Federal Council of the Churches of Christ in America and two other groups. Out of twenty-two denominations surveyed, only seven granted women full equality with men. But even in the instances where women were granted full equality, women fell far behind in leadership positions in the church. Yet, women had a great deal of influence in their respective churches, and the committee made an interesting observation along these lines:

> It seems to be generally admitted that women frequently contribute the largest proportion of attendance at meetings, the majority of Sunday school teachers, the largest missionary intelligence and interest, the greatest spiritual power and loyalty, the largest devotion to personal needs, to visitation and philanthropy, the keenest value of team work and responsibility,

the encouragement of the highest ideals, in addition to those duties once designated as "woman's church work" which consisted of furnishing flowers, serving food, raising funds by the "chore method."[72]

Roman Catholics

In most mainline Protestant denominations women fared far better at the turn of the twentieth century than they did in the Roman Catholic Church. On such issues as women's suffrage, the church took a hard line. Archbishop Sebastian Messmer's views were typical. His rationale against women's suffrage was simply "the essential inequality of man and woman." The widely read Catholic writer, John Boyle O'Reilly, expressed similar views: "Woman suffrage is an unjust, unreasonable, unspiritual abnormality. . . . It is a quack bolus to reduce masculinity even by the obliteration of femininity."[73]

Some Catholic women rose to the occasion and defended their sex. In 1910 British Catholic women founded the St. Joan's International Alliance to support women's suffrage. Although Rosemary Ruether calls it the "original Catholic feminist organization," it was hardly a radical group. Not until 1961 did it make an appeal for the diaconate to be opened up to women, and even then it was in mild terms. A call for women's ordination to the priesthood two years later was equally mild: "St. Joan's International Alliance re-affirms its loyalty and filial devotion and expresses its conviction that should the Church in her wisdom and in her good time decide to extend to women the dignity of the priesthood, women would be willing and eager to respond."[74]

Because of the powerful male-dominated hierarchical structure of the Roman Catholic Church, women have found themselves overwhelmed by a clergy and by dogma that are slow to change. Indeed, some of the commentary relating to women sounds more like that of the Middle Ages than of the twentieth century. Are the souls of women equal to the souls of men? This issue actually made its way into the 1913 edition of the *Catholic Encyclopedia*. One of the articles presented the position that "the female sex is in some respects inferior to the male sex, both as regards body and soul."[75]

Whether women should sing in choirs was also an issue that was raised by church leaders. In 1927 Bishop William Hickey of Providence called for priests, in keeping with the teachings of Pius X, to eliminate women from choirs. "In *Motu Propino*, issued in 1903, the Pope had affirmed that church singers filled a 'real liturgical office' and that 'women, being incapable of exercising such office, cannot be admitted to form part of the choir'; soprano and contralto parts must be sung by boys."[76]

While such views were not characteristic of the church as a whole, they do illustrate the opposition women confronted when raising the issue of sexual equality in the church. But the issue could not remain in the clerical camp forever. Spurred on by the liberating forces of Vatican II and the feminist movement of the 1960s, Catholic women along with some sympathetic male voices began demanding equality in ministry. This was in part due to a statement contained in a Vatican II document that gave renewed hope to some women who had feared the church had forgotten them: "With respect to the fundamental rights of the person, every type of discrimination, whether social or cultural, whether based on sex, race, colour, social condition, language, or religion, is to be overcome and eradicated as contrary to God's intent."[77]

By the 1970s, widespread rumblings of dissatisfaction began to shake the church. In response, the Vatican issued the *Declaration on the Question of the Admission of Women to the Ministerial Priesthood* in 1977.

> The statement makes a rather amazing effort to separate the tradition of exclusion of women from priesthood from the concepts of women's natural inferiority and status of subjection. . . . It asserts that, following Jesus, the Church has always believed in the equality of women with men in the natural order. Exclusion from priesthood is not based on any such concept of inferiority or subjection, but rather on some mysterious sacramental bond between Christ, maleness and priesthood.[78]

American Catholic laity, according to a Gallup poll, reacted against the Declaration. Support for women priests jumped from 29 percent to 41 percent immediately following its release.[79] But wholly unmoved by Gallup polls, the Catholic Church remains firmly committed to a secondary role for women in ministry, and in that sense it stands alone among major denominations.

Anglicans (Church of England)

The early twentieth century was one of slow but steady progress for women in the Church of England. Although women had actively lobbied for official recognition, they had no voting privileges in church affairs at the turn of the century. When the matter was brought before the church in 1903, little headway was made, and Charles Gore (later Bishop of Oxford) referred to the efforts as a "positively and definitely retrograde step." The following year a committee was appointed to investigate a limited form of franchise, "so as not wholly to exclude women." Further extension of the franchise was granted in 1914, when women were "admitted to the parochial lay franchise on the same terms as men" and permitted to serve as representatives on the parochial councils, though they were barred from higher councils. One of the fears of men regarding the increased power of women was the fact that women so heavily outnumbered men in the local parishes—sometimes by as many as seven to one. "The women, by sheer weight of numbers will be able to capture the whole government of the Church," wrote one opponent of equality for women. The opposition was strong, and it was a hard-fought battle, but finally in 1919, the church granted full lay rights for churchwomen, and the following year, more than 10 percent of the lay representatives at the National Assembly were women.[80]

An issue that took far longer to settle in the Anglican Church was the status of women in ministry—an issue that was very unclear in the early twentieth century. A general convention ruled in 1889 that deaconesses would be "set apart" for ministry, and in 1920 the Lambeth Conference ruled that "ordination of a deaconess confers on her holy orders," but a decade later Lambeth reversed the ruling, maintaining that a deaconess could not be ordained to holy orders.[81]

A strong voice against sex discrimination among the Anglicans of the early twentieth century was that of Dr. A. Maude Royden, who conceded that women were allowed certain privileges as long as their ministry was couched in the proper terminology. She described this situation from her own standpoint in England: "In the Church of England I have myself been allowed to preach in churches so long as I was not said to 'preach' but to 'give an address.' Only a priest or deacon can preach; not a layman or woman. Did John the Baptist then give addresses on the banks of the Jordan? What nonsense is this?" The situation in the Church of England was not so different from the situation in other denominations in the British Isles, according to Royden. "I myself have been invited to preach in Free Churches. Yet women are rarely called to take charge of a church."[82] Even after the Lambeth Conference voted to permit women to preach "at non-statutory services," Bishop Winnington-Ingram forbade Royden to speak at a nonstatutory service because "it was a specially sacred service."[83]

Royden was a staunch Anglican who was singled out by one of her contemporaries as being the "world's greatest woman preacher." In her early career she served in various capacities in religious work—as an inter-city social worker, as curate to an Anglican minister, and as the first woman lecturer in the extension program at Oxford University. Then in 1917 she accepted a call to become an assistant pastor at the City Temple, a Congregational church, in London, and that launched her into her preaching ministry. After only two years, she left and founded a new independent mission work with another pastor. During her seventeen-year tenure in this ministry, she conducted regular meetings, except for Sunday morning, so as not to compete with Anglican Church services. She also "established a radio ministry and traveled on preaching and lecture tours to the United States, Australia and New Zealand, India, and China."[84]

Although she could not be ordained in the Anglican Church and was forbidden by the church to preach on a number of occasions, Royden continued to be loyal to that church all her life. In addition to her speaking ministry, she wrote a number of books, including *The Church and Women*. She was ever optimistic about the future of women's role in the church, as is evident in a tract she wrote, entitled *The Ministry of Women*.

The advance of feminism within the Church of England has already been very great. When the question of women missionaries was first raised, the great principle that women might preach the gospel was at once established. People, knowing only of the decision, and being perfectly accustomed to the idea of women missionaries, have forgotten how the battle raged, and with what earnestness and sincerity religious people pointed out that our Lord had only sent out men, chosen men apostles, and never even suggested that women could preach. . . . In fact the controversy followed lines now exquisitely familiar, and reached its cheerfully inevitable end in the defeat of the opponents of women missionaries.[85]

During Royden's years of ministry, changes were slowly being made in the Anglican Church—partly as a result of feminists such as Royden who fought for equal status in the church. The long struggle for voting rights came to fruition in 1919, when the church followed the lead of the government and extended the franchise to women. The next battle to be waged concerned the ordination of women, and the League of the Church Militant was formed to pressure the church in this matter. After only a decade of existence, the League published an optimistic overview of the situation:

Since the League started its work of education and propaganda, thought on women's service in the Church has advanced so rapidly that it was felt that ordination to the priesthood must inevitably follow in due time, and that the best way that women of this and future generations could further this cause was by prayer for its fulfillment and by preparing themselves mentally and spiritually to meet those opportunities and responsibilities of service in the Church that may open up to them in the future.[86]

Ordination of women did follow in "due time"—but not until more than a half century later, and even then it included only the lowest clerical office in the Anglican Church—that of deacon. In July of 1985 the General Synod finally passed the measure that allowed the church's 350 deaconesses to "take their place alongside male deacons, performing marriages and assisting priests in other ways."[87]

The Protestant Episcopal Church

On the American scene, Episcopalian women also struggled long and hard for recognition. In 1946 a female delegate was seated at the General Convention of the Protestant Episcopal Church, but three years later three more convention delegates were denied voting privileges. Then, in 1952, the House of Deputies "ruled for the third time against giving women the right to vote on church legislation."[88]

Ordaining women to the priesthood, however, was the most controversial issue the denomination confronted. Indeed, one of the most newsworthy events to occur in the twentieth century regarding women in ministry was the "irregular" ordination of eleven women to the Episcopal priesthood in 1974. The service took place before a crowd of nearly two thousand at the Church of the Advocate located in an economically depressed section of Philadelphia, and was presided over by bishops who supported the women's cause. After that, things moved quickly in the Episcopal Church—though not without heated debates and many closed-door meetings. In 1975, four more women were ordained in the Washington D. C. diocese, and at the 1976 General Convention the leading church officials, realizing the issue would not lose its volatility, decided in favor of women's ordination.[89]

Voting in favor of legalizing the ordination of women in the church was a simpler matter than deciding the fate of the fifteen women who had already been "illegally" ordained.

The irregularly ordained women had always raised emotional hackles as well as theological questions. Not only had they gone "beyond" the institutional Church's normal procedures to obtain ordination to the priesthood, but they had subsequently proclaimed that priesthood with baptisms, weddings and public celebrations of the eucharist. These were not contrite women recognizing the "error" of their ways but priests who had grown quickly and deeply in their sense of spiritual power.[90]

But that issue, too, was settled in favor of the women, and the fifteen women were recognized as priests in the Episcopal Church.[91]

Presbyterians

The Presbyterians were among the most restrictive of the mainline Protestant denominations in the early twentieth century regarding women in ministry. Like women in other denominations, Presbyterian women had formed their own mission boards in the late nineteenth century, but even in their mission work they had very little autonomy. But in 1923 "Presbyterian women received a shattering blow . . . when a denominational reorganization resulted in the termination of the woman's Board of Home Missions and the Woman's Board of Foreign Missions." For many women it was a devastating ordeal. "Apart from the disappointment in seeing their power base destroyed, the women bitterly resented the fact that they had been excluded from any vote in the entire reorganizational process."[92]

Katharine Bennett was one of the leading women in the Presbyterian Church in the early twentieth century, and it was through her initiative and persistence that the Woman's Board of Home Missions had been independently incorporated in 1915. She and other women had worked so hard to win independence that it naturally was a blow when it was taken away. They "watched the absorption of their mission societies without an outcry, but within two years morale and revenues plummeted."[93]

It was not just in the area of organizing for missions that women had difficulty. The "Women of the Church" was organized in 1912. Although this was a duly recognized organization, the chief officer was not permitted, because of her sex, to read the annual report before the General Assembly. Instead it was read by a male member of that body. In 1925, a woman was allowed to read the report, but the following year when some of the "brethren" took a public stand against female participation, the report was voluntarily turned over to a man. In 1927, the issue was finally settled in favor of the women.[94] It is interesting to note that time and again women deferred to men over such issues—and were far from what could be termed "women's rights" activists.

The general dissatisfaction of women did not go unnoticed by church officials, but the modernist-fundamentalist controversy of the 1920s threw the church into so much turmoil that the problems of women seemed very low on the list of priorities. Indeed, when a committee was formed in 1926 to identify the issues causing divisiveness in the church, "the last item in the long list of contributing factors was the status of

women." The report of the committee noted that there were "many women in the church who are not satisfied with present administrative conditions" and that "some of them fear the loss of organization through which they worked so long. Likewise, "some regard as unjust the lack of representation of women in the church."[95]

Because of the findings of the committee, Katharine Bennett and Margaret Hodge were appointed by the General Council to study the reasons for dissatisfaction among women. Their findings, entitled *Causes of Unrest Among Women of the Church*, told more about the character of the Presbyterian women than about the restrictiveness of the church polity. They "candidly admitted that most churchwomen were either unaware or uninterested in issues of freedom and equality," and those who were concerned about such matters "preferred to accept the status accorded them rather than to criticize the church openly." Yet they concluded their report by calling for equality for women in the church, and warning the leadership that beneath the surface there was real unrest: "Her mind rebels even if her heart keeps her tongue quiet."[96]

But if her mind was rebelling, it was not over the issue of ordination—at least not in the 1920s. When Robert Speer, an ardent advocate of women's ministry and the head of the Presbyterian Board of Foreign Missions, suggested the possibility of ordaining women as evangelists, Margaret Hodge was not particularly enthusiastic. The issue disturbing women, she reminded him "is not so much a desire to be admitted to the diaconate, the eldership, or even the ministry, as it is to have removed all discrimination against them as women." Katharine Bennett responded similarly.[97]

It is significant to note that Speer was far more open to the full ministry of women than were the vast majority of female "feminists" in the church. He argued that

> it would be strange and anomalous to deny to women equality in the church, which is the very fountain of the principle of equality. It is Christ who has made women free and equal. Is she to be allowed this freedom and equality elsewhere and denied it in the Church, where freedom and equality had their origin?[98]

Likewise, he had high praise for "the Christian Churches on the foreign mission field" that were "apprehending the measure of the Gospel in this better than we.... God shuts no doors to His daughters which He opens to His sons."[99] Speer's influence had a significant impact on the course of events leading to equal status for Presbyterian women.

The issue of equality was debated in committee at some length before it was put before the General Council in 1929, and at that time, by a significant margin a resolution was passed to remove from the church rules "any form of speech which is inconsistent with the recognition of the complete equality of men and women in the life and work of the Church." The council then sent the resolution to the presbyteries. It was at this point that bitter strife ensued. David S. Kennedy, editor of the *Presbyterian*, referred to the proposal as "ungodly and unscriptural" and called on God to give the church a "full and prompt deliverance from this violence and sin." Kennedy quickly rallied conservatives against the measure, and when the final tally of presbytery votes came in, the measure lost, as did a proposal to license women as evangelists. The supporters of women, however, won a major victory in the passage of a proposal permitting women ordination as ruling elders in the local churches.[100]

During the 1930s and 1940s, following this decision on women, "the subject of ordination of women disappeared almost immediately," and very few women became ruling elders in the churches. In 1940, a survey indicated that fewer than 7 percent of the churches had any women elders at all. By the mid 1950s the number of women elders in the Presbyterian Church in the U.S.A. had increased, but their numbers were still a small fraction of the total—that being less than 5 percent. Why the ranks of women elders did not immediately swell is a thought-provoking question. It is true that in many cases men were not eager to share their authority with women, but "in most Presbyterian congregations, women outnumbered men three to one." It would seem, then, that the women themselves were largely responsible for their lack of leadership positions in the churches. Most women were satisfied working as they had in the past in ministries to women and children and for missions and humanitarian causes.[101]

In spite of the strong male opposition and the lack of female aggressiveness regarding the issue of ordination of women, the Presbyterian Church of the U.S.A. granted women equal status with men in 1956, before many of the other mainline denominations were willing to make such a controversial move. The following year, when the church merged with a smaller Presbyterian denomination that did not ordain women, the officials of the new United Presbyterian Church upheld the equal status of women in the church, but made it clear that "no congregation would be forced to accept women elders or ministers against their will."[102] Nevertheless, it was a major advance for those women who had long been struggling for greater equity in church affairs. Few would deny that Presbyterian women had made considerable progress during the twentieth century. Indeed, of all the major denominations it is "one of the few in which women in the past seventy years moved from having no status, except as church members, to full ecclesiastical equality."[103]

Even though women had achieved full equality with men in the church, their influence continued to be far less than that of men—a reality that is reflected in the title of Elizabeth Verdesi's book *In But Still Out*. Although they had been permitted ordination in 1956, in 1975 there were fewer than two hundred ordained women ministers out of a total of some thirteen thousand, and only about 10 percent of those had pastorates of their own.[104] Prior to the 1956 ruling, Presbyterian women, like women in other denominations, had been able to circumvent tight restrictions against their sex by finding alternatives to an ordained ministry or by seeking ordination outside their church. Daisy Billings, who became the wife of Oswald J. Smith, is an example of the former. In 1914 she became a deaconess at the Dale Presbyterian Church in Toronto—a position that entailed mainly visitation and counseling. Her preaching ability, however, did not escape the attention of J. D. Morrow, the senior pastor. Indeed, "her greatest delight was taken in the fact that her pastor allowed her to preach once each month to his congregation, for she loved to preach." These opportunities to preach, however, came to a sudden end when Morrow decided to hire a full-time assistant pastor— Oswald J. Smith. Her later decision to marry him was a difficult one, for she knew it meant giving up her preaching and independent ministry.[105]

Some Presbyterian women sought ordination outside the Presbyterian Church. Jessie Bartlett Hess is an example. She and her husband started twelve churches in Colorado, Idaho, and Washington during their early married life. Although she was a full partner in the ministry as a pastor's wife, she was not recognized as such. She sought ordination in the Presbyterian church where her husband held his credentials, but her request was denied, so she turned to the Congregational-Christian Church, one of the few churches that ordained women in the 1930s. While her husband ministered in a Presbyterian church, she served as the pastor of a nearby Congregational church. After he retired from the ministry, she continued serving in churches. Following her retirement from the pastoral ministry, she taught several large women's Bible studies in the New York Metropolitan area, and continued this ministry past the age of seventy.[106]

Reformed Churches

The Reformed Churches, like some of the smaller more conservative Presbyterian denominations, continued to place tight restrictions on women in ministry well beyond the mid-twentieth century. In Europe the situation was resolved sooner than in America, but controversy was hardly less bitter. This is illustrated in the life and ministry of Elisabeth Schmidt, the first woman ordained by the French Reformed Church. She tells her story in her book *When God Calls a Woman: The Struggle of a Woman Pastor in France and Algeria*. Her decision to seek seminary training and a pastoral ministry was motivated by a "compelling call which required complete availability and thus the abandonment of my teaching career."[107]

Elisabeth Schmidt, the First Woman Ordained by the French Reformed Church. From Elisabeth Schmidt, *When God Calls a Woman* (New York: Pilgrim, 1981).

It was in 1945, after she had served

for a number of years in parishes in a Reformed Church in France that the Presbyterial Council requested that she be ordained by the synod. She waited two years before she herself became involved in the struggle, and even then she made her noncombative position regarding her ordination very clear:

> I have never asked for it in the twelve years in which parishes have been entrusted to me. I have refused to write or publicly debate on this question. I have imposed these twelve years of silence on myself, asking God to keep me from all error and to lead me. Today I believe that the hour has come for breaking this silence. I have not been able to shed God's call, nor to avoid the charge to minister which he has entrusted to me. And I feel constrained to put this question to the church.[108]

For her the issue was solely one of spiritual ministry, and she completely dissociated herself from those who sought to make her struggle a feminist issue. "The notorious feminists, men and women who were preoccupied with the promotion of womanhood, did not care what took place in Synod meetings and were not looking for victories in Christian milieus."[109]

Schmidt's request for ordination was placed before the National Synod in 1948. Although the highly respected president of the synod, Pastor Boegner, made the motion, it was turned down by the assembly at large. Schmidt was personally devastated. "I left the temple, sliding noiselessly into the sacristy, where I let my tears pour out. I felt that between my church and myself there was a break." The following year there were enough votes mustered at the National Synod to sanction her ordination—though without making any precedent-setting decisions for any other women in the future. It was not until 1965 that women in general were permitted to be ordained. Schmidt continued to maintain a low profile until 1972, when she retired after thirty-seven years of pastoral ministry.[110]

The Reformed Church in America also took a strong stand against ordaining women ministers, but in 1979 the General Synod voted to open the door for women's ordination. Still, vocal and latent opposition remained. In 1982, James I. Cook, president of the General Synod, wrote:

Although we have opened the offices to women, we have been notably reluctant to open our pulpits to them on an equal basis. Congregations have sent their daughters as candidates to New Brunswick and to Western [seminaries] but have been less willing to receive them back in ministry. Little wonder that these candidates often experience feelings of frustration, rejection, anger, and despair!"[111]

In the Christian Reformed Church there was even stronger opposition to an expanded role for women in the church. It was the debate over this issue more than anything else that prompted the decade of the 1970s to be called the "decade of unrest" in the church. "No other issue . . . appeared on the agenda of the Christian Reformed Church so regularly, so vigorously, as the so-called 'women's issue.'" In 1957, the synod gave women the right to vote in congregational meetings, but it was a limited privilege because

"questions of *whether* and *when* women should be invited to participate were left to the judgment of each consistory." In 1978 the synod "decided that the consistories may ordain qualified women as deacons, provided their work" was "distinguished from that of elders," but the following year, because of strong protests, the synod "instructed consistories to defer implementing the 1978 decision."[112]

Lutherans

The high priority placed on doctrine by Lutherans made the issue of women's ordination a difficult one. Prior to the 1970s, the idea of women preachers was repugnant to most Lutherans. Their theology ruled out women in such a role by "orders of creation" if for no other reason. Likewise, Lutherans, unlike most other Protestants, had a profound reverence for the clerical office—a position inappropriate for a woman. An alternative to pastoral ministry for women in the Lutheran church was the diaconate, an institution revived by Theodore Fliedner in the 1830s. In Europe the deaconess movement thrived for more than a century, but in America the situation was entirely different. Although the movement grew during the early decades of the twentieth century, by 1940 there were still fewer than five hundred Lutheran deaconesses in the United States. In the years following, interest waned even though there were efforts to make the ministry more meaningful. Many women considered the diaconate a demeaning role for women in the church in comparison to the roles that were available to men. Yet, until the 1960s it was the only official ministry open to Lutheran women.[113]

Despite longstanding opposition, European Lutherans began ordaining women in the 1960s, and in 1970 the Americans followed suit. In that year both the American Lutheran Church and the Lutheran Church in America voted to ordain women. The much more conservative Missouri Synod, however, strongly rejected the trend. By a vote of 674 to 194, this synod ruled that "the Word of God does not permit women to the pastoral office."[114]

Methodists

Methodists, like most other mainline denominations, have split and merged over the centuries, and thus the historical roots are sometimes fragmented. The Methodist Episcopal Church was the largest body of Methodists, and it was not until 1906, after considerable struggle by women's groups, that that body officially recognized women as lay people in the church. Women would wait another half century, until 1956, before they were granted full clerical privileges involving ordination. Long before this, however, there were Methodist women preachers. Indeed, it was two Methodist women who organized "An American Association of Women Preachers" in 1919. The official organ of the new organization was the *Woman's Pulpit*, so the specter of women in the pulpit in 1956 was not a new phenomena in Methodist circles. By 1970 there were nearly four hundred ordained female ministers, and five years later that figure had surpassed six hundred.[115]

Disciples of Christ

The Disciples of Christ illustrate the significant change in attitude toward women in ministry that occurred during the first half of the twentieth century. In 1905, J. W. McGarvey, president of the College of the Bible in Lexington, Kentucky, defended the admission of women students to opponents who feared the school would soon be turning out women preachers. His response was reassuring: "I replied, that by the time they [the women students] studied the Scriptures with us they will learn that women are not to be preachers." A half century later the scene had changed considerably. Riley B. Montgomery, the president of the college at the time of an inquiry in 1953, issued the following response:

> We believe that women should have the same right to ordination for any position in the church that is accorded to men. Our educational program is planned on the basis of this belief. Although the function of ordination among Disciples of Christ is a function of the local church, The College of the Bible shares in this responsibility with the local churches when they are ordaining graduates from our institutions. *We should recommend women to the local churches for ordination as readily as we would men.*[116]

By mid-century, the Disciples of Christ were giving more than rhetorical support to women in ministry. In 1952, the denomination elected a woman as first vice-president of their International Convention, and she opened the convention that year with the president's address because the president himself was ill. Yet, as with most other denominations, the role of women in the church was largely one involving traditional "women's work"—that being foreign missions, humanitarian endeavors, and church women's societies. Lorraine Lollis' book, *The Shape of Adam's Rib: A Lively History of Women's Work in the Christian Church*, gives the impression that women's work in the church is the work that is organized by women and serves women. "Our story," she writes, "is that of our organized life in various forms as the 'better half' of the church."[117]

Baptists

The various Baptist denominations are more diverse than the Methodists, and their policy on women has varied considerably. The American Baptist Convention, the most liberal of the large Baptist denominations, began ordaining women in the nineteenth century and has since permitted women great latitude in ministry. In fact, so open was the denomination toward women that by the 1950s three women—Mrs. Leslie Swain, Mrs. H. G. Colwell, and Mrs. Helen Barrett Montgomery—had held its highest executive office.[118] The most well known of these was Montgomery. She was a leading figure in the women's missionary movement, a prolific writer, and the first woman translator of the New Testament from the Greek. She served only one term as president, in 1910, but "it was the first time that any woman had held this position in any large Christian body, and when the name of Mrs. Montgomery was presented to the convention, the shouts made the rafters ring." Although not ordained,

Montgomery was a licensed preacher and took an active part in the preaching ministry of her church. She also served for forty-four years as the teacher of the Barrett Memorial class, "one of the most influential women's classes in the city of Rochester." The class numbered as high as 250 members.[119]

The giant Southern Baptist Convention remained adamantly opposed to equalizing roles for women in the church. It was not until 1929 that the president of the Woman's Missionary Union of that denomination was permitted to report directly to the Convention. On that occasion "a number of male delegates walked out, necessitating a compromise whereby the session was held in the Sunday school rooms of the host church rather than violate the dictum of St. Paul."[120]

The first woman to be officially ordained in a Southern Baptist church was Addie Davis. The service took place in Durham, North Carolina, in 1964. Although she was a graduate of Southeastern Baptist Theological Seminary and had served as an assistant pastor and as a supply pastor, there was bitter opposition to what was perceived as a new course of action. Warren Carr, the pastor of the church where her ordination took place, did not seek to justify women's ordination in general but he did strongly defend his action in her case, claiming it "was almost solely due to her personal testimony." As had been true of so many women before her, it was a "call" that propelled her into the ministry. It was that aspect of her testimony that was most convincing to Carr and his colleagues: "We took her seriously when she said that God had called her to the ordained ministry and that she could not rest until she answered that call."[121]

Despite the fears of some of the Southern Baptist "brethren," the ordination of Davis did not unleash a deluge of women clamoring for ordination. In fact, the next female ordination did not occur until 1971, when Shirley Carter was ordained in Columbia, South Carolina, by the Kathwood Baptist Church. So controversial was the ordination, however, that the following year the church rescinded it.[122]

In the years that followed a few more women were ordained, and controversy continued to rage. In February of 1984 an article in the *Chicago Tribune*, under the title, "Women Pastors Split Southern Baptists," told of the opposition to the installation of the Reverend Susan Wright as the pastor of a small Baptist church in the Chicago area. Several pastors from nearby Southern Baptist churches were seeking to disqualify the church that installed her from membership in the Chicago Metropolitan Baptist Association. When motion to that effect was defeated, some churches withdrew their membership in protest. [123] In June of 1984, spurred on by a conservative swing toward fundamentalism, the Southern Baptist Convention voted to deny women ordination in order "to preserve a submission God requires because man was first in creation and woman was first in the Edenic fall."[124] Although individual churches remained autonomous, the vote was nevertheless symbolic of a mood that was evident elsewhere in both evangelical and fundamentalist circles.

Mennonites

The position of Mennonites toward women in the church is illustrated by the life and ministry of Ann J. Allebach (1874–1918). She grew up in a Mennonite community in Pennsylvania, attended normal school, became a school teacher and later principal, took university and seminary training, and finally threw herself into a full-time ministry with the poor and down-trodden of New York City. It was when she was in her early thirties, "after her years of education and her intensive training in church work at the Chapel, after her years of preaching and evangelizing at the Missions," that she contacted two old friends—both Mennonite ministers—"and asked to be ordained by her own people—the General Conference Mennonite Church." Their willingness to comply led to controversy within the movement, but she did not back down. "On a cold, gray Sunday, January 15, 1911, some 270 people parked their buggies in the rain at the first Mennonite Church" in Philadelphia. Her own pastor preached the ordination sermon, which dealt very specifically with women in ministry and Paul's admonitions for women to be silent—an admonition that he argued had been determined by Greek culture.[125]

Alleback's ordination made the newspaper headlines: "WOMAN ORDAINED AS MENNONITE PASTOR: Miss Allebach Is First of Her Sex So to Act in America; SHE IS A SUFFRAGIST." The publicity no doubt only harmed her cause, and she soon discovered that ordination did not translate into open doors of ministry. Her qualifications and experience were not enough to overcome long-held negative attitudes of congregations toward women pastors. She did receive several pastoral calls from congregations outside the Mennonites, but she turned them down, choosing to remain in nondenominational humanitarian and organizational work. In 1916, however, five years after her ordination, she accepted a pastoral call to Sunnyside Reformed Church. Her ministry there was different from that of many of her male counterparts. She sought to reach out to hurting people who were often neglected in fashionable religious circles. An article in the *New York World* captured the essence of her ministry:

> Should you chance some Sunday morning to visit the Sunnyside Reformed Church, do not be surprised if the service opens thus: "If any of you here present are sick or hungry and need employment or help in your homes, come to me after the service and I will help you." And the Rev. Miss Allebach does help. There are many men and women in New York City who can corroborate this, men and women who know that this woman minister not only preaches but practices the Gospel.[126]

Her pastoral ministry, however, was short. She died suddenly of an apparent heart attack in 1918.

> The local Mennonites, even after her death, did not quite know what to make of this woman so unlike her kind. Ann's name never appeared in any of the standard Mennonite leadership lists. It was penciled in, as an afterthought, on an ordination list of "Men Ordained. . . ." They shook their heads and marveled, and in several years, they forgot.[127]

The opposition to an equal role for women in the church continued, and few other women sought to break the barriers. Barbara Bender Reber summed up the situation in 1982: "Although Mennonite women, almost without exception, have been excluded from ordination, their ministry has been essential to the growth of the home, the church, and the communities in which they lived and worked."[128]

Fundamentalists and Free Churches

It was not uncommon for the women's issue to be associated with liberalism during the early twentieth century when the controversy between modernism and fundamentalism was raging. Yet with few exceptions it was the more conservative sectarian movements that permitted women the most latitude in ministry, and in many such churches women also sat on governing boards.

The Free Church Movement

The openness to women in ministry was seen in the Free Churches that broke away from European State Churches in the late nineteenth century. In Fredrik Franson, the Free Church movement in Scandinavia and the United States had a staunch advocate of women in ministry. But what he was advocating was a limited ministry—one that was focused on the foreign mission field. Although Donald Dayton and others have asserted that in his widely read pamphlet, *Prophesying Daughters*, Franson "defended the right of women to preach," such an interpretation is unwarranted. Franson seems clearly to be defending women's evangelistic work, especially on the foreign mission field, and he distinguished that from "preaching" per se.

When we realize that nearly two-thirds of all converted people in the world are women, then the question of women's work in evangelization is of great importance. In China each day 30,000 people go into eternity without having heard the gospel. There is no prohibition in the Bible against women's public work, and we face the circumstance that the devil . . . has been able to exclude nearly two-thirds of the number of Christians from participation in the Lord's service. . . . The loss for God's cause is so great that it can hardly be described."[129]

In regard to women "preaching," Franson appears to have had serious reservations about it and cautioned women against it:

One matter that all missionary sisters in the homeland should be especially careful about is that they not seek to defend preaching by women, especially in public. As soon as they would do so, they would appear as teachers concerning questions in dispute and would be in a field where their place, to say the least, is ambiguous. It is enough that they themselves in their heart have assurance concerning God's Word, that they have the right to evangelize, and they don't need to talk much about it.[130]

What should women do when they confront opposition? "If mission houses or churches sometimes are closed against them, they should accept this as from God in that it helps them to come just to those places where the need is the greatest and which opportunities would be lost to them if too much acceptance was theirs."[131]

The history of the role of women in the Free Churches is one that needs further study. Della E. Olson, in her book *A Woman of Her Times*, writes that "it appears from writings of the early church leaders that the participation of women in preaching and teaching had a high period just before and after the turn of the century," and that "the practice did not actually stop." Yet the vast majority of examples she cites relate to women doing home missionary work in the West, particularly among the Mormons and those doing itinerant evangelistic work, such as Alma Olson, who in the 1920s conducted tent meetings and held "services and Sunday school in the homes or in a hired hall."[132]

But despite their often lowly position, these lay preachers were crucial to the early development of the Free Church movement.

Although few of these women were gifted speakers, they were sincere, God-fearing persons with a passion for souls. In view of the fact that this movement was a new phenomenon, still the women evangelists drew crowds for many years and many people were won to the Lord through their simple testimonies and songs of faith.[133]

Another early writer stated:

A notable portion of our work in North Dakota was launched by women workers. With one or two exceptions they were the only workers who had ventured into the sparsely populated Dakota districts. . . . Meetings were held mostly in homes; now and then a schoolhouse would be available. The gatherings could not have been large at any time, yet seasons of refreshing were frequently sent from God."[134]

Although few people denied the contribution that women evangelists made to the spread of the Free Churches, there was strong resentment against their work among certain factions in the movement. This antagonism is evident in the book by Frank Lindberg on the Swedish Evangelical Free Church of America, *Looking Back Fifty Years*. He introduces a section entitled "Women Evangelists" by focusing on the controversial nature of the subject:

Now we come to a period within the Free Church work which I dread to write about, because mention of the matter is so apt to cause irritation. . . . This was the period in which women ministers were active. It was started by Franson who conceived the idea that women ought to preach, and published a book entitled "Prophesying Daughters" . . . [which] contained only the passages of Scripture that he thought were fitting.[135]

Lindberg conceded that there were others besides Franson who supported women's ministry: "The first of these interested ministers was Axel Nordin, who got some sisters from Chicago to come to Phelps County, Nebraska. August Davis also approved the idea, and being President of the Scandinavian Mission Society of the U.S.A., he arranged that women might secure clergy fare on various railroads." According to Lindberg, that single act had such a powerful impact that "the movement went forward by leaps and bounds." "I am not stretching the truth," he wrote, "when I say that at least fifty were out on the field. It went so far that at one

Sunday service about ten of us preachers sat listening to one woman preach." Although many of them were trained in Bible school, Lindberg ridiculed the qualifications of the women: "If a girl could play the guitar, it was taken as a sure sign that God had called her to preach." The solution, in Lindberg's mind, however, was certainly not further education. He clearly was not among those who supported Ellen Modin's fundraising efforts for a school for women preachers. Indeed, he lamented that "Free church ministers . . . had fallen so deeply that God no longer could use them but must call out the women."[136]

Independent Fundamentalist Churches of America

Another movement that took a strong stand against "modernism" and yet allowed women to have an active role in ministry during its formative years was a movement that became known as the Independent Fundamentalist Churches of America. This organization dates its origins to the early 1920s when the American Conference of Undenominational Churches was formed in Iowa. Its purpose was to be a "fundamental fellowship" free of modernism and denominationalism. In the ACUC, the forerunner of the IFCA, women were permitted full membership, and the constitution used the phrase "his or her" in specifying its requirements for membership. "Most women members," according to IFCA historian James Henry, "were listed either as pastors or as assistants to their husbands who were pastors." But such egalitarianism was not to endure. "In 1930, when the name was changed to the IFCA," continues Henry, "it was evident there was a need for some 'tightening of the reins' in the area of membership. . . . The first major change was the elimination of women from membership."[137]

Mid-Century Evangelical Church Women

Although opportunities for women in evangelical churches were decreasing as the century wore on, a number of women continued to work effectively within the church or in close association with the church. One means was to give lip service to the authority of men in the church, as the ordained Kathryn Kuhlman did, while at the same time preaching, performing marriage ceremonies, and conducting baptisms. Another means of carrying out such a ministry was to assume a nonpastoral title, such as Henrietta Mears did as Director of Christian Education. And still another means was to accept less desirable work within the church. An example is that of Dr. Hilda Ives. She was the mother of four children and was left alone to rear them after the death of her attorney husband following World War I. As the responsibilities for her children lessened, Ives sought personal fulfillment through church ministry. She became an ordained minister herself and then began traveling back and forth across New England, preaching and working with floundering rural churches and establishing men and women pastors in parishes that needed them.[138]

Kathryn Kuhlman

The age of dynamic women evangelists did not end with the death of Aimee Semple McPherson. By mid-century, hundreds of thousands of Americans had become enamored with another Pentecostal healing evangelist, Kathryn Kuhlman. She began preaching at age sixteen, after she "felt a definite call to the ministry," and for most of two decades she did itinerant evangelistic work in the rural Midwest. In 1946, after experiencing the "baptism of the Holy Spirit," Kuhlman began preaching. Following one of her sermons that same year, a woman reported that her tumor had miraculously disappeared. This testimony launched Kuhlman into her thirty-year healing ministry.[139]

Like other prominent women in the church, Kuhlman faced strong opposition. A particularly harsh attack came in 1952, when she conducted tent meetings in Akron, Ohio, at the invitation of Rex Humbard, another well-known Pentecostal evangelist. Her flamboyant antagonist was Dallas Billington, pastor of the large fundamentalist Akron Baptist Temple. Besides "exposing" her as a divorcée, he lambasted her for her healing ministry: "There is no greater racket in America, whether it be horse jockeying, dog races, or the numbers racket, than the so-called divine healers of our day." But even if divine healing was valid, it was not an activity for women: "Nowhere was the power of divine healing ever given to be administered by any woman. Women have their rightful places but when you put one in the pulpit it is unscriptural." The efforts to silence her, however, only increased interest in her meetings, and the Sunday following Billington's attacks, more than twenty thousand attended her meeting. [140]

Kuhlman did not seek to defend her ministry scripturally, as was the case with so many women before her. She had no desire for a public ministry, and she cautioned other women against it:

> I'd give anything if I could have just been a good housewife, a good cook. And I'd like to have had a big family. It would have been nice to have a man boss me around. . . . Let women be sure—very sure—that they have a call from God before they ever decide to enter such a ministry. If you are not definitely called, don't do it.[141]

Kuhlman was not a feminist, and she went to great lengths to convince her followers of that:

> I never think of myself as a woman preacher, I tell you the truth. I am a woman; I was born a woman, and I try to keep my place as a woman. And I want to say to the women here in this auditorium: please, whatever you do, don't try to be a man. . . . I recognize the fact that I was born a woman, and with it I try to be a lady. I never try to usurp the place of authority of a man—never! That's the reason I have no church. I leave that to the man. I am a woman. I know my place. . . . I do not believe that those who know me best think of me as being a woman preacher.[142]

Yet Kuhlman did not object to her followers calling her "pastor," and she "wanted to be known as a Bible teacher, not a miracle worker." And indeed she was—at least by a select few. "Her Monday night Bible studies at the First Presbyterian Church in Pittsburgh were attended by some of the most elite Bible scholars in the city." And, although she did not want people to think of her as a "woman preacher," she was "an ordained minister of the Gospel" and she sometimes baptized her new converts in mass outdoor baptismal services. She also performed marriages and conducted funerals. And despite her disclaimers about women in authority, there was little doubt in her inner circle of associates who was in control. She was a strong leader who demanded high performance from those who worked with her.[143]

Henrietta Mears

One of the most influential women in mid-twentieth-century religious life was Henrietta Mears, the founder of Gospel Light Publications and the Hollywood Christian Group, Director of Christian Education at Hollywood Presbyterian Church, developer of Forest Home Conference Center, and a respected Bible teacher who "produced more than one generation of some of the most prominent Presbyterian ministers in America."[144]

Mears was deeply involved in Christian ministry long before she became nationally known. As a high school chemistry teacher in Minneapolis in the 1920s, she accepted the challenge of teaching a Sunday school class at the First Baptist Church. It was a class of eighteen-year-old girls—a clique of five—who referred to themselves as "The Snobs." From that unpretentious beginning developed a class of over five hundred, for which a special hall was built to accommodate them.[145]

In 1928, Mears accepted a position

as Director of Christian Education at the prestigious Hollywood Presbyterian Church, and from that time on she was involved in full-time Christian ministry. When she began her ministry there, the Sunday school enrollment was four hundred and fifty; in two and one half years that number increased to more than four thousand. It was soon after she began her ministry in Hollywood that she developed her own Sunday school curriculum, and within a few years orders for her "homemade" Sunday school lessons were coming in from all over the country. It was out of this humble beginning that Gospel Light Press was born.[146]

Next to her publishing ministry, Mears' most lasting impact was in the realm of her teaching—particularly her teaching of young men. Among her protégés were Bill Bright, the founder of Campus Crusade for Christ and Richard Halverson, pastor of the influential Fourth Presbyterian Church in Washington, D.C. Harold Ockenga, the noted evangelical leader in Boston, wrote a moving tribute to her:

> What a work you have done! There is no young peoples' work in this nation equal to yours. When I think of the tens of thousands who have studied the Bible under your leadership, of the thousands who have faced the claims of Christ and made a commitment to Him, of the hundreds of young men who have gone into the ministry, and other young people into Christian service, I cannot but be struck with amazement.[147]

The late Clarence Roddy, a professor of homiletics at Fuller Seminary, used to refer to Mears as the best preacher in Southern California. "She was not ordained and had no formal theological training, but the impact of her life and teaching on her boys was comparable to the influence some of the world's greatest theologians had on their students."[148]

Itinerant Speakers Outside the Church

Kathryn Kuhlman's refusal to acknowledge that she was a "preacher" who wielded authority in the church was perhaps a natural response to the turnaround that had occurred in evangelical circles as denominations that had emerged out of the holiness, Pentecostal, and fundamentalist movements matured. There had been a backlash against women in leadership positions in the church, and one way to circumvent the opposition was to publicly acknowledge the "headship" of men. Another way to circumvent opposition was to work outside the parameters of the church. Indeed, most women who sought full-time Christian ministry found their opportunities outside the church. This was certainly not a new concept. Women such as Phoebe Palmer and Hannah Whithall Smith, had wielded powerful influence outside the church a century earlier. They were able to sustain an unprecedented ministry to large mixed audiences in middle-class circles with biblical and theological subject matter.

In the mid-twentieth century a new breed of female speakers arose—women whose subject matter came primarily out of their own struggles in the Christian life. And in virtually every instance the speaking ministry was supplemented by a writing career—the one ministry that has always been safe for Christian women. Two well-known examples of such ministry are those of Corrie ten Boom and Joni Eareckson.

Corrie ten Boom

Born in Holland and raised in a Christian family, Corrie ten Boom lived an inauspicious life until World War II broke out—when she was in her fifties. Her family home became "the hiding place" for Jews who were seeking to escape Nazi terror. As a result of her involvement Corrie herself spent time in a Nazi concentration camp. It was that story along with her vivacious Christian witness that propelled her into an international speaking and writing ministry. Her first major work *The Hiding Place*, detailing her wartime activities, was an immediate bestseller. Her second successful book, *Tramp for the Lord*, detailed her ministry following the war, though the ministry actually began while she was still interned at Ravensbruck, "the notorious women's death camp." There she held "clandestine Bible study groups for an ever-growing group of believers, and Barracks 28 became known throughout the camp as 'the crazy place, where they hope.' "[149]

Corrie's ministry entailed travel and involved more than three decades of speaking in more than sixty countries, beginning in the United States. After her release from the death camp, she set out for the United States—"to carry the Gospel as a missionary to the Americans." The opportunities for speaking, however, did not come easily. "The Americans were polite and some of them

were interested, but none wanted me to come and speak. . . . As the weeks slipped by, I found more and more resistance to my ministry. No one was interested in a middle-aged spinster woman from Holland who wanted to preach." That situation suddenly changed after she was introduced to an influential Christian man, whose recommendation led to a flood of speaking requests, which in turn opened up even more opportunities not only in churches, but also on college campuses and in prisons and women's clubs.[150]

Corrie ten Boom, Internationally known Speaker, and Author of *The Hiding Place*.

Following her speaking tour in the United States, Corrie returned to Europe—specifically to Germany, the place she most dreaded to go. There, with the help of the Lutheran Sisterhood of Mary, she rented an abandoned concentration camp and turned it into a refugee home. "Barbed wire disappeared. Flowers, light-colored paint and God's love in the hearts of the people changed a cruel camp into a refuge where people would find the way back to life again." From Germany she began traveling and speaking throughout the world. She visited Eastern Europe, the Soviet Union, Africa, Latin America, and Southeast Asia. She stayed in Korea three months, and while there had more than 250 speaking engagements. From there she went to New Zealand and then on to India. Although she told her story time and again, it was always with an evangelistic thrust, and always with a personal interest in individuals. She was straightforward and blunt and was quick to offer counsel to people with special needs—from a political prisoner in Africa who could not forgive his captors to a Christian university student in Korea who was struggling with doubts after having read the works of the liberal biblical scholar, Rudolph Bultmann.[151]

Joni Eareckson

Joni Eareckson, a quadriplegic as a result of a diving accident in 1967, has, like Corrie ten Boom, developed her ministry from her personal struggles. Initially life seemed not worth living. But "after waves of depression and a phase of reading existentialists and atheists, she gradually came back to a deepened version of the orthodox Christianity in which she had been raised." She began sharing her experience publicly and soon became a "popular speaker on the Evangelical Protestant celebrity cir-

cuit." In addition to having a speaking ministry, she became a "successful commercial artist, a bestselling author and the star of a two-hour, $2 million film version of her life." She also founded a ministry, "Joni and Friends," that reaches out to people who are disabled and suffering.[152]

Joni Eareckson Tada, Author and Public Speaker, Pictured With Her Husband, Ken Tada.   Photo by Arthur Tilley.

Parachurch and Independent Ministries

Through the burgeoning increase of parachurch organizations and independent ministries women have become more visible in religious endeavors than they ever had been before. By the mid-twentieth century, "respectability" no longer permitted middle-class evangelical women to be "called" to "preach" or conduct a revival ministry, but a wide variety of new ministries opened up to accommodate their desire to publicly serve God.

Youth and Children's Ministries

The area outside the church in which women found ample opportunity for career Christian ministry was in parachurch organizations. Although women were often barred from leadership roles, they were eagerly accepted for lower staff positions in such campus and youth ministries as Campus Crusade for Christ, InterVarsity Christian Fellowship, Campus Life, and The Navigators and in such children's ministries as Child Evangelism Fellowship and the Bible Club Movement. Although these organizations have required staff members to be trained professionals, they have not generally paid salaries but rather have required their staff to do deputation in order to raise their own financial support. Thus, while parachurch ministries have been open to women, the positions they have offered have not been comparable to those positions that have been easily available to men in salaried church ministries. Further study needs to be done on this issue, but on the surface it seems that a much higher percentage of women than men have been restricted to ministries requiring the "faith" concept of personal finances.

Self-Help Ministries to Women

During the 1960s and 1970s a number of ministries were founded that were focused specifically on women. Unlike the voluntary associations of women in the nineteenth century that were primarily service oriented, many of these associations of evangelical women were "self-help" groups, with an emphasis on health and exercise, marriage enrichment, or political action.

Overeaters Anonymous and Overeaters Victorious are examples of groups that focus primarily on self-help. The latter was founded by Neva Coyle in 1977. "She weighed 248 pounds and always gained back what she lost—until she used her born-again Christian faith in her fight against fat." By 1980 some sixteen hundred people had finished the program.[153] Like the diet ministries, marriage-enrichment groups often focused on women—often telling them that it was their spiritual responsibility as godly wives to insure a happy marriage. Helen Andelien, the founder of Fascinating Womanhood, and Marabel Morgan, author of *The Total Woman*, were the most prominent in spreading this antifeminist message across American during the 1970s.

Also coming from a strong antifeminist position were political action organizations that appealed directly to conservative Christian women. Phyllis Schlafly, head of Eagle Forum, and, for a time, Anita Bryant were in the forefront of such movements. But even more closely tied to conservative religious values was the movement founded by Beverly LaHaye, Concerned Women for America, which claimed well over one hundred thousand members in 1980, one year after it was founded. By 1985, it boasted a membership of some five hundred thousand. The thrust of the movement has been antiabortion, antigay, and profamily, its leaders blaming the feminist movement for much of the failure of modern-day society. "The philosophy of rebellion and hatred underlying the modern-day feminism," points out LaHaye, "has been largely responsible for the destruction of the American nuclear family."[154]

Women's Conference and Retreat Speakers

Paralleling the growth of various parachurch organizations was the increase of women's retreats and conferences, which offered women spiritual self-help and opened opportunities for women to travel the speaking circuit. Well-known authors such as Joyce Landorf and Jill Briscoe received more invitations than they could accept, while less-well-known women tried desperately to obtain a hearing. Some conferences and retreats have been denominationally related, while others have been sponsored by such groups as Christian Women's Clubs, an organization known mainly for its monthly women's luncheons with celebrity speakers and an evangelistic focus.

The role of women's speakers has been one that has brought new opportunities for women since the 1960s. But even that ministry role was viewed by some as too elevated to be spiritually proper. Jo Berry, the founder and director of Creative Ministries, which trains women to "discover and develop their gifts," relates in her book *Growing, Sharing, Serving* how she initially "quenched" the "Spirit-planted desire" the Lord had given her to be a women's speaker:

> The first time I was aware of a Spirit-planted desire, I thought I was sinning.

My dear friend Georgia Lee, who is a Christian actress and speaker, was standing in the podium at a large conference center, speaking to about eight hundred women. As I watched her I remember thinking, "Someday I want to do what she is doing. I want to talk to huge groups of women about the Lord."

Immediately she felt guilty for such thoughts, but later, after she herself had become involved in a speaking ministry, she became convinced that the desire for the ministry was from God.[155] It was on that basis that she founded her Creative Ministries training center.

Women's Bible Studies

Like the retreats and Bible conferences, women's Bible studies have mushroomed since the 1960s, and have involved vast numbers of women in the United States and world-wide. Many of these groups have been church related or entirely independent, but a significant number have been part of organized movements such as Bible Study Fellowship or Neighborhood Bible Studies. Both organizations focus primarily on women but have entirely different philosophies of approach to Bible study. The former, founded by A. Wetherell Johnson in 1952, has offered extensive training for its teachers and has been highly structured, with uniform lessons for all Bible study groups. During its first twenty years the movement grew from five to over one hundred thousand class members who had completed the five-year course.[156]

Neighborhood Bible Studies, on the other hand, has been loosely organized with an emphasis on small discussion groups. It was founded in 1960 by Marilyn Kunz and Catherine Schell, and by 1985 there were thousands of such groups meeting worldwide, using the organization's various study guides that were available in some thirty languages.[157]

Christian Feminist Organizations

The "creative" ministries that Jo Berry has recommended for women involved ministries to other women, as have the vast majority of week-day Bible studies. Not all evangelical women, however, have accepted such boundaries for women's ministries or the prescribed marriage role recommended by such women as Marabel Morgan or Beverly LaHaye. In reaction to such traditional approaches and in an effort to provide support networks, conferences, and literature, feminist organizations have arisen in evangelical circles. The Evangelical Women's Caucus and the Daughters of Sarah are examples, both of which are small organizations—the Evangelical Women's Caucus having fewer than six hundred members in 1984.[158] Outside evangelical circles, church women have organized for various functions, but most notably for humanitarian efforts. The largest such interdenominational organization is Church Women United, which rallies to the cause of the oppressed, and specifically to oppressed women.

A Century of Opening and Closing Doors

In spite of the official gains women have made in the church since the mid-twentieth century, women in the 1980s continued to be in a minority in leadership positions—particularly in the evangelical churches that have grown most rapidly since the 1950s. Even in parachurch ministries, where women were theoretically granted equal status, they fall far behind their male counterparts. That has been due in part to a conservative reaction that developed not only among evangelicals but in society as a whole in the late 1970s and 1980s. By that time the issue of women in the church became a hotly debated topic that often created splits in individual churches and denominations. Seminaries and Bible colleges continued to bar women from certain exclusively male areas of study, and mission boards tightened their restrictions on women, who had long been involved in extensive teaching and preaching ministries overseas. The stricter controls on women's ministries among evangelicals appears to have developed largely as a reaction to the feminist movement. The trend manifested itself in many ways—one notable example being the introduction of a bachelor's degree in marriage and motherhood by the fundamentalist Hyles-Anderson College.[159]

Chapter 11

The Contemporary Church Faces the Issues

Introduction

This history of women's contributions to the church and its ministries has reached the present era. Not only what women did, but their relationships to the church and the world have been unfolded. Changing perspectives on women in the church have been observed, and sometimes (depending on one's *own* perspective) these perspectives have improved, sometimes worsened; they have often undulated and have even returned in circular fashion to a previous stage.

As the contemporary church faces the issues, probably most of the attitudes that have existed over the centuries, excepting those extreme concepts of women as mindless consorts and lustful deceivers of mankind, still exist somewhere today. In some denominations and religious organizations the "women's issue" has become a battleground and even (though few would say it out loud) a test of orthodoxy. Some people who are willing to tolerate others who hold opposing views on, say, Calvinism or baptism are not able to serve in an organization, teach in a seminary, or minister in a church alongside those differing on this matter.

To gain further historical perspective with a view to increasing mutual understanding in the contemporary church, it will be helpful to identify some of the recent currents of thought and to isolate some of the most troublesome issues and difficult questions.

Late Nineteenth- to Early-Twentieth-Century Writers

The avalanche of literature and a corresponding increase in activism can now be seen to have had their origin in the deep recesses of church history. But in the history of feminist ideas, certain significant contributions are worthy of note. The opinions of a few earlier observers, even if named already, are worth citing here in order to pick up the thread of ideas.

Antoinette Brown Blackwell

Antoinette Blackwell, a pioneer woman seminarian and cleric of the late nineteenth century, had expressed her convictions as follows:

> I assert that every woman, in the present state of society, is bound to maintain her own independence and own integrity of character; to assert herself, earnestly and firmly, as the equal of man, who is only her peer. [If she consents to being subject to her husband because of civil law] I do insist that she consents to degradation; that this is sin and it is impossible to make it other than sin.[1]

A. J. Gordon

The esteemed spiritual and missionary leader, A. J. Gordon (after whom Gordon-Conwell Divinity School is partially named) wrote an article that was originally published in 1894 and has recently been recirculated. Entitled "The Ministry of Women," it begins with the promise in Acts 2 about the ministry of women as prophets under the new covenant. It continues with the discussion of 1 Timothy 2:8–11, offering the suggestion that such notable scholars as Chrysostom and Alford had previously made, namely, that Paul expected us to understand that when he said "in like manner," the reader was to assume the repetition of the word "pray." Therefore this passage does not exclude women from praying but assumes that they do. Gordon's article continues with 1 Corinthians 11, where he follows Bengel's terse comment: "Therefore women were not excluded from these duties." As for 1 Corinthians 14:34–35, Gordon suggests that this is a particular circumstance, one of several instances in the chapter where those who are speaking need at certain times to to silent, and that it should be interpreted in the context of "the entire New Testament teaching." He then refers to Romans 16 and Paul's female associates, noting that the word *diakonos*, which is used of Phoebe,

> is rendered "minister" when applied to Paul and Apollos (I Corinthians iii:5), and "deacon" when used of other male officers of the Church (I Timothy iii:10,12,13). Why discriminate against Phoebe simply because she is a woman? . . . "Phoebe, a *servant*" might suggest to an ordinary reader nothing more than the modern church drudge, who prepares sandwiches and coffee for an ecclesiastical sociable.

The rest of the article is in the same incisive style.[2]

Gordon's article sounds remarkably up-to-date and surely should help lay to rest the idea that evangelical feminism is simply a modern reaction to "women's lib."

Katherine C. Bushnell

In the early years of this century a vigorous appeal was made by Dr. Katherine C. Bushnell in a book entitled *God's Word to Women*. This was abridged and summarized by Jessie Penn-Lewis in *The Magna Charta of Women* in 1919 and was reprinted in 1923. Bushnell and Penn-Lewis have both been criticized at certain points, but Bushnell's work was considered significant enough to warrant republication in 1976.[3] Among the contributions that these authors have made is their suggestion regarding 1 Corinthians 14:

We are driven to believe *the Apostle was not uttering his own views* in verses 34 and 35 of 1 Cor. ch. 14, ... we believe this is the language of Judaizers at Corinth, which has been reported to Paul, and which Paul quotes to answer back in the words: "What! Came the word of God out from you? or came it unto you only?" ... [4]

This interpretation has been picked up by several recent scholars as the most likely explanation of the passage.

Margaret Sanger

The early decades of this century witnessed much activism leading up to the ratification in 1920 of Amendment 19 on Woman Suffrage. Attention then turned increasingly from the woman's role in society to that in her own home. A leading voice in this was Margaret Sanger. One memorable line expresses her concern. Declared Sanger, "Woman's role has been that of an incubator and little more."[5]

The Mid-Twentieth Century

Simone de Beauvoir

In her work *The Second Sex*,[6] Simone de Beauvoir articulated ideas that have found expression in countless subsequent writings:

Woman herself recognizes that the world is masculine on the whole; those who fashioned it, ruled it, and still dominate it today are men. ... The lot of women is a respectful obedience. ... Many of the faults for which women are reproached—mediocrity, laziness, frivolity, servility—simply express the fact that their horizon is closed. ... Sexually unsatisfied, doomed to male

crudeness, ... she finds consolation in creamy sauces, heady wines, velvets. ... If she seems to man so "physical" a creature, it is because her situation leads her to attach extreme importance to her animal nature.[7]

The following two quotations from de Beauvoir show the beginnings of what was to become a strong link between the concerns of women and their perception of the role of religion in their dilemma.

Woman is asked in the name of God not so much to accept her inferiority as to believe that, thanks to Him, she is the equal of the lordly male; even the temptation to revolt is suppressed by the claim that the injustice is overcome. ... Although subordinated to the law of men by the will of God Himself, woman none the less finds in Him a mighty refuge from them. ... With the heavenly Father's connivance, woman can boldly lay claim to the glory of her femininity in defiance of man.[8]

Religion sanctions women's self-love. ... But, above all, it confirms the social order, it justifies her resignation, by giving her the hope of a better future in a sexless heaven.[9]

Others were shortly to bring judgment on religion in different and even more severe words.

The material presented thus far should help the Christian reader to penetrate behind what has seemed to many to be hostile activism among those they often call "radical feminists." Modern feminism had its roots at least partly in the frustrations of women who felt that—whether in bed, business, society, or school—their lives were inordinately dominated by men. The frequent response of the church was to reaffirm male leadership rather than to give evidence of a desire to understand the perspective of women. Such a response could hardly have failed to fortify the impression that the church was a, if not the, major opponent of women.

A scientific issue lies behind much of the contemporary discussion: Are there demonstrable differences between males and females? A number of tests were conducted on this subject in the 1960s and 1970s. For a survey of these, see Eleanor Emmons Maccoby and Carol Nagy Jacklin, *The Psychology of Sex Differences*.[10] Research continues, some of it connected with the lateralization of the brain, with inquiries centered on whether some of the apparent male-female differences are related not only to the dominance of either part, but also to the way they function together.[11] One influential work that offered an opinion of research up to the early 1950s was Montagu's *Natural Superiority of Women*.[12] Montagu attempted to show that although men may have certain physical advantages over women, there are other ways, including intellectual ability, in which women are superior.

John R. Rice

It would be difficult to find a greater contrast between the foregoing works and the widely distributed book by a popular evangelist of that day, John R. Rice. Its title told the story: *Bobbed Hair, Bossy Wives, and Women Preachers*.[13] Enhanced by pictures of the author's daughters with their long hair, the book addressed what Rice thought were infractions of biblical practice. His opinion comes through loudly: "I have no doubt that millions will go to Hell because of the unscriptural practice of women preachers."[14]

Rice did not even approve of women teaching men on the mission field. He especially decried deputation at home by women missionaries who so often "prattle about dress and customs and food."[15] All this is part of "modern sissified churches."[16] After all, "God is a masculine God . . . God is not effeminate."[17] One of John R. Rice's daughters, Elizabeth Rice Handford, followed in the tradition with a book, *Me Obey Him?*[18] The answer, she says, is yes. However difficult it may be, wives must obey their husbands.

But to stop there would leave a one-sided picture of a truly remarkable man and his family. Rice wanted his daughters to learn theology and Greek. He encouraged theological discussions in their home. In time he strongly encouraged more women to enter active ministries. To that end, Rice, his wife, and three of their daughters with their husbands founded the Joyful Woman Ministries. These ministries include conferences for the instruction and encouragement of women—"Jubilees." A periodical, *The Joyful Woman*, begun in 1977, reached a circulation of 12,000–14,000 ten years later. Rice's surviving daughters—Jessie Sandford, Elizabeth Handford, and Joy Martin—are all in active ministries, as are their husbands.

P. B. Fitzwater, Charles C. Ryrie

Two works by evangelical scholars appeared at about this time. The significance of the first is that the author was the esteemed professsor of systematic theology at Moody Bible Institute, P. B. Fitzwater. Fitzwater distinguished between teaching with authority and other ministries. The former is not permitted to women, but Fitzwater did not consider other ministries to be forbidden. "Paul does not exhort all women to aspire to be preachers for he well knew that according to their constitution and sphere as wives and mothers, women of proper endowment, leisure, and undivided consecration, would be always the exception, rather than the rule."[19] For Fitzwater the reason women were not to be preachers was not some biblical prohibition, but rather their circumstances. "She may, if the gifts be hers, and she observe due restrictions, pray and speak to edification, exhortation and comfort in all suitable places except at the Lord's Table, where it is quite evident silence is her bound and duty." Thus, he affirms, "she may be . . . instructor of men . . . in short, in whatever she has ability for, except a pastoral head."[20] For Fitzwater the command to silence in 1 Corinthians 14 is not absolute: "He [Paul] is simply reproving abuses. . . ."[21]

For Charles C. Ryrie, on the other hand, "the exception was permitting women to speak in any capacity in public worship."[22] As for the subject of women's praying and prophesying in 1 Corinthians 11:5, "it appears that the fact the women prayed and prophesied at all was very extraordinary and probably limited to the Corinthian congregation. As has been pointed out, Corinth was a city of very loose standards."[23]

Thus we conclude . . . that the early church did not make a practice of permitting women to speak in their public meetings. That it may have been done in prayer and prophesying cannot be absolutely denied in every case, but it was decidedly the exception and not the general practice."[24]

Ryrie's opinion became widely influential. Fitzwater's moderate views seem to have been overshadowed by Ryrie's opinions, perhaps even at Fitzwater's own Moody Bible Institute.

The 1960s

Several significant contributions to the discussion on women were made during the 1960s. Germaine Greer's book *The Female Eunuch* appeared in 1971. The following quotations express her concern that women had allowed themselves to be demeaned: "Women are reputed never to be disgusted. The sad fact is that they often are, but not with men; following the lead of men, they are most often disgusted with themselves."[25] "The universal sway of the feminine stereotype is the single most important factor in male and female womenhatred."[26] "Self-sacrifice is the leitmotif of most of the marital games played by women. . . ."[27]

Karl Barth

At the other end of the spectrum were the opinions of the great neo-orthodox theologian Karl Barth. Although he had written his volume on the doctrine of creation more than ten years earlier, the English translation of this work did not appear until 1960. Barth's views on women were traditional. He affirmed a distinction between men and women both "physiologically and biblically." Barth's concept of the "I-Thou" encounter is discernible here. Man has strength, woman has weakness, but she is not inferior. There is "super- and subordination." God has established an order (taxis), with man having headship over woman, but woman must decide this freely on her own. Her subordination is primarily to the Lord.[28] Judging from a comment in Barth's How I Changed My Mind, this is one subject on which he did not change his mind.[29]

Betty Friedan

It was The Feminine Mystique by Betty Friedan,[30] however, that captured the widest attention. The "mystique" is an ideal of femininity that, Friedan felt, universally plagued women. It is a role that is defined by her relationship to her family and her service in the home. Friedan did what many others had not done: she listened. She heard the same things over and over again. "Sometimes a woman would say, 'I feel empty somehow, . . . incomplete.' Or she would say, 'I feel as if I don't exist.' . . . 'I call it the housewife's blight,' said a family doctor in Pennsylvania."[31] Friedan compared the plight of the woman in her home to that of prisoners in Nazi concentration camps. The solution was not to keep urging women to love their children more or to be more "feminine." Women have "autonomous interests of their own" that need to be recognized and fulfilled.

Naturally this apparent attack on traditional values of the home and of motherhood infuriated many people, especially Christians. The reactions were, to a large degree, justified, and Friedan later modified her views. But once again the tendency of Evangelicals was to react rather than to listen. If Friedan was right in regard to women's feelings about their traditional role as housewife, the mere restatement of that role by Christian teachers and preachers could hardly have been expected to win these disaffected women.

Krister Stendahl

Although specific interaction by Evangelicals was still to come, discussion was underway among biblical scholars. At about the time that Friedan's work appeared, Krister Stendahl, Dean of Harvard Divinity School, became the first New Testament scholar of international reputation to address this issue positively in a full-length book. The Bible and the Role of Women appeared in 1966 in a popular series of seminal works.[32]

Mary Daly

In the next several years the published flow of ideas increased dramatically. Shortly after the United Nations' "Declaration of Women's Rights," Kate Millett's turbulent book Sexual Politics was published. But this explosive work with its indictment of male use and abuse of women did not have as direct an effect on the church as did Mary Daly's work The Church and the Second Sex, first published in 1968 and published in a new edition in 1975 with a "New Feminist Post Christian Introduction."[33] Her work was directed to the situation in the Catholic Church, a situation that needed to "be purified of antifeminist notions and practices."[34]

Daly built on the ideological foundation of Simone de Beauvoir. She opened her first chapter with one of de Beauvoir's succinct comments: "Christian ideology has contributed no little to the oppression of women."[35] Daly noted that "those engaged in the struggle for the equality of the sexes have often seen the Catholic Church as an enemy. This view is to a large extent justified, for Catholic teaching has prolonged a tradition of woman which at the same time idealizes and humiliates her."[36]

A further statement by Daly ought to be heard because so much Christian literature on women attempts to affirm women simply by stressing positive words about their feminine qualities and their important role as wives and mothers. This can be patronizing and can miss the real feelings of women. Daly wrote:

> Proponents of equality charge that there is inexcusable hypocrisy in a species of ecclesiastical propaganda which pretends to put woman on a pedestal but which in reality prevents her from self-fulfillment and from active, adult-size participation in society. They point out that symbolic idealization tends to dupe women into satisfaction with the narrow role imposed upon them. Made to feel guilty or "unnatural" if they rebel, many have been condemned to a restricted or mutilated existence in the name of religion . . . so effective has the conservative pressure and propaganda been, that this idealizing ideology is accepted and perpetuated not only by countless members of the clergy, but

indeed by many women. Fascinated by an exalted symbol of "Woman," they are not disposed to understand the distress imposed upon countless real, existing women.[37]

Daly had originally intended to develop a restatement of essential Christian theology in feminist form. However, between the writing of *The Church and the Second Sex* and *Beyond God the Father: Toward a Philosophy of Women's Liberation*,[38] she became convinced that the male symbolism of God and Christ is impossible to separate from ontology. Revision of the language itself is insufficient. In a review, Carol P. Christ says:

> Daly views the characteristics of absolute transcendence and absolute power as reflections of a hierarchal and ultimately imperialistic patriarchal mentality. The Father, Son, and Spirit legitimate an "Unholy Trinity" of Rape, Genocide, and War in which unrestrained power forces the submission of "the other."[39]

Even to think of God as feminine is unsatisfactory because doing so maintains a sexual distinction that ought to be abrogated.

In her book *Beyond God the Father*, Daly included a chapter entitled, "Beyond Christolatry: A World Without Models." She claimed that it would "become less plausible to think of Jesus as 'the Second Person of the Trinity' who 'assumed' a human nature in unique 'hypostatic union.' Indeed, it is logical that the prevalent emphasis upon the total uniqueness and supereminence of Jesus will become less meaningful."[40] She then referred to the "Christian idolatry concerning the person of

Jesus" and said that it was "not likely to be overcome except through revolution that is going on in women's consciousness."[41]

Such a statement can lead an Evangelical who may hear of it to assume that all feminism is theologically heretical. Yet there are devout Evangelical thinkers today who do believe that some modification of sexist language is possible even as applied to God, but without destroying Christian orthodoxy. They would, however, reject the radical surgery that Mary Daly desires to perform on the doctrine of God and of Christology.

Naomi R. Goldenberg

Goldenberg wrote on the same issues that provoked Mary Daly. Her challenging book is called *Changing of the Gods: Feminism and the End of Traditional Religions*.[42] In a section entitled "What will happen to God?" she says:

> *I saw a problem.* How could women represent a male God? Everything I knew about Judaism and Christianity involved accepting God as the ultimate in male authority figures. . . . "and what would these women priests, ministers, and rabbis read to their communities?" I wondered. They could certainly not use the Bible. . . . "God is going to change," I thought. "We women are going to bring an end to God. . . . we will change the world so much that he won't fit in anymore."[43]

In this incisive, cleverly written analysis Goldenberg continues with a section entitled "Feminists are cooking up Götterdämmerung."[44] She begins, "The feminist movement in Western culture is engaged in the slow execution of Christ and Yahweh.

Yet very few of the women and men now working for sexual equality within Christianity and Judaism realize the extent of their heresy." Further, she says, "As a psychologist of religion, I do not agree that improving the position of women is a minor alteration in Judaeo-Christian doctrine. . . . The psychology of the Jewish and Christian religions depends on the masculine image that these religions have of their God. Under the heading "New Gods are coming," she says:

> There will of course be nothing to prevent people who practice new religions from calling themselves Christians or Jews. Undoubtedly many followers of new faiths will still cling to old labels. But a merely semantic veneer of tradition ought not to hide the fact that very nontraditional faiths will be practiced.[45]

Something of the flavor of Goldenberg's book can be gained by reading her comments on the Virgin Mary. She tells of seeing a statue of the Virgin Mary in Zurich on which someone had painted genitals. The artist, she muses,

> probably did not realize the political statement he or she was making. Mary has certainly been desexed in Christian tradition. The painter was restoring her sexuality. Obsession with purifying Mary of any taint of womanhood has occupied Christian scholars for centuries. Treatises on the Holy Mother's hymen abound in every Catholic research library. Theologians have insisted that Mary remained "intact" before, during [!] and after the birth of Jesus. . . . Mary is certainly the good girl of Christianity. . . . because of her absolute purity and obedience, she is the only pinup girl who has been

permitted in monks' cells throughout the ages. . . . Mary has been castrated by popes, cardinals, priests and theologians, by all who feel the sexual and emotional power of natural womanhood. We must be suspicious of all modern efforts to tout Mary as the "liberated woman of Christianity" as Pope Paul suggested in 1974.[46]

Goldenberg's racy language brings the point home. Whatever one may conclude about the varying viewpoints (they are certainly not uniform), they accomplish their avowed goal of "consciousness raising."

The Decade of the 1970s

The 1970s witnessed an increasing flow of substantial contributions to the subject of women in ministry. Rosemary Radford Ruether published her *Liberation Theology*[47] in 1972 and *New Woman, New Earth*[48] in 1975. In *Liberation Theology* Ruether presented a sequence of essays on various aspects of that subject. For Ruether, women's liberation was not to be isolated from other liberation concerns. Over the next decade, Ruether and others developed a hermeneutic (to be discussed in appendix A) that approaches the biblical texts in a way that we are now familiar with from liberation theology—i.e., from the standpoint of a disadvantaged people. One theological charge Ruether made in this earlier work was against Augustine for holding that woman possesses the image of God only together with man. This is an idea Ruether attributed to an underlying misogyny that characterizes Christianity in general.[49] Ruether's work will be discussed below in connection with her further writings.

The contrast between the different concepts of the issues and their solutions that marked the emerging literature of that period is seen in a comparison of Ruether's work with two others. In the same year that *Liberation Theology* appeared, Gladys Hunt published *Ms Means Myself*.[50] This was one of the first Evangelical Christian books intended to foster self-esteem among women. Her work was noncontroversial and personal, rather than confrontational and social. But in the next year an extreme work was published, the sort that provoked the ire of both traditionalists and Christian feminists. This was Jill Johnston's *Lesbian Nation*. Her statement that "the lesbian is *the* revolutionary feminist"[51] is the kind of language that has fostered the idea that lesbianism is a natural by-product of feminism.

C. S. Lewis

Hidden away in a book called *God in the Dock*, C. S. Lewis' essay "Priestesses in the Church" did not draw the attention it might have in another format.[52] Lewis, writing as an Anglican who believed in the ministry of the priest to represent not only people before God but God before people, could not conceive of a woman priest. Masculine imagery is appropriate for God. He is not like a woman and, therefore, a woman cannot represent him. Lewis did not enter into exegetical arguments on the nature and ministry of women. His extraordinary gift of imagination and his commitment to an Anglican view of priesthood dominated his thinking. That marvelous imagination also took over in his perceptions of sexuality in

Perelandra and *That Hideous Strength*. One feels rather than discerns the image of melody and rhythm for sexual differences.[53]

Gloria Steinem

One of the best-known names in the feminist movement is that of Gloria Steinem. One of her observations on women's employment parallels what has long been acknowledged with respect to the struggle of blacks for equal opportunity:

> We hear a lot about the first jockey or the first television anchorwoman, the first coal miner or Episcopal priest. What we don't hear is that these exceptions mean almost nothing to the lives of most women because they are still confined to female job ghettos. And so we get a false sense of progress from hearing only about the few exceptions allowed to enter almost totally male worlds.[54]

Since that article was written (in 1977) women have been able to attain to increasingly higher levels of business and professional life, but feminists see much more that needs to be accomplished. This situation has been paralleled in some, but far from all, religious hierarchies. During the period when Steinem and others were pressing for egalitarianism throughout society, evangelical works urging egalitarianism in church and home relationships began appearing with some frequency.

The Boldreys

In 1972 Richard and Joyce Boldrey wrote an article entitled "Women in Paul's Life,"[55] which was published as a book in 1976.[56] The Boldreys argued that although Paul's teaching is somewhat ambiguous, it is clear that the attitude of submission is intended to be mutual, an attitude all Christians should have to each other. The Boldreys believed in a totally egalitarian marriage and equality in ministry. In their opinion the prohibitions Paul placed on women's teaching were for the specific circumstances of women who had not yet matured in their doctrinal understanding. The quietness enjoined on them was the same as that commanded of the ignorant teachers in Titus 1:10–16 (who surely included males). In fact, the Boldreys pointed out, the verb Paul uses for silence in the Titus passage is stronger than the verbs he used for the silence he enjoins on women.[57] For the Boldreys, Paul was a radical, but his radicalism goes beyond not only traditionalism but feminism as well.

Robin Scroggs

Dialogues concerning women and the church, like those on other controversial issues, have been carried on in many different circumstances and media, such as books, articles, seminars, unpublished papers, and scholarly conventions. While the general public has often been aware only of well-advertised books, progress toward the understanding, if not the resolution, of issues continues unseen in quiet discussion. An example of this was the scholarly interaction with Robin Scroggs, whose significant article "Paul and the Eschatological Woman" appeared in 1972.[58] This was followed two years later by "Paul and the Eschatological Woman Revisited."[59]

Scroggs' second article was originally presented as a paper delivered at a panel discussion in the 1973 meeting of the American Academy of Religion. Elaine Pagels gave a paper at the same discussion in which she interacted with Scroggs' earlier work. The panel included several notable New Testament scholars. Both the AAR and the Society of Biblical Literature have for some years now had regular sectional meetings devoted to the study of women. The field was thus no longer confined to secularist writers and only a few biblical specialists. Biblical and theological scholars were recognizing increasingly the importance of this field of study.

Marabel Morgan

On the popular side, Marabel Morgan aired her ideas on husband-and-wife relationships in the now famous handbook *The Total Woman*. Reviewers enjoyed citing such passages as "For an experiment [greeting her husband at the door] I put on pink baby-doll pajamas and white boots after my bubble bath. . . . [He] chased me around the dining room table."[60] More telling than such descriptions, however, is the book's approach to wife-husband relationships. "I do believe it is possible," claimed Morgan, "for almost any wife to have her husband absolutely adore her in just a few weeks' time. . . . It really is up to her. She has the power."[61] Morgan has produced another book, *Total Joy*, but it has not gained the attention *The Total Woman* did.

Letha Scanzoni and Nancy Hardesty

In 1974 Scanzoni and Hardesty published their often cited work, *All We're Meant to Be*.[62] The title page describes this as "A Biblical Approach to Women's Liberation." Rather than being an academic study of the biblical texts or merely an Evangelical reaction to women's liberation, it was a persuasive presentation of the authors' understanding of Christian women in many dimensions. Topics such as singleness, menstruation, and masturbation found their way into the text. It boldly called for egalitarianism in marriage and in ministry. The arguments were not confined to a biblical or logical structure; a good deal of the material was drawn from life itself. For more traditional Christians, it posed a threat to what they considered biblical values. It still remains one of the most controversial books on the subject, but it has had considerable influence.

Ten years after the publication of this work, Scanzoni was interviewed by *Radix*. Asked about developments during this period, one troubling observation she offered was that "even the *single* woman is not to make any decision without a male head."[63] Scanzoni urged a balance between autonomy and attachment in relationships and a closer relationship between men and women without thoughts of subordination or dominance. Along with other observations she spoke of the strong opposition she and co-author Hardesty received on the publication of their book ten years previously.

Within a year after *All We're Meant to Be* appeared, Scanzoni's husband,

John, a sociologist, published a book entitled *Sex Roles, Life Styles, and Childbearing: Changing Patterns in Marriage and the Family*.[64] This scholarly, technical work suggested, among other things, that sex roles were largely formed before marriage but in some cases could be modified thereafter.

A growing phenomenon in the early 1970s was the proliferation of seminars on various topics, notably the "Institute in Basic Youth Conflicts," a creation of Bill Gothard. Gothard had realized that young people who were experiencing conflicts, particularly with their parents, needed help. He had considerable success in counseling young people and their parents, and his ministry developed into a continuing series of seminars across the country. At the very time when biblical scholars were questioning the traditional hierarchal view of the dominance of the husband over the wife, Gothard was teaching the "chain-of-command." His manual showed a symbol of God with two arms, one holding a hammer and the other holding a chisel under the hammer. The hammer was labeled "father," and the chisel, "mother." At the bottom was a diamond labeled "teen-ager." Gothard's teachings were sometimes radical; he taught, for example, that a twenty-one-year-old girl who was supporting herself and living away from home should follow the wishes of her non-churchgoing parents about marriage rather than her own judgment and that of her Christian boyfriend.[65]

Larry Christenson

The strong hierarchical views that characterized Gothard were also set forth in a book by Larry Christenson called *The Christian Family*.[66] His aim was to determine the biblical teachings about the family and to apply them appropriately. He began with a chapter on "God's Order for the Family," the first page of which incorporated a chart showing Christ as the head of the husband; the husband as head of the wife and authority over the children; the wife as the "help-meet" to the husband and "secondary authority" over the children; and then the children, who are obedient to their parents.

For Christenson the wife is "vulnerable" physically, emotionally, psychologically, and spiritually (although he later says that women's "stamina and emotional endurance are often greater" than men's). Because of this vulnerability, she "needs a husband's authority and protection."[67] "The wife is subject to spiritual attack." Her submissiveness to her husband is part of a "shield of protection against Satan's devices."[68] Women should not be "burdened with the authority and responsibility of decision."[69]

But suppose a woman has a husband who is not a believer. Rather than preaching to him, a wife might follow the suggestion of C. S. Lovett, says Christenson, to use "light" and "works" like the jaws of a nutcracker to "crack" his resistance. Above all, although a wife might take her husband to "hear the preaching of the Gospel," he warns that she should "not attempt to teach him herself. SUCH AN ATTEMPT WILL AND SHOULD FAIL"[70] (capital letters his).

Thus Christenson made a consistent application of his principle of women's subordination. The chapter concluded with this advice, "Wives, rejoice in your husband's authority over you! Be subject to him in all things. It is your special privilege to move under the protection of his authority."[71]

In a later chapter, "God's Order for Husbands," Christenson describes his views on the husband's authority: "It is a divine and spiritual authority which is rooted in the sacrifice of one's self."[72] Also "a husband who falls to lecturing his wife on her duty to be submissive to his authority has already yielded the ground of his authority."[73]

Paul K. Jewett

Thus far, the evangelical contributions assumed the integrity and complete authority of the Scriptures. A new dimension entered, however, when Paul K. Jewett published his work *Man as Male and Female*.[74] For Jewett the Pauline arguments for the restriction of women were inconsistent with the larger views expressed elsewhere in his epistles. The solution for him was that Paul's vision was at times limited by his own rabbinic training. He followed the insights of Karl Barth, that to be male and female is not merely an aspect of marriage but is especially what it means to be created in the image of God.

The implications that Jewett's appraisal of Paul's rabbinic viewpoint had for biblical infallibility were unacceptable to many Evangelicals, and this tended to blunt the effectiveness of his strong arguments. Nevertheless, Jewett made an important contribution to the discussion from the perspective of theology.

Jewett's related work, *The Ordination of Women*, published in 1980, contains mainly theological arguments rather than biblical exegesis on the subject. Jewett argues from the nature of women, the nature of the ministerial office, and the nature of God himself. Harvie M. Conn suggests that Jewett may have made a "tactical mistake" in trying to address both Protestants and Catholics in this book. "I personally suspect," says Conn, "that the understanding of ordination may be more central than Jewett has made it."[75] This point needs to be emphasized and will be taken up in appendix C. With the increasing discussion on the nature of ordination itself, the issue of women's ordination cannot be solved without a clear understanding of what that means and entails.

Dorothy Pape

In a totally different vein, Dorothy Pape wrote the fascinating book *In Search of God's Ideal Woman*.[76] The subtitle, *A Personal Examination of the New Testament*, accurately describes her approach. Drawing on her experience in a third-world country, Pape used common-sense arguments for the dignity and ministry of Christian women. She wrote in a first-person style, allowing the reader to follow her thoughts as she interacted with various scholars. One example: "With the exception of James Hurley's recent article, no commentator I have read has attempted to explain how exactly woman is the glory of man, though one suggested 'she is as moonlight to his sunlight' which does not sound very glorious."[77]

Pape pitted one scholar against another, a device that, despite her own acknowledged lack of skills to provide detailed exegetical analysis herself, does help the reader to understand the issues. Thus she quoted the Boldreys on the equality of Adam and Eve and set against their opinion that of Calvin in his declaration that women are "born to obey."[78] A good example of her approach is chapter 14, "Woman: The Weaker and More Sinful Sex?" She cited the Scriptures that are often mentioned in this connection and surrounded these with an array of opinions from commentaries, books, and a newspaper article and of insights from the values expressed in various contemporary cultures.

Elisabeth Elliot

Let Me Be a Woman, by Elisabeth Elliot was cast in the format of a series of essays addressed to her daughter, Valerie, in view of Valerie's approaching marriage.[79] The popularity of this author, along with the way the book enshrines traditional values in her superb literary style, gained for it a large readership. Among a variety of practical and devotional thoughts, Elliot offered some observations on differences between men and women: "Doesn't it seem strange that male dominance has been universal if it's purely social conditioning?"[80] There is no reference here to the statement that it is a consequence of the Fall that the husband would rule over his wife (Gen. 3:16). She dealt again, and more specifically, with the matter of hierarchy in a subsequent chapter: "The notion of hierarchy comes from the Bible. The words superior and inferior refer originally to position, not to intrinsic worth. A person sitting in the top of the stadium would be superior to—higher up than—a person on the front row."[81] She then showed that throughout the created universe there is orderliness and harmony.

Equality, in Elliot's opinion, is not a Christian ideal. She considered the idea that "all men are created equal" to be a "political one" but "marriage is one place where it doesn't belong at all. Marriage is not a political arena."[82] Quoting Aristotle on justice and "graded shares of honor, power, liberty, and the like," she illustrated the application of this in her own home where her father had the best chair in the living room. She concluded that "household justice was based on household authority."[83]

Elliot claimed that "submission for the Lord's sake does not amount to servility. It does not lead to self-destruction, the stifling of gifts, personhood, intelligence and spirit. . . . God is not asking anybody to become a zero."[84] Yet more recently she has said, "I believe all women are called to be spiritual mothers. By that, I mean prepared to give their lives for the life of the world, to be available to do the so-called dirty jobs, the menial jobs, the jobs nobody else wants to do."[85]

Virginia Ramey Mollenkott

On the other side, Virginia Ramey Mollenkott brought her analytical and literary mind to bear on feminist problems. She faces the question of sex language with regard to God. Her conclusion on this subject is moderate:

It might serve to remind us of the metaphoric nature of God-language if we follow the biblical practice of picturing God in feminine terms every once in a while. But it would serve no real purpose to switch completely to feminine pronouns and feminine references, because not only would we have to rewrite the Bible, but after a while we might forget all over again and begin to think of God as literally female.[86]

But Mollenkott alienated many Evangelicals by her contention that "some of the apostle Paul's arguments reflect his personal struggles over female subordination and show vestiges of both Greek philosophy (particularly Stoicism) and the rabbinical training he received from his own socialization and especially from Rabbi Gamaliel."[87] She restates this later in another context, suggesting that "according to his rabbinical training Paul believed in female subordination but according to his Christian vision he believed that the gospel conferred equality on all believers."[88]

Mollenkott is open in her recognition that such a view is a problem to many Evangelicals, who fear that "the admission will undercut the authority of Scripture and the doctrine of divine inspiration."[89] She specifically refers to the problems Jewett faced after the publication of his first book, but she was willing to put her own views on the line.

Patricia Gundry

The challenge launched by Patricia Gundry in *Woman, Be Free!*[90] concisely set forth both the concerns of contemporary Christian women and the issues churchmen tend to raise on the basis of various biblical texts. After discussing what woman is and what she is not, Gundry listed three "threats" to hold women down: "If you step outside your sphere (or role), (1) you will lose your femininity"; (2) "you will disrupt and destroy society"; and (3) "you are denying the inspiration of the Bible."[91]

Gundry sought to show how certain Scriptures have been used to deny women participation in church meetings and ministries. One example is 1 Timothy 2:11–15, which she calls the "single most effective weapon to keep women from active and equal participation in the church."[92] She pointed out that even those who are sure of the meaning of the first part and use it "as a proof text to prove woman's unsuitability for the public ministry" are uncertain as to verse 15. "Such snatch and chop prooftexting violates sound interpretive principles."[93] She proceeded to survey various interpretations offered, purposefully trying to show why one should not automatically accept the traditional understanding. Two works followed this—*Heirs Together, The Complete Woman* (based on Proverbs 31), and *Neither Slave nor Free.*[94]

Kevin Giles

In the same year a lesser-known but carefully thought-out study was published in Australia, under the title, *Women and Their Ministry: A Case for Equal Ministries in the Church Today.*[95] The author, Kevin Giles, writes lucidly in defense of women's ministry in the church. It is clear that his overriding concern is a proper interpretation of Scripture and a proper understanding of ministry. He is abreast of modern scholarship and is clearly Evangelical. His conclusion is that ministry is servanthood, the clergy-laity distinction is invalid, and the present rethinking of these issues should lead to a clearer picture of the place of women in ministry.

Don Williams

Yet another contribution to this theme appeared in 1977, *The Apostle Paul and Women in the Church*, by Don Williams.[96] Taking a plunge into the stream of thought that was current at the time of his writing, Williams started with a summary of several other books. His brief survey is worth paralleling here as a means of further summarizing some of the options that were available to writers in the 1960s and 70s and then hearing his response as one of the observers of the scene. He began with the "celestial love" that Helen Andelin says women should have for their husbands.[97] "The message is simple," says Williams: "Find out what a man wants and needs, give it to him and he will worship you forever." He notes that this book was in its twenty-second printing by 1973. Williams also offered Marabel Morgan's book *Total Woman* as an exhibit. This book, noted above, had appeared some eight years after Andelin's. Another popular Evangelical work touching on the relationship of a woman to her husband that Williams reviewed was Larry Christenson's *Christian Family*. By this time it had sold over 800,000 copies. Williams also reviewed Friedan, Scanzoni, and

Hardesty, and Jewett's book *Man as Male and Female*, all of which have been discussed above.

Williams asked several penetrating questions: If woman's role is "God-ordained to be that of wife and mother (Andelin, Morgan, Christenson), . . . what of the increasing number of single and professional women?"[98] If the wife derives all authority from the husband (Christenson), "how can there be spiritual equality and authority for the wife directly from Christ Himself: 'There is neither male nor female for you are all one in Christ Jesus' (Gal. 3:28)?"[99] Williams challenged Friedan's idea that women must be "liberated from wife/mother roles today to find their own identity" with this question: "If so, does this mean that personhood is found in new roles, rather than in the self and especially in the self related to God?"[100] To Scanzoni and Hardesty he directed this question: "Is the Biblical ideal the transcendence of our sexuality . . . ? If so, why did God create us male and female to begin with?"[101] The question he asked of Jewett was: "Does Paul's understanding of 'hierarchy' stand in conflict with the idea of 'partnership'. . . . If so, on what ground may we choose one over the other?"[102]

Williams's work shows the kind of issues that were developing in the late 1970s. His response was to go through the major New Testament texts relating to women in the church. His interpretation of these texts was essentially feminist, but, it is important to note, it was also moderate. Examples: 1 Corinthians 11 teaches that "in the realization of redemption the old orders of creation and nature have been broken through. Women now have spiritual gifts to be exercised in the church and in the Lord. Their equality with men is understood."[103] The veiling of women is a "cultural custom . . . against radical assertion of women's freedom which would offend both Jew and Gentile and make Christian women scandalous to the culture."[104] With regard to Ephesians 5 and the submission of the wife, William's position is that "while Paul maintains the traditional hierarchal structure of the submission of wives to their husbands he modifies it by mutual submission and changes the content."[105]

Further, for Williams, 1 Timothy 2 is a temporary restriction on women. Paul is not saying, "I never permit," but rather, "I am not permitting"—a conclusion based on Paul's use of the present tense. Like many interpreters since, Williams thought that there were certain reasons why women in that situation only were not permitted to teach. In his judgment this is because the women converts would have had very little previous instruction and therefore would not be suitable teachers.[106]

In spite of his moderately feminist understanding of the texts, in his concluding chapter Williams did not completely abandon traditional ideas: "It is clear from Paul's letters that women are to function in the hierarchy of authority."[107] However, since men are to follow the example of Christ in their headship, they give themselves to women and therefore "rather than the subjugation of women under the male ego, women are lifted to a new position as the hierarchy is infused with new content by Christ Himself."[108] He there-fore advocated a new "partnership" between men and women in the church. To bar women from "the pulpit, the seminary lecture hall, and the pastor's office only weakens the church. . . ."[109] Williams, like Giles, challenges the barring of women from ordination. " 'Ordination' as we understand it today is far different from [that of] the early church where there was no clergy-laity distinction. There was only a distinction in gifts, and since women as well as men were and are gifted for ministry, they must be allowed to use their gifts."[110]

Lucia Sannella

In stark contrast to the more mild approaches stands a challenge by Lucia Sannella in her book *The Female Pentecost*.[111] A brief sample will suffice:

> The assumption here is that the male is naturally endowed by reason of his genitals with a superior spiritual perception with which he must lead the frail and sin-prone woman. . . . Woman's so-called "sin" must never be forgiven or forgotten. Her subjection is to be an eternal prison; a cosmic criminal. . . . Now here is where Eve gets decapitated so as to hand over her head (her intellect), intelligence, and spiritual discernment to Adam. Woman has . . . become a mindless womb."[112]

These strong words serve to alert those who teach and preach a traditional view of women to the way their proclamations are being perceived by those who do not share their convictions. What seems fair to some preachers because it seems biblical and familiar is often conceived of by many others as totally unfair, unreasonable, and dehumanizing to women.

George W. Knight III

What George Knight has written concerning the New Testament teaching on the role relationship of men and women[113] provides, in the opinion of Harvie Conn, an example of this problem. Conn wrote with concern of the "narrowing of perceptions" that "gives the 'traditionalist' more the appearance of a knee-jerk reaction agent. And for those outside any Christian camp at all it reduces further any desire to listen."[114]

Knight's material was on two related topics, the only ones mentioned in the table of contents: "submission and headship." Man is to rule both at home and in the church. These concerns, which provide occasion for considerable criticism of opposing views, were addressed with a particular ecclesiastical structure in mind, that of the Reformed tradition. His inclusion of an appendix discussing the Reformed Ecumenical Synod show his special concern for a particular segment of the church with its own view of church polity. The sharpness and defensiveness of Knight's arguments must be seen against that concern. (James Hurley has similar concerns in his more moderate and comprehensive work.)

Knight's appendix deals especially with the concept of "office." For Knight the concept of "office" in the church is important in assigning the role of women. In large measure, those who hold to a traditional view of office and of ordination (especially Roman Catholics, though not Anglicans) seem to have a greater difficulty with the ministry of women than do those who stress servanthood and spiritual function over office. Entire denominations of various theological persuasions are making decisions about the ministry of women and are seeking guidelines for these decisions. Those outside the Christian faith are observing the discussion, often allowing their perception of the sensitivity of Christian writers to women's concerns to shape their opinion of Christianity itself. Harvie Conn, according to the comments referred to above, is clearly worried about the impression that Evangelical works such as Knight's are making on those of other persuasions.

Knight's work has been reissued in a revised edition.[115] There is little revision except for an appendix by Wayne Grudem on the meaning of headship. Knight also published an article on the verb *authenteō* in 1 Timothy 2:12.[116]

Phyllis Trible and John Otwell

Although traditionalists have sometimes failed to distinguish between differing feminist positions, feminists have certainly not been united on their approach to Scripture. Some have consciously departed from the Judeo-Christian tradition and its Scriptures. Others, like Phyllis Trible, have sought to understand both positive and what they considered negative patriarchal attitudes in the Bible. Still others focused on what they saw as positive biblical passages. Trible pioneered feminist study of the Old Testament in her book *God and the Rhetoric of Sexuality*.[117] She sought to uphold feminism but also to retain the relevance of the Old Testament. Trible continued her feminist study of the Old Testament with a book published in 1984, *Texts of Terror*.[118]

The Old Testament had also received attention in John Otwell's book *And Sarah Laughed*.[119] Otwell seeks to show that the Old Testament is not as negative as some have proposed. One of the assumptions of feminists in their study of Scripture is that the outlook of the biblical writers (as well as that of the characters in the biblical narratives) is patriarchal. That is to say, male dominance of the family and of society in general was considered the norm, and thus all the biblical writings are colored (if not distorted, as many claim) by this outlook.

Leonard and Arlene Swidler and Evelyn and Frank Stagg

The Swidlers edited a collection of biblical, theological, and historical articles relating to the Roman Catholic priesthood, specifically women priests.[120] Leonard Swidler had previously published a book entitled *Women in Judaism*[121] and later surveyed the whole body of biblical literature, including the so-called intertestamental works, to gather positive material on women in *Biblical Affirmations of Women*.[122] A further source book for biblical material, this time on the New Testament, and one that was likewise co-authored by a man and a woman was *Woman in the World of Jesus* by Frank and Evelyn Stagg.[123] This book offered useful information on the ministry and teachings of Jesus.

The works by these four authors took their place among the growing number of co-authored works by men and women who combined their insights to broaden the dimensions of their publications. The Staggs and the Swidlers also contributed to the breadth of the discussion by providing insights from Roman Catholic and Southern Baptist viewpoints respectively.

S. Scott Bartchy

The former director of the Institute for the Study of Christian Origins at Tübingen in Germany, S. Scott Bartchy, touched on some basic issues in his article "Power, Submission, and Sexual Identity Among the Early Christians."[124] Bartchy focused on the misuse of power, not only by women, but also by men, as being antithetical to the spirit of Christian service as taught by both Jesus and Paul. Paul's restrictions in 1 Timothy 2:12 had to do, not with women teachers as such, but with the content of their teaching. Bartchy followed that up with some unpublished materials and also with "Human Sexuality and Our Identity," a remarkably succinct presentation of the topic in an expanded outline form.[125] A somewhat similar outline emphasizing the same theme of the rejection of hierarchical power appeared the next year in the *TSF Bulletin*.[126]

Linda Mercadante

The history of interpretation can be a useful check of the validity of one's own approach to problematic texts. Reference is sometimes made, in the course of a discussion of some disputed point, to "the commentaries" that support this or that position. But commentaries are human productions and tend to reflect ideas prevailing at the time. A survey of commentaries on a particular text over a long period of time can reveal such settings and the resultant (sometimes subjective) conclusions. Linda Mercadante, a student at Regent College at that time, published a penetrating thesis on the history of the interpretation of the 1 Corinthians passages on women.[127] It has deservedly received wide attention.

Catherine and Richard Kroeger

Several stimulating and original articles have appeared from the pens of the Kroegers. Two essays appeared in 1978: "Pandemonium and Silence at Corinth" and "Sexual Identity in Corinth."[128] Catherine Kroeger followed these in the next year with the article "Ancient Heresies and a Strange Greek Verb."[129] The purpose of these articles was to show how an understanding of the cultural background helps to explain the restrictions Paul placed on women. The first two dealt with the religion and society of Corinth, the third with 1 Timothy 2:12 and the rare verb *authentein*, usually translated "to have [or "usurp," KJV] authority." She suggested that *authentein*—which had at times been associated with sexual aggression, suicide, and murder—signified here a crude or hostile attitude. This last article drew both positive and negative reactions and has had considerable influence. Kroeger has continued her research into the use of *authentein* in Greek literature but, apart from a brief treatment in an essay on 1 Timothy,[130] she has not published her conclusions.

The Shaping of Issues in the 1980s

Stephen B. Clark

Several comprehensive works appeared in the early 1980s. The longest of these, having 753 pages, was a work by Stephen B. Clark, *Man and Woman in Christ*.[131] Clark, a Roman Catholic, seeks to apply the social sciences to feminist issues. In his preface he claims that "much of the modern feminist movement in church and society is advocating measures that would destroy social roles that have performed a useful function in all of past societies. At the same time they seem to be unaware that their proposals lead to a restructuring of the very bases of our society."[132]

A volume of this length is difficult to work through, and it is also difficult for a nonspecialist in the social sciences to evaluate. It seems almost unfair to relate his conclusions without providing some of the substance of his argumentation. Nevertheless, conclusions are important, and among his are these:

There should be a system for raising people in the Lord with men having primary responsibility for men, and women for women. . . . There should be a system of personal subordination among the Christian people with the elders (heads) of the community chosen from among the men and the husbands serving at the head of the family, with women in complementary positions of leadership and subordinate government. . . . The role of "deaconess" and other female leadership roles should be restored in the Christian community. . . . There should be cultural expressions of role differences for men and women. . . . Each attempt to apply the scriptural teaching on men's and women's roles, inside or outside the Christian community, should be guided by local cultural considerations.[133]

It is interesting that this proponent of hierarchical relationships thinks contemporary Christians should "be guided by local cultural considerations," while some others of the same viewpoint think culture can play no role in the understanding of the first-century biblical texts.

Elizabeth Tetlow

A slender volume next to Clark's massive work, *Women and Ministry in the New Testament*, is a concisely written book by Elizabeth Tetlow.[134] Clark's work touched on ordination but that was not its focus; Tetlow, on the other hand, was concerned with the issue of ministry. Clark is traditional, Tetlow is feminist, and she uses what has come to be known as "feminist hermeneutics." Her work will be discussed further in appendix A.

Susan T. Foh and James B. Hurley

Two books by conservative writers, both graduates of Westminster Seminary, appeared within a year of each other. Susan Foh wrote *Women and the Word of God* as a response to Christian feminism.[135] Foh is more traditional than Hurley, but not so strongly so as Knight. Hurley's *Man and Woman in Biblical Perspective* is more comprehensive in its sweep of Scripture and has gained more attention.[136]

Both Foh and Hurley showed themselves capable of careful exegesis, although in taking a traditionalist stand on complex and controversial passages it is not surprising that they have been heavily challenged. Foh acknowledged the cultural dimensions of women's roles, but minimized the importance of culture in the interpretation of Scripture (see appendix A). Foh did interact with other scholars, though, as Harvie Conn observed with regard to Foh and the issue of Evangelical egalitarianism: "It is here she cannot match the scope of Scanzoni and Hardesty's work. She has not really seen the cultural woods for the egalitarian trees."[137]

This same reviewer called Hurley's work "by far, the fairest and best of the hierarchical statements. . . ." Hurley takes the reader through a survey of ancient Near Eastern culture and the Old Testament, through Judaism in New Testament times and the role of women in the New Testament, through detailed discussion of various key texts, and toward the discussion and attempted resolution of basic issues. Having written an article on head coverings,[138] he naturally included a fine discussion of that in this book. A useful feature at the end of his work is a series of case studies in which he describes several hypothetical situations involving the role of women and seeks to apply his principles to them.

The issue of culture is important in connection with Hurley's work as with others just cited. Linda Mercadante wrote:

There is clear evidence of a distinct accommodation to the cultural realities of the changing, improving status

421

of women. This is reflected in the exegesis of the very theologians who would be the first to throw the stones of "cultural accommodation" at those who insist the Bible does not support female subordination.[139]

In her review of Hurley, Mercadante noted that Calvin "justified the subordination of women by claiming the innate superiority of men" and that "Charles Hodge based this same hierarchy on the contention that man, but not woman, was given dominion over creation." She noted that Hurley holds, as they did, the subordination of women to a God-ordained male dominance, but disagrees with their reasons.[140]

Mercadante offered trenchant criticisms of Hurley's work, and some of these will be mentioned here to illustrate several of the issues that need careful consideration. She cited Hurley's failure to recognize a different verbal formula in the pre- and post-Fall instances of Adam's naming of Eve, thereby missing the fact that "dominance of man over woman will now be one of the sinful conditions of fallen humanity." She is uneasy with such terminology as "dominant partner" and "to whom submission is due." In addition, she claimed that Hurley did not apply his own observations on Jesus' example to the issues.

Kari Torjesen Malcolm

Another European has written a work in English. Kari Torjesen Malcolm had Norwegian parents but was born in China. Her work, *Women at the Crossroads* sought to avoid both the traditional and the feminist viewpoints:

Each side has its cheerleading squad. The conservative church waves her arms with the traditionalists and shouts, "Men, be men. Don't give an inch. God is on your side . . . your side . . . your side." Women's liberation also has its cheerleaders. They shout with even more vehemence, "Women, it's your turn to run the show. Don't lose the ground we've gained. Stand firm . . . stand firm . . . stand firm."[141]

Malcolm combined references to women in church history, some comments on Scripture, observations from her broad international experience, and a good deal of warm spiritual encouragement to women. She expressed concern about the number of women who desire to serve God, while, at the same time, there are desperate needs in the world that are not being fulfilled. If women were given more scope for ministry, there would be both a greater fulfillment of their desire to serve and a greater filling of the vast existing needs. Malcolm believes that the Great Commission is calling women from lesser involvements to world evangelization. She has a concern for single as well as married women. The book is not intended to stir controversy. Feminists would think it too mild, but it brings a challenge and encouragement to Christian women.

E. Margaret Howe

Women and Church Leadership by E. Margaret Howe[142] is different from any other work considered thus far. Howe devotes part of the book to considering the major biblical texts. There is little that is ideologically new in Howe's work; its value lies in its appraisal of the contemporary scene. Although one reviewer found reason to criticize her exegesis and statistical methods in gathering information,[143] Howe made a valuable contribution in providing a chapter on the feelings of women in seminary, and another chapter on the present-day attitudes toward the ordination of women in various church groups, along with some historical and biblical material and the personal observations of the author.

The book represents an important phase in changing perspectives on women. The numbers of women in seminaries have been increasing significantly. Many of them are frustrated both in seminary and on graduation as they face severely limited opportunities for ministry. Many of these women find themselves in a tension between traditional teachings and denominational positions on the one hand and an inner sense of the call of God on the other. It must be granted that the latter can be subjective and false, whether it is in the experience of women or of men. But it remains true, as is abundantly illustrated in the preceding chapters, that many women have been convinced that God has given them gifts and called them, whatever church officials may say. In the quest for trends and patterns, one reality certainly stands out beyond question: the dilemma of the woman who feels called of God but who is refused opportunity to respond to her sense of call.

Mary J. Evans

In 1983 Mary J. Evans' survey appeared, advertised as an "overview of all the crucial passages on women's roles," a work that David M. Scholer called "the best book in support of women in ministry written from an evangelical perspective with a commitment to careful exegesis."[144] Originally written as a thesis under the direction of Donald Guthrie at London Bible College, it deals briefly and thoughtfully with a great many Scriptures on the topic. Evans takes pains to present opposing views, deal with exegetical data, and reach conclusions on an impressive number of key passages. The footnotes and bibliography are extensive, making this a good reference work for further study.[145]

Willard M. Swartley

A unique contribution was made by Willard M. Swartley in a book called *Slavery, Sabbath, War, and Women*, published in 1983.[146] Swartley reviewed arguments on different sides of the issues named in his title. He found remarkably similar approaches used in the discussions. Those who upheld slavery in the nineteenth century, for example, believed they had Scripture on their side, that it was "divinely sanctioned among the patriarchs," and that it was "recognized and approved by Jesus Christ and the apostles." Proof texts from the Bible were freely quoted, just as certain texts are today regarding the role of women. Abolitionists, by contrast, "gave priority to theological principles and basic moral imperatives, which in turn put slavery under moral judgment. The point we should learn from this is that theological principles and basic moral imperatives should be primary biblical resources for addressing social issues today."[147]

Such a statement naturally will be welcomed by those who emphasize that the general tenor of Scripture supports women's ministry. Swartley, however, did not sell out to one side or the other. Rather, he issued a caution:

> It is striking to note how one's position affects and even determines what one sees in the text. The emphasis on female subordination permeated the hierarchical commentary, but the word "subordination" occurs *only once* in the texts cited above, and that is in a text (I Cor. 14:34) which counts least in the hierarchical argument, precisely because its apparent call for women to be silent in worship is an injunction that even the most thoroughgoing hierarchical interpreters cannot accept as normative policy. On the other hand, emphasis on equality permeates the liberationist's commentary, but such a word occurs nowhere in the various texts cited. One may argue, however, that the concept of equality is present, but this raises an even longer agenda [i.e., the meaning of equality].[148]

Rosemary Radford Ruether

One of the most prominent theologians of the feminist movement is Rosemary Radford Ruether. Mention was made earlier of her 1972 work, *Liberation Theology* and of *New Woman, New Earth* (1975). Among many of her other contributions, she has authored an article entitled "Misogynism and Virginal Feminism in the Fathers,"[149] co-edited *Women of Spirit: Female Leadership in the Jewish and Christian Traditions*,[150] written *Sexism and God-Talk*,[151] contributed a chapter, "Feminist Theology and Spirituality" to the volume *Christian Feminism*[152] and compiled

Womanguides: Readings Toward a Feminist Theology.[153]

Like other feminists, Ruether views the Bible as clothed in patriarchy, yet she does not want to discard Christianity as she understands it. For her, God is "the transcendent matrix of Being that underlies and supports both our own existence and our continual potential for being." The task of the feminist theologian is laid out as follows:

> The sexist bias of patriarchal theology . . . must be evaluated as blasphemous ratification of sin in God's name. . . . Feminist theology engages in a systematic reconstruction of all the symbols of human relation to God to delegitimize sexist bias and to manifest an authentic vision of redemption as liberation from sexism.[154]

Other religions also provide insights for Ruether. She finds "usable tradition" in a number of religious sources. As with many other feminists who remain within the sphere of Christianity, she is not at ease with some orthodox concepts that many consider crucial. Regarding the maleness of Christ, she distinguishes between "Jesus as the Christ thought of as an ontological necessity" and "as a historical particularity." "The symbol of Christ must not be encapsulized in Jesus, as though he alone represented a perfect kind of humanity. . . . Jesus' humanity points beyond himself to the new humanity that is indeed both male and female and includes all people of every time and place."[155] It is difficult to summarize or typify the ideas of such a prolific thinker in a few words, but, as with others surveyed on these pages, a few sentences can provide some idea of the distinctive perspectives of significant scholars as well those as of popular commentators on the present scene.

Elisabeth Schüssler Fiorenza

There is probably no feminist theologian and biblical scholar whose works, especially *In Memory of Her*[156] have been as widely discussed today as that of Elisabeth Schüssler Fiorenza.[157] An idea of the focus of her studies in this area can be gained by mention of several titles of articles published over a period of years. One of these, which provided copious references to source materials, was "Women in the Pre-Pauline and Pauline Churches."[158] Another, which was published in Germany, was *"Die Beitrag der Frau zur urchristlichen Bewegung. Kritische Überlegung zur Rekonstruction urchristlicher Geschichte."*[159] She also published a collection of her essays, including "Women–Church: The Hermeneutical Center of Feminist Biblical Interpretation"; "The Functions of Scripture in the Liberation Struggle: A Critical Feminist Hermeneutics and Liberation Theology"; "Remembering the Past in Creating the Future: Historical-Critical Scholarship and Feminist-Critical Interpretation"; and "Toward a Critical-Theological Self-Understanding of Biblical Scholarship."[160]

The title of Fiorenza's major work, *In Memory of Her*, was taken from Jesus' comment about the woman who anointed him, of whom he said, "Truly I say to you, wherever the gospel is preached in the whole world, what she has done will be told in memory of her" (Mark 14:9 RSV).

Fiorenza began by noting that although the name of the man who betrayed Jesus is well known, the name of the woman who did this is forgotten because she was a woman. Fiorenza's approach is indicated by the subtitle: *A Feminist Theological Reconstruction of Christian Origins.* She uses what has come to be called a "feminist hermeneutic." This calls for careful attention, and so will be considered further in appendix A.

An Inclusive-Language Lectionary

This lectionary[161] is a selection of readings for the church year produced by the National Council of Churches and is intended for "experimental and voluntary use in churches." It has stirred a large amount of controversy because of its substitution of inclusive (i.e., nonsexist) language for God. It is important to read the appendix, repeated at the back of each volume, which explains the reasons for the wording, along with examples. Wherever the term *Father* is used for, or in connection with other terms for, *God,* the *Lectionary* has "[*God*] the Father [*and Mother*]." (The italics are not for emphasis but, as in some versions of the Bible, to indicate added words.) "Lord" becomes "Sovereign"; "Son of God" is rendered "Child of God"; "Son of Man" is now "Human One." In addition, "Kingdom," because of the masculine, "king-," becomes "Realm"; "Brethren" (which, as an address usually applies to both men and women) is variously translated "Sisters and Brothers," "Friends," or "Neighbors." Where a man's name is used in connection with the birth or descent of children, the wife's name is added to the text. Thus Matthew 3:9 becomes "We have Abraham as our Father [*and Sarah and Hagar as our mothers*]."[162]

The effect of these changes is seen especially in doctrinal passages. John 1:18 now reads in part, "We have beheld the Word's glory, glory as of the only Child from [*God*] the Father [*and Mother*]. Such renderings are related to the issue of feminine characteristics of God, a subject that will receive attention in appendix A on theology.

Beverly LaHaye

This energetic national director of Concerned Women of America and wife of a popular minister has written several books from a traditionalist and strongly antifeminist viewpoint. Her concerns and opinions developed largely from her observation of the agendas of those involved in the International Women's Year, the International Year of the Child, and of course, the ERA movement.[163] In *The Restless Woman*[164] LaHaye described the present period as "the last days" and challenged the feminist activists who appealed to restless women searching for their identity. She selected several early feminists as examples and found some "common threads of thought," such as "hatred of God and authority figures," "rebellion based on selfishness," "disdain for family life and children," and "a commitment to atheism or spiritualism."[165] One of LaHaye's major thrusts has been to lay the blame for the breakdown of the family at the door of the feminists. Concern for the family also led her husband, Tim LaHaye, to write *The Battle for the Family*.[166] In *The Restless Woman* venereal disease, divorce, abortion, and teenage suicide are all blamed on feminism or on the sexual revolution.[167] Career women are especially vulnerable. LaHaye's work takes its place in the succession of concerned writings over the past many decades that saw deterioration developing from such changes as women having the right to vote, working outside the home, and gaining higher education. The complexity of social issues makes simple cause-and-effect hard to determine. Many Evangelicals would, however, identify with LaHaye's troubled spirit over present conditions.

Not all, on the other hand, would agree with LaHaye's attitudes toward the feminists themselves. She writes about the "sick ideas espoused by the leaders of the feminist movement. . . . They have grown up filled with paranoia and impulsive hatred. . . . In a very real sense these women are mentally disturbed. . . . This kind of disturbed woman puts our society in danger. . . . The unhappy women are all feminists."[168] In contrast to this, one might note the comment of another Evangelical woman who shares LaHaye's concerns over the need of contemporary women for a sense of self-identity. Dee Jepsen, who, as a special assistant to President Reagan, had many opportunities to interact with women of different viewpoints, said, "Labeling each other liberal, conservative, feminist, traditionalist, only divides; it does not unite. People don't fit into neat, tidy little labeled boxes. We are not merchandise. We are human beings, unique, special—each one of us."[169]

John W. Robbins

Whereas LaHaye is a traditionalist against feminists, John W. Robbins is a traditionalist against traditionalists. He cites several writers who are well to the "right" of most scholars dealing with women's issues today and castigates them for not being conservative enough. In his *Scripture Twisting in the Seminaries, Part I: Feminism*,[170] Robbins heavily criticized George W. Knight III, Susan T. Foh, and James B. Hurley for what is in his opinion a distortion of Scripture. Others were likewise criticized, while the revered Benjamin Warfield was quoted against "heretics," presumably in reference to those with whom Robbins disagrees. Prior to the introduction, on a separate page, there is a quotation from Benjamin Warfield, a staunch conservative theologian of an earlier day at Princeton. Warfield wrote that anyone who "modifies the teachings of the Word of God" is "already, in principle, a 'heretic.'" Robbins did not provide the source of this quotation, so it is impossible to know if Warfield had the subject of women's ministry in mind when he wrote it. The implication, however, is that those who disagree with Robbins' interpretation of Scripture are heretics. He also quotes his late associate, Gordon H. Clark, in a statement that begins with such phrases as "the persuasive influence of liberalism" and "apostate denominations," and then he warns, "Too many seminaries and denominations slip into apostasy almost imperceptibly."[171]

Eminent Christian leaders—such as James Packer, Carl Armerding, John Gerstner, and W. A. Criswell— who endorse Hurley's book "either did not read Hurley's book" or "their understanding of and adherence to Scripture is as defective and inconsistent as Hurley's." Robbins thought it necessary to introduce the former views of Westminster Seminary professor Bruce Waltke on the subject of Exodus 21 and abortion into a discussion on whether Paul's teaching on women applies only to church meetings. Although Hurley had affirmed three times in his book on women that he accepts the Bible as the "Word of God, written," Robbins asserted, in oversize boldface type, "Nowhere in his book of 271 pages does Hurley affirm that the Bible is infallible and inerrant." Further, "neither George Knight nor James Hurley believes what the Bible teaches about the silence of women in church."[172]

Robbins showed a concern for careful exegesis, though he centered attention on the restrictive verses rather than viewing the whole sweep of the Scriptures relative to women. Unlike LaHaye, who thought that the sexual revolution shared blame with the feminist movement for contemporary social abuses, Robbins wrote sweepingly of the "women's movement, with all its attendant evils— child abuse, promiscuity, adultery, homosexuality, abortion and divorce."[173] Robbins' position is based in part on his particular concept of authority. He thinks Foh is wrong for holding that the diaconate does not possess authority as do elders and teachers. He also believes that Knight and Hurley are wrong for thinking that Paul distinguished preaching from prophesying, allowing women to do the latter.[174]

At the end of the book Robbins

appended two articles by Gordon H. Clark, one on the ordination of women and the other on the Presbyterian doctrine of ordination. It is here that one can place Clark and Robbins in their proper stream of thought. "Note well that ordination confers authority to preach, administer the sacraments, and exercise discipline."[175] This concept of ordination and its relevance to the ordination of women is crucial in Robbins' thought and in that of several other scholars who have been previously noted.

Sheldon Vanauken

Much to the chagrin of Bible scholars, popular opinion is typically formed, not by detailed exegesis, but by forceful writing and first-person sincerity. The author of the widely acclaimed book *A Severe Mercy*, Sheldon Vanauken, has chronicled his departure from feminism in a thirty-eight-page chapter of narrative and observations in *Under the Mercy*.[176] The change began in the last year of his wife, Davy's, life, when she "began to desire to be, not a 'comrade-lover' but a *wife*."[177] His own transformation took time. The strength of his growing convictions regarding women and the church was already seen in the title of an article he wrote in 1978: "Since God Doesn't Make Mistakes: WOMEN'S 'ORDINATION' DENIES THE INCARNATION" (emphasis his).[178]

The line of argument seems to be that Jesus was God incarnate and did his Father's will perfectly. Since he did not appoint any women apostles, it is clearly not God's will for a woman to be a priest. If Jesus were wrong in that matter, he could not be God incarnate. Vanauken insisted,

> I am not . . . hostile to women. I do not for a moment believe that men are superior to women—only different. . . . [They are] equal in importance as a nut and bolt are entirely equal without being identical—and doing a job together that neither two bolts nor two nuts could do.[179]

This kind of metaphor is appealing. But an evaluation of Vanauken's work must put alongside this analogy the kind of reasoning that assumes that the absence of women apostles necessarily means there can be no women priests. Whether or not one accepts the conclusion, the way it is reached is part of the package.

Ronald and Beverly Allen

Yet another example of Evangelicals who are trying to assess the contemporary scene and provide guidance for Christians is the husband-and-wife team of Ronald and Beverly Allen. They produced a comprehensive, easy-to-read survey of feminism and biblical texts.[180] Their book, *Liberated Traditonalism*, is significant in being an attempt by Evangelicals to provide a guide through conflicting claims. The book is part of the *Critical Concerns* series of Multnomah Press. It is not intended to be a study of the biblical texts. Rather, it offers clear opinions under clever captions without discussion of the exegetical data. This helps the reader to grasp the authors' interpretation of the key texts without getting bogged down in working through the issues. The authors tend to be warmer to traditionalists than to feminists, but depart from the traditionalist position in significant ways.

Gilbert Bilezikian

Gilbert Bilezikian's book *Beyond Sex Roles*[181] was attracting considerable attention among Evangelicals shortly after its publication. The reason for this is undoubtedly that Bilezikian wrote a clear, forthright argument for a Christian feminist position. This characteristic has also drawn criticism, as some consider the clearly stated conclusions to be at times overdrawn. A minor, but significant example is in a section on the appearance of women in the parables and other teachings of Jesus: Bilezikian concluded, "In His own teaching ministry, Jesus made use of women as teachers."[182] One reader, in a personal comment, remarked that actually the women were examples and illustrations, not teachers. Taken as a point of detail, the use of the word *teacher* is perhaps unfortunate. Seen, however, as part of the whole, the fact that Jesus did refer so often to women in his teachings *does* have significance, as Bilezikian recognizes.

It is this kind of insight that will commend the book to many who are looking for support in their concept of women. Although debate over the book will probably center on the interpretation of specific texts, one section has special value that may be overlooked. The conclusion offers practical and sensitive suggestions for the improvement of mutual attitudes and relationships between men and women. This is transparently the goal of the author.

Elaine Storkey

The same concern that Bilezekian had is expressed in one of a number of penetrating chapters in the outright Christian feminist work *What's Right With Feminism* by Elaine Storkey.[183] Her discussion of the question "Is God the Father?" is, like the rest of her book, conducted in a balanced, sensitive manner. While not a theological work, it does not neglect theology.[184]

Storkey is not ready for easy answers. Her recognition of complexity where it truly exists helps the reader to break through ideological patterns in the search for truth. The following statement illustrates this: "It has often been supposed that a discussion of women and the Church is, in the end, about the ordination of women. I hope I have shown that the issues are more complex than that."[185] She has indeed shown the complexity of the issues, working through early chapters like "The Feminist Case" to "Some Christian Responses" and what she calls "A Third Way." This last chapter presents not only her synthesis, but also a posing of yet more questions. This invitation to think and to apply characterizes Storkey's approach—a needed one.

David Scholer

The dean of Northern Baptist Seminary, David Scholer, has been in the forefront of Christian feminist studies for some years. Since his contributions have been in the form of articles and scholarly dialogues, rather than in a single book, the significance of his work may not be as apparent to the nonspecialist as it is to those who have interacted with him in scholarly circles. One example of his approach to the issues is found in a series of articles he has written.[186] These covered a number of the relevant passages in an open dialogic manner. Scholer concluded that it was his "deepest conviction that the full evidence of Scripture and an understanding of balance and consistency in interpretation mean that we must rethink some of our traditions and reaffirm with clarity and conviction the biblical basis for the full participation of women in the ministries of the church."[187]

Scholer wrote an informative article entitled "Women's Adornment," which provided excellent background materials for understanding references in Scripture to the clothing, jewelry, and hair styles of women.[188] But the fullest presentation of his exegetical research is in an essay, "1 Timothy 2:9–15 and the Place of Women in the Church's Ministry."[189] Scholer investigated the background of 1 Timothy 1:12–15, holding that Paul's prohibition of women's teaching is directly related to the problem of false teaching at Ephesus. His conclusion was that the restriction of women in that passage is not applicable universally.

Aída Besançon Spencer

In Beyond the Curse[190] Spencer combined a high view of Scripture with exegetical ability to produce a series of interpretive studies supporting women's ministry in the church. Spencer worked carefully through major texts and phases of biblical history, beginning in Eden. She presented references to women in Scripture—women who are often overlooked—including women in the Gospels, Paul's associates, and the women mentioned as possible over-

seers of house churches. In the last category she discussed the question of whether the "elect lady" of 2 John is merely a metaphor for a church or an actual female leader. Spencer opted for the second alternative.[191]

Spencer had already published an article on 1 Timothy 2:11–15.[192] In that study, which was further pursued in her book Beyond the Curse[193] she stressed the importance of the fact that Paul did want women to learn and that their quietness and submission in this context had to do with learning (not a submission in every sphere). Their restriction was temporary: "When women anywhere, including Ephesus, grow beyond a resemblance to Eve in this respect, then the analogy is no longer valid."[194]

In connection with the issue of women leaders in the apostolic church, Spencer made the following observation: "Similarly, the New Testament also does not record any example of a woman pastor. Yet, neither does it record any example of an individual male pastor."[195] One assumes that she considers Timothy and Titus to have been apostolic delegates rather than "pastors" in the modern sense. She continued with the observation that on looking into the New Testament for evidence, "one notices that present church practices and first-century church practices often jar against one another." For Spencer, the matter of women in leadership must include the probability that "the functional equivalents of today's 'head' pastor was yesterday's overseer of church communities."[196]

Roman Catholic Writers

Contributions to the discussion on women and the church have not to this point been categorized according to ecclesiastical position, but the discussions among scholars in this large sector of Christendom call for particular attention. Among those with a Catholic background, Rosemary Radford Ruether, Elisabeth Schüssler Fiorenza, and the Swidlers have already been mentioned. Many other scholars and publications could be mentioned. Several significant representatives of scholars and their works will be discussed here.

In 1965 Charles R. Meyer wrote a careful study entitled, "Ordained Women in the Early Church."[197] Meyer maintained that there is evidence for the ordination of deaconesses in the early church equal to that of deacons. He also cited materials indicating that ecclesiastical responsibilities were accorded women beyond what has traditionally been supposed. This work has been selected for attention here because of the immense significance that the practices of the early church has for Catholics (and, in varying degrees, for others). Scholars have disagreed on the implications of some of the evidence. It seems clear that certain women servants of the church in the early years (see chapter 3) were given ecclesiastical recognition, even with the laying on of hands. But it has been difficult for Catholics to identify this with ordination to the priesthood and the right to administer the sacraments. The material Meyers has provided requires intense study.

Sister Agnes Cunningham, a semi- nary professor, theological and patristics scholar, and former president of the Catholic Theological Society of America, has written a number of papers and articles on women and the church. She has been a consultant to bishops on the matter and is sensitive to the biblical, historical, and theological evidence and to the complexities of the ecclesiastical situation. Her titles express her concerns and include the following: "Ecclesial Ministry for Women,"[198] "The Role of Women in Church and Society,"[199] *Women in Ministry: A Sister's View* [200] (a work that includes contributions from scholars in such varied fields as sociology, psychology, and pastoral theology, as well as in different ethnic groups), *The Role of Women in Ecclesial Ministry: Biblical and Patristic Foundations,* [201] and "Women in Ministry: A Roman Catholic View."[202]

In these works, Cunningham considered the ministry of women in the Catholic church from a number of different perspectives. She showed the rich ministry of women in the church's early history. She stressed that the gifts of the Spirit have been given to women and that their ministry enriches the church. Among the issues she addressed are those of authority and the sacraments. It is precisely at these sensitive places that agreement becomes most difficult. In one observation of interest to both Catholics and Protestants who are concerned with the significance of ordination, she observed, "There seems to be some basis for admitting an association between women's exclusion from formal ecclesial ministry and the rise of 'clericalism,' " a subject that she cautions needs careful handling.[203]

431

The following four books serve to indicate the kinds of resources available to those investigating the Catholic situation. One deals with canon law: Ida Raming, *The Exclusion of Women from the Priesthood: Divine Law of Sex Discrimination.*[204] Another contains the proceedings of the Detroit Ordination Conference: *Women and Catholic Priesthood: An Expanded Vision.*[205] A vigorous discussion is carried on by Haye van der Meer, SJ, in *Women Priests in the Catholic Church? A Theological-Historical Investigation.*[206] This work is packed with information and opinions relating to both sides of the issue. The *Concilium* series now has a section on feminist theology. The first contribution was *Women: Invisible in Church and Theology.*[207] This project is supervised by an international advisory committee of women scholars. A further work, already cited earlier, is the compilation of articles concerning the Vatican Declaration on the admission of women to the priesthood, edited by Leonard and Arlene Swidler.

Similar collections could be cited in connection with discussion among Anglicans and other denominations. With few exceptions, the church is confronting the issues openly. In some quarters there is a greater acknowledgment that women do possess the gifts of the Spirit and should have far greater scope for ministry than has been granted, even if certain official positions are still closed to them. Some consider this minimal progress and perhaps for some a means of terminating the discussion quickly; others are more hopeful—or fearful—of further developments. But it is difficult to deny the increased study of Scripture and of church history and the value of open dialogue among scholars of both fields.

Scholars in Dialogue

Help in understanding differing positions on women and the church is found in various compilations. Among these are a collection of papers and responses given at a 1984 colloquium and in books published as parts of two series on current issues.

One of these publications, *Women, Authority and the Bible,*[208] consists of papers delivered at an "Evangelical Colloquium on Women and The Bible," held in the Chicago area in October 1984. The participants included prominent theologians and Bible scholars from diverse backgrounds, such as James I. Packer, Richard N. Longenecker, Berkeley Mickelsen, and Roger Nicol, to name just a few. Subjects included discussions of the key biblical passages and of major issues, such as authority, headship, and hierarchy.

The British Inter-Varsity Press has approached significant current issues in a series entitled, "When Christians Disagree." One volume is *The Role of Women.*[209] The participants in the discussion include several persons well known in the United States, such as I. Howard Marshall, Michael Griffiths, and James B. Hurley. Topics range from relationships in the home to women in church ministries.

One aspect of the discussion is of special importance with respect to the ministry of women in church leadership. In the dialogue between New Testament scholars I. Howard

Marshall and James B. Hurley, the question of "office" occupies an important place. Hurley sees a more firm organizational structure in the early church than does Marshall, but he acknowledges that there have been abuses in the limiting of certain church functions only to those who hold specific offices. For his part, I. Howard Marshall notes that

> the modern concept of "the minister" in the sense of one person ordained by the laying on of hands to be (usually) the chief functionary in the local church and (usually) the one person authorized to celebrate the sacrament of the Lord's Supper, has no single counterpart in the New Testament.[210]

Marshall also observes that

> the trajectory which apparently leads through the Pastoral Epistles to the rigid clamping down on the place of women in the postapostolic church and on into many modern churches is a false one; rather, recognizing that the Pastoral Epistles were concerned to deal with a real abuse in their time, we may argue that the true line of advance should be traced from Jesus through the earlier epistles and onwards in the direction of the equality of God's people in His church. There were good social and cultural reasons why the early church "hastened slowly" in giving women a vital role in the church and its ministry, thus restraining potentially dangerous developments at the time. In the world of today, we can move more readily to a full appreciation to the part that women can play in the church.[211]

The British series in which this volume appeared was being somewhat paralleled by a series published by the American InterVarsity Press. A volume in this series, as yet forthcoming at the date of this writing, sets forth four views, with responses, on various positions on women, ranging from traditional to feminist.

These dialogues are a significant development in the publication of books on women and the church. After years marked by individualistic expressions of opinion, both in print and in pulpits, Evangelicals are talking together publicly, willing to have their ideas critiqued by respected representatives of opposing views.

A significant example of this was the 1986 annual meeting of the Evangelical Theological Society, held just as the present work was undergoing final editing. Evangelical scholars of traditionalist, centrist, and feminist persuasions were invited to present papers pertaining to male-female relationships, including church roles and ministries. Just previously the October 3, 1986, issue of the Evangelical magazine *Christianity Today* contained a supplement from the Christianity Today Institute on "Women in Leadership." The contributions were from various perspectives but included some perhaps unexpectedly strong support for women's ministry and church leadership. Subsequent letters to the editor demonstrated strong reactions as well as agreement. Thus between the Evangelical Theological Society and *Christianity Today* the dialogue has now come strongly before the Evangelical public. There is promise of further open conversation on the subject with an increasing awareness of the reasons and the serious studies that lie behind the various viewpoints.

Conclusion

During the period just surveyed, the church has devoted increasing attention to the ministry of women. Whatever position a particular denomination may take, it is certain that there is now an intense awareness of the issues among its leadership and people. The amount and diversity of material written during the decades just surveyed—not only by the exegetes and theologians but also by lay people of all sorts—is astounding. And it is long overdue.

It is difficult to draw conclusions from such a sequence of varied and often opposing viewpoints. Both the opinions themselves and the methodologies for reaching them defy simplistic categorization. To be sure, the approach of some has been ideological. That is to say, the views one holds regarding women are seen as part of a closed structure of beliefs that are considered of extreme importance. For others, conclusions are tentative, subject to further illumination from historical and exegetical research. But traditionalists and feminists can be found in both groups, and of course there are many who cannot be categorized, either as to position or as to methodology.

There is no doubt that some earlier exegetical decisions need to be reviewed in the light of continuing research. New lexical information, aided by computer data banks, new insights into ancient literary form and syntactical structure, and a better understanding of ancient society contribute to this need. Although some opinions have naturally been more a reaction either to strong feminism or to a patriarchal mentality than they have been a carefully worked out position, exposure to the recent work of those scholars who at least strive for objectivity should open new perspectives for all.

CONCLUSION

Historical Conclusions

The conclusions one reaches with regard to women and the church, are essentially of two kinds. First, historically, women have had far more involvement in the church's mission and other ministries than has generally been realized. This has been true in some periods of history more than in others. It is always difficult to discern trends. It has not been the purpose of this book to set forth any kind of developmental theory. Nevertheless, certain observations seem justified. One is that there have been clear instances in which women have begun ministries, missionary endeavors, or Christian organizations only to be later displaced by men in leadership positions. Rather than men taking the initiative and women then trying to seize authority, which is the scenario that one might expect from some viewpoints, there are repeated occasions where the reverse has been true.

Another observation is that the equality and freedom of women discerned by many in the New Testament record seems to have diminished as church organization and hierarchical structure increased. This is not a simple linear decline as some have supposed, but an irregular development both geographically and chronologically. One fact stands out: where authoritarian and priestly roles emerged, women tended to be excluded. Where, however, ministry was emphasized as service rather than authority, there were outstanding examples of active women. Orders of virgins and widows and the emergence of monasticism provided circumstances for the exercise of various spiritual gifts for the good of the church and of people in need.

Contrary to a popular contemporary supposition, no examples were found of heresy or other evil effects of women's ministry that were the clear, sole result of the sex of the instigator. Cults have had their share of women members, but the leaders have usually been men. The proportion of

435

cults originated by women are fewer than has been claimed. The major heresies of the early church were, of course, launched by men. It is impossible, therefore, to prove from history that women are more easily deceived than men, as some think 1 Timothy 2:11–15 teaches.

Practical Questions

The second kind of conclusion one might reach with regard to women and the church has to do with qualifications for ministry, and especially for ordination. Conclusions in this respect are inevitably affected to some degree by the way the questions are posed. It is sometimes claimed, for example, that there is only one question: Should Christian ministry, which by all testimony of Scripture is *spiritual* in nature, be limited by the sex of the minister, which is by nature a *human* distinction? That is certainly a basic and straightforward way of putting it. It puts the burden of proof on those who would imply that there is some distinction—physical, mental, social, or spiritual—that disqualifies a woman for certain aspects of ministry. It confronts them with one apparently unambiguous text: "There is neither . . . male nor female, for you are all one in Christ Jesus" (Gal. 3:28).

The opposite approach is to cite the key passages that impose restrictions: ". . . women should remain silent in the churches" (1 Cor. 14:34) and "I do not permit a woman to teach or to have authority over a man" (1 Tim. 2:12). Then the argument runs: Woman is not inferior, but God himself has ordained a submissive role for her that excludes certain church activities.

The way the question has been posed naturally has varied from generation to generation. How was it posed in the first century? Some contemporary observers find it hard to suppose that Christians in the early years of the church thought in terms of restrictions at all. While, on the one hand, some emphasize that Jesus did not appoint any female apostles, others do not find that strange, given the disdain and lack of credence a woman apostle would have faced in that society. They emphasize the fact that Jesus did, contrary to custom, have women disciples. Jesus' Great Commission, which church and missionary leaders usually repeat with great fervor, applies to all believers and includes discipling, baptizing, and teaching. (One looks in vain for any biblical prohibition against women baptizing, yet in how many churches can a woman baptize a person she has led to the Lord?)

With the emphasis in Paul on the bestowal of spiritual gifts on *all* believers completely apart from any mention of sexual distinction, could anyone in the New Testament church, it may be asked, have doubted that spiritual ministry was egalitarian? Given the number of women who were associated with Paul in his ministry, it seems to have been normal for women to be actively engaged in evangelism and associated ministries in the young churches. Paul did, after all, use the same language to describe female co-workers that he used for males.

Would there have been any challenge except from those whose Jewish or conventional Gentile moralistic sensitivities may have caused them to balk at the idea of women spokespersons? Is it possible that the restrictions Paul placed on women were made with this largely in mind? The reference in 1 Timothy 2:12–15 to the order of creation and the deception of Eve must not be neglected in such an approach. (See appendixes A and B.)

Some see in Paul's references to the other churches in 1 Corinthians 11:16 and 14:33 an indication that anything the New Testament may say elsewhere about women's spiritual ministries must forever be modified by Paul's restrictions. Others see them simply as encompassing the churches that existed during the period of transition in which the early church was developing. Actually Jesus broke with custom in allowing women to learn and to follow with him in ministry, and Paul had female associates. The apparent restrictions in 1 Corinthians and 1 Timothy relate, on this view, to particular circumstances; therefore Paul did not foresee or intend a universal and timeless application. However, as time went on, and the church imposed various restrictions on women, the church fathers often cited Paul's words.

One's conclusions regarding the appropriate extent and nature of women's ministries today tend to lean heavily not only on prior conclusions concerning the meaning and application of certain biblical texts, but also on ecclesiastical assumptions. These include perceptions of the significance of certain contemporary church activities and how they relate to those in past ages of the church's history.

The Importance of Perspective and Perception

It has become clear in the course of this survey of church history that one's own perspective, on the one hand, and the way various ministries are perceived, on the other, greatly affect the conclusions reached.

Is preaching perceived simply as sharing one's faith? Is it something equivalent to the prophesying Paul permitted women to do (1 Cor. 11)? Or does preaching by definition always include teaching? Is teaching to be seen as an act of authority or is it simply the proclamation of the Scriptures, in which the only true authority resides? Is teaching today the same as teaching in the New Testament period?

Such questions need to be placed alongside the questions concerning the meaning of the relevant biblical texts. Attention is sometimes directed to those texts in isolation, with little acknowledgment that the forms and perceptions of ministry today may be far different from what they were in the New Testament church. It is too easily assumed that all teaching today has the same weight that it did in the period before the New Testament was readily available, when teaching involved carrying the apostolic traditions of the words and deeds of Christ. The early teachers affirmed the truth of this tradition, bearing a witness that would not have been acceptable from the lips of women. Also in the early church, men who listened to a woman who taught or evaluated the teaching of others in the church would have had a far different perception of her than would men listening to a woman

437

today. For we live in an age when women are educated and when whatever biblical text she might read is already in our hands, its meaning already widely taught in commentaries and other sources.

It is also important to recognize the variety of perceptions concerning the nature of authority. Although in many churches authority is vested, not in the preacher, but in an elderhood or some other board or council, or perhaps in the congregation itself, the preacher is still perceived as an, if not *the*, authority. It is strange that churches that claim Scripture as their only authority still tend to bar women from preaching or teaching on the grounds that they should not exercise authority. Observation of the contemporary scene even suggests that some who hold to the inerrancy of Scripture are in danger of setting up a parallel authority in the person of a Correct Interpreter of Scripture. This is especially strange when the same people insist on the perspicuity of Scripture (i.e., the clarity of its basic teachings) over against those who claim that it needs an authoritative interpreter.

In Jesus' day there was a similar danger. Many gave the oral tradition of the rabbis equal status with the Scriptures. Jesus showed how in some cases tradition even had the effect of nullifying Scripture (Mark 7:13). One of the issues of the Reformation had to do with the authority of the Scriptures over against church tradition. One may well ask whether there is a subtle trend in some quarters of contemporary evangelicalism to elevate the pastor (or TV preacher, cassette-tape teacher, seminary professor) to a position of authority, a sort of Protestant magesterium. It is not unusual to find among Fundamentalists and Evangelicals a concept of the ministry that vests as much de facto authority in the pastor as do some hierarchical denominations. Most earnest preachers would recoil at that idea. But if women are barred from ministry because it is thought they should not have authority, one needs to ask what kind of authority is in mind.

Of course, if, as the most recent evidence seems to indicate, the "authority" Paul denied women by the use of the unusual verb *authenteō* in 1 Timothy 2:12 was not ordinary authority but an inordinate assumption of authority or some other unwarranted intrusion, the whole matter of women in contemporary positions of authority must be seen in a different light. The same would be true if it is established that Paul's instructions were for a specific situation only. This would also affect the question of whether women should serve as elders or in other official capacities. In addition, those parachurch organizations that now bar women from positions involving teaching or leadership would need to rethink their policies.

It is not sufficiently recognized that in churches with a congregational form of government, if more than half the membership is female, women are already in authority. Here again the minister may be the one *perceived* to have authority, but in actuality, the minister's very tenure could be in the hands of a female majority.

Other questions of perspective and perception include the matter of music ministry. Those who believe that women's ministries must be restricted need to decide on what basis any restrictions are to be justified and where they should end. There was a time when boy sopranos were used so that women would not take the lead by singing the melody. Such restrictions would be unheard of today. But if a church holds that women are to be silent and not teach, that church will need to decide whether a woman should be allowed to sing a solo or be a choir director, when such ministries involve deciding what hymns to use. After all, hymns contain theology, and many were written by women. In most churches, of course, even traditional ones with respect to women's ministries, music is (rightly or wrongly) not perceived as a teaching ministry.

Similar questions may be asked about the ministry of Christian education in a church that forbids a full teaching ministry to women. Would it be wrong for a woman to chair the Christian education committee? Does that responsibility mainly involve doctrinal teaching, or is it rather the use of administrative and educational skills? How is the position perceived? Does it bear any relation to the kind of teaching that Paul forbade (whether temporarily or permanently) to women?

What is the perception of women's intelligence today? Not long ago there were reports of a new insistence in Iran that women thoroughly cover all but their hands and faces. The reason offered was that, after all, women have "smaller brains and smaller hearts" than men. Such perceptions are rare today. One that does persist, however (that women are more easily deceived than men), is based on an interpretation of Scrip-

ture (1 Tim. 2:14). This is nothing more than an inference from the historical fact that Eve was the one deceived; Paul did not say that women were deceivable by nature.

Nevertheless, some today not only accuse women of being the ones to start heretical cults (a charge rebutted above) but also use this as a reason for not permitting women to teach men. Once again, perceptions enter in. What would be the difference between a woman teaching a man and her teaching a woman? One might well suppose that women should not teach other women, who, on the assumption that women are more easily deceived, would be unable to know if they were being deceived by their women teachers. Should children and new converts on mission fields and at home be protected from women teachers? Yet it is these who most proponents of the deceivability theory would allow to be taught by women. Thus once again it is easy to lose perspective.

It is clear that perceptions about women's ministries today are far from uniform, objective, or even necessarily theologically related. One needs perspective, the ability to stand back and study a scene in proper relation and proportion to its background. That is what a historical work should facilitate. It is also important to view one's own position, not in comparison with a few selected representatives of other positions, but with the whole spread of opinions. It is possible, for example, for a moderate traditionalist to appear extreme when compared with a Mary Daly but not when compared with a John Robbins. The same is, of course, true in reverse, with people who are nowhere near an extreme position being called "radical feminists."

This book has been written from an open centrist position. It has sought to present fairly the entire range of views from, say, a Mary Daly or Naomi Goldberg to a John Robbins. Our own views are at neither end of the scale. We think it is important to open windows of understanding for the reader, windows on women in the history of the church and on the changing perspectives from which they have been viewed. We also consider it important to gain a new perspective from the standpoint of history on contemporary viewpoints. This helps one to understand better the reasons for differing positions and also to evaluate one's own position more objectively.

One conclusion that seems inevitable from the preceding survey is that dogmatism is no longer an appropriate way to approach the subject of women and the church. Positions must, of course, be taken by those in responsibility, but even a strong position need not exclude the acknowledgment of legitimate and sincere differences. These differences concern both the interpretation of Scripture and its application to contemporary circumstances. This is not a matter of conservatism versus liberalism. That terminology is erroneous both as regards theology (one's view of women and the church cannot be predicted simply from one's view of major doctrines, including the doctrine of Scripture) and as regards history (theological conservatives have been feminist, and liberals have been traditional with respect to women).

Today there are some independent Fundamentalists who grant a great deal of freedom to women in various ministries, including teaching in Bible schools, while there are others who claim that one cannot hold to the inerrancy of Scripture and be a feminist. The terms *conservative* and *liberal* should be discarded with respect to the question of women and the church. Since for the greater part of church history it has been assumed that ordination should be restricted to men, it is accurate to call those who agree with that point of view traditionalists. If labels must be used, the alternative position is perhaps best called feminist or, within the church, Christian feminist.

Differing Views of Ordination

The fact that the ordained ministry is something of a touchstone in these discussions calls for a few comments on the subject at this point.

One major problem regarding women in ordained ministry is the divergence of views among Christians as to what ordination actually means and implies. Is it a recognition of spiritual gifts? Is it permission to preach or to teach? Is it permission to preside at the Lord's Supper? Does it bestow a rank and grant authority over the church? Who should be ordained—pastors, bishops, elders, Sunday-school superintendents, missionaries? Can a female commissioned missionary carry on a teaching ministry not allowable by ordination to a woman at home? It is apparent that no single sweep of the pen can underline the right answer to the question of women in ordained ministry. Different denominations will answer the question in different ways.

The vigorous discussions among both Roman Catholics and Protestants are well known. Some further consideration is needed on ordination and authority so that informed decisions can be made. It is important to know some of the exegetical and historical factors involved. These will be presented in appendix C.

Ministry and Servanthood

The purpose of this book has not been to press arguments but to survey history and open windows of insight. It is clear that women have had significant ministries in a remarkable variety of ways throughout the history of the church. It can reasonably be suggested on the basis of this survey that when men have severely restricted the ministry of women, one of the possible causes was a loss of the concept of ministry as servanthood and the substitution

of an understanding of ministry as the possession of rank and authority. It has been easy for the church to forget that the Greek term for ministry (*diakonia*) is related to the verb "to serve" (*diakonein*). Jesus took a towel and washed the disciples' feet. When his disciples asked about their ranking in the coming kingdom, Jesus reminded them that Gentiles sought power and status. Christians—both male and female—should, like the Son of Man, come to serve, not to be served. Questions about authority in the church, and particularly about the ministry of women, might be resolved more biblically if attention were given to the fact that "ministry" means "serving."

With that definition in mind, a most appropriate response to the biblical and historical survey just completed is not for either men or women to grasp at ministerial status or authority, but rather to encourage one another in faithful service to the glory of God.

APPENDIX A

HERMENEUTICS AND THEOLOGY

The differences between biblical interpreters on the key texts about women and the church are so great that it seems impossible at present to arrive at a full consensus. One crucial area of disagreement is on the foundational matter of hermeneutics, that aspect of biblical study that deals with principles of interpretation. Another area, theology, includes significant issues that, when probed, reveal underlying presuppositions that often affect exegesis and the resultant positions on women and the church. The following survey may help to clarify such matters and bring about a better mutual understanding and, perhaps, a greater measure of agreement as well.

Hermeneutics

Much could be said about recent developments in hermeneutics. These have included such topics as the meaning of language and the impingement of the "horizon" of the interpreter on the meaning of the text. But there are two distinct developments with respect to scriptural passages that refer to women, and they deserve special mention here. First, new attention has been given to the hermeneutics of these passages by Evangelicals. Second, feminists have developed an entirely new approach called "feminist hermeneutics."

Evangelical Scholarship

Evangelical writers on the subject of women, especially those who might be called "traditionalists," have long been accused of merely using "proof texts" to support their position. While this has not been true of all, there certainly has been need for a more careful use of hermeneutical principles. One attempt, that of Paul K. Jewett, to bring a new approach to the writings of Paul drew considerable criticism: he saw an intrusion of Paul's rabbinic background into his comments on women. Others, however, also sought to take background factors into consideration. A significant Evangelical contribution regarding texts on women appeared in 1977 when Grant Osborne published an article entitled, "Hermeneutics and Women in the Church."[1] Osborne was concerned about serious instances of the neglect of sound interpretive principles in some treatments of the key texts about women. He urged recognition of the distinction between what is truly an expression of principle and what is merely cultural in the biblical text.

The matter of culture was also taken up, along with a number of other topics, in an essay by Robert K. Johnston, "The Role of Women in the Church and Home: An Evangelical Testcase in Hermeneutics."[2] Johnston provides a series of hermeneutical principles that should prevent the twisting of Scripture in order to extract support for one's position.

Not all Evangelicals agreed that the role of culture is a necessary factor in determining the meaning and application of a text. Susan T. Foh referred to "the hermeneutical principle of deculturalization" as "the means by which passages that make distinctions between men and women can be removed."[3] She continued with the objection that it is difficult to determine "what parts of the Bible are culturally conditioned and therefore nonauthoritative." The word "therefore" is significant in that sentence; whatever is culturally conditioned simply cannot, in Foh's opinion, be authoritative. In such an approach, she thinks, "any absolute standard is impossible." Further, "if Paul's teaching about women in the church is cultural, maybe his teaching on justification or his faith in God is, too."[4]

The issue here is whether the role of women is a purely theological matter, like faith and justification, or whether in the ancient world the way women appeared and what they did in public had a social significance that doctrines per se did not. But if it was improper in the eyes of some moralists of the first century (such as Plutarch) for a woman to speak publicly, the biblical teachings about women are not disembodied truths suspended, as it were, above the real world in some timeless abstract proposition. There is a qualitative distinction between the doctrines of faith and justification and the social role of women. What many fear, and this is probably part of Foh's concern, is that readers of the Bible may fail to make the proper cultural transition and application today.

Actually, the role of culture and, to expand the issue, both the role of social history and the employment of contemporary social theory are major subjects of discussion among scholars today. Much information is being gathered from ancient literature and archaeology, such as inscriptions, artwork, the remains of synagogues, and the like. These provide insights into social strata, methods of itinerant preachers, roles of women in non-Christian religions, family structure, concepts of authority, and other matters pertaining to women in the church. Some applications of contemporary social and anthropological *theory* have been questionable, but solid progress is being made in the field of social *history*.

Many Evangelicals today would contend that it is not a matter of *whether* one uses cultural or social considerations in the interpretation and application of the passages on women, but *how* this is best done. For the Evangelical student of Scripture the key question is how these can be used to determine, rather than erode, that which is transcultural and theologically binding.

It is important to recognize that the use of cultural factors in interpretation does not assume that the biblical message is culturally *relative*, but rather that it is culturally *relevant*, both in its own times and today. Even basic word study requires the consideration of cultural factors in order for one to know what common understanding (based on common usage and inner context) the biblical writers could assume between themselves and their readers. Also it may help if recognition is given to the difference between Scripture *being modified* by culture and Scripture *addressing* culture.

If the term *cultural* is threatening to some, at least an attempt should be made to determine from the context of a passage what *circumstances* evoked it. What, for example, were the circumstances under which women were to wear head coverings at Corinth? Under what circumstances did Paul refuse to allow women to teach at Ephesus? What did teaching involve? What was the connection between Paul's prohibitions of women's teaching and the problem of false teaching, which was so prominent in 1 Timothy? Such questions may or may not involve the cultural background, but they certainly require some reconstruction of the circumstances behind the particular epistle.

It is sometimes difficult, of course, to distinguish what is, in fact, connected with cultural factors. The beards of hippies in the 1960s had a significance that Dwight L. Moody's beard did not have. Therefore a book that might have been published in, say, 1968, urging Christian young men for the sake of the glory of God not to wear beards, would make no sense if the background were not known. Christians seem at ease with this way of dealing with culture when they substitute a handshake for the five New Testament commands to Christians to give one another a holy kiss.[5] Some who take Paul's teaching about women in 1 Timothy 2:12 as a universal rule interpret the words a few verses earlier about men raising holy hands in prayer, as well as the extensive instructions a few chapters later about widows, as cultural. Many Christians today (rightly or wrongly) refrain from footwashing on the same basis, even though Jesus based the command on doctrine—i.e., that he was their Savior and Lord (John 13:3, 13–14). Were these matters any less cultural than Plutarch's idea that for a woman to speak publicly was an indecent exposure of her mind?[6]

Another approach to hermeneutics in connection with the issue of women in the church was taken by the Evangelical scholar Willard Swartley in his work *Slavery, Sabbath, War and Women*.[7] In this he showed the similarity of approaches followed in discussions of each of these controversial topics and suggested some guidelines to prevent skewed interpretations. It has often been suggested that the use of arguments from selected texts to support slavery is paralleled by those used against women's ministries today. Swartley has categorized the materials under several arguments, including these: "Slavery was divinely sanctioned among the patriarchs" and "Slavery was recognized and approved by Jesus Christ and the apostles."[8]

Swartley offered a number of hermeneutical conclusions, including the following: (1) "Quoting the Bible does not in itself guarantee correctness of position." (2) "To avoid selective use of evidence, the entire biblical witness on a given subject should be considered." (3) "Each particular text or section of the Bible should be used for its main emphasis, not for its attendant features." (4) "The interpreter should give priority to theological principles and basic moral imperatives rather than to specific council on particular topics when these two contradict." (5) "The interpreter needs to examine carefully the factors that influence his/her use of Scripture. Religious, social, political, and economic factors affect our use of the Bible. Behind these are psychic forces related to our own lives, loves, values, and circles of friendship."[9] The list is long (there are twenty-two items in all) and includes the following important principle: "The biblical interpreter should recognize the temporal and cultural distance that exists between the world of the Bible and the world of the believer today, especially when addressing social issues. Whether the topic be slavery, war, or the role of women, the meaning of the same word, command, or instruction may differ significantly, depending on the historical and cultural place and time in which it was and is spoken."[10]

Feminist Hermeneutics

This approach to the Bible is based on the growing consensus among modern hermeneutical theorists that it is impossible to interpret Scripture with complete objectivity. Although generations of conservative scholars have followed a methodology they call "grammatical-historical" (the exact wording varies) and thereby attempted to be rigorously objective and consequently accurate in their interpretation, it is now seriously doubted whether such objectivity is really obtainable. This naturally has a bearing on the way one interprets passages about women. Evangelicals, however, including those who recognize the existence of what has been called two "horizons" (the author's and the reader's vantage points)[11] and even those who hold that biblical authors did write from a patriarchal perspective, still normally believe that what the Bible *teaches* is true and authoritative.

The approach of feminist hermeneutics, however, is not only to dispute objectivity but purposefully to acknowledge a feminist standpoint of interpretation. This is similar to (and many consider it a part of) the hermeneutics of liberation theology. Rosemary Radford Ruether included a chapter on women in her book on liberation theology.[12] It is contended that women—like blacks, the disenfranchised poor, and other minorities—have been victimized by those in power. Those holding to male priority and dominance have shaped religious thought and structures from biblical times through today Therefore a radical new look at Scripture is needed. Mary Ann Tolbert summarizes the essence of feminist hermeneutics when she writes, "Whereas patriarchal hermeneutics grounds its perceptions in the ideological assurance of 'reality' or 'the way things are,' feminist hermeneutics self-consciously attempts to ground its analyses in the experience of women's oppression."[13]

Some feminists whose contributions were surveyed above, such as Mary Daly, have reached extremely negative views of Christianity. Others have tried to remain within a generally Christian framework. It is difficult for those with an Evangelical stance to understand the struggles of a Phyllis Trible, a Rosemary Radford Ruether, or an Elisabeth Schüssler Fiorenza in grappling with feminist concerns on the one hand and with Christianity on the other. Fiorenza, for one, works on the premise that "all early Christian texts are formulated in an androcentric language and conditioned by their patriarchal milieu and histories."[14] Yet she also contends that "feminists cannot afford to disown androcentric biblical texts and patriarchal history as their own revelatory texts and history."[15]

How then can one appropriate Scripture at all when it speaks of women? Fiorenza's answer is: "Biblical revelation and truth are given only in those texts and interpretive models that transcend critically their patriarchal frameworks and allow for a vision of Christian women as historical and theological subjects and actors."[16] The implications of this position are immense. Passages of Scripture that do not say what the contemporary reader determines to be true from a feminist perspective are simply not accepted as "biblical revelation and truth." If one were to charge that this is subjective, the answer is that it is consciously and deliberately so, to balance the patriarchal interpretations of centuries. It is not surprising that a work of the magnitude and importance of Fiorenza's *In Memory of Her* has received wide attention. Some of the titles or subtitles of reviews reveal the radical nature of her proposals: "A Feminist Re-reads the New Testament,"[17] "A Feminist Reconstruction of Christian Origins,"[18] and "The Reconstruction of Christian Origins."[19]

For Fiorenza and many other feminists, Jesus himself was not androcentric or patriarchal in his attitude and teaching, but this was not true of all his followers. It is usual to consider Mark and John as more positive about the contribution of women than Luke.[20] In fact, Luke, although traditionally thought of as very sensitive to, and appreciative of, women, has a low place in the opinion of contemporary feminists. This opinion was observed and challenged in the excursus to chapter 1. The view is expressed in comments such as these: "Luke characteristically qualified every mention of women by a reference to some negative aspect of their character. . . . This is a literary device used throughout the gospel of Luke to present women as both weak and sinful."[21] For some scholars this builds on the assumption that Luke wrote late in the first century, during a period marked also by the writing of the Pastoral Epistles by a follower of Paul, when restrictions were being placed on the freedom women had earlier to minister.[22]

The issues are complex, as with many other aspects of women and the church, but clearly in feminist hermeneutics any acknowledgment of the authority of a given Scripture depends on the judgment of the reader.

The Citation of Scripture and Biblical Doctrine .

As in John 13:3, 13–14, where Jesus based the footwashing command on his lordship and saviorhood, so several commands or instructions about women are accompanied by references to theology or to the Old Testament. Paul refers to the order of creation in 1 Corinthians 11 and 1 Timothy 2, to headship in 1 Corinthians 11 and Ephesians 5, to the deceit of Eve in 1 Timothy 2, and to the obedience of Sarah in 1 Peter 3. The issue is whether such citations require that the instructions be understood as timeless and universal. Many doubt that this is the case with John 13. Is it so with other commands?

To some extent the answer involves details of exegesis. For example, is the word usually translated "for" (Greek gar) in 1 Timothy 2:13 to be interpreted as introducing an explanation of, or the grounds for, his conclusion?[23] The options are discussed in appendix B in connection with 1 Timothy 2:12. However the grammar is understood, further questions have to be asked. One is whether the validity of a command is greater if it is supported by a reference to the creation narrative. If all Scripture is inspired and true, one might expect that it does not need a reference back to itself to be authoritative. Is it, therefore, right to insist on a universal and timeless application simply because it is accompanied by a secondary biblical reference? A traditionalist response might be that what is established by the referent is not the validity of the command but its nature.

Another question is how to understand such a directive when compared with Old Testament commands that are also based on revealed truth. For example, in Leviticus 19 a series of commands, including universals—such as "Do not steal," "Do not lie"— are based on the words "Be holy because I, the LORD your God, am holy" (v. 2), and "I am the LORD your God" (v. 3). Among these commands, however, are "Do not plant your field with two kinds of seed" and "Do not wear clothing woven from two kinds of material" (v. 19). Although the transition of covenants or dispensations is generally assumed to be reason to ignore these directives, the fact remains that they are based on the nature of God. We may therefore question whether a theological basis in itself is reason to consider a command timeless and universal.

A third question is whether a reference to creation makes Paul's teachings about women any more universally or permanently binding than is the Sabbath command, which is certainly part of the creation order. In fact, one might argue that the latter is even more foundational because it is part of the basic seven-day structure of the creation. Yet it is argued from the New Testament, with relatively few dissenters, that the Sabbath need not be observed now in the same way that it had been. Without entering into that discussion, we can observe several things. If one is considering order in creation, the sequence of days and the matter of the Sabbath certainly must not be overlooked. The concept of the Sabbath is found throughout Scripture. Hebrews 4:1–11 bases the idea of a Christian "rest" on the creation order of the Sabbath. At the same time, Jesus characteristically considered human need above the observance of a particular day, in spite of the unquestionable importance of the Sabbath. Yet Luke, emphasizing, as he often did, the fact that Jesus and the early Christians were faithful

Jews, made a point of the fact that Jesus went to the synagogue on the Sabbath "as was his custom" (Luke 4:16). The point is made even more strongly when Luke writes that after the crucifixion the women went home to prepare spices, "But they rested on the Sabbath in obedience to the commandment" (Luke 23:56). It is certainly appropriate to ask, therefore, whether it is not hermeneutically proper to conclude that a reference can be made in Scripture to the order of creation to support a *particular* action without such a reference implying that the action must be repeated *universally* and *permanently.*

A fourth question is whether a biblical or theological allusion leads necessarily to the specific command given in the context, or whether it leads to a principle (perhaps unexpressed) that could be fulfilled in other ways in different circumstances. An illustration may be drawn from a culture in which it is considered improper for a woman to appear on the street unescorted. A woman who does so is suspected of being a prostitute. Perhaps Paul would have written the Christians there: "Because we are to show the holiness of God in our lives, I do not permit a woman to walk on the street unescorted." The proper interpretation would be to understand the writer to mean, "Do not do anything that appears indecent, such as. . . ." The obvious parallel here is the fact that unbound, uncovered hair in Paul's world signified prostitution.[24] The very act of a woman's speaking in public was *in itself* a message (cf. Marshall McLuhan's famous dictum, "The medium is the message"). Conversely, today the *absence* of women from positions of responsibility in a contemporary Christian church or organization constitutes in itself a message to our generation. Obedience to a principle may, therefore, require a different action today from what it required in the New Testament period. This procedure must, of course, be clearly distinguished from that of "situational ethics," which tends to ignore clear moral teachings.

In summary, great care is called for in applying proper principles of interpretation to the biblical passages about women. Perspectives on women and the church are inevitably affected by hermeneutics. But along with hermeneutics stands theology, and it is likewise inevitable that each person's interpretation of matters has been modified to some extent as a result of previous theological conditioning. There are also some misconceptions that call now for correction.

Theology

Inerrancy

The topic of inerrancy relates both to hermeneutics and to theology. It is a subject under considerable debate today. Many, including the authors of this volume, consider it an essential element in discussions on Scripture. But it needs careful definition. It is rightly argued that defective hermeneutics can result in the term's being applied too narrowly. In fact, the International Council on Biblical Inerrancy considered the matter of hermeneutics so important that a "summit" conference was held on the subject and the results were later published.[25]

One sometimes hears it said, however, that it is impossible to allow the ordination of women and still hold to biblical inerrancy, or that to approve such ordination one must be either exegetically incompetent or disobedient to Scripture. It would seem that differences in opinion concerning such matters as baptism, eschatology, and the Calvinist-Arminian debate are often tolerated more graciously than differences about women. Even a high view of Scripture does not guarantee proper hermeneutics. It is not only unfortunate, therefore, but theologically faulty, so to identify an exegete's opinion with the inspired Scriptures themselves that any deviation from that opinion is thought of as a deviation from biblical authority.

A serious question is raised, therefore, by such statements as the following by Susan Foh:

> Biblical feminists see irreconcilable contradictions in the Bible's teaching on women. . . . Biblical feminists do not believe that God has given us his word true and trustworthy, the unchanging standard for beliefs and practices. . . . The biblical feminists criticize the Old Testament and question its authority. . . . The biblical feminists have abandoned the biblical and historic position of the God-breathed, inerrant Scriptures. . . . A faulty conception of Scriptures produces apostasy.[26]

Remarks like these may be true of some feminists, especially those whom traditionalists call "radical," but there are many biblical feminists today of whom the statements are not only untrue but also a very serious misrepresentation. Such language can have the unfortunate effect of leading readers to conclude that anyone who holds to views other than Foh's regarding women's ministries has abandoned inerrancy and become apostate. Further, her description of alleged error includes "a contradiction resulting from the culturally determined opinions of one of its human authors."[27] The transparent fact is, however, that any apparent contradictions between, for example, 1 Corinthians 11 and 14, face the inerrantist as much as they do anyone else. They exist within the text itself. The introduction of cultural considerations may actually provide a solution that *supports* the concept of inerrancy. Without wanting to minimize Foh's positive contributions, a call for caution is in order regarding these issues that require such delicate and balanced evaluation.

Inclusive Language and the Nature of God

Chapter 11 described the *Inclusive Language Lectionary*, an attempt to delete from the Bible all "improper" masculine terminology. Criticism of this revisionary text has centered on the use of inclusive terminology for God, extending even to referring to him as "Mother" as well as "Father." The Lectionary itself is only one expression of a growing feminist theology that rejects all patriarchal ideas of God. Hymnology has come under scrutiny as a number of hymns not only assume male singers but address God in male terms (e.g., "High King of Heaven"). The Doxology has repeated references to "Him." Some feminists find it difficult to say the Lord's Prayer with its ascription of Fatherhood to God.

Among the biblical texts to which appeal is made are Genesis 2:28 (the creation of male and female in the image of God), passages that attribute motherly characteristics to God (e.g., Num. 11:12; Deut. 32:11–12; Isa. 49:15; 66:13), and the verse that gives a description of Jesus' yearning for Jerusalem in terms of a mother hen's desire to gather her chicks (Matt. 23:37). Difficult hermeneutical questions are involved here. Is a given masculine description of God metaphorical or analogical? If it is merely metaphorical, is it therefore legitimately balanced by the use of a feminine metaphor, on the assumption that had the Bible not been written in an androcentric, patriarchal society, it would have used some feminine terminology? Is the masculine terminology analogical and thereby expressive of a closer comparison between expression and subject? Do the terms *Father* and *Son* describe the nature of the Persons of the Trinity, or are they only figurative terms that can be modified without diminishing the truth of God's nature?

Such questions go far beyond the scope and intention of this book. Nevertheless the subject is crucial. God, by any orthodox definition, transcends human masculinity and femininity. Therefore even core terms like "Father" cannot reduce God to our concepts of manhood. If there is a problem with such terminology, it does not lie in the nature of God nor in the words of Scripture, but in any meaning we ascribe to them that goes beyond the biblical intention and restricts God to human categories. Correspondingly, metaphors that ascribe feminine characteristics to God should be recognized as descriptive instruments to help us understand the depths of God's character and care for us. Pagan deities were either masculine or feminine. God is infinitely greater than such categories.

The whole issue, described here only in broad strokes, requires theologically sophisticated discussion. Therefore some references are provided in a footnote for those who desire to pursue the matter further.[28] But in spite of the complexity of the subject, the questions may be reduced to three: (1) How far can one remove or minimize certain expressions, such as "Father," without distorting the nature of God? (2) What does one's view of the inspiration and authority of the Scripture say to the proposal that biblical language descriptive of God (as distinguished from words of instruction relating to human circumstances such as were discussed earlier) reflect, not immutable truth, but patriarchal ideas? (3) Where is the boundary between metaphorical language that helps us understand God in terms appropriate to our own sphere of reference and language that conveys absolutes about the nature of God? Once again, hermeneutics and theology are joined together.

Creation, the Fall, and Redemption

This also is a topic that bridges hermeneutics and theology. The hermeneutical aspect, i.e., the citation of Old Testament events in the New Testament, was discussed above. The theological issues are whether woman was subordinate before the Fall, as part of the created order, and whether redemption in Christ removes any inferior position, restoring a pristine position of equality. First, many now dispute whether Genesis indicates that woman was created subordinate to man, or whether that state came about as a result of the Fall. It is sometimes claimed that the helper must be subordinate to the one helped, and that to name another is to show control or authority. Others hold that a proper understanding of the Hebrew word for "helper" and of the naming of Eve does not support the idea of subordination. A brief exegetical explanation is needed here: The word, "helper" (Gen. 2:18), is used for God a number of times, and this shows that the word does not in itself indicate subordination. Adam named the animals, but he did so before Eve was created, and, further, it was necessary for this to take place in order for his need for a woman to become clear to him. Adam did not name his wife "Eve" before the Fall but only called her a "woman" (Gen. 2:23). He named her "Eve" after the Fall (Gen. 3:20), and the Hebrew indicates the distinction in the naming process. Therefore, some scholars claim, it is not proper to deduce inferiority or subordination prior to the Fall. Further, the roles and functions given man and woman in the garden prior to the Fall appear to be undifferentiated. Adam's responsibility in the garden was given before woman appeared. Furthermore, Adam seems incomplete without woman, not sufficient in himself. Within the Genesis account, therefore, there seems little ground for assuming women's subordination before the Fall. (That man became domineering as a result of the Fall can hardly be disputed given Genesis 3:16.)

Paul, however, does refer back to the order of creation as a reason for the restriction he places on women's teaching, as noted elsewhere. In 1 Corinthians 11:8−9 and in

1 Timothy 2:13 this order constitutes part of Paul's argument. Some find it noteworthy that when Paul seeks to impose a restriction on women, he reverts back to the Old Testament, particularly to the early part of Genesis. But when he proclaims that there is no difference between male and female in the Lord, he bases this on redemption— specifically, on justification by faith through grace (Gal. 3:28).[29] This seems to vindicate the view that redemption makes a difference as to the position of women in Christian theology. The arguments from Genesis are useful when addressing a Jewish situation where restriction of some sort is necessary, but, it can be argued, the curse has been superseded by redemption. If so, it has been argued, just as farm machinery is used to alleviate the curse on the ground, and just as anesthesia is used to alleviate the pain of the woman in childbirth, so Christians should do everything possible to alleviate the effect of the Fall on male-female relationships, especially in the church.

Headship and the Relation Between Home and Church Roles

The main text is Ephesians 5:22–33. The occurrence of the concept of headship occurs also in 1 Corinthians 11:3 (discussed elsewhere), but here it is in a context that deals with the relationship of husband and wife. In neither case is the concept of headship applied to women's ministry as such. It is useful to inquire when studying Ephesians 5 how the notion of headship is developed in the context. Put in other terms, if one did not know what "head" meant, what would one learn from its use here? More specifically in terms of the role of the husband, does it set forth the idea of authority or rulership? In verse 23 the mention of head is immediately followed by a reference to Christ's being the "Savior" of the body. The idea of salvation includes, among other ideas, salvation from sin, rescue from danger, healing, and making one whole. Certainly the first of these is most prominent with respect to Christ. Some take it to be simply a descriptive phrase unrelated to the context; others think it suggests that Christ sets an example for husbands by bringing wholeness or completeness to the church. The passage goes on to speak of Christ's loving the church, giving himself up for her, making her holy, cleansing her, making her radiant, feeding and caring for her (vv. 25–29). It must be acknowledged that nowhere does Paul mention rulership or authority. Yet the initial mention of Christ as head occurs between two statements that the wife is to submit to the husband. It seems, therefore, that we are less than honest with the text if we ignore the fact that even though the husband is not pictured as ruling, the portrayal of the wife as submitting is related to the husband's headship.

This brings the discussion around to the matter of submission. In addition to questions discussed elsewhere, the following are relevant here: First, if, as many suggest today, Ephesians 5:22–33 teaches mutual submission (cf. v. 21) rather than a hierarchical relationship between husband and wife, does that mean that there is no hierarchy in the church? If a marriage is completely egalitarian, should men and women share leadership roles in the church equally?

Second, if on the other hand there is a divinely established hierarchical role relationship in marriage, whereby the wife submits to her husband in a way that the husband does not submit to the wife, in what form, if any, is this carried over to the church? Furthermore, would all women be submissive to all men in the church? What is the meaning of 1 Corinthians 14:34: "[Women] must be in submission"? (Appendix B will include reference to theories that this does not represent Paul's teaching, but if this is Paul's injunction, the question must be answered.) The options are (1) submission to all men, (2) submission to their own husbands, and (3) having a submissive attitude, particularly with regard to church order.

The first of these three options is not taught elsewhere in Scripture. The second would fit in with the idea that in this passage Paul may have been concerned lest women challenge their own husbands with questions during the judging of the prophets. The third is rendered likely by the fact that the Greek omits the usual mention of a person or persons *to whom* submission is given. Therefore, it may be reasonably supposed that they were being told to have a submissive attitude, in contrast to speaking out in challenge to others. This all introduces the question of the nature of the early church. Recent studies have probed the question of how the house churches were viewed socially. Were they perceived as a household unit under the leadership of the host? Did males, who were dominant in the households of that society, also lead in the house churches? If a church met in a household lacking a strong Christian husband, did the hostess take the lead when the Christians gathered there? What are we to conclude from, for example, the reference to "Nympha and the church in *her* house" (Col. 4:15) (italics mine)? Further study remains to be done on this whole issue.

The instructions Paul gave concerning qualifications for elders and deacons do link, in contrast to Ephesians 5:22–33, the life of these leaders at home and in the community to their role in the church. The elder "must manage his own family well and see that his children obey him with proper respect. (If anyone does not know how to manage his own family, how can he take care of God's church?)" (1 Tim. 3:4–5). A deacon "must be the husband of but one wife and must manage his children and his household well" (1 Tim. 3:12). There is a clear relationship between the man's role in the church as a leader and his role at home. Does this text imply that the man is the authority in the home? Can only males have authority in the church on this analogy, or does it mention men only because at that time it would have been unthinkable that women could be elders?

The Greek word translated "manage" in 1 Timothy 3:5, 12 means "to be up front," "to exercise leadership." But the word used two chapters later when Paul tells the young widows to marry and "manage their homes" (1 Tim. 5:14) is a much stronger word (*oikodespotein* [*despotēs* is the source of our word "despot"]). The noun form is the normal word used in the New Testament for the ruler of a house (Matt. 10:25; 13:27, 52; 21:11; 21:33; 24:43; Mark 14:14; Luke 12:39; 13:25; 14:21; 22:11.) Figuratively it is also used of God.[30] The word group also had strong meanings of mastery and predominance in the classical period.[31] If a widow, left without the help of a man, is told to exercise such strong household management, one must assume that women were not by nature incapable of leadership. Would that then apply to a house *church* that lacked strong male leadership?

Such questions are theological in that they involve general concepts of headship, leadership, and the nature of the early church, and they are not easily answered simply on the basis of individual texts of Scripture. Appendix B will discuss exegetical issues, but resolution of those would not abrogate the need to reflect carefully on the preceding matters before applying the exegesis to contemporary situations.

APPENDIX B

EXEGETICAL ISSUES

Volumes of exegetical studies cannot possibly be compressed into a few lines, but some attention to the history of exegesis will be useful. The following is an indication of where matters presently stand with regard to certain key texts. In the preceding historical survey, the texts were included as part of the flow of New Testament history. Although some lines of interpretation were suggested in passing, there was no intention to reach final conclusions, and few technical issues were discussed. Some of these details will now be outlined.

Galatians 3:28

This is a crucial passage. It tends to be seen either as an absolute statement that abrogates all differences and governs the interpretation of all other New Testament texts on women or, on the other hand, as only indicating that justification is without regard to racial, social, or sexual differences.

It is important to understand this verse in its context. In Galatians, Paul is dealing with such matters as the law, justification, and the liberty of the Spirit. The immediate context is a contrast between past times under law and the new family relationship we have with God through faith as "sons." This new relationship is also indicated by the terminology of baptism and of being "clothed with Christ." Clothing symbolism occurs in two other passages that speak of new life in Christ. Both Ephesians 4:20–24 and Colossians 3:9–14 speak of "putting on" the new man like new clothing. This seems to have been common language to describe the new life in Christ. The use of clothes as a figure of behavioral characteristics goes back to the Old Testament.[1] It is crucial to recognize that in Colossians 3:9–11 the putting off of the old and putting on of the new affects the believers' *social relationships*: "Here there is no Greek or Jew, circumcised or uncircumcised, barbarian, Scythian, slave or free" (Col. 3:11). The implication of this is seen in the exhortations that immediately follow those words, exhortations that relate to mutual forbearance and love (vv. 12–14).

It is obvious in the Colossians passage that when one has put on the new clothing of Christ, the obliteration of differences in Christ affects not only *position* but also *practice*. There seems to be no reason why the same direction of thought is not to be understood also in Galatians. F. F. Bruce noted in his commentary on Galatians that the removal of restrictions did not pertain only to baptism or only to the Jew-Gentile and slave-freeman relationships. He raises a pertinent question: "If in ordinary life existence in Christ is manifested openly in church fellowship, then, if a Gentile may exercise spiritual leadership in church as freely as a Jew, or a slave as freely as a citizen, why not a woman as freely as a man?"[2]

In summary, some people, noting the theme of justification in the context, hold that Paul's point in this particular passage is that anyone can receive the promised salvation and be clothed with Christ in spite of racial, social, and sexual differences. The biblical use of the clothing metaphor, however, seems to give support to the view that being clothed with Christ rules out these differences, not merely with respect to justification but also in subsequent personal relationships.[3]

1 Corinthians 11:2–16

The exegetical issues involved in this passage are extraordinarily complex. They relate to vocabulary, syntax, circumstances in the Corinthian church, and social background. An introductory issue is whether Paul does or does not approve of women prophesying and praying publicly. If the Corinthians were unspiritual (1 Cor. 3:1) and subject to Paul's correction in a number of matters, could it not be assumed that they were wrong in allowing women to speak in church? Also those who understand 1 Corinthians 14:34 to forbid any spoken words by women in the church must deny that Paul allows it in chapter 11. This involves some difficulties, such as the fact that Paul would then have invested a good amount of space regulating a practice he rejects shortly afterwards.

One bit of internal evidence has sometimes been overlooked in this discussion. Paul begins his instructions in 1 Corinthians 11 with the words "I praise you." The same words are repeated, but in a negative construction, in verse 17, where Paul refuses to praise them for the way they were celebrating the Lord's Supper. Given the importance of the Lord's Supper, it is significant that he withholds praise in that connection but offers praise in connection with the prophetic ministry of women in the first part of the same chapter. One might have thought that if women should not have been taking any audible part in the service, Paul would have withheld praise here as he did in verse 17. Incidentally, the structure of the parallel "praise" phrases, as well as the general context and the reference in verse 10 to angels (thought by some first-century Jews to be present at worship), makes it fairly certain that Paul is describing a meeting of the church, not just a women's meeting as some have suggested. There seems to be no evidence against the supposition. Were it not for the apparent conflict with 14:34b–35 it may be questioned whether anyone would have doubted that 11:1–16 was describing a church meeting.

In addition to these considerations is the fact that Paul introduces some heavy theological concepts (such as headship and the image and glory of God) in this passage to support his regulation of women's participation. This would be strange if the practice were wrong to begin with.

Headship

This is a major issue that also affects other passages such as Ephesians 5:22–33 and consequently impinges on one's concept of the marriage relationship. It is common among those who hold a "traditional" view of women and the church to understand the Greek word for "head," *kephalē*, to signify authority or rule. Not only is this typical in older commentaries, but it is also found in most of the early church fathers as well.[4]

This view is currently under vigorous debate. One reason is that this meaning was *not* characteristic of the metaphorical use of *kephalē* in ancient Greek literature. Another has to do with the Septuagint, the Greek translation of the Hebrew Old Testament done a couple of centuries before Christ. In this translation, when the

Hebrew word for "head" (rōsh) meant rule or authority, the translators tended to avoid using the Greek *kephalē*, using a stronger word, *archōn*, to convey that meaning. A third reason is that some scholars think that "source" conveys the meaning better than rulership or authority in at least some secular and also biblical passages.[5] For example, the idea of source is in the context of 1 Corinthians 11: "For man did not come from woman, but woman from man" (v. 8) and the reverse, "For as woman came from man, so also man is born of woman" (v. 12).

That proposal was challenged in one study on the basis of a survey of over two thousand occurrences of the word.[6] This study concluded that there were no instances in ancient Greek literature where *kephalē* means "source." It also suggested the meaning of "rule" or "authority" in various nonbiblical writings around the New Testament period. More recent research, however, has turned up evidence, previously unrecognized or unacknowledged, that *kephalē* was indeed used to mean "source." It seems difficult to ignore this evidence, especially when some of it is found in ancient medical writings. Also some of the alleged instances of the meaning "rule" or "authority" have been questioned.[7] This illustrates the importance of helpful interaction among scholars.

Another metaphorical use of *kephalē* in ancient Greek literature was to represent the whole person. The head was the most easily visible and prominent part of the body. It was natural to refer to the "head of X," meaning that person. To disgrace one's head (v. 4) is the same as bringing disgrace on oneself (v. 14). Even today one speaks of shame being heaped on the head of someone. First Corinthians 11 may have the idea of prominence at least partially in view when it uses the term "head." In the very next chapter, following a mention of "head" and "feet," Paul refers to those parts of the body that people *think* are more or less honorable, even if they are not really so (1 Cor. 12:21–23).

The result of all this has been to bring into serious question whether, even if authority or rulership is a legitimate metaphorical meaning of *kephalē* in other literature, that is its main use here. In any case, the application of headship in the context of 1 Corinthians 11 is to the covering of the woman's head during ministry, not to her ministry as such. Whatever meaning one assigns to headship, its use in this passage cannot be claimed to exclude women from prophetic ministry in the church. In this conclusion many traditionalist as well as feminist scholars would agree.

Related to this is the question of whether 1 Corinthians 11 is teaching a "chain of command" in which woman is under man. Actually the order in which Paul lists the various relationships is not from God to women, as a chain of command theory would imply, but refers to man and Christ, woman and man, Christ and God. There is certainly order within the pairs, but not some overall movement from greatest (God) to least (woman).

Veiling

Clearly for a woman to have her head uncovered (or hair not modestly bound up)[8] brought disgrace (v. 5). Words about honor, dishonor, shame, and glory are prominent in this passage. Such terms were in common use among moralists in Paul's day to brand what was or was not acceptable morality. Without becoming involved in the many details of the passage, it should be apparent that when Paul writes about headcovering or the binding up of hair, he is dealing with a common symbol of what was honorable in that society.

Authority

Verse 10 says that a woman should have authority (or "right," *exousia*) over her head. Since the publication of a significant study on this verse twenty-five years ago,[9] exegetes have generally accepted its conclusion that "to have authority" means here, as elsewhere in the New Testament, to *possess* authority, not to be under it. The noun *exousia* followed, as in 1 Corinthians 11:10, by *epi*, "over," appears with (1) the verb "to have," as in our passage (cf. Luke 9:1; Rev. 11:6; 14:18; 16:9; 20:6), (2) "to give" (Matt. 28:18; Rev. 2:26; 6:8; 13:7) and (3) the simple verb "to be" (Rev. 22:14, declaring that there is a "right" to the tree of life that the blessed ones will have). In none of these instances is the idea passive—that is, that one is *subject* to authority.

The Greek word *exousia* in 1 Corinthians 11:10 probably does not mean ecclesiastical authority in this context, but simply the right to do something. It is common now to conclude that Paul was giving a woman the right to speak if she had the appropriate hair style or covering. However, it could also be argued on the basis of syntax and context that the right she has is to decide whether or not to wear a head covering.[10] The entire structure of the passage has been the subject of much study.[11]

The small Greek word *plēn* that introduces verses 11ff. indicates some sort of break in the argument. It could be translated "however." The question is whether the word is used in a strong sense to indicate that Paul is setting aside the previous argument or whether it is used simply to indicate a modification or shift in emphasis. In either case, the implication is that what follows expresses elements of Paul's theology that did not appear in the first part. These elements are, first, that (whatever authority a woman may have) woman is not independent of man, nor is man independent of woman. Second, in support or explanation of this, just as the woman came from man (Adam), so, in reverse, man comes through woman (by birth). Neither can argue preference; all is "from God." This reciprocal idea has a parallel in 1 Corinthians 7:4, where Paul teaches that a man and his wife "rule" (*exousiazō*) over each other's bodies.

By using the word for "however" or "nevertheless," Paul gives a hint that while what has preceded is appropriate behavior (perhaps the way for a woman to maintain honor in accordance with both biblical principles and conventional morality), yet fundamentally there is a reciprocal relationship between men and women, as indicated in verses 11 and 12.

In any event, Paul calls the appropriate binding up or covering of the hair, not doctrine, but "custom" (v. 16, NIV "practice"). This fact suggests that a reasonable understanding of the passage is that Paul has established a practice or custom that is an appropriate application of biblical doctrine. Such an understanding bridges two polar positions: one is that the passage contains a timeless command that is to be universally obeyed in the form in which it was given (i.e., women are to wear headcoverings). The other is that the passage is to be interpreted as culture-bound and, therefore, not applicable today. If the above understanding is correct, the passage *does* contain a theological principle about the relationship of men and women. It is associated with the concept of headship on the one hand, and with an appropriate application (the "custom") to all the Pauline churches on the other.

It is increasingly recognized today (even apart from the "women's issue") that Paul was concerned that Christian practice not run counter to the accepted moral norms in society. His concern was that unbelievers would not think that Christians were behaving inappropriately and therefore be repulsed by the behavior and dress of their women. What Paul counsels is not capitulation or conformity to culture, much less a personal lapse into old rabbinic modes of thought, but a deliberate theologically based approach to his society in conformity to biblical principles. By being properly attired, a woman would avoid criticism from conservative Jews and pagans. It might also, if some recent research on the matter is correct, avoid any appearance of homosexuality or a ritual sex change.[12] Paul seems to be showing that the church must not be drawn into pagan ways, while, at the same time, it should make sure that its moral distinctives are not so unconventionally displayed that they *appear* to be immoral.

In the preceding chapters (1 Cor. 8–10) Paul had shown that some of the freedom he passionately argued for in Galatians must be yielded so that he would be like "those under the law" (Jews) or "those without law" (pagans) "in order to win some" (9:18–23). It may be worth considering whether this is an appropriate approach to other passages as well. Few Christians today insist on a headcovering for women, reasoning that this is a cultural matter. Yet the same Christians may insist on women's silence in the church, not realizing that a woman's presence, especially if she spoke, likewise communicated something symbolically to her own society. If the above approach is correct, avoiding the extremes both of culturalizing Paul's instructions on the one hand and of absolutizing them on the other could draw Christians together in an understanding of his instructions, not only regarding women, but on other topics as well.

1 Corinthians 14:34–35

In 1 Corinthians 14 the issue is whether Paul commands permanent silence on the part of women in the church. No one debates that the verb itself means absolute silence. The question is whether women were to be silent under certain circumstances only or at all times. The references to "all the congregations of the saints" in verse 33 and to "law" in verse 34 suggest a universal application. On the other hand, the fact that the two other groups (tongues-speakers and prophets) who were told in the same context (vv. 28, 30) to be silent obviously did normally speak suggests that women likewise normally spoke but had to be silent under some specific circumstances.

It is important to note that the issue here is not over whether the silence of women is irksome today, but whether this passage contradicts the privilege Paul seems to give women to pray and prophesy publicly in chapter 11. Further, that privilege (or, better, ministry) is in accord with the declaration of Peter in Acts 2:17–18, quoting Joel 2:28–29, that a major characteristic of the new age of the Spirit was that both men and women would prophesy. (Some distinguish between the infallible prophecies of Old Testament prophets and the prophecies given in New Testament churches which are to be evaluated [1 Cor. 14:29].) Therefore, three options are available: (1) It is a misunderstanding that Acts 1:17–18 and 1 Corinthians 11:2–16 permit women to prophesy in the church. (2) It is a misunderstanding that 1 Corinthians 14:34b–35 forbids all vocal, audible participation in the church by women. (3) Scripture contradicts itself. For the Evangelical, at least, this is not simply a "feminist" issue, but an exegetical one that relates to the integrity of Scripture.

Several solutions have been proposed:

1. Verses 34–35 were not originally in this passage at this place, and perhaps were not even written by Paul. There is some textual evidence that they originally occurred later in the passage. Manuscripts in the so-called "Western" tradition, that is, used in the churches in the western part of the Roman Empire, had the verses at the end of what we know as chapter 14. This suggests that the verses originally constituted a comment some scribe wrote in the margin of a manuscript, which were then

incorporated into the body of the text by different scribes at different places. In support of this it has been observed that, if that section is omitted, the wording of the text flows very smoothly from verse 33 to verses 36 and following. This solution has naturally been considered with great caution. It is difficult for many people to realize that there are words, phrases, and even entire verses in the present text of the Bible that were introduced into the manuscripts after the originals were completed. But that is the case, and it is a matter of careful judgment on the part of skilled textual scholars, not the feelings of the reader, whether a given text is original or not. That is where the decision on verses 34–35 must rest.[13]

2. The word "law" in verse 34 refers to rabbinic tradition.[14] In support of this theory it is proposed that the first word in verse 36 (usually translated "or") indicates strong disagreement with what precedes.[15] The theory based on these observations is that, as happens occasionally elsewhere in this epistle, Paul is quoting something said by people at Corinth, something he proceeds to reject.

This theory faces some difficulties: (1) Paul never elsewhere uses the word *law* to refer to rabbinical tradition. (2) Although the word that begins verse 36 in the Greek is indeed used elsewhere to indicate a disjunction of thought, there is no context that is an exact parallel. In the closest parallel, 1 Corinthians 6:18–19, what precedes is not an opponent's view but Paul's own command. It is reasonable to infer that what is negated in the present passage is, as in 6:18–19, the implied disobedience to Paul's command.

As for the meaning of "law," the reason some have suggested that it refers to rabbinical tradition is that there is no clear text in the Old Testament to which this refers. Another possibility to be kept in mind is that it may refer both to the Jewish laws and to various provisions in civil legislation to keep women "in their place." This latter theory avoids the argument against "law" referring to rabbinic tradition, for, although Paul would probably not dignify rabbinic tradition with the term *law* (something he does nowhere else), he may well have used the term in a more general way. It is important to observe that what the "law" commands is "submission." This is seen as the opposite of speaking. There is no Old Testament text that specifically commands a woman to be submissive or to be silent. The consequence of the Fall was male domination (Gen. 3:16), but this is expressed, not as a command, but as a description of the way things would be. It is possible that Paul had in mind the insubordination and consequent judgment of Miriam and Aaron (Num. 12:1–15). Miriam was a leader and prophetess in her own right, but she should not have opposed Moses.[16] Perhaps Paul is suggesting that although women could minister in the church, they should assume a submissive attitude in regard to judging or evaluating the prophecies others gave.

3. Paul restricted women only in the matter of participating in the evaluation of the prophets' words. Paul had commanded silence twice previously in this chapter: first, in verse 28 to those speaking in tongues if no interpreter were present and, second, in verse 30 to prophets if a revelation came to another. It is reasonable to ask whether there were some circumstances under which women were to be silent. These circumstances could be the evaluation of prophecies, which was mentioned in verse 29. The structure of the passage can be analyzed as follows: Paul gave instructions (1) for prophesying (v. 29a), then (2) for weighing what was said (v. 29b), followed by (3) further instructions in verses 30–33 concerning the prophesying described in #1 and (4) further instructions in verses 34–36 concerning the weighing of the prophecies described in #2. Some scholars today are tending to see a reference to the "judging of the prophets" as the best solution presently in view, but the matter is by no means settled.[17]

Whatever the case may be, it may be significant that when Paul summarizes his teaching at the end of chapter 14, he refers to prophesying and to speaking in tongues but makes no mention of women's silence. If it were a major point in his teaching, one would expect that he would mention it in his summary.

Ephesians 5:21–33

The main issues in this passage are the meanings of "submit" and of "head." The latter has already been discussed. The word *submit* does not occur in verse 22 in the manuscripts generally considered more dependable. It was probably assumed there from the preceding use in verse 21. In turn verse 21 is actually part of the construction that begins in verse 18. The filling of the Spirit is to be accompanied by speaking to one another with psalms, hymns, and spiritual songs, singing and making music to the Lord, giving thanks, and submitting to one another (vv. 19–21).

The approach adopted by many today, therefore, is that the submission of wives to husbands is part of a mutual submission, reciprocated by the husband, rather than a one-directional submission, as it is usually understood. The traditional understanding is that submission is in one direction only, with some holding that it implies obedience. The verb *submit* can, in fact, be used in situations where one obediently yields to the authority of another, but some traditionalists soften the obedience idea by suggesting that a voluntary, not a forced obedience is taught here. While it is hard to see how the fulfillment of a command can be voluntary, what they mean is that the wife is to do this willingly for the Lord's sake, not in cringing obedience to the husband.

Traditionalists argue that submission can be in only one direction, because it is inconceivable, on Paul's analogy in verse 23, that Christ should be subject to the church. The other point of view is that for Christ to give himself in death for the church was actually a voluntary kind of submission. By analogy, the husband should be willing to forgo claim over his own life, and to yield his life for his wife.

The response on the part of traditionalists would again be that this is not the usual meaning of submission. That is true; we should note, however, that in each of the other two cases, children and parents, slaves and masters, there is a reciprocal, if not submissive, action on the part of the one who demands obedience. Fathers are not to exasperate their children (6:4), and masters are not to threaten their slaves (6:9). It is suggested that Paul is asking fathers and masters to modify their response in a way that was not normal in the ancient world. It is further noted that the word *obey*, which occurs with regard to children and to slaves, is conspicuously absent in the section about wives. In addition, not one of the instructions to the husbands pertains to ruling. All have to do with caring for and enhancing one's wife.

Probably the arguments on both sides have been overstated. A realistic observation is that women in the first century did not need a command to tell them to be submissive to their husbands. That was already expected of them in their pagan society. The point of the passage on this view is that the expected social relationships were to be carried out "in the Lord" by Christians. Paul is not merely repeating a pagan "household code" (as scholars call this type of instruction) but is presenting a theologically based teaching. Far beyond expectations, the relation of husband and wife are revealed to be based on the mystical relation of Christ and the church.[18]

1 Timothy 2:11–15

This passage is another center of controversy. Some of the issues have already been discussed in this volume, specifically (1) the issue of Paul's reference to the order of creation; (2) the question of Paul's intent, that is, whether he intended this as a permanent universal command; and (3) the semantic problem revolving around the words "teach" and "assume authority." Extensive exegetical work has been done on the issues.[19]

One of the major issues is the meaning of *authentein*, translated "usurp authority" in the King James Version, but simply "have authority" in the New International Version. Countless churches have barred women from ministry on the basis of this verb. It is reasoned that if it forbids any kind of authority over men, and if a given church ministry is understood to carry authority, women must be excluded from that ministry.

Interaction thus far has been vigorous. The problem is that the verb is used nowhere else in the New Testament and only rarely in other Greek literature. It is not the common word for exercising authority. Perhaps the first of the contemporary studies on the meaning of *authentein* was Catherine Kroeger's article, "A Strange Greek Verb."[20] The author cited such meanings of the *authent-* word group in ancient Greek usage as sexual aggression, murder, and suicide. The very mention of such meanings, which seem far removed from the context of 1 Timothy, caused many to be skeptical of her conclusions, but it served to open up the discussion and to caution against assuming that Paul was denying any authority at all to women.

A subsequent article by George W. Knight, III, offered material that, in his opinion, proved the simple meaning, "to have authority."[21] Kroeger has continued her own study on the passage itself[22] but, although she has made some telling points against the meaning "to have authority," she has not yet published a full response to Knight.

Some problems have surfaced relating to Knight's citations and interpretations, and more careful study is needed before the matter can be considered settled. This applies especially to the context and dating of some of the occurrences of the verb *authenteō*; around the time of the writing of the New Testament there is evidence of its use in a strong sense of assertiveness (such as "to originate" or "to take authority to oneself"). In the meantime, it would seem premature to conclude that this rare verb has the simple meaning, normally expressed by *exousiazō*, "to have authority."

As for the word "teach" (Greek, *didaskō*), insufficient attention has been given to the fact that this word and others drawn from the same root diminished in church usage while the use of *katecheō* increased. The latter verb related more narrowly to the instruction of converts rather than to teaching in a broader sense. "This marked change in vocabulary from the early to the later Patristic Period seems to correlate with the disappearance of the independent teacher who was responsible for accurately passing on the teachings of the apostles and prophets."[23]

The *didaskō* word group seems to have been used in a more formal sense—that is, for the teaching of doctrine—than was true of the teaching that occurred during the ministry of prophesying (1 Cor. 14:3, 4, 31). There were teachers who carried the authoritative traditions of Jesus and of the apostles to the multiplying and growing churches of the first decades of the church. It was necessary that they be received as authoritative conveyers of the tradition. They were witnesses to what had been said and done. Jewish people would not accept women, nor would pagans. It has been shown that the ancient Greeks accepted women *prophets* but rejected women *teachers*.[24]

Another way to look at the word "teach" is to ascribe a particular authority to the role of teaching. Those who have that viewpoint think in terms of a "teaching office," a concept that led to the teaching "magisterium" of the Catholic church. One problem with this is that the idea of a separate clerical "office" was, according to present evidence, a late development. There will be further discussion on ecclesiastical authority and office in appendix C.

Yet another possibility is that Paul is not permitting women to teach *in such a way* as to *authentein* a man.[25] This takes *didaskō* and *authentein*, not as similar but as related. This takes into account that the word *didaskō* is widely separated grammatically from the word of woman, which seems to indicate that it is not a man teaching a woman that Paul objects to.

We must emphasize that Greek scholars differ among themselves on the relationship of these words. This should serve as a caution against taking a strong position on the basis of one interpretation.

One exegetical datum considered important especially by traditionalists is Paul's reference back to the order of the creation of men and women and to the deception of Eve. The order of creation also constitutes part of Paul's argument in 1 Corinthians 11:8-9. The alternatives would appear to be whether Paul (1) is lapsing into a rabbinic method of thinking (and is wrong), (2) is employing the creation narrative simply as an explanation (showing that this restriction is supported, though not required, by Scripture), (3) is using a legitimate method of argumentation (meaningful to his immediate readership to validate his principle and approach, but not necessarily leading only to the particular application he makes in that context), or (4) is grounding a permanent injunction on a fact that can never lead to any other conclusion. There is yet another option, but it is not a hermeneutical one. That is the critical theory that Paul was not the originator of the teaching in that verse.

The approach represented by option 1 was mentioned in chapter 10 in connection with the work of Paul K. Jewett. Option 2 takes the word "for" in Paul's statement to introduce an illustration or explanation, rather than introducing a reason. This is a usage familiar in classical Greek and continued in Paul's time, as the noted scholar of the history of Greek grammar, A. T. Robertson, pointed out.[26]

Option 3 and option 4 take the word "for" in the text as expressing cause, or logical grounds. That is, Paul is basing his argument on the creation order, not just using that as an illustration or explanation, as in number 2. The difference between options 3 and 4 may be explained as follows: in the former, while Paul's restrictions are derived from creation order, that order could conceivably be honored and followed by other actions in other circumstances. View 4 insists, however, that there can never be any other way to express the order of creation; the restriction of women must be continued exactly as designated, no matter what the circumstances.

Another factor must be kept in mind in arriving at a decision concerning the significance of what is often called creation order. That is the hermeneutical approach of the New Testament to the keeping of the Sabbath, which was certainly a basic element in creation order. The discussion of that and of the whole matter of redemption and the new creation in appendix A should be read in conjunction with the present study of 1 Timothy 2.

Regarding the deception of Eve, it may be useful to keep in mind that in 2 Corinthians 11:3 Paul addresses the entire church with a warning lest they be led astray "just as Eve was deceived by the serpent's cunning." So man as well as woman can be deceived as Eve was.

The matter of circumstances and cultural factors also arises once again in connection with 1 Timothy 2. Several theories have been proposed, among them (1) that women were as yet so uneducated that they should not teach, (2) that the women converts in the church at Ephesus where Timothy was had not yet become mature or proved themselves sufficiently to be able to teach, (3) that among the heretical teachers at Ephesus were women who needed to be silenced, and (4) that the women at Ephesus were caught up with some kind of cultic or heretical doctrines that appealed especially to women. Suggestions regarding this last proposal have included an incipient form of gnosticism that exalted the role both of Eve and of other women and that postulated prominent female elements in a hierarchy of divine beings, and cultic activities that included the symbolism of the snake, with its obvious connection with the garden of Eden. The fourth proposal especially seeks to give due regard to the reference in 1 Timothy 2:13 to the deception of Eve. It is suggested that there is some possibility that ideas concerning the priority of Eve at creation were circulating and needed to be countered by a strong affirmation about the priority of Adam.[27]

A correct interpretation and application of the 1 Timothy 2:8–15 passage must take into consideration *all* of the exegetical data and whatever knowledge of the background can be accurately determined. The passage has tended to attract some careless and subjective interpretations. Disagreement is understandable, but carefulness and honesty in handling the Word of God is an absolute requirement of any who would seek to teach and apply such a crucial passage.

1 Peter 3:1–6

This passage seems to present fewer problems, because the submissive attitude required of the woman has a clear purpose. The believing wife of an unconverted man is to fulfill the expectations of submission in order that she might win him to the Lord. This purpose is in accordance with Titus 2 where Paul says that the young women are to be subject to their husbands "so that no one will malign the word of God" (v. 5). Likewise young men are to show integrity "so that those who oppose you may be ashamed because they have nothing bad to say about us" (v. 8), and slaves are to be subject to their masters "so that in every way they will make the teaching about God our Savior attractive" (v. 10).

This emphasis on submission in personal relationships for the sake of winning the unconverted probably also lies behind 1 Corinthians 11 with respect to the appearance of women when participating publicly in the church. The emphasis on shame versus honor in that section of Corinthians likewise supports this probability, along with Paul's injunction at the end of 1 Corinthians 14 that all things should be done "decently and in order." Some take that to mean spiritual orderliness, but in view of the context, it very likely refers to an orderliness that will commend itself to the outsider. Paul also showed his concern for visitors to the church meeting in 1 Corinthians 14:23–25, where he is worried about such people hearing unintelligible speech. So then the general direction of 1 Peter 3 is clear.

It was said above that this passage *seems* to present fewer problems than the previous. There are issues relating to the setting of the book and this passage. It is generally agreed that Peter, like Paul (Eph. 5:22–33; Col. 3:18–25; cf. Titus 2:2–10), has utilized a form common in the ancient world to list various mutual responsibilities within households (including slaves). Scholars today usually call such a domestic code by the German term *Haustafel*. There is some debate over the reason why Peter takes over this form. One suggestion is that persecuted Christians do not seek the highest places but are willing to take subordinate positions, welcoming and giving a home to those who are the disadvantaged, disinherited "strangers" of that society.[28]

Another approach is to see the domestic code as an expression of conformity to certain generally accepted secular conventions of behavior.[29] Was Peter accommodating to the generally accepted norms of role relationships? Most likely where this was in accordance with biblical principle, he emphasized it so that the gospel would indeed commend itself to the outsider. But that does not mean that Peter modified biblical principles to suit society. In fact, it is assumed in the passage that the wife chose Christianity though her husband did not. But this was already in contrast to the idea of both Dionysius of Halicarnassus and Plutarch that a wife should keep to her husband's religion.[30] Plutarch said that "it is becoming for a wife to worship and to know only the gods that her husband believes in."[31] Therefore the Christian women addressed by Peter would seem to have already been in danger of being charged with insubordination because of their taking an independent stand religiously. They had to demonstrate that by submitting in other ways they were following accepted moral standards.

The other issue in this passage relates to Sarah and Abraham. One may understand the statement "as Sarah obeyed Abraham calling him lord" (v. 6 KJV) as defining submission as obedience. But it would seem that if this requires obedience, it also requires calling the husband "lord." If, however, it is objected that the term "lord" was only the way Sarah expressed her obedience in that culture and need not be be used by Christian wives today, is it not logical to extend the point and say that obedience itself was only the way Sarah expressed her submission in that culture and need not be required of Christian wives today? It is probably best to understand Sarah's obedience (including the term "lord") as an illustration of her submission in a manner that was appropriate to her own society but not to ours.

APPENDIX C

ORDINATION AND AUTHORITY

Importance of the Topic

The ministry of women can, as amply demonstrated in the foregoing historical survey, be exercised in many different ways. Inevitably, however, the question of ordination presses itself to the forefront. The reason for this is clear enough. If ordination admits one to the ranks of the clergy and qualifies that person to perform the church's highest ministries (such as teaching, preaching, and the administration of the ordinances or sacraments), the admittance of women to that office is an unambiguous statement that sex is of no consequence whatsoever in Christian ministry. Conversely, no matter what other ministries might be open to women in a given church or denomination, if women are barred from ordination, a hierarchical position in which women are subordinate to men is thereby affirmed. But the matter is not that simple.

Diversity of Viewpoints

Concepts of ordination differ from denomination to denomination and church to church. Any resolution of the question depends on two variables: (1) one's ecclesiology, particularly the definition and the significance of ordination with regard to the functions it permits, and the qualifications it requires, and (2) one's interpretation of Scripture with regard to the ministries a woman is permitted to perform. The second of these has been touched on earlier under several categories; so attention will now be directed to the meaning of ordination and also to the related matters of church office and the locus of authority.

Recent years, especially since Vatican II, have witnessed many dialogues, spoken and in writing, on the subject of ordination. Discussions about ordination have occasionally resulted in rather extreme positions, just as the practice has been subject to extreme abuses. It is well known that there have been times in history when ordination itself has been challenged, as in such groups as the Quakers and the Plymouth Brethren. One of the early spokesmen for the latter, John Nelson Darby, put the matter into clear and strong terms in a booklet he wrote: "The Notion of a Clergyman: The Sin against the Holy Ghost in This Generation."[1] His thesis was simple: If the Holy Spirit has bestowed spiritual gifts on all believers, for a clergyman to arrogate to himself the sole right to preside at communion and direct the entire service is to deny the work of the Holy Spirit.

Approaching the matter on a different level, Marjorie Warkentin wrote a monograph on the subject, in which she challenged ordination from both a biblical and a historical perspective.[2] Her work explores the rise of the clergy, the assumptions that made this possible, and the biblical issues involved.

One example of dialogue on this subject is a work jointly published in Germany by Catholics and Lutherans in which the arguments raised included reference to such topics as the priesthood of all believers, the theology of ministry, and the pastoral role.[3]

For a sample of traditional thought on ordination the following statement may be quoted:

A new theology of ministry cannot (as some Reformation traditions intended) turn ministry into laity nor eliminate ordination and liturgy as excessively cultic. Just the opposite is needed. The social and animal facets of our human nature call for sacramental liturgy. Ordination is a visible affirmation and invocation of charism, a celebration of the church's diverse life and risky mission, a symbol of the Spirit truly present in the church.[4]

The Ordination of Women

With such diversity of viewpoints on ordination, it is not surprising that there is no unity on the matter of the ordination of women. Recent years have seen publication of various "pro and con" articles and books.[5] A survey of these contributions reveals that proponents of women's ordination characteristically speak to the matter of women's equality as human beings, their equality as Christians, the pouring out of the Spirit on both men and women (Acts 2), their equality in the reception of spiritual gifts (the biblical passages on the subject—such as Romans 12, 1 Corinthians 12, and Ephesians 4:7–13—make no sexual distinction), and the long history of women's varied ministries in Scripture and in the church age. Opponents tend to focus on such matters as the restrictive passages (1 Cor. 14:34–36: 1 Tim. 2:11–15), the headship of the man or husband (1 Cor. 11:3; Eph. 5:22–24), the idea that women are more easily deceived, the qualifications for elders that are couched in male terms (e.g., "husband of one wife"), the exclusively male priesthood in the Old Testament, the fact that Jesus did not appoint any women apostles, and theories about the nature of Christian ministry and priesthood.

Related Issues

In order to clarify the issues further, three related subjects need attention. One is the nature of authority in the church, including teaching authority. A second is the question of what the term "office" implies and whether women occupied church offices in the New Testament period. The third is the laying on of hands and its relation to ordination. The literature on these subjects is vast, but for the present purposes only summaries of each topic will be offered, with occasional references to pertinent scholarly contributions.

Authority

The reason this is a subject for consideration is that if 1 Timothy 2:12 precludes women having any authority in the church, it is essential to know what that does or does not entail. Of course, if the verb authenteō in that passage refers to some wrongful way of assuming authority rather than to the normal exercise of authority, then it is not necessary to determine where ecclesiastical authority lies. Those, however, who have concluded that women ought not to be in any position of authority need to define what positions are involved.

Several questions call for serious consideration: Where did authority lie in the New

Testament church? Was authority attached to an office, such as that of elder or overseer, to the teaching ministry, to the prophetic ministry, to the apostolate, or to some combination of these? Is it appropriate to distinguish between two kinds of authority, that of office and that of personal influence? What kind of authority, if any, did a teacher or prophet have? Was authority inherent in teaching itself? If so, in what kind or level of teaching was it found? Did teaching in the New Testament church include some dimension of judgment or of exercising discipline that it does not have today? Even if the words *didaskō* ("teach") and *authenteō* ("assume authority") are grammatically independent in 1 Timothy 2:12, were they so closely entwined in people's minds that the former implied the latter, with the result that it was better for women not to do either?

While these are important questions, something of great significance can easily be lost in the discussion. The great fear many have today about women having authority is based on several questionable assumptions, such as that (1) 1 Timothy 2:12 totally prohibits women from having authority, (2) certain individuals in the church have authority over others, (3) there is an "office" of ministry whose incumbents are vested with authority, and (4) teaching is always an exercise of authority. In all this discussion an important fact is usually overlooked. This fact is that attention is focused almost exclusively on governmental authority of church leaders over other Christians, whereas in the New Testament the greater emphasis is on authority in the spiritual realm.

It may help, therefore, to summarize briefly some of the occasions in the New Testament where it is said that authority was exercised. These include (1) the right of Jesus to forgive sin (Matt. 9:6; Mark 2:10; Luke 5:24); (2) the teaching of Jesus (Matt. 7:29; Mark 1:22, 27; Luke 4:32); (3) the disciples' casting out demons (Matt. 10:1; Mark 3:15; 6:7; Luke 4:36; 9:1); (4) healing (Matt. 10:1; Luke 9:1); (5) the activities of Jesus in the temple, and, in comparison, the ministry of John the Baptist (Matt. 21:23–25; Mark 11:27–33; Luke 20:1–8); (6) authority over snakes, scorpions, and all the power of the Enemy (Luke 10:19–20); (7) the authority God gave to the Son to judge (John 5:27); (8) power to cast into hell (Luke 12:5); (9) the "rights" Paul had as an apostle (1 Cor. 8:9; 9:4–6, 12, 18; 11:10; 2 Thess. 3:9); (10) the apostolic authority to build up the church (2 Cor. 10:8; 13:10); and (11) the right to eat at the altar in contrast to those who ministered at the tabernacle (Heb. 13:10). To these may be added the problematic matter of the keys of the kingdom, though the word *exousia* does not occur in Jesus' statement about that (Matt. 16:19). Also Jesus said that all authority was given to him, and on the basis of that he gave the Great Commission. We generally apply the Commission to all believers, not just to the apostles. In that case, should we not assume that whatever kind of authority is thereby conveyed to those who go, make disciples, baptize, and teach, is given to women as well as to men?

But even with respect to the circumstance of church activities, a distinction should be made at this point between *actual* authority and *perceived* authority. A church, for example, that has a congregational form of government has vested its authority in the congregation itself. If the church membership has a majority of women, these women can actually be in control of the church, even if that church does not admit women to church office. The pastor would be accountable to this female majority and could be dismissed by them. But in some churches, as is the case with some baptistic "superchurches" today, the pastor dominates the scene. Sometimes he (in such cases it is probably a man) has a great deal of designated authority, such as the power to veto board appointments. But often *perceived* authority also has great significance. That is, the pastor is thought of as an authority figure even without official bestowal of power.

Because of the aura around the figure in the pulpit, it would be difficult for those who withhold all authority from women to accept a woman preacher, even if church polity officially vests authority in the congregation, not in the pastor.

Given not only the fact that the contemporary church is divided today in its concept of authority, but also the humbling probability that all churches have beliefs and practices that depart in some way from those of the New Testament church, it is difficult to lay down simple rules as to lines of authority and the relation of authority to teaching. But it is safe to say that a person teaching the Bible to a local congregation today can hardly be said to have the same authority that a teacher had in New Testament times, especially before the New Testament was completed and readily available.

In ancient times the teacher was highly honored. Jesus noted that those "to whom the word of the Lord came"—i.e., the judges in ancient Israel whose legal decisions were based on their interpretation of divine law—were called "gods" (Ps. 82:6; John 10:34–35). But today, although a teacher may speak in an authoritative manner, no one is bound (with the possible exception of some legalistic sects) to obey every word of that teacher on pain of excommunication. What authority there is resides in the Scripture that is being taught, not in the teacher.

Some question is raised in this respect by Titus 2:15, which is typically translated, as in the NIV: "Encourage and rebuke with all authority." But the word here is not the familiar *exousia*, but *epitagē*. This word was often used in ancient times to refer to a command from God (or, in paganism, from a god) that is to be passed on. Paul uses it to refer to God's command to himself (1 Tim. 1:1). Revelation came through the prophets by the command of God (Rom. 16:26). On some matters Paul had received a specific command of God, probably in the sense of a saying of Jesus (1 Cor. 7:6). The apostle himself had the right to issue a command (2 Cor. 8:8); Timothy and Titus were apostolic delegates. The terminology, therefore, seems not to indicate that Titus was vested with ongoing ecclesiastical authority as an individual, but that he was to convey God's commands in their full force.

One may ask, then, at what point authority enters into ministry. Apart from, say, the sacramental authority of the Catholic priesthood, is there anything about breaking bread at the Lord's Supper that involves authority? What about baptizing? And at what point does pastoral counseling become authoritative? If a woman may teach a boy, how is the age beyond which this is wrong determined? What dimension of teaching or authority is inappropriate for a woman? Is it telling people what the Bible says? Is it telling them what the Bible says Christians should do? Is it telling them what they should identify as sin and therefore not do or repent of having done? Is it explaining doctrine? Is it telling them of the nature and attributes of God? Is it telling them they should be baptized? Can they teach in the home but not in church? What is the theological or spiritual difference between the two? Is one authoritative and the other not? If so, in what sense? What kind of spiritual authority does a preacher have that a Sunday school superintendent does not? Such questions deserve consideration. To rethink the matter of authority may result in an allayment of some fears over the ministry of women.

Office

Was there such an institution as "office" in the New Testament church, or did the churches function through charismatic (i.e., gifted) ministries? Was the situation clear-cut, or was there a blend of office and charisma, with churches differing in their emphasis, depending on their stage of development and other circumstances? This has been the object of ongoing study. Further, is office something that exists independent of the incumbent, continuing even when the office-holders change, or does office exist only when a capable and designated person is performing the indicated ministry?

Contemporary studies on office and ecclesiastical power have isolated several elements that are considered characteristic. These include the idea of permanency just indicated, recognition by the church, a separation of the designated people from the rest (a separation that exists today in the separation of clergy and laity), an act of commissioning (such as ordination), and financial remuneration.[6] But even where there was a ranking of importance of gifts (as Paul seems to do in 1 Corinthians 12:27–31—according to their value in edifying the church), it has to be said that "in reality there hardly existed any *hierarchical* differentiation between the various functions or, in other words, no function at the time of Paul's letter-writing was legally subordinated to any other."[7]

Concepts of power developed rapidly in the early church, however, and Jesus' words about being servants instead of "lords" like those among the Gentiles were being forgotten. But what about ordination? If that is attested in the New Testament and marked by a distinctive act, such as the laying on of hands, it would seem to establish a separate office of authority to which, as some view the Scriptures on women, only men can be admitted.

A related topic is elderhood and similar governing bodies. The New Testament speaks in terms of a plurality of leadership, rather than of individual authority. Some elders lead well and some are good at teaching (1 Tim. 5:17), but there is no indication that elders in the New Testament church exercised authority as individuals over others. On the contrary, elders were not to "lord it over the flock" (1 Peter 5:3). If a denomination does vest ultimate authority in its elders individually and also holds that 1 Timothy 2:12 precludes authority of any kind whatsoever to women, that denomination would understandably bar women from being elders. But if the biblical picture of elders is seen as shepherding and guarding the flock rather than disciplining it, or if *authenteō* in 1 Timothy 2:12 describes, not normal, but some kind of inordinate authority, then matters are different.

A contemporary arrangement may be worth citing here. One large church has recently restructured its organization into a church council that includes all members of the full-time staff and a number of parishioners chosen by the congregation. The members of this group in turn are divided among various specialized ministries in the church. There are no elders or deacons as such, but the functions of elders and deacons are faithfully carried out by the specialized groups. The church is congregational in government; so the ultimate authority does not reside either with the professional staff or with the council, but with the people themselves. Under this arrangement, women may function on the council and in the various ministries groups. In this way it is possible for them to serve, for example, in some of the ministries that elders normally carry on, but without the problems of "authority" that membership on an elder board as such might bring. What such an arrangement accomplishes, in addition to being a practical and efficient way to carry on the work of a large church, is to return to the New Testament emphasis of function and spiritual ministry rather than to center attention on elevation to an "office."

However one may evaluate this arrangement, it can serve to stimulate fresh thinking on the matter. The ultimate question is whether the form of government a particular congregation or denomination holds represents biblical principles as closely as possible. Only when that question has been addressed honestly can the participation of women in church ministries and government be properly discussed.

The Laying on of Hands

It is almost universally assumed that the laying on of hands in 1 Timothy 4:14 and 2 Timothy 1:6 (possibly also 1 Tim. 5:22) is an example of ordination to Christian ministry. Calvin, for example, claimed, "It was the custom and ordinary practice of the Apostles to ordain ministers by the laying on of hands."[8] A further common assumption is that the laying on of hands in the Pastoral Epistles takes its meaning from a Jewish custom of ordaining rabbis and thereby bestowing authority to teach and to render judgments. But the assumption that rabbinic ordination was being performed by the laying on of hands at the time of the New Testament is being challenged today. This naturally brings into question the laying on of hands for Christian ordination.

Lest the task of evaluating the evidence seem easy, the observation of a Catholic scholar, may be noted, that "almost every issue related to the subject remains unsolved."[9] A Jewish scholar concludes his study of Jewish ordinations by saying, "The real question, or questions, have yet to be asked. . . . The real challenge of investigating authority structures in Jewish societies past and present should now begin."[10]

The laying on of hands was practiced from earliest biblical times (cf. Gen. 48:14–22). It is sometimes overlooked, however, that the practice was used for a number of different reasons, including identification with sacrifices. Perhaps the most familiar use was when Moses designated his successor, Joshua (Num. 27:18–23; cf. Deut. 34:9). In the former passage, it says that Joshua was already filled with the Holy Spirit; in the latter that he became filled with the Spirit. Acts 6:1–6 is reminiscent of the former, 1 Timothy 4:14 and 2 Timothy 1:6 of the latter. In neither New Testament instance, however, is it related to the choice of a successor. Hands were also laid on the Levites to set them apart for the Lord (Num. 8:5–14), but not on the seventy elders to whom Moses gave authority to judge (Num. 11:16–25). Therefore the attempt of the medieval Jewish scholar Maimonides to trace rabbinic ordination to the installation of the seventy elders is not valid, at least as regards the rite used.

It seems significant that the Gospels do not record that Jesus laid hands on the apostles, as one might have expected if this were the way the church should convey authority. There is no instance of it being done either with the group or with individual disciples, in spite of the attention given to Jesus' call of the disciples. Neither did he lay hands on the disciples to whom he gave the Great Commission (Matt. 28:16–20).

There are several occasions of the laying on of hands in Acts. Twice the laying on of hands conveyed, or appears to have conveyed, the gift of the Holy Spirit (8:17; 19:6). The appointment in Acts 6:1–6, already noted, was for a particular work in serving others, not to a position of authority. Ananias laid his hands on Paul, having been sent so that Paul might regain his vision and be filled with the Holy Spirit (Acts 9:17). In Acts 13:1–3 Barnabas and Paul were commissioned with the laying on of hands for a particular mission, which they are said to have fulfilled at the end of Acts 14. This was not an "ordination" as it is known today. They had already been in Christian ministry. It was not a commissioning to a position but to a particular task. That task was not within the church, but external to it—that is, to missionary work.

The clear impression gained thus far is that the laying on of hands had to do with service, not rank. The appointment of elders by Paul and Barnabas on the return leg of the first missionary journey (Acts 14:23) offers no further data, since it did not include the laying on of hands. In place of the laying on of hands, however, we find a significant expression: to "stretch out the hand" (as one did in voting in the ancient Greek assemblies or in pointing out someone or something). It came to mean "to appoint," and was used of the appointment of the high priest and of church officials. In 2 Corinthians 8:19 it is used of the appointment of Titus to assist in the offering Paul was taking to Jerusalem. After apostolic times the term came to be used for ordination, a use it did not have in the New Testament. This is not the term used in 1 Timothy 4:14 and 2 Timothy 1:6. Instead, we find the familiar laying on of hands. A spiritual gift was imparted at this time. There is no indication that Timothy was installed into some office or position of authority.

Thus the laying on of hands was different from the later practice of Jewish ordination. Ordination of rabbis meant the conferral of judicial authority. This was also the case with a different practice that was going on at the time of the New Testament: the appointment of the Sanhedrin by the laying on of hands. That was purely judicial and unrelated to teaching ministry. As regards rabbinic ordination, no saying referring to the laying on of hands is attributed to any rabbi prior to the time of Rabina (4th century, C.E.), who asked R. Ashi, "Is ordination practiced by the laying on of hands?" (B. Sanhedrin 13.b).

Perhaps the strongest position on Jewish antecedents to Christian ordination has been taken by Hoffman, who says, "In modern times, the analogy with Christian ordination has led to a search for something comparable in early Jewish tradition. So scholars have built an elaborate structure of notions presumed to correspond to early ordination ceremonial. There is no evidence to support any of this."[11] Any conclusion has to be expressed with caution, but it would seem that 1 Timothy 4:14 and 2 Timothy 1:6 do *not* describe an ordination as we think of it today, nor did Acts 6:6 or 13:3. The laying on of hands was a charismatic act that had points of comparison with various other impositions of hands in Scripture, but it cannot be identified with any uniform rite practiced in New Testament times. Therefore it would appear that while arguments concerning women's ordination (whether pro or con) may be meaningful with regard to denominational polity, there is no passage within the New Testament dealing with ordination to clerical office as usually conceived today on which such arguments can be based.

NOTES

Preface

[1] Patricia Hill, *The World Their Household: The American Woman's Foreign Mission Movement and Cultural Transformation, 1870–1920* (Ann Arbor: University of Michigan, 1985), 2, quoted in James J. Kenneally, "Eve, Mary, and the Historians," in Janet Wilson James, ed., *Women in American Religion* (Philadelphia: University of Pennsylvania, 1980), 206.

[2] Catherine Booth, "Female Ministry; or, Woman's Right to Preach the Gospel," in *Papers on Practical Religion* (London: S. W. Partridge, 1978), 122–23.

[3] John R. Rice, *Bobbed Hair, Bossy Wives and Women Preachers* (Murfreesboro, Tenn.: Sword of the Lord, 1941), 59.

[4] Peter Berger, *The Sacred Canopy; Elements of a Sociological Theory of Religion* (Garden City: Doubleday, 1967), 108.

[5] Frances Willard, *Women in the Pulpit* (Boston: Lathrop, 1888), 73.

Chapter 1

[1] Luke 1:5–22, 26–38.

[2] Luke 1:20.

[3] Luke 1:45.

[4] The patriarchal nature of Old Testament society—that is, the assumption of male superiority common in Ancient Near Eastern society—is now assumed by many interpreters. The following works will provide an introduction to the various approaches to the way women are pictured in the Old Testament: Phyllis Trible, *God and the Rhetoric of Sexuality* (Philadelphia: Fortress, 1978) and *Texts of Terror* (Philadelphia: Fortress, 1984); John H. Otwell, *And Sarah Laughed: The Status of Women in the Old Testament* (Philadelphia: Westminster, 1977); Leonard Swidler, *Biblical Affirmations of Women* (Philadelphia: Westminster, 1979).

[5] Judith 10:5; 11:2; 12:7–9; Judith 4:12; 8:31; 9:2–14; 12:6, 8; 13:4, 5, 7; 16:1–17; Judith 10:6–12:20.

[6] G. W. E. Nickelsburg in Michael E. Stone, ed., *Jewish Writings of the Second Temple Period. Compendia Rerum Iudicarum ad Novum Testamentum.* Section 2 (Philadelphia: Fortress, 1984), 50–51.

[7] Tobit 8:5–6.

[8] We are assuming that Luke is reproducing essentially what Mary said, although this is disputed by some scholars who assume it comes from another source or is his own creation.

[9] Both Mary J. Evans (*Woman in the Bible* [Downers Grove: InterVarsity, 1983], 57–60) and James B. Hurley (*Man and Woman in Biblical Perspective* [Grand Rapids: Zondervan, 1981], 112–14) devote an extra section to Mary. This indicates their recognition of her importance, but neither sees as much in the narratives concerning her as does Ben Witherington III (*Women in the Ministry of Jesus.* Society for New Testament Studies, monograph series 51 [Cambridge: Cambridge University Press, 1984], 80–100). In his opinion Mary was in the process of becoming a disciple.

[10] See, for example, Raymond E. Brown, *The Gospel According to John I–XII,* Anchor Bible 29 (Garden City: Doubleday, 1966), 99; Ernst Haenchen, *A Commentary on the Gospel of John,* trans. Robert W. Funk (Philadelphia: Fortress, 1980), 173; Leon Morris, *Commentary on the Gospel of John,* The New International Commentary Series (Grand Rapids: Eerdmans, 1971), 180–82.

[11] Brown, *The Gospel According to John,* 99.

[12] Witherington, *Women in the Ministry of Jesus,* 95.

[13] Mark 3:21.

[14] Matthew 12:46–50; Mark 3:31–35; Luke 8:19–21.

[15] Luke 11:27–28.

[16] Luke 12:13–14.

[17] Luke 1:39–45; 2:36–38.

[18] Luke 1:5–7.

[19] Luke 2:25–38.

[20] Luke 2:36.

[21] Luke 10:38–42.

[22] Leonard Swidler, *Biblical Affirmations of Woman* (Philadelphia: Westminster, 1979), 192. Cf. Hurley, *Man and Woman in Biblical Perspective*, 88–89; Evelyn and Frank Stagg, *Woman in the World of Jesus* (Philadelphia: Westminster, 1978), 118–19, 140–41.

[23] Luke 10:39.

[24] Mishnah Aboth 1.4.

[25] Acts 22:3.

[26] 1 Timothy 2:11.

[27] Aída Besançon Spencer, *Beyond the Curse* (Nashville: Nelson, 1985), 59.

[28] John 11:17–44.

[29] Matthew 16:16.

[30] It is remarkable that the verbal identity has been virtually overlooked by commentators. Leon Morris, while not mentioning the parallel, does underscore the theological significance of Martha's words (*Commentary on the Gospel of John*. New International Commentary [Grand Rapids: Eerdmans, 1971], 551–52). Raymond E. Brown observes that her statement is "quite like" Peter's confession (*The Gospel According to John (I–III)*. Anchor Bible [Garden City: Doubleday, 1966], 425).

[31] Elizabeth M. Tetlow, *Women and Ministry in the New Testament* (New York: Paulist, 1980), 111.

[32] Witherington, *Women in the Ministry of Jesus*, 109. Witherington points out, in response to critical scholars, that Martha's response does not include all one might have expected if the conversation were totally editorial work on the author's part rather than a true representation of what actually transpired. Martha's answer does not specifically refer to the question Jesus asks in verse 26 (p. 106). He affirms that we have here "not an idealized portrait of two women disciples, but a portrait that indicates women are capable of faith and an accurate confession, and are worthy recipients of the teaching of Jesus."

[33] Matthew 16:21–23.

[34] John 12:3.

[35] Matthew 26:12.

[36] Matthew 26:13. The words of Jesus became the title of one of the most influential works on feminist biblical theology: Elisabeth Schüssler Fiorenza, *In Memory of Her* (New York: Crossroad, 1983).

[37] Luke 8:1–3.

[38] Matthew 19:29; Mark 10:29–30; Luke 18:29–30; cf. Luke 14:26.

[39] Matthew 19:12.

[40] Luke 7:12.

[41] Luke 7:36–50.

[42] Luke 13:10–13.

[43] Witherington, *Women in the Ministry of Jesus*, 71.

[44] Luke 13:16. Witherington (*Women in the Ministry of Jesus*, 70) says that this term is never applied to an individual elsewhere in the Bible or in rabbinic literature.

[45] Witherington, *Women in the Ministry of Jesus*, 70.

[46] Mark 12:41–44; Luke 21:1–4.

[47] John 4:1–26, 39.

[48] John 17:20.

[49] Raymond E. Brown, "Roles of Women in the Fourth Gospel," *Theological Studies* 36 (1975): 691. See also the comments by Ben Witherington, *Women in the Ministry of Jesus*, 57–63.

[50] Matthew 8:14–15; Mark 1:29–31; Luke 4:38–39.

[51] Witherington, *Women in the Ministry of Jesus*, 67.

[52] Ibid., 68.

[53] John 7:53–8:11. See Bruce M. Metzger, *Textual Commentary on the Greek New Testament* (London and New York: United Bible Societies, 1971), 219–22.

[54] Matthew 9:18–26; Mark 5:21–43; Luke 8:40–56.

[55] Cf. Leviticus 15:25–39.

[56] Janice Capel Anderson, "Matthew: Gender and Reading," *Semeia* 28 (1983): 11.

[57] Evans, *Woman in the Bible*, 51.

[58] Anderson, "Matthew: Gender and Reading," 14–15.

[59] Matthew 15:21–28; cf. 14:13–21; 15:29–39; Mark 7:24–30; cf. 6:30–44; 8:1–13.

[60] D. A. Carson, "Matthew," in *The Expositor's Bible Commentary*, Frank E. Gaebelein, ed., 12 vols. (Grand Rapids: Zondervan, 1984), 8:355.

[61] Matthew 27:55–56.

[62] Mark 15:40–41.

[63] Luke 23:49.

[64] Ibid.

[65] John 19:25–26.

[66] This has long been taken as a technical term describing the rabbi-student relationship in the Talmud. It has also been claimed that it is a late term, mainly brought into the Gospel

tradition after the time of Jesus. (H. D. Betz, *Nachfolge und Nachahmung Jesu Christi im Neuen Testament* [1967], discussed in Martin Hengel, *The Charismatic Leader and His Followers*, James Greig, trans. [New York: Crossroad, 1981], 84–86.) But no less a scholar than Martin Hengel has concluded, after an intensive study, that in the rabbinic tradition the idea of following refers concretely to the student walking after the teacher in a subordinate relationship, "without any more profound sense" (Martin Hengel, *The Charismatic Leader*, 52). Following after Jesus has "primarily the concrete sense of following him *in his wanderings and sharing with him his uncertain and indeed perilous destiny* and becoming his pupils only in a derivative sense" (p. 54, italics his). This direction of research makes it perilous to read too much into the fact that women "followed" Jesus. But at the same time, whatever limitations must be recognized will apply to both men and women "followers." The more significant facts in this regard are that (1) no woman is ever called a "disciple" (*mathētēs*) and that (2) no women are included among the Twelve.

[67] Mark 15:41.

[68] Tetlow, *Women and Ministry in the New Testament*, 97.

[69] Luke 23:55–56.

[70] Dorothy Pape, *In Search of God's Ideal Woman* (Downers Grove: InterVarsity, 1976), 47–48.

[71] John 19:39.

[72] Gilbert Bilezikian, *Beyond Sex Roles* (Grand Rapids: Baker, 1985), 104.

[73] Evans, *Woman in the Bible*, 54.

[74] Acts 4:13.

[75] See Warren C. Trenchard, *Ben Sira's View of Women: A Literary Analysis*, Brown Judaic Studies 38 (Chico, Calif.: Scholars, 1982).

[76] Trenchard, *Ben Sira's View of Women*, 19ff.

[77] Ibid.

[78] Ibid., 169.

[79] Ibid., 58.

[80] 1 Timothy 2:14.

[81] Romans 5:12.

[82] Genesis 3:16.

[83] The former position has been taken by such Old Testament scholars as C. F. Keil and Franz Delitzsch, *Biblical Commentary on the Old Testament*, vol. 1, Pentateuch (Edinburgh: T. & T. Clark, 1964), 103; E. J. Young, *Genesis 3* (London: Banner of Truth Trust, 1966), 122–29. The latter interpretation has been expounded

most clearly by Susan B. Foh, "What is the Woman's Desire?" *Westminster Theological Journal* 37 (1974): 376–83; idem, *Women and the Word of God: A Response to Biblical Feminism* (Grand Rapids: Baker, 1981), 67–69. A key issue is the meaning of the rare word *teshukah*, usually translated "desire." Many think it indicates an inordinate dependence on, or sexual desire for, another. Foh interprets it in parallel with Genesis 4:7, where sin's desire is for Cain, who should rule over it. She interprets the word according to Arabic etymology, which is now a questionable method linguistically. In my judgment, she fails to see the significance of the only other use of *teshuka* (Song of Songs 7:10). She understands its meaning there to be affected by the idea of possession ("I am my beloved's"), whereas the point seems to be that it is the bridegroom, not the possessed bride, who has the "desire" for the other. The use of the word for the feelings of the *male* would seem to raise a question about the theory that in Genesis the word indicates competition for rulership, in spite of its use in 4:7. Also Foh understands the clauses in Genesis 3:16b to be antithetical because of the use of the pronoun and the *vav*. That is questionable. There is also an issue as to whether the whole statement is to be taken imperatively as a curse or whether it is essentially a declaration of consequences. In the latter case it is proper both to alleviate the fallen situation, as with medical help at childbirth (a controversy long since settled), and to seek an understanding as to how the redemptive work of Christ in believers' lives modifies the distorted relationship between fallen man and fallen woman.

[84] E.g., Sirach 26:7, "A bad [or evil] wife is a chafing yoke." Statements like this are balanced by others, such as "A good wife is a generous gift" (26:3). See the translation by Bruce Vawter in *The Book of Sirach*, part 2 with commentary (New York: Paulist, 1962).

[85] Trenchard, *Ben Sira's View of Women*, 73.

[86] Ibid., 79.

[87] In the introduction to the published revision (1984) of his dissertation (1981) on women in the ministry of Jesus, Ben Witherington rejects the positive conclusions of R. Loewe, *The Position of Women in Judaism* (London: S.P.C.K., 1966), as well as those of George Foote Moore, *Judaism in the First Centuries of the Christian Era*, vols. 1 and 2 (New York: Schocken, 1971). On the other hand, he finds

J. Jeremias, *Jerusalem in the Time of Jesus Christ,* trans. F. H. and C. H. Cave (Philadelphia: Fortress, 1969) and J. Bonsirven, *Palestinian Judaism in the Time of Jesus Christ,* trans. W. Wolf (New York: Holt, Rinehart and Winston, 1964) too negative. He does not comment at that point on the works we have referred to above by Swidler (1976, 1979), Stagg, or Biale, which were probably published too late for his use.

Leonard Swidler's summary of the evidence is this: "Simply stated, the clear conclusion . . . is that in the formative period of Judaism the status of women was not one of equality with men, but rather, severe inferiority, and that even intense misogynism was not infrequently present. . . . In drawing this conclusion . . . Judaism was not simply following the pattern of the societies and cultures around it. On the contrary, it appears to be running quite counter to the trends of at least the surrounding (Egyptian), Hellenistic, and Roman cultures" (Leonard Swidler, *Women in Judaism* [Metuchen, N. J.: Scarecrow, 1967], 167).

The reason for gathering and dating these works at this point is to show something of the swing from one opinion to another and the fact that right up to the present the picture is not uniform. At the time of this writing, Witherington's book is the most recent on the subject. His conclusion, after several brief but compact and well-documented pages is that "there was no monolithic entity . . . though it appears that by the first century of the Christian era a negative assessment was predominant among the rabbis" (p. 10).

[88] Luke 15:11–32.

[89] Luke 15:3–10.

[90] Luke 18:1–8.

[91] Walter Bauer, William F. Arndt, F. Wilbur Gingrich, and Frederick W. Danker, *A Greek-English Lexicon of the New Testament,* 2d ed., revised and augmented (Chicago and London: University of Chicago Press, 1979), s.v. *hypōpiazō,* 848.

[92] Matthew 25:1–13.

[93] Matthew 13:31–32, 33–35.

[94] Matthew 12:42; Luke 11:31.

[95] Bilezikian, *Beyond Sex Roles,* 86.

[96] Bauer, Arndt, Gingrich, Danker, *Greek-English Lexicon of the New Testament,* 412.

[97] Luke 17:34–35.

[98] Witherington says that grinding was also done at night, just before dawn (p. 45).

[99] Acts 1:15–26.

[100] Pape, *In Search,* 47–49, quoting Ryrie, *The Place of Women,* 38.

[101] Dorothy L. Sayers, *Are Women Human?* (Grand Rapids: Eerdmans, 1971), 47.

[102] Tetlow, *Women and Ministry,* 103.

[103] Luke 1:6.

[104] E.g., Acts 2:17–18; 18:18–28.

[105] Luke 19:10.

[106] Luke 13:10–17.

[107] Matthew 2:18, from Jeremiah 31:15.

[108] Matthew 8:14–15; Mark 1:29–31; Luke 4:38–39.

[109] Matthew 9:18–26; Mark 5:21–43; Luke 8:40–56.

[110] Matthew 14:3–12; Mark 6:17–29.

[111] Matthew 18:24–25.

[112] John 7:53–8:11. The overwhelming mass of manuscript evidence places it here or else omits it completely; two minuscules place it in Luke, one following 21:38, the other (a very late minuscule) following 24:53. Were Luke looking for an incident that illustrated a woman's sinfulness, this would have served well. The evidence that it was originally in his Gospel is too slight and too late to consider. Whether he knew of it is impossible even to conjecture.

[113] Matthew 21:31.

[114] Mark 12:41–44; Luke 21:1–4.

Chapter 2

[1] The following are useful works on women in the classical world: Helene P. Foley, *Reflections of Women in Antiquity* (New York, London, Paris: Gordon and Breach Science Publishers, 1981); Mary R. Lefkowitz and Maureen B. Fant, eds., *Women's Life in Greece and Rome* (Baltimore: Johns Hopkins University Press, 1982); and Sarah B. Pomeroy, *Goddesses, Whores, Wives, and Slaves: Women in Classical Antiquity* (New York: Schocken, 1975).

[2] Pomeroy, *Goddesses,* 35–38.

[3] Ibid., 74.

[4] James Sigountos and Myron Shank, "Public Roles for Women in the Pauline Church: A Reappraisal of the Evidence," *Journal of the Evangelical Theological Society* 26 (1983): 283–95.

[5] This transition is described by Pomeroy, *Goddesses,* 93–148.

[6] J. P. V. D. Balsdon, *Roman Women: Their History and Habits* (Westport, Conn.: Greenwood, 1962), 226–29.

[7] Livy, *History of Rome* 34.1–8, quoted in Mary R. Lefkowitz and Maureen B. Fant, eds., *Women's Life in Greece and Rome: A Source Book in Translation* (Baltimore: Johns Hopkins University Press, 1982), 177.

[8] Susan Bell, ed., *Women: From the Greek to the French Revolution* (Stanford: Stanford University Press, 1973), 36.

[9] Balsdon, *Roman Women*, 77–78.

[10] Juvenal Satire VI, "The Ways of Women," 83–136 (Loeb Translation).

[11] Balsdon, *Roman Women*, 63.

[12] See Balsdon, *Roman Women*, 45–62, "Female Emancipation," for examples of the situations described in this paragraph.

[13] On Musonius Rufus, see S. A. Cook, F. E. Adcock, and M. P. Charlesworth, eds., *The Cambridge Ancient History*, 11:752; on Seneca see Anna Lydia Motto, "Seneca on Women's Liberation," *Classical World* 65 (1972): 155–57; J. N. Sevenster, *Paul and Seneca* (Leiden: Brill, 1961), 192-96.

[14] Diodorus Siculus *Library of History* 1.27.1–2, quoted in David Balch, *Wives Be Submissive: The Domestic Code in 1 Peter*, Society of Biblical Literature Monograph Series 26 (Chico, Calif.: Scholars, 1981), 71.

[15] Dio Cassius, *Roman History* 50.28.3, quoted in Balch, *Wives Be Submissive*, 71.

[16] Rachel Biale, *Women and Jewish Law: An Exploration of Women's Issues in Halakhic Sources* (New York: Schocken, 1984), 12.

[17] Biale, *Women and Jewish Law*, 17–24.

[18] Mishnah Sotah 3.4; B. Sotah 20a.

[19] Leonard Swidler, *Women in Judaism: The Status of Women in Formative Judaism* (Metuchen, N. J.: Scarecrow, 1976), 93–95.

[20] Biale, *Women and Jewish Law*, 34.

[21] Sotah 3.4.

[22] Jerusalem Talmud, Sotah 3:16a, quoted in Biale, *Women and Jewish Law*, 35.

[23] B. Pesahim 62b.

[24] B. Berakhoth 10a.

[25] B. Shabbath 152a.

[26] Tosephta Berakhoth 7, 8.

[27] B. Berokhoth 13b.

[28] B. Manakhoth 43b. See L. Swidler, *Biblical Affirmations of Women* (Philadelphia: Westminster, 1979), 155.

[29] R. Kiddushin 7a. See Biale, *Women and Jewish Law*, 49.

[30] Ben Witherington III, *Women in the Ministry of Jesus*, SNTS Monograph Series 51 (Cambridge: Cambridge University Press, 1984), 3–4.

[31] Swidler, *Women in Judaism*, 159–60.

[32] Such situations included the failure of the husband to consummate the marriage and unusual circumstances such as the husband's occupation, contraction of leprosy, and inability to provide support. Witherington, *Women in the Ministry of Jesus*, 5.

[33] Louis M. Epstein, *Sex Laws and Customs in Judaism* (New York: Ktav, 1967), 16, citing for these and other similar prohibitions Ber. 24a; 61a–b; 'Erub. 18b; Sab. 33a; 64b; Ket. 17a; Ned. 20a; B.K. 16b; B.B. 55a; Gen. R. 60, 13; Der. Er. Ch. 1; Kallah, Ch. 1; Yer. Hal. 58c; Yer. Sotah 18c.

[34] Bernadette J. Brooten, *Women Leaders in the Ancient Synagogue*, Brown Judaic Studies 36 (Chico, Calif.: Scholars, 1982), 5–33.

[35] Brooten deals with this, though in my judgment she fails to meet the force of the objection. As for the actual evidence, of over thirty Greek and Latin inscriptions that refer to a head of a synagogue, ranging from 70 B.C. to the Byzantine period, only three (all in Greek) mention a woman. None is known prior to or during the life of Christ. Brooten understands a rare term, *peristeria archēgisis*, as possibly indicating the female founder of a Jewish community. Any connection this might have with New Testament times is not clarified; Brooten does not discuss dating. She cites six inscriptions that list women as elders. All are too late for our period except for one that she dates somewhere between the first century B.C. and the third century A.D. In that inscription the word *presbytēs*, could mean simply "aged woman," though in one of the later inscriptions a woman so designated was only thirty-eight. Six inscriptions refer to a woman as mother of the synagogue. All are after the first century. There is one inscription, dated at 28 B.C., that refers to a woman priest. Not surprisingly this comes from Egypt, where women were far less restricted (apart from Philo's opinion) than in Palestine. It also relates to one of the rare instances of a temple outside of Jerusalem.

[36] Brooten, *Women Leaders*, 104–6.

[37] Ibid., 107–8.

[38] Pomeroy, *Women in Hellenistic Egypt*, 48–49.

[39] Philo, *The Special Laws*, Book III, 169 (Loeb translation).

[40] Philo, *Questions on Genesis*, Book IV, 15.

[41] *Questions on Genesis*, Book I, 33.

[42] Josephus *Antiquities* 11.3.5.

[43] Elizabeth M. Tetlow, *Women and Ministry in the New Testament* (Ramsey, N.J.: Paulist, 1980), 106–9.

44 W. M. Ramsay, *St. Paul the Traveller and Roman Citizen*, 102, quoted in F. F. Bruce, *The Book of Acts*, NICNT (Grand Rapids: Eerdmans, 1954), 284.

45 For observations on these changes see Bruce M. Metzger, *Textual Commentary on the Greek New Testament* (London and New York: United Bible Societies, 1971), 453–54, 459–60.

46 Acts 16:1.

47 2 Timothy 1:5.

48 2 Timothy 3:15.

49 In Bernadette Brooten's discussion of women active in synagogues (*Women Leaders*, 140), she understands *proslambanō* in Acts 18:26 simply as "took," inferring that Priscilla taught Apollos "in a synagogue context." The Greek word strongly implies taking aside or even into one's home.

50 Gillian Clark, "Roman Women," *Greece and Rome* 28 (1981): 206–7.

51 Philippians 4:3.

52 Colossians 4:15.

53 Romans 16:3; 1 Corinthians 16:19.

54 Peter Richardson, "From Apostles to Virgins: Romans 16 and the Roles of Women in the Early Church," forthcoming article.

55 Henry George Liddell and Robert Scott, *A Greek English Lexicon*, rev. by Henry Stuart Jones (Oxford: Oxford University Press, 1940, with supplement, 1968), s.v. *prostatis*, 1527; cf. word group on 1526–27.

56 Liddell and Scott, *Lexicon*, s.v. *thea*, 786.

57 E. A. Judge, "Cultural Conformity and Innovation in Paul: Some Clues From Contemporary Documents," *Tyndale Bulletin* 35 (1984): 21.

58 Origen, *Epistolam ad Romanos Commentariorum* 10.26; 39, cites early commentators who assumed Junia was a woman. John Chrysostom, *Homily on the Epistle of St. Paul the Apostle to the Romans* 31; Jerome, *Liber Interpretationis Hebraicorum Nominum* 72, 15. See the discussion in Aída Besançon Spencer, *Beyond the Curse: Women Called to Ministry* (Nashville: Nelson, 1985), 101–02. She also explains why the text means that Junia was considered outstanding *among*, rather than *by*, the apostles, as some contend.

59 C. E. B. Cranfield, *The Epistles to the Romans*, vol. 2, International Critical Commentary (Edinburgh: T. & T. Clark, 1979, 1983), 788.

60 Spencer, *Beyond the Curse* (Nashville: Nelson, 1985), 109–12.

61 Livy, *History of Rome* 34, 1–8, quoted in Lefkowitz and Fant, *Women's Life in Greece and Rome*, 177.

62 Plutarch, *Moralia: Advice to Bride and Groom*, 31.

63 Ibid., 32–33, 48.

64 Robert Banks, *Paul's Idea of Community* (Grand Rapids: Eerdmans, 1980), 160, citing Plutarch, *Advice on Marriage* 19.32 and 48, and Seneca *Ad Helvium* 17.2–5.

65 Sirach 26:14.

66 Richard and Catherine Kroeger, "Sexual Identity in Corinth," *Reformed Journal* 28 (1978): 12.

67 James B. Hurley, "Did Paul Require Veils or the Silence of Women? A Consideration of I Cor. 11:2–16 and I Cor. 14:33b–36," *Westminster Theological Journal* 35 (1973): 190–220.

68 Kroeger, "Sexual Identity in Corinth," 11–15.

69 Richard Kroeger and Catherine Kroeger, "Pandemonium and Silence at Corinth," *Reformed Journal* 28 (June 1978): 11–15.

70 E. A. Judge, "Cultural Conformity and Innovation."

71 1 Corinthians 11:16.

72 1 Corinthians 14:40.

73 H. C. Kee, "The Linguistic Background of 'Shame' in the New Testament" in Matthew Black and W. A. Smalley, eds., *On Language, Culture, and Religion* (The Hague: Mouton, 1974), 135–47.

74 Richardson, "From Apostles to Virgins."

75 1 Corinthians 9:20.

76 For this background, see David L. Balch, *Let Wives Be Submissive: The Domestic Code in I Peter* (Chico, Calif.: Scholars, 1981), 1–62, and David C. Verner, *The Household of God: The Social World of the Pastoral Epistles*, SBL Dissertation Series 71 (Chico, Calif.: Scholars, 1983), 1–81.

77 Balch, *Wives Be Submissive*, 63–121.

78 Two opposing views are found in Catherine Kroeger, "Ancient Heresies and a Strange Greek Verb," *Reformed Journal* 29 (March 1979): 12–15, along with her article "1 Timothy 2:12—A Classicist's View" in Alvera Mickelson, ed., *Women, Authority and the Bible* (Downers Grove: InterVarsity, 1986), 225–44; and George W. Knight III, "AUTHENTEO in Reference to Women in 1 Timothy 2:12," *New Testament Studies* 30 (1984): 143–47.

79 See Sigountos and Shank, "Public Roles for Women," 285–95.

80 Spencer, *Beyond the Curse*, 71–95.

81 J. N. D. Kelly, *A Commentary on the Pastoral Epistles* (London: A. C. Black, 1963; reprint, Grand Rapids: Baker, 1981), 112.

[82]A. T. Hanson, *The Pastoral Epistles*, New Century Bible Commentary (Grand Rapids: Eerdmans, 1982), 81.

[83]Kelly, *Pastoral Epistles*, 83.

[84]Hanson, *Pastoral Epistles*, 80.

Chapter 3

[1]Patricia Wilson-Kastner et al, *A Lost Tradition: Women Writers of the Early Church* (New York and London: University Press of America, 1981).

[2]Some of the relevant studies are: Jean Daniélou, *The Ministry of Women in the Early Church*, trans. Glyn Simon (London: Faith, 1961); Roger Gryson, *The Ministry of Women in the Early Church*, trans. J. LaPorte and Mary Louise Hall (Collegeville, Minn.: Liturgical, 1976); Leonard Swidler and Arlene Swidler, eds., *Women Priests: A Catholic Commentary on the Vatican Declaration* (New York: Paulist, 1977); Haye van der Meer, S.J., *Women Priests in the Catholic Church?* trans. Leonard and Arlene Swidler (Philadelphia: Temple University Press, 1973).

[3]Edith Deen, *Great Women of the Christian Faith* (New York: Harper & Brothers, 1959).

[4]Julia Kavanagh, *Women of Christianity* (1891), cited in Deen, *Great Women*, xvii.

[5]Elizabeth A. Clark, *Women in the Early Church. Message of the Fathers of the Church, no. 13* (Wilmington: Glazier, 1983), 15.

[6]Agnes Cunningham, S.S.C.M., *The Role of Women in Ecclesial Ministry* (Monograph published by the United States Catholic Conference in 1976), 3.

[7]E. Margaret Howe, *Women and Church Leadership* (Grand Rapids: Zondervan, 1982), 83–104.

[8]Gryson, *Ministry of Women*, xi–xvi and passim.

[9]Daniélou, *Ministry of Women*, 14, quoting Polycarp, *Epistle to the Philippians* 4.3.

[10]Ibid., quoting Ignatius, *To Smyrna*, 13.1.

[11]Stevan L. Davies, *The Revolt of the Widows: The Social World of the Apocryphal Acts* (Carbondale: Southern Illinois University Press, 1980).

[12]Cunningham, *Role of Women*, 4.

[13]*New Documents Illustrating the New Testament* (North Ryde, Australia: Ancient History Document Centre, Macquarie University, 1978), section 79.

[14]Ibid.

[15]Dorothy Irwin, "The Ministry of Women in the Early Church: The Archaeological Evidence," *Duke Divinity School Review* 45 (1980): 83.

[16]1 Clement 1:3. Kirsopp-Lake, trans., *The Apostolic Fathers* (New York: Putnam, 1912), 10–11.

[17]1 Clement 6:2.

[18]Epistle to the Philippians, chap. 4.

[19]1 Timothy 5:3–16.

[20]Epistle to Polycarp, chap. 4.

[21]Ibid., chap. 5.

[22]Ibid., chap. 7.

[23]Ibid., chap. 8.

[24]Eusebius *Ecclesiastical History* V.1.

[25]Ibid.

[26]Pliny to *Trajan* Letter X.96.

[27]Daniélou, *Ministry of Women*, 15.

[28]Patricia Wilson-Kastner in *A Lost Tradition*, ix.

[29]Roger Gryson, *Ministry of Women*, 15.

[30]Eusebius, *Ecclesiastical History* 3.18. See also W. H. C. Frend, *The Rise of Christianity* (Philadelphia: Fortress, 1984), 148 and note 134 on p. 160; "Domitilla, Flavia" in F. L. Cross and E. A. Livingstone, eds., *The Oxford Dictionary of the Christian Church*, 2nd ed. (London: Oxford University Press, 1974), 418–19.

[31]Irenaeus *Against Heresies* 3.22.4.

[32]*Similitudes* 2.

[33]Ibid.

[34]Ibid.

[35]See Gryson, *Ministry of Women*, 12.

[36]Ibid., 13–14.

[37]Tatian *Address to the Greeks*, 33.

[38]Athenagoras *A Plea for the Christians* 32.

[39]Ibid., 33.

[40]*Dialogue with Trypho*, chap. 288; *Ante-Nicene Fathers*, 1:242.

[41]Clement of Alexandria, *The Instructor*, book 2, chaps. 11–13.

[42]Ibid., book 3, chap. 11.

[43]*Stromata (Miscellanies)*, book 2, chap. 12.

[44]Ibid., book 4, chap. 8.

[45]Ibid., chap. 11.

[46]Ibid., chap. 23.

[47]Clark, *Women in the Early Church*, 47.

[48]*Stromata* 3, chap. 1, as quoted in Clark, *Women in the Early Church*, 48–49.

[49]Jean LaPorte, *The Role of Women in Early Christianity: Studies in Women and Religion* (Lewiston, N.Y.: Mellon, 1982), 7:30.

[50]*Stromata* book 4.7–8, 19.

[51]The name Noria recurs in different spellings and contexts as daughter of Eve, Noah's

wife, a divine figure, and source of knowledge. "The Hypostasis of the Archons" (II, 4:91–92) and "The Thought of Norea" (IX, 2:27–29), *Nag Hammadi Library*, trans. the members of the Coptic Gnostic Library Project of the Institute for Antiquity and Christianity, James M. Robinson, Director (San Francisco: Harper & Row, 1977), 156, 404–5; and Irenaeus, *Against Heresies* I.XXX.9.

[52] The gnostic Jesus taught women (see, e.g., "Sophia" [III.4:114–18] in *The Nag Hammadi Library*, 225), and women were commended for their understanding (e.g., "This word she spoke as a woman who knew the All." "The Dialogue of the Savior" [III.5:139]; ibid., 235).

[53] Elaine Pagels, *The Gnostic Gospels* (New York: Random, 1979), 48–69.

[54] Ibid., 67.

[55] "Gospel of Thomas," (II.2), Logion 114, *Nag Hammadi Library*, 130. The text is cited by Pagels in her *Gnostic Gospels*, 49.

[56] *Concordia Journal* 8 (1982): 12–18.

[57] See "The Dialogue of the Savior" (III.5) in *The Nag Hammadi Library*, 229–38.

[58] "The Gospel of Mary" (BG 8502.1), ibid., 471–74.

[59] Irenaeus, *Against Heresies* I.XXIII.2.

[60] Ibid., I.I.1.

[61] Ibid., I.IV.1.

[62] Ibid., I.V.1.

[63] Ibid., I.XIII.1–2.

[64] Ibid., I.XII.3–5.

[65] Ibid., I.XIII.4.

[66] Ibid., I.XIII.5–6.

[67] Ibid., I.XI.5.

[68] Louis A. Brighton, "The Ordination of Women: A Twentieth-Century Gnostic Heresy?" *Concordia Journal* 8 (1982): 16.

[69] Pagels, *Gnostic Gospels*, 62–63.

[70] Quoted in LaPorte, *Role of Women*, 57.

[71] *The Martyrdom of Perpetua and Felicitas*, 5. The translation used here is that of Wilson-Kastner, 4. See also the selections in Clark, *Women in the Early Church*, 98–106, and in LaPorte, *The Role of Women*, 13–21.

[72] Ibid., quoted from Wilson-Kastner, 30.

[73] An excellent thesis on "Tertullian's Understanding of Human Sexuality" was submitted as a master's thesis to Trinity Evangelical Divinity School by Ernest B. Manges in 1975. It has a fine bibliography. Of particular interest are the works that "attempt to trace such dynamics as the history of the status of women or the history of misogyny or the roots of cultural sexual roles." Some examples the author cites are: Simone de Beauvoir, *The Second Sex* (New York: Vintage, 1974), 110 and 189, which first appeared in French: *Le Deuxième Sexe* (Librairie Gallimard, 1949); Vern L. Bullough and Bonnie Bullough, *The Subordinate Sex: A History of Attitudes Toward Women* (Urbana: University of Illinois Press, 1973), 114–15; Kathrine M. Rogers, *The Troublesome Helpmate* (Seattle: University of Washington Press, 1966), 14–15; and Reay Tannahill, *Sex in History* (Briarcliff Manor, N.Y.: Stein and Day, 1980), 141, 146–47. Specific to the history of sexuality in the church (excluding the many works on the history of women in ministry) are: Derrick Sherwin Bailey, *Sexual Relation in Christian Thought* (New York: Harper & Brothers, 1959), 20, 24; Mary Daly, *The Church and the Second Sex* (New York: Harper & Row, 1975), 87; and Rosemary Radford Ruether, "Misogynism and Virginal Feminism in the Fathers," in Rosemary Radford Ruether, *Religion and Sexism: Images of Women in the Jewish and Christian Traditions* (New York: Simon and Schuster, 1974), 157.

[74] Gryson, *Ministry of Women*, 17.

[75] Tertullian, *On the Apparel of Women* I.1 (ANF 4:14).

[76] Manges, "Tertullian's Understanding," 13.

[77] *On the Apparel of Women* 2:1 (ANF 4:18).

[78] *On the Veiling of Virgins*, chap. 3 (ANF 4:28–29).

[79] *De Corona*, chap. 4 (ANF 3:95).

[80] Ibid., chap. 6 (ANF 3:96).

[81] Ibid., chap 14 (ANF 3:102).

[82] *To His Wife* I.1 (ANF 4:40).

[83] Ibid. (ANF 4:43).

[84] *On Exhortation to Chastity*, chap. 1 (ANF 4:50).

[85] *Against Marcion* I.29; V.7 (ANF 3:293–94; 443).

[86] Ernest B. Manges, *Tertullian*, 112–25.

[87] Manges, 121.

[88] Tertullian *Against Marcion*, V.8 (ANF 3:445). See the discussion of this by Ruth A. Tucker in *Women, Authority and the Bible*, Alvera Mickelsen, ed. (Downers Grove: InterVarsity, 1986), 113. The key clause is "*auctoritas autem non alterius erit quam auctoris*," literally: "Now [or "however" or "but"] authority will not be other than of the originator." This is somewhat ambiguous and needs to be interpreted with reference to the whole context.

[89] Ibid. V.8 (ANF 3:446).

[90] *On Baptism*, chap. 1 (ANF 3:677).

[91]*On the Veiling of Virgins*, chap. 3 (ANF 4:33).

[92]Ibid., chap. 7 (ANF 4:31).

[93]See the discussion and quotations in Gryson, *Ministry of Women*, 19.

[94]Tertullian, *On Prescription Against Heretics*, chap. 6 (ANF 3:246).

[95]Ibid., chap. 30 (ANF 3:257).

[96]Ibid., chap. 41:263 (ANF 3:263).

[97]Origen, *Fragments on 1 Corinthians*, 74, quoted in Gryson, *Ministry of Women*, 28–29.

[98]Origen, *Commentary on Romans*, 10, 17, quoted in Gryson, *Ministry of Women*, 31.

[99]Elisabeth Schüssler Fiorenza, "Word, Spirit and Power: Women in Early Christian Communities," in Rosemary Ruether and Eleanor McLaughlin, eds., *Women of Spirit: Female Leadership in the Jewish and Christian Traditions* (New York: Simon and Schuster, 1979), 56.

[100]Origen, *On Song* I.1, as quoted in Jean LaPorte, *The Role of Women*, 140.

[101]Hippolytus, *Refutation of All Heresies*, VIII.19, as quoted by Elizabeth A. Clark, in *Women in the Early Church*, Wilmington: Glazier, 1983), 161.

[102]Hippolytus, *Apostolic Tradition*, XIII, quoted in LaPorte, *The Role of Women*, from G. Dix, *The Apostolic Tradition of Hypolytus* (London, 1968), 70.

[103]Ibid., XI.1.4.5 quoted in LaPorte, *The Role of Women*, 59, from Dix, *The Apostolic Tradition*, 20.

[104]Gryson, *Ministry of Women*, 24.

[105]Hippolytus, *Refutation of All Heresies*, VII (ANF 5:129–30).

[106]Kurt Aland, *A History of Christianity* 1, trans. James L. Schaaf (Philadelphia: Fortress, 1985), 59; W. H. C. Frend, *The Rise of Christianity* (Philadelphia: Fortress, 1984), 561–62.

[107]Frend, *The Rise of Christianity*, 562.

[108]Cyprian *Epistle* LXI, *To Pomponius, Concerning Some Virgins* (ANF 5:356–58; *On the Dress of Virgins* (ANF 5:430–36); *Head* 36 (ANF 5:544). Cyprian also argued on the bases of 1 Corinthians 14:34–35 and 1 Timothy 2:11–14 that women ought to be silent in the church. He quoted these verses but did not comment on them.

[109]Fiorenza, "Word, Spirit and Power," 55.

[110]Quoted in Daniélou, *Ministry of Women in the Early Church*, 11.

[111]LaPorte, *The Role of Women*, 60–64 on widows, and 111–14 on deaconesses.

[112]*Didascalia* 3.13.1.

[113]Ibid., 3.12.1–13.1.

[114]Gryson, *Ministry of Women*, 42.

[115]Mary Lawrence McKenna, S.C.M.M., *Women of the Church* (New York: McKenna, n.d.), 66. Cf. pages 64–93 for a general survey of deaconesses in the early church.

[116]Haye van der Meer, *Women Priests in the Catholic Church?* 87.

[117]Ibid., 86–87.

[118]Charles R. Meyer, "Ordained Women in the Early Church," *Chicago Studies* (1965) 4:302.

[119]Chaps. 14–15, quoted in LaPorte, *The Role of Women*, 60–64; see also Daniélou, *Ministry of Women*, 19.

[120]Gryson, *Ministry of Women*, 39.

[121]Dionysius, "Epistle to Bishop Basilides," Canon II. (ANF 6:96).

[122]Howe, *Women and Church Leadership*, 99.

[123]Palladius, *Lausiac History* 55, quoted in Clark, *Women in the Early Church*, 133.

[124]LaPorte, *The Role of Women*, 71.

[125]Ibid., 103.

[126]*The Banquet of the Ten Virgins*, Discourse I.2 (ANF VI 3.11).

[127]Ibid.

[128]Eusebius, *Ecclesiastical History*, VI.41.

[129]Ibid., VI.41.

[130]Ibid.

[131]Ibid., VIII.12.

[132]Ibid., VI.5.

[133]Ibid., VIII.14.

[134]Ibid.

[135]Ibid.

[136]Ibid., IV.17.

[137]Ibid., V.13.1–2.

[138]*History*, V.14.1; V.16.12–22; V.17.4.

[139]Ibid., V.18.3.

[140]The edition of John Foxe, *Foxe's Book of Martyrs* used here is that by J. Milner (London: Thynne and Jarvis, n.d.).

[141]Ibid., 30–31, 33.

[142]Ibid., 44–45.

[143]Ibid., 48–49.

[144]Ibid., 56–59.

[145]Ibid., 66–68.

[146]Ibid., 69–70, 72–73, 77.

[147]Peter Toon, "Epiphanius," in J. D. Douglas, rev. ed., *The New International Dictionary of the Christian Church* (Grand Rapids: Zondervan, 1978), 346.

[148]Quoted in Daniélou, *The Ministry of Women in the Early Church*, 25.

[149]Excerpted from the quotation in Wilson-Kastner, *A Lost Tradition*, 45–68.

[150]Jerome *Epistle* 127.2–7, as quoted in Clarke, *Women in the Early Church*, 205–8.

[151] Ibid., 208.

[152] Ibid., 127.10, as quoted in Clarke, *Women in the Early Church*, 163.

[153] *Epistle* 108.5–6, 26, quoted in LaPorte, *The Role of Women*, 88–90, and in A. Clarke, *Women in the Early Church*, 209–13.

[154] For a brief sketch of her life, see Rosemary Ruether, "Mothers of the Church: Ascetic Women in the Late Patristic Age" in Rosemary Ruether and Eleanor McLaughlin, eds., *Women of Spirit: Female Leadership in the Jewish and Christian Traditions* (New York: Simon and Schuster, 1979, 83–85. For full details in the early sources, see the following footnote.

[155] Palladius, *Lausiac History* 55, quoted in Clark, *Women in the Early Church*, 164–65. See also the excerpts from Palladius on pages 213–16 and 221–23 of the same work.

[156] *Epistle* 29, quoted in Clark, *Women in the Early Church*, 217.

[157] Palladius, *Lausiac History*, 55, quoted by Rosemary Ruether, "Mothers of the Church: Ascetic Women in the Late Patristic Age" in Ruether and McLaughlin, *Women of Spirit*, 87.

[158] Rosemary Ruether, "Mothers of the Church," 91.

[159] Palladius, *Lausiac History*, quoted in Clark, *Women in the Early Church*, 223.

[160] *Life of Olympias, Deaconess*, quoted in Clark, *Women in the Early Church*, 227.

[161] For a summary of the career of Olympias, see McKenna, *Women of the Church*, 84–89.

[162] Gregory of Nyssa, *Life of St. Macrina*, I.6, quoted in Clark, *Women in the Early Church*, 235–43. See also LaPorte, *The Role of Women*, 81–88.

[163] LaPorte, *Role of Women*, 100–101.

[164] *On Virginity*, 14.1. See Clark, *Women in the Early Church*, 118–22.

[165] Gryson, *Ministry of Women*, 46–48.

[166] *Canons of Hippolytus* 9, quoted in Gryson, *Ministry of Women*, 50.

[167] *Apostolic Constitutions* VIII.19–20.

[168] Ibid., VIII.24.

[169] Ibid., I.3.

[170] Ibid., III.5.

[171] Ibid., III.6.

[172] Ibid., III.7.

[173] Ibid., III.9.

[174] Ibid.

[175] Ibid., III.10.

[176] Ibid., III.11.

[177] Augustine, *Confessions* 2.3.

[178] Ibid., 8.12.

[179] Ibid., 3.11–12.

[180] Ibid., 9.10–12.

[181] Augustine, *Literal Commentary on Genesis* IX.5.

[182] Ambrose, *On Paradise* X.48.

[183] Augustine, *The City of God* XIV.26.

[184] *On the Sermon on the Mount* I.15.41, as quoted in Elizabeth A. Clark, *Women in the Early Church*, 65.

[185] Rosemary Ruether, *Liberation Theology: Human Hope Confronts Christian History and American Power* (New York: Paulist, 1972), 100.

[186] John Chrysostom, *Homily* XX.

[187] John Chrysostom, *Discourse 4 on Genesis* I.2.

[188] John Chrysostom, *The Kind of Women Who Ought to Be Taken as Wives*, IV, quoted in Clark, *Women in the Early Church*, 37.

[189] John Chrysostom, *Discourse 4 on Genesis*, as quoted in Clark, *Women in the Early Church*, 44.

[190] *Homily 9 on 1 Timothy*, as quoted in Clark, *Women in the Early Church*, 15, 157–58.

[191] John Chrysostom, *Greet Priscilla and Aquila* I.3, as quoted in Clark, *Women in the Early Church*, 159.

[192] John Chrysostom, *Homily 7 on Matthew*, 6.

[193] Ibid.

[194] John Chrysostom, *The Epistle to the Romans*, 31, quoted in Aída Besançon Spencer, *Beyond the Curse* (Nashville: Nelson, 1985), 101, 132.

[195] Rosamond Nugent, *Portrait of the Consecrated Woman in Greek Christian Literature of the First Four Centuries* (Washington, D.C.: Catholic University Press, 1941), 62–64.

[196] See *On the Priesthood* III.17.

[197] John Chrysostom, *Homily on I Corinthians 7:2*, as quoted in Clark, *Women in the Early Church*, 64.

[198] Ibid., 72–73

[199] John Chrysostom, *Homily 19 on I Corinthians*.

[200] Quoted in Henry Alford, *The New Testament for English Readers* (Chicago: Moody, n.d.), 1243–44.

[201] John Chrysostom, *On Virginity* 15.1, as quoted in Clark, *Women in the Early Church*, 124.

[202] *On the Necessity of Guarding Virginity*.

[203] *Exhortation to Chastity*, IX.

[204] John Chrysostom, *On Not Marrying Again*.

[205] Clark, *Jerome, Chrysostom and Friends* (Champaign, Ill.: University of Illinois Press, 1982).

[206]Ibid., 48–59.

Chapter 4

[1]Eleanor McLaughlin, "Women, Power and the Pursuit of Holiness in Medieval Christianity," in *Women of Spirit: Female Leaders in the Jewish and Christian Traditions*, ed. Rosemary Ruether and Eleanor McLaughlin (New York: Simon and Schuster, 1979), 101.

[2]Ibid., 102.

[3]Marlys Taege, *And God Gave Women Talents!* (St. Louis: Concordia, 1978), 86.

[4]Susanne F. Wemple, *Women in Frankish Society: Marriage and the Cloister, 500 to 900* (Philadelphia: University of Pennsylvania Press, 1981), 141; Taege, *And God Gave Women Talents!* 86.

[5]Will Durant, *The Age of Faith* (New York: Simon and Schuster, 1950), 896.

[6]Joan Morris, *The Lady Was a Bishop: The Hidden History of Women With Clerical Ordination and the Jurisdiction of Bishops* (New York: Macmillan, 1973), 110.

[7]Ibid., 110–11.

[8]Susan M. Stuard, ed. *Women in Medieval Society* (Philadelphia: University of Pennsylvania Press, 1976), 9.

[9]Wemple, *Women in Frankish Society*, 139.

[10]Ibid., 140; Philip Schaff, *History of the Christian Church*, vol. 3, *Nicene and Post-Nicene Christianity*, A.D. *311–600* (Grand Rapids: Eerdmans, 1979), 259–60.

[11]Quoted in Schaff, *History of the Christian Church*, 3:260–61.

[12]Wemple, *Women in Frankish Society*, 141; Schaff, *History of the Christian Church*, 3:259, 262–63.

[13]Wemple, *Women in Frankish Society*, 133, 159.

[14]Lina Eckenstein, *Woman Under Monasticism* (New York: Russell & Russell, 1896), 48.

[15]Wemple, *Women in Frankish Society*, 163.

[16]Frances and Joseph Gies, *Women in the Middle Ages* (New York: Crowell, 1978), 65; Susan G. Bell, ed. *Women: From the Greeks to the French Revolution* (Stanford: Stanford University Press, 1973), 96; Durant, *Age of Faith*, 805.

[17]Eckenstein, *Woman Under Monasticism*, 67–68.

[18]Ibid., 69.

[19]Nancy Hardesty, *Great Women of the Christian Faith* (Grand Rapids: Baker, 1980), 37;

Joan M. Ferrante, "The Education of Women" in *Beyond Their Sex*, 9.

[20]Eckenstein, *Woman Under Monasticism*, 93.

[21]Wemple, *Women in Frankish Society*, 193.

[22]Eckenstein, *Woman Under Monasticism*, 128, 135, 138; Hardesty, *Great Women*, 35.

[23]Edith Deen, *Great Women of the Christian Faith* (New York: Harper & Row, 1959), 307; McLaughlin, "Women, Power and the Pursuit of Holiness," 105.

[24]McLaughlin, "Women, Power and the Pursuit of Holiness," 106.

[25]Ibid., 107.

[26]Wemple, *Women in Frankish Society*, 168, 170–71.

[27]Bell, *Women*, 97; Stuard, *Women in Medieval Society*, 8.

[28]Quoted in Wemple, *Women in Frankish Society*, 145.

[29]Ibid., 145.

[30]Schaff, *History of the Christian Church*, vol. 5, *The Middle Ages*, A.D. *1049–1294*, 266-68.

[31]Thomas Aquinas, *Summa Theologica*, Supplement, 64, 6, ad 1, quoted in Eleanor McLaughlin, "Equality of Souls, Inequality of Sexes: Woman in Medieval Theology," in Rosemary Ruether, *Religion and Sexism: Images of Woman in the Jewish and Christian Traditions* (New York: Simon and Schuster, 1974), 226–27.

[32]David Herlihy, "Land, Family, and Women in Continental Europe, 701–1200," in Stuard, *Women in Medieval Society*, 25.

[33]Schaff, *History of the Christian Church*, vol. 4, *Medieval Christianity*, A.D. *590–1073*, 265; Peter Toon, "Joan, Pope," in J. D. Douglas, ed., *New International Dictionary of the Christian Church*, rev. ed. (Grand Rapids: Zondervan, 1978), 536.

[34]Schaff, *History of the Christian Church*, 4:265.

[35]R. W. Southern, *Western Society and the Church in the Middle Ages* (New York: Penguin, 1970), 310.

[36]Gies, *Women in the Middle Ages*, 64.

[37]Laurel Braswell, "Saint Edburga of Winchester: A Study of Her Cult, A.D. 950–1500," *Medieval Studies*, (1971), 23:310.

[38]Durant, *Age of Faith*, 805; Bell, *Women*, 97. So it is not unreasonable to assume that a significant number of women were either forced to be at convents or were there as a last resort. By the same token, some women—particularly young noblewomen—found the intellectual stimulation and independence of

convent life more appealing than the prospects of an arranged marriage.

[39] Gies, *Women in the Middle Ages*, 70.

[40] Durant, *The Age of Faith*, 807; Gies, *Women in the Middle Ages*, 65.

[41] Caroline W. Bynum, *Jesus as Mother: Studies in the Spirituality of the High Middle Ages* (Berkeley: University of California Press, 1982), 14; Gies, *Women in the Middle Ages*, 64; Durant, *Age of Faith*, 757.

[42] Mclaughlin, "Equality of Souls," in *Religion and Sexism*, 238.

[43] Brenda M. Bolton, "Mulieres Sanctae" in Stuard, *Women in Medieval Society*, 143.

[44] Ibid., 142; Schaff, *History of the Christian Church*, 5:368–69.

[45] McLaughlin, "Equality of Souls," 239.

[46] Bolton, "Mulieres Sanctae," 142.

[47] Eckenstein, *Woman Under Monasticism*, 184; Bell, *Women*, 96.

[48] McLaughlin, "Women, Power and the Pursuit of Holiness, 106; Mary Daly, *The Church and the Second Sex* (New York: Harper & Row, l968), 54.

[49] "Abbesses," *Dictionaire de Theologie Catholique*, vol. 1, col. 18, quoted in Daly, *The Church and the Second Sex*, 54.

[50] Durant, *Age of Faith*, 805.

[51] Eckenstein, *Woman Under Monasticism*, 204.

[52] Morris, *The Lady Was a Bishop*, 19, 55.

[53] Bell, *Women*, 97.

[54] Eckenstein, *Woman Under Monasticism*, 356.

[55] Durant, *Age of Faith*, 515.

[56] Quoted in Gies, *Women in the Middle Ages*, 67.

[57] Eckenstein, *Woman Under Monasticism*, 181.

[58] Bell, *Women*, 108.

[59] Eckenstein, *Woman Under Monasticism*, 238–39.

[60] Morris, *The Lady Was a Bishop*, 91.

[61] Durant, *Age of Faith*, 806.

[62] Nesta de Robeck, *St. Clare of Assisi* (Chicago: Franciscan Herald, 1980), 162.

[63] Donald Weinstein and Rudolph M. Bell, *Saints & Society: The Two Worlds of Western Christendom, 1000–1700* (Chicago: University of Chicago Press, 1982), 156.

[64] Rudolph M. Bell, *Holy Anorexia* (Chicago: University of Chicago Press, 1985), passim.

[65] Braswell, "Saint Edburga of Winchester," 301–2.

[66] Weinstein and Bell, *Saints and Society*, 220; Bynum, *Jesus as Mother*, 137.

[67] Weinstein and Bell, *Saints and Society*, 177, 107.

[68] Durant, *Age of Faith*, 806–7.

[69] Ibid., 806; Bynum, *Jesus as Mother*, 18.

[70] Schaff, *History of the Christian Church*, 5:371.

[71] Quoted in Deen, *Great Women of the Christian Faith*, 310.

[72] Quoted in Henry Osborn Taylor, *The Mediaeval Mind* (Cambridge: Harvard University Press, 1949), 466–67.

[73] Schaff, *History of the Christian Church*, 5:372.

[74] Quoted in Taylor, *The Mediaeval Mind*, 470–71.

[75] Bynum, *Jesus as Mother*, 174–81.

[76] Ibid., 181, 194.

[77] Ibid., 197.

[78] Ibid., 172–3.

[79] Ibid., 184.

[80] George Williams and Edith Waldvogel, "A History of Speaking in Tongues and Related Gifts," in Michael P. Hamilton, ed., *The Charismatic Movement* (Grand Rapids: Eerdmans, 1975), 70.

[81] Morris, *The Lady Was a Bishop*, 12.

[82] Weinstein and Bell, *Saints and Society*, 155.

[83] Edmund College and James Walsh, "Editing Julian of Norwich's *Revelations*: A Progress Report," *Medieval Studies* (1976) 38:421.

[84] Jennifer P. Heimmel, *"God Is Our Mother": Julian of Norwich and the Medieval Image of Christian Feminine Divinity* (Salzburg: University of Salzburg Press, 1952), 48.

[85] McLaughlin, "Women, Power and the Pursuit of Holiness," 108–11.

[86] Ibid., 112.

[87] Deen, *Great Women of the Christian Faith*, 316; Elizabeth Clark and Herbert Richardson, eds., *Women and Religion: A Feminist Sourcebook of Christian Thought* (New York: Harper & Row, 1977), 107.

[88] Bolton, "Mulieres Sanctae," in Stuard, *Women in Medieval Society*, 150–52.

[89] Bynum, *Jesus as Mother*, 14.

[90] McLaughlin, "Equality of Souls," in *Religion and Sexism*, 242, 251–52.

[91] Ibid., 244.

[92] Schaff, *History of the Christian Church*, 5:399.

[93] Quoted in de Robeck, *St Clare*, 40, 84–85.

[94] Ibid., 103.

[95]St. Francis, *Little Flowers of St. Francis* (New York: Dutton, 1947), 62.

[96]Michael De La Bedoyere, *Catherine: Saint of Siena* (London: Hollis and Carter, 1947).

[97]Weinstein and Bell, *Saints & Society*, 39.

[98]Schaff, *History of the Christian Church*, 6:195; De La Bedoyere, *Catherine*, 29, 33.

[99]Quoted in De La Bedoyere, *Catherine*, 40.

[100]De La Bedoyere, *Catherine*, 41, 44.

[101]Ibid., 46.

[102]Schaff, *History of the Christian Church*, 6:196.

[103]Quoted in De La Bedoyere, *Catherine*, 56 57.

[104]De La Bedoyere, *Catherine*, 136–40.

[105]Ibid., 140, 236.

[106]Quoted in ibid., 186.

[107]McLaughlin, "Women, Power and the Pursuit of Holiness," 117.

[108]De La Bedoyere, *Catherine*, 240.

[109]Quoted in McLaughlin, "Women, Power and Pursuit of Holiness," 119.

[110]Schaff, *History of the Christian Church*, 6:204.

[111]Ibid., 199.

[112]Ibid., 109.

[113]Bynum, *Jesus as Mother*, 14–15; Schaff, *History of the Christian Church*, 5:490.

[114]Schaff, *History of the Christian Church*, 5:490.

[115]Robert E. Lerner, *The Heresy of the Free Spirit in the Later Middle Ages* (Berkeley: University of California Press, 1972), 45.

[116]Ibid., 46.

[117]McLaughlin, "Women, Power and the Pursuit of Holiness," 124.

[118]Schaff, *History of the Christian Church*, 5:500–504.

[119]Ibid., 177, 476.

[120]Ibid., 509, 511.

[121]Rudolph Heinze, "Taborites," in the *New International Dictionary of the Christian Church*, 951; Schaff, *History of the Christian Church*, 6:393.

[122]Durant, *Age of Faith*, 973.

[123]Ibid., 826.

[124]Francine Cardman, "The Medieval Question of Women and Orders," *The Thomist* (October 1978), 42:586–91.

[125]Ibid., 596.

[126]Emma T. Healy, *Woman According to Saint Bonaventure* (New York: Georgian, 1956), i–ii, 46.

[127]Schaff, *History of the Christian Church*, 6:524.

[128]Ibid., 525–26.

[129]Quoted in Durant, *Age of Faith*, 986.

[130]Ibid., 986.

[131]Schaff, *History of the Christian Church*, 5:611–12.

[132]Quoted in ibid., 612.

[133]Ibid., 614–15.

[134]Quoted in Durant, *Age of Faith*, 943.

[135]Bell, *Women*, 97.

[136]Schaff, *History of the Christian Church*, 5:531–32.

[137]Durant, *Age of Faith*, 806.

[138]Ibid.

[139]Schaff, *History of the Christian Church*, 5:837–38.

[140]Ibid., 831, 840, 842.

[141]McLaughlin, "Equality of Souls," in *Religion and Sexism*, 246–54.

[142]Durant, *The Age of Faith*, 747.

[143]Quoted in Schaff, *History of the Christian Church*, 5:832.

[144]Durant, *Age of Faith*, 826.

[145]Ibid., 505.

[146]Bell, *Women*, 159.

[147]de Robeck, *St. Clare*, 102, 111.

Chapter 5

[1]Natalie Z. Davis, *Society and Culture in Early Modern France* (Stanford: Stanford University Press, 1975), 76–77.

[2]Roland H. Bainton, *Erasmus of Christendom* (New York: Scribner, 1969), 22–23.

[3]Jane D. Douglass, "Christian Freedom: What Calvin Learned at the School of Women," *Church History*, 53 (June 1984): 167.

[4]Julia O'Faolain and Lauro Martines, eds, *Not in God's Image* (New York: Harper & Row, 1973), 180.

[5]Charmarie J. Blaisdell, "Response to 'The Role and Status of Women in the Writings of John Calvin,'" in Peter De Klerk, ed., *Renaissance, Reformation, Resurgence* (Grand Rapids: Calvin Theological Seminary, 1976), 21.

[6]O'Faolain and Martines, *Not in God's Image*, 194.

[7]Martin Luther, *Notes on Ecclesiastes* in Jaroslav Pelikan, ed., *Luther's Works* (St. Louis: Concordia, 1972), 15:130.

[8]Martin Luther, *The Christian in Society*, in Helmut T. Lehmann, ed., *Luther's Works* (Philadelphia: Muhlenberg, 1962), 45:37.

[9]Quoted in Will Durant, *The Reformation: A History of European Civilization from Wycliffe*

to Calvin, 1300–1564 (New York: Simon and Schuster, 1957), 416.

[10] Quoted in O'Faolain and Martines, *Not in God's Image,* 196–97.

[11] Quoted in Ian Siggins, *Luther and His Mother* (Philadelphia: Fortress, 1981), 73.

[12] Luther, *Christian in Society,* 2:368.

[13] Joyce L. Irwin, *Womanhood in Radical Protestantism, 1525–1675* (New York: Mellen, 1979), 128.

[14] Martin Luther, *Luther's Commentary on Genesis,* (Grand Rapids: Zondervan, 1958), 1:34.

[15] Ibid., 55.

[16] Martin Luther, "The Babylonian Captivity of the Church," in *Primary Works,* trans. and ed. by H. Wace and C. A. Buchheim (London, 1896), 103–4, quoted in O'Faolain and Martines, *Not in God's Image,* 195.

[17] Quoted in Irwin, *Womanhood,* 159.

[18] Luther, *Church and Ministry,* 2:154.

[19] Constance M. Coltman, "Post-Reformation: The Free Churches" in A. Maude Royden, *The Church and Woman* (New York: Doran, 1924), 83.

[20] Charmarie J. Blaisdell, "Calvin's Letters to Women: The Courting of Ladies in High Places," *Sixteenth Century Journal* 13 (Fall 1982): 67–71.

[21] Willis P. DeBoer, "Calvin on the Role of Women," in David E. Holwerda, ed., *Exploring the Heritage of John Calvin* (Grand Rapids: Baker, 1976), 236–72; Douglass, "Christian Freedom," 155–73.

[22] Douglass, "Christian Freedom," 156, 158.

[23] Ibid., 158–59.

[24] Quoted in ibid., 162.

[25] Douglass, "Christian Freedom," 166.

[26] Ibid., 157.

[27] John Calvin, *Commentaries on the Gospel of John,* trans. William Pringle (Grand Rapids: Eerdmans, 1956), 260–61.

[28] David Laing, ed. *The Works of John Knox* (Edinburgh: Stevenson, 1855), 4:351, 357–58.

[29] John Knox, "The First Blast of the Trumpet Against the Monstrous Regiment of Women" (1558) in Laing, ed., *Works,* 4:365.

[30] Ibid., 374, 377.

[31] Roland H. Bainton, *Women of the Reformation From Spain to Scandanavia* (Austin: Augsburg, n.d.), 91.

[32] Irwin, *Womanhood,* 49.

[33] John Cairncross, *After Polygamy Was Made a Sin: The Social History of Christian Polygamy* (London: Routledge & Kegan Paul, 1974), 25, 9.

[34] Quoted in ibid., 9.

[35] Irwin, *Womanhood,* 55.

[36] Menno Simons, *The True Christian Faith,* from John C. Wenger, ed., *The Complete Writings of Menno Simons (c. 1496–1561),* trans. Leonard Verduin (Scottsdale, Pa.: Herald, 1956), 376–83, quoted in Irwin, *Womanhood,* 55.

[37] Irwin, *Womanhood,* 202–3.

[38] Quoted in Douglass, "Christian Freedom," 172.

[39] Bainton, *Women of the Reformation From Spain to Scandanavia, . . . in France and England, . . . in Germany and Italy.*

[40] Susan C. Karant-Nunn, "Continuity and Change: Some Effects of the Reformation on the Women of Zwickau," *Sixteenth Century Journal,* 12 (Summer 1982): 35.

[41] Richard Friedenthal, *Luther: His Life and Times,* trans. John Nowell (New York: Harcourt Brace Jovanovich, 1970), 437.

[42] Roland H. Bainton, *Here I Stand: A Life of Martin Luther* (New York: Mentor, 1950), 223.

[43] Quoted in Roland H. Bainton, *Women of the Reformation in Germany and Italy* (Minneapolis: Augsburg, 1971), 24.

[44] Friedenthal, *Luther,* 438.

[45] Quoted in Philip Schaff, *History of the Christian Church,* (Grand Rapids: Eerdmans, 1979), 8:417.

[46] Quoted in Theodore J. Kleinhans, *Martin Luther, Saint and Sinner* (London: Marshall, Morgan & Scott, 1959), 105.

[47] Quoted in Bainton, *Women of the Reformation in Germany and Italy,* 27.

[48] Quoted in Friedenthal, *Luther,* 439–40.

[49] Bainton, *Women of the Reformation in Germany and Italy,* 45–50.

[50] Quoted in ibid., 51–52.

[51] Quoted in O'Faolain and Martines, eds., *Not in God's Image,* 204.

[52] Mariam V. Chrisma, "Women of the Reformation in Strasburg, 1490–1530," *Archive for Reformation History* (1972), 63:152–53.

[53] Quoted in Bainton, *Women of the Reformation in Germany and Italy,* 55.

[54] Schaff, *History of the Christian Church,* 7:633.

[55] Bainton, *Women of the Reformation in Germany and Italy,* 65, 73.

[56] Quoted in ibid., 66–67.

[57] Quoted in ibid., 72.

[58] Quoted in ibid.

[59] Chrisma, "Women in Reformation Strasburg," 157–58.

[60] Bainton, *Women of the Reformation in Germany and Italy,* 84.

61 Ibid., 97, 100, 105.

62 Ibid., 97−98.

63 Quoted in ibid., 97.

64 Bainton, *Women of the Reformation in Germany and Italy*, 107.

65 Ibid., 105.

66 Ibid., 105−6.

67 Quoted in ibid., 106.

68 Bainton, *Women of the Reformation in Germany and Italy*, 108.

69 Blaisdell, "Calvin's Letters to Women," 74−75.

70 Quoted in Bainton, *Women of the Reformation in France and England*, 29.

71 Quoted in Douglass, "Christian Freedom," 169.

72 Bainton, *Women of the Reformation in France and England*, 25.

73 Nancy Roelker, "The Appeal of Calvinism to French Noblewomen of the Sixteenth Century," *Journal of Interdisciplinary History* 2 (Spring 1972): 408.

74 Bainton, *Women of the Reformation in France and England*, 54.

75 Quoted in Ibid., 60−61.

76 Bainton, *Women of the Reformation in England and France*, 62-69; Nancy Hardesty, *Great Women of the Christian Faith* (Grand Rapids: Baker, 1980), 54.

77 Blaisdell, "Calvin's Letters to Women," 78.

78 Roelker, "The Appeal of Calvinism," 408.

79 Quoted in Bainton, *Women of the Reformation in Germany and Italy*, 241.

80 Blaisdell, "Calvin's Letters to Women," 80.

81 Charmarie Jenkins-Blaisdell, "Renée de France Between Reform and Counter-Reform," *Archive for Reformation History* 63 (1972): 198.

82 Bainton, *Women in the Reformation in Germany and Italy*, 246, 248−49.

83 Quoted in ibid., 247, 249.

84 John Foxe, *Foxe's Christian Martyrs of the World* (Chicago: Moody, n.d.), 542−46.

85 Ibid., 511, 521−22.

86 Ibid., 404.

87 Ibid., 405.

88 Ann Askewe, *The First Examination of the Worthy seruant of God, Mistress Anne Askew . . . lately Martyred in Smithfield* (London: Robert Waldegraue, 1585), 3−4.

89 Bainton, *Women of the Reformation in France and England*, 247.

90 Ibid., 10−11.

91 George Huntston Williams, *The Radical Reformation* (Philadelphia: Westminster, 1962), 184, 506−7.

92 Johannes Kessler, *Sabbata*, ed. Emil Egli and Rudolf Schoch (St. Gall, 1902), 154, quoted in Irwin, *Womanhood*, 203.

93 Ibid., 204−5.

94 Karant-Nunn, "Continuity and Change," 37−40.

95 Quoted in Bainton, *Women in the Reformation From Spain to Scandanavia*, 163.

96 Ibid., 28−29.

97 Ibid., 29−30.

98 Ibid., 29−31.

99 Ibid., 34−37.

100 Ibid., 37−39.

101 Douglass, "Christian Freedom," 169−70.

102 Roelker, "Appeal of Calvinism," 407.

103 Karant-Nunn, "Continuity and Change," 19.

104 Ibid., 28.

105 Jane D. Douglass, "Women and the Continental Reformation" in Rosemary Ruether, *Religion and Sexism: Images of Women in the Jewish and Christian Traditions* (New York: Simon and Schuster, 1974), 310.

106 Quoted in ibid., 310−11.

107 Quoted in Lina Eckenstein, *Woman Under Monasticism* (New York: Russell and Russell, 1896), 471.

108 Karant-Nunn, "Continuity and Change," 22−23.

109 Quoted in Eckenstein, *Woman Under Monasticism*, 463, 465.

110 Ibid., 467.

111 Eckenstein, *Woman Under Monasticism*, 470−71, 473.

112 Ibid., 475.

113 Blaisdell, "Calvin's Letters to Women," 73.

114 Hugo Rahner, *Saint Ignatius Loyola: Letters to Women* (London: Nelson, 1956), 12, 14n, 19.

115 Ibid., 18.

116 Denise L. Carmody, *Women and World Religions* (Nashville: Abingdon, 1979), 132.

117 Quoted in Victoria Lincoln, *Teresa: A Woman, A Biography of Teresa of Avila* (Albany: State University of New York Press, 1984), 37, 40.

118 Ibid., 49.

119 Ibid., 52.

120 Stephen Clissold, *St Teresa of Avila* (New York: Seabury, 1982), 56.

121 Ibid., 67, 195.

122 Edith Deen, *Great Women of the Christian Faith* (New York: Harper & Row, 1959), 100−101.

123 Quoted in Caroline Marshall, "Teresa of Avila" in *Eerdmans' Handbook to the History of Christianity*, ed. Tim Dowley (Grand Rapids: Eerdmans, 1977), 417.

[124] Deen, *Great Women*, 102–7.

[125] Quoted in Bainton, *Women of the Reformation from Spain to Scandanavia*, 56.

[126] Quoted in Clissold, *St Teresa*, 113.

[127] Bainton, *Women of the Reformation from Spain to Scandanavia*, 56-57.

[128] Quoted in Deen, *Great Women*, 102.

[129] Quoted in Hugo Rahner, *Saint Ignatius*, 25.

[130] Ibid., 25.

[131] Don Sharkey, *The Woman Shall Conquer* (New York: All Saints, 1962), 7.

Chapter 6

[1] Selma Williams, *Divine Rebel: The Life of Anne Marbury Hutchinson* (New York: Holt, Rinehart and Winston, 1981), 35.

[2] Antonia Fraser, *The Weaker Vessel* (New York: Knopf, 1984), 122.

[3] Fraser, *Weaker Vessel*, 2; Williams, *Divine Rebel*, 56.]

[4] John Chamberlain, *The Chamberlain Letters: A Selection of the Letters of John Chamberlain Concerning Life in England From 1597–1626*, ed. Elizabeth M. Thomson (London: John Murray, 1966), 271.

[5] Williams, *Divine Rebel*, 70.

[6] Quoted in David J. Latt, "Introduction," in Margaret Fell, *Women's Speaking Justified* (Los Angles: University of California Press, 1979), xi.

[7] Quoted in Keith Thomas, *Religion and the Decline of Magic* (New York: Scribner, 1971), 137.

[8] Fraser, *Weaker Vessel*, 251.

[9] Ibid., 154–55.

[10] Thomas, *Religion and the Decline of Magic*, 137–38.

[11] Norman Penney, ed., *Experiences in the Life of Mary Penington* (London, 1911), quoted in Jessamyn West, ed., *The Quaker Reader* (New York: Viking, 1962), 132.

[12] Ibid., 133–34.

[13] Ibid.

[14] Ibid., 142.

[15] Quoted in Jonathan L. Pearl, "French Catholic Demonologists and Their Enemies in the Late Sixteenth and Early Seventeenth Centuries," *Church History* (December 1983), 461.

[16] Judith C. Brown, *Immodest Acts: The Life of a Lesbian Nun in Renaissance Italy* (London: Oxford University Press, 1985), passim.

[17] Fraser, *Weaker Vessel*, 127.

[18] Beatrix M. Couch, "Sor Juana Ines de la Cruz: The First Woman Theologian in the Americas," in John and Ellen Webster, eds. *The Church and Women in the Third World* (Philadelphia: Westminster, 1985), 51–52.

[19] Quoted in Anne Fremantle, *Woman's Way to God* (New York: St. Martin's, 1977), 129.

[20] Ibid.

[21] Couch, "Sor Juana," 52.

[22] Ibid., 53.

[23] Quoted in Deen, *Great Women of the Christian Faith* (New York: Harper & Row, 1959), 130.

[24] Jeanne Guyon, *The Autobiography of Madame Guyon*, trans. Thomas Allen (New Canaan, Conn.: Keats, 1980), 133.

[25] Ibid.

[26] Thomas C. Upham, *The Life and Religious Opinions and Experience of Madame Guyon* (London: Allenson, 1905), 185–86.

[27] Guyon, *Autobiography*, 231.

[28] Upham, *Life of Madame Guyon*, 187–89.

[29] Ibid., 191.

[30] Guyon, *Autobiography*, 236.

[31] Upham, *Life of Madame Guyon*, 264–65.

[32] Ibid., 229, 264–65.

[33] Deen, *Great Women*, 132.

[34] Ronald A. Knox, *Enthusiasm: A Chapter in the History of Religion* (New York: Oxford University Press, 1961), 325ff.

[35] Guyon, *Autobiography*, 323.

[36] Quoted in Richard L. Greaves, "The Role of Women in Early English Nonconformity," *Church History* (September 1983), 307.

[37] Rita Mancha, "The Woman's Authority: Calvin to Edwards," *Journal of Christian Reconstruction*, vol. 6, no. 2 (Winter 1979–80), 86–98, 93.

[38] Quoted in Edmund S. Morgan, *The Puritan Family* (New York: Harper & Row, 1966), 44.

[39] Thomas Edwards, *Gangraena*, (London, 1646), quoted in Joyce L. Irwin, *Womanhood in Radical Protestantism, 1525–1675* (New York: Mellen, 1979), 218.

[40] Margo Todd, "Humanists, Puritans and the Spiritualized Household," *Church History* (March 1980), 29.

[41] Quoted in ibid., 29.

[42] Keith Thomas, "Women and the Civil War Sects," in Trevor Aston, ed., *Crisis in Europe, 1560–1660* (New York: Basic Books, 1965), 317–40.

[43] Latt, "Introduction," ix.

[44] Fraser, *Weaker Vessel*, 246.

[45] Greaves, "The Role of Women," 302, 306–7.

46 Quoted in Constance M. Coltman, "Post-Reformation: The Free Churches," in A. Maude Royden, *The Church and Woman* (New York: George H. Doran, 1924), 95.

47 John Robinson, *A Justification of Separation From the Church of England* (n.p., 1610), 150, quoted in Irwin, *Womanhood*, 163.

48 Ibid., 163.

49 Irwin, *Womanhood*, 165.

50 Richard Mather, *Church Government and Church Covenant Discussed* (London, 1643), 60, quoted in Irwin, *Womanhood*, 167.

51 R. Baillie, *A Dissuasive From the Errours of the Time* (London, 1645), 110, in Irwin, *Womanhood*, 168.

52 Thomas Hutchinson, "The Examination of Mrs. Anne Hutchinson at the court at Newtown. November 1637," in Thomas Hutchinson, ed., *The History of the Colony and Province of Massachusetts-Bay* (1767; reprint, Cambridge: Harvard University Press, 1936), 366–91, quoted in Williams, *Divine Rebel*, 73.

53 Williams, *Divine Rebel*, 79–81.

54 Ibid., 91–92.

55 Ibid., 97–98.

56 John Cotton, "The Way of the Congregational Churches Cleared" (1648), in David D. Hall, ed., *The Antinomian Controversy* (Middletown, Conn.: Wesleyan University Press, 1968), 412.

57 John Winthrop, "Short Story" (1644), in Hall, *Antinomian Controversy*, 205–13.

58 Williams, *Divine Rebel*, passim, 54–114.

59 John Winthrop, *Winthrop's Journal: History of New England, 1630–1649*, 2 vols., ed. James K. Hosmer (New York: Scribner, 1908), 1:240.

60 Quoted in Williams, *Divine Rebel*, 2–3.

61 Ibid., 142, 127–28.

62 Williams, *Divine Rebel*, 121.

63 Franklin B. Dexter, ed., "A Report of the Trial of Mrs. Anne Hutchinson before the Church in Boston, 1638." Massachusetts Historical Society Proceedings. 2nd series (1889), 4:173, quoted in Williams, *Divine Rebel*, 178.

64 Winthrop, "Short Story," 274.

65 Williams, *Divine Rebel*, 121, 4; John Winthrop, *Life and Letters of John Winthrop*, 2 vols. (Boston: Little, Brown, 1869), 2:207.

66 Thomas Weld, quoted in Winthrop, "Short Story," 214.

67 Ibid., 218.

68 Donald G. Mathews, "Women's History/Everyone's History," in Thomas and Keller, *Women in New Worlds*, 33.

69 Quoted in Leon McBeth, *Women in Baptist Life* (Nashville: Broadman, 1979), 29.

70 Fraser, *Weaker Vessel*, 245.

71 Greaves, "Role of Women," 308; Irwin, *Womanhood*, 218.

72 Fraser, *Weaker Vessel*, 245.

73 Coltman, "Post-Reformation," 97.

74 Ibid., 97.

75 Greaves, "Role of Women," 302–3.

76 John Rogers, *Ohel or Beth-shemesh* (London, 1653), quoted in Joyce Irwin, *Womanhood*, 171, 174.

77 Irwin, *Womanhood*, 170.

78 B. S. Capp, *The Fifth Monarchy Men* (London: Faber and Faber, 1972), 174, 142, 184.

79 Ibid., 102, 189, 183.

80 George H. Williams and Edith Waldvogel, "A History of Speaking in Tongues and Related Gifts," in Michael P. Hamilton, ed., *The Charismatic Movement* (Grand Rapids: Eerdmans, 1975), 75–80.

81 John Wesley, *The Journal of John Wesley*, 4 vols. (New York: Dutton, 1907), 1:171.

82 Ibid., 172.

83 Thomas, "Women and the Civil War Sects," 324–25.

84 George Fox, *The Works of George Fox*, 8 vols. (New York: Isaac T. Hopper, 1831; reprint ed., New York: AMS, 1975), 4:106, 109.

85 Elaine C. Huber, "'A Woman Must Not Speak': Quaker Women in the English Left Wing," in Ruether and McLaughlin, *Women of Spirit*, 167.

86 Quoted in Emily Manners, *Elizabeth Hooton: First Quaker Woman Preacher* (London: Headley Brothers, 1914), 30, 41.

87 Horatio Rogers, *Mary Dyer of Rhode Island* (Providence: Preston and Rounds, 1896), quoted in West, *Quaker Reader*, 169; Huber, "A Woman Must Not Speak," 169.

88 G. T. Paine, ed., *A Call from Death to Life, being an account of the sufferings of Marmaduke Stephenson, William Robinson and Mary Dyer in New England, in the year 1659* (Printed by Friends in London, 1660), 46, quoted in Huber, "A Woman Must Not Speak," 171.

89 Ibid.

90 Rogers, *Mary Dyer*, 175.

91 West, *Quaker Reader*, 219.

92 Latt, "Introduction," in Fell, *Women's Speaking Justified*, iii–iv.

93 Margaret Fell, *The Examination and Tryall of Margaret Fell and George Fox* (London, n.p.: 1664), 15–16.

94 West, *Quaker Reader*, 219.

⁹⁵Latt, "Introduction," in Fell, *Women's Speaking Justified*, v.

⁹⁶Fell, *Women's Speaking Justified*, 10.

⁹⁷Ibid., 18.

⁹⁸George Fox, "An encouragement to all the faithful women's meetings," (Letter CCCXX) in *Works*, 8:97.

⁹⁹Quoted in West, *Quaker Reader*, 221–22.

¹⁰⁰Joseph Besse, *A Collection of the Sufferings of the People Called Quakers*, 2 vols. (London, 1753), 1:84ff., quoted in Julia O'Faolain and Lauro Martines, eds., *Not in God's Image* (New York: Harper & Row, 1973), 264.

¹⁰¹Pamela Volkman, *From Heroics to Dissent: A Study of the Thought and Psychology of English Nonconformity, 1660–1700, Through Autobiography* (Ph.D. dissertation, University of Rochester, 1982, quoted in Greaves, "The Role of Women," 299.

¹⁰²Thomas, "Women and the Civil War Sects," 325.

¹⁰³Ibid., 326–27.

¹⁰⁴Cotton Mather, *Ornaments for the Daughters of Zion* (Delmar, N.Y.: Scholars' Facsimiles & Reprints, 1978), 46.

¹⁰⁵Pattie Cowell, "Introduction," in Mather, *Ornaments*, xv–xvi, 85.

¹⁰⁶Laurel T. Ulrich, *Good Wives: Image and Reality in the Lives of Women in Northern New England, 1650–1750* (New York: Knopf, 1982), 224–25.

¹⁰⁷Alexander V. G. Allen, *American Religious Leaders: Jonathan Edwards* (Cambridge: Riverside, 1890), 197.

¹⁰⁸Rita Mancha, "The Woman's Authority: Calvin to Edwards," 96.

¹⁰⁹Jonathan Edwards, "Sarah Pierrepont," in *Jonathan Edwards: Representative Selections*, ed. Clarence H. Faust and Thomas H. Johnson (New York: Hill and Wang, 1935), 56.

¹¹⁰Jonathan Edwards, "A faithful Narrative," in Faust and Johnson, *Jonathan Edwards*, 85–87.

¹¹¹Jonathan Edwards, *The Works of Jonathan Edwards*, ed. John E. Smith, 7 vols. *The Great Awakening* (New Haven: Yale University Press, 1972), 4:428.

¹¹²F. Ernest Stoeffler, *Continental Pietism and Early American Christianity* (Grand Rapids: Eerdmans, 1976), 58.

¹¹³Quoted in ibid., 59.

¹¹⁴Stoeffler, *Continental Pietism*, 59.

¹¹⁵Rebecca L. Harmon, *Susanna: Mother of the Wesleys* (Nashville: Abingdon, 1968), 20.

¹¹⁶Harmon, *Susanna*, 47–49.

¹¹⁷Quoted in ibid., 47.

¹¹⁸*Proceedings of the Wesley Historical Society*, 29:50–57, quoted in Robert G. Tuttle, Jr., *John Wesley: His Life and Theology* (Grand Rapids: Zondervan, 1978), 41–42.

¹¹⁹Quoted in Harmon, *Susanna*, 89.

¹²⁰John Wesley, *The Works of John Wesley*, 14 vols. (Grand Rapids, Zondervan, 1958), 1:385–86.

¹²¹Ibid., 386.

¹²²Ibid.

¹²³Ibid.

¹²⁴Earl Kent Brown, "Standing in the Shadow: Women in Early Methodism," *Nexus*, vol. 17, no. 2 (Spring 1974), 22.

¹²⁵Earl Kent Brown, *Women of Mr. Wesley's Methodism* (New York: Mellen, 1983), 99.

¹²⁶Ibid., 105.

¹²⁷Ibid., 185–98.

¹²⁸John Wesley, *The Letters of the Rev. John Wesley*, 8 vols., ed. John Telford (London: Epworth, 1931), 2:118–20.

¹²⁹John Wesley, *Explanatory Notes Upon the New Testament* (London: Wesleyan-Methodist Book-Room, 1754), n.p.

¹³⁰Brown, *Women of Mr. Wesley's Methodism*, 20.

¹³¹Wesley, *Letters*, 8:190; 4:133, 164.

¹³²Ibid., 5:130.

¹³³Ibid., 5:257.

¹³⁴Quoted in Brown, "Women of the Word," 76.

¹³⁵*A Discoverie of Six women preachers, in Middlesex, Kent, Cambridgeshire, and Salisbury* (London, 1641), quoted in Irwin, *Womanhood*, 211.

¹³⁶Brown, "Women of the Word," 76.

¹³⁷Quoted in ibid., 78.

¹³⁸Brown, "Women of the Word," 80.

¹³⁹Brown, *Women of Mr. Wesley's Methodism*, 174–75.

¹⁴⁰Ibid., 77.

¹⁴¹John R. Weinlick, *Count Zinzendorf* (Nashville: Abingdon, 1956), 200.

¹⁴²Ibid., 200, 205.

¹⁴³Thomas, "Women and the Civil War Sects," 327–28.

Chapter 7

¹Quoted in Mary D. Irvine and Alice L. Eastwood, *Pioneer Women of the Presbyterian Church, United States* (Richmond: Presbyterian Committee of Publication, 1923), 18.

[2] Lawrence Foster, *Religion and Sexuality: The Shakers, The Mormons, and the Oneida Community* (Urbana: University of Illinois, n.d.), 25.

[3] Terry D. Bilhartz, ed., *Francis Asbury's America: An Album of Early American Methodism* (Grand Rapids: Zondervan, 1984), 85, 39.

[4] Rosemary Ruether and Rosemary Keller, eds., *Women and Religion in America: The Nineteenth Century*, 3 vols. (New York: Harper & Row, 1981), 1:2–3, 6.

[5] Martha T. Blauvelt, "Women and Revivalism," in Rosemary Ruether and Skinner, *Women and Religion*, 1:32.

[6] William G. McLoughlin, *Revivals, Awakenings, and Reform: an Essay on Religion and Social Change in America, 1607–1977* (Chicago: University of Chicago Press, 1978), 132–33.

[7] Emily Hahn, *Once Upon a Pedestal* (New York: Crowell, 1974), 40.

[8] Page P. Miller, "Women in the Vanguard of the Sunday School Movement," *Journal of Presbyterian History* 58 (Winter 1980): 311.

[9] Ford K. Brown, *Fathers of the Victorians* (Cambridge: University Press, 1961), 327–28.

[10] Quoted in Charles Edwin Jones, *Perfectionist Persuasion: The Holiness Movement and American Methodism, 1867–1936* (Metuchen, N.J.: Scarecrow, 1974), 189–94.

[11] Quoted in Ian Bradley, *The Call to Seriousness: The Evangelical Impact on the Victorians* (New York: Macmillan, 1976), 49–50.

[12] Bradley, *The Call to Seriousness*, 49.

[13] Martin E. Marty, *The Pro and Con Book of Religious America* (Waco: Word, 1975), 98.

[14] Bradley, *Call to Seriousness*, 48.

[15] Ibid.

[16] Edwin W. Rice, *The Sunday-School Movement and the American Sunday-School Union, 1780–1917* (Philadelphia: American Sunday-School Union, 1917), 20; William Roberts, *Memoirs of Hannah More*, 2:63ff., quoted in Rice, *Sunday-School Movement*, 20; Robert Lynn and Elliott Wright, *The Big Little School: Sunday Child of American Protestantism* (New York: Harper & Row, 1971), 9.

[17] George W. Bethune, *Memoirs of Mrs. Joanna Bethune* (New York: Harper & Brothers, 1863), 88, 120.

[18] Edwin Wilbur Rice, *The Sunday-School Movement*, 57; Nancy Hardesty, *Great Women of the Christian Faith* (Grand Rapids: Baker, 1980), 74.

[19] Quoted in Miller, "Women in the Vanguard," 313.

[20] Lynn and Wright, *Big Little School*, 12.

[21] Rice, *The Sunday School Movement*, 59–60.

[22] Lynn and Wright, *Big Little School*, 69.

[23] Rice, *The Sunday School Movement*, 209–10.

[24] Ibid., 33.

[25] Charles G. Finney, *Memoirs* (New York: Revell, 1876), 214.

[26] Quoted in Donald Dayton, *Discovering an Evangelical Heritage* (New York: Harper & Row, 1976), 88.

[27] Dayton, *Discovering an Evangelical Heritage*, 88.

[28] Finney, *Memoirs*, 214, 321–22, 438, 444; Nancy Hardesty, *Women Called to Witness: Evangelical Feminism in the 19th Century* (Nashville, Abingdon, 1984), 47.

[29] Lois A Boyd and R. Douglas Brakenridge, *Presbyterian Women in America: Two Centuries of a Quest for Status* (London: Greenwood, 1983), 94.

[30] Quoted in Hardesty, *Great Women*, 102.

[31] Finney, *Memoirs*, 421, 443.

[32] Charles G. Finney, *Revivals of Religion* (London: Revell, n.d.), 291.

[33] E. Glenn Hinson, "The Church: Liberator or Oppressor of Women?" *Review and Expositor*, 73 (Winter 1975): 22.

[34] Harriette F. Cooke, *Mildmay: Or, The Story of the First Deaconess Institution* (London: Elliot Stock, 1892), 47.

[35] A. Maude Royden, *The Church and Woman* (New York: Doran, 1924), 139.

[36] Frederick S. Weiser, "The Origin of the Modern Diaconate for Women," in *Servants of Christ: Deaconesses in Renewal*, ed. Donald G. Bloesch (Minneapolis: Bethany, 1971), 32.

[37] Janet James, ed., *Women in American Religion* (Philadelphia: University of Pennsylvania, 1980), 12.

[38] Rosemary S. Keller, "Lay Women in the Protestant Tradition," in Ruether and Keller, *Women and Religion in America*, 1:247.

[39] Virginia L. Brereton, "Preparing Women for the Lord's Work," in *Women in New Worlds: Historical Perspectives on the Wesleyan Tradition*, ed. Hilah F. Thomas and Rosemary Keller (Nashville: Abingdon, 1981), 184–87.

[40] Christian Golder, "Mission and Aim of the Female Diaconate in the United States," in Ruether and Keller, *Women and Religion in America*, 1:272–73.

[41] Amanda Porterfield, *Feminine Spirituality in America: From Sarah Edwards to Martha Graham* (Philadelphia: Temple University Press, 1980), 122.

[42] Quoted in Allan Coppedge, "Entire Sanctification in Early American Methodism: 1812–1835," *Wesleyan Theological Journal* (Spring 1978), 46.

[43] Thomas Coke, *The Experience and Spiritual Letters of Mrs Hester Ann Rogers: With a Sermon Preached on the Occasion of Her Death* (London: Milner, n.d.), 200–201.

[44] Bradley, *Call to Seriousness*, 42.

[45] Clark Griffith, "Emily Dickinson," *The World Book Encyclopedia*, 22 vols. (Chicago: World Book, 1983), 5:157.

[46] Porterfield, *Feminine Spirituality in America*, 130.

[47] Erik Routley, *A Panorama of Christian Hymnody* (Collegeville, Minn.: Liturgical, 1979), 115.

[48] Kenneth W. Osbeck, *Singing With Understanding* (Grand Rapids: Kregel, 1979), 180.

[49] Ibid., 136.

[50] Routley, *Panorama*, 116.

[51] Bernard Ruffin, *Fanny Crosby* (n.p.: United Church Press, 1976), 78.

[52] Ibid., 129.

[53] Dale A. Johnson, *Women in English Religion, 1700–1925* (New York: Mellen, 1983), 87.

[54] I. D. Stewart, *The History of the Freewill Baptists*, 2 vols. (Dover: Freewill Baptist Printing Establishment, 1862), 1:191.

[55] Ibid., 188, 191.

[56] Ibid., 308–10, 318, 338, 377, 391.

[57] Jerena Lee, *Religious Experiences and Journal* (Philadelphia: Jerena Lee, 1849), 14–17, quoted in Ruether and Keller, eds., *Women and American Religion*, 212.

[58] Ibid., 213.

[59] Almond Davis, *The Female Preacher; or Memoir of Salome Lincoln, Afterwards the Wife of Elder Junia S. Mowry* (Providence: Elder J. S. Mowry, 1843), 36–37, 43–44.

[60] Ibid., 53.

[61] Mary Cole, *Trials and Triumphs of Faith* (Anderson, Ind.: Gospel Trumpet, 1914), 50–51, 85, 106.

[62] Timothy L. Smith, *Called Unto Holiness: The Story of the Nazarenes, the Formative Years* (Kansas City, Mo.: Nazarene, 1962), 12, 20.

[63] Timothy L. Smith, *Revivalism*, 124; Jones, *Perfectionist Persuasion*, 3.

[64] Smith, *Revivalism*, 169.

[65] Hardesty, *Women Called*, 73.

[66] Jones, *Perfectionist Persuasion*, 4–5; Smith, *Revivalism*, 125.

[67] Jones, *Perfectionist Persuasion*, 3; Nancy Hardesty, "The Wesleyan Movement and Women's Liberation," in Theodore Runyon, ed., *Sanctification and Liberation*, (Nashville: Abingdon, 1981), 167.

[68] Phoebe Palmer, *Promise of the Father; or, A Neglected Speciality of the Last Days* (Boston: Henry V. Degen, 1859), 2.

[69] Smith, *Revivalism*, 67–68.

[70] Smith, *Called Unto Holiness*, 23.

[71] Catherine Booth, *Female Ministry; Or, Woman's Right to Preach the Gospel* (New York: Salvation Army, 1975), 14; F. de L. Booth-Tucker, *The Life of Catherine Booth*, 2 vols. (London: Salvation Army, 1892), 1:86.

[72] Catherine Bramwell-Booth, *Catherine Booth: The Story of Her Loves* (London: Hodder and Stoughton, 1970), 185.

[73] Quoted in Norman H. Murdoch, "Female Ministry in the Thought and Work of Catherine Booth" *Church History* 53 (September 1984): 351.

[74] Quoted in Bramwell-Booth, *Catherine Booth*, 185.

[75] Margaret Troutt, *The General Was a Lady: The Story of Evangeline Booth* (Nashville: Holman, 1980), 22.

[76] Catherine Booth, *Papers on Aggressive Christianity* (London: Partridge, 1980), 11, 14.

[77] Catherine Booth, *The Salvation Army in Relation to the Church and State* (London: Partridge, n.d.), 17–18.

[78] Quoted in Catherine Booth, *Female Ministry*, 3.

[79] Flora Larsson, *My Best Men Are Women* (London: Hodder and Stoughton, 1974), 17, 19–22.

[80] Ibid., 22.

[81] Troutt, *The General Was a Lady*, 55–56.

[82] Catherine Booth, *Life and Death, Being Reports of Addresses Delivered in London* (London: Salvation Army, 1883), 11.

[83] Murdoch, "Female Ministry," 354.

[84] Smith, *The Christian's Secret of a Happy Life* (Grand Rapids: Zondervan, 1984), 38.

[85] Henry, *The Secret Life*, 86.

[86] Smith, *The Christian's Secret of a Happy Life*, 171.

[87] Melvin Dieter, *The Holiness Revival of the Nineteenth Century* (Metuchen, N.J.: Scarecrow, 1980), 26.

[88] Ibid., 163.

[89] Quoted in Benjamin B. Warfield, *Perfectionism* (Philadelphia: Presbyterian and Reformed, 1958), 261.

[90] Melvin E. Dieter, "The Smiths—A Biographical Sketch With Selected Items From the

Collection," *The Asbury Seminarian* 38 (Spring 1983): 33.

[91] Elliott Wright, *Holy Company: Christian Heroes and Heroines* (New York: Macmillan, 1980), 41; Ruether and Keller, *Women and Religion in America*, 8.

[92] Frances E. Willard, *Glimpses of Fifty Years: The Autobiography of an American Woman* (Chicago: Smith, 1889), 219–20.

[93] Leon McBeth, *Women in Baptist Life* (Nashville: Broadman, 1979), 60–61.

[94] Wright, *Holy Company*, 39–40.

[95] Amanda Smith, *An Autobiography: The Story of the Lord's Dealings with Mrs. Amanda Smith, the Colored Evangelist* (Chicago: Meyer & Brothers, 1893), 19–20.

[96] Ibid., 199–200.

[97] Ibid., 281, 321.

[98] Quoted in Wright, *Holy Company*, 42.

[99] Quoted in Elinor Rice Hays, *Those Extraordinary Blackwells: The Story of a Journey to a Better World* (New York: Harcourt, Brace & World, 1967), 119–20.

[100] Mother Stewart, *Memoirs of the Crusade: A Thrilling Account of the Great Uprising of Women of Ohio in 1873, Against the Liquor Crime* (Columbus: Williams & Hubbard, 1889), 10.

[101] Frances E. Willard, *Woman and Temperance; or, The Work and Workers of The Women's Christian Temperance Union* (Hartford: Park, 1883), 208–11.

[102] Ibid., 57–58.

[103] Quoted in Ruth Bordin, *Woman and Temperance: The Quest for Power and Liberty, 1873–1900* (Philadelphia: Temple University Press, 1981), 49.

[104] Anna A. Gordon, *The Beautiful Life of Frances E. Willard* (Chicago: Woman's Temperance Publishing Association, 1898), 147–49.

[105] Ray Strachey, *Frances Willard: Her Life and Work* (New York: Revell, 1913), 208.

[106] Willard, *Glimpses of Fifty Years*, 356–59.

[107] Frances E. Willard, *Woman in the Pulpit* (Boston: Lothrop, 1888), 62.

[108] Willard, *Glimpses of Fifty Years*, 359–60.

[109] Carry A. Nation, *The Use and Need of the Life of Carry A. Nation* (Topeka: Stevens, 1909), 126.

[110] Ibid., 130, 133–34.

[111] Ibid., 292.

[112] Walter Martin, *The Kingdom of the Cults: An Analysis of the Major Cult Systems in the Present Christian Era* (Minneapolis: Bethany, 1982), 223, 225.

[113] Lawrence Foster, *Religion and Sexuality*, 32, 37.

[114] Ronald L. Numbers, *Prophetess of Health: A Study of Ellen G. White* (New York: Harper & Row, 1976), 15–21.

[115] Ibid., 200–201.

[116] Mary Ewens, "The Leadership of Nuns in Immigrant Catholicism," in Ruether and Keller, *Women in American Religion*, 101.

[117] Edith Deen, *Great Women of the Christian Faith*, 364–65.

[118] Joseph I. Dirvin, *Mrs. Seton: Foundress of the American Sisters of Charity* (New York: TAN, 1975), 138, quoted in Porterfield, *Feminine Spirituality*, 112–13.

[119] Ewens, "Leadership of Nuns," 115, 128.

[120] Ibid., 132.

[121] Mary Ewens, "Removing the Veil: The Liberated American Nun," in Rosemary Ruether and Eleanor McLaughlin, eds., *Women of Spirit: Female Leadership in the Jewish and Christian Traditions* (New York: Simon and Schuster, 1979), 263.

[122] Willard, *Woman in the Pulpit*, 95.

[123] Ibid., 96, 98–99.

[124] Hays, *Those Extraordinary Blackwells*, 117–18.

[125] Ibid., 118–19.

[126] Barbara B. Zikmund, "The Struggle for the Right to Preach," in Ruether and Keller, eds., *Women and Religion in America*, 214.

[127] Luther Lee, *Woman's Right to Preach the Gospel*, quoted in Ruether and Keller, *Women and Religion in America*, 217.

[128] Hays, *Those Extraordinary Blackwells*, 120.

[129] Ibid., 121–22.

[130] Hardesty, *Great Women*, 101–2.

[131] Frances E. Willard and Mary A Livermore, eds., "Olympia Brown," in *A Woman of the Century: Fourteen Hundred-Seventy Biographical Sketches of Leading American Women* (Chicago: Moulton, 1893), 130.

[132] Arthur T. Jennings, *History of American Wesleyan Methodism* (Syracuse: Wesleyan Methodist Publishing Association, 1902), 4.

[133] James, *Women in American Religion*, 19; Hardesty, *Called*, 22.

[134] Hardesty, *Called*, 23; James, *Women*, 19.

[135] James, *Women in American Religion*, 19–20.

[136] Willard, *Woman in the Pulpit*, 38.

[137] Boyd and Brackenridge, *Presbyterian Women in America*, 98.

[138] Ibid., 91.

139 Ibid., 112, 116.

140 Alan Graebner, "Birth Control and the Lutherans: The Missouri Synod as a Case Study," in James, *Women in American Religion*, 231.

141 Ibid., 231.

142 Velma M. Ferrell, "Called to Serve: Women in the Southern Baptist Convention," *Faith and Mission* 2 (Fall 1984): 22; McBeth, *Women in Baptist Life*, 109–11.

143 McBeth, *Women in Baptist Life*, 112, 110.

144 Ibid., 113.

145 Margaret Bacon, *As the Way Opens: The Story of Quaker Women in America* (Richmond, Ind.: Friends United, 1980), 58.

146 Dana Greene, ed., *Lucretia Mott: Her Complete Speeches and Sermons* (New York: Mellen, 1980), 4–8.

147 Greene, *Lucretia Mott*, 17; Hinson, "The Church: Liberator or Oppressor of Women?" 26.

148 Luther Lee, *Five Sermons and a Tract*, ed. Donald W. Dayton (Chicago: Holrad, 1975), 16–17.

149 Arthur T. Jennings, *History of American Wesleyan Methodism* (Syracuse: Wesleyan Methodist Publishing Association, 1902), 113, 124.

150 B. T. Roberts, *Ordaining Women* (Rochester: Earnest Christian, 1891), 159.

151 Ibid., 52.

152 Lucille Sider Dayton and Donald W. Dayton, "Your Daughters Shall Prophesy: Feminism in the Holiness Movement," *Methodist History* (January 1976), 87.

153 Jerry R. Flora, "Ninety Years of Brethren Women in Ministry," *Ashland Theological Journal* 17 (Fall 1984): 4–5.

154 Leslie Andrews, "Restricted Freedom: A. B. Simpson's View of Women in Ministry" in *Birth of a Vision*, ed. David Hartzveld and Charles Nienkirchen (Beaverlodge, Alta.: Horizon, 1986), 219.

155 Ibid., 220.

156 A. B. Simpson, *When the Comforter Came* (New York: Christian Publications, 1911), 11.

157 Ibid.

158 Carrie Judd Montgomery, *"Under His Wings": The Story of My Life* (Oakland: Triumphs of Faith, 1936), 98–102.

159 Dayton and Dayton, "Your Daughters," 88; John W. Smith, *Heralds of a Brighter Day: Biographical Sketches of Early Leaders in the Church of God Reformation Movement* (Anderson, Ind.: Gospel Trumpet, 1955), 125.

160 Charles W. Conn, *Like A Mighty Army— Moves the Church of God, 1886–1955* (Cleveland, Tenn.: Church of God Publishing House, 1955), 73, 93, 245-46.

161 George Garrison, "The Sanctificationists of Belton," *The Charities Review* 3 (November 1893): 29, quoted in Ruether and Keller, *Women and Religion in America*, 95.

162 Ibid., quoted in Ruether and Keller, *Women and Religion in America*, 99–100.

163 Boyd and Brackenridge, *Presbyterian Women in America*, 117.

164 Gayle Kimball, *The Religious Ideas of Harriet Beecher Stowe: Her Gospel of Womanhood* (New York: Mellen, 1982), 161.

Chapter 8

1 Patricia R. Hill, *The World Their Household: The American Woman's Foreign Mission Movement and Cultural Transformation, 1870–1920* (Ann Arbor: University of Michigan Press, 1985), 3.

2 Hill, *The World Their Household*, 2.

3 Ruth A. Tucker, *From Jerusalem to Irian Jaya: A Biographical History of Christian Missions* (Grand Rapids: Zondervan, 1983).

4 Albert L. Vail, *Mary Webb and the Mother Society* (Philadelphia: American Baptist Publication Society, 1914), ii.

5 R. Pierce Beaver, *American Protestant Women in World Mission: A History of the first Feminist Movement in North America* (Grand Rapids: Eerdmans, 1980), 13–14.

6 Ibid., 34.

7 Ibid., 53.

8 Jane Hunter, *The Gospel of Gentility: American Women Missionaries in Turn-of-the-Century China* (New Haven: Yale University Press, 1984), 44.

9 Quoted in A. E. Thompson, *The Life of A. B. Simpson* (New York: Christian Alliance Publishing, 1920), 121.

10 Quoted in Mary Drewery, *William Carey: A Biography* (Grand Rapids: Zondervan, 1979), 71.

11 Drewery, *William Carey*, 81.

12 Quoted in ibid., 94, 123.

13 Quoted in Marshall Broomhall, *Robert Morrison: A Master-builder* (New York: Doran, 1924), 59.

14 George Seaver, *David Livingstone, His Life and Letters* (New York: Harper, 1957), 276; Oliver Ransford, *David Livingstone: The Dark Interior* (New York: St. Martin's, 1978), 118.

[15] Norman Grub: *Once Caught, No Escape: Norman Grubb's Life Story* (Fort Washington, Pa.: Christian Literature Crusade, 1970), 49.

[16] Quoted in Drewery, *William Carey*, 94; quoted in H. and G. Taylor, *J. Hudson Taylor: God's Man in China* (Chicago: Moody, 1978), 208.

[17] Rufus Anderson, "The Marriage of Missionaries" (1842) in R. Pierce Beaver, ed., *To Advance the Gospel: Selections From the Writings of Rufus Anderson* (Grand Rapids: Eerdmans, 1967), 210–15.

[18] Quoted in Courtney Anderson, *To the Golden Shore: The Life of Adoniram Judson* (Grand Rapids: Zondervan, 1972), 84.

[19] Jonathan Allen, in a sermon delivered at Haverhill, Massachusetts, February 5, 1812, quoted in Joan Jacobs Brumberg, *Mission for Life: The Story of the Family of Adoniram Judson* (New York: Macmillan, 1980), 82.

[20] *American Baptist Magazine*, 4 (January 1823): 19, quoted in Brumberg, *Mission for Life*, 87.

[21] *American Baptist Magazine*, 4 (January 1923): 20, quoted in Brumberg, *Mission for Life*, 87.

[22] *Boston Evening Transcript*, 17 (March 27, 1846): 4807, quoted in Brumberg, *Mission for Life*, 41.

[23] William Dean, *Memoir of Mrs. Lucy T. Lord of the Chinese Baptist Missions* (Philadelphia, 1854), 123, quoted in Barbara Welter, "She Hath Done What She Could: Protestant Women's Missionary Careers in Nineteenth-Century America," in Janet Wilson James, ed., *Women in American Religion* (Philadelphia: University of Pennsylvania Press, 1980), 115–16.

[24] Winifred Mathews, *Dauntless Women: Stories of Pioneer Wives* (Freeport, N.Y.: Friendship, 1947), 146, 163; Mrs. Horace G. Underwood, "Woman's Work for Women in Korea," *Missionary Review of the World* 18 (July 1905): 498–500.

[25] Brumberg, *Mission for Life*, 115.

[26] John C. Pollock, *Hudson Taylor and Maria: Pioneers in China* (Grand Rapids: Zondervan, 1962), 171.

[27] H. and G. Taylor, *Hudson Taylor's Spiritual Secret* (Chicago: Moody, 1932), 210–11.

[28] Daniel Eddy, *Heroines of the Missionary Enterprise: Sketches of Prominent Female Missionaries* (London: Arthur Hall, Virtue, and Co., 1858), 124.

[29] Dorothy Clarke Wilson, *Dr. Ida: The Story of Dr. Ida Scudder of Vellore* (New York: McGraw-Hill, 1959), 221.

[30] Beaver, *American Protestant Women*, 59.

[31] Hill, *The World Their Household*, 47, 49.

[32] Beaver, *American Protestant Women*, 38.

[33] Edwin M. Bliss, *The Missionary Enterprise: A Concise History of Its Objects, Methods and Extension* (New York: Revell, 1908), 253.

[34] Ibid., 88.

[35] Beaver, *American Protestant Women*, 87-88.

[36] Welter, "She Hath Done What She Could," 124.

[37] Beaver, *American Protestant Women*, 88.

[38] Carma Van Liere, "Sarah Doremus. Reformed Church Saint," *The Church Herald* (October 4, 1985), 16–17.

[39] Hill, *The World Their Household*, 45–47.

[40] Rosemary Keller, "Lay Women in the Protestant Tradition," in Rosemary Ruether and Rosemary Keller, eds., *Women and Religion in America: The Nineteenth Century, A Documentary History*, 3 vols. (New York: Harper & Row, 1981), 1:242–43.

[41] Quoted in Hunter, *The Gospel of Gentility*, 13–14.

[42] Irwin Hyatt, *Our Ordered Lives Confess: Three Nineteenth-Century American Missionaries in East Shantung* (Cambridge, Mass.: Harvard University Press, 1976), 104–5.

[43] James Thoburn, *Life of Isabella Thoburn* (Cincinnati: Jennings and Pye, 1903), quoted in Welter, "She Hath Done What She Could," 120.

[44] Elisabeth Elliot Leitch, "The Place of Women in World Missions," in David M. Howard, ed., *Jesus Christ: Lord of the Universe, Hope of the World*, (Downers Grove: InterVarsity, 1974), 124–25.

[45] Hyatt, *Our Ordered Lives*, 104–5.

[46] Beaver, *American Protestant Women*, 63, 102.

[47] Hunter, *The Gospel of Gentility*, 88.

[48] Mrs. Ethan Curtis, "The Reflex Influence of Missions," *Missionary Review of the World* 5 (March 1892): 183.

[49] Hyatt, *Our Ordered Lives*, 135–37.

[50] Robert Speer, *Servants of the King* (New York: Interchurch, 1909), 144.

[51] Frances E. Willard, *Woman in the Pulpit* (Boston: Lothrop, 1888), 81, 100.

[52] Leecy A. Barnett, *Pioneers, Pedagogues, and Preachers: Expanding Opportunities for Women in Presbyterian Missions to the American Indians, 1833–1893*, M.A. Thesis, Trinity Evangelical Divinity School, Deerfield, Ill. (December 1985), 117, 127, 129.

[53] Hyatt, *Our Ordered Lives*, 99.

[54] Beaver, *American Protestant Women*, 179.

[55] Frank Houghton, *Amy Carmichael of Dohnavur* (London: Society for the Propagation of Christian Knowledge, 1954), 62.

[56] Ibid., 217–21.

[57] Kenneth Scott Latourette, *A History of the Expansion of Christianity: Three Centuries of Advance, 1500–1800*, 7 vols. (Grand Rapids: Zondervan, 1970), 3:100.

[58] Francis Parkman, *The Jesuits in North America in the Seventeenth Century*, (Boston: Little, Brown, 1868), 278.

[59] Stephen Neill, *A History of Christian Missions* (New York: Penguin, 1964), 423.

[60] Glenn D. Kittler, *The Woman God Loved* (Garden City: Hanover, 1959), 58.

[61] Henri Daniel-Rops, *The Heroes of God* (New York: Hawthorn, 1959), 154–55.

[62] Ibid., 162–63.

[63] E. R. Pitman, *Lady Missionaries in Many Lands* (London, Pickering & Inglis, n.d.), 5.

[64] Tucker, *From Jerusalem to Irian Jaya, 161.*

[65] Carol Christian and Gladys Plummer, *God and One Redhead: Mary Slessor of Calabar* (Grand Rapids: Zondervan, 1970), 177.

[66] Maria Nilsen, *Malla Moe* (Chicago: Moody, 1956), 143–46.

[67] Ibid., 135.

[68] C. S. Winchell, "Mary Clarke Nind," *Woman's Missionary Friend*, 37 (November 1905): 382–83, quoted in Hill, *The World Their Household*, 85.

[69] Hill, *The World Their Household*, 85.

[70] Louise A. Cattan, *Lamps Are for Lighting: The Story of Helen Barrett Montgomery and Lucy Waterbury Peabody* (Grand Rapids: Eerdmans, 1972), 38.

[71] Quoted in Hill, *The World Their Household*, 136.

[72] Helen Barrett Montgomery, *Western Women in Eastern Lands* (New York: Macmillan, 1910), 243–44.

[73] Valentin H. Rabe, "Evangelical Logistics: Mission Support and Resources to 1920" in John K. Fairband, ed., *The Missionary Enterprise in China and America*, (Cambridge, Mass.: Harvard University Press, 1974), 72.

[74] Delavan L. Leonard, *A Hundred Years of Missions: The Story of Progress Since Carey's Beginning* (New York: Funk & Wagnalls, 1895), 181–82.

[75] A. T. Pierson, "The Outlook for the Twentieth Century," *Missionary Review of the World* 14 (March 1901): 167–68.

[76] Hill, *The World Their Household*, 167.

[77] Cattan, *Lamps Are for Lighting*, 56-57.

[78] Hill, *The World Their Household*, 163.

[79] Ibid., 148–49.

[80] Ibid., 51–53.

[81] McBeth, *Women in Baptist Life*, 88, 94.

[82] Bobbie Sorrill, *Annie Armstrong: Dreamer in Action* (Nashville: Broadman, 1984), 93–94.

[83] McBeth, *Women in Baptist Life*, 95, 97.

[84] Alma Hunt, *History of the Woman's Missionary Union* (Nashville: Convention, 1964), 24, quoted in McBeth, *Women in Baptist Life*, 92.

[85] Hyatt, *Our Ordered Lives*, 114.

[86] Donald Mathews, "Women's History/ Everyone's History," in Thomas and Keller, eds., *Women in New Worlds*, 47.

[87] Augustus R. Buckland, *Women in the Mission Field: Pioneers and Martyrs* (New York: Whittaker, 1895), 11, 13; Geoffrey Moorhouse, *The Missionaries* (London: Methuen, 1973), 274.

[88] Buckland, *Women in the Mission Field*, 23; Moorhouse, *The Missionaries*, 275.

[89] Buckland, *Women in the Mission Field*, 28.

[90] Hill, *The World Their Household*, 169.

[91] *Missionary Review of the World* 11 (November 1898): 873.

[92] Ibid., 874.

[93] Evelyn Stenbock, *Miss Terri: The Story of Maude Cary, Pioneer GMU Missionary in Morocco* (Lincoln, Neb.: Good News Broadcasting Association, 1970), 99–103.

[94] Norman P. Grubb, *C. T. Studd: Cricketer and Pioneer* (Chicago: Moody, 1962), 210–11.

[95] Lorry Lutz, *Born to Lose, Bound to Win: The Amazing Journey of Mother Eliza George* (Irvine, Calif.: Harvest, 1980), 138–39, 144, 169, 190.

[96] Mrs. Ethan Curtis, "A generation of 'Woman's Work for Woman,'" *Missionary Review of the World* 23 (July 1910): 535.

[97] Dorothy Clarke Wilson, *Palace of Healing: The Story of Dr. Clara Swain, First Woman Missionary Doctor and the Hospital She Founded* (New York: McGraw Hill, 1968), passim.

[98] Quoted in Sherwood Eddy, *Pathfinders of the World Missionary Crusade* (New York: Abingdon-Cokesbury, 1945), 131.

[99] Dorothy Clarke Wilson, *Dr. Ida: The Story of Dr. Ida Scudder of Vellore* (New York: McGraw Hill, 1959), 273–75.

[100] Ibid., 298.

[101] Ibid., 286.

[102] Alan Burgess, *Daylight Must Come: The Story of a Courageous Woman Doctor in the Congo* (New York: Dell, n.d.), 135.

[103]"Interview with Helen Roseveare," *HIS* (January 1977), 18.

[104]Ibid., 19.

[105]She is the subject of a biography, Allan Burgess, *Daylight Must Come,* and has written her own accounts of her missionary experience in *Give Me This Mountain, He Gave Me a Valley,* and *Living Sacrifice.* She has also become a leading spokeswoman for evangelical foreign missions.

[106]Ethel Wallis and Mary Bennett, *Two Thousand Tongues to Go* (New York: Harper & Row, 1959), 98.

[107]Eunice V. Pike, *Not Alone* (Chicago: Moody, 1964), 10.

[108]Clarence W. Hall, "Two Thousand Tongues to Go," in *Adventurers for God* (New York: Harper, 1959), 119.

[109]Ethel E. Wallis, *The Dayuma Story: Life Under Auca Spears* (New York: Harper & Row, 1960), passim.

[110]Tucker, *From Jerusalem to Irian Jaya,* 363.

[111]Phyllis Thompson, *Count It All Joy: The Story of Joy Ridderhof and Gospel Recordings* (Wheaton: Shaw, 1978), 143–44.

[112]"Miss Betty Greene: First Lady of MAF," *Christian Times* (January 15, 1967): 3.

[113]Hill, *The World Their Household,* 175.

[114]Kenneth Cragg, "Constance E. Padwick (1886—1968)," *The Muslim World* 59 (January 1969): 29–34.

[115]Constance E. Padwick, "North African Reverie," *International Review of Missions* 17 (1938): 346–47.

[116]Marguerite Kraft to Ruth A. Tucker, Personal Correspondence, January 5, 1986.

[117]Ruth A. Tucker, "Female Mission Strategists: A Historical and Contemporary Perspective," *Missiology* 15 (1987): 87.

[118]E. Thomas Brewster and Elizabeth S. Brewster, "Bonding and the Missionary Task: Establishing a Sense of Belonging," in Ralph Winter and Steven Hawthorne, eds., *Perspectives of the World Christian Movement* (Pasadena: William Carey Library, 1981), 458, 462.

[119]Fatima Mahoumet, "Ann Croft and the Fulani," in *Perspectives on the World Christian Movement,* 721.

[120]Phyllis Thompson, *A Transparent Woman: The Compelling Story of Gladys Aylward* (Grand Rapids: Zondervan, 1971), 183.

Chapter 9

[1]Margaret Burton, *The Education of Women in China* (New York: Revell, 1911), 90, quoted in Shirley S. Garrett, "Images of Chinese Women," in John and Ellen Webster, eds., *The Church and Women in the Third World* (Philadelphia: Westminster, 1985), 26–27.

[2]Garrett, "Images of Chinese Women," 27.

[3]Ibid., 27–29.

[4]Charles W. Forman, " 'Sing to the Lord a New Song': Women in the Churches of Oceania," in Denise O'Brien and Sharon W. Tiffany, eds., *Rethinking Women's Roles: Perspectives From the Pacific* (Los Angeles: University of California Press, 1984), 156.

[5]Helen Barrett Montgomery, *Western Women in Eastern Lands: An Outline of Fifty Years of Women's Work in Foreign Missions* (New York: Macmillan, 1910), 211.

[6]Ibid., 213.

[7]J. Waskom Pickett, *Christ's Way to India's Heart* (Lucknow: Lucknow Publishing House, 1938), 69.

[8]J. Waskom Pickett, *Christian Mass Movements in India* (New York: Abingdon, 1933), 193.

[9]J. B. Schuyler, "Conceptions of Christianity in the Context of Tropical Africa: Nigerian Reactions to Its Advent," in C. G. Beata, ed., *Christianity in Tropical Africa* (London: Oxford University Press, 1968), 216–17.

[10]Jane Hunter, *The Gospel of Gentility: American Women Missionaries in Turn-of-the-Century China* (New Haven: Yale University Press, 1984), 181.

[11]David B. Barrett, *Schism and Renewal in Africa: An Analysis of Six Thousand Contemporary Religious Movements* (London: Oxford University Press, 1968), 146–47.

[12]Quoted in Frances Hiebert, "Missionary Women as Models in the Cross-Cultural Context," *Missiology* 10 (October 1982): 458.

[13]Joyce Siwani, "Mission Issues in South Africa," *International Review of Mission* 73 (July 1984): 329.

[14]Penelope Campbell, "Presbyterian West African Missions: Women as Converts and Agents of Social Change," *Journal of Presbyterian History* 52 (Summer 1978): 123; M. Louise Pirouet, "Women Missionaries of the Church Missionary Society in Uganda, 1896–1920," in Torben Christensen and William R. Hutchison, eds., *Missionary Ideologies in the Imperialist Era: 1880–1920* (Denmark: Aros, 1982), 236–37.

[15]Barrett, *Schism and Renewal,* 147.

[16] Campbell, "Presbyterian West African Missions," 128.

[17] Ibid., 124.

[18] Mercy Amba Oduyoye, "Standing on Both Feet: Education and Leadership Training of Women in the Methodist Church, Nigeria," *Ecumenical Review* 33 (January 1981): 61.

[19] Montgomery, *Western Women in Eastern Lands*, 210.

[20] Kathleen Bliss, *The Service and Status of Women in the Churches* (London: SCM, 1952), 18.

[21] Barrett, *Schism and Renewal*, 147.

[22] Rose Marie Cecchini, "A Witness for Peace: The Experience of Japan YWCA," *International Review of Mission* 73 (July 1984): 336–39.

[23] Christiana Tsai, *Queen of the Dark Chamber* (Chicago: Moody, 1953), 35.

[24] Ibid., 67–68.

[25] Ibid., 71–72.

[26] Ibid., 77–78.

[27] Ibid., 83–88.

[28] Ibid., 184.

[29] B. V. Subbamma, *New Patterns for Discipling Hindus* (Pasadena: William Carey Library, 1970), 36.

[30] Oduyoye, "Standing on Both Feet," 69.

[31] Virginia R. Jones, "A Sketch of Women of the Good News," unpublished paper, May, 1985.

[32] Ibid.; Ruth A. Tucker, "African Women's Movement Finds Massive Response," *Evangelical Missions Quarterly* 22 (July 1986): 290.

[33] Virginia R. Jones, "Information Sheet for Women of the Good News Program," Minute # 7 of committee meeting, June 27–28, 1979, 1.

[34] Ibid., 2.

[35] Virginia Jones to Ruth Tucker, personal correspondence, Napopo Zaire, August 22, 1985.

[36] Montgomery, *Western Women in Eastern Lands*, 114.

[37] Winburn T. Thomas, *Protestant Beginnings in Japan: The First Three Decades, 1859–89* (Rutland, Vt.: Tuttle, 1959), 107; Rosalind Goforth, *Climbing: Memories of a Missionary's Wife* (Chicago: Moody, n.d.), 155.

[38] Kenneth Scott Latourette, *A History of Christian Missions in China* (New York: Macmillan, 1929), 648; Edith G. Dreyer, *Light and Shadow in China* (London: China Inland Mission, n.d.), 59–63.

[39] Margaret E. Burton, *Women Workers of the Orient* (West Bedford, Mass.: Central Committee on the United Study of Foreign Mission, 1918), 37.

[40] Ruth A. Tucker, "The Role of Bible Women in World Evangelism," *Missiology* 13 (April 1985): 142–43; Goforth, *Climbing*, 33.

[41] Montgomery, *Western Women in Eastern Lands*, 233.

[42] Winburn T. Thomas, *Protestant Beginnings in Japan: The First Three Decades, 1859–1889* (Rutland, Vt.: Tuttle, 1959), 107–8.

[43] James L. Barton, "Bible Women in Ceylon and India," *Life and Light* 32 (May 1902): 204.

[44] Ibid., 205.

[45] John L. Nevius, "Planting and Development of Missionary Churches," in Francis M. DuBose, ed., *Classics of Christian Missions* (Nashville: Broadman, 1979), 259; Bliss, *The Service and Status of Women*, 110.

[46] Pickett, *Christ's Way to India's Heart*, 70–71.

[47] Pandita Ramabai, *The High-Caste Hindu Woman* (London: George Bell, 1888), xxi.

[48] Quoted in Helen S. Dyer, *Pandita Ramabai: Her Vision, Her Mission and Triumph of Faith* (London: Pickering & Inglis, n.d.), 24.

[49] Ibid., 26.

[50] Shamsundar Manohar Adhav, *Pandita Ramabai* (Madras: The Christian Literature Society, 1979), 6–8.

[51] Ibid., 131.

[52] Quoted in ibid., 131.

[53] Ibid., 141.

[54] Ibid., 141–42.

[55] Adhav, *Pandita Ramabai*, 42.

[56] Pandita Ramabai, *The High-Caste Hindu Woman* (London: George Bell, 1888), 62.

[57] Nancy Hardesty, *Great Women of Faith* (Grand Rapids: Baker, 1980), 128.

[58] Quoted in Adhav, *Pandita Ramabai*, 19.

[59] Russell T. Hitt, *Sensei: The Life Story of Irene Webster-Smith* (New York: Harper & Row, 1956), 131.

[60] Eunice V. Pike, *Not Alone* (Chicago: Moody, 1964), 59.

[61] Ibid., 78.

[62] Forman, "Sing to the Lord a New Song," 160–61.

[63] Quoted in Alice Chai, "Korean Women in Hawaii, 1903-1945," in Hilah Thomas and Rosemary Keller, eds., *Women in New Worlds* (Nashville: Abingdon, 1981), 331.

[64] Allen Finley and Lorry Lutz, *Mission: A World-Family Affair* (San Jose: Christian National Press, 1981), 110–11.

[65] Bliss, *The Service and Status of Women*, 64.

[66] Ibid.

[67] Montgomery, *Western Women in Eastern Lands*, 222.

[68] Dorothy Clarke Wilson, *Dr. Ida: The Story of Dr. Ida Scudder of Vellore* (New York: McGraw Hill, 1959), 320–21.

[69] Flora Larsson, *My Best Men Are Women* (London: Hodder and Stoughton, 1974), 33–34.

[70] Quoted in ibid., 35.

[71] Frank Houghton, *Amy Carmichael of Dohnavur* (London: Society for the Propagation of Christian Knowledge, 1954), 217–21, 355–58.

[72] John Webster, "Assumptions About the Indian Woman Underlying Protestant Church Policies and Programs, 1947–1982," in Webster and Webster, *The Church and Women*, 40–42.

[73] Ibid., 43.

[74] Ibid.

[75] Anne Fremantle, *Woman's Way to God* (New York: St. Martin, 1977), 251.

[76] Eileen Egan, *Such a Vision of the Street: Mother Teresa—The Spirit and the Work* (Garden City: Doubleday, 1985), p. 369.

[77] Mia Brandel-Syrier, "The Role of Women in African Independent Churches," *Missionalia* 12 (April 1984): 14–15; Peter Falk, *The Growth of the Church in Africa* (Grand Rapids: Zondervan, 1979), 459–60.

[78] Ibid., 16.

[79] Barrett, *Schism and Renewal*, 148.

[80] Dorothea A. Lehmann, "Women in the Independent African Independent Churches," in Victor E. W. Hayward, ed., *African Independent Church Movements* (London: Edinburgh House, 1963), 68.

[81] Adrian Hastings, *A History of African Christianity, 1950–1975* (London: Cambridge University, 1979), 75.

[82] Kurt Koch, *The Revival in Indonesia* (Grand Rapids: Kregel, 1970), 219.

[83] Ibid., 245–46.

[84] Bliss, *The Service and Status of Women*, 98.

[85] Forman, "Sing to the Lord a New Song," 170, 153.

[86] Bliss, *The Service and Status of Women*, 134–38.

[87] Cecchini, "A Witness for Peace," 336.

[88] Norene Carter, "The Episcopalian Story," in Rosemary Ruether and Eleanor McLaughlin, eds., *Women of Spirit: Female Leadership in the Jewish and Christian Traditions* (New York: Simon and Schuster, 1979), 357.

[89] Siwani, "Mission Issues in South Africa," 329.

[90] Ada Maria Isasi-Diaz, "Silent Women Will Never Be Heard," *Missiology* 7 (July 1979): 195–96.

[91] Katherine Gilfeather, "Coming of Age in a Latin Church," in Webster and Webster, *The Church and Women*, 62.

[92] Subbamma, *New Patterns for Discipling Hindus*, 201.

[93] Hiebert, "Missionary Women," 460.

[94] Montgomery, *Western Women in Eastern Lands*, 227–29.

[95] Elisabeth F. Isais, "The Problems Facing Latin American Women in Leadership," *INTERLIT* (September 1981), 8.

Chapter 10

[1] Vinson Synan, *The Holiness-Pentecostal Movement in The United States* (Grand Rapids: Eerdmans, 1971), 101; Agnes N. O. LaBerge, *What God Hath Wrought* (New York: Garland, 1985), 29.

[2] John T. Nichol, *The Pentecostals* (Plainfield, N.J.: Logos, 1966), 63.

[3] Sarah E. Parham, *The Life of Charles F. Parham, Founder of the Apostolic Faith Movement* (Joplin, Mo.: Hunter, 1930), 161–62.

[4] *A Historical Account of The Apostolic Faith* (Portland, Ore.: Apostolic Faith, 1965), 59, quoted in Nichol, *The Pentecostals*, 35.

[5] Ibid., 35.

[6] Robert B. Mitchell, *Heritage and Horizons: The History of Open Bible Standard Churches* (Des Moines: Open Bible Publishers, 1982), 30; *A Historical Account of the Apostolic Faith*, 21, quoted in Nichol, *The Pentecostals*, 98–99, 144.

[7] Ibid., 144.

[8] Synan, *The Holiness-Pentecostal Movement*, 114.

[9] Mitchell, *Heritage and Horizons*, 41.

[10] Quoted in ibid., 47.

[11] Mitchell, *Heritage and Horizons*, 47–48.

[12] Janet Wilson James, "Women in American Religious History: An Overview," in Janet Wilson James, ed., *Women in American Religion* (Philadelphia: University of Pennsylvania Press, 1980), 22.

[13] Mary B. Woodworth-Etter, *Signs and Wonders: God Wrought in the Ministry for Forty Years* (Tulsa: Harrison, 1916), 21, 28, 32.

[14] Ibid., 35–36.

[15] Ibid., 138.

[16] Ibid., 151.

[17] Ibid., 120.

[18] Ibid., 139.

[19] Ibid., 142.

[20] Ibid., 151–56.

21 Ibid., 45, 157, quoted in Nichol, *The Pentecostals*, 59.

22 Quoted in Woodworth-Etter, *Signs and Wonders*, 7.

23 Quoted in Charles H. Barfoot and Gerald T. Sheppard, "Prophetic Vs. Priestly Religion: The Changing Role of Women Clergy in Classical Pentecostal Churches," *Review of Religious Research* 22 (September 1980): 8.

24 Ibid., 14.

25 Barfoot and Sheppard, "Prophetic Vs. Priestly Religion," 14.

26 *Time*, October 9, 1944.

27 Aimee Semple McPherson, *The Story of My Life* (Waco: Word, 1973), 26.

28 Ibid., 52–67.

29 Aimee Semple McPherson, *This Is That* (Los Angeles: Echo Part Evangelistic Association, 1923), 73–76.

30 Robert Barr, *Least of All Saints: The Story of Aimee Semple McPherson* (Englewood Cliffs, N.J.: Prentice-Hall, 1979), 115, 120–21.

31 Barr, *Least of All Saints*, 150–51.

32 Quoted in ibid., 161.

33 Quoted in Synan, *The Holiness-Pentecostal Movement*, 198.

34 Barr, *Least of All Saints*, 212–16, vi.

35 McPherson, *Story of My Life*, 232–39.

36 Quoted in Barr, *Least of All Saints*, 282.

37 Quoted in Barfoot and Sheppard, "Prophetic Vs. Priestly Religion," 15.

38 U.S. Bureau of the Census, Census of Religious bodies, 1936, quoted in Barfoot and Sheppard, "Prophetic vs. Priestly Religion," 3.

39 See section below on Anglicans.

40 Seth Cook Rees, *The Ideal Pentecostal Church* (Cincinnati: Knapp, 1897), 41.

41 Byron Rees, *Hulda A. Rees: The Pentecostal Prophetess* (Philadelphia: Christian Standard, 1898, 11–25; Paul S. Rees, *Seth Cook Rees: The Warrior-Saint* (Indianapolis: Pilgrim Book Room, 1934), 41.

42 Alma White, *Looking Back from Beulah* (Bound Brook, N.J.: The Pentecostal Union, 1910), 50–51; Ford Hendrickson, *Martyrs and Witnesses* (Detroit: Protestant Missionary, 1917), 297.

43 Hendrickson, *Martyrs and Witnesses*, 297.

44 J. Gordon Melton, *Encyclopedia of America's Religions* (Wilmington, N.C.: McGrath, 1978), 231.

45 Alma White, *Demons and Tongues* (Zaraphath, N.J.: Pillar of Fire, 1949), 43, 56, 68–69, 82–84, 112–15.

46 Hendrickson, *Martyrs and Witnesses*, 298.

47 Melton, *Encyclopedia*, 213.

48 Synan, *The Holiness-Pentecostal Movement*, 111.

49 Alma White, *The New Testament Church* (Bound Brook, N.J.: Pentecostal Union, 1912), 217, 223, 227, 230.

50 Timothy L. Smith, *Called Unto Holiness* (Kansas City, Mo.: Nazarene, 1962), 113.

51 Ibid., 155.

52 Ibid., 157–58.

53 Ibid., 156.

54 Flora Larsson, *My Best Men Are Women* (London: Hodder and Stoughton, 1974), 170.

55 Margaret Troutt, *The General Was a Lady: The Story of Evangeline Booth* (Nashville: Holman, 1980), 313–15.

56 Ibid., 55–63.

57 Ibid., 74–78.

58 Ibid., 184.

59 Edward H. McKinley, *Marching to Glory: The History of the Salvation Army in the United States* (New York: Harper & Row, 1980), 94–95.

60 Troutt, *The General Was a Lady*, 263.

61 McKinley, *Marching to Glory*, 185.

62 James, *Women in American Religion*, 22.

63 Max Weber, *The Sociology of Religion*, trans. E. Fischoff (Boston: Beacon, 1963), 104.

64 Mary Agnes Dougherty, "The Social Gospel According to Phoebe," in Hilah F. Thomas and Rosemary Keller, eds., *Women in New Worlds*, (Nashville: Abingdon, 1981), 202.

65 Gladys G. Calkins, *Follow Those Women: Church Women in the Ecumenical Movement* (New York: National Council of the Churches of Christ in the U.S.A., 1961), 19.

66 James, "Women in American Religious History," in James, *Women in American Religion*, 10.

67 Quoted in Rebecca P. Garber, *The Social Gospel and Its View of Women and the Women's Movement, 1880–1919* (Trinity Evangelical Divinity School: M. A. Thesis, 1978), 88–91.

68 Ibid., 94–95, 126.

69 Garber, *The Social Gospel and Its View of Women*, 123, 125.

70 Ibid., 81.

71 Lyman Abbott, *The Home Builder* (New York: Houghton-Mifflin, 1908), 3.

72 "General Findings from the Survey of the Relative Place of Women in the Church" (April 7, 1927), 1, quoted in Elizabeth Howell Verdesi, *In But Still Out: Women in the Church* (Philadelphia: Westminster, 1975), 100.

73 Quoted in James J. Kenneally, "Eve, Mary, and the Historians: American Catholicism and

Women," in James, *Women in American Religion,* 194.

74 Quoted in Rosemary Ruether, "Entering the Sanctuary: The Roman Catholic Story," in Ruether and McLaughlin, *Women of Spirit,* 373–74.

75 Augustine Rossler, "Woman," in *The Catholic Encyclopedia* ed. Charles G. Herbermann, 16 vols. (New York: Encyclopedia, 1913), 15: 687.

76 Kenneally, "Eve, Mary, and the Historians," in James, *Women and American Religion,* 201.

77 Mary Luke Tobin, "Women in the Church: Vatican II and After," *The Ecumenical Review* 37 (July 1985): 295.

78 Ruether, "Entering the Sanctuary," 380.

79 Ibid., 381.

80 Brian Heeney, "The Beginning of Church Feminism," *Journal of Ecclesiastical History* 33 (January 1982): 101–5.

81 "Daughters of Prophecy," *The Witness* (Special Issue, 1984), 4.

82 Mossie A. Wyker, *Church Women in the Scheme of Things,* (St. Louis: Bethany, 1953), 46.

83 A. Maude Royden, *A Threefold Cord* (New York: Macmillan, 1948), 59–61.

84 Dale Johnson, *Women in English Religion,* 309–10.

85 Quoted in ibid., 311.

86 Ibid., 300.

87 "Women Deacons: A New Anglican Church Policy," *Time* (July 15, 1985), 51.

88 Wyker, *Church Women,* 35.

89 Barbara C. Harris, "Pentecost Revisited," *The Witness* (Special Issue, 1984), 10.

90 Heather Huyck, "Indelible Change: Woman Priests in the Episcopal Church," *Historical Magazine of the Protestant Episcopal Church* 51 (December 1982): 397.

91 Ibid.

92 Lois A. Boyd and R. Douglas Brackenridge, *Presbyterian Women in America: Two Centuries of a Quest for Status* (London: Greenwood, 1983), 124.

93 Janet Wilson James, ed., *Women in American Religion* (Philadelphia: University of Pennsylvania Press, 1980), 23–24.

94 Wyker, *Church Women,* 34.

95 Boyd and Brackenridge, *Presbyterian Women,* 125.

96 Ibid., 125–26.

97 Ibid., 130.

98 W. Reginald Wheeler, *A Man Sent From God: A Biography of Robert E. Speer* (London: Revell, 1956), 163.

99 Ibid.

100 Ibid., 132–37.

101 Ibid., 140–41.

102 Ibid., 153.

103 Verdesi, *In But Still Out,* 18.

104 Ibid., 19.

105 Hope Evangeline, *Daisy* (Grand Rapids: Baker, 1978), 74–76, 78, 84.

106 "In Memoriam: Jessie Bartlett Hess," 1881–1969, unpublished paper.

107 Elisabeth Schmidt, *When God Calls a Woman: The Struggle of a Woman Pastor in France and Algeria,* trans. Allen Hackett (New York: Pilgrim, 1981), 15.

108 Ibid., 35.

109 Ibid., 97.

110 Ibid., 102, 108, 215.

111 James I. Cook, "The President's Commentary," *Church Herald* (October 1, 1982), 19.

112 Gordon J. Spykman and Lillian V. Grissen, *Men and Women: Partners in Service* (Grand Rapids: Christian Reformed Church, 1981), 11, 115, 120–21.

113 Frederick S. Weiser, *Love's Response: A Story of Lutheran Deaconesses in America* (Philadelphia: United Lutheran Church in America, 1962), 70–82.

114 Virginia Brereton and Christa Klein, "American Women in Ministry: A History of Protestant Beginning Points," in Ruether and McLaughlin, *Women of Spirit,* 320; E. Clifford Nelson, *Lutheranism in North America, 1914–1970* (Minneapolis: Augsburg, 1972), 261.

115 Brereton and Klein, "American Women," 315, 322.

116 Wyker, *Church Women,* 13–15.

117 Wyker, *Church Women,* 33; Lorraine Lollis, *The Shape of Adam's Rib: A Lively History of Women's Work in the Christian Church* (St. Louis: Bethany, 1970), 11.

118 Wyker, *Church Women,* 33.

119 Albert W. Beaven, "Helen of Rochester," in Helen Barrett Montgomery, *Helen Barrett Montgomery: From Campus to World Citizenship* (New York: Revell, 1940), 92.

120 James, "Women in American Religious History," 20.

121 Leon McBeth, *Women in Baptist Life* (Nashville: Broadman, 1979), 153.

122 McBeth, *Women in Baptist Life,* 155.

123 Bruce Buursma, "Women Pastors Split Southern Baptists," *Chicago Tribune,* February 18, 1984.

124 Quoted in Aida B. Spencer, *Beyond the Curse: Women Called to Ministry* (Nashville: Nelson, 1985), 19.

[125] Mary Lou Cummings "Ordained into Ministry: Ann J. Allebach," in Mary Lou Cummings, ed., *Full Circle: Stories of Mennonite Women*, (Newton, Kansas: Faith and Life, 1978), 2–8.

[126] Quoted in ibid., 9–10.

[127] Cummings, *Full Circle*, 10.

[128] Elaine S. Rich, *Mennonite Women: A Story of God's Faithfulness, 1683–1983* (Scottdale, Pa.: Herald, 1983), 9.

[129] Dayton, *Discovering an Evangelical Heritage*, 93; Fredrick Franson, *Prophesying Daughters: A Few Words Concerning Women's Position in Regard to Evangelization* (Stockholm: n.p., 1897), 2.

[130] Franson, *Prophesying Daughters*, 20.

[131] Ibid., 21.

[132] Della E. Olson, *A Woman of Her Times* (Minneapolis: Free Church, 1977), 31, 77.

[133] Quoted in ibid., 45

[134] Ibid., 46.

[135] Frank T. Lindberg, *Looking Back Fifty Years* (Minneapolis: Franklin, n.d.), 58.

[136] Ibid., 59.

[137] James O. Henry, *For Such a Time as This: A History of the Independent Fundamental Church of America* (Westchester, Ill.: IFCA, 1983), 49.

[138] Wyker, *Church Women*, 48–49.

[139] James Morris, *The Preachers* (New York: St. Martin's, 1973), 242.

[140] Jamie Buckingham, *Daughter of Destiny: Kathryn Kuhlman . . . Her Story* (Plainfield, N. J.: Logos, 1976), 125–26.

[141] Helen Kooiman Hosier, *Kathryn Kuhlman* (Old Tappan, N. J.: Revell, 1971), 99.

[142] Morris, *The Preachers*, 246.

[143] Buckingham, *Daughter of Destiny*, 158, 198–99; Kathryn Kuhlman, *I Believe in Miracles* (Englewood Cliffs, N. J.: Prentice-Hall, 1962), 7.

[144] Richard Quebedeaux, *By What Authority: The Rise of Personality Cults in American Christianity* (New York: Harper & Row, 1982), 39.

[145] Ethel M. Baldwin and David V. Benson, *Henrietta Mears and How She Did It* (Glendale, Calif.: Gospel Light, 1966), 46.

[146] Ibid., 77.

[147] Quoted in Dorothy R. Pape, *In Search of God's Ideal Woman* (Downers Grove: InterVarsity, 1976), 245.

[148] Quoted in Richard Quebedeaux, *I Found It!: The Story of Bill Bright and Campus Crusade* (New York: Harper & Row, 1979), 10.

[149] Corrie ten Boom, *Tramp for the Lord* (Old Tappan, N. J.: Revell, 1974), 16, 18.

[150] Ibid., 9, 35, 42, 46.

[151] Ibid., 47, 127, 79, 134.

[152] Richard N. Ostling, " 'This Is a God I Can Trust': Joni Eareckson's Special Ministry for the Disabled." *Time* (December 29, 1980), 67.

[153] Karen Mills, "Christian Faith Helps People Reduce," *Grand Rapids Press*, August 10, 1980.

[154] Richard N. Ostling, "Jerry Falwell's Crusade," *Time* (September 2, 1985), 57; Beverly LaHaye, *The Restless Woman* (Grand Rapids: Zondervan, 1984), 89.

[155] Jo Berry *Growing, Sharing, Serving* (Elgin, Ill.: Cook, 1979), 66–67.

[156] A. Wetherell Johnson, *Created for Commitment* (Wheaton: Tyndale, 1982), 225.

[157] "Neighborhood Bible Studies: 25 Years of Ministry, 1960–1985,"(Dobbs Ferry, N.Y.: Neighborhood Bible Studies, 1985). A pamphlet.

[158] *EWC Update* 8 (June–August 1984): 4.

[159] Ostling, "Jerry Fallwell's Crusade," 57.

Chapter 11

[1] Woman's Rights Convention, 1860, *History of Woman Suffrage*, I, 1881, quoted in *Feminist Quotations: Voices of Rebels, Reformers, and Visionaries*, compiled by Carol McPhee and Ann Fitzgerald (New York: Crowell, 1979), 235.

[2] *Missionary Review of the World* 7:12, New Series (December 1894): 910–21.

[3] Katherine C. Bushnell, *God's Word to Women* (1919; reprint, North Collins, N.Y.: Munson, 1976).

[4] Ibid., lesson 27, para. 203.

[5] Margaret Sanger, *Women and the New Race*, 1920, quoted in McPhee and Fitzgerald, *Feminist Quotations*, 70.

[6] Trans. H. M. Parshley (New York: Knopf, 1953).

[7] Ibid., 598, 603.

[8] Ibid., 621–22.

[9] Ibid., 624.

[10] Stanford: Stanford University Press, 1974; see also Alexandra G. Kaplan and Joan P. Bean, eds., *Beyond Sex-Role Stereotypes: Readings Toward a Psychology of Androgyny* (Amherst: University of Massachusetts Press, 1976) and Alice G. Sargent *Beyond Sex Roles* (St. Paul: West, 1977).

[11] See, for example, Barbara Hilkert Andolsen, "Gender and Sex Roles in Recent Religious

Ethics Literature," *Religious Studies Review* 11 (1985): 217–23; Richard D. Kahoe, "Social Science of Gender Differences: Ideological Battleground," *Religious Studies Review* 11 (1985): 223–28.

[12] Ashley Montagu *The Natural Superiority of Women*, rev. ed. (New York: Macmillan, 1952).

[13] John R. Rice *Bobbed Hair, Bossy Wives, and Women Preachers* (Murfreesboro, Tenn.: Sword of the Lord, 1941).

[14] Ibid., 59.

[15] Ibid., 63.

[16] Ibid., 65.

[17] Ibid., 68.

[18] Elizabeth Rice Handford, *Me Obey Him?* (Murfreesboro, Tenn.: Sword of the Lord, 1972).

[19] P. B. Fitzwater, *Women: Her Mission, Position, and Ministry* (Grand Rapids: Eerdmans, 1949), 66.

[20] Ibid., 67.

[21] Ibid., 72.

[22] Charles C. Ryrie, *The Place of Women in the Church* (New York: Macmillan, 1958), 76.

[23] Ibid., 77.

[24] Ibid., 78.

[25] Quoted in McPhee and Fitzgerald, *Feminist Quotations*, 11.

[26] Ibid., 19.

[27] Ibid., 80.

[28] Karl Barth, *Church Dogmatics*, vol. 3, sec. 2, ed. & trans. G. W. Bromiley and T. F. Torrance (Edinburgh: T. & T. Clark, 1960), 286–96; sec. 4 (1961), 172–74.

[29] Karl Barth, *How I Changed My Mind* (Richmond: John Knox, 1966), 58. On Barth's views on women, see also Elizabeth Clark and Herbert Richardson, eds., *Women and Religion: A Feminist Sourcebook of Christian Thought* (New York: Harper & Row, 1977), 239–58. (The chapter title is "The Triumph of Patriarchalism in the Theology of Karl Barth.")

[30] Betty Friedan, *The Feminine Mystique* (New York: Norton, 1963).

[31] Ibid., quoted in Agonito, *History of Ideas on Women*, 378.

[32] Krister Stendahl, *The Bible and the Role of Women: A Case Study in Hermeneutics*, Biblical Series 15 (Philadelphia: Fortress, Facet, 1966).

[33] Mary Daly, *The Church and the Second Sex* (New York: Harper & Row, 1975).

[34] Ibid., 9.

[35] Ibid., 11.

[36] Ibid.

[37] Ibid., 11–12.

[38] Mary Daly, *Beyond God the Father: Toward a Philosophy of Women's Liberation* (Boston: Beacon, 1973).

[39] *Religious Studies Review* 3:4 (October 1977): 205.

[40] Daly, *Beyond God the Father*, 69–70.

[41] Ibid., 71.

[42] Naomi R. Goldenberg, *Changing of the Gods: Feminism and the End of Traditional Religions* (Boston: Beacon, 1979).

[43] Ibid., 3.

[44] Ibid., 4–5.

[45] Ibid., 9

[46] Ibid., 75–76.

[47] Rosemary Radford Ruether *Liberation Theology* (New York: Paulist, 1972).

[48] Rosemary Radford Ruether *New Woman, New Earth* (New York: Seabury, 1975).

[49] Ruether, *Liberation Theology*, 100.

[50] Gladys Hunt, *Ms Means Myself* (Grand Rapids: Zondervan, 1972).

[51] As quoted in McPhee and Fitzgerald, *Feminist Quotations*, 231.

[52] C. S. Lewis, "Priestesses in the Church," in W. Hooper, ed., *God in the Dock* (Grand Rapids: Eerdmans, 1970).

[53] W. Andrew Hoffecker and John Timmerman, " 'Watchmen in the City': C. S. Lewis's View of Male and Female," *The Cresset* (February 1978), 16–21.

[54] Gloria Steinem, "Pink-Collar Workers," *Progressive* (May 1977), quoted in McPhee and Fitzgerald *Feminist Quotations*, 110.

[55] Richard Boldrey and Joyce Boldrey, "Women in Paul's Life," *Trinity Studies* 22 (1972): 1–36.

[56] Richard Boldrey and Joyce Boldrey, *Chauvinist or Feminist: Paul's View of Women* (Grand Rapids: Baker, 1976).

[57] Boldrey, *Chauvinist or Feminist*, 63.

[58] *Journal of the American Academy of Religion* 40 (1972): 283–303.

[59] Ibid., 42 (1974): 532–49.

[60] Marabel Morgan, *The Total Woman* (Old Tappan, N. J.: Revell, 1973), 94.

[61] Ibid., 27.

[62] Letha Scanzoni and Nancy Hardesty, *All We're Meant to Be* (Waco: Word, 1974).

[63] "Women, Men and Change: A Reflection on the Last 10 Years," An interview with Letha Scanzoni, *Radix* (March/April 1984), 5.

[64] John Scanzoni, *Sex Roles, Life Styles, and Childbearing: Changing Patterns in Marriage and the Family* (New York: Free Press, 1975).

[65] Bill Gothard, *Manual,* copyright 1969, section entitled "Principles of God's Chain-of-Command," 1–2.

[66] Larry Christenson, *The Christian Family* (Minneapolis: Bethany, 1970).

[67] Ibid., 35; cf. 47.

[68] Ibid., 36–37.

[69] Ibid., 44.

[70] Ibid., 50–51, 53.

[71] Ibid., 54.

[72] Ibid., 127.

[73] Ibid., 133.

[74] Paul K. Jewett, *Man as Male and Female* (Grand Rapids: Eerdmans, 1975).

[75] Harvie M. Conn, "Evangelical Feminism: Reflections on the State of the 'Union,'" *TSF Bulletin* (November–December 1984), 20.

[76] Dorothy Pape, *In Search of God's Ideal Woman: A Personal Examination of the New Testament* (Downers Grove: InterVarsity, 1976).

[77] Ibid., 165.

[78] Ibid., 179.

[79] Elisabeth Elliot, *Let Me Be a Woman* (Wheaton: Tyndale, 1976).

[80] Ibid., 58.

[81] Ibid., 122–23.

[82] Ibid., 125–27.

[83] Ibid., 132–33.

[84] Ibid., 144.

[85] "Biblical Woman: But What Can She Do? Six Opinions on the Role of Women in the Church," from interviews by Sharon Johnson, *Moody Monthly* (February 1983): 13.

[86] Virginia Ramey Mollenkott, *Women, Men and the Bible* (Nashville: Abingdon, 1977), 68.

[87] Ibid., 95.

[88] Ibid., 103.

[89] Ibid., 103.

[90] Patricia Gundry, *Woman Be Free!* (Grand Rapids: Zondervan, 1977).

[91] Ibid., 29–39.

[92] Ibid., 75.

[93] Ibid.

[94] Patricia Gundry, *Heirs Together: Mutual Submission in Marriage* (Grand Rapids: Zondervan, 1980); idem, *The Complete Woman* (New York: Jove, 1984); idem, *Neither Slave nor Free: Helping Women Answer the Call to Church Leadershsip* (San Francisco: Harper & Row, 1987).

[95] Kevin Giles, *Women and Their Ministry: A Case for Equal Ministries in the Church Today* (Victoria, Australia: Dove, 1977).

[96] Don Williams, *The Apostle Paul and Women in the Church* (Van Nuys, Calif.: BIM, 1977).

[97] Helen Andelin, *Fascinating Womanhood* (Santa Barbara, Calif.: Pacific, 1965).

[98] Williams, *The Apostle Paul and Women in the Church,* 29.

[99] Ibid.

[100] Ibid.

[101] Ibid.

[102] Ibid.

[103] Ibid., 69.

[104] Ibid., 68.

[105] Ibid., 92.

[106] Ibid., 111–14.

[107] Ibid., 138.

[108] Ibid., 140.

[109] Ibid., 146.

[110] Ibid., 147.

[111] Lucia Sannella, *The Female Pentecost* (Port Washington, N.Y.: Ashley, 1976).

[112] Ibid., 122–24.

[113] George W. Knight III, *The New Testament Teaching on the Role Relationship of Men and Women* (Grand Rapids: Baker, 1977).

[114] Harvie M. Conn, "Evangelical Feminism," 21.

[115] Chicago: Moody, 1985.

[116] "AUTHENTEO in Reference to Women in 1 Timothy 2:12," *New Testament Studies* 30 (1984): 143–47.

[117] Phyllis Trible, *God and the Rhetoric of Sexuality* (Philadelphia: Fortress, 1978).

[118] Phyllis Trible, *Texts of Terror: Literary-Feminist Readings of Biblical Narratives* (Philadelphia: Fortress, 1984).

[119] John Otwell, *And Sarah Laughed: The Status of Woman in the Old Testament* (Philadelphia: Westminster, 1977).

[120] Leonard Swidler and Arlene Swidler, *Women Priests: A Catholic Commentary on the Vatican Declaration* (New York: Paulist, 1977).

[121] Metuchen: Scarecrow, 1976.

[122] Philadelphia: Westminster, 1979.

[123] Frank Stagg and Evelyn Stagg, *Woman in the World of Jesus* (Philadelphia: Westminster, 1978).

[124] In C. Robert Wetzel, ed., *Essays on New Testament Christianity* (Cincinnati: Standard, 1978).

[125] *Mission Journal* 17:5 (November 1983): 10–14.

[126] "Jesus, Power, and Gender Roles," *TSF Bulletin* 7 (1984): 2–4.

[127] Linda Mercadante, *From Hierarchy to Equality: A Comparison of Past and Present Interpretations of 1 Corinthians 11:2–16 in Relation to the Changing Status of Women in*

Society (Vancouver, B.C.: G.M.H. Books, Regent College Press, 1978).

128 *The Reformed Journal* 28 (June 1978): 6–11; (December 1978): 11–15.

129 *The Reformed Journal* 29 (March 1979): 12–15.

130 "1 Timothy 2:12—A Classicist's View" in Alvera Mickelsen, ed., *Women, Authority and the Bible* (Downers Grove: InterVarsity, 1986), 225–43.

131 Stephen B. Clark, *Man and Woman in Christ* (Ann Arbor, Mich.: Servant, 1980).

132 Ibid., x.

133 Ibid., 602, 605–7, 616.

134 Elizabeth Tetlow, *Women and Ministry in the New Testament* (New York: Paulist, 1980).

135 Susan T. Foh, *Women and the Word of God: A Response to Biblical Feminism* (Grand Rapids: Baker, 1981).

136 James B. Hurley, *Man and Woman in Biblical Perspective* (Grand Rapids: Zondervan, 1981).

137 Conn, "Evangelical Feminism," 22.

138 Harvie Conn, "Did Paul Require Veils or the Silence of Women?" *Westminster Theological Journal* 35 (1973): 190–220.

139 *TSF Bulletin* (January–February 1983), 21.

140 Ibid.

141 Kari Torjesen Malcolm, *Women at the Crossroads* (Downers Grove: InterVarsity, 1982), 171–72.

142 Grand Rapids: Zondervan, 1982.

143 Review by Wayne Grudem, *Trinity Journal* 27 (1984): 223–27.

144 From the jacket blurb of Mary J. Evans, *Women in the Bible.*

145 Mary J. Evans, *Women in the Bible* (Downers Grove: InterVarsity, 1983).

146 Willard M. Swartley, *Slavery, Sabbath, War, and Women: Case Issues in Biblical Interpretation* (Scottdale, Pa., and Kitchener, Ont.: Herald, 1983).

147 Ibid., 61.

148 Ibid., 183–84.

149 In *Religion and Sexism: Images of Women in the Jewish and Christian Traditions* (New York: Simon and Schuster, 1974).

150 Co-edited with Eleanor McLaughlin (New York: Simon and Schuster, 1979).

151 Boston: Beacon, 1983.

152 Judith L. Weidman, ed., *Christian Feminism* (San Francisco: Harper & Row, 1984), 9–32.

153 Boston: Beacon, 1985.

154 "Feminist Theology and Spirituality," 9, 11–12.

155 "Of One Humanity," interview with the editors of *Sojourners* (January 1984), 17–18.

156 New York: Crossroad, 1983.

157 In addition to a number of reviews of her major work, *In Memory of Her*, by various scholars in prestigious journals, a symposium on her book was held at the 1983 meeting of the American Academy of Religion. The symposium has been published in *Anima* 10 (1984): 95–112.

158 *Union Seminary Quarterly Review* 33 (1978): 153–66.

159 In Willy Schottroff and Wolfgang Stegemann, *Tradition der Befreiung*, Band 2, *Frauen in der Bibel* (Munich: Kaiser and Gelnhausen: Burckhardthaus-Laetare, 1980), 60–90.

160 In *Bread Not Stone: The Challenge of Feminist Biblical Interpretation* (Boston: Beacon, 1984).

161 Produced by the National Council of Churches in two volumes, *Readings for Year A* and *Readings for Year B* (published for The Cooperative Publication Association; Atlanta: John Knox, and other publishers, 1983, 1984).

162 See discussion in the appendix of either volume.

163 LaHaye chronicled her increasing concern and her own agenda in *Who But a Woman?* (Nashville: Nelson, 1984).

164 Beverly LaHaye, *The Restless Woman*, (Grand Rapids: Zondervan, 1984).

165 Ibid., 53.

166 Tim LaHaye, *The Battle for the Family* (Old Tappan, N.J.: Revell, 1982).

167 LaHaye, *Restless Woman*, 93–110.

168 Ibid., 85–86.

169 Dee Jepsen, *Women: Beyond Equal Rights* (Waco: Word, 1984), 86.

170 John W. Robbins, *Scripture Twisting in the Seminaries, Part I: Feminism* (Jefferson, Md.: Trinity Foundation, 1985).

171 Ibid., quoted on an unnumbered page just prior to the introduction and attributed to Gordon H. Clark's *Pastoral Epistles* (1984) without further data.

172 Ibid., 3, 5, 5n, 9, 38–39.

173 Ibid., xi.

174 Ibid., 44, 47ff.

175 Ibid., 91.

176 Sheldon Vanauken, *Under the Mercy* (Nashville: Nelson, 1985).

177 Ibid., 179.

178 Quoted in ibid., 181.

[179]Vanauken, *Under the Mercy*, 214.

[180]Ronald Allen and Beverly Allen, *Liberated Traditionalism: Men and Women in Balance* (Portland: Multnomah, 1985).

[181]Gilbert Bilezikian, *Beyond Sex Roles* (Grand Rapids: Baker, 1985).

[182]Ibid., 87.

[183]Elaine Storkey, *What's Right With Feminism* (Grand Rapids: Eerdmans, 1985).

[184]Ibid., 123–26.

[185]Ibid., 53.

[186]David Scholer, in *The Covenant Companion* (December 1, 1983, December 15, 1983, January 1, 1984, February 1984).

[187]Quoted from ibid. (reprint of February 1984), 15.

[188]David Scholer, "Women's Adornment," *Daughters of Sarah* 6 (1980): 3–6.

[189]In Alvera Mickelsen, ed., *Women, Authority and the Bible*, (Downers Grove: InterVarsity, 1986), 193–224.

[190]Aída Besançon Spencer, *Beyond the Curse: Women Called to Ministry* (Nashville: Nelson, 1985).

[191]Ibid., 109.

[192]Aída Besançon Spencer, "Eve at Ephesus," *Journal of the Evangelical Theological Society* 17 (Fall 1984): 215–22.

[193]Spencer, *Beyond the Curse*, 71–95.

[194]Spencer, "Eve at Ephesus," 220.

[195]Spencer, *Beyond the Curse*, 108.

[196]Ibid.

[197]*Chicago Studies* 4 (1965): 285–308.

[198]In R. McCormick and G. Dyer, eds., *Future Forms for Ministry* (1971), 103–11.

[199]In W. Burghardt et al., *Catholic Theological Society 28th Convention* (1973), 219–23.

[200]Chicago: National Association of Women Religious, 1972.

[201]Published by the United States Catholic Conference, n.d. (c. 1977).

[202]Unpublished papers (1979).

[203]Agnes Cunningham, *The Role of Women in Ecclesial Ministry* (Monograph published by the United States Catholic Conference in 1976), 21.

[204]The subtitle indicates that this is a historical investigation concerning the Code of Canon Law, canon 978, par. 1., trans. Norman R. Adams (Metuchen, N.J.: Scarecrow, 1976).

[205]Edited by Anne Marie Gardiner (New York: Paulist, 1976).

[206](Philadelphia: Temple University Press, 1973).

[207]Edited by Elisabeth Schüssler Fiorenza and Mary Collins (Edinburgh: T. & T. Clark, 1985).

[208]Alvera Mickelsen, ed., *Women, Authority and the Bible* (Downers Grove: InterVarsity, 1986).

[209]Shirley Lees, ed., *The Role of Women* (Leicester: Inter-Varsity, 1984).

[210]Quoted in ibid., 178.

[211]Ibid., 196.

Appendix A

[1]*Journal of the Evangelical Theological Society* 20 (1977): 337–52.

[2]In W. Ward Gasque and William Sanford LaSor, eds., *Scripture, Tradition and Interpretation* (Grand Rapids: Eerdmans, 1978), 234–59.

[3]Susan T. Foh, *Women and the Word of God: A Response to Biblical Feminism* (Grand Rapids: Baker, 1981), 44.

[4]Ibid., 46.

[5]Romans 16:16; 1 Corinthians 16:20; 2 Corinthians 13:12; 1 Thessalonians 5:26; 1 Peter 5:14.

[6]Plutarch, *Moralia: Advice to Bride and Groom*, 31.

[7]Willard Swartley, *Slavery, Sabbath, War and Women* (Scottdale, Pa.: Herald, 1983).

[8]Ibid., 31–37.

[9]Ibid., 229–30.

[10]Ibid., 231.

[11]See Anthony C. Thiselton, *The Two Horizons* (Grand Rapids: Eerdmans, 1980).

[12]Rosemary Radford Ruether, *Liberation Theology* (New York: Paulist, 1972), 95–114.

[13]Mary Ann Tolbert, "Defining the Problem: The Bible and Feminist Hermeneutics," *Semeia* 28 (1983): 119.

[14]Elisabeth Schüssler Fiorenza, *In Memory of Her* (New York: Crossroad, 1983), 30.

[15]Ibid., 29.

[16]Ibid., 30.

[17]Jerome Murphy-O'Connor, *Doctrine and Life* 34 (1984): 398–404, 495–99.

[18]Cornell West and Ross S. Kraemer, *Religious Studies Review* 11 (1985): 1–9.

[19]Robert M. Grant, *Journal of Religion* 65 (1985): 83–88.

[20]Elizabeth Struthers Malbon, "Fallible Followers: Women and Men in the Gospel of Mark," *Semeia* 28 (1983): 29–48; Fiorenza, *In Memory of Her*, 316–33.

[21] Elizabeth M. Tetlow, *Women and Ministry in the New Testament* (New York and Ramsey: Paulist, 1980), 103, cf. 101–9. This allegation is discussed in the excursus to chapter 1, pages 41–42.

[22] Ibid., 109.

[23] See the discussion between Philip B. Payne ("Libertarian Women in Ephesus: A Response to Douglas J. Moo's article, '1 Timothy 2:11–15: Meaning and Significance,' " *Trinity Journal*, 2 NS [1981]: 175–77) and Douglas J. Moo, "The Interpretation of 1 Timothy 2:11–15: A Rejoinder," *Trinity Journal* 2 NS [1981]: 202–4. A surrejoinder by Payne was eventually published privately and is available from the author (c/o Gordon Conwell Divinity School, South Hamilton, MA 01982).

[24] Cf. appendix B on 1 Corinthians 11:2–16.

[25] Earl D. Radmacher and Robert D. Preuss, eds., *Hermeneutics, Inerrancy and the Bible* (Grand Rapids: Zondervan, 1984).

[26] Foh, *Women and the Word of God*, 6–7, 14, 19–20.

[27] Ibid., 20.

[28] Donald G. Bloesch, *The Battle for the Trinity* (Ann Arbor: Servant, 1985); Mary Daly, *Beyond God the Father: Toward a Philosophy of Women's Liberation* (Boston: Beacon, 1973); James R. Edwards, "Does God Really Want to Be Called 'Father'?" *Christianity Today* (February 21, 1986): 27–29; Naomi R. Goldenberg, *Changing of the Gods: Feminism and the End of Traditional Religions* (Boston: Beacon, 1979); Margaret Hebblethwaite, *Motherhood and God* (London: Goeffrey Chapman, 1984); *An Inclusive Language Lectionary*, vols. 1 and 2, produced by the National Council of Churches; *Readings for Year A* and *Readings for Year B* (published for the Cooperative Publication Association, Atlanta: John Knox and other publishers, 1983, 1984); Paul K. Jewett, *Man as Male and Female* (Grand Rapids: Eerdmans, 1975); Alan E. Lewis, "The Biblical Witness to our Motherly Father," *Irish Biblical Studies* 7 (1984): 8–45; Sally McFague, *Metaphorical Theology: Models of God in Religious Language* (Philadelphia: Fortress, 1982); Celine Mangan, O.P., *Can We Still Call God "Father"?* (Wilmington, Del.: Glazier, 1984); Virginia Ramey Mollencott, *The Divine Feminine* (New York: Crossroad, 1983); Ralph Quere, " 'Naming' God 'Father,' " *Currents in Theology and Mission* 12 (1985): 5–14. The strongest Evangelical protest against inclusive language and theology is the work by Donald Bloesch.

[29] Cf. Richard N. Longenecker, *New Testament Social Ethics for Today* (Grand Rapids: Eerdmans, 1984), 87.

[30] Walter Bauer, *A Greek English Lexicon of the New Testament*, ed. and rev. by William F. Arndt, F. Wilbur Gingrich, and Frederick W. Danker (Chicago and London: University of Chicago Press, 1957, 1979), s.v. *oikodespotēs*, 558.

[31] Henry George Liddell and Robert Scott, *A Greek-English Lexicon*, rev. by Henry Stuart Jones and Roderick McKenzie (Oxford: Oxford University Press, 1940), s.v. *oikodespotēs*, 1204

Appendix B

[1] Job 29:14; Psalm 35:26; 109:29; 132:9; Isaiah 11:5; 59:17; cf. Romans 13:12, 14; 1 Thessalonians 5:8. See F. F. Bruce, *Epistle to the Colossians*, The New International Commentary on the New Testament (Grand Rapids: Eerdmans, 1984), 145–46, and note 72.

[2] F. F. Bruce, *Commentary on Galatians*, New International Greek New Testament Commentary (Grand Rapids: Eerdmans, 1982), 190.

[3] In addition to the various commentaries on Galatians, the following two articles provide recent surveys of the issues involved and useful references to the current literature: Ben Witherington, "Rite and Rights for Women," *New Testament Studies* 27 (1981): 593–604; Klyne Snodgrass, "Galatians 3:28—Conundrum or Solution?" in Alvera Mickelsen, ed., *Women, Authority and the Bible* (Downers Grove: InterVarsity, 1986), 161–80.

[4] See Ruth A. Tucker, "Response" to Berkeley and Alvera Mickelsen, "What Does *Kephalē* Mean in the New Testament?" in Alvera Mickelsen, ed., *Women, Authority and the Bible* (Downers Grove: InterVarsity, 1986), 111–17.

[5] S. Bedale, "The Meaning of *kephalē* in the Pauline Epistles," *Journal of Theological Studies*, n.s. 5 (1954): 211–15. Cf. the modification of this in Berkeley and Alvera Mickelsen, "The 'Head' of the Epistles," *Christianity Today* (1981), 264–67; and "What Does *Kephalē* Mean in the New Testament?" in Alvera Mickelsen, ed., *Women, Authority and the Bible* (Downers Grove: InterVarsity, 1986).

[6] Wayne Grudem, "Does *Kephalē* ('Head') Mean 'Source' or 'Authority Over' in Greek Literature? A Survey of 2,336 Examples," published both as an appendix in George W. Knight III, *The Role Relationship of Men and*

Women (1977, 1985) and in the *Trinity Journal*, 6 NS, no. 1 (1985): 38–59.

[7] These studies have not, at the time of this writing, been published. For an earlier work on the meaning of the word *kephalē* in Colossians, a work that also contains material pertinent to other passages, see the unpublished dissertation by R. Weldon Crabb, "The *kephalē* concept in the Pauline tradition, with special emphasis on Colossians" (San Francisco Theological Seminary, 1968), available through University Microfilms.

[8] James P. Hurley, "Did Paul Require Veils or the Silence of Women? A Consideration of I Cor. 11:2–16 and I Cor. 14:33b–36," *Westminster Theological Journal* 35 (1973): 190–220.

[9] Morna D. Hooker, "Authority on Her Head: An Examination of I Cor 11:10," *New Testament Studies* 10 (1963/64): 410–16, reinforced by another article by A. Jaubert, "La voile des femmes," *New Testament Studies* 18 (1972): 419–30.

[10] Philip B. Payne has been studying this option, but had not published his conclusions at the date of this writing.

[11] See Walter L. Liefeld, "Women, Submission and Ministry in First Corinthians," in Alvera Mickelsen, ed., *Women Authority and the Bible*, 134–53.

[12] Richard and Catherine Kroeger, "Sexual Identity in Corinth," *The Reformed Journal* 28 (December 1978): 11–15.

[13] A paper presented by Gordon Fee at the Evangelical Theological Society's annual meeting in November 1986 offered reasons for this conclusion. This study will be available in his forthcoming commentary on 1 Corinthians.

[14] This solution was proposed many years ago by Katherine C. Bushnell, *God's Word to Women* (privately reprinted by Ray B. Munson, Box 52, North Collins, NY 14111, n.d.), lessons 25–28, sections 189–215.

[15] One proponent of this theory is David W. Odell-Scott, "Let the Women Speak in Church: An Egalitarian Interpretation of I Cor 14: 33b–36," *Biblical Theology Bulletin* 13 (1983): 90–93.

[16] This possibility was suggested to me by one of my students, David Banks.

[17] See David Aune, *Prophecy in Early Christianity* (Grand Rapids: Eerdmans, 1983), 217–22, on evaluation of prophecy; and Wayne A. Grudem, *The Gift of Prophecy in 1 Corinthians* (Washington, D.C.: University Press of America, 1982), 245–55.

[18] The opinions cited here are found in a number of commentaries, books, and articles on the subject. An extensive presentation of the position of woman's subordination is found in Stephen Clark, *Man and Woman in Christ* (Ann Arbor: Servant, 1980), 72–87. John C. Howell in *Equality and Submission in Marriage* (Nashville: Broadman, 1979) advocates mutual submission toward the meeting of one another's needs. The book is a mixture of biblical study and counseling and avoids a critical attitude toward more traditional views. Peter DeJong and Donald R. Wilson have written a thoughtful, informed book that blends biblical and sociological insights, *Husband and Wife* (Grand Rapids: Zondervan, 1979). The authors advocate avoiding "gender roles," which are stereotyped and limiting, but holding to "sex roles," which flow from the natural physical characteristics of men and women in their pre-Fall, created state. Some of the arguments relating to 1 Peter 3 by David Balch and by John H. Elliott, pertain also to this passage. (Cf. footnotes 24–26 below.) Most commentaries hold a traditionalist position, often with a comment that the submission of the wife must be accompanied by sacrificial love on the part of the husband.

[19] See especially, Douglas J. Moo, "1 Timothy 2:11–15: Meaning and Significance," *Trinity Journal*, 1, n.s. (1980): 62–83; Philip B. Payne, "Libertarian Women in Ephesus: A Response to Douglas J. Moo's Article, "1 Timothy 2:11–15: Meaning and Significance" *Trinity Journal* 2, n.s. (1981), 169–97; Douglas J. Moo, "The Interpretation of 1 Timothy 2:11–15: A Rejoinder," *Trinity Journal* 2, n.s. (1981): 198–222; M. D. Roberts, "Women Shall Be Saved: A Closer Look at 1 Timothy 2:15," *TSF Bulletin* 5 (1981): 4–7; Aída Besançon Spencer, "Eve at Ephesus," *Journal of the Evangelical Theological Society* 17 (1974): 215–22; Catherine Clark Kroeger, "1 Timothy 2:12—A Classicist's View," and David M. Scholer, "1 Timothy 2:9–15 and the Place of Women in the Church's Ministry" in Alvera Mickelsen, ed., *Women, Authority and the Bible* (Downers Grove: InterVarsity, 1986), 225–44, followed by response by Walter L. Liefeld, 244–47. See also the privately printed surrejoinder to Douglas J. Moo by Philip B. Payne listed in note 23 to appendix A.

[20] *Reformed Journal* 29 (1979): 12–15.

[21] George W. Knight III, "AUTHENTEŌ in Reference to Women in 1 Timothy 2:12," *New Testament Studies* 30 (1984): 143–57.

[22]"1 Timothy 2:12—A Classicist's View," in Mickelsen, *Women, Authority and the Bible*, 225–43. Cf. the response by Walter L. Liefeld that follows on 244–47.

[23]Donna Peterson, unpublished paper, "Women and Biblical Teaching," Trinity Evangelical Divinity School, 1983.

[24]James Sigountos and Myron Shank, "Public Roles for Women in the Pauline Church: A Reappraisal of the Evidence," *Journal of the Evangelical Theological Society* 26 (1983): 283–95.

[25]This position was presented in a paper by Philip B. Payne at the annual meeting of the Evangelical Theological Society in Novermber 1986.

[26]Robertson wrote in his *Grammar of the Greek New Testament in the Light of Historical Research:* "It is a mistake . . . to approach the study of [gar] with the theory that it is always or properly an illative, not to say causal, particle. It is best, in fact, to note the explanatory use first. . . . In general the N.T. use of [gar] is in accord with that of the classical period. The explanatory use is common in Homer. The N.T. examples are numerous." (Nashville: Broadman, 1923), 1190–91. We should keep this in mind when we are confronted with the assertion that the illative use is common in Paul. Also the term, "illative," has to do basically with inference, not cause, and it is the "causal" use that traditionalists need to defend here.

[27]Kroeger, "1 Timothy 2:12—A Classisist's View," in Mickelsen, *Women, Authority, and the Bible,* 232–38.

[28]John H. Elliott, *A Home for the Homeless* (Philadelphia: Fortress, 1981).

[29]David L. Balch, *Let Wives Be Submissive: The Domestic Code in 1 Peter*, Society of Biblical Literature Monograph Series, 26 (Chico, Calif.: Scholars, 1981).

[30]See David L. Balch, "Early Christian Criticism of Patriarchal Authority: 1 Peter 2:11–3:12," *Union Seminary Quarterly Review* 39 (1984): 165–66.

[31]Plutarch, *Advice to Bride and Groom*, in Plutarch's *Moralia*, trans. Frank Cole Babbitt, Loeb Classical Library (Cambridge: Harvard University Press, 1928), 19 (140D).

Appendix C

[1]Privately published, no date; sometime in the mid-nineteenth century.

[2]Marjorie Warkentin, *Ordination: A Biblical-Historical View* (Grand Rapids: Eerdmans, 1982).

[3]Peter Bläser et al, *Ordination und Kirchliches Amt*, (Paderborn: Verlag Bonifacius-Druckerei and Bielefeld: Luther-Verlag, 1976).

[4]Thomas Franklin O'Meara, *Theology of Ministry* (New York: Paulist, 1983) 187.

[5]Some of the books pertaining to the ordination of women are: Michael Bruce and G. E. Duffield, *Why Not? Priesthood and the Ministry of Women* (Appleford, Abingdon: Marcham, 1976); Anne Marie Gardiner, ed., *Women and Catholic Priesthood: An Expanded Vision* (New York: Paulist, 1976); Elsie Gibson, *When the Minister Is a Woman* (New York, Chicago: Holt, Rinehart and Winston, 1970); Michael P. Hamilton and Nancy S. Montgomery, eds., *The Ordination of Women: Pro and Con* (New York: Morehouse-Barlow, 1975); Paul King Jewett, *The Ordination of Women* (Grand Rapids: Eerdmans, 1980); Ida Raming, *The Exclusion of Women From the Priesthood: Divine Law or Sex Discrimination?* Norman R. Adams, trans. (Metuchen, N.J.: Scarecrow, 1976); Carroll Stuhlmueller, ed., *Women and Priesthood: Future Directions* (Collegeville, Minn.: Liturgical Press, 1978); Leonard Swidler and Arlene Swidler, eds., *Women Priest: A Catholic Commentary on the Vatican Declaration* (New York: Paulist, 1977); and Haye van der Meer, *Women Priests in the Catholic Church? A Theological-Historical Investigation* (Philadelphia: Temple University Press, 1973).

[6]For a summary and discussion of these see Bengt Holmberg, *Paul and Power* (Philadelphia: Fortress, 1978) 109–12.

[7]Ibid., 119.

[8]John Calvin, *Commentaries on the Epistles to Timothy, Titus and Philemon*, trans. W. Pringle (Grand Rapids: Eerdmans, 1948), 116.

[9]Edward J. Kilmartin, "Ministry and Ordination in Early Christianity against a Jewish Background," *Studia Liturgica* 13 (1979): 45.

[10]Lawrence A. Hoffman, "Jewish Ordination on the Eve of Christianity," *Studia Liturgica* 13 (1979): 36.

[11]Hoffman, "Jewish Ordination," 35.

BIBLIOGRAPHY

GENERAL

Note: Many of the following works also appear in one of the specialized categories below. They are included here because they are significantly broader than those categories.

Allen, Ronald and Beverly. *Liberated Traditionalism: Men and Women in Balance.* Portland, Ore.: Multnomah, 1985.

Bilezikian, Gilbert. *Beyond Sex Roles.* Grand Rapids: Baker, 1985.

Bowie, Walter R. *Women of Light.* New York: Harper & Row, 1963.

Bullough, Vern L. and Bonnie. *The Subordinate Sex: A History of Attitudes Toward Women.* Urbana: University of Illinois Press, 1973.

Carmody, Denise L. *Women and World Religions.* Nashville: Abingdon, 1979.

Clark, Elizabeth, and Herbert Richardson, eds. *Women and Religion: A Feminist Sourcebook of Christian Thought.* New York, Hagerstown, San Francisco, London: Harper & Row, 1977.

Clark, Stephen B. *Man and Woman in Christ.* Ann Arbor, Mich.: Servant, 1980.

Deen, Edith. *Great Women of the Christian Faith.* New York: Harper & Brothers, 1959.

Evans, Mary J. *Women in the Bible.* Downers Grove: InterVarsity, 1983.

Fiorenza, Elisabeth Schüssler. *In Memory of Her.* New York: Crossroad, 1983.

Foh, Susan T. *Women and the Word of God: A Response to Biblical Feminism.* Grand Rapids: Baker, 1981.

Giles, Kevin. *Women and Their Ministry: A Case for Equal Ministries in the Church Today.* Victoria, Australia: Dove Communications, 1977.

Gundry, Patricia. *Woman Be Free.* Grand Rapids: Zondervan, 1977.

Howe, E. Margaret. *Women and Church Leadership.* Grand Rapids: Zondervan, 1982.

Jewett, Paul K. *Man as Male and Female.* Grand Rapids: Eerdmans, 1975.

Lees, Shirley, ed. *The Role of Women: When Christians Disagree.* Leicester, England: Inter-Varsity, 1984.

MacHaffie, Barbara J. *Her Story: Women in Christian Tradition.* Philadelphia: Fortress, 1986.

Malcolm, Kari Torjesen. *Women at the Crossroads.* Downers Grove: InterVarsity, 1982.

Michelsen, Alvera, ed. *Women, Authority and the Bible.* Downers Grove: InterVarsity, 1986.

Pape, Dorothy. *In Search of God's Ideal Woman.* Downers Grove: InterVarsity, 1976.

Royden, A. Maude. *The Church and Women.* New York: Doran, 1924.

Ruether, Rosemary Radford. *Womanguide: Readings Toward a Feminist Theology.* Boston: Beacon, 1985.

Ruether, Rosemary, and Eleanor McLaughlin, eds. *Women of Spirit: Female Leadership in the Jewish and Christian Traditions.* New York: Simon and Schuster, 1979.

Sayers, Dorothy. *Are Women Human?* Grand Rapids: Eerdmans, 1971.

Scanzoni, Letha and Nancy Hardesty. *All We're Meant to Be.* Waco: Word, 1974.

Scholer, David M. "Women in Ministry." *The Covenant Companion* (December 1, 1983): 8–9; (December 15, 1983): 14–15; (January 1984): 12–13; (February 1984): 12–15.

Spencer, Aída Besençon. *Beyond the Curse: Women Called to Ministry.* Nashville: Thomas Nelson, 1985.

Storkey, Elaine. *What's Right With Feminism?* Grand Rapids: Eerdmans, 1985.

Taves, Isabella. *The Widow's Guide.* New York: Schocken, 1984.

Wright, Elliott. *Holy Company: Christian Heroes and Heroines.* New York: Macmillan, 1980.

CHAPTERS 1 AND 2
THE NEW TESTAMENT AND ITS BACKGROUND

Note: Most of the resources for appendix B are included in this section. This bibliography does not list commentaries on the New Testament or, for the most part, primary sources in Graeco-Roman or intertestamental Jewish literature. Relevant materials are cited in detail in the footnotes. Likewise it omits articles in the Theological Dictionary of the New Testament, *in the* New International Dictionary of New Testament Theology, *and in other encyclopedias, which can easily be located by topic.*

Almlie, Gerald L. "Women's Church and Communion Practice." *Christian Brethren Review* 33 (December 1982): 40–56.

Anderson, Janice Capel. "Matthew: Gender and Reading." *Semeia* 28 (1983): 3–27.

Balch, David. *Wives, Be Submissive: The Domestic Code in 1 Peter.* Society of Biblical Literature Monograph, Series 26. Chico, Calif.: Scholars, 1981.

Balge, Richard D. "An Exegetical Study of Galatians 3:28–There Is no Male and Female . . . in Christ Jesus." *Wisconsin Lutheran Quarterly,* 78 (1981): 168–75.

Balsdon, J. P. V. D. *Roman Women: Their History and Habits.* Westport, Conn.: Greenwood, 1962.

Banks, Robert. *Paul's Idea of Community.* Grand Rapids: Eerdmans, 1980.

Becker, Siegbert W. "An Exegetical Study of 1 Corinthians 14:33b–36." *Wisconsin Lutheran Quarterly* 78 (1981): 176–84.

Bedale, S. "The Meaning of *kephalē* in the Pauline Epistles." *Journal of Theological Studies,* n.s. 5 (1954): 211–15.

Bell, Susan, ed. *Women: From the Greek to the French Revolution.* Stanford: Stanford University Press, 1973.

Biale, Rachael. *Women and Jewish Law: An Exploration of Women's Issues in Halakhic Sources.* New York: Schocken, 1984.

Birney, Leroy. "The Role of Women in the New Testament Church," with "Response" by Mary J. Evans. *Christian Brethren Review* 33 (December 1982): 15–40.

Bonsirven, J. *Palestinian Judaism in the Time of Jesus Christ.* Translated by W. Wolf. New York: Holt, Rinehart and Winston, 1964.

Boucher, Madeleine. "Some Unexplored Parallels in I Cor. 11:11–2 on Gal. 3:28: The New Testament on the Role of Women." *Catholic Biblical Quarterly* 31 (1969).

_____. "New Data on Ordination: A Rejoinder." *America* 143 (1980): 306–7.

Brennan, Irene. "Women in the Gospels." *New Blackfriars* 52, part 2 (July 1971): 291–99.

Brooten, Bernadette J. *Women Leaders in the Ancient Synagogue.* Brown Judaic Studies 36. Chico, Calif.: Scholars, 1982.

Brown, John Pairman. "The Role of Women and the Treaty in the Ancient World." *Biblische Zeitschrift* 25 (1981): 1–3.

Brown, Raymond E. "Roles of Women in the Fourth Gospel." *Theological Studies* 36 (1975): 688–99.

Bruce, F. F. "Women in the Church: A Biblical Survey." *Christian Brethren Review* 33 (December 1982): 7–14.

Cameron, Averil. "Neither Male nor Female." *Greece and Rome* 27 (1980): 60–68.

Cameron, Averil, and Amélie Kuhrt. *Images of Women in Antiquity.* Detroit: Wayne State University Press, 1983.

Clark, Gillian. "Roman Women." *Greece and Rome* 28 (1981): 206–7.

_____. "The Women at Corinth." *Theology* (1982): 256–62.

Cook, S. A.; F. E. Adcock; and M. P. Charlesworth, eds. *The Cambridge Ancient History,* 12 vols. Cambridge: Cambridge University Press, n.d. Vol. 11.

Craven, Toni. "Tradition and Convention in the Book of Judith." *Semeia* 28 (1983): 49–61.

Davis, John Jefferson. "Some Reflections on Galatians 3:28: Sexual Roles and Biblical Hermeneutics." *Journal of the Evangelical Theological Society* 19 (1976): 202–4.

Derrett, J. Duncan M. "Miscellanea: A Pauline Pun and Judas' Punishment." *Zeitschrift für die Neustamentliche Wissenschaft* 72 (1981): 131–33.

Donaldson, J. *Woman: Her Position in Ancient Greece and Rome and Among the Early Christians.* London, 1907.

Ellis, E. Earle. "Paul and His Co-Workers." *New Testament Studies* 17 (1970–71): 437–52.

Epstein, Louis M. *Sex Laws and Customs in Judaism.* New York: KTAV, 1948, 1967.

Evans, Mary J. *Women in the Bible.* Downers Grove: InterVarsity, 1983.

Feuillet, A. "La Dignite' et le Role de la Femme d'aprés quelques textes Pauliniens: Comparison avec l'Ancien Testament." *New Testament Studies* 21 (1975): 157–91.

Fiorenza, Elisabeth Schüssler. *In Memory of Her.* New York: Crossroad, 1983.

_____. "Women in the Pre-Pauline and Pauline Churches." *Union Seminary Quarterly Review* 33 (1978): 153–66.

Fitzmeyer, J. A. "A Feature of Qumran Angelory and the Angels of I Cor. XI. 10." *New Testament Studies* 6 (1957–58): 48ff.

Flanagan, Neal M., O.S.M., and Edwina Hunter Snyder. "Did Paul Put Down Women in 1 Cor 14:34–36?" *Biblical Theology Bulletin* 11 (1981): 10–12.

Flory, M. "Where Women Precede Men: Factors Influencing the Order of Names in Roman Epitaphs." *Classical Journal* 79 (1984): 216–24.

Foh, Susan. "What Is the Woman's Desire?" *Westminster Theological Journal* 37 (1974): 376–83.

_____. *Women and the Word of God: A Response to Biblical Feminism.* Grand Rapids: Baker, 1981.

Ford, P. J. "Paul the Apostle: Male Chauvinist?" *Biblical Theology Bulletin* 4 (1975): 302–11.

Freeman, David. "Woman, a Power Equal to Man." *Biblical Archaeology Review,* 9 (1983): 56–58.

Grudem, Wayne. "Does *kephalē* ("head") Mean 'Source' or 'Authority Over' in Greek Literature? A Survey of 2336 Examples." *Trinity Journal* 6 (Spring 1985): 38–59.

Heard, Warren. "The Meaning and Implications of the Subordination Directive to Women in 1 Timothy 2:11–15: Understanding the Ethical Tradition Employed." Unpublished article.

Hengel, Martin. *The Charismatic Leader and His Followers.* Translated by James Greig. New York: Crossroad, 1981.

House, H. Wayne. "Paul, Women, and Contemporary Evangelical Feminism." *Bibliotheca Sacra* 136 (1979): 40–53.

Howard, George. "The Head/Body Metaphors of Ephesians." *New Testament Studies* 20 (1973–74): 350–56.

Howard, J. Keir. "Neither Male nor Female." *The Evangelical Quarterly* 40 (1983): 31–42.

Hurley, James B. "Did Paul Require Veils or the Silence of Women? A Consideration of 1 Cor. 11:2–16 and 1 Cor. 14:33b–36." *Westminster Theological Journal* 35 (1973): 190–220.

————. *Man and Woman in Biblical Perspective.* Grand Rapids: Zondervan, 1981.

Jeremias, J. *Jerusalem in the Time of Jesus.* Translated by F. H. and C. H. Cave. Philadelphia: Fortress, 1969.

Judge, E. A. "Cultural Conformity and Innovation in Paul: Some Clues from Contemporary Documents." *Tyndale Bulletin* 35 (1984): 3–24.

————. "St. Paul as a Radical Critic of Society." *Interchange* (Sydney, Australia) 16 (1974): 191–203.

Kähler, Else. *Die Frau in den Paulinischen Briefen unter Besonderer Berücksichtung des Begriffes der Unterordnung.* Zurich: Gotthelf-Verlag, 1960.

Karris, R. J. "The Role of Women According to Jesus and the Early Church." In C. Stuhlmueller, ed., *Women and Priesthood: Future Directions.* Collegeville: Liturgical, 1978, 47–57.

Knight, George W., III. "*Authenteō* in Reference to Women in I Timothy 2:12." *New Testament Studies* 30 (1984): 143–47.

————. *The Role Relationship of Men and Women: The New Testament Teaching.* 1977. Rev. ed. Grand Rapids: Baker, 1985.

Kraemer, Ross S. "Women in the Religions of the Greco-Roman World." *Religious Studies Review* 9 (1983): 127–39.

Kroeger, Catherine. "Ancient Heresies and a Strange Greek Verb." *Reformed Journal* 29 (March 1979): 12–15.

————. "1 Timothy 2:12—A Classicist's View." In Alvera Mickelsen, ed. *Women, Authority and the Bible.* Downers Grove: InterVarsity, 1986.

Kroeger, Richard, and Catherine C. "Pandemonium and Silence at Corinth." *Reformed Journal* 28 (June 1978): 6–11.

————. "Sexual Identity in Corinth." *Reformed Journal* 28 (December 1978): 11–15.

Kuske, D. "Exegesis of 1 Corinthians 11:3–16." *Wisconsin Lutheran Quarterly* 78 (1981): 83–103.

Laurentin, René. "Jesus and Women: An Underestimated Revolution." *Concilium* (Religion in the Seventies) 134 (1980): 80–92.

Lefkowitz, Mary R., and Maureen B. Fant, eds. *Women's Life in Greece and Rome: A Source Book in Translation.* Baltimore: Johns Hopkins University Press, 1982.

Leslie, William H. "The Concept of Women in the Pauline Corpus in the Light of the Social and Religious Environment of the First Century." Ph.D. Dissertation, Northwestern University, 1976.

Lewis, Robert M. "The 'Women' of I Tim. 3:11." *Bibliotheca Sacra* 136 (1979): 167–75.

Lightman, Marjorie, and William Zeisel. "Univira: An Example of Continuity and Change in Roman Society." *Church History* 46 (1977): 19–32.

Loewe, Raphael. *The Position of Women in Judaism*. London: SPCK, 1966.

Malbon, Elizabeth Struthers. "Fallible Followers: Women and Men in the Gospel of Mark." *Semeia* 28 (1983): 29–48.

Martin, W. J. "I Cor 11:2–16: An Interpretation." In Ward Gasque and Ralph P. Martin, eds. *Apostolic History and the Gospel*. Grand Rapids: Eerdmans, 1970, 231–34.

Mercadante, Linda. *From Hierarchy to Equality: A Comparison of Past and Present Interpretations of 1 Corinthians 11:2–16 in Relation to the Changing Status of Women in Society*. Vancouver, B.C.: G.M.H. Books, Regent College, 1978.

Mickelsen, Berkeley, and Alvera Mickelsen. "The 'Head' of the Epistles." *Christianity Today* (1981), 264–67.

Moltmann-Wendel, Elizabeth. *The Women Around Jesus: Reflections on Authentic Personhood*. New York: Crossroad, 1982.

Moo, Douglas J. "I Timothy 2:11–15: Meaning and Significance." *Trinity Journal* 1 n.s. (1980): 62–83.

————. "The Interpretation of I Timothy 2:11–15: A Rejoinder." *Trinity Journal* 2 n.s. (1981): 198–220.

Motto, Anna Lydia. "Seneca on Women's Liberation." *Classical World* 65 (1972): 155–57.

Murphy-O'Connor, Jerome. "The Non-Pauline Character of 1 Corinthians 11:2–16." *Journal of Biblical Literature* 95 (1976): 615–21.

————. "Sex and Logic in I Corinthians 11:2–16." *Catholic Biblical Quarterly* 42 (1980): 482–500.

Odell-Scott, David W. "Let the Women Speak in Church: An Egalitarian Interpretation of 1 Cor. 14:33b–36." *Biblical Theological Bulletin* 13 (1983): 90–93.

Odom, William Lee. *A Study of Plutarch: The Position of Greek Women in the First Century After Christ*. Charlottesville: University of Virginia Press, 1961.

Otwell, John. *And Sarah Laughed: The Status of Woman in the Old Testament*. Philadelphia: Westminster, 1977.

Pagels, Elaine H. "Paul and Women: A Response to Recent Discussion." *Journal of the American Academy of Religion* 42 (1974): 538–49.

Payne, Philip B. "Libertarian Women in Ephesus: A Response to Douglas Moo's Article, 'I Tim. 2:11–15: Meaning and Significance.'" *Trinity Journal* 2 n.s. (1981): 169–97.

Plutarch. *Moralia: Advice to Bride and Groom*. Translated by Frank Cole Babbitt. Cambridge, Mass.: Harvard University Press, 1962.

Pomeroy, Sarah B. *Goddesses, Whores, Wives, and Slaves: Women in Classical Antiquity*. New York: Schocken, 1975.

————. *Women in Hellenistic Egypt: From Alexander to Cleopatra*. New York: Schocken, 1984.

Reinhold, Meyer. *The Golden Age of Augustus*. Toronto and Sarasota: Samuel Stevens, 1978.

Richardson, Peter. *Paul's Ethic of Freedom*. Philadelphia: Westminster, 1979.

Sayers, Dorothy. *Are Women Human?* Grand Rapids: Eerdmans, 1971.

Scholer, David M. "1 Timothy 2:9–15 & the Place of Women in the Church's Ministry." In Alvera Mickelsen, ed. *Women, Authority and the Bibe*. Downers Grove: InterVarsity, 1986.

Schottroff, Willy, and Stegemann, Wolfgang. *Traditionen der Befreiung: Sozialgeschichtliche Bibelauslegungen*. Band 2. *Frauen in der Bibel*. München: Chr. Kaiser Verlag & Gelnhausen; Berlin, Stein: Burckhardthaus-Laetare, 1980.

Sevenster, J. N. *Paul and Seneca*. Leiden: Brill, 1961.

Sigountos, James, and Myron Shank. "Public Roles for Women in the Pauline Church: A Reappraisal of the Evidence." *Journal of the Evangelical Theological Society* 26 (1983): 283–95.

Spencer, Aída Besançon. *Beyond the Curse: Women Called to Ministry*. Nashville: Thomas Nelson, 1985.

————. "Eve at Ephesus." *Journal of the Evangelical Theological Society* (1974), 215–22.

Stagg, Evelyn, and Frank Stagg. *Woman in the World of Jesus*. Philadelphia: Westminster, 1978.

Swidler, Leonard. *Biblical Affirmations of Women*. Philadelphia: Westminster, 1979.

————. *Women in Judaism: The Status of Women in Formative Judaism*. Metuchen, N.J.: Scarecrow, 1976.

Tetlow, Elizabeth. *Women and Ministry in the New Testament*. New York and Ramsey: Paulist, 1980.

Theissen, Gerd. *The Social Setting of Pauline Christianity*. Philadelphia: Fortress, 1982.

Trenchard, Warren C. *Ben Sira's View of Women: A Literary Analysis*. Brown Judaic Studies 38. Chico, Calif.: Scholars, 1982.

Trible, Phyllis. *God and the Rhetoric of Sexuality*. Philadelphia: Fortress, 1978.

————. *Texts of Terror: Literary-Feminist Readings of Biblical Narratives*. Philadelphia: Fortress, 1984.

————. "Depatriarchalizing in Biblical Interpretation." *Journal of the American Academy of Religion* 41 (1973): 30–48.

Verner, David C. *The Household of God: The Social World of the Pastoral Epistles,* SBL Dissertation Series 71. Chico, Calif.: Scholars, 1983.

Waltke, Bruce. "I Cor. 11:2–16: An Interpretation." *Bibliotheca Sacra* 135 (1978): 46–57.

————. "Relationship of the Sexes in the Bible." *CRUX* 19:3 (September 1983): 10–16.

Williams, Don. *The Apostle Paul and Women in the Church*. Van Nuys, Calif.: BIM, 1977.

Witherington, Ben, III. *Women in the Ministry of Jesus*. SNTS Monograph Series 51. Cambridge: Cambridge University Press, 1984.

Young, E. J. *Genesis 3*. London: Banner of Truth Trust, 1966.

CHAPTER 3
THE EARLY CHURCH

Note: This bibliography does not contain references to individual church fathers. Many of those cited can be found in the Ante-Nicene Fathers, *listed below. Specific citations will be found in the footnotes.*

The Ante-Nicene Fathers, Alexander Roberts and James Donaldson, eds., American Reprint of Edinburgh edition by Cleveland Coxe, ed. Christian Literature Publishing Company. New York: Scribner, 1925. Cited as ANF.

Bailey, Derrick Sherwin. *Sexual Relation in Christian Thought*. New York: Harper & Brothers, 1959.

Brighton, Louis A. "The Ordination of Women: A Twentieth Century Gnostic Heresy?" *Concordia Journal* 8 (1982): 16ff.

Bullough, Vern L., and Bonnie Bullough. *The Subordinate Sex: A History of Attitudes Toward Women*. Urbana: University of Illinois, 1973.

Clark, Elizabeth A. *Jerome, Chrysostom, and Friends.* Champaign, Ill.: University of Illinois Press, 1982.

————. *Women in the Early Church.* Message of the Fathers of the Church No. 13. Wilmington: Michael Glazier, 1983.

Crook, Margaret Brackenburg. *Women and Religion.* Boston: Beacon, 1964.

Cunningham, Agnes, S.S.C.M. *The Role of Women in Ecclesial Ministry.* Monograph published by the United States Catholic Conference, 1976.

Daniélou, Jean. *The Ministry of Women in the Early Church.* Translated by Glyn Simon. London: Faith, 1961.

Davies, Stevan. *The Revolt of the Widows.* Carbondale: Southern Illinois University Press; London: Feffer & Simons, 1980.

Deen, Edith. *Great Women of the Christian Faith.* New York: Harper & Brothers, 1959.

Fiorenza, Elisabeth Schüssler. "Word, Spirit and Power: Women in Early Christian Communities." In *Women of Spirit: Female Leadership in the Jewish and Christian Traditions,* edited by Rosemary Ruether and Eleanor McLaughlin. New York: Simon and Schuster, 1979.

Foley, Helene P. *Reflections of Women in Antiquity.* New York, London, Paris: Gordon and Breach Science, 1981.

Gryson, Roger. *The Ministry of Women in the Early Church.* Translated by J. LaPorte and Mary Louise Hall. Collegeville, Minn.: Liturgical, 1976.

Irvin, Dorothy. "The Ministry of Women in the Early Church: The Archaeological Evidence." *Duke Divinity School Review* 45 (1980): 76–86.

Karris, R. J. "The Role of Women According to Jesus and the Early Church." In *Women and Priesthood: Future Directions,* edited by C. Stuhlmueller. Collegeville: Liturgical, 1978, 47–57.

LaPorte, Jean. *The Role of Women in Early Christianity: Studies in Women and Religion 7.* Lewiston, N.Y.: Mellen, 1982.

Manges, Ernest B. "Tertullian's Understanding of Human Sexuality." Unpublished master's thesis, Trinity Evangelical Divinity School, 1975.

McKenna, Mary Lawrence, S.C.M.M. *Women of the Church.* New York: McKenna, n.d.

McPhee, Carol, and Ann FitzGerald, compilers. *Feminist Quotations: Voices of Rebels, Reformers, and Visionaries.* New York: Crowell, 1979.

Meyer, Charles R. "Ordained Women in the Early Church." *Chicago Studies* 4 (1965): 285–308.

Michelsen, Alvera, ed. *Women, Authority and the Bible.* Downers Grove: InterVarsity, 1986.

Nag Hammadi Library in English. Translation directed by James M. Robinson. New York: Harper & Row, 1977.

Nugent, Rosamond. *Portrait of the Consecrated Woman in Greek Christian Literature of the First Four Centuries.* Washington, D.C.: Catholic University Press, 1941. (University Microfilms, 1979).

Osiek, Carolyn. "The Widow as Altar: The Rise and Fall of a Symbol." *The Second Century* 3 (1983): 159–69.

Pagels, Elaine. *The Gnostic Gospels.* New York: Random, 1979.

Rader, Rosemary. *Breaking Boundaries: Male/Female Friendship in Early Christian Communities.* New York: Paulist, 1983.

Rogers, Kathrine M. *The Troublesome Helpmate.* Seattle: University of Washington Press, 1966.

Ruether, Rosemary, and Eleanor McLaughlin, eds. *Women of Spirit: Female Leadership in the Jewish and Christian Traditions.* New York: Simon and Schuster, 1979.

Ruether, Rosemary Radford. "Misogynism and Virginal Feminism in the Fathers." *Religion and Sexism: Images of Women in the Jewish and Christian Traditions.* New York: Simon and Schuster, 1974.

Swidler, Leonard, and Arlene Swidler, eds. *Women Priests: A Catholic Commentary on the Vatican Declaration.* New York: Paulist, 1977.

Tannahill, Reay. *Sex in History.* Briarcliff Manor, N.Y.: Stein and Day, 1980.

Tavard, George. *Women in the Christian Tradition.* Notre Dame University Press, 1973.

Toon, Peter. "Ephiphanius." In *The New International Dictionary of the Christian Church.* Revised edition by J. D. Douglas. Grand Rapids: Zondervan, 1978.

van der Meer, Haye, S. J. *Women Priests in the Catholic Church?* Translated by Arlene and Leonard Swidler. Philadelphia: Temple University Press, 1973.

Wilson-Kastner, Patricia et al. *A Lost Tradition: Women Writers of the Early Church.* Lanham, New York and London: University Press of America, 1981.

CHAPTER 4
THE MIDDLE AGES

Abelard and Heloise. *The Letters of Abelard and Heloise.* Translation and introduction by Betty Radice. New York: Scholars', 1986.

Bell, Rudolph M. *Holy Anorexia.* Chicago: University of Chicago Press, 1985.

Bell, Susan G., ed. *Women: From the Greeks to the French Revolution.* Stanford: Stanford University Press, 1973.

Borresen, Kari Elisabeth. *Subordination and Equivalence: The Nature and Role of Women in Augustine and Thomas Aquinas.* Washington, D.C.: University Press of America, 1981.

Braswell, Laurel. "Saint Edburga of Winchester: A Study of Her Cult, A.D. 950–1500." *Medieval Studies* 23 (1971): 292–333.

Bynum, Caroline W. "Jesus as Mother: Studies in the Spirituality of the High Middle Ages." Berkeley: University of California Press, 1982.

Cardman, Francine. "The Medieval Question of Women and Orders." *The Thomist* 42 (October 1978): 582–99.

Colledge, Edmund and James Walsh. "Editing Julian of Norwich's *Revelations:* A Progress Report." *Medieval Studies* 28 (1976): 404–27.

Collins, Louise. *Memoirs of a Medieval Woman: The Life and Times of Margery Kempe.* New York: Crowell, 1964.

Clark, Elizabeth, and Herbert Richardson, eds. *Women and Religion: A Feminist Sourcebook of Christian Thought.* New York: Harper & Row, 1977.

de La Bedoyere, Michael. *Catherine: Saint of Siena.* London: Hollis and Carter, 1947.

Dean, Edith. *Great Women of the Christian Faith.* New York: Harper & Row, 1959.

Durant, Will. *The Age of Faith.* New York: Simon and Schuster, 1950.

Eckenstein, Lina. *Woman Under Monasticism.* New York: Russell & Russell, 1896.

Ferrante, Joan M. "The Education of Women" in Patricia H. Labalme, *Beyond Their Sex.* New York: New York University Press, 1980. Pages 9–42.

————. *Woman as Image in Medieval Literature From the Twelfth-Century to Dante.* Durham, N.C.: Labyrinth, 1985.

Gies, Frances, and Joseph Gies. *Women in the Middle Ages.* New York: Crowell, 1978.

Goodich, Michael. "The Contours of Female Piety in Later Medieval "Hagiography." *Church History* 50 (March 1981): 20–32.

Hardesty, Nancy. *Great Women of the Christian Faith.* Grand Rapids: Baker, 1980.

Healy, Emma T. *Woman According to Saint Bonaventure*. New York: Georgian, 1956.

Heimmel, Jennifer P. *"God is Our Mother: Julian of Norwich and the Medieval Image of Christian Feminine Divinity*. Salzburg: University of Salzburg Press, 1952.

Julian of Norwich. *Revelations of Divine Love*. Translated by Clifton Walters. New York: Scholars', 1986.

Kempe, Margery. *The Book of Margery Kempe*. Translated, with introduction, by Barry Windeatt. New York: Scholars', 1986.

Lerner, Robert E. *The Heresy of the Free Spirit in the Later Middle Ages*. Berkeley: University of California Press, 1972.

McDonnell, Ernest W. *The Beguines and the Beghards in Medieval Culture*. New York: Octagon, 1969.

McLaughlin, Eleanor. "Equality of Souls, Inequality of Sexes. Woman in Medieval Theology" in Rosemary Ruether, *Religion and Sexism: Images of Woman in the Jewish and Christian Traditions*. New York: Simon and Schuster, 1974. Pages 213–66.

McLaughlin, Eleanor. "Women, Power and the Pursuit of Holiness in Medieval Christianity." In Rosemary Ruether and Eleanor McLaughlin. *Women of Spirit: Female Leaders in the Jewish and Christian Traditions*. New York: Simon and Schuster, 1979. Pages 99–130.

Morris, Joan. *The Lady Was a Bishop: The Hidden History of Women With Clerical Ordination and the Jurisdiction of Bishops*. New York: Macmillan, 1973.

Petroff, Elizabeth A., ed. *Medieval Women's Visionary Literature*. New York: Oxford University Press, 1986.

Robeck, Nesta de. *St. Clare of Assisi*. Chicago: Franciscan Herald, 1980.

Schaff, Philip. *History of the Christian Church*. Vol. 3, *Nicene and Post-Nicene Christianity*, A.D. *311–600*. Grand Rapids: Eerdmans, 1979.

————. *History of the Christian Church*. Vol. 5, *The Middle Ages*, A.D. *1049–1294*. Grand Rapids: Eerdmans, 1979.

Southern, R. W. *Western Society and the Church in the Middle Ages*. New York: Penguin, 1970.

St. Francis. *Little Flowers of St. Francis*. New York: Dutton, 1947.

Stuard, Susan M., ed. *Women in Medieval Society*. Philadelphia: University of Pennsylvania Press, 1976.

Taylor, Henry Osborn. *The Medieval Mind*. Cambridge: Harvard University Press, 1949.

Taege, Marlys. *And God Gave Women Talents*. St. Louis: Concordia, 1978.

Weinstein, Donald, and Rudolph Bell. *Saints and Society: The Two Worlds of Western Christendom, 1000–1700*. Chicago: University of Chicago Press, 1982.

Wemple, Susanne F. *Women in Frankish Society: Marriage and the Cloister, 500 to 900*. Philadelphia: University of Pennsylvania Press, 1981.

Williams, George, and Edith Waldvogel. "A History of Speaking in Tongues and Related Gifts," in *The Charismatic Movement*. Edited by Michael P. Hamilton. Grand Rapids: Eerdmans, 1975. Page 70.

CHAPTER 5
THE REFORMATION ERA

Alexander, J. H. *Ladies of the Reformation*. Harpenden, England: Gospel Standard, 1978.

Askewe, Anne. *The First Examination of the worthy seruant of God, Mistress Anne Askew . . . lately martyred in Smithfield.* London: Robert Waldgraue, 1585.

Bainton, Roland H. *Erasmus of Christendom.* New York: Scribners, 1969.

_____. *Here I Stand: A Life of Martin Luther.* New York: Mentor, 1950.

_____. *Women of the Reformation in France and England.* Minneapolis: Augsburg, 1973.

_____. *Women of the Reformation in Germany and Italy.* Minneapolis: Augsburg, 1971.

_____. *Women of the Reformation in Spain to Scandanavia.* Minneapolis: Augsburg, 1977.

Blaisdell, Charmarie J. "Response to 'The Role & Status of Women in the Writings of John Calvin.' " In Peter De Klerk, ed. *Renaissance, Reformation, Resurgence.* Grand Rapids: Calvin Theological Seminary, 1976. Pages 19–32.

_____. "Calvin's Letters to Women: The Courting of Ladies in High Places." *Sixteenth Century Journal* 13 (Fall 1982): 67–84.

Cairncross, John. *After Polygamy Was Made a Sin: The Social History of Christian Polygamy.* London: Routledge & Kegan Paul, 1974.

Calvin, John. *Commentaries on the Gospel of John.* Translated by William Pringle. Grand Rapids: Eerdmans, 1956.

Chrisman, Mariam V. "Women of the Reformation in Strasburg, 1490–1530." *Archive for Reformation History* 63 (1972): 143–68.

Clissold, Stephen. *St. Teresa of Avila.* New York: Seabury, 1982.

Coltman, Constance M. "Post-Reformation: The Free Churches." In A. Maude Royden, *The Church and Woman.* New York: Doran, 1924.

Davis, Natalie Z. *Society and Culture in Early Modern France.* Stanford: Stanford University Press, 1975.

Douglass, Jane D. "Christian Freedom: What Calvin Learned at the School of Women." *Church History* 53 (June 1984): 155–73.

_____. "Women and the Continental Reformation." In Rosemary Ruether, *Religion and Sexism: Images of Women in the Jewish and Christian Traditions.* New York: Simon and Schuster, 1974. Pages 292–318.

Durant, Will. *The Reformation: A History of European Civilization From Wycliff to Calvin, 1300–1564.* New York: Simon and Schuster, 1957.

Foxe, John. *Foxe's Christian Martyrs of the World.* Chicago: Moody, n.d.

Friedenthal, Richard. *Luther: His Life and Times.* Translated by John Nowell. New York: Harcourt Brace Jovanovich, 1970.

Irwin, Joyce L. *Womanhood in Radical Protestantism, 1525–1675.* New York: Mellen, 1979.

Karant-Nunn, Susan C. "Continuity and Change: Some Effects of the Reformation on the Women of Zwickau." *Sixteenth Century Journal* 12 (Summer 1982): 17–42.

Kleinhans, Theodore J. *Martin Luther, Saint and Sinner.* London, Marshall, Morgan & Scott, 1959.

Knox, John. *The First Blast of the Trumpet Against the Monstrous Regiment of Women.* 1558. In David Laing, ed., *The Works of John Knox.* 6 vols. Edinburgh: Stevenson, 1855.

Laing, David, ed. *The Works of John Knox,* vol. 4. Edinburgh: Stevenson, 1855. Pages 351, 357–58.

Lincoln, Victoria. *Teresa: A Woman, A Biography of Teresa of Avila.* Albany: State University of New York Press, 1984.

Luther, Martin. *The Christian in Society*. In Helmut T. Lehmann, ed., *Luther's Works*. 45 vols. Philadelphia: Muhlenberg, 1962.

————. *Luther's Commentary on Genesis*. Translated by J. Theodore Mueller. 2 vols. Grand Rapids: Zondervan, 1958.

————. *Notes on Ecclesiastes*. In Jaroslav Pelikan, ed., *Luther's Works*. 54 vols. St. Louis: Concordia, 1972.

O'Faolain, Julia, and Lauro Martines, eds. *Not in God's Image*. New York: Harper & Row, 1973.

Rahner, Hugo. *Saint Ignatius Loyola: Letters to Women*. London: Nelson, 1956.

Roelker, Nancy. "The Appeal of Calvinism to French Noblewomen of the Sixteenth Century." *Journal of Interdisciplinary History* 2 (Spring 1972): 391–413.

Schaff, Philip. *History of the Christian Church*. Grand Rapids: Eerdmans, 1979. Vol. 8.

Siggins, Ian. *Luther and His Mother*. Philadelphia: Fortress, 1981.

Simons, Menno. *The True Christian Faith*. From *The Complete Writings of Menno Simons (c. 1496–1561)*. Translated by Leonard Verduin. Edited by John C. Wenger. Scottsdale, Pa.: Herald, 1956.

Walsh, Walter. *The Women Martyrs of the Reformation*. London: Religious Tract Society, 1912.

Williams, George Huntston. *The Radical Reformation*. Philadelphia: Westminster, 1962.

CHAPTER 6
POST-REFORMATION ERA

Besse, Joseph. *A Collection of the Sufferings of the People Called Quakers*. 2 vols. London, 1753. Vol. 1.

Brailsford, Mabel Richmond. *Quaker Women, 1650–1690*. London: Duckworth, 1915.

Brown, Earl Kent. *Women in Mr. Wesley's Methodism*. New York: Mellen, 1983.

————. "Standing in the Shadow: Women in Early Methodism." *Nexus* 17 (Spring 1974): 22–31.

————. "Women of the Word: Selected Leadership Roles of Women in Mr. Wesley's Methodism." In Hilah Thomas and Rosemary Keller, eds. *Women in New Worlds: Historical Perspectives on the Wesleyan Tradition*. Nashville: Abingdon, 1981. Pages 69–81.

Brown, Judith C. *Immodest Acts: The Life of a Lesbian Nun in Renaissance Italy*. London: Oxford University Press, 1985.

Capp, B. S. *The Fifth Monarchy Men*. London: Faber and Faber, 1972.

Coltman, Constance M. "Post-Reformation: The Free Churches." In A. Maude Royden. *The Church and Woman*. New York: Doran, 1924.

Cotton, John. "The Way of the Congregational Churches Cleared." 1648. In David D. Hall, ed., *The Antinomian Controversy*. Middletown, Conn.: Wesleyan University Press, 1968.

Couch, Beatriz M. "Sor Juana Ines de la Cruz: The First Woman Theologian in the America." In John and Ellen Webster, eds. *The Church and Women in the Third World*. Philadelphia: Westminster, 1985. Pages 51–57.

Dexter, Franklin B., ed. "A Report of the Trial of Mrs. Anne Hutchinson before the Church in Boston, 1638." Massachusetts Historical Society Proceedings. 2d series, vol. 4, 1889.

Edwards, Jonathan. "Sarah Pierrepont." In *Jonathan Edwards: Representative Selections*. Edited by Clarence H. Faust and Thomas H. Johnson. New York: Hill and Wang, 1935.

―――――. *The Works of Jonathan Edwards*. Edited by John E. Smith, vol. 4: *The Great Awakening*. New Haven: Yale University Press, 1972.

Fell, Margaret. *Women's Speaking Justified*. Introduction by David J. Latt. Los Angeles: University of California Press, 1979.

Fox, George. *The Works of George Fox*. 8 vols. 1831; reprinted New York: AMS, 1975.

Fraser, Antonia. *The Weaker Vessel*. New York: Knopf, 1984.

Fremantle, Anne. *Woman's Way to God*. New York: St. Martin's, 1977.

Greaves, Richard L. "The Role of Women in Early English Nonconformity." *Church History* 52 (September 1983): 299–311.

Guyon, Jeanne. *The Autobiography of Madame Guyon*. Translated by Thomas Allen. New Caanan, Conn.: Keats, 1980.

Harmon, Rebecca L. *Susanne: Mother of the Wesleys*. Nashville: Abingdon, 1968.

Huber, Elaine C. "'A Woman Must Not Speak': Quaker women in the English Left Wing." In Ruether and McLaughlin, eds. *Women of Spirit*. New York: Simon and Schuster, 1979. Pages 153–81.

Hutchinson, Thomas, ed. "The Examination of Mrs. Anne Hutchinson, at the Court at Newtown. November 1637." In Thomas Hutchinson, *The History of the Colony and Province of Massachusetts-Bay* 2 (1767): 366–91. Reprint, Cambridge: Harvard University Press, 1936.

Irwin, Joyce L. *Womanhood in Radical Protestantism, 1525–1675*. New York: Mellen, 1979.

Knox, Ronald A. *Enthusiasm: A Chapter in the History of Religion*. New York: Oxford University Press, 1961.

Latt, David J. "Introduction." In Margaret Fell, *Women's Speaking Justified*. Los Angeles: University of California Press, 1979.

Mancha, Rita. "The Woman's Authority: Calvin to Edwards." *Journal of Christian Reconstruction* 6:2 (Winter 1979–80): 86–98.

Manners, Emily. *Elizabeth Hooton: First Quaker Woman Preacher*. London: Headley, 1914.

Mather, Cotton. *Ornaments for the Daughters of Zion*. Delmar, N.Y.: Scholars' Facsimiles & Reprints, 1978.

Matthews, Donald G. "Womens' History/Everyone's History." In Hilah Thomas and Rosemary Keller, eds. *Women in New Worlds: Historical Perspectives on the Wesleyan Tradition*. Nashville: Abingdon, 1981. Pages 29–47.

Morgan, Edmund S. *The Puritan Family*. New York: Harper & Row, 1966.

Paine, G. T., ed. *A Call From Death to Life, being an account of the sufferings of Marmaduke Stephenson, William Robinson and Mary Dyer in New England, in the year 1659*. Printed by Friends in London, 1660.

Pearl, Jonathan L. "French Catholic Demonologists and the Enemies in the Late Sixteenth and Early Seventeenth Centuries." *Church History* 52 (December 1983): 457–67.

Penny, Norman, ed. *Experiences in the Life of Mary Penington*. London, 1911.

Rogers, Horatio. *Mary Dyer of Rhode Island*. Providence: Preston and Rounds, 1896.

Ruether, Rosemary, and Rosemary Keller. *Women and Religion in America; The Colonial and Revolutionary Periods*. San Francisco: Harper & Row, 1983.

Stoeffler, F. Ernest. *Continental Pietism and Early American Christianity*. Grand Rapids: Eerdmans, 1976.

Thomas, Keith. *Religion and the Decline of Magic.* New York: Scribner, 1971.

————. "Women and the Civil War Sects." In Trevor Aston, ed. *Crisis in Europe, 1560–1660.* New York: Basic, 1965. Pages 317–40.

Todd, Margo. "Humanists, Puritans and the Spiritualized Household." *Church History* 49 (March 1980): 18–34.

Ulrich, Laurel T. *Good Wives: Image and Reality in the Lives of Women in Northern New England, 1650–1750.* New York: Knopf, 1982.

Upham, Thomas C. *The Life and Religious Opinions and Experience of Madam Guyon.* London: Allenson, 1905.

Volkman, Pamela. *From Heroics to Dissent: A Study of the Thought and Psychology of English Nonconformity, 1660–1700, Through Autobiography.* Ph.D. dissertation, University of Rochester, 1982.

Wesley, John. *Explanatory Notes Upon the New Testament.* London: Wesleyan-Methodist Book Room, 1754.

————. *The Journal of John Wesley.* 4 vols. New York: Dutton, 1907.

————. *The Letters of the Rev. John Wesley.* 8 vols. Edited by John Telford. London: Epworth, 1983.

————. *The Works of John Wesley.* 14 vols. Grand Rapids: Zondervan, 1958.

West, Jessamyn, ed. *The Quaker Reader.* New York: Viking, 1962.

Williams, George H., and Edith Waldvogel. "A History of Speaking in Tongues and Related Gifts." In Michael P. Hamilton, ed. *The Charismatic Movement.* Grand Rapids: Eerdmans, 1975. Pages 61–113.

Williams, Selma. *Divine Rebel: The Life of Anne Marbury Hutchinson.* New York: Holt, Rinehart and Winston, 1981.

Winthrop, John. *Winthrop's Journal: History of New England, 1630–1649.* 2 vols. Edited by James K. Hosmer. New York: Scribner, 1908.

CHAPTER 7
THE NINETEENTH-CENTURY

Andrews, Leslie. "Restricted Freedom: A. B. Simpson's View of Women in Ministry." In *Birth of a Vision.* Edited by David Hartzveld and Charles Nienkirchen. Beaverlodge, Alta.: Horizon, 1986.

Bacon, Margaret. *As the Way Opens: The Story of Quaker Women in America.* Richmond, Ind.: Friends, 1980.

Barley, Fred A. "Woman's Superiority in Disciple Thought, 1865–1900." *Restoration Quarterly* 23 (First Quarter 1980): 151–60.

Bethune, George W. *Memoirs of Mrs. Joanna Bethune.* New York: Harper, 1863.

Blauvelt, Martha T. "Women and Revivalism." In Rosemary Ruether and Rosemary Keller, eds. *Women and Religion in America.* 3 vols. New York: Harper & Row, 1981. 1:1–45.

Booth, Catherine. *Female Ministry: Or, Woman's Right to Preach the Gospel.* New York: Salvation Army, 1975.

————. *Life and Death, Being Reports of Addresses Delivered in London.* London: Salvation Army, 1883.

————. *Papers on Aggressive Christianity.* London: Partridge, 1980.

————. *The Salvation Army in Relation to the Church and State.* London: Partridge, n.d.

Booth-Tucker, Frederick. *The Life of Catherine Booth.* London: Salvation Army, 1892.

Bordin, Ruth. *Woman and Temperance: The Quest for Power and Liberty, 1873–1900.* Philadelphia: Temple University Press, 1981.

Boyd, Lois A., and Douglas R. Brakenridge. *Presbyterian Women in America: Two Centuries of a Quest for Status.* London: Greenwood, 1983.

Bradley, Ian. *The Call to Seriousness: The Evangelical Impact on the Victorians.* New York: Macmillan, 1976.

Bramwell-Booth, Catherine. *Catherine Booth: The Story of Her Loves.* London: Hodder and Stoughton, 1970.

Brereton, Virginia L. "Preparing Women for the Lord's Work." In Hilah F. Thomas and Rosemary Keller, eds. *Women in New Worlds: Historical Perspectives on the Wesleyan Tradition,* Nashville: Abingdon, 1981. Pages 178–99.

Brown, Ford K. *Fathers of the Victorians.* Cambridge: Cambridge University Press, 1971.

Brown, Kenneth O. " 'The World-Wide Evangelist'—The Life and Work of Martha Inskip." Methodist History 21 (July 1983): 170–91.

Coke, Thomas. *The Experience and Spiritual Letters of Mrs. Hester Ann Rovers: With A Sermon Preached on the Occasion of Her Death.* London: Miller and Company, n.d.

Cole, Mary. *Trials and Triumphs of Faith.* Anderson, Ind.: Gospel Trumpet, 1914.

Cooke, Harriette. *Mildmay: Or, The Story of the First Deaconess Institution.* London: Elliot Stock, 1892.

Cott, Nancy F. *The Bonds of Womanhood: "Women's Sphere" in New England 1780–1835.* New Haven: Yale University Press, 1977.

————. "Young Women in the Second Great Awakening in New England." *Feminist Studies* 3 (1975): 15–29.

Davis, Almond. *The Female Preacher: Or, Memoir of Salome Lincoln, Afterwards the Wife of Elder Junia S. Mowry.* Providence: Mowry, 1843.

Dayton, Donald. *Discovering an Evangelical Heritage.* New York: Harper & Row, 1976.

Dayton, Lucille Sider, and Donald W. Dayton " 'Your Daughters Shall Prophesy': Feminism in the Holiness Movement." *Methodist History* 14 (January 1976): 67–92.

Dieter, Melvin, E. *The Holiness Revival of the Nineteenth Century.* Metuchen, N.J.: Scarecrow, 1980.

————. "The Smiths—A Biographical Sketch With Selected Items From the Collection." *The Asbury Seminarian* 38 (Spring 1983): 6–41.

Dirvin, Joseph I. *Mrs. Seton: Foundress of the American Sisters of Charity.* New York: Farrar, Straus, & Giroux, 1975.

Ewens, Mary. "Removing the Veil: The Liberated American Nun." In Rosemary Ruether and Eleanor McLaughlin. *Women of Spirit: Female Leadership in the Jewish and Christian Traditions,* New York: Simon and Schuster, 1979. Pages 253–78.

Fell, Margaret. *The Examination and Tryall of Margaret Fell and George Fox.* London, n.p.: 1664.

Flora, Jerry R. "Ninety Years of Brethren Women in Ministry." *Ashland Theological Journal* 17 (Fall 1984): 4–21.

Foster, Lawrence. *Religion and Sexuality: The Shakers, the Mormons, and the Oneida Community.* Urbana: University of Illinois, 1981.

Gordon, Anna A. *The Beautiful Life of Frances E. Willard.* Chicago: Woman's Temperance Publishing Association, 1898.

Golder, Christian. "History of the Deaconess Movement in the Christian Church. Cincinnati: Jennings & Pye, 1903.

Graebner, Alan. "Birth Control and the Lutherans: The Missouri Synod as a Case Study." In Janet Wilson James, ed. *Woman in American Religion*. Philadelphia: University of Pennsylvania Press, 1980.

Greene, Dana, ed. *Lucretia Mott: Her Complete Speeches and Sermons*. New York: Mellen, 1980.

Hardesty, Nancy. "The Wesleyan Movement and Women's Liberation." In Theodore Runyon, ed. *Sanctification and Liberation*. Nashville: Abingdon, 1981. Pages 164–73.

———. *Women Called to Witness: Evangelical Feminism in the 19th Century*. Nashville: Abingdon, 1984.

Harrison, Beverly W. "The Early Feminists and the Clergy: A Case Study in the Dynamics of Secularization." *Review and Expositor* 73 (Winter 1975): 41–51.

Hays, Elinor R. *Those Extraordinary Blackwells: The Story of a Journey to a Better World*. New York: Harcourt, Brace & World, 1967.

Henry, Marie. *The Secret Life of Hannah Whitall Smith*. Grand Rapids: Zondervan, 1984.

Hinson, E. Glenn. "The Church: Liberator or Oppressor of Women." *Review and Expositor* 73 (Winter 1975). Pages 19–29.

Irvine, Mary S., and Alice L. Eastwood. *Pioneer Women of the Presbyterian Church, United States*. Richmond: Presbyterian Committee of Publication, 1923.

Johnson, Dale A. *Women in English Religion, 1700–1925*. New York: Mellen, 1983.

Jones, Charles Edwin, quoted in *Perfectionist Persuasion: The Holiness Movement and American Methodism, 1867–1937*. Metuchen, N. J.: Scarecrow, 1974.

Keller, Rosemary, "Lay Women in the Protestant Tradition." In Rosemary Ruether and Rosemary Keller, eds. *Women and Religion in America*. 3 vols. New York: Harper & Row, 1981. Pages 242–57.

Kimball, Gayle. *The Religious Ideas of Harriett Beecher Stowe: Her Gospel of Womanhood*. Lewiston, N.Y.: Mellen, 1982.

Larsson, Flora. *My Best Men Are Women*. London: Hodder and Stoughton, 1974.

Lawson, Ellen. *The Three Sarahs: Documents of Black Antebellum College Women*. Lewiston, N.Y.: Mellen, 1985.

Lee, Jerena. *Religious Experiences and Journal*. Philadelphia: Jerena Lee, 1849.

Lynn, Robert and Elliott Wright. *The Big Little School: Sunday Child of American Protestantism*. New York: Harper & Row, 1971.

McBeth, Leon. *Women in Baptist Life*. Nashville: Broadman, 1979.

McLoughlin, William G. *Revivals, Awakenings, and Reform: An Essay on Religion and Social Change in America, 1607–1977*. Chicago: University of Chicago Press, 1978.

Miller, Page P. "Women in the Vangard of the Sunday School Movement." *Journal of Presbyterian History* 58 (Winter 1980): 311–25.

Montgomery, Carrie Judd. *"Under His Wings": The Story of My Life*. Oakland: Triumphs of Faith, 1936.

Murdoch, Norman H. "Female Ministry in the Thought and Work of Catherine Booth." *Church History* 53 (September 1984): 348–62.

Nation, Carry A. *The Use and Need of the Life of Carry A. Nation*. Topeka: Steves, 1909.

Numbers, Ronald L. *Prophetess of Health: A Study of Ellen G. White*. New York: Harper & Row, 1976.

Palmer, Phoebe. *Promise of the Father: Or, A Neglected Speciality of the Last Days*. Boston: Segen, 1859.

Porterfield, Amanda. *Feminine Spirituality in America: From Sarah Edwards to Martha Graham*. Philadelphia: Temple University Press, 1980.

Rice, Edwin W. *The Sunday-School Movement and the American Sunday-School Union, 1780–1917.* Philadelphia: American Sunday-School Union, 1917.

Roberts, B. T. *Ordinary Women.* Rochester: Earnest Christian, 1981.

Roberts, William. *Memoirs of Hannah More.* 2 vols. London: Seely and Burnside, 1834.

Rodgers, Margaret. "Attitudes to the Ministry of Women in the Diocese of Sidney: An Historical Study, 1834–1839." *The Reformed Theological Journal* 29 (1980): 73–82.

Royden, Maude A. *The Church and Woman.* New York: Doran, 1924.

Ruether, Rosemary and Rosemary Keller, eds. *Women and Religion in America.* 3 vols. New York: Harper & Row, 1981.

Ruffin, Bernard. *Fanny Crosby.* n.p.: United Church Press, 1976.

Smith, Amanda. *An Autobiography: The Story of the Lord's Dealings With Mrs. Amanda Smith, the Colored Evangelist.* Chicago: Meyer, 1893.

Smith, Hannah Whitall. *The Christian's Secret of a Happy Life.* Grand Rapids: Zondervan, 1984.

Smith, John W. *Heralds of a Brighter Day: Biographical Sketches of Early Leaders in the Church of God Reformation Movement.* Anderson, Ind.: Gospel Trumpet, 1955.

Smith, Timothy L. *Called Unto Holiness: The Story of the Nazarenes, the Formative Years.* Kansas City, Mo.: Nazarene, 1962.

Stewart, I. D. *History of the Freewill Baptists.* 2 vols. Dover: Freewill Baptist Establishment, 1862.

Stewart, Mother. *Memoirs of the Crusade: A Thrilling Account of the Great Uprising of Women of Ohio in 1873, Against the Liquor Crime.* Columbus: Williams & Hubbard, 1889.

Strachey, Ray. *Frances Willard: Her Life and Work.* New York: Revell, 1913.

Synan, Vinson. *The Holiness-Pentecostal Movement in the United States.* Grand Rapids: Eerdmans, 1971.

Tanis, James. "Reformed Pietism in Colonial America." In F. Ernest Stoeffler, ed. *Continental Pietism and Early American Christianity.* Grand Rapids: Eerdmans, 1976. Pages 34–73.

Tatum, N. *A Crown of Service: A Story of Women's Work in the Methodist Episcopal Church South 1878–1940.* Nashville: Parthenon, 1960.

Terrell, Velma M. "Called to Serve: Women in the Southern Baptist Convention." *Faith and Mission* 2 (Fall 1984): 18–29.

Troutt, Margaret. *The General Was a Lady: The Story of Evangeline Booth.* Nashville: Holman, 1980.

Wall, Ernest. "I Commend Unto You Phoebe." *Religion in Life* 24 (Summer 1957): 396–408.

Warfield, Benjamin B. *Perfectionism.* Philadelphia: Presbyterian and Reformed, 1958.

Weiser, Frederick S. "The Origin of the Modern Diaconate for Women." In Donald G. Bloesch, ed. *Servants of Christ: Deaconesses in Renewal.* Minneapolis: Bethany, 1971. Pages 17–43.

Welter, Barbara. "The Feminization of American Religion, 1800–1860." In (editor???) *Clio's Consciousness Raised.* New York: Harper Colophon, 1974.

Willard, Frances E. *Glimpses of Fifty Years: The Autobiography of an American Woman.* Chicago: Smith, 1889.

————. *Woman and Temperance: Or, The Work and Workers of The Woman's Christian Temperance Union.* Hartford, Conn.: Park, 1883.

————. *Woman in the Pulpit.* Boston: Lothrop, 1888.

Willard, Frances E., and Mary A. Livermore, eds. *A Woman of the Century: Fourteen Hundred-Seventy Biographical Sketches of Leading American Women.* Chicago: Moulton, 1893.

Zikmund, Barbara B. "The Struggle for the Rights to Preach." In Rosemary Ruether and Rosemary Keller, eds. *Women and Religion in America*. New York: Harper & Row, 1981. Vol. 1, pages 208–41.

CHAPTER 8
WOMEN IN MODERN MISSIONS

Allen, Catherine. *The New Lottie Moon Story*. Nashville: Broadman, 1980.

Anderson, Courtney. *To the Golden Shore: The Life of Adoniram Judson*. Grand Rapids: Zondervan, 1972.

Anderson, Rufus. "The Marriage of Missionaries" (1842). In R. Pierce Beaver, ed. *To Advance the Gospel: Selections From the Writings of Rufus Anderson*. Grand Rapids: Eerdmans, 1967. Pages 210–15.

Barnett, Lucy A. *Pioneers, Pedagogues, and Preachers: Expanding Opportunities for Women in Presbyterian Missions to the American Indians, 1833–1893*. Trinity Evangelical Divinity School. M.A. thesis. 1985.

Beaver, R. Pierce. *American Protestant Women in World Mission: A History of the First Feminist Movement in North America*. Grand Rapids: Eerdmans, 1980.

Bliss, Edwin M. *The Missionary Enterprise: A Concise History of the Feminist Movement in North America*. New York: Revell, 1908.

Brumberg, Joan Jacobs. *Mission for Life: The Story of the Family of Adoniram Judson*. New York: Macmillan, 1980.

Buckland, Augustus R. *Women in the Mission Field: Pioneers and Martyrs*. New York: Thomas Whittaker, 1895.

Burgess, Alan. *Daylight Must Come: The Story of a Courageous Woman Doctor in the Congo*. New York: Dell, n.d.

————. *The Small Woman*. New York: Sutton, 1957.

Cattan, Louise A. *Lamps Are for Lighting: The Story of Helen Barrett Montgomery and Lucy Waterbury Peabody*. Grand Rapids: Eerdmans, 1972.

Christian, Carol, and Gladys Plummer. *God and One Redhead: Mary Slessor of Calabar*. Grand Rapids: Zondervan, 1970.

Cragg, Kenneth. "Constance E. Padwick (1886–1968)." *The Muslim World* 59 (January 1969): 29–39.

Curtis, Mrs. Ethan. "A Generation of 'Woman's Work for Woman.' " *Missionary Review of the World* 23 (July 1910): 535.

————. "The Reflex Influence of Missions." *Missionary Review of the World* (March 1892). Page 183.

Daniel-Rops, Henri. *The Heroes of God*. New York: Hawthorn, 1959.

Dean, William. *Memoir of Mrs. Lucy T. Lord of the Chinese Baptist Missions*. Philadelphia: n.p., 1854.

Drewery, Mary. *William Carey: A Biography*. Grand Rapids: Zondervan, 1979.

Eddy, Daniel. *Heroines of the Missionary Enterprise: Sketches of Prominent Female Missionaries*. London: Arthur Hall, Virtue, and Co., 1858.

Eddy, Sherwood. *Pathfinders of the World Missionary Crusade*. New York: Abingdon-Cokesbury, 1945.

Garrett, Shirley S. "Sisters All: Feminism and the American Women's Missionary Movement." In Torben Christensen and William R. Hutchinson, eds. *Missionary Ideologies in the Imperialist Era: 1800–1920*. Denmark: Aros, 1982.

Hill, Patricia R. "Heathen Women's Friend: The Role of Methodist Episcopal Women in Women's Foreign Mission Movement, 1869–1915." *Methodist History.* Pages 146–54.

————. *The World Their Household: The American Woman's Foreign Mission Movement and Cultural Transformation, 1870–1920.* Ann Arbor: University of Michigan Press, 1985.

Houghton, Frank. *Amy Carmichael of Dohnavur.* London: Society for the Propagation of Christian Knowledge, 1954.

Hull, Eleanor. *Women Who Carried the Good News: The History of the Woman's American Baptist Home Mission Society.* Valley Forge: Judson, 1975.

Hunt, Alma. *History of the Woman's Missionary Union.* Nashville: Convention, 1964.

Hunter, Jane. *The Gospel of Gentility: American Women Missionaries in Turn-of-Century China.* New Haven: Yale University Press, 1984.

Hyatt, Irwin. *Our Ordered Lives Confess: Three Nineteenth-Century American Missionaries in East Shantung.* Cambridge: Harvard University Press, 1976.

Jacobs, Sylvia M. "Their 'Special Mission': Afro-American Women as Missionaries to the Congo, 1894–1937." In Sylvia M. Jacobs, ed. *Black Americans and the Missionary Movement in Africa.* Westport, Conn.: Greenwood, 1982.

Kellersberger, Julia. *A Life for the Congo: The Story of Althea Brown Edmiston.* New York: Revell, 1947.

Kittler, Glenn D. *The Woman God Loved.* Garden City: Hanover, 1959.

Latourette, Kenneth Scott. *A History of the Expansion of Christianity: Three Centuries of Advance, 1500–1800.* Vol. 3. Grand Rapids: Zondervan, 1970.

Leitch, Elisabeth Elliot. "The Place of Women in World Missions." In David M. Howard, ed. *Jesus Christ: Lord of the Universe, Hope of the World.* Downers Grove: InterVarsity, 1974.

Leonard, Delavan L. *A Hundred Years of Missions: The Story of Progress Since Carey's Beginning.* New York: Funk & Wagnalls, 1895.

Lutz, Lorry. *Born to Lose, Bound to Win: The Amazing Journey of Mother Eliza George.* Irvine, Calif.: Harvest, 1980.

Mahoumet, Fatima. "Ann Croft and the Fulani." In Ralph D. Winter and Steven C. Hawthorne, eds. *Perspectives on the World Christian Movement.* Pasadena: William Carey, 1981.

Mathews, Winifred. *Dauntless Women: Stories of Pioneer Wives.* Freeport, N.Y.: Friendship, 1974.

Montgomery, Helen Barrett. *Western Women in Eastern Lands.* New York: Macmillan, 1910.

Moorhouse, Geoffrey. *The Missionaries.* London: Methuen, 1973.

Neill, Stephen. *A History of Christian Missions.* New York: Penguin, 1964.

Nilsen, Maria. *Malla Moe.* Chicago: Moody, 1956.

Parkman, Francis. *The Jesuits in North America in the Seventeenth Century.* Boston: Little, Brown, 1868.

Pierson, A. T. "The Outlook for the Twentieth Century." *Missionary Review of the World* 14 (March 1901): 167–68.

Pitman, E. R. *Lady Missionaries in Many Lands.* London: Pickering & Inglis, n.d.

Pollock, John C. *Hudson Taylor and Maria: Pioneers in China.* Grand Rapids: Zondervan, 1962.

Ransford, Oliver. *David Livingston: The Dark Interior.* New York: St. Martin's, 1978.

Roseveare, Helen. "Interview With Helen Roseveare." *His* (January 1977).

————. *Give Me This Mountain.* London: Inter-Varsity, 1966.

_____. *He Gave Us a Valley.* Downers Grove: InterVarsity, 1976.

Seaver, George. *David Livingstone: His Life and Letters.* New York: Harper & Brothers, 1957.

Sorrill, Bobbie. *Annie Armstrong: Dreamer in Action.* Nashville: Broadman, 1984.

Speer, Robert. *Servants of the King.* New York: Interchurch, 1909.

Stenbock, Evelyn. *Miss Terri: The Story of Maude Cary, Pioneer GMU Missionary in Morocco.* Lincoln, Neb.: Good News Broadcasting, 1970.

Thoburn, James. *Life of Isabella Thoburn.* Cincinnati: Jennings and Pye, 1903.

Thomas, E., and Elizabeth S. Brewster. "Bonding and the Missionary Task: Establishing a Sense of Belonging." In Ralph Winter and Steven Hawthorne, eds. *Perspectives of the World Christian Movement.* Pasadena: William Carey, 1981.

Thompson, A. E. *The Life of A. B. Simpson.* New York: Christian Alliance, 1920

Thompson, Phyllis. *A Transparent Woman: The Compelling Story of Gladys Aylward.* Grand Rapids: Zondervan, 1971.

_____. *Count It All Joy: The Story of Joy Ridderhof and Gospel Recordings.* Wheaton: Shaw, 1978.

Tucker, Ruth A. "African Women's Movement Finds Massive Response." *Evangelical Missions Quarterly* 22 (July 1986): 282–90.

_____. "Female Mission Strategists: A Historical and Contemporary Perspective." *Missiology* 15 (January 1987): 73–89.

_____. *From Jerusalem to Irian Jaya: A Biographical History of Christian Missions.* Grand Rapids: Zondervan, 1983.

Underwood, Mrs. Horace G. "Woman's Work for Women in Korea." *Missionary Review of the World* 18 (July 1905): 498–500.

Vail, Albert L. *Mary Webb and the Mother Society.* Philadelphia: American Baptist Publication Society, 1914.

Van Liere, Carma. "Sarah Doremus: Reformed Church Saint." *The Church Herald* (October 4, 1985), 16–17.

Wallis, Ethel E. *The Dayuma Story: Life Under Auca Spears.* New York: Harper & Row, 1960.

Wallis, Ethel, and Mary Bennett. *Two Thousand Tongues to Go.* New York: Harper & Row, 1959.

Welter, Barbara. "She Hath Done What She Could: Protestant Women's Missionary Careers in Nineteenth-Century America." In Janet Wilson James, ed. *Women in American Religion.* Philadelphia: University of Pennsylvania Press, 1980. Pages 111–25.

Wilson, Dorothy Clarke. *Dr. Ida: The Story of Dr. Ida Scudder of Vellore.* New York: McGraw, 1959.

_____. *Palace of Healing: The Story of Dr. Clara Swain, First Woman Missionary Doctor and the Hospital She Founded.* New York: McGraw-Hill, 1968.

CHAPTER 9
WOMEN IN THE THIRD-WORLD CHURCH

Adhav, Shamsundar Manohar. *Pandita Ramabai.* Madras: Christian Literature Society. 1979.

Barrett, David. *Schism and Renewal in Africa.* Nairobi: Oxford University Press, 1968.

Barton, James L. "Bible Women in Ceylon and India." *Life and Light* 32 (May 1902): 203–8.

Bliss, Kathleen. *The Service and Status of Women in the Churches.* London: SCM, 1952.

Brandel-Syrier, Mia. "The Role of Women in African Independent Churches." *Missionalia* 12 (April 1984): 14–15.

Burton, Margaret, E. *The Education of Women in China.* Old Tappan, N. J.: Revell, 1911.

————. *Women Workers of the Orient.* West Bedford, Mass.: Central Committee on the United Study of Foreign Mission, 1918.

Campbell, Penelope. "Presbyterian West African Missions: Women as Converts and Agents of Social Change." *Journal of Presbyterian History* 52 (Summer 1978): 121–32.

Cecchini, Rose Maria. "A Witness for Peace: The Experience of Japan YWCA." *International Review of Mission* 73 (July 1984): 336-39.

Chai, Alice. "Korean Women in Hawaii, 1903–1945." In Hilah Thomas and Rosemary Keller, eds. *Women in New Worlds.* Nashville: Abingdon, 1981. Pages 328–44.

Ching, Lucy. *One of the Lucky Ones.* Hong Kong: Gulliver, 1980.

Dreyer, Edith G. *Light and Shadow in China.* London: China Inland Mission, n.d.

Dyer, Helen S. *Pandita Ramabai: Her Vision, Her Mission and Triumph of Faith.* London: Pickering & Inglis, n.d.

Egan, Eileen. *Such a Vision of the Street: Mother Teresa—The Spirit and the Work.* Garden City: Doubleday, 1985.

Falk, Peter. *The Growth of the Church in Africa.* Grand Rapids: Zondervan, 1979.

Finley, Allen and Lorry Luta. *Mission: A World-Family Affair.* San Jose: Christian National, 1981.

Forman, Charles W. " 'Sing to the Lord a New Song': Women in the Churches of Oceania." In Denise O'Brien and Sharon W. Tiffany, eds. *Rethinking Women's Roles: Perspectives From the Pacific.* Los Angeles: University of California Press, 1984.

Garret, Shirley S. "Images of Chinese Women." In John Webster and Ellen Webster, eds. *The Church and Women in the Third World.* Philadelphia: Westminster, 1985. Pages 21–34.

Gilfeather, Katherine. "Coming of Age in a Latin Church." In John Webster and Ellen Webster, eds. *The Church and Women in the Third World.* Philadelphia: Westminster, 1985. Pages 58–73.

Goforth, Rosalind. *Climbing: Memories of a Missionary's Wife.* Chicago: Moody, n.d.

Hastings, Adrian. *A History of African Christianity, 1950–1975.* London: Cambridge University Press, 1979.

Hiebert, Frances. "Missionary Women as Models in the Cross-Cultural Context." *Missiology* 10 (October 1982): 455–60.

Hitt, Russell T. *Sensei: The Life Story of Irene Webster-Smith.* New York: Harper & Row, 1956.

Houghton, Frank. *Amy Carmichael of Dohnavur.* London: Society for the Propagation of Christian Knowledge, 1954.

Hunter, Edward. *The Story of Mary Liu.* New York: Tarrar, Straus and Cudahy, 1957.

Hyo-Jae, Yi. "Christian Women and the Liberation of Korean Women." *The International Review of Missions* 74 (January 1985): 93–102.

Isais, Elizabeth F. "The Problem Facing Latin American Women in Leadership." *Interlit* (September 1981).

Isasi-Diaz, Ada Maria. "Silent Women Will Never Be Heard." *Missiology* 7 (July 1979): 295–301.

Kellersberger, Julia. *Congo Crosses: A Study of Congo Womanhood.* Boston: Central Committee on the United Study of Foreign Missions, 1936.

Koch, Kurt. *The Revival in Indonesia.* Grand Rapids: Kregal, 1970.

Latourette, Kenneth Scott. *A History of Christian Missions in China.* New York: Macmillan, 1929.

Lehmann, Dorothea A. "Women in the African Independent Churches." In Victor E. W. Hayward, ed. *African Independent Church Movements.* London: Edinburgh House, 1963. Pages 65–69.

Li, Jeanette. *The Autobiography of a Chinese Christian.* Translated by Rose Huston. London: Banner of Truth, 1971.

Montgomery, Barrett. *Western Women in Eastern Lands: An Outline of Fifty Years of Women's Work in Foreign Missions.* New York: Macmillan, 1910.

Oduyoye, Mercy Amba. "Standing on Both Feet: Education and Leadership Training of Women in the Methodist Church, Nigeria." *Ecumenical Review* 33 (January 1981): 60–71.

Picket, J. Waskom. *Christian Mass Movements in India.* New York: Abingdon, 1933.
————. *Christ's Way to India's Heart.* Lucknow: Lucknow, 1938.

Pirouet, Louise M. "Women Missionaries of the Church Missionary Society in Uganda." In Torben Christenson and William R. Hutchinson, eds. *Missionary Ideologies in the Imperialist Era: 1880–1920.* Denmark: Aros, 1982. Pages 231–39.

Ramabai, Pundita. *The High-Caste Hindu Woman.* London: Bell, 1888.

Siwani, Joyce. "Mission Issues in South Africa." *International Review of Mission* 73 (July 1984): 328–34.

Subbamma, B. V. *New Patterns for Discipling Hindus.* Pasadena: William Carey Library, 1970.

Thomas, Winburn R. *Protestant Beginnings in Japan: The First Three Decades, 1859–1889.* Rutland, Vt.: Tuttle, 1959.

Tsai, Christiana. *Queen of the Dark Camber.* Chicago: Moody, 1953.

Tucker, Ruth A. "The Role of Bible Women in World Evangelism." *Missiology* 13 (April 1985): 133–46.

Webster, John. "Assumptions About the Indian Woman Underlying Protestant Church Policies and Programs, 1947–1982." In John Webster and Ellen Webster, eds. *The Church and Women in the Third World.* Philadelphia: Westminster, 1985. Pages 35–47.

Wilson, Dorothy Clarke. *Dr. Ida: The Story of Dr. Ida Scudder of Vellore.* New York: McGraw-Hill, 1959.

CHAPTER 10
THE TWENTIETH CENTURY

A Historical Account of the Apostolic Faith. Portland, Ore.: The Apostolic Faith, 1965.

Abbott, Lyman. *The Home Builder.* New York: Houghton-Mifflin, 1908.

Baldwin, Ethel M., and David V Benson. *Henrietta Mears and How She Did It.* Glendale, Calif.: Gospel Light, 1966.

Barfoot, Charles H., and Gerald T. Sheppard. "Prophetic vs. Priestly Religion: The Changing Role of Women Clergy in Classical Pentecostal Churches." *Review of Religious Research* 22 (September 1980): 2–17.

Barr, Robert. *Least of All Saints: The Story of Aimee Semple McPherson.* Englewood Cliffs, N. J.: Prentice-Hall, 1979.

Berry, Jo. *Growing, Sharing, Serving.* Elgin, Ill.: David C. Cook, 1979. Pages 66–67.

Boyd, Lois A., and R. Douglas Brackenridge. *Presbyterian Women in America: Two Centuries of a Quest for Status.* London: Greenwood, 1983.

Brereton, Virginia and Christa Klein. "American Women in Ministry: A History of Protestant Beginning Points." In Rosemary Ruether and Eleanor McLaughlin. *Women of Spirit: Female Leaders in the Jewish and Christian Traditions.* New York: Simon and Schuster, 1979. Pages 301–32.

Buckingham, Jamie. *Daughter of Destiny: Kathryn Kuhlman . . . Her Story.* Plainfield, N. J.: Logos, 1976. Pages 125–26.

Buursma, Bruce. "Women Pastors Split Southern Baptists," *Chicago Tribune,* February 18, 1984.

Calkins, Gladys G. *Follow Those Women: Church Women in the Ecumenical Movement.* New York: National Council of the Churches of Christ in the U.S.A., 1961.

Cummings, Mary Lou. "Ordained Into Ministry: Ann J. Allebach." In Mary Lou Cummings, ed. *Full Circle: Stories of Mennonite Women,* Newton, Kansas: Faith and Life, 1978. Pages 2–8.

Dougherty, Mary Agnes. "The Social Gospel According to Phoebe." In Hilah F. Thomas and Rosemary Keller. *Women in New Worlds.* Nashville: Abingdon, 1981. Pages 200–216.

Evangeline, Hope. *Daisy.* Grand Rapids: Baker, 1978.

Fredrick Franson. *Prophesying Daughters: A Few Words Concerning Women's Position in Regard to Evangelization.* Stockholm, 1897.

Garber, Rebecca P. *The Social Gospel and Its View of Women and the Women's Movement, 1880–1919.* Trinity Evangelical Divinity School: M. A. Thesis, 1978.

Hardesty, Nancy, Lucille Dayton, and Donald Dayton, "Women in the Holiness Movement: Feminism in the Evangelical Tradition." In Rosemary Ruether and Eleanor McLauhglin, eds. *Women of Spirit.* New York: Simon and Schuster, 1979. Pages 225–54.

Harris, Barbara C. "Pentecost Revisited." *The Witness* (Special issue, 1984), 10.

Heeney, Brian, "The Beginning of Church Feminism." *Journal of Ecclesiastical History* 33 (January 1982): 101–5.

Hendrickson, Ford. *Martyrs and Witnesses.* Detroit: Protestant Missionary, 1917.

Henry, James O. *For Such a Time as This: A History of the Independent Fundamental Church of America.* Westchester, Ill.: IFCA, 1983. Page 49.

Huyck, Heather. "Indelible Change: Women Priests in the Episcopal Church." *Historical Magazine of the Protestant Episcopal Church* 51 (December 1982).

James, Janet Wilson, ed. *Women in American Religion.* Philadelphia: University of Pennsylvania Press, 1980.

Johnson, Dale A. *Women in English Religion, 1700–1925.* New York: Mellen, 1983.

Kenneally, James. J. "Eve, Mary, and the Historians." In Janet James, ed. *Women in American Religion.* Philadelphia: University of Pennsylvania Press, 1980.

Klinglesmith, Sharon. "Women in the Mennonite Church, 1900–1920." *The Mennonite Quarterly Review* 54 (July 1980): 163–207.

Kuhlman, Kathryn. *I Believe in Miracles.* Englewood Cliffs, N.J.: Prentice-Hall, 1962.

LaHaye, Beverly. *The Restless Woman.* Grand Rapids: Zondervan, 1984. Page 89.

Larsson, Flora. *My Best Men Are Women.* London: Hodder and Stoughton, 1974.

Lindberg, Frank T. *Looking Back Fifty Years.* Minneapolis: Franklin Printing, n.d.

McBeth, Leon. *Women in Baptist Life.* Nashville: Broadman, 1979.

McKinley, Edward H. *Marching to Glory: The History of the Salvation Army in the United States.* New York: Harper & Row, 1980.

McPherson, Aimee Semple. *The Story of My Life.* Waco: Word, 1973.

_____. *This Is That.* Los Angeles: Echo Part Evangelistic Association, 1923.

Mitchell, Robert B. *Heritage and Horizons: The History of Open Bible Standard Churches.* Des Moines: Open Bible Publishers, 1982.

Morris, James. *The Preachers.* New York: St. Martin's, 1973.

Nelson, E. Clifford. *Lutheranism in North America, 1914–1970.* Minneapolis: Augsburg, 1972.

Nichol, John T. *The Pentecostals.* Plainfield, N.J.: Logos, 1966.

Olson, Della E. *A Woman of Her Times.* Minneapolis: Free Church, 1977.

Pape, Dorthy R. *In Search of God's Ideal Woman.* Downers Grove: InterVarsity, 1976.

Parham, Sarah E. *The Life of Charles F. Parham, Founder of the Apostolic Faith Movement.* Joplin, Mo.: Hunter, 1930.

Rees, Byron. *Hulda A. Rees: The Pentecostal Prophetess.* Philadelphia: Christian Standard, 1898.

Rees, Seth Cook. *The Ideal Pentecostal Church.* Cincinnati: Knapp, 1897.

Rich, Elaine S. *Mennonite Women: A Story of God's Faithfulness, 1683–1983.* Scottdale, Pa.: Herald, 1983.

Ruether, Rosemary. "Entering the Sanctuary: The Roman Catholic Story." In Rosemary Ruether and Eleanor McLaughlin, eds. *Women of Spirit.* New York: Simon and Schuster, 1979. Pages 373–83.

Schmidt, Elisabeth. *When God Calls a Woman: The Struggle of a Woman Pastor in France and Algeria.* Translated by Allen Hackett, N.Y.: Pilgrim, 1981.

Smith, Timothy L. *Called Unto Holiness.* Kansas City, Mo.: Nazarene, 1962.

Spykman, Gordon J., and Lillian V. Grissen. *Men and Women: Partners in Service.* Kalamazoo: Christian Reformed Church, 1981.

Synan, Vinson. *The Holiness-Pentecostal Movement in the United States.* Grand Rapids: Eerdmans, 1971.

ten Boom, Corrie. *Tramp for the Lord.* Old Tappan, N.J.: Revell, 1974. Pages 16, 18.

Tobin, Mary L. "Women in the Church: Vatican II and After." *Ecumenical Review* 37 (July 1985): 295–305.

Troutt, Margaret. *The General Was a Lady: The Story of Evangeline Booth.* Nashville: Holman, 1980.

Verdesi, Elizabeth Howell. *In But Still Out: Women in the Church.* Philadelphia: Westminster, 1975.

White, Alma. *Demons and Tongues.* Zaraphath, N.J.: Pillar of Fire, 1949.

_____. *The New Testament Church.* Bound Brook, N.J.: Pentecostal Union, 1912.

Woodworth-Etter, Mary B. *Marvels and Miracles.* Indianapolis: Woodwarth-Etter, 1922.

_____. *Signs and Wonders: God Wrought in the Ministry for Forty Years.* Tulsa: Harrison, 1916.

Wyker, Mossie A. *Church Women in the Scheme of Things.* St. Louis: Bethany, 1953.

CHAPTER 11 AND APPENDIXES
THE CONTEMPORARY CHURCH FACES THE ISSUES

Note: Most of the resources for studying the exegetical issues in appendix B are listed in the bibliography for chapters 1 and 2.

Abel, Elizabeth, and Emily K. Abel. *The Signs Reader: Women, Gender and Scholarship*. Chicago: University of Chicago Press, 1983.

Achtemeier, Elizabeth. *The Feminine Crisis in Christian Faith*. New York: Abingdon, n.d.

Adeney, Miriam. "Women of Fire: A Response to Waltke, Nolland and Gasque." *CRUX* 19:3 (September 1983): 24–31.

Allen, Ronald, and Beverly Allen. *Liberated Traditionalism: Men and Women in Balance*. Portland, Ore.: Multnomah, 1985.

Andelin, Helen. *Fascinating Womanhood*. Santa Barbara, Calif.: Pacific, 1965.

Anderson, Ray S. "The Resurrection of Jesus as Hermeneutical Criterion (part 2): A Case for Sexual Parity in Pastoral Ministry." TSF Bulletin 9, no. 4 (1986): 15–20.

Andolsen, Barbara Hilkert. "Gender and Sex Roles in Recent Religious Ethics Literature." *Religious Studies Review* 11 (1985): 217–23.

Barnhouse, Ruth Tiffany, and Urban T. Holmes, III, eds. *Male and Female: Christian Approaches to Sexuality*. New York: Seabury, 1976.

Bartchy, S. Scott. "Human Sexuality and Our Identity." *Mission Journal* 17:5 (November 1983): 10–14.

————. "Jesus, Power, and Gender Roles." *TSF Bulletin* 7 (1984): 2–4.

————. "Power, Submission, and Sexual Identity Among the Early Christians." In *Essays on New Testament Christianity*. Edited by C. Robert Wetzel. Cincinnati: Standard Publishing, 1978.

Barth, Karl. *Church Dogmatics* 3, sec. 4. Edited and translated by G. W. Bromily and T. F. Torrance. Edinburgh: T. & T. Clark, 1961.

————. *How I Changed My Mind*. Richmond: John Knox, 1966.

de Beauvoir, Simone. *The Second Sex*. Translated by H. M. Parshley. New York: Alfred A. Knopf, 1952.

Bilezikian, Gilbert. *Beyond Sex Roles*. Grand Rapids: Baker, 1985.

Bloesch, Donald G. *Is the Bible Sexist?* Westchester, Ill.: Crossway, 1982.

————. *The Battle for the Trinity*. Ann Arbor: Servant, 1985.

Boldrey, Richard, and Joyce Boldrey. *Chauvinist or Feminist: Paul's View of Women*. Grand Rapids: Baker, 1976.

Borker, Ruth. "To Honor Her Head: Hats as a Symbol of Women's Position in Three Evangelical Churches in Edinburgh, Scotland." *Women in Ritual and Symbolic Roles,* Judith Hoch-Smith and Anita Spring, eds. New York: Plenum, 1978.

Boucher, Madeleine. "Some unexplored parallels in 1 Cor.11,11–12 on Gal. 3,28: The NT on the Role of Women." *Catholic Biblical Quarterly* 31 (1969).

————. "New Data on Ordination: A Rejoinder." *America* 143 (1980) 306–7.

Briscoe, Jill. "The Biblical Woman: But What Can She Do?" *Moody Monthly* (February 1983), 15.

Briscoe, Stuart. "The Biblical Woman: We've Buried a Treasure." *Moody Monthly* (February 1983), 5–6.

Bruce, Michael, and G. E. Duffield, eds. *Why Not? Priesthood and the Ministry of Women*. Appleford, Abingdon, Berkshire: The Marcham Manor, 1976.

Bullough, Vern L. *The Subordinate Sex*. Urbana: University of Illinois Press, 1973.

Burghardt, S.J., Walter, ed. *Woman: New Dimensions*. New York: Ramsey; Toronto: Paulist, 1975.

Bushnell, Katherine C. *God's Word to Women*. 1919. Privately reprinted by Ray B. Munson.

Catholic Biblical Association of America's Task Force on the Role of Women in Early Christianity. "Women and Priestly Ministry: The New Testament Evidence." *Catholic Biblical Quarterly* 41 (1979).

Cerling, C. E., Jr. "Women Ministers in the New Testament Church." *Journal of the Evangelical Theological Society* 19 (1976): 209–15.

Christ, Carol P. "The New Feminist Theology: A Review of the Literature." *Religious Studies Review* 3 (1977): 203–12.

Christ, Carol P., and Judith Plaskow, eds. *Womanspirit Rising*. San Francisco: Harper & Row, 1979.

Christenson, Larry. *The Christian Family*. Minneapolis: Bethany, 1970.

Clark, Elizabeth, and Herbert Richardson, eds. *Women and Religion: A Feminist Sourcebook of Christian Thought*. New York: Harper & Row, 1977.

Clark, Stephen B. *Man and Woman in Christ*. Ann Arbor, Mich.: Servant, 1980.

Conn, Harvie M. "Evangelical Feminism: Reflections on the State of the 'Union.'" *TSF Bulletin* 8 (November–December 1984): 20–23, (January–February 1985): 18–21.

Craston, Colin. "The Case for the Ordination of Women: Reasons for Acting Now." *Churchman* 92 (1978): 294–309.

Cunningham, Sr. Agnes, S.S.C.M. "Ecclesial Ministry for Women." In *Future Forms for Ministry*. Edited by R. McCormick and G. Dyer (1971). Pages 103–11.

————. "The Role of Women in Church and Society." In *Catholic Theological Society 28th Convention*. Edited by W. Burghardt et al. (1973). Pages 219–23.

————. *Women in Ministry: A Sister's View*. Chicago: National Association of Women Religious, 1972.

————. *The Role of Women in Ecclesial Ministry: Biblical and Patristic Foundations*. Published by the United States Catholic Conference, n.d., about 1976/77.

Daly, Mary. *The Church and the Second Sex*. New York: Harper & Row, 1968.

————. *Gyn/Ecology*. Boston: Beacon, 1978.

————. *Beyond God the Father: Toward a Philosophy of Women's Liberation*. Boston: Beacon, 1973.

————. *Pure Lust: Elemental Feminist Philosophy*. Boston: Beacon, 1984.

Davis, John Jefferson. "Some Reflections on Galatians 3:28: Sexual Roles and Biblical Hermeneutics." *Journal of the Evangelical Theological Society* 19 (1976): 202–4.

DeJong, Peter, and Donald R. Wilson. *Husband and Wife*. Grand Rapids: Zondervan, 1979.

Donelson, Elaine, and Jeanne E. Gullahorn. *Women: A Psychological Perspective*. New York: Wiley, 1977.

Dorff, Elliott N. "Equality With Distinction." *University Papers*. The University of Judaism. (March 1984), 12–23.

Duberman, Lucile. *Gender and Sex in Society*. New York: Praeger, 1975.

Edwards, James R. "Does God Really Want to be Called 'Father'?" *Christianity Today* (February 21, 1986), 27–29.

Elliot, Elisabeth. *Let Me Be a Woman*. Wheaton: Tyndale, 1976.

————. "The Biblical Woman: But What Can She Do?" *Moody Monthly* (February 1983): 12.

Evans, Mary J. *Women in the Bible*. Downers Grove: InterVarsity, 1983.

Fiorenza, Elisabeth Schüssler. *Bread, Not Stone: The Challenge of Feminist Biblical Interpretation*. Boston: Beacon, 1984.

————. "Die Beitrag der Frau zur urchristlichen Bewegung, Kritische Überlegung zur Rekonstruction unchristlicher Geschichte." In Willy Schottroff and Wolfgang Stegemann, *Tradition der Befreiung*, Band 2, *Frauen in der Bibel*. Munich: Kaiser and Gelnhausen: Burckhardthaus-Laetare, 1980.

————. *In Memory of Her*. New York: Crossroad, 1983.

————. "The Study of Women in Early Christianity." *Women Priests: A Catholic Commentary on the Vatican Declaration.* New York: Paulist, 1977, 114–23, 135–40.

Fiorenza, Elisabeth Schüssler, and Mary Collins, eds. *Women: Invisible in Church and Theology,* Concilium 182. Edinburg: T. & T. Clark, n.d.

Fitzwater, P. B. *Women: Her Mission, Position, and Ministry.* Grand Rapids: Eerdmans, 1949.

Foh, Susan. *Women and the Word of God: A Response to Biblical Feminism.* Grand Rapids: Baker, 1981.

Friedan, Betty. *The Feminine Mystique.* New York: Norton, 1963.

Gardiner, Anne Marie, S.S.N.D. *Women and Catholic Priesthood: An Expanded Vision.* Proceedings of the Detroit Ordination Conference. New York: Paulist, 1976.

Gasque, Ward. "The Role of Women in the Church, in Society, and in the Home." *CRUX* 19:3 (September 1983): 3–9.

Gibson, Elsie. *When the Minister Is a Woman.* New York: Holt, Rinehart and Winston, 1970.

Giles, Kevin. *Women and Their Ministry: A Case for Equal Ministries in the Church Today.* Victoria, Australia: Dove, 1977.

Glass, Judith. "Beyond Sex Roles." *University Papers.* University of Judaism. (March 1984), 1–11.

Goldenberg, Naomi R. *Changing of the Gods: Feminism and the End of Traditional Religions.* Boston: Beacon, 1979.

Gordon, A. J. "The Ministry of Women." *Missionary Review of the World* 7:12, New Series (December 1894): 910–21.

Gothard, William. Manual, copyrighted in 1969, Section entitled "Principles of God's Chain-of-Command." Privately circulated.

Greer, Germaine. *The Female Eunuch.* New York: McGraw-Hill, 1971.

Gundry, Patricia. *Neither Slave nor Free: Helping Women Answer the Call to Church Leadership.* San Francisco: Harper & Row, 1987.

————. *The Complete Woman.* Garden City: Doubleday, 1981.

————. *Woman Be Free.* Grand Rapids: Zondervan, 1977.

Hagemann, A. L., ed. *Sexist Religion and Women in the Church.* New York: Association, 1974.

Hamilton, Michael P., and Nancy S. Montgomery, eds. *The Ordination of Women: Pro and Con.* New York: Morehouse-Barlow, 1975.

Harkness, Georgia. *Women in Church and Society: A Historical and Theological Inquiry.* Nashville: Abingdon, 1972.

Harper, Joyce. *Women and the Gospel.* Christian Brethren Research Fellowship Paper, 5. Middlesex: CBRF Publications, 1974.

Harrison, B. W. "The New Consciousness of Women: A Socio-Political Resource." *Cross-Currents* 24 (1975): 445–62.

Hebblethwaite, Margaret. *Motherhood and God.* London: Goeffrey Chapman, 1984.

Hestenes, Roberta, ed. *Women and Men in Ministry.* Pasadena, Calif.: Fuller Theological Seminary and Westminster, 1984.

Hewitt, Emily C., and Suzanne R. Hiatt. *Women Priests: Yes or No?* New York: Seabury, 1973.

Hommes, N. J. "Let Women Be Silent in the Church." *Calvin Theological Journal* 4 (1969): 5–22.

Howard, J. Keir. "Neither Male nor Female: An Examination of the Status of Women in the New Testament." *Evangelical Quarterly* 40 (1983): 31–42.

Howe, E. Margaret. "The Positive Case for the Ordination of Women." *Perspectives on Evangelical Theology: Papers From the Thirtieth Annual Meeting of the Evangelical Theological Society.* Edited by K. S. Kantzer and S. N. Gundry. Grand Rapids: Baker, 1979.

_____. *Women and Church Leadership.* Grand Rapids: Zondervan, 1982.

Hunt, Gladys. *Ms. Means MySelf.* Grand Rapids: Zondervan, 1972.

Hurley, James B. *Man and Woman in Biblical Perspective.* Grand Rapids: Zondervan, 1981.

An Inclusive Language Lectionary, vols. 1 and 2. Produced by National Council of Churches. *Readings for Year A* and *Readings for Year B.* Published for the Cooperative Publication Association, Atlanta: John Knox and other publishers, 1983, 1984.

Jepsen, Dee. *Women Beyond Equal Rights.* Waco: Word, 1971.

Jewett, Paul K. *Man as Male and Female.* Grand Rapids: Eerdmans, 1975.

_____. *The Ordination of Women: New Testament Perspectives.* Grand Rapids: Eerdmans, 1980.

Johnston, Robert K. "The Role of Women in the Church and Home: An Evangelical Test Case in Hermeneutics." *Scripture, Tradition, and Interpretation.* Essays presented to Everett F. Harrison. Edited by W. Gasque and William Sanford LaSor. Grand Rapids: Eerdmans, 1978.

Kahoe, Richard D. "Social Science of Gender Differences: Ideological Battleground." *Religious Studies Review* 11 (1985): 223–28.

Kaiser, Walter C. "Paul, Women and the Church." *Worldwide Challenge* (1976), 9–12.

Kaplan, Alexandra G., and Joan Bean. *Beyond Sex-Role Stereotypes: Readings Toward a Psychology of Androgyny.* Boston: Little Brown, 1976.

Knight, George W., III. "The Ordination of Women: No." *Christianity Today* 25 (1981): 260–63.

_____. *The Role Relationship of Men and Women: The New Testament Teaching.* Grand Rapids: Baker, 1977, 1985.

Kroeger, Catherine Clark, "1 Timothy 2:12—A Classicist's View." In Alvira Mickelsen, ed., *Women, Authority and the Bible* (Downers Grove: InterVarsity, 1968), 232–38.

LaHaye, Beverly. *I Am a Woman by God's Design.* Old Tappan, N.J.: Revell, 1980.

_____. *The Restless Woman.* Grand Rapids: Zondervan, 1984.

LaHaye, Tim. *The Battle for the Family.* Old Tappan, N.J.: Revell, 1982.

Lees, Shirley, ed. *The Role of Women: When Christians Disagree.* Leicester, England: Inter-Varsity, 1984.

Leipoldt, J. *Die Frau in der Antike Welt und im Urchristentum.* Leipzig, 1954.

Lewis, Alan E. "The Biblical Witness to Our Motherly Father." *Irish Biblical Studies* 7 (1984): 8–45.

Litfin, A. Duane, "Evangelical Feminism: Why Traditionalists Reject It." *Bibliotheca Sacra* 136 (1979): 158–271.

Loesch, Juli. "Weaknesses of Feminist Theology." *New Oxford Review* 51 (1984): 8–12.

Longenecker, Richard N. *New Testament Social Ethics for Today.* Grand Rapids: Eerdmans, 1984.

_____. "Authority, Hierarchy and Leadership Patterns in the Bible." In Alvera Mickelsen, ed. *Women, Authority and The Bible.* Downers Grove: InterVarsity, 1986, 66–84, with responses by Willard Swartley and Marianne Meye Thompson, 85–96.

Maccoby, Eleanor Ammons, and Carol Nagy Jacklin. *The Psychology of Sex Differences.* Stanford: Stanford University Press, 1974.

McFague, Sallie. *Metaphorical Theology: Models of God in Religious Language.* Philadelphia: Fortress, 1982.

McKenna, Mary Lawrence, S.C.M.M. *Women of the Church.* New York: McKenna, n.d.

McPhee, Carol, and Ann FitzGerald, compilers. *Feminist Quotations: Voices of Rebels, Reformers, and Visionaries.* New York: Thomas Y. Crowell, 1979.

Malbon, Elizabeth Struthers. "Fallible Followers: Women and Men in the Gospel of Mark," *Semeia* 28 (1983): 29–48.

Malcolm, Kari Torjesen. *Women at the Crossroads.* Downers Grove, Ill.: InterVarsity, 1982.

Mangan, O.P. Celine. *Can We Still Call God "Father"?* Wilmington, Del.: Glazier, 1984.

Mercadante, Linda. *From Hierarchy to Equality: A Comparison of Past and Present Interpretations of 1 Corinthians 11:2–16 in Relation to the Changing Status of Women in Society.* Vancouver, B.C: G.M.H. Books, Regent College, 1978.

Meyer, Charles R. "Ordained Women in the Early Church." *Chicago Studies* 4 (1965): 285–308.

Mickelsen, Alvera, ed. *Women, Authority and the Bible.* Downers Grove: InterVarsity, 1986.

Mickelsen, A. Berkeley, and Alvera Mickelsen. "Does Male Dominance Tarnish Our Translations?" *Christianity Today* (October 1979), 23–29.

Micks, Marianne H., and Charles P. Price, eds. *Toward a New Theology of Ordination: Essays on the Ordination of Women.* Summerville, Mass.: Greeno, Hadden, 1976.

Millett, Kate. *Sexual Politics.* Garden City, N.Y.: Doubleday, 1970.

Mollenkott, Virginia Ramey. *Women, Men and the Bible.* Nashville: Abingdon, 1977.

————. *The Divine Feminine.* New York: Crossroad, 1983.

Moltmann-Wendel, Elisabeth. *Liberty, Equality, Sisterhood.* Translated by Ruth C. Gritsch. Philadelphia: Fortress, 1978.

Montagu, Ashley. *The Natural Superiority of Women.* New York: Collier, 1970.

Morgan, Marabel. *The Total Woman.* New York: Pocket, 1975.

————. *Total Joy.* Old Tappan, N. J.: Revell, 1971.

Munro, W. "Patriarchy and Charismatic Community in 'Paul.'" In Plaskow and Romero, eds. *Women and Religion,* Missoula: Scholars, 1974, 189–98.

Neff, David. "What's a Woman to Do in Your Church or Your Chapter?" *HIS* (April 1985), 1–4.

Nolland, John. "Women in the Public Life of the Church." *CRUX* 19:3 (September 1983): 17–23.

Olthuis, James H. *I Pledge You My Troth.* New York: Harper & Row, 1975.

O'Meara, Thomas Franklin, O.P., *Theology of Ministry.* New York: Paulist, 1983.

Osborne, Grant R. "Hermeneutics and Women in the Church." *Journal of the Evangelical Theological Society* 20 (1977): 337–52.

Otwell, John. *And Sarah Laughed: The Status of Woman in the Old Testament.* Philadelphia: Westminster, 1977.

Pape, Dorothy. *In Search of God's Ideal Woman.* Downers Grove: InterVarsity, 1976.

Penn-Lewis, Jessie. *The Magna Charta of Woman.* Minneapolis: Bethany, 1919.

Quere, Ralph. "'Naming' God 'Father.'" *Currents in Theology and Mission* 12 (1985), 5–14.

Raming, Ida. *The Exclusion of Women From the Priesthood: Divine Law or Sex Discrimination?* Translated by Norman R. Adams. Metuchen, N.J.: Scarecrow, 1976.

Religion in America—1981. The Gallup Organization and the Princeton Religion Research Center, 1981.

Rice, John R. *Bobbed Hair, Bossy Wives, and Women Preachers.* Murfreesboro, Tenn.: Sword of the Lord Publishers, 1941.

Robbins, John W. *Scripture Twisting in the Seminaries,* Part I: Feminism. Jefferson, Md.: Trinity Foundation, 1985.

Rogers, Olive. "The Role of Women in the Church." *Christian Brethren Review* 33 (December 1982): 57–68.

Ruether, Rosemary Radford. *Liberation Theology: Human Hope Confronts Christian History and American Power.* New York: Paulist, 1972.

————. *New Woman, New Earth.* New York: Seabury, 1975.

————. "Of One Humanity." *Sojourners* (January 1984), 17–18.

————. *Religion and Sexism: Images of Women in the Jewish and Christian Traditions.* New York: Simon and Schuster, 1974.

————. *Sexism and God-Talk.* Boston: Beacon, 1983.

————. *Womanguide: Readings Toward a Feminist Theology.* Boston: Beacon, 1985.

Ruether, Rosemary Radford, and Eleanor McLaughlin, eds. *Women of Spirit: Female Leadership in the Jewish and Christian Traditions.* New York: Simon and Schuster, 1979.

Russell, Letty M. *Human Liberation in a Feminist Perspective: A Theology.* Philadelphia: Westminster, 1974.

Ryrie, Charles C. *The Place of Women in the Church.* New York: Macmillan, 1958.

Sannella, Lucia. *The Female Pentecost.* Port Washington, N.Y.: Ashley, 1976.

Sargent, Alice G. *Beyond Sex Roles.* St. Paul: West, 1977.

Saucy, Robert L. "The Negative Case Against the Ordination of Women." In K. S. Kantzer and S. N. Gundry, eds. *Perspectives on Evangelical Theology: Papers From the Thirtieth Annual Meeting of the ETS.* Grand Rapids: Baker, 1979. Page 278.

Scanzoni, John. *Sex Roles, Life Styles, and Childbearing: Changing Patterns in Marriage and the Family.* New York: Free, 1975.

Scanzoni, Letha, and Nancy Hardesty. *All We're Meant to Be.* Waco: Word, 1974.

————. Interview in *Radix* (March–April 1984), 4–9.

Scholer, David M. "Women in Ministry." *The Covenant Companion* (December 1, 1983), 8–9; (December 15, 1983), 14–15; (January 1984), 12–13; (February 1984), 12–15.

————. "Women's Adornment." *Daughters of Sarah* 6 (1980): 3–6.

Spencer, Aída Besançon. *Beyond the Curse: Women Called to Ministry.* Nashville: Nelson, 1985.

Stagg, Frank, and Evelyn Stagg. *Woman in the World of Jesus.* Philadelphia: Westminster, 1978.

Stendahl, Krister. *The Bible and the Role of Women: A Case Study in Hermenutics.* Facet Books—Biblical Series 15. Philadelphia: Fortress, 1966.

Steinem, Gloria. "Pink-Collar Workers." *Progressive* (May 1977).

Storkey, Elaine. *What's Right With Feminism.* Grand Rapids: Eerdmans, 1985.

Stouffer, Austin H. "The Ordination of Women: Yes." *Christianity Today* 25 (1981): 12–15.

Stuhlmueller, Carroll, ed. *Women and Priesthood.* Collegeville, Minn.: Liturgical, 1978.

Swartley, Willard M. *Slavery, Sabbath, War, and Women: Case Issues in Biblical Interpretation.* Scottdale, Pa., and Kitchener, Ont.: Herald, 1983.

Swidler, Leonard, and Arlene Swidler, eds. *Women Priests: A Catholic Commentary on the Vatican Declaration.* New York: Paulist, 1977.

Swidler, Leonard, and Arlene Swidler, trans. *Women Priests in the Catholic Church?: A Theological-Historical Investigation.* Philadelphia: Temple University Press, 1973.

Teitelbaum, Michael S., ed. *Sex Differences*. Garden City: Anchor/Doubleday, 1976.

Tetlow, Elizabeth. *Women and Ministry in the New Testament*. New York and Ramsey, N. J.: Paulist, 1980.

Tetlow, Elizabeth, and Louis Mulry Tetlow. *Partners in Service*. Lanham, Md.: University of America, 1983.

Theology News and Notes: Women in Ministry (1985). Published for the Fuller Theological Seminary Alumni/ae.

Thrall, M. E. *The Ordination of Women to the Priesthood: A Study of the Biblical Evidence*. London: SCM, 1958.

Tolbert, Mary Ann. "Defining the Problem: The Bible and Feminist Hermeneutics." *Semeia* 28 (1983): 113–26.

Trible, Phyllis. *God and the Rhetoric of Sexuality*. Philadelphia: Fortress, 1978.

————. *Texts of Terror: Literary Feminist Readings of Biblical Narratives*. Philadelphia: Fortress, 1984.

Vanauken, Sheldon. *A Severe Mercy*. Nashville: Nelson, 1985.

van der Meer, Haye, S.J. *Women Priests in the Cathoic Church?* Translated by Arlene and Leonard Swidler. Philadelphia: Temple University Press, 1973.

Walker, William O., Jr. "1 Corinthians and Paul's Views Regarding Women." *Journal of Biblical Literature* 94 (1975): 94–110.

Warkentin, Marjorie. *Ordination: A Biblical-Historical View*. Grand Rapids: Eerdmans, 1982.

Weidman, Judith L. *Women Ministers*. San Francisco: Harper & Row, 1981.

Weidman, Judith L., ed. *Christian Feminism: Visions of a New Humanity*. San Francisco: Harper & Row, 1984.

Wenham, Gordon. "The Ordination of Women: Why Is It So Divisive?" *Churchman* 92 (1978): 310–19.

White, Richard C. "Inclusive Language: A Personal Interpretation." *Lexington Theological Quarterly* 20 (1985): 51–57.

Williams, Don. *The Apostle Paul and Women in the Church*. Van Nuys, Calif.: BIM, 1977.

Woman's Pulpit. This is the official journal of the International Association of Women Ministers.

Yamauchi, Edwin, M. "Cultural Aspects of Marriage in the Ancient World." *Bibliotheca Sacra* 135 (1978): 241–52.

SUBJECT INDEX

SCRIPTURE INDEX

DAUGHTERS OF THE CHURCH